P9-CNC-776

OUR NATURAL WORLD

OTHER BOOKS BY HAL BORLAND

The Outdoors

COUNTRYMAN: A SUMMARY OF BELIEF
AN AMERICAN YEAR
THIS HILL, THIS VALLEY
THE ENDURING PATTERN
BEYOND YOUR DOORSTEP
SUNDIAL OF THE SEASONS

People and Places

HIGH, WIDE AND LONESOME
THE DOG WHO CAME TO STAY

Fiction

THE AMULET
THE SEVENTH WINTER
WHEN THE LEGENDS DIE
KING OF SQUAW MOUNTAIN

Folklore

ROCKY MOUNTAIN TIPI TALES
THE YOUNGEST SHEPHERD

Poetry

AMERICA IS AMERICANS

Our Natural World

THE LAND AND WILDLIFE OF AMERICA
AS SEEN AND DESCRIBED BY WRITERS
SINCE THE COUNTRY'S DISCOVERY

COMPILED AND EDITED
WITH COMMENTS BY

Hal Borland

WITH DRAWINGS BY RACHEL S. HORNE

Doubleday & Company, Inc., Garden City, New York
1965

Library of Congress Catalog Card Number 65-19914

Printed in the United States of America
First Edition

Grateful acknowledgment is made to the following for the use of copyrighted material:

Mrs. Robert P. Allen, for "The Whooping Crane's World" by Robert P. Allen, from *Discovery*, published 1961 by J. B. Lippincott Company. Reprinted by permission.

Hal Borland, for "Flowers: Pollen and Seed" from *The Enduring Pattern* by Hal Borland, published 1959 by Simon & Schuster, Inc. Reprinted by permission.

Morgan Bulkeley, for "Neighbors of the Night" by Morgan Bulkeley, from the *Berkshire Eagle*. Reprinted by permission.

University of Chicago Press, The, for "White Oak and Blue Heron" from *Stars Upstream* by Leonard Hall, copyright © 1959 by The University of Chicago Press. Reprinted by permission.

Margaret Mowery DeWire, for "Out of the Soft, Black Night" by William Byron Mowery, originally published in *Audubon Magazine*. Reprinted by permission.

Dodd, Mead & Company, for "Winter Isolation" from *Hawks Aloft* by Maurice Broun, copyright 1949 by Maurice Broun; "The Rainy Day" from *Land of the Snowshoe Hare* by Virginia S. Eifert, copyright © 1960 by Virginia S. Eifert; "Consider the Egg" from *A Multitude of Living Things* by Lorus J. and Margery J. Milne, copyright 1945, 1946, 1947 by Lorus J. Milne and Margery J. Milne; "Ghoulies and Ghoosties" from *Birds over America* by Roger Tory Peterson, copyright © 1948, 1964 by Roger Tory Peterson; and "Grasshopper Road" from *Journey into Summer* by Edwin Way Teale, copyright © 1960 by Edwin Way Teale. All reprinted by permission.

Down East and Olin Sewell Pettingill, Jr., for "The Woodcock" by Olin Sewell Pettingill, Jr., from *Down East*, May 1963, No. 8, Vol. IX. Reprinted by permission.

Doubleday & Company, Inc., for "The Ordeal" from *Folded Hills* by Stewart Edward White, copyright 1932, 1934 by Stewart Edward White; "Mountain Winter" from *Bent's Fort* by David Lavender, copyright 1954 by David Lavender; "Olympic Mountains" from *My Wilderness: The Pacific West* by William O. Douglas, copyright © 1960 by William O. Douglas; "The Social Register" from *Wasp Farm* by Howard Ensign Evans, copyright © 1963 by Howard Ensign Evans; and "Which Way Did the Dinosaurs Go?" from *The Elderberry Tree* by Irving Petite, copyright © 1964 by Irving Petite. All reprinted by permission.

Don Eckelberry, for "On the Heels of the Dodo" by Don Eckelberry, from *Discovery*, published 1961 by J. B. Lippincott Company. Reprinted by permission.

Funk & Wagnalls Company, Inc., for "Boom or Bust" from *Our Wildlife Legacy* by Durward L. Allen. Reprinted by permission.

Mary Devoe Gwinn, for "The World of the Chipmunk" by Alan Devoe, originally published in *Audubon Magazine*. Reprinted by permission.

Harper & Row, Publishers, for "Autumn Harvest" from *The Landbreakers* by John Ehle, copyright © 1964 by John Ehle; "A Short Life but a Full One" from *Lives* by Gustav Eckstein, copyright © 1960 by Gustav Eckstein; "Sea of Grass" from *Face of North America* by Peter Farb, copyright © 1963 by Peter Farb; and "Spring in Washington" from *Spring in Washington* by Louis J. Halle, Jr., copyright © 1957 by Louis J. Halle, Jr. All reprinted by permission.

Victor Paul Hass, for "Mystique" by Victor Paul Hass, from the *Omaha World-Herald*. Reprinted by permission.

Holt, Rinehart & Winston, Inc., for "Shame to Waste a Boy" from *The Old Man and the Boy* by Robert Ruark, copyright 1953, 1954, © 1956, 1957 by Robert C. Ruark; "Great River: Prologue" from *Great River: The Rio Grande* by Paul Horgan, copyright 1954 by Paul Horgan; and "The Year at High Tide" from *The Outermost House* by Henry Beston, copyright 1928, 1949, © 1956 by Henry Beston. All reprinted by permission.

Houghton Mifflin Company, for "The Enduring Sea" from *The Edge of the Sea* by Rachel Carson, copyright © 1955 by Rachel Carson; "Life Cycle of a Fern" from *A Field Guide to the Ferns* by Boughton Cobb, copyright © 1956 by Boughton Cobb; "Mammals Within the City Gates" from *Natural History of New York City* by John Kieran, copyright © 1959 by John Francis Kieran; "Peregrine Falcon" from *The Peregrine Falcon* by Robert Murphy, copyright © 1963 by Robert Murphy; and "Wolves" from *Mountain Cattle* by Mary Kidder Rak, copyright 1936 by Mary Kidder Rak. All reprinted by permission.

Bessie F. Johnson, for "A Time Remembered." Reprinted by permission.

Alfred A. Knopf, Inc., for "The Deer Mouse" from *One Day on Beetle Rock* by Sally Carrighar, copyright 1944 by Sally Carrighar; "Wild Rice" from *Runes of the North* by Sigurd F. Olson, copyright © 1963 by Sigurd F. Olson; and "The Island" from *Goodbye to a River* by John Graves, copyright © 1950 by the Curtis Publishing Company, © 1960 by John Graves. All reprinted by permission.

J. B. Lippincott Company, for "Beaver" from *The World of the Beaver* by Leonard Lee Rue III, copyright © 1964 by Leonard Lee Rue III and John K. Terres; and "A Pond in His Life" from *The Wonders I See* by John K. Terres, copyright © 1964 by John K. Terres. Both reprinted by permission.

Little, Brown & Company, for "Like Crusoe, I Discover an Island" from *Enchanted Streets* by Leonard Dubkin, copyright 1947 by Leonard Dubkin. Reprinted by permission.

Macmillan Company, The, for "New England's Mountains" from *The Changing Face of New England* by Betty Flanders Thomson, copyright © 1958 by Betty Flanders Thomson; and "Marshes and Fall" from *Of Men and Marshes* by Paul L. Errington, copyright © 1957 by Paul L. Errington. Both reprinted by permission.

William Morrow and Company, for "Adirondack Hunt" from *One Man's Pleasure, a Journal of the Wilderness World* by Hugh Fosburgh, copyright © 1960 by Hugh Fosburgh. Reprinted by permission.

W. W. Norton & Company, Inc., for "Wind and Weather" from *The House on Nauset Marsh* by Wyman Richardson, copyright 1955 by W. W. Norton & Company, Inc. Reprinted by permission.

Oxford University Press, Inc., for "Wilderness" from *A Sand County Almanac: and Sketches Here and There* by Aldo Leopold, copyright 1949 by Oxford University Press, Inc. Reprinted by permission.

G. P. Putnam's Sons, for "The Nest in the Cave" from *Singing in the Wilderness* by Donald Culross Peattie, copyright 1935 by D. C. Peattie. Reprinted by permission.

Random House, Inc., for an excerpt from "The Secret of Life," copyright 1953 by Loren C. Eiseley from the book, *The Immense Journey*, by Loren Eiseley. Reprinted by permission.

Aretas A. Saunders, for "Bird Songs" from *The Lives of Wild Birds* by Aretas A. Saunders, copyright 1954 by Aretas A. Saunders. Reprinted by permission.

Charles Scribner's Sons, for "Big Storm" from *The Yearling* by Marjorie Kinnan Rawlings, copyright 1938 by Marjorie Kinnan Rawlings. Reprinted by permission.

William Sloane Associates, for "The Contemplative Toad" from *The Desert Year* by Joseph Wood Krutch, copyright 1952 by Joseph Wood Krutch. Reprinted by permission.

George Miksch Sutton, for "Caught in a Dust Storm" by George Miksch Sutton, from *Discovery*, published 1961 by J. B. Lippincott Company. Reprinted by permission.

United States Department of Agriculture, for "Where We Get Our Water" by William C. Ackerman, E. A. Colman, and Harold O. Ogrosky, from *Water: Yearbook of Agriculture 1955*; "The Importance of Seeds" by Victor R. Boswell, from *Seeds: Yearbook of Agriculture 1961*; "The Settlement of Grasslands" by Everett E. Edwards, from *Grass: Yearbook of Agriculture 1948*; and "A Tree Is a Living Thing" by N. T. Mirov, from *Trees: Yearbook of Agriculture 1949*. All reprinted by permission.

Viking Press, Inc., The, for "Let Nature Grow Her Own" from *Cream Hill* by Lewis Gannett, copyright 1938, 1944 by Lewis Gannett, 1949 by Lewis Gannett and Ruth Gannett; and "A Promise Land" from *The Great Meadow* by Elizabeth Madox Roberts, copyright 1930 by The Viking Press, Inc. Reprinted by permission.

Foreword

This is a book about America, the look of it and the color and sound and smell of it, the almost incredible variety of the land and the life that is native to it. It is a book written by many people, because it is a selection from the writing about America that has been done since the first literate Europeans saw its shores. Almost ninety writers are represented here, and among them they present a composite picture of outdoor America over almost four centuries. Even so, this is not intended to be a definitive selection, which would be impossible within the scope of a single volume. This is too big a country and it has been too extensively written about to be crammed into one book. So I have picked and chosen and often been arbitrary in my selections, which represent personal preferences from many years of reading. I am sure there are omissions that some readers will regret; I hope there are choices that will surprise and please them as well.

I have divided the book into two major parts, The Scene, and The Life. These, of course, are arbitrary divisions and inevitably overlap, since the setting and the life within it cannot really be separated. This overlapping is also true of the subdivisions within each of the major parts. Rivers and swamps, for instance, are usually accompanied by woodlands, often by mountains or plains. And plants, birds, animals and insects invariably are interrelated and interdependent. So the subdivisions are for convenience and not to be taken as inflexible boundaries.

Since this was not intended to be a book of quotations, of snippets and pieces, most of the selections are either whole chapters or long excerpts from books. One reason is that I wished to give the writers room to turn around and have their say. A few of the selections are from works of fiction, but in every instance the author was a good field naturalist as well as a good storyteller. I have minimized the excerpts from technical writers. This book, after all, is intended for reading, not for technical study.

Finally, this is not an esoteric collection from books and documents to be found only in specialized libraries. Many of the selections are from books on my own shelves, and the others are from books in the public libraries within an hour's reach of the rural New England valley where I live. Virtually all of them are available to almost any reader in the United States.

In assembling this collection I have spent many days and months in the company of good companions and able naturalists who, over the years, have taught me much and made my life incalculably richer. I hope the reader will be equally rewarded.

H.B.

Salisbury, Connecticut, 1965

Contents

PART I. THE SCENE

The Woodlands

The Watery Places

The Plains and Deserts

The Mountains

The Woodlands

Until there were trees, the newly risen land was a place of rocks and sand, scarred by wind and rain, seared by the unrelieved scorch of the sun. Then there were forests. Trees clothed the hills, cleansed the air, checked erosion, shaped the continents, made the land hospitable. And when man's earliest ancestors achieved reason and dreams they found the makings of tomorrow on the forest floor, saw the future's shape in the long shadows of the woodland.

Man's cultures had their beginnings in the forests, where trees provided shelter and fire and food and, eventually, a degree of safety and time for thought. There he found both gods and demons. There he found himself. In time, he cut the trees to become a farmer, and he pushed back the woodlands to build his cities. But when the hive-cities threaten to devour his dreams, he turns back to the forests in search of peace and replenishment. For deep in the race memory is the knowledge that cities crumble and die, but trees remain and creep back to heal the scars and nourish new beginnings.

Trees are the oldest living things we know. Rooted in the earth and reaching for the stars, they partake of immortality. In spring, the trees are life resurgent, bud and leaf and blossom. In summer, they are a cooling canopy of chlorophyll, more miraculous than all the fractured atoms. In autumn, the woodland is both beauty and bounty, glory and replenishment beyond measure. In winter, the trees are the elemental shape of life and enduring growth. Without the woodlands the earth would be rocks and sand and desolation, as it was in the beginning.

H.B.

AUTUMN HARVEST

BY JOHN EHLE

John Ehle (1925 —) is a native Carolinian whose roots reach back to the first settlers in the mountains of western North Carolina. Born in Asheville and educated at the University of North Carolina, he has been on the University's staff almost ever since, with time off for special assignments as assistant to the state's Governor. From boyhood he has steeped himself in Carolina history and the land itself, particularly the mountains and their wildlife, material that permeates his writing. He has written two biographies, four novels, and a series of radio plays for the "American Adventure" program broadcast by Radio Free Europe, Voice of America, and the Armed Forces Network. He has received two Freedom Foundation awards. This selection is from The Landbreakers, *a novel about the earliest pioneers in the Carolina mountain country that re-creates the time, the place, and the settler's relationship to the wilderness with notable vigor and reality. In this selection the time is 1781 and Mooney, the first settler in the valley, has been there two years. Lorry is his common-law wife and the two boys are her sons. It is fall, harvest time.*

(*The Landbreakers*, by John Ehle; Harper & Row, 1964.)

On the morning when the first witch hazel flowers appeared, at a time when they often heard the thumping of the pheasants in the woods, both signs of coming frost, Mooney told the boys to pull the blades from the sorghum cane, and he went down the rows himself and selected from the tallest canes the best of the big brown tassels of seeds, which he took to the house and put in a gourd, to be saved until the future planting time.

The boys pulled the blades, then cut armloads of the stalks near the ground and brought them to Mooney, who was busy contriving a press out of two oak boards. In the bottom one of the two he had cut grooves so that the sorghum juice would drip down into the iron pot.

There had been so much rain during the last part of the growing season that the yield wasn't as large as he had hoped it would be, and his press wasn't as good as a geared press, but the stalks gave up their sweetness, nonetheless; the sirup dripped into the pot in spurts as he crushed and turned and crushed again each hand of cane. The bees and flies and wasps gathered, coated themselves with juice; they fell onto the ground from heaviness, and into the pot of green liquid.

When the pot was two-thirds full, he helped Lorry carry it to the fire. One of the boys fetched a long pole, and she stirred the sirup as it thickened. A green skim formed and she removed it, brushing it onto the ground. When the green skim stopped forming, she reduced the heat, and after a while a white foam gathered to the top. This she ladled off carefully and put into a bowl, to be twisted later into candy.

"I declare, if I get the molasses too thick," she told Mooney, "they'll clabber on me and sour." It was a complaint, a gentle complaint, for it was a pleasure to make sirup and she didn't intend to get it too thin. Better to have it too thick, even though it might be gummy. The steam rose about her, dampening her face and dress. The bees buzzed everywhere, infesting the bath of steam, toppling into it as often as not, to boil in the sirup.

She made two gallons of the molasses that day, and more the next, and put it in gourds to keep.

On the third night of the molasses-making, which brought them to the end of their cane crop, they were in the cabin working with the pot of white foam, working it until it was thick enough to be cut. They were doing this when the pup began to growl and nose about the door. Almost every night the pup had barked, later to be answered by wolves from the edge of the clearing, or by a fox, but her growl tonight was not for wolves. She had come to have a rather casual growl for wolves, for she had found that Mooney was not much concerned about them, only annoyed with them. This was a different growl, and it indicated that a more dangerous animal was near the clearing.

Mooney unlatched the door. He saw in the moonlight two good-size black bears, one of them moving around the black pot, trying to get the last bit of molasses out of it, the other licking molasses from the ground, licking even the two boards which Mooney had used for a press.

He watched them as they tasted the green waste which had been scattered about. It had a bitter taste, Mooney knew, and addled the brain for a time. He watched curiously as the bears began to waddle about, seeking more of it.

They found all there was. Then, either because of the effect of the herb or, more likely, because of their disappointment at having found so little molasses, they began to fight one another. They fought for several minutes, knocking each other down, rolling over on the ground, before one went away, walking off in a rambling manner. The other licked the pot again, then left in a different direction.

The chestnut trees had released their harvest of nuts; the pigs filled their bellies with them, and the boys gathered them for the winter and fed them by handfuls to the two fattening hogs. Acorns, beechnuts and chinkapins rattled always across the forest floor, and the chipmunks and whistle-pigs gorged themselves until they were fat and wobbly.

When the first warblers and thrushers stopped at the valley on their way south, Lorry and the boys pulled the main harvest of gourds from the vines, cleaned them out and set them to dry. On a dry day the flax was pulled and laid out on the ground; the weeds were sorted out of it, the flax was tied, and the boys stacked it in the loft of the cabin, near the loom and wheel.

By now the frost had touched the mountain peak and was moving down the mountainside. The balsam forest didn't change, nor did the slicks of rhododendron, but the trees below them took on tones of red and yellow.

The wash of color flowed down toward the clearing, reached it in the sharpness of an early morning. And about them now the woods were changed into a fairyland of color. The buckeye turned yellow and dropped its eye-shaped seeds. The box elder near the spring turned into a bank of yellow leaves and pods; the maple in the valley just to the edge of the clearing got red as fire and beside it a white oak turned into the color of old wine; the sourwood was a rich red, the red oak was orange, and the possums climbed higher every night into the persimmon trees.

The salamander laid her eggs in the stream. The poplars finally turned from green to shades of yellow and gold.

Mooney and Lorry pulled the corn. The boys hauled it to the newly made crib and stacked it away. It was safe now; it was stored beyond bears or seasons, and all that day the warmest elation possessed them. They pulled the corn leaves from the stalks and stacked them, Mooney uprooted the corn stalks, cut them into pieces with the ax and stacked them near the stable.

The sun set blood-red each day, and rose as brilliantly from upriver every morning. Autumn, Lorry thought, in these lush, water-fed lands, was more colorful than springtime. And the air was clear; there was no haze at all. One afternoon she was able to make out high on the mountain an elk standing near the crest of a rock, and on another day she pointed out to Mooney a herd of deer. Often of a day she would see ravens leaving the mountain peaks in dizzying flights, feeling winter, swooping down from the high rocks where they had their summer nests. The crows were dismayed by their arrival and argued with them about it, but the ravens, as if to show their right to nest where they pleased, would fly in mated pairs into the air and do acrobatic stunts that ended in the clouds. Then from the clouds they would appear, and dip and twist, plunge, roll sideways in the air, and finally land near where the crows unhappily were perched on tree limbs, trembling.

The winter wren moved down to the valley, too, and the white-throated sparrow came back to the valley. Winter was in the woods, but suddenly the coolness left and it was warm of a day. The violets bloomed again. Streamers of gossamers, woven by spiders and set loose on the wind, waved from the trees.

At night the foxes barked at the moon. The owl sometimes kept them awake, too, and the wolves had gathered into packs and could be heard high on the mountain chasing down elk and deer. The trees dropped their leaves, and the streams were glutted with them and the water in the streams would disappear under them, then appear again near the rocks, and would sometimes flow over a bed of them. A family of pheasants could sometimes be seen, Fate said, lying on colored leaves not far beyond the spring.

Paul and Nancy Larkins worked on their cabin. Mooney helped them chop and cut, and Mina helped the boys gather rock for the chimney and hearth. A chill returned to the air, suggesting approaching bitterness. The groundhog sniffed the wind and went back to his den, there to stay until spring.

"It's time to kill the hogs," Mooney said one night. He was sitting by the fire talking and waiting for that utter weariness which came to him before sleep. The boys had been quiet, listening to the wind and playing with the dog. "Which one you want first, Lorry?"

"It seems to me like the red one is the fattest."

"I think so," he said. "Might as well do the hard one now. You boys get poles and separate those two hogs in the pen tomorrow morning."

The boys watched him expectantly.

"And don't feed that red hog tomorrow, but give it water."

The boys nodded.

"And don't feel sorry for it," Mooney said. "I've told you afore about making pets out of stock."

The boys pressed their lips together and stared at the fire.

"They told me up in Pennsylvania that it's a sign of bad luck to have pity on what you've got to kill. It's not right to the hog, or sheep, or whatever. So drag saplings tomorrow morning and separate them two and just feed one, you hear?"

He went outdoors and went down to the fattening pen, where the two hogs were. The boar heard him coming and began to grunt, so he spoke to him and the boar got quiet again.

He looked down at the two big hogs, lying on their sides on the ground, too fat to want to rise. "How you, Poppy?" he said to the big red one, then turned away. It didn't do to pity them, he knew that.

Two mornings later he took his ax and went down to the pen. He removed the roof logs from the place where the big red one was.

The hog got to his feet and looked up at him.

"You boys go get the horse and chain," he said.

He spat on his hands and lifted the ax. Swiftly he brought the ax down, striking the hog between the eye and the ear, and the hog crumpled to the ground.

He took the side logs out of the pen, hooked the chain onto the hog and dragged the carcass out. He bled the hog, then pulled it on up to the black pot, where Lorry was heating water.

The water was steaming but not boiling. He tested the water the way he had learned in Pennsylvania: he dipped his finger into it quickly several times in succession, to see how many times it took before the water scalded his skin. It scalded him slightly on the third time, so it was all right, as he told Lorry. If it burned on the first or second time, it was too hot for hog-singeing and might cause the hair and bristles on the hog's skin to set.

He and Verlin lifted the hog and set its rear end into the water. He had a smile at the sight, for the hog seemed to be resting there, taking a bath, its front hoofs poking out.

When the rear half was steamed hot, they put the head half in, then he and the boys scraped the skin while Lorry emptied the pot.

He cut through the skin and cleanly cut off the hams and shoulders. He cut out the spare ribs and side meat, and Lorry took each section as he gave it to her and laid it in the rinsed-out pot, which was set on the ground and was cool. He cut off the leaf fat and she put that into the pot. It came off easily, for the carcass was still warm. He gave Lorry the heart and she put that into the pot.

He pulled the hide off the carcass, what was left of it, and told the boys to grain it before it hardened, then he went up on the side of the hill and sat down near the grave and rested, for he was tired. He hated worse than anything slaughtering stock.

When he got back to the cabin, there was the smell of fresh pork coming from the hearth pot, and Lorry had a bowl of honey on the table. She had taken some of the dried corn and had milled it. A pone of bread was on the heat rock, and the promise of the place, of the farm and of the valley and of the family, came to him, and he welcomed it. They fell to eating and ate all that was cooked, and talked in pleasure about what they had.

That afternoon they tended the stock, and it was evening when they carried the pieces of pork up the loft steps and laid them out on a board. Salt was rubbed into the hams and shoulders until the meat sweated and caked the salt. The slabs of bacon, which weighed forty pounds apiece, were cut into three parts each and were salted and stacked. The hams, which weighed over twenty pounds apiece, were placed skin side down next to the shoulders.

When this was done, at the last light of day, they stood back and looked on at the sight, at the white meat which had pink in it and which looked gray because of the whiteness of the salt. "It makes you feel wealthy," Lorry said.

"Those hams and shoulders look like little animals cuddled down for the winter," Mooney said.

"How long will they stay like that?" Verlin asked.

"Forty, fifty days," Mooney said. "The colder it is, the longer they stay. They get the salt in them to the bone, then they can't spoil."

"Not ever?" the boys said.

"For years, anyway, especially if you smoke them when they're cured."

"I like it smoked might nigh as well as plain," Lorry said.

"No need," he said, "no need to smoke them here, though smoking keeps the flies off."

"It's a pretty sight," she said. They stood there looking at the store of meat, until at last they went down the ladder and ate another meal of fresh meat, field beans and hot bread.

That night a bear came to the clearing and ate the scraps that were left. The boys had hung the pigskin on the side of the crib, and the bear sniffed about that. Mooney shouted at it from the door, trying to scare it away, and the bear turned toward the cabin, bewildered by what he saw—a yellow-lighted doorway, open like the mouth of a giant animal, and in the mouth a creature as thin and sharp as a snake's tongue.

The bear growled and tore at the pigskin.

"Get gone, get gone," Mooney said angrily.

The bear woofed and ignored him.

"Hold that dog," Mooney told the boys. "Don't let her get free." Both boys had ahold of her.

The bear waddled off to the side of the crib and stopped there, but it looked back at the cabin, then began to sniff around the crib.

"He's still hungry for meat," Mooney said. "You boys bury what we have left of that other hog tomorrow, you hear?"

"The bears will still smell it," Verlin said.

"I don't need advice right now," Mooney said.

The bear backed away from the crib, then went close to it again, struck it a mighty blow with his paw, and the sound of the blow echoed back from across the river. He sucked at his paw, then struck the crib again, and the side of the crib trembled.

The horses began to move about inside the shed, frightened now, and to press against the shed door. The sheep moved in their pen, seeking a way out.

Mooney raised his rifle to his shoulder, braced his arm against the doorjamb, and fired.

He closed the door and Larry bolted it with a pole. He went to the bed quickly and began to load. The bear struck the door with his paw, and the door trembled in its holds.

The bear struck the door again. Chinking fell from behind the logs on that side of the cabin and the door flew open. The bear started forward and Mooney fired from beside the bed. The bear hurtled backward, for the shot hit a bone. At the same moment the young dog tore loose from the boys and moved toward the bear, leaped against it, trying to grab hold of its jaw with her mouth. There was a heap of bear and dog tumbling about in the yard. The bear got up and started back for the house, but Lorry threw a lighted piece of firewood at it, and the bear turned and started across the clearing, the dog snapping at it. Mooney took up the ax and ran after them, calling to the dog, but the dog went on.

Mooney stumbled over a piece of a sapling log and fell heavily to the ground. He got up, feeling of his shin, which was paining. Far off he heard his dog, baying.

He limped back to the house. "Where's the gun?"

Lorry handed it to him and he loaded it. "You stay here," he said to the boys, and turned and ran up through the clearing. Verlin moved to the door, but Lorry caught hold of him and held him. "You do what he told you," she ordered.

Verlin pulled free of her. "I'm going," he said, and fleet as a small animal, he dashed away.

Way off they heard the dog and moved toward it, seeking to stay on the trail in the darkness. "That bear'll tear my dog up," Mooney said.

Verlin was huffing for breath. "Will he kill her?"

"If she's got no better sense than she's shown so far, he will. I didn't know she would go chasing after a bear. She's not even of full size yet."

"I tried to hold her."

"A female's not usually so prompt to fight."

The path was steep. He moved with heavy breathing. Prickly limbs of bushes slashed at him, but that only made him more determined.

High on the mountain he stopped at the laurel slicks, a matted jungle of rhododendron bushes. The bear had gone into it.

He looked off to the right, up above the slick, toward where the dog was still baying. "I'm going through it," he said. "You want to come?"

"I think so," Verlin said.

"Stay close then."

The trails twisted and turned, and all he could see were the tall, stiff bushes around him, closing in even the sky above him, closing out the moon and stars. Now he was in the world of mountain secrets, of lost ways and weasels.

The dog's voice came from uphill, so he went that way. He reached the end of a path, had to back up and find another way. "Get in these hills and can't get out," he said. "Can't see a speck of light even."

Verlin was holding to his shirt now, for he couldn't see to follow. Mooney was stumbling over bush roots and sticks, and the loose rocks slipped under his feet sometimes.

He walked until he had little strength left. His breathing was coming hard, for he was tense as well as weary, and he was angry at all that was wrong. "You ever want to kill something, boy?" he said.

The boy's teeth were chattering from fear and the cold.

"I'd kill these bushes. They're pretty when they bloom, but they're hells all year along. What's pretty is not allus safe, I tell you."

"Are we going on?"

"Yes. I'm just listening. That dog has moved, ain't she?"

"I don't know. Maybe we moved."

"But that dog moved across the ridge there, didn't she?"

"I don't know."

"She must have, for she's not within sound of us now."

The wind felt noisily of the rocks, but in the limbs of the bushes not even a whisper was made. "There's a big open space at the top of this slick," he said.

"The mountaintop, it's clear."

"Uh huh," Mooney said. "I'm going on up there."

He pushed his way along the narrowing path, moving until the bushes stopped him. He braced himself and pushed hard and the bushes let him advance a short way. He moved on, but the bushes began to come lower over his head, so that he had to bend to get through. He fell to his hands and knees and, pushing his gun ahead of him, began to crawl. "Don't you ever come alone in one of these, you hear me?"

"Yes," Verlin said breathlessly.

"Come in here and not be able to get out by yourself." The bushes began to close tighter around him. Branches poked at his face and eyes and throat. His body was aching. "We're almost to the top of it."

"How you know?"

"I know when I get to the top of a laurel slick, don't you worry about that." He rubbed his torn skin with his fingers. "Huh," he said, grunting. "I'll tan that dog's hide if I ever catch her."

He crawled until the bush limbs pressed down so tightly he had to lie on his belly. He slithered through, pushing the gun ahead, pulling himself forward by grasping at bush trunks. He tried to get back on his hands and knees, but the limbs wouldn't let him.

He stopped. He lay there on his belly on the ground, panting for breath. He wanted to start fighting the slicks, try to break through, but he knew that wouldn't do any good.

Something moved in the bushes. It went away, breaking through the bushes. Some beast or other.

"We're about at the top," he said to the boy. "Not far to go." He began creeping forward, pulling at the bushes. He grasped at a bush, and something damp moved from his fingers, went away, and he froze on the ground. A small beast, he guessed. A rat, maybe.

He forced himself to reach for the bush trunk once more. He pulled himself forward. He tried to push himself to his hands and knees but couldn't. He reached out and grasped a trunk and pulled himself forward. He forced himself to grasp another trunk, and another, until he stopped thinking about it, and he went on until there was no trunk to grab hold of.

His mind returned to thought and he asked himself what had happened. He lay there wondering. He reached out, feeling, seeking. There was no bush to grasp. He turned his head, looked up and saw the stars near where the mountain stopped.

"I told you we was near the top," he said.

They lay there side by side until they had their breath. The boy got up slowly. "I lost my shirt," he said.

"Huh?" Mooney said. He sniffed the chilly air. "Law, that was something."

"I'm bleeding some."

"Don't never go into one of those slicks," he said. Painfully he took a few steps toward the gap.

They were on a rock shelf and there was light now, drifting down from the moon. The rock shelf was near the mountaintop, which was a deer and elk pasture; the moonlight reflected on the rock and the pasture. Being here was like being small in a great land. Here a man was no bigger than a gnat on the belly of a horse, he thought.

They came to the balsam woods and stopped, awed by the utter darkness before them. They moved into them slowly. The wind whined, the trees moaned and solemnly honed their limbs.

He heard the dog again, far off. The hound note held, then shifted in a changing breeze.

"She's some'ers on beyond the mountain."

He backed away from the great trees and moved into the open once again. Clouds were racing by, not far above their heads.

Verlin was close enough to brush against him. Mooney put his hand on the boy's head. A boy was like a pup, he thought, a friendly pup and it whining. "Your mama's down there worried about us. We go tearing off like crazy men, chasing a bear. Look a there, you tore your shirt off your back, Verlin."

"I told you I done it."

"Look at you. You got no pants on, either. Verlin, you ain't got a stitch left on yer back."

Verlin looked solemn. He had been scared nigh to death in that slick, and there was no humor in any of it to him.

"Your mama's going to skin you alive. My Lord in heaven, boy."

"I didn't mean to," Verlin said grumpily.

"Well, we're going to get you out of the cold." He found a crevice which he poked about in for snakes; he crept into it and Verlin followed. Mooney gave him his hunting shirt to put on. "Verlin, don't you tell your mama we went in a laurel slick, you hear?" he said.

"What am I going to say?"

"You think of a way to explain it. Look a there," he said, pointing toward the top of the mountain where now white clouds were passing. "Huh," he said. He huddled against the rock. "You see the settlement? See down there. One cabin is sending up sparks. Might be Paul Larkins', or maybe the German's." He rubbed his arms to warm them. "We'll stay here safe," he said, "until we warm, then we'll go find the dog."

They moved along the side of the mountain, high up near the peak. They followed the sound, hurrying, slapping into tree limbs, moving fast. They came to another, smaller laurel slick and stopped, then sighed, moved on, seeking an opening. He found one and went into it, holding the rifle before him.

He crashed his way along, the boy behind him. The barking had a closer sound to it now.

They came to the end of the slick, and before them was a great rock. He climbed the slope of it, tapping the gun stock against it to warn the snakes. He got to the top, the boy following, and stopped to rest. The barking was close by.

They moved quickly and quietly until they saw the dog sitting near the trunk of a hickory tree. She saw him approach, but no change came into her howl. Like music, it was very much like music, he thought.

He crept close. He saw nothing above, then abruptly high up he saw two eyes sparkle as the bear looked down. He aimed and fired.

There was a grunt. Nothing more.

He took out tow, took off the ramrod and was ramming home the shot when there came a sound of cracking limbs above. The bear was coming down. The bear fell, fell on his stomach and didn't move.

The dog came over to the mound of fur, her tongue hanging out. She sat down near the bear's head and considered it speculatively. She stretched out on her stomach, so tired she could scarcely move, and with a lazy, weary motion, fastened her mouth to the bear's neck.

"I'll tell you this," Mooney said quietly to Verlin, "we've got us a good dog there."

Small pieces of pigskin, fat and cracklin's, which had been put back, Lorry boiled outdoors in the pot, then left to cool. By evening there was a layer of white grease on the top of the pot, and she ladled that off to keep.

She emptied the pot and put lye water in it, water which she had let soak through hickory ashes overnight. She boiled the lye water until it would float an egg. She put the grease into it and stirred it with a sassafras stick.

When the bark on the stick began to get stringy, she set the grease to cool.

Mooney put the boys to work on a log, scooping it out. He and the boys lifted it onto the pile of wood next to the door of the cabin. That done, he went over to where she was. "I'll say this," he said, "you stay with your work."

"I do no more'n I have to."

"You don't lose a day, and act like every one is a race to sunset," he said.

"I don't know why you tell me that," she said, pleased.

She helped Mooney on another day tan the leather he had made. The tanning trough was where oak bark had been soaked in water for most of the year, the bark being changed from time to time. On the tanning day she brought ashes from the hearth, dumped them into it for lye, and stirred the mixture.

He fetched the pigskins and the bear hide, and two deerskins. He left them in the trough until the hair would slip, then laid them over a barked log and worked them until they were pliable. "I'm going to cut new harness from the best of this bearskin," he told her. "I'll need new harness if I'm to clear more land this winter."

"You need you a good pair of boots," she told him.

"I'd like to have a pair of boots," he admitted.

"Verlin is still nigh about naked," she said.

He glanced at her to see how angry she was with him. "We can cut him a pair of pants out of a deerskin."

"If you cut one boy's pants, you've got to cut the other'n a pair."

He thought about that. He needed leather; he needed twangs and slings, harness and shoes.

"I can make them a linen shirt apiece this winter," she said, "or one of linsey, if we use part of the wool."

"We'll get them clothed," he said. "Cut each boy deerskin pants, and we'll use the hogskins for a shirt apiece. Maybe we can split them."

"What about yourself?" she said. "You need a shirt."

"I'll kill a deer or two when I can."

It would be well to shear the lambs, yes, and shear the ewes again, Lorry thought. She had put off mentioning it earlier. Her mother had told her that no lamb's fleece should be cut without the woman saying what the fleece would be used for. Lorry was waiting, hoping she could have a baby started in her womb before lamb-shearing had to be done.

There was herb-gathering yet to do, too, even though late fall was not as good a time as spring for it. Any number of illnesses and afflictions might strike them during the winter, however, and they needed to do what they could to prepare. She had learned from her mother how to cure the agues, which chill and fever a body, the cahexia, diarrhea, dysentery; she knew how to tonic a colic or a cholera morbus, how to stop convulsions or web-treat a wound; she knew the symptoms of ringworm and whooping cough; she had cures for rashes, prickly heats and the itch. Her mind was busy with information about cures, spells, roots and bark. "We've got herbs to gather soon," she had said many a night since summer, but there had always been something else Mooney wanted to do first. "We ought to get the herbs afore all the leaves fall," she told him many times. He would nod and promise her a day, but it all went by somehow. Then one night she said they must gather the herbs next morning if they planned to do so at all, and Mooney didn't say any different.

So she brought baskets from the loft and shook them out. She got gourds ready, too. She came to the fire and sat down, and quietly but firmly said, "Verlin, you stay here tomorrow; Fate, you come with us."

Mooney looked up sharply, startled by her interference, but she returned his gaze firmly. After all, herb-gathering was a woman's task and she should be able to choose the child she wanted to help her.

Mooney turned from her. He studied the birch flames on the hearth, aware that both boys were waiting for his view. "Verlin, tomorrow while you're stock-watching, you can weave me a trap for coons," he said. "Get some canes and split them into twos and fours."

Boneset they found in the valley near the roots of a chestnut tree. Boneset tea was good for colds. Lorry told Mooney they needed tar of the pine, ooze of the sweet gum, and spirit of the beech, so he tapped three trees and fastened half-gourds to their bark. Pennyroyal, the best thing in the world for pneumonia, they found in plenty. They came upon a bed of galax and Fate bundled a hundred waxen leaves with honeysuckle vine. Mooney noticed a stand of ginseng and Lorry dug them up carefully so as not to break the roots.

They looked for pokeroot, which was needed for the itch, and red alder, which could be made into a tea for hives. They gathered dock leaves, which would make a poultice to draw the soreness out of boils.

She needed belladonna for lessening pain, so they sought the deadly night-shade plant. She needed leopard's bane. She needed acid from the prickly ash and the roots of the blackberry briar.

They walked on up the mountain, gathering and discussing and thinking about where they might eat the lunch Lorry had brought. Now and then they would stop to rest, or to gather a kind of leaf or bark. "I declare, I thought I saw a flash of cloth through the woods over there," Lorry said at one point, looking off toward a stand of tulip trees.

Mooney looked in that direction. So did Fate. "What do you suppose it might be, Fate?" he asked him.

The boy's big dark eyes turned up to him questioningly.

"Looked like a swish of colored cloth," Lorry said.

It might be Mina, Mooney thought. "Mina, you over there?" he called. There was no answer. "She's probably hiding out from us," he said.

They cut a length of wild-cherry bark and wound it into a roll. They climbed higher on the mountain, cutting a patch of seneca along the way. They stopped to rest near the balsam grove high up. Balsam was the best herb for kidney ailments, he knew, and he cut bark from a tree on the edge of the woods. He didn't want to go into the woods, if he could help it, for such places were houses of spirits and the devil. Only a few shafts of light filtered through the heavy branches. On the floor were not bushes or shrubs, only moss and ferns, which had moisture clinging to them. A balsam woods was a coffin, he thought; there was no way for a beast to live in there, or even for a flower to bloom. It was the place old beasts most likely went to die, when they had lorded over the wilderness as long as they cared to and were weary of warding off death, when they were ready to find death and say to him: Do what you have in mind to do. Then the moss would cushion them on itself. Perhaps a buzzard would find a way along one of the shafts of light to tear away the flesh. The moss someday would cover the bones.

There was a ledge nearby with a path leading up to it. As they climbed the path, they caught glimpses of the valley below them. Past limbs of beech trees, they saw the Harrison clearing, a patch of brown in a thickly green sea. Mooney saw his own smaller place, with a smoky chimney, a shed, a lambing pen, and below the house the pigpens. He could see Verlin and the dog walking across the lower part of the clearing. From the last bend on the path, he could see the German's clearing.

Still looking and talking, they went on up the little path, and from the top of the ledge they could see it all, see every clearing, see the river, see the trail in the valley and decide where the trail must be that went along the mountainside, and where the valley trail, which was becoming a road it was used so often. He was caught up in wondering at the sights, in marveling at the sense of accomplishment it gave him, when he noticed Fate's eyes widen with surprise. Mooney turned, and there, sitting at the back of the ledge, was Mina Plover, a big smile on her face. She began to giggle at the looks on the faces of the three people who were so startled to see her.

She walked home with them, and helped them cut aspen bark, for it would relieve muscle pain. They cut a root from an elm tree and peeled off the bark. The bark could be beaten into a pulp and dried in the cabin chimney; it would heal wounds, Lorry said.

From the edge of their clearing, they collected holly berries, which could be used to purge with—eight or ten berries for a single dose, Lorry said. They cut sassafras bark and sassafras roots, which would make a strengthening tea.

They arrived home and dumped down their store of supplies in the far fireplace corner, and at once the cabin smelled richly of sap and bark, of roots and moldy earth. A person could feel safe to live here now, Mina said, with such herb smells to drive away sickness.

Even Fate was pleased. Normally he was shy and reticent about anything Mooney did, but he was happy with the store of herbs and even smiled at Mooney now and was pleasant to him. After Mina was gone, Mooney asked Fate a good many questions about their tour of the mountains, and the boy answered them and told Verlin, often with enthusiasm, about what they had done and where they had gone. The change in the boy pleased Mooney and surprised him.

After supper he went outdoors and stood near the lambing pen, where he often went to listen to the night creatures, and directly Fate came outside, too, and began to walk about, waiting for Mooney to speak to him. Mooney went on up to Imy's grave and sat down there on a rock, and he began to talk, not to the boy, who was a fair distance away, but to the grave. He had done so before once in a while, telling Imy what had happened of a day; and Lorry, though she always frowned when she saw him sitting up there, had never objected.

He told Imy what had happened gathering the herbs. He was talking along that way when he saw Fate move up along the west border of the clearing, stopping from time to time as if he were listening for something.

"Imy, we been out gathering herbs," Mooney said quietly. Out the corner of his eye he saw that Fate had heard him talking. "One spring you and me got a few, but today we harvested a stock that will carry us for a long while, more'n a year, though we'll collect others along in the spring when sap comes easier."

The boy was trying to hear him.

"Verlin stayed home and tried to make a trap. He fashioned a piece of one. It's not going to do, but we'll weave it again tonight or tomorrow night. A boy learns by trying, and when he's tried and not done well, he can be taught easier. A man can't teach a boy much that the boy's not tried to do for himself."

He heard Fate moving slowly up behind him in the bushes.

"Fate was with us today, Imy. We don't ordinarily say more'n a dozen words to each other in a day, and they're not words that pry into a matter, but we got along today without argument."

Down below, the doorway of the cabin was yellowing from firelight. He could see Lorry moving about inside, putting the herbs away. Below the cabin, Verlin was leading the ram up toward the pen.

"I can't talk to Fate about some matters. I can't tell him why it is his mama needed to marry again, for that's something a person grows up to know in feeling more than in mind. I can't tell him why his papa left and didn't come back, for I don't know. Lord, it's not something I can figure out, for it's unlikely that man would do something like that. Fate and me can't sit down and reason out these matters, not yet, and maybe not ever, for it's chancey to talk about another person."

He was quiet and listening.

"I can see some matter we might discuss, him and me. I'm thinking of such as my coming into his house down there in the valley and making things over my way, when he had been taking care of his mama right along. I couldn't a been more plain and blunt than I was, and he had a right to play an angry part with me for it. He had a nice farm there for his mama. He had sheep and chickens, and there I come and changed it all around, took everything off to my place, without talking it over, showing him and his mama and Verlin my place, how it all was bigger here and better. I went in there and whacked my way through. A man can do that. A man as big as me is accustomed to doing his work that way, accustomed to telling stock what to do, to wade in on anything and lash out, moving whatever is in his way, cutting down or plowing up. A man works that way, but I needed to show a difference here, for the boy wasn't a piece of stock or land. He was a man, not grown yet, but accustomed to his own way, and I wish I had gone about it differently."

He was silent and waiting. He could hear the boy breathing, that was all. Then he heard a catch in the boy's breathing, and that tiny sound went through him like a shaft of pain. He closed his eyes tightly, hoping the boy would not sob, would not give in to the pity inside him.

The breathing steadied. Mooney was grateful for that. "I saw where some of the chinking has come out near the chimney, Imy," he said simply. "We need to put little rocks in there and some wet clay. I suppose we can use that clay out of the branch, that of it which is gray, and there's plenty of rocks about." He let the words settle and the night sounds sweep over him. He stood, brushed the dirt off his pants. "It would be a big help to get that chinking done," he said quietly, then went down the path, walking slowly, went to the lambing pen, where Verlin was working. He glanced back only once and saw the huddled figure of the boy, there just above Imy's grave.

On the next afternoon, in the cool of the day, when he was free for a little while from sheep-tending, Fate went down to the creek and brought back rocks and some of the light-gray clay, and mended the chimney.

The family got the sheep into the pen and one by one Mooney and Lorry hobbled and sheared the ewes. When it came time for the lambs, Lorry hesitated for a moment before cutting on the first one, then quietly, firmly, she said, "The wool's to be used for a baby's things." She noticed the barest flicker of a glance which revealed that Mooney had heard her.

"When's it to be?" he said.

"It's not far along," she said.

"Summer then, is that it?" he said.

"Summer might be," she said. Yes, he was pleased, she could tell, and so was she, for this was another way to hold the family together, and was an answer to any question of their right to live together.

"These lambs are going to be cold as a bare-bottomed baby in the snow," he said, suddenly cheerful. "But they don't have as much feeling as a man for coldness, anyhow. Not much feeling or sense, either. A lamb is a fool-stunted thing, and so is a ram."

"I don't know as they are," she said, gently patting the head of the frightened, shivering animal.

"They're pretty, I'll admit that, and cute as a pearl button, but they're not sensey."

He's talking about sheep, she thought, but he's wondering about the baby, what it will be in kind, how it will grow, how he will tend to it and I will tend to it.

They washed the wool in the pool below the spring. The next day they washed it again. On the third day she sent the boys to the top of the cabin with it, to spread it out on the roof boards in the sun. There it lay, drying and growing fluffy, setting off the cabin prettily, she thought. She walked up the hill a ways and looked down at it and at the boys, scampering about, chasing the naked sheep off to the grazing places in the woods.

Mooney came up the hill to where she was. "I've not seen such a sight in years," he said.

"Nor I," she said.

He gazed down at the house, proud and comfortable to see everything so well done.

THE RAINY DAY

BY VIRGINIA S. EIFERT

Virginia S. Eifert (1911 —) was born and educated in Illinois and has made the Midwest her special field as an all-round naturalist. In love with the outdoors from childhood, she has written about birds, animals, insects, trees, flowers and aquatic life, and as editor of The Living Museum, *monthly publication of the Illinois State Museum, she has dealt with all phases of natural science. Her interest in waterways led to* River World, *a book about wildlife along the Mississippi. She has written several books for young readers about Abraham Lincoln and the Lincoln country. Her experience as guide and nature teacher in the Canadian border country provided material for* Land of the Snowshoe Hare, *from which this selection is taken. She is an able, versatile naturalist of broad interest and knowledge, a conservationist and ecologist who has found the whole world of nature in her own region. An artist and photographer as well as a writer, she has illustrated several of her own books.*

(*Land of the Snowshoe Hare*, by Virginia S. Eifert; Dodd, Mead & Company, 1960.)

It was too dry for June. The duff under the pines had grown tinderous; a spark could start a conflagration. The balsams had a resinous smell, and their new growth looked wilted. The back roads with their border of moosewood, spruces, dogwood, wild raspberry bushes and ferns were dusty, and the deer now fed far from their usual roadside browse. The forest trails were dry. Old logs were no longer moist and soggy, but crumbled at a touch. The white flowers of bunchberry looked meager and stunted, and the wintergreen berries, usually so plump by summer, were small and parched.

The bogs had grown so dangerously low in water that the sphagnum in the muskeg hummocks was drying out, bleaching white under the heat; the large cells in the spongy plants were empty now of the reserve moisture which they usually held. Even these water conservators were in danger of fire, and the long rainless spell menaced the vulnerable coolness and life-preserving dampness in the land of the snowshoe hare.

Fire warnings were out. There had already been two bad fires in the forests near Lake Superior, and it could happen again at any time, at any place. Up in their far-seeing towers above the forest, men were on tense twenty-four hour duty. It was an uncomfortable, taut time of waiting, of hoping for rain, yet praying that it would be a steady soaker instead of a sudden thunderstorm whose carelessly cast lightning could strike flame from a pine and start the forest-fire which everyone feared.

And then one morning dawned to a sky which was beautifully gray and overcast, the air deliciously cool. A soft, diffused light lay through the woods. The lake was quiet as ice, the bog misty and remote, the forest shadowy. Everything seemed to be waiting, relaxed, mouths held up for moisture.

Rain did not begin until night. Even when it pattered on the cabin roof I could not be sure that it was really rain and not the endless chattering and clacking of the quaking aspen leaves which can give the gay illusion of a hard shower in the midst of the worst drouth. I went out into the soft night, then, and knew that at last it was really raining.

The exciting smell of moisture on dry earth and sand was a tonic to breathe. It brought out latent perfumes from fallen needles and old leaves, from the chemical properties of dead wood and the earth itself. At that moment, the scent of rain was the most glorious aroma in the world.

Morning was even more perfumed, revived, wet, wonderful—safe; and still it rained. The fire watchers went home. The forest and bog and meadow could live with renewed vigor.

In spite of a night of rain, there were few puddles and almost no mud. Into this glacier-laid fine sand, the water had soaked gently, had not rushed off to erode slopes and be lost in ditches and rivers, for the North makes the most of its moisture. The forest was obviously drinking up, savoring and treasuring every drop.

Rain fell with the greatest force and quantity on the tops of the tallest trees, ran in rivulets down trunks and branches. Leaves of the sugar maples, as if waxed or oiled, held droplets in puddles on the surface, drops which merged and ran down the hollows of the veins to the tips of the lobes. On each lobe a crystal drop poised, and let go, and splashed to another leaf under it, to diffuse with drops that ran down other leaves, and to finally patter upon the ferns. The fern fronds channeled rain down their midribs or let it drip slowly from curving pinnae. Although the rain might have come down fast on to the top levels, it grew slower as it passed through the lower parts of the forest. A drop that fell on the topmost maple leaf or balsam tip might not reach the ground for half a day, while those cast in a rush on meadow and bog came down and landed in moments.

Rain on the pines slid down upright needles, clung silverly where the needle bundles joined the twigs, ran one by one or in a smooth stream down the branch, slid down the smooth bark. Water followed bending twigs and ran into drooping needle clusters. The end of each soft, curving, blue-green needle held one raindrop, a silvery gazing-globe, which finally slipped from its mooring and fell . . . and fell . . . and fell . . . and was replaced by another.

Balsams and spruces channeled water down their twigs, let drops go off one at a time from the needles, from tips or undersides, funneled them down the twigs to the terminal buds, and off. Waxen aspen leaves, held in a slanting or sharply vertical position, lost their rain quickly, though each leaf was filmed with fine moisture which gathered, little by little, upon the lowermost notches in the leaf. Each tree had its own way of handling the rain, of producing its own little rainfall by means of its own kind of leafage or branching. Instead of the concerted pounding made by water pouring upon the meadow or roof, the tune of the raindrops was gentle and varied as they passed downward through the woods—a tinkling, pattering, splashing, that made a sort of concerto of wetness.

Each thing took to itself the rain, or cast it off. Cones on pine and spruce, on balsam and hemlock and cedar, were all tightly closed against the moisture, and a knife-point could not pry them open. Cones have the power to open and close—open in dry weather, shut firmly against the wet, protecting seeds from mildew and ruin. Many flowers resisted the water. Twinflowers and starflowers nodded to protect their pollen. Orange hawkweeds along the logging trail were shut, and so were the pearly everlastings, and the white and pink Pyrolas were naturally bent.

Other things received wetness in abundance. Mosses took it in like sponges. Lichens on tree trunks, branch and slope had absorbed water all night and by morning were soft and pliable. They were almost twice the size they had been when the drouth parched them. Strong and enduring lichens can withstand long periods of cold, heat and dryness, yet can revive in a half a day of blessed rain when it finally comes.

Lichens are no strangers to hardship. They developed in rigorous times, evidently were created in the necessity which came of primeval poverty. They came about as a combination of two plants, in the lowest phylum of plants, the Thallophytes, yet quite dissimilar. No one knows exactly how or when or why it happened, but it did happen—an alga with green coloring, and a little whitish blob of fungus, which had no chlorophyll, got together.

In a sort of botanical alliance called symbiosis, the alga was enabled to live more successfully by mingling its cells with the tangled hyphae of the fungus than it had on its own. The fungus, unable to make any food for itself and having had to live as a formless little saprophyte —perhaps the dead material it required as food was scarce at that time—found a reliable source of nourishment in the alga's chlorophyll. Together they built up form and substance as a plant which was neither fungus nor alga, but lichen. The fungal mass held moisture; the algal cells made food. It was and still is a successful union which has lasted since some of the earliest days of life on earth, and seems to be in no hurry to end or change. With this combination of power and resource, lichens in their many variations and forms have proved they can live in almost any situation on land.

They are the pioneers which contrive to subsist on the uncrowded, barren, hungry areas of the world, finding sustenance and anchorage on such unlikely habitats as bare rock, tree trunks, dead branches, or sterile soil. They are abundant in the North Country, to which they came on the heels of the last glacier, yet are inconspicuous until a day of rain brings them into delightful freshness and prominence again.

That day in the rain, the once-shrivelled, charred-looking lungwort lichens on the trees took on a fresh, green, spinach-like look. Dog lichens, like small, tattered pieces of blackened green paper with white undersides in sharp contrast, freshened on the ground. The lovely rosettes of gray-green Parmelias on bark looked newly minted. Cladonias on moss banks held up their gray, powdery, cup-in-cup arrangements of fruiting bodies, the pyxie-cups of the woods, while the scarlet caps and knobs on British Soldier Cladonias were magnificent small spots of color against the gray-green of the lichen mass—as bright as the tanager which was singing in the rain.

Reindeer lichens in curled, many-branched, coralline masses four inches high covered yards of earth in the coniferous woods, where the deer often came to eat. The lichens here had been so crisp that they had snapped off when I stepped on them only two days before, and now, like cool seaweeds freshly emerged from the tide, they were soft and springy and pliable, and bounced back into shape as I walked there.

Even so quickly after the lifeless drouth, mushrooms, triggered by moisture, were coming up. There were half a dozen little peaked caps in deepest crimson-scarlet with gold stems and gills, poking up among the moss; a few fragile coral mushrooms; three orange Chanterelles among the reindeer lichens; while the old fungi on stump and ground, the woody brackets and Polypores, had a freshly washed, alive look, though they might have been several years old and deeply rooted in solid wood.

In all my rambling that day in the rain along the forest trail, the path was without puddles. The sand was absorbing the raindrops when they finally reached it, and it was percolating slowly through the matting of old decayed pine needles and forest litter of years past. But the rain filled every blueberry bush with hundreds of drops. The simple way to get wet, I discovered suddenly, was to brush against a blueberry bush, or through bracken, each of whose flat, triangular fronds seemed to hold at least a pint of loosely attached water. They and the blueberry bushes were soakers.

In the rain, the diffused light of the forest was much the same above as below. There was none of that spotlighting of sunshine from openings in the forest canopy or the dark gloom of woods in full shade. In a rain it was all shade, yet not as dark as with the contrast of a sunny day outside. Skylight was the same everywhere. On a sunny day, the sunshine is largely held on the tops of the trees; light-rays bounce off the polished leaf-surfaces and only a portion is absorbed. Much of the rest is cast back into the atmosphere, while only about ten percent of the sun's rays gets to the ground. But on a rainy day I found a soft illumination everywhere, skylight reflected from gas molecules, moisture droplets and dust particles, suffusing it gently. The temperature also was more equal. On a sunny day, the heat on the tops of the trees might be almost thirty degrees greater than the temperature down among the ferns.

But the ferns themselves are responsible for some of that floor-level coolness. They are probably among the coolest plants in the woods. All plants give off moisture in a sort of inverted rain, but ferns exude it almost visibly. When I held my hand under a fern frond on a warm day, I could feel the cool, transpired, invisible moisture. If I multiplied many ferns and their natural built-in air-conditioning, it was no wonder the forest floor could be so much lower in temperature even when it is above ninety degrees upstairs on the tops of the trees or out on the sun-baked open meadow.

Because the rain was so much heavier on the upper levels, many birds which normally feed up there had moved down to the lower parts of the woods where the force of the rain was reduced to a pleasant dripping and splatting. Pewees and least flycatchers sat on dead twigs a few yards above the ground, in woods openings where they could see well all around them, and zipped out now and again to snap up a mosquito. The red-eyed vireo, singing his over-and-over conversational soliloquies which never wait for an answer, was poking about in a little aspen sapling whose loosely hung, slippery leaves had shed most of their water.

So, also, had the vireo's nest. I had discovered it a week ago, suspended compactly and securely in a forking crotch some twenty feet up in a maple, plainly visible from below though well thatched above with maple leaves. The nest had that special embellishment which vireo nests in the North Woods may have—curls of tissue-thin white birchbark, plucked one by one from the nearby trees and woven into the astonishing structure of the little basket nest. Birchbark in itself is waterproof and, whatever else the nest was made of, it apparently had not gathered enough wetness to show. From where I stood and examined it with binoculars, the vireo's nest under its canopy of leaves looked as dry as it had been on the days of drouth. But something new had been added since I last walked here. As the adult flew with a beakful of insects, four heads shot above the edge of the nest, and four bright red mouths opened wide.

It was the time of year when young birds were in most of the woodland nests and few were placed to get any of the force of rain. Most of them, also, were quite hidden from my prying curiosity. I could only guess at their presence. A few, like that of the vireo, the ruffed grouse, and the crested flycatcher had been located, each one quite by accident, which is usually the way of the woods.

The flycatchers were nesting in an old woodpecker hole in a tottering birch stub which was only a shell, really, still standing but most of its inner substance and strength rotted. I could make it rock a bit simply by touching it and had done so one day. A furious female flycatcher had come steaming out of the hole and had set up a great racket.

Early in June I had heard a commotion from these big handsome flycatchers and found them near this old birch stub. The birds were almost robin-sized, with a stubby russet crest, sulphur-yellow breast and green-brown and red-brown back and wings. The two were doing an unnecessary amount of loud shrieking and *wheeping*, wings moving faster than needful, whirring up to a hemlock from which long beards of lichen hung. The birds were gathering the lichens—filling their beaks until they appeared to have long trailing mustaches, then flying to the hole in the old stub. Here was something new to me—no bird-book I had ever read had mentioned that crested flycatchers filled their nest holes with lichens, but they were doing just that. I wondered what else would be in that nest with the polished olive-brown eggs.

Farther south in snake country, the crested flycatcher likes to drape a cast snake skin at the entrance to the hole. Up here in the North Woods, reptiles are few. I had seen only the slim little emerald-green grass snake which lived under a big old charred stump at the entrance to the Big Woods, and the ribbon snake among the rocks at the Burnt Rollway Dam. Surely there weren't enough cast skins to supply the crested flycatchers, which are abundant in these woods with their numerous woodpecker-hewn dead trees. Perhaps up here, therefore, the birds use lichens.

As I left the shaky old snag with its flycatcher nest, the male ruffled his crest and screeched out an eloquent *wheep!*, then dashed out into the lightly falling drops, turned a double summersault, and caught a small moth which had ventured out into the wet. He came back to the nest hole, moth wings standing out like strange whiskers on either side of his beak, to poke the catch inside.

From another hole, young yellow-bellied sapsuckers thrust their heads, all crowding to get their beaks out and fussing and fizzing with impatience and hunger. There was a great ado of buzzing among them when the hard-working female, her feathers draggled in the rain, swooped up to the hole in the aspen and hastily stuffed the food inside.

In the balsams, warblers were in constant motion which set up small secondary rain showers from the loaded needles and twigs. The little birds themselves appeared as waterproof as their pictures in books—the Canadas and magnolias in the balsams, a brilliant Blackburnian warbler in a birch, the black-throated green warblers working high in the hemlocks and pines, where they are almost always to be found in their nesting grounds. Energetically the little birds flitted and called, nipped up small insects and spiders, darted like little flycatchers into the rain.

A ruby-crowned kinglet, even smaller than the diminutive warblers, zipped out of a soaking-wet spruce and caught gnats which it carried to a matted nest high in the spire of the tree. The chickadees, also with nests nearby, were hunting in the rain but were saying very little about it. Birds were reaching that period in the year when songs grew less. Some, like most of the hermit thrushes, may have sung their last songs until next spring. The woods were occupied by birds which were all very busy hunting food for their ever-hungry young; the time for ardent song was past.

Other creatures avoided the rain as well as they could. The barred owl, below the busy warblers in the hemlock, dozed on the sheltered side of the dark trunk. Now and again, in a preoccupied way, he gave his feathers a quick shake to knock off the water; now and again a drop coursed down his forehead and dripped from his curved beak onto his barred chest.

The chipmunks stayed in their burrows until hunger drove them out. I came upon one which perched himself on the bending bough of a hazel bush where he was eating green buds. Neither he nor his fellows seemed concerned with making the usual alarm racket in announcing my intrusion in their domain. It was too wet even for scolding. The brown snowshoe hare was pretty damp under a young balsam, but shrugged it off, though one which slopped across the trail looked uncomfortably soggy in the tail and hind quarters.

As I followed the trail at the foot of the hemlock hill where it meets the little bog, there was a rackety snorting and splashing as a large buck, his young antlers in the velvet, his russet back darkened in the rain and steaming a little, wheeled from where he had been drinking, knee-deep in bog. He tore off up the hill, snorting and whistling all the way, kicking up clods of wet earth as he went and rumpling the contours of the reindeer lichen beds.

Then the red squirrel, which had evidently kept an eye on me during the walk but had not found it worth while to make a fuss, now started a fearful chittering and snickering, flapping his tail about like a wet rag, and leaping from branch to branch. In so doing he set up a heavy shower all the way, managing while just above me to send down a good sprinkling.

Between the wetness of the blueberry bushes and brackens, and the showers sent down by the squirrel, I had become literally part of the rainy-day world by the time I got back to the cabin. But I had satisfied myself as to what this rain had done. It had brought the bog back to its normal water level, had quickly revived the sphagnum, had brought up lake levels, and the creek, too; had soaked the meadow, saturated the woods, dampened all the conifers which had been so greatly in danger from a single spark. All about me I could feel a good relaxing of the tensions brought on by drouth. The North was itself again, cool, moist and fragrant. As the last raindrops shook themselves off the maples, and a lifting of clouds came far across the muskeg and its rim of tapered spruces, a pallid sun looked through and set up a gentle steaming from the bog.

PINE WOODS

BY WILSON FLAGG

(Thomas) Wilson Flagg (1805–1884) was born, grew up and spent nearly all his life within fifty miles of Boston. Educated at Harvard Medical School, he never practiced; shy and retiring by nature, he welcomed a clerkship in the Boston customs office and seems to have spent his leisure wandering the nearby graveyards and countryside, about which he wrote many essays. He was a moody writer, rather morbidly romantic, not too well informed as a naturalist but a good observer. He admitted that he shrank from "personal adventure." His copious writing is now largely forgotten, but he represented a minor current of nature-writing typical of his day. This selection is from his The Woods and By-Ways of New England. *In it he refers to a trip to the South, probably the only venture he ever made far beyond the borders of Massachusetts.*

(*The Woods and By-Ways of New England*, by Wilson Flagg, 1872.)

I have often thought of the pleasure I should feel on entering a forest of tree-ferns, and observing their elegant fronds spread out above my head, displaying a form of vegetation never witnessed except in a tropical country. Yet I doubt whether an assemblage of tree-ferns, a grove of magnolias, or an island of palms could equal a forest of pines in the expression of grandeur and solemnity. A pine wood expresses characters entirely unique, and affects us with sensations which nothing else in nature seems capable of inspiring. Whether this arises from the contrast between the light outside and the darkness within,—a certain harmonious blending of cheerfulness and gloom,—or from the novelty of the whole scene, there comes up from every deep recess and shadowy arbor, every dripping dell, every mossy fountain, and every open glen throughout the wood, an indescribable charm. Notwithstanding the darkness of its interior, and the sombre character of its dense masses of evergreen foliage, as seen from without,—and whence the name of *black timber*, which has been applied to it,—yet the shade and shelter it affords, and the sentiment of grandeur it inspires, cause it to be allied with the most profound and agreeable sensations.

In a pine wood Nature presents one of her most remarkable features; and there is so much that is healthful and delightful in its emanations, and in the atmosphere that is diffused around it, that she has not denied its benefits to any clime. Pines are found in every latitude save the equatorial region, where the broad-leaved palms supply the same enduring shade. Even there pines are distributed over mountains at a height corresponding with the northern temperate zone. Nature has spread these trees widely over the earth, that the inhabitants of the sunny South and the inhospitable North may equally derive benefit from their protection and their products. There is not a region this side of the equator, where a man may not kneel down under the fragrant shade of a pine wood, and thank the Author of nature for this beneficent gift.

In New England the white pine usually predominates in our evergreen woods, mixed in greater or less degree with pitch-pine and fir. In the gracefulness of its foliage, in its lofty stature and the beautiful symmetry of its wide-spread branches, the white pine exceeds all other species. But the balsamic fragrance that is so agreeable to travellers when journeying over the sandy tracts of some parts of New England comes from the homely pitch-pine. These odors greet our senses at all seasons, but chiefly during the prevalence of a still south-wind, and are in a different manner almost as charming as a beautiful prospect.

In a dense pine wood we observe certain peculiarities of light and shade seldom seen in a deciduous wood. The foliage that forms the canopy over our heads is so closely woven, that, whenever an opening occurs, the light pours into it with distinct outlines of shadow, very much as it shines into a dark room through a half-opened shutter. These sudden gleams of light, blending with the all-pervading shadow in which we are involved, deepen all our sensations, and cause us to feel a little of the religious awe which is inspired when passing under the interior arches of a cathedral. The presence of a group of deciduous trees always becomes apparent at some distance before we reach it, by the flickering light among their loose foliage, and a general brightness and cheerfulness in the space occupied by the group.

There are many agreeable circumstances connected with a pine wood. The foliage that drops from the trees, after the new growth of leaves has been put forth, covers the ground with a smooth brown matting, as comfortable to the footsteps as a gravel walk, while it savors only of nature. The acicular foliage of the pine is so hard and durable, that in summer we always find the last year's crop lying upon the ground in a state of perfect soundness, and under it that of the preceding year only partially decayed. This bed of foliage is so compact as to prevent the growth of underbrush; and it keeps the space open under the trees, whose tall shafts resemble pillars rising out of the floor of a magnificent temple. Hence a pine wood is pleasantly accessible to the rambler and the student of nature; and the absence of a woody undergrowth permits many plants of a peculiar character to thrive upon this carpeted ground. The purple cypripedia is common here, pushing up its leaves through this mass of decayed foliage, and displaying its beautiful inflated blossoms like some bright flower of a fairer clime. Mushrooms of various species and of divers fantastic shapes are frequent as we pass, some spreading out their hoods like a parasol, some with a dragon-like aspect, others perfectly globular, all having a great diversity of hues. In the deeper wood, where there is no sunshine to green the sprouting herbs, appears that rare genus of plants resembling the pale and sickly slaves of the mine,—the grotesque and singular monotropa.

In an old pine wood our attention is diverted by the great variety of lichens that incrust the bark of the trees and hang from their boughs. Many rare species decorate the trees with their tufts, circles and protuberances, and their curiously painted dots and patches. All green herbs, however, are checked in their growth by the darkness of the wood. The verdure of a pine wood is chiefly over our heads; there is but little under our feet. But the few plants whose habits permit them to grow here are the more conspicuous because they are not mingled with a crowded assemblage of different species. Hence the little creeping michella, with its checkered green leaves, its twin flowers resembling heath-blossoms, and its scarlet fruit, is very beautiful, clustering at the roots of some tall pine, or garlanding some prostrate tree covered with mosses that mark its decay. . . .

The pine barrens of the Southern States are celebrated as health retreats for the inhabitants of the seaports, whither they resort in summer to escape the prevailing fevers. They are generally of a mixed character, consisting of the Northern pitch-pine, the long-leafed pine, and a few other species, intermixed with the Southern cypress, occasional red maples, and a few other deciduous trees. Pines, however, constitute the dominant growth; but the trees are, for the most part, widely separated, so that the surface is green with herbs and grasses, and often covered with flowers. The thinness of these woods may be attributed to the practice, for two centuries past, of tapping the trees for turpentine, causing their gradual decay. Their tall forms and branchless trunks show that they obtained their principal growth in a dense wood.

The first visit I made to the pine barrens was after a long ride by railroad through the plains of North Carolina. It was night; and I often looked from the car windows into the darkness, made still more affecting by the sight of the tall pines that raised their heads almost into the clouds, like monsters watching the progress of our journey. The prospect was rendered almost invisible by the darkness that gave prominence to the dusky forms of the trees as they were pictured against the half-luminous sky. At length the day began to break, and the morning beams revealed to my sight an immense wilderness of giant spectres. The cars made a pause at this hour, allowing the passengers to step outside; and while absorbed in the contemplations of this desolate region, suddenly the loud and mellow tones of the mocking-bird came to my ears, and, as if by enchantment, reversed the character of my thoughts. The desert, no longer a solitude, inspired me with emotions of unspeakable delight. Morning never seemed so lovely as when the rising sun, with his golden beams and lengthened shadows, was greeted by this warbling salutation, as from some messenger of light who seemed to announce that Nature over all scenes has extended her beneficence, and to all regions of the earth dispenses her favors and her smiles.

At the end of my journey I took a stroll into the wood. It was in the month of June, when vegetation was in its prime, before it was seared by the summer drought. Many beautiful shrubs were conspicuous with their flowers, though the wood contained but a small proportion of shrubby undergrowth. During my botanical rambles in this wood I was struck with the multitude of flowers in its shady arbors, seeming the more numerous to me as I had previously confined my observations to Northern woods. The phlox grew here in all its native delicacy, where it had never known the fostering hand of man. Crimson rhexias—called by the inhabitants deerweed—were distributed among the grassy knolls, like clusters of picotees. Variegated passion-flowers were conspicuous on the bare white sand that checkered the green surface, displaying their emblematic forms on their low repent vines, and reminding the wanderer in these solitudes of that faith which was founded on humility and crowned with martyrdom. Here too the spiderwort of our gardens, in a meeker form of beauty and a paler radiance, luxuriated under the protection of the wood. I observed also the predominance of luxuriant vines, indicating our near approach to the tropics, rearing themselves upon the tall and naked shafts of the trees, some, like the bignonia, in a full blaze of crimson, others, like the climbing fern, draping the trees in perennial verdure.

ADIRONDACK HUNT

BY HUGH FOSBURGH

Hugh Fosburgh (1927 —) is a native New Yorker, Yale-educated, who grew up knowing intimately the wild country of the Adirondack State Forest Preserve, where his family still owns a share of a 5000-acre private reservation. After an apprenticeship of magazine writing and wartime service in the Air Force, he turned to fiction writing, chiefly novels and stories with an Adirondack wilderness background. One Man's Pleasure, *from which this selection is taken, however, is nonfiction, the journal of a year spent at the house in the forest, and of "the world of nature as it interested and affected me." Fosburgh is an informed outdoorsman, a good field naturalist, a hardheaded conservationist and an able, no-nonsense writer about the natural world around him. In this book he has disguised the names of some of the characters, but the man he calls Maunton in this selection is, as Fosburgh says, "Little Ed Maunton, a trapper and aerial game observer for the Conservation Department, also a dangerous man with a rifle or an airplane."*

(*One Man's Pleasure,* by Hugh Fosburgh; William Morrow and Company, 1960.)

November 12th.

This morning early, Maunton and I headed for Peaked Mountain with the announced intention of waylaying a bear.

Going down Splitrock, there were more ducks and of greater variety than I have ever seen on that pond—ruddies, blacks, buffleheads, hooded mergansers, wood ducks and grebes—perhaps seventy-five in all. (When we returned that evening, most of them had moved out.)

It was a clear, sunny, too-warm day and not much of anything was stirring. I hunted up the ravine under Peaked, seeing few signs of deer and none whatever of bears, despite the fact that this is usually a favorite beechnut ground. From there I worked up the side of the mountain through rugged country to the first notch that commands a fine view of the sheer ledges and the mountainside, and presently spotted two deer below me. It took some time to determine that one of these was a small buck—a crotch-horn, I think—and some more time to decide what to do about it, which was nothing. Then Maunton's rifle went off, just once.

I was in a quandary. Maunton is lucky—when he shoots, he usually, for some nonsensical reason, gets what he's aiming at. I have known him to fail only once. Furthermore, when he shoots something, it is always in the most inaccessible place that he can discover for my personal inconvenience, and it has got to the point that he takes for granted, and counts heavily upon, my strong back and obliging personality. So, while eating my lunch, I seriously considered ignoring the shot and heading quickly for another area where a man couldn't possibly hear any calls for assistance that might be forthcoming; but curiosity overcame my prudence, and I went to discover what outrage he had perpetrated.

I was prepared to assist in hauling out a buck, even a very large buck. Or even a small bear. I was not prepared, mentally or physically, to have any part of a very large bear—which is precisely the thing with which I was confronted, nor did Maunton's smug satisfaction make me feel any better about it. ("I said I was going to kill a bear, didn't I?")

His story, at the time, was that he had been coming up through a steep narrow ravine with many boulders and rocky ledges along one side, and had stopped to lean against a large maple tree while he smoked and surveyed the ravine ahead. Seeing what appeared to be bear troughs in the beech leaves up there, he moved up to investigate. They *were* bear troughs, so he started looking for the responsible party, and saw it. It was crawling out of the rocks not twenty feet from the tree he had been leaning against. (Whether it had been asleep or hiding in there, we were unable to determine.) Anyway, he broke the bear's neck with one shot, the bear rolled over with its feet in the air, and Maunton sat down, with the greatest confidence, to await my arrival. That was his story at the time. The theme he is presently circulating to anybody fool enough to listen is that he just glimpsed the bear two hundred yards away, running through the brush, and had merely a snap shot, and furthermore, he says, he carried the bear almost to Splitrock before I made a belated attempt to assist him.

For the record, nobody carried that bear one inch and nobody but six mules and a boy would have had the stupidity to try. We dragged it a mile and a quarter through swamps, blow-downs, and rocks, to Splitrock, and for my share in this enterprise I expect, and intend to get, two hindquarters, the loins, and the saddle. Maunton can have the rest, including the fat, and should be well satisfied.

November 16th.

Despite a painful right knee—a tricky prop that occasionally gives out on me—I went with Maunton to the Splitrock country.

The deer there had the beech grounds thoroughly dug up during the night and had then moved somewhere else, so when I encountered Maunton at noon, neither of us had seen anything. We separated again and tried to locate them.

There is a high rocky knob between Splitrock and Frank Pond which is a fine place for bucks to lie—many terraced ledges and open grassy places, and spruce thickets where the deer can hide and dodge. I went there and was immediately certain that I had come to the right place—it was tracked up like a pigpen and there were fresh buck rubs everywhere.

Twenty minutes later I saw a buck, only I didn't know for sure that it was a buck. He was a hundred yards ahead of me, a little higher up than I, and facing away. Then he smelled me, whirled about, and let out a great whistle. One jump downwind would have taken him out of my sight but like almost every buck, he wouldn't go downwind on a bet. Instead he quartered toward me, running like sixty and going between me and Frank Pond, which was directly below. On two good legs I could have cut down there and intercepted him and at least got a close-up running shot, but all I could do was hobble. For some reason he stopped in a thicket right by the shore of the pond, out of sight, so I sat down and waited for his next move. This was some time in coming—a minute perhaps—then he burst out and went catapulting along the lake shore, too fast and far away to try a shot to kill, so I put a bullet in front of him, thinking it might confuse him into stopping again, but it only strengthened his determination to get out of there.

I massaged my knee for an hour and crawled home.

November 18th.

This has been the poorest weather for deer-hunting that I ever remember. The season has been on now for twenty-three days—eighteen of these have been rainy, with high temperatures and constant fog. There has been almost no frost and a total lack of snow. As a consequence the deer have done a minimum of moving and feeding, and what they have done has been mostly at night, or late in the afternoon. In the daytime I believe they frequent the swamps to keep cool.

In weather like this, few animals, except the water animals—mink, beaver, otter and muskrat—seem to be at all active. Nothing whatever has monkeyed around my traps, which I took up yesterday. This may very well reflect on my prowess as a trapper, but it seems strange that nothing got interested in the two-porcupine set—they are there just as I left them on October 25th and not even a weasel has touched them. It may be that there are enough dead deer and cleanings of bucks around the woods to keep all the predators glutted and happy, but I doubt it. I'm sure the sick weather accounts for it.

November 19th.

It cleared and turned cold last night, and today was an interesting and lovely day in the woods. Maunton leaves tomorrow so he was determined to get a buck.

We decided to try for the enormous animal that has been frequenting the sawmill hill for several years, so at seven o'clock we were down there. Standing in the middle of the road, looking at us, was the buck. In the half-light, Maunton refused to shoot—he couldn't be sure, he said, and anyway he was damned if he'd kill a deer that way. The buck loped up onto the hill and we sat there till it got light enough to shoot. Then he started around one side of the hill and I went around the other.

Almost immediately I became entangled with two does and a small buck that were feeding on beechnuts. I couldn't get by without alerting them; so, stymied, I waited there for something to happen. It did—Maunton shot once, on the other side of the hill, and right away a big buck came careening into sight and vanished in the swamp. The three deer I had been watching scampered off.

I was certain Maunton hadn't shot at the big buck. It was equally certain that he had killed something. I was determined not to make an ass of myself again by rushing pellmell to his assistance. So I sat there for a good hour, admiring the scenery and the fine weather—enough time and more for any moron to gut a deer and drag it two miles—and then I sauntered over.

I found the little oaf reclining on his butt, smoking his pipe, and admiring a fine ten-point buck, not the monster we were after, but a lean, rutting ridge-runner of a buck that is going to make tough chewing indeed. He had been, said Maunton, prepared to sit it out on these terms if it took me all day to get there. He had been sure, he said, that sooner or later my belief in the buddy system would get me there to help him, and he didn't care at all whether it was sooner or later. We had some words about reciprocity in such matters, and dragged the buck out.

After breakfast, I started off to hunt in the vicinity of Splitrock. Two hundred yards from the clearing, I came on something that I had been half-expecting to encounter since the end of October—the dead doe which we were sure one of the guests had shot. It was lying some twenty feet from the trail, shot twice, and the slob who killed it had done his best to conceal it with leaves and branches. A weasel had been eating on it and bitten part of its white tail off, leaving it where I could see it.

Under way again, I was in such a state of frustrated anger that I walked within fifty feet of a buck and a doe, standing in plain sight, and didn't see them until they crashed off. They headed toward the Middle Beaver swamp, not very fast, and I believe I could have got another crack at them but I wasn't in the mood to try.

Brune and Maunton met me at Splitrock and we paddled down to the hunting camp for lunch. At this particular time, after two rum drinks and with Brune as a witness, Maunton stated that he would remain in the vicinity for the rest of the afternoon and come immediately to my assistance at the sound of a shot. With this assurance, I took off.

I suppose everyone who has hunted a certain area of country over a long period of time has a particular place, or maybe two or three places, where he feels especially confident of seeing a buck. If he really wants to get one he goes to such a place.

Although I wasn't particularly anxious to shoot one—I wanted to wait for a tracking snow—I headed for the west side of Splitrock ridge, which is such a place for me. This side of the ridge has everything that beguiles a deer—fine food in the way of beechnuts, ferns and browse; fine lying and standing around places among the steep ledges and promontories and hillocks; easy escape into the evergreen swamp that lies at the bottom. Deer are always there at this time of year and I don't remember ever failing to see some.

The leaves were noisy so I could move only when the wind rose up to deaden the sound. I worked around the side of the ridge, low enough to see to the edge of the swamp, and sat down to smoke a cigarette and watch. Nothing happened for some time, then a huge doe that had been lying hidden sprang up with a snort, took three jumps and stopped out of sight. (Although the wind was in my favor, I imagine a stray gust had brought her a whiff of me.) She stood there, silent and apparently perplexed, for at least five minutes. Then another stray gust must have confirmed her suspicion, because she started blowing again—great deep snorts—at spaced intervals, then presently I heard her crashing down toward the swamp, then she came into sight in an open place down there, and the last I saw was her waving white tail.

Then I heard another deer going off—I thought surely it would be a buck—but when it leaped through the open space it was another outsize doe. It followed as the first had gone, then a third deer took off—it was as if they were running a handicap and being started by a referee—and I was certain this one was going to have horns. It didn't—another enormous mother shot through the open place.

I sat there pondering what these fat-bottomed, bosomy females—I have never seen three bigger does in my life—would have in common. I had just concluded that I had probably broken up a chapter meeting of the local D.A.R., when I saw another deer down there, going fast.

It didn't take the route of the others and it didn't go through the open place, so all I saw was a waving tail and enough of a rear end to let me know that this animal was at least as big as the other three.

I became avidly interested in this fourth deer and wanted nothing but to get another and better look at it.

To follow their trail and attempt to get up on them in that swamp would have been fruitless. They would have stopped in thick cover and be watching their back track, and the buck (if that last deer was a buck) would most surely have fixed things so that the does were between him and danger.

Fosburgh, alias D. Boone, did some profound and astute reasoning. He figured that in an hour or so, if nothing further happened to alarm them, the deer would quiet down and go about their normal business. At that time it would be near sundown and at sundown the normal business of deer is to move toward the feeding grounds. Where would they feed? They would come out of the swamp and back to the ridge. Where, precisely, would they come out of the swamp?

I concluded they would come out at a place we used to call "the corner drugstore" but which we have renamed "Frankie's Bones." (My Uncle Frankie, who was the most enthusiastic deer hunter I ever knew, first named this place "the corner drugstore," because deer, especially the bucks, were always hanging around there. It was not only his favorite place to hunt, it was the place, he always told us, that he loved best in the world; so when he died we put his ashes there, and renamed it.)

It is, indeed, a lovely quiet place.

You sit high up in the rocks on the ridge-side and look down on a long beaver meadow of bear grass. Through the meadow winds a deep slow-moving stream, lined with a thick tangle of alders, and beyond the meadow, on the far side, is what we call the "old burn"—acres and acres of rolling ground covered with blueberry bushes and occasional clumps of stunted spruce and gnarled old pines that somehow survived the fire of a century ago.

At one time or another, sitting at Frankie's Bones, I have seen just about every species of Adirondack wildlife, and deer by the dozen.

Today, I was quite sure my four deer would appear there. Specifically, I thought they would come through the alders that line the stream because, having been alerted once, I presumed they would move in the thickest possible cover to get back on the ridge.

It took me a good hour, moving as quietly as possible, to get there, so it was about thirty minutes before sundown when I arrived. I picked the spot on top of the cliff that gave me the best view down into the alders and began the vigil.

There wasn't a dull moment. First, a small deer appeared on the ridge above, picked its way down and went out of sight to my right.

A red fox—as glossy and red as a fox can be—appeared way over in the burn, trotted into the alders, crossed the stream on an old beaver dam, and passed twenty feet from me, climbing up on the ridge. It was going someplace with quiet determination.

Another deer appeared briefly, way down in the beaver meadow.

And then one of my does—I was sure of it—walked into sight; but she wasn't in the alders, she was in the old burn way out beyond them. She was moving across the hillside, in sight one moment, hidden the next. Once she looked back, and I began to get excited.

She had moved maybe seventy-five yards across the hillside when matron number two appeared, exactly where number one had come, and promenaded sedately after her.

I was trying to watch three things at once—the two does and the place where the third would appear if it followed the others—and it wasn't easy or good for the state of my nerves, which were rapidly going to pot.

Number three came out of the thicket at the proper place and at the appointed interval—just seventy-five yards behind number two—but number four had no knowledge of, or interest in, his proper place in the parade. The first I saw of him were his gleaming white horns about one foot behind the upraised tail of his female associate, then the rest of him came into view, and he was a dandy. He followed behind, almost nudging her, as if she had him on a leash.

It was now a question of getting a shot at him before I had a helpless case of buck fever, so I watched the first does to see if the parade route might take him through an opening where I could stop him and get a shot. (I wasn't going to shoot at that distance unless I could first make him stand.)

Both does passed through a little clearing, about 250 yards away, directly opposite. I would try for him there.

I waited in a state of suspense until the Judas doe led him into the opening, then I yelled "Whoa"—as sharply and as loud as I could. He whoaed all right and stood there, baffled. I aimed for the top of his shoulder and at the shot he slammed over and never moved again.

I sat there, tense and suspicious that he might get up, then finally I relaxed and lived it all over again, and began to feel pleased and more than a little conceited, and wished that Maunton had been there to see that shot, and thought that old Uncle Frankie would have loved every second of it, and maybe did.

Then I worked down off the ridge and got myself through the alders and across the stream, and went out to him on the burn, and he was just as fine and exciting as he had looked to be as he shambled across the hillside, except he was dead.

November 20th.

It was dusk yesterday afternoon by the time I had dressed-out and hung up the buck. I started for home, with no particular effort to be quiet, and on the ridge at the head of Middle Beaver Pond I flushed what appeared to be a large doe. I stopped to watch until it was out of sight, then started again, and instantly recoiled—there was a sock-walloper buck not twenty feet away, standing broadside in the open, looking at me. It had its head down, low to the ground, and it seemed to be peering at me, sizing me up in a quiet, deadly way. Even in the almost-total dark his great horns stood out gleaming. He hulked there like a sullen bull.

I will admit to cocking my rifle, just in case. I was as close to that animal as I wanted to be.

I don't know how long we looked at each other—probably not fifteen seconds—then he let out one blood-chilling whistle and pounded downhill into the swamp.

I suppose my nervousness at this incident was ridiculous. I know of no authenticated record of a wild unwounded buck attacking a man, but it surprises me that there are no such records. Bucks in captivity are notorious man-killers during the rut, and I don't see why the maniacal sex-induced urge which prompts them to do this in a pen shouldn't occasionally induce them to attack a man in the wild.

Of one thing I am sure—at certain times during the rut, certain bucks, maybe all bucks, get so insensate with lust that they have no other senses at all. Once, bear-hunting on Peaked Mountain in mid-November, I encountered such an animal.

I was going through a narrow ravine when a doe came running

down it, directly toward me. She was the most desperate animal I have ever seen—utterly exhausted, with her flanks heaving and her tongue hanging out. She must have been running for miles. She didn't see me until she almost ran me down, then she stopped, braced her feet wide to keep from falling, and looked at me as if I were the last straw about to be loaded on her back. Then she heard the buck coming behind her and staggered up the side of the ravine.

He came along on her track with his head down, sniffing like a hound dog. He too almost ran me down, then he braked to a halt and looked at me with stupid eyes, and did the damnedest thing I ever saw a deer do—he turned his back on me and forgot I was there. If I had been fool enough to try I could have jumped on his back or tackled him by the hind legs. He stood there, looking around and sniffing for the doe, long enough for me to tell that he was as thin and bony as any buck could be and probably as old. His horns were like billy clubs—two massive spikes with rough knobs, instead of tines, at the top. He stood there until he located the doe up on the side of the ravine, then he took after her like a grim fury.

I don't like to think what might have happened if I had tried to interfere with his purpose. Probably nothing, but I wasn't about to try.

It was an hour after total dark when I reached the clearing last night, and I was greeted by the sound of Maunton, hooting like a barred owl from the front porch. This ridiculous noise brought to a boil a resentment that had been simmering inside me for some time —Maunton had been conspicuous by his absence when I needed him the most, and after he had faithfully promised to come. By the time I reached the house I was in no mood to prevaricate—I told him that if his definition of mutual assistance was to sleep under my roof, eat my food, drink my liquor—which he was at that moment doing—and then to stand on the porch and hoot like a fool owl, then he could make himself another attachment.

He was all injured innocence. He hadn't heard the shot, he said, really he hadn't. (Brune, who happened to be there also, and who happened to be drinking my liquor at Maunton's invitation, and who obviously was in some sort of debt to Maunton, attested to the truth of this palpable lie.) This confirmation bloated Maunton with such smugness that he resembled a liverish toad. He is a little pipsqueak of a thing—scarcely big enough to climb out of a flowerpot—so I refrained from hurting him. Brune has no knowledge whatever of the truth, which isn't really his fault, so I didn't molest him either. I just quietly put some kerosene in their vodka bottle and got out another for myself.

It had been a long day.

November 23rd.

Yesterday, hobnobbing with Kelly in his tent, he told me that a friend of his had wounded a big buck the day before, had followed it into the Mink outlet swamp, and there given up the chase. The buck wasn't badly hit, the man told Kelly. (That's what almost everybody says when they hit and lose a deer, probably because they hope it's true and want to believe it, but in almost every case in my experience, it isn't true at all—any rifle or shotgun-slug wound that isn't a mere crease-shot is a terrible thing which few deer survive.)

Anyway I told Kelly I'd have a look for it.

It was important to get my own buck back to camp before the bears got at it, so it was almost two thirty when I arrived at the general area where the hunter had abandoned his buck. I was lucky—almost immediately I found a clot of blood where the deer had stopped for a while, and there were enough tracks leaving that place to indicate the general direction he was headed—which was toward a much bigger, almost impenetrable swamp about a quarter of a mile away.

After that, there was no more blood that I could see, and so many different tracks that it was impossible to follow the one I was after; so I gave up trying to trail it and began hunting very slowly toward the big swamp.

Presently I saw a buck lying down and, on the instant, concluded it was the hurt one. I came within one finger twitch of shooting it, and wish to God, now, that I had. But I got to thinking—maybe this wasn't the deer. The more I thought about it, and watched it, the more doubtful it seemed. This buck was lying out in the open and a wounded deer usually lies in the thickest cover he can find. The hunter had said he had hit a big buck and there was nothing big about this one—he was smaller than average with pinched little horns. And he was lying there quietly, like any deer taking a siesta. (Usually a wounded deer's head will sway from side to side and up and down, as he fights the pain.)

I worked to a place, about twenty-five yards from him, where I could see his whole body. It was clean of blood so far as I could tell.

I had now convinced myself that it wasn't the wounded buck. To make absolutely certain, I wanted to see him on his feet so, with this in mind, I tossed a stick into the thicket in front of him. It was a mistake—he caught the movement of my arm, heaved up, took one three-legged stumbling lunge, and was out of sight. I knew, then and there, I would never see him again.

I never did. After I had looked at his bed (it appeared from the blood smear that he had been shot square in the right hip), I followed his track to where it went into the big swamp. It was dusk then and beginning to snow, so I went home.

I was back at daylight this morning. There were eight inches of snow by that time, with more coming down, so it was hopeless from the start; but I criss-crossed the swamp all morning before I gave up, leaving one more deer to slow death and the carrion eaters.

This buck was the fourth, that I have heard of or know about, to be hit and escape, in this general area, since the opening of the season. There are undoubtedly twice as many more that I don't know of, which would indicate that about as many deer have escaped as have been carried out of the woods. It is appalling and disgusting, but true.

I do some trapping, so perhaps I am not a proper person to inveigh against the careless and needless cruelty inflicted by deer hunters, and perhaps it wouldn't do any good anyway. Certain it is that no amount of inveighing is going to influence the thousands of would-be butchers who take to the woods with one thought in mind—butcher something. These goons take sound shots, snap shots, running shots, long shots—any kind of shot at almost anything they see so long as there is the barest possibility of inflicting injury on it—and nothing is going to stop them.

There is another disheartening and, so far as I can see, insoluble aspect to this business—every hunter starts out as a neophyte and there is only one way to progress from this stage and that is by experience—plenty of it—and along the way every best-intentioned would-be hunter in the world is going to learn the hard way—by grisly mistakes.

So as long as there is deer-hunting there is going to be horrible cruelty inflicted.

But I think certain things could be done that would eliminate much of it.

For one thing, there could be education and legislation about the weapons that should be used. Take, for instance, the measly little .30 caliber army carbine that was turned out during World War II. (Half a dozen local citizens use these for deer.) It shoots a bullet that was never intended for deer and should never be used on them. They should be outlawed for such purposes.

Take also the use of shotguns, with either slugs or buckshot. (I won't go into the human-safety factor, which in some states and in some areas of this state has prompted legislation which forbids hunters to shoot deer with anything but shotguns, except to say that I think the reasoning behind it is usually fallacious.) Except in the hands of the very few hunters who know when to shoot and, more important, when *not* to shoot, shotguns will maim half a dozen deer for every one they kill cleanly. Buckshot, praise be, is outlawed in this area but slugs are bad enough—particularly since it is mostly gunners who don't know any better that use them. If these guns can't be outlawed, at least the sporting magazines and clubs could educate the people about them.

Then there are the auto-loading or semi-automatic rifles. I suppose there is nothing inherently bad about them; it is just that a man who selects one to shoot deer with—on the theory that the more lead a rifle can spray around the woods the more effective it is—doesn't know the first thing about deer-hunting and will do just that: spray lead, often with devastating but seldom with effective results. I don't know a single good hunter who uses one. They too should be outlawed.

The figures may not prove anything, but in the years I have been hunting, five men have been killed or seriously wounded in the forty-odd square miles to the south of us, and in every case the weapon involved was either a shotgun or a semi-automatic. I suspect that the wounded-deer toll statistics would be similar, and for the same reasons: ignorance and carelessness.

I won't go extensively into what *does* constitute a good deer rifle —there are many of them that fire effective hard-hitting bullets, and each one is good for certain people under certain conditions. For me, here, there is nothing better than the thirty-thirty I have been using for twenty-nine years.

I believe there is another way that this useless maiming of wild game can be reduced and that is to downgrade the notion that shooting something is sport. The sport is in the hunting, and when the shooting starts it is a dead-serious business that shouldn't be taken lightly. But it often is—I know a man who kills a buck every year but I have never known him to kill one cleanly; he is always shooting the legs out from under them, or paunching them, or shooting them in the rear end, but so long as he gets them eventually he doesn't seem to care. A great many hunters are that way—they remember and talk about the fantastic, miraculous, stupendous shots they've made, and they forget, or don't talk about, the shots that were almost fantastic and miraculous and stupendous, but not quite, because the animal got away with some lead in it.

The essence of being a really good hunter is, paradoxically, to love the particular species of game you're after and to have enormous respect and consideration for it; and the practical application of this essence is knowing when to shoot and when not to shoot. You shoot to kill, and when you're not sure you can kill, you don't shoot.

To me, the perfect way to kill a deer is to trail it to its bed and come upon it lying down twenty-five yards away, or maybe less; then you shoot it in such a way that it never knows you were there, or what happened to it. When you've done that, you've hunted well and made a perfect shot and done more to be pleased about than all the fantastic shots, put together, that you ever made in your life.

WILDERNESS

BY ALDO LEOPOLD

Aldo Leopold (1887–1948) was a gifted writer, a noted naturalist and a militant conservationist. As a boy he hunted, fished and roamed the outdoors in his native Iowa. After graduation from the Yale Forestry School he joined the U. S. Forestry Service and eventually became Chief of Operations in the Arizona-New Mexico District. He helped establish basic policies of management for all the national forests. At thirty-seven he became Associate Director of the U. S. Forest Products Laboratory at Madison, Wisconsin, and after four years there turned to the field of wildlife management, in which he made many surveys of wildlife population and problems. In 1933 the chair of Game Management was created for him at the University of Wisconsin and he was still at that post when, at the age of sixty-one, he died while helping fight a grass fire on a neighbor's farm. He wrote hundreds of articles but only a few books. His last book, A Sand County Almanac, *was compiled by him but published after his death. It is now a classic. This selection from it illustrates his trenchant style as a writer and his dedication as a naturalist and conservationist.*

(*A Sand County Almanac*, by Aldo Leopold; Oxford University Press, 1949.)

Wilderness is the raw material out of which man has hammered the artifact called civilization.

Wilderness was never a homogeneous raw material. It was very diverse, and the resulting artifacts are very diverse. These differences in the end-product are known as cultures. The rich diversity of the world's cultures reflects a corresponding diversity in the wilds that gave them birth.

For the first time in the history of the human species, two changes are now impending. One is the exhaustion of wilderness in the more habitable portions of the globe. The other is the world-wide hybridization of cultures through modern transport and industrialization. Neither can be prevented, and perhaps should not be, but the question arises whether, by some slight amelioration of the impending changes, certain values can be preserved that would otherwise be lost.

To the laborer in the sweat of his labor, the raw stuff on his anvil is an adversary to be conquered. So was wilderness an adversary to the pioneer.

But to the laborer in repose, able for the moment to cast a philosophical eye on his world, that same raw stuff is something to be loved and cherished, because it gives definition and meaning to his life. This is a plea for the preservation of some tag-ends of wilderness, as museum pieces, for the edification of those who may one day wish to see, feel, or study the origins of their cultural inheritance.

The Remnants

Many of the diverse wildernesses out of which we have hammered America are already gone; hence in any practical program the unit areas to be preserved must vary greatly in size and in degree of wildness.

No living man will see again the long-grass prairie, where a sea of prairie flowers lapped at the stirrups of the pioneer. We shall do well to find a forty here and there on which the prairie plants can be kept alive as species. There were a hundred such plants, many of exceptional beauty. Most of them are quite unknown to those who have inherited their domain.

But the short-grass prairie, where Cabeza de Vaca saw the horizon under the bellies of the buffalo, is still extant in a few spots of 10,000-acre size, albeit severely chewed up by sheep, cattle, and dry-farmers. If the forty-niners are worth commemorating on the walls of state capitals, is not the scene of their mighty hegira worth commemorating in several national prairie reservations?

Of the coastal prairie there is one block in Florida, and one in Texas, but oil wells, onion fields, and citrus groves are closing in, armed to the teeth with drills and bulldozers. It is last call.

No living man will see again the virgin pineries of the Lake States, or the flatwoods of the coastal plain, or the giant hardwoods; of these, samples of a few acres each will have to suffice. But there are still several blocks of maple-hemlock of thousand-acre size; there are similar blocks of Appalachian hardwoods, of southern hardwood swamp, of cypress swamp, and of Adirondack spruce. Few of these tag-ends are secure from prospective cuttings, and fewer still from prospective tourist roads.

One of the fastest-shrinking categories of wilderness is coastlines. Cottages and tourist roads have all but annihilated wild coasts on both oceans, and Lake Superior is now losing the last large remnant of wild shoreline on the Great Lakes. No single kind of wilderness is more intimately interwoven with history, and none nearer the point of complete disappearance.

In all of North America east of the Rockies, there is only one large area formally reserved as a wilderness: the Quetico-Superior International Park in Minnesota and Ontario. This magnificent block of canoe-country, a mosaic of lakes and rivers, lies mostly in Canada, and can be about as large as Canada chooses to make it, but its integrity is threatened by two recent developments: the growth of fishing resorts served by pontoon-equipped airplanes, and a jurisdictional dispute whether the Minnesota end of the area shall be all National Forest, or partly State Forest. The whole region is in danger of power impoundments, and this regrettable cleavage among proponents of wilderness may end in giving power the whip-hand.

In the Rocky Mountain states, a score of areas in the National Forests, varying in size from a hundred thousand to half a million acres, are withdrawn as wilderness, and closed to roads, hotels, and other inimical uses. In the National Parks the same principle is recognized, but no specific boundaries are delimited. Collectively, these federal areas are the backbone of the wilderness program, but they are not so secure as the paper record might lead one to believe. Local pressures for new tourist roads knock off a chip here and a slab there. There is perennial pressure for extension of roads for forest-fire control, and these, by slow degrees, become public highways. Idle CCC camps presented a widespread temptation to build new and often needless roads. Lumber shortages during the war gave the impetus of military necessity to many road extensions, legitimate and otherwise. At the present moment, ski-tows and ski-hotels are being promoted in many mountain areas, often without regard to their prior designation as wilderness.

One of the most insidious invasions of wilderness is via predator control. It works thus: wolves and lions are cleaned out of a wilderness area in the interest of big-game management. The big-game herds (usually deer or elk) then increase to the point of over-browsing the range. Hunters must then be encouraged to harvest the surplus, but modern hunters refuse to operate far from a car; hence a road must be built to provide access to the surplus game. Again and again, wilderness areas have been split by this process, but it still continues.

The Rocky Mountain system of wilderness areas covers a wide gamut of forest types, from the juniper breaks of the Southwest to the 'illimitable woods where rolls the Oregon.' It is lacking, however, in desert areas, probably because of that under-aged brand of esthetics which limits the definition of 'scenery' to lakes and pine trees.

In Canada and Alaska there are still large expanses of virgin country

> Where nameless men by nameless rivers wander
> and in strange valleys die strange deaths alone.

A representative series of these areas can, and should, be kept. Many are of negligible or negative value for economic use. It will be contended, of course, that no deliberate planning to this end is necessary; that adequate areas will survive anyhow. All recent history belies so comforting an assumption. Even if wild spots do survive, what of their fauna? The woodland caribou, the several races of mountain sheep, the pure form of woods buffalo, the barren ground grizzly, the freshwater seals, and the whales are even now threatened. Of what use are wild areas destitute of their distinctive faunas? The recently organized Arctic Institute has embarked on the industrialization of the Arctic wastes, with excellent chances of enough success to ruin them as wilderness. It is last call, even in the Far North.

To what extent Canada and Alaska will be able to see and grasp their opportunities is anybody's guess. Pioneers usually scoff at any effort to perpetuate pioneering.

Wilderness for Recreation

Physical combat for the means of subsistence was, for unnumbered centuries, an economic fact. When it disappeared as such, a sound instinct led us to preserve it in the form of athletic sports and games.

Physical combat between men and beasts was, in like manner, an economic fact, now preserved as hunting and fishing for sport.

Public wilderness areas are, first of all, a means of perpetuating, in sport form, the more virile and primitive skills in pioneering travel and subsistence.

Some of these skills are of generalized distribution; the details have been adapted to the American scene, but the skill is world-wide. Hunting, fishing, and foot travel by pack are examples.

Two of them, however, are as American as a hickory tree; they have been copied elsewhere, but they were developed to their full perfection only on this continent. One of these is canoe travel, and the other is travel by pack-train. Both are shrinking rapidly. Your Hudson Bay Indian now has a put-put, and your mountaineer a Ford. If I had to make a living by canoe or packhorse, I should likely do likewise, for both are grueling labor. But we who seek wilderness travel for sport are foiled when we are forced to compete with mechanized substitutes. It is footless to execute a portage to the tune of motor launches, or to turn out your bell-mare in the pasture of a summer hotel. It is better to stay home.

Wilderness areas are first of all a series of sanctuaries for the primitive arts of wilderness travel, especially canoeing and packing.

I suppose some will wish to debate whether it is important to keep these primitive arts alive. I shall not debate it. Either you know it in your bones, or you are very, very old.

European hunting and fishing are largely devoid of the thing that wilderness areas might be the means of preserving in this country. Europeans do not camp, cook, or do their own work in the woods if they can avoid doing so. Work chores are delegated to beaters and servants, and a hunt carries the atmosphere of a picnic, rather than of pioneering. The test of skill is confined largely to the actual taking of game or fish.

There are those who decry wilderness sports as 'undemocratic' because the recreational carrying capacity of a wilderness is small, as compared with a golf links or a tourist camp. The basic error in such argument is that it applies the philosophy of mass-production to what is intended to counteract mass-production. The value of recreation is not a matter of ciphers. Recreation is valuable in proportion to the intensity of its experiences, and to the degree to which it *differs from* and *contrasts with* workaday life. By these criteria, mechanized outings are at best a milk-and-water affair.

Mechanized recreation already has seized nine-tenths of the woods and mountains; a decent respect for minorities should dedicate the other tenth to wilderness.

Wilderness for Science

The most important characteristic of an organism is that capacity for internal self-renewal known as health.

There are two organisms whose processes of self-renewal have been subjected to human interference and control. One of these is man himself (medicine and public health). The other is land (agriculture and conservation).

The effort to control the health of land has not been very successful. It is now generally understood that when soil loses fertility, or washes away faster than it forms, and when water systems exhibit abnormal floods and shortages, the land is sick.

Other derangements are known as facts, but are not yet thought of as symptoms of land sickness. The disappearance of plants and animal species without visible cause, despite efforts to protect them, and the irruption of others as pests despite efforts to control them, must, in the absence of simpler explanations, be regarded as symptoms of sickness in the land organism. Both are occurring too frequently to be dismissed as normal evolutionary events.

The status of thought on these ailments of the land is reflected in the fact that our treatments for them are still prevailing local. Thus when a soil loses fertility we pour on fertilizer, or at best alter its tame flora and fauna, without considering the fact that its wild flora and fauna, which built the soil to begin with, may likewise be important to its maintenance. It was recently discovered, for example, that good tobacco crops depend, for some unknown reason, on the preconditioning of the soil by wild ragweed. It does not occur to us that such unexpected chains of dependency may have wide prevalence in nature.

When prairie dogs, ground squirrels, or mice increase to pest levels we poison them, but we do not look beyond the animal to find the cause of the irruption. We assume that animal troubles must have animal causes. The latest scientific evidence points to derangements of the *plant* community as the real seat of rodent irruptions, but few explorations of this clue are being made.

Many forest plantations are producing one-log or two-log trees on soil which originally grew three-log and four-log trees. Why? Thinking foresters know that the cause probably lies not in the trees, but in the micro-flora of the soil, and that it may take more years to restore the soil flora than it took to destroy it.

Many conservation treatments are obviously superficial. Flood-control dams have no relation to the cause of floods. Check dams and terraces do not touch the cause of erosion. Refuges and hatcheries to maintain the supply of game and fish do not explain why the supply fails to maintain itself.

In general, the trend of the evidence indicates that in land, just as in the human body, the symptoms may lie in one organ and the cause in another. The practices we now call conservation are, to a large extent, local alleviations of biotic pain. They are necessary, but they must not be confused with cures. The art of land doctoring is being practiced with vigor, but the science of land health is yet to be born.

A science of land health needs, first of all, a base datum of normality, a picture of how healthy land maintains itself as an organism.

We have two available norms. One is found where land physiology remains largely normal despite centuries of human occupation. I know of only one such place: north-eastern Europe. It is not likely that we shall fail to study it.

The other and most perfect norm is wilderness. Paleontology offers abundant evidence that wilderness maintained itself for immensely long periods; that its component species were rarely lost, neither did they get out of hand; that weather and water built soil as fast or faster than it was carried away. Wilderness, then, assumes unexpected importance as a laboratory for the study of land-health.

One cannot study the physiology of Montana in the Amazon; each biotic province needs its own wilderness for comparative studies of used and unused land. It is of course too late to salvage more than a lopsided system of wilderness study areas, and most of these remnants are far too small to retain their normality in all respects. Even the National Parks, which run up to a million acres each in size, have not been large enough to retain their natural predators, or to exclude animal diseases carried by livestock. Thus the Yellowstone has lost its wolves and cougars, with the result that elk are ruining the flora, particularly on the winter range. At the same time the grizzly bear and the mountain sheep are shrinking, the latter by reason of disease.

While even the largest wilderness areas become partially deranged, it required only a few wild acres for J. E. Weaver to discover why the prairie flora is more drouth-resistant than the agronomic flora which has supplanted it. Weaver found that the prairie species practice 'team work' underground by distributing their root-systems to cover all levels, whereas the species comprising the agronomic rotation overdraw one level and neglect another, thus building up cumulative deficits. An important agronomic principle emerged from Weaver's researches.

Again, it required only a few wild acres for Togrediak to discover why pines on old fields never achieve the size or wind-firmness of pines on uncleared forest soils. In the latter case, the roots follow old root channels, and thus strike deeper.

In many cases we literally do not know how good a performance to expect of healthy land unless we have a wild area for comparison with sick ones. Thus most of the early travelers in the Southwest describe the mountain rivers as originally clear, but a doubt remains, for they may, by accident, have seen them at favorable seasons. Erosion engineers had no base datum until it was discovered that exactly similar rivers in the Sierra Madre of Chihuahua, never grazed or used for fear of Indians, show at their worst a milky hue, not too cloudy for a trout fly. Moss grows to the water's edge on their banks. Most of the corresponding rivers in Arizona and New Mexico are ribbons of boulders, mossless, soil-less, and all but treeless. The preservation and study of the Sierra Madre wilderness, by an international experiment station, as a norm for the cure of sick land on both sides of the border, would be a good-neighbor enterprise well worthy of consideration.

In short all available wild areas, large or small, are likely to have value as norms for land science. Recreation is not their only, or even their principal, utility.

Wilderness for Wildlife

The National Parks do not suffice as a means of perpetuating the larger carnivores; witness the precarious status of the grizzly bear, and the fact that the park system is already wolfless. Neither do they suffice for mountain sheep; most sheep herds are shrinking.

The reasons for this are clear in some cases and obscure in others. The parks are certainly too small for such a far-ranging species as the wolf. Many animal species, for reasons unknown, do not seem to thrive as detached islands of population.

The most feasible way to enlarge the area available for wilderness fauna is for the wilder parts of the National Forests, which usually surround the Parks, to function as parks in respect of threatened species. That they have not so functioned is tragically illustrated in the case of the grizzly bear.

In 1909, when I first saw the West, there were grizzlies in every major mountain mass, but you could travel for months without meeting a conservation officer. Today there is some kind of conservation officer 'behind every bush,' yet as wildlife bureaus grow, our most magnificent mammal retreats steadily toward the Canadian border. Of the 6000 grizzlies officially reported as remaining in areas owned by the United States, 5000 are in Alaska. Only five states have any at all. There seems to be a tacit assumption that if grizzlies survive in Canada and Alaska, that is good enough. It is not good enough for me. The Alaskan bears are a distinct species. Relegating grizzlies to Alaska is about like relegating happiness to heaven; one may never get there.

Saving the grizzly requires a series of large areas from which roads and livestock are excluded, or in which livestock damage is compensated. Buying out scattered livestock ranches is the only way to create such areas, but despite large authority to buy and exchange lands, the conservation bureaus have accomplished virtually nothing toward this end. The Forest Service has, I am told, established one grizzly range in Montana, but I know of a mountain range in Utah in which the Forest Service actually promoted a sheep industry, despite the fact that it harbored the sole remnant of grizzlies in that state.

Permanent grizzly ranges and permanent wilderness areas are of course two names for one problem. Enthusiasm about either requires a long view of conservation, and a historical perspective. Only those able to see the pageant of evolution can be expected to value its theater, the wilderness, or its outstanding achievement, the grizzly. But if education really educates, there will, in time, be more and more citizens who understand that relics of the Old West add meaning and value to the new. Youth yet unborn will pole up the Missouri with Lewis and Clark, or climb the Sierras with James Capen Adams, and each generation in turn will ask: Where is the big white bear? It will be a sorry answer to say he went under while conservationists weren't looking.

Defenders of Wilderness

Wilderness is a resource which can shrink but not grow. Invasions can be arrested or modified in a manner to keep an area usable either for recreation, or for science, or for wildlife, but the creation of new wilderness in the full sense of the word is impossible.

It follows, then, that any wilderness program is a rearguard action, through which retreats are reduced to a minimum. The Wilderness Society was organized in 1935 'for the one purpose of saving the wilderness remnants in America.'

It does not suffice, however, to have such a society. Unless there be wilderness-minded men scattered through all the conservation bureaus, the society may never learn of new invasions until the time for action has passed. Furthermore a militant minority of wilderness-minded citizens must be on watch throughout the nation, and available for action in a pinch.

In Europe, where wilderness has now retreated to the Carpathians and Siberia, every thinking conservationist bemoans its loss. Even in Britain, which has less room for land-luxuries than almost any other civilized country, there is a vigorous if belated movement for saving a few small spots of semi-wild land.

Ability to see the cultural value of wilderness boils down, in the last analysis, to a question of intellectual humility. The shallow-minded modern who has lost his rootage in the land assumes that he has already discovered what is important; it is such who prate of empires, political or economic, that will last a thousand years. It is only the scholar who appreciates that all history consists of successive excursions from a single starting-point, to which man returns again and again to organize yet another search for a durable scale of values. It is only the scholar who understands why the raw wilderness gives definition and meaning to the human enterprise.

A TREE IS A LIVING THING

BY N. T. MIROV

N. T. Mirov is a plant physiologist, one of the able specialists in the U. S. Department of Agriculture who can write about his subject with clarity and simplicity as well as scientific accuracy. When this selection was written he was Plant Physiologist of the Institute of Forest Genetics, a branch of the California Forest and Range Experiment Station. It appeared originally in Trees, *the Department of Agriculture yearbook for 1949.*

(*Trees: The Yearbook of Agriculture,* 1949. Government publication.)

From the seed that in the autumn falls to the ground and is covered with leaves and soil, a tree is born. The seed is a thing to marvel at.

Pick up a pine nut; crack it open. The rich kernel, called endosperm, is packed with starch, fat, and proteins. Inside the kernel is cradled the ivory rod that is an embryo pine, a baby tree. On one end of the miniature stem is a tuft of pale leaves; the tapering opposite end of the rod will develop into a root.

Cut open a mellow acorn. In it the baby tree does not rest inside rich, nutritional tissue. The starch and fat and proteins are packed in

the two seed leaves of the embryo, which are plump and round like the two halves of a peanut. The whole acorn inside the shell is an embryo.

In the spring, when the soil gets warm enough and moisture is abundant, deep changes begin to take place in the dormant seed, already conditioned by the low winter temperatures. The embryo tree awakens from its sleep and begins to grow. What causes this awakening of life is not exactly known, and what is known is complicated, indeed. The growth hormone is activated; the enzymes, whose part is to direct and hasten living processes, start their work feverishly. The insoluble stored fats and starch begin to break down to soluble sugars, mainly dextrose. The stored proteins are split by the enzymes into some 20 soluble compounds called amino acids. Both sugars and amino acids are rushed to the growing points, where still different enzymes rearrange them into building material to be used by the germinating embryo. Proteins are formed again from the amino acids, and dextrose is partly used for building the body of the tree and partly burned up to provide necessary energy for the process.

The embryo grows fast. Soon the seed shell becomes too small and splits open. The newly born tree emerges above the ground. Its shoot begins to grow straight up and its roots straight down. The root has important work to do; it provides water for the young seedling. As soon as the little root of a seedling penetrates the ground, the tree is permanently anchored, for better or for worse, to the place where, unless it is transplanted, it has to stay all its life. From now on the tree has to depend on the nutrients available in that particular place and to develop under climatic conditions found there, which cannot be changed. In nature, however, a seedling generally begins its life in a place where its ancestors have been growing for a long time, so the little tree is well adapted to the existing conditions.

As it emerges from the ground, a young tree seedling is as tender as a blade of grass. Its seed leaves may remain in the shell below the ground, as in oak, or they may be carried above the ground, as in maple. In pine, the seed leaves pull themselves out from the endosperm and spread above the seedling like the crown of a miniature palm tree. On the tip of the little stem, tucked between the seed leaves, is the growing point or terminal bud that gives origin to the shoot; its growth continues as long as the tree lives.

Besides the root and stem tips, another important growing region is soon established in the seedling. It is called the cambium layer and is found between the wood and the bark. It makes the tree grow in girth. The cambium consists of a single layer of cells that retain their capacity to divide throughout the life of the tree. This single layer of cells has a peculiar property in that it gives origin both to the wood and to the bark. In the spring, when the cambium layer becomes active, it begins to split off rows of wood cells to the inside and rows of bark cells to the outside. Generally speaking, the bark part of the tree is much thinner than the woody part, or the stem. Bark continuously sloughs off, while the wood accumulates. In the soft inner bark, or bast, are formed sieve tubes, through which manufactured sugar dissolved in water flows from the foliage to storage tissues in stem and root.

The wood formed in the spring consists of light-colored, thin-walled cells; toward the end of the season smaller cells are formed—their walls are heavier and darker, and thus summer wood is formed. This alternation of spring wood and summer wood causes the concentric structure of the tree trunk known as annual rings; they are seen clearly on the cross section of a tree. By counting the annual rings of a tree, one can determine fairly closely its age. When growth conditions are favorable and food and water are abundant, the rings are wide. When drought occurs, the growth slows down and the rings are narrow. By reading a cross section of an old tree, one can determine what growth conditions prevailed during any particular year of the past.

In the cross section of the hardwood trees there may be seen numerous dots. These are canals, so-called vessels, that serve for conducting water along the trunk. In the conifers, like pines or firs, there are no vessels and water moves painstakingly up the trunk through minute holes from one cell to another.

Sixty percent of the wood in a tree is cellulose—by far the most important ingredient. The structure of cellulose is well understood and is rather simple. Molecules of dextrose are linked in pairs to form a more complex sugar cellobiose, and these units are hooked up to form long chains of cellulose molecules. This structure of cellulose may be easily changed by action of even a weak acid; cellulose then falls apart into the original dextrose molecules, providing an enormous source of sugar that can be used for many purposes, from fattening hogs to production of industrial alcohol. Most of the cellulose used at present, however, is converted into pulp and paper.

The rest of the wood consists mostly of lignin, which is a binding material composed, like the cellulose, of carbon, oxygen, and hydrogen, but of an entirely different and more complicated chemical structure than cellulose. Lignin is not so useful as cellulose at present, but there is little doubt that valuable products will be made from it.

Besides cellulose and lignin, wood contains a small quantity of different substances—starch, fats, sugar, resins, tannins, and many others—and is literally saturated with water.

About 10 percent of the wood mass of a tree is found underground in the form of roots. The root system of a large tree is enormous. The total length of all roots of a big spreading oak tree amounts to many hundreds of miles. The function of the root is to provide water and minerals for the tree and to anchor it securely to the ground. It is important to keep in mind that the roots are part of a living organism and that they need air, food, and water for growing. Mistreatment of roots, such as tramping the soil above them, flooding them for long periods of time, or burying them too deeply, will affect the welfare of the whole tree.

The tree comes of age. Our tree gradually becomes taller and broader, and in the course of time it reaches maturity. The complicated mechanism functions with the precision of a machine, and its many vital processes are well coordinated. Some of the processes, such as respiration or digestion of fats, are strikingly similar in both plants and animals. Others, as mineral nutrition, are found only in the plants.

Let us consider first the process of photosynthesis—that is, the building with the energy of light. In this process, organic matter is formed literally from thin air and water. The air contains minute amounts of carbon dioxide (0.03 percent by volume or three parts in 10,000 parts of air). Through millions of small pores, or stomata, on the leaf surfaces, air penetrates the leaves and gives up about 10 percent of its meager supply of precious carbon dioxide to the tree. In the leaf cells are found small particles called chloroplasts; these contain a green substance, chlorophyll, similar in structure to the hemoglobin of the blood. In fact, in reflected light chlorophyll appears not green but blood red.

Carbon dioxide unites with the chlorophyll and in a chain of reactions, regulated by the enzymes, it combines with oxygen and hydrogen of water to form sugar. An excess of oxygen is released in this process. The energy that is needed for transformation of carbon dioxide and water into the organic substance (sugar) is supplied by sunlight. Only about 1 percent of the solar energy that falls on a leaf is used for photosynthesis. The sugar formed in the process of photosynthesis is dextrose. From it 95 percent of the body of the tree is ultimately made by a series of complicated reactions. Dextrose may be converted into other sugars or it may be combined with nitrogen to form the amino acids, the building blocks from which proteins are made and on which all life, both plant and animal, depends. Part of the dextrose is also used for other purposes, such as conversion into starch, fats, and other substances.

The most favorable conditions for photosynthesis are mild temperatures (about 70° F.) and diffused, moderate light. On hot, bright, summer days the efficiency of photosynthesis goes down. An ample supply of water is essential. When the soil is dry and not enough water is delivered to the crown, the rate of photosynthesis declines. Fertility of the soil is also important, for the building of the tree body requires an ample supply of mineral elements.

Respiration is another life process. Like other living organisms, a tree must respire. The process of respiration consists of oxidizing (burning at low temperature) dextrose sugar; although some energy is lost as heat, most of the energy released during the process is used by the organism for its vital processes. Thus sugar is a source of energy for a tree just as it is for a football player. The chemical reaction of respiration is a reversal of the chemical reaction of photosynthesis, as seen from the following scheme:

Photosynthesis: Carbon dioxide + water + energy expended = dextrose + oxygen;

Respiration: Dextrose + oxygen = carbon dioxide + water + energy released.

In daytime both photosynthesis and respiration occur at the same time.

Oxygen liberated in photosynthesis is used for respiration, while the carbon dioxide exhaled by the tree is used in photosynthesis. As photosynthesis is a more intensive process than respiration, during a normal day an excess of oxygen is eliminated and an excess of carbon dioxide is absorbed by the tree. When, under adverse conditions, daytime respiration is more intensive than the body-building photosynthesis, the tree loses weight instead of gaining. At night, because of the absence of light, photosynthesis is at a standstill, but respiration continues—just as in humans, oxygen is taken in and carbon dioxide is eliminated. Respiration is going on at all times in all living cells, in the leaves, the roots, and in the stem and bark.

While photosynthesis has its optimum in cool days and decreases when the weather becomes too hot, respiration does not have such an optimum. The warmer it gets, the more intense is the respiration. Respiration is less sensitive to the lack of water than photosynthesis; that is why during droughts, when photosynthesis stops, respiration still continues and causes great harm to the tree. Inside temperatures of 120° and 130° F. are deadly.

Nitrogen is needed by a tree for making its proteins. Without proteins a cell cannot grow and cannot divide. Generally speaking, an abundance of nitrogen promotes vegetative growth of a tree. Animals have no capacity for producing proteins from nitrogen; they depend on plants for the needed proteins.

A tree has the capacity to absorb inorganic nitrogen and with it to make its own proteins. Although four-fifths of the air consists of nitrogen, less than 1 percent of the element is found in the wood of a tree. And to get that little bit of nitrogen is an extremely difficult task for a tree. Nitrogen as found in the atmosphere cannot be used by the tree; it has to be converted into ammonia or into nitrates and only in this form (mostly as nitrates) can nitrogen be absorbed by the roots. Let us see how a tree manages its nitrogen economy.

Traces of ammonia are found in the air, and some of the nitrogen oxide is formed there, especially after thunderstorms. These substances are carried by the rain to the soil, but their quantity is altogether too meager to contribute much to the nitrogen nutrition. A few trees, such as the locust or alder, have on their roots nodules formed by bacteria that are capable of assimilating nitrogen from the air and converting it into nitrates, but most trees have no nitrogen-fixing nodules. There are free bacteria that live in the soil and can use atmospheric nitrogen. But these bacteria are not abundant and they like warmth, so that in cooler climates they are not active. Fallen leaves, if not burned, contain some proteins. These proteins are gradually decomposed into amino acids, ammonia, and eventually into nitrates. But fallen leaves contain only about 1 percent of nitrogen—slightly more in the hardwood leaves and slightly less in pine needles.

Animals waste a great deal of nitrogen, which they obtain from the plants. Fur, hair, nails, and skin, being made of proteins, contain nitrogen that cannot be used again by the organism. Large amounts of nitrogen are eliminated by the animals as waste. Trees, however, are frugal with their nitrogen. They do not waste it, but use it over and over. A tree that is well supplied with nitrogen has lush, dark-green foliage, and its growth is luxuriant—a tree deprived of nitrogen is stunted and its leaves are pale green. An overdose of nitrogen is also bad for a tree. Conditions of nitrogen excess are extremely rare in nature, but might occur occasionally, for instance, in a tree grown in a chickenyard where supply of nitrogen is in excess.

How can you help a tree in its nitrogen nutrition? Growing nitrogen-fixing legumes, such as clover, near your trees will enrich the soil with nitrogen. The addition of leafmold to the soil would serve the same purpose. Remember, too, that removing or burning fallen leaves from around the trees deprives the trees of the much-needed nitrogen. If burning or removing must be done, it is wise to replace the loss by applying some nitrogen fertilizer. One word of caution in feeding trees with nitrogen. Nitrate fertilizers are leached rapidly from the soil; they are not absorbed by the soil as readily as, say, the phosphates. It is advisable therefore to add nitrates in small quantity and often, rather than to apply a large quantity at one time.

In applying fertilizer one should keep in mind that trees do not grow so fast as field crops, and thus their demand for nitrogen and for other nutrients is comparatively smaller.

Besides oxygen, hydrogen, carbon, and nitrogen, which are obtained from water and air, for proper functioning a tree needs several other elements, which it obtains from the minerals found in the soil.

Some of these mineral elements—potassium, phosphorus, and calcium—are needed in relatively large amounts. Other elements—magnesium, sulfur, and iron—are needed in relatively smaller quantities. Still others, called trace elements—such as manganese, copper, zinc, boron, or molybdenum—are necessary only in minute quantities. The need even of major elements is very small indeed. The total amount of the mineral elements in dry wood is less than one-half of 1 percent, and the need for the trace elements is so small that generally they are found in sufficient quantity in any soil.

Occasionally there may be a complete absence or too small a supply of the trace elements in a particular soil. In that case, a tree will not grow properly unless the lacking element is introduced. Great care should be exercised not to apply too much of the trace elements, lest great damage be done to the tree. For instance, while potash or phosphorus may be added to soil at the rate of, say, 1,000 pounds an acre, about 5 or 10 pounds an acre of a trace element is enough. More than that might be harmful to the trees. A specialist should be consulted before any trace element is added to the soil.

When wood is burned, all these and many other elements are found in the ashes, but some sulfur and phosphorus and all nitrogen are lost in smoke. Twenty-seven elements, including silver, titanium, and nickel, are found in the ashes of white pine. That does not mean that all these elements are necessary for the life of the tree. Some minerals that may be found in a tree, such as common salt, apparently are not needed for its proper functioning. These are absorbed by the roots simply because they happened to be in the soil; the tree has no way of telling the useful minerals from the useless or even harmful ones. For example, arsenic, though very poisonous to the tree, is as readily absorbed as phosphorus.

Mineral elements are needed by a tree to perform various vital functions. Phosphorus is found in some plant proteins; seeds and growing points are especially rich in phosphorus. Lack of phosphorus often manifests itself in purpling or bronzing of foliage, which is easy to detect. Sulfur also enters into the building of certain proteins. It is well distributed throughout the plant. Calcium apparently is somehow involved in the carbohydrate translocation. It enters into the construction of the cell wall; crystals of calcium oxalate are found often in the tissues of plants. Magnesium is a constituent of the chlorophyll molecule. It is also probably related to fat formation and to the synthesis of some proteins. Potassium is especially abundant in young growing parts of the tree; it has something to do with synthesis and translocation of sugars; in the absence of potassium, cells do not divide. Iron is needed to keep the tree green. Iron is not a part of the chlorophyll molecule, but without it chlorophyll cannot be formed. Iron is also needed in respiration. Generally, there is enough iron in any soil, but sometimes in alkaline soils it is found in an insoluble state. Iron-deficient trees lack the healthy color.

The physiological role of minor elements is little known, but symptoms of their deficiency are pronounced. At present our concept of the physiology of plant nutrition is in the process of revision. With the recent advances of nuclear physics, it is possible to prepare radioactive mineral salts. "Tagged" radioactive phosphorus or potassium can be followed as soon as it is absorbed by a plant; it can be traced to its destination and its function in plant life can be determined.

Water is contained in all tissues of a tree, both dead and alive. Young leaves or tips of roots contain up to 90 percent of water; tree trunks contain as much as 50 percent. Water is indispensable to the tree. All living processes take place in water. Sugars are built from carbon dioxide and water. Mineral nutrients are carried from the soil to the top of the tree in a stream of water. In the spring the organic materials in the form of sugars and amino acids are rushed in a stream of water from their places of winter storage to the bursting buds.

And there is the dramatic process called transpiration. In that process, water is absorbed by the roots, pushed into the sapwood, and then pulled up to the leaves (as high as 350 feet in redwood) above the ground. The energy needed for transpiration, as for photosynthesis, is supplied by the sun. About one-half of the solar energy falling on a leaf is used for transpiration. Through the same openings (the stomata) that admit carbon dioxide to the inner tissues of the leaf, the water is evaporated to the atmosphere, and this evaporation creates a tremendous pull on the minute, continuous strands of water in the sapwood and thereby causes a movement of water from the roots to the treetop. There is no such process in the tree as circulation of the sap similar to circulation of the blood in animals. Only a trifle of water is transported from the crown downward and comparatively little is retained by the tissues. The terms "the sap is up" and "the sap is down" are not correct and are misleading.

The formation of 100 grams of cellulose requires 55 grams of water. But while a tree increases its weight by 100 grams, it loses in transpiration nearly 100,000 grams (that is, 1,000 times more) of water.

Transpiration brings water from the soil to the leaves so that photosynthesis can be carried on. To enter through the cell walls, carbon dioxide must be dissolved in water. The surface of the chlorophyll containing cells must be moist at all times.

The leaves have a water-regulated mechanism that permits a tree to shut off the stomata and thus prevent loss of water. But the very same stomata have to be open in order to admit carbon dioxide for the photosynthesis. When stomata are open, the tree loses water; when they are closed, the tree cannot assimilate carbon dioxide. A balance between the two processes must be maintained by the tree.

The stomata open their little shutters early in the morning. At noon they begin to close, and just before sunset they are closed tight for the night. In some trees, stomata may open at night. During excessively hot and dry days the stomata are open only for a short time in the early morning and then close for the rest of the day. Under these conditions the tree cannot make much sugar from the carbon dioxide.

What can a man do to help a tree in its water economy? Not more than to supply it with water by irrigation, by preserving the natural mulch on the ground and thus reducing evaporation from the soil, and by not planting trees too close to each other or exposing the shade-loving trees to full sunlight.

The physiology of growth is this: Through the process of photosynthesis and with the help of nitrogen and the mineral elements, the tree builds up its body. In some trees, such as the giant sequoias, as much as 50,000 cubic feet of organic matter, mostly wood, may accumulate in this way. But the growth of a tree is not merely an accumulation of organic matter. Growth is an involved physiological process, in which the use of building materials is regulated by the growth substances or hormones.

Growth of a tree is retarded if mineral nutrition is held at a minimum and water is withheld. This is the method used by the Japanese in dwarfing trees; some of their dwarf trees, grown in small pots, may be several hundred years old. In fact, any pot-bound young tree is checked in its growth and thus is more or less dwarfed.

Growth of the tree depends not only on the correlation of its physiological functions but also on external factors like temperature, light, and moisture. Within a certain range, an increase of temperature of 18° F. nearly doubles the rate of growth of plants; but when temperatures are either too low or too high for a proper functioning of the organism, many disturbances may occur in the tree. In that case the growth of the tree is retarded, and although life may still continue there is no coordination between the different vital functions. The tree ceases to grow. The optimum temperature for growth is not necessarily the same as the optimum temperature for general development of the plant. Many trees need a low temperature period for their normal development; when this cold period is eliminated, they do not grow.

Light must also be available in the proper amount and quality.

When light is lacking, the tree cannot manufacture organic matter and will eventually die. Light also retards the growth of the tree. In the dark, the shoots grow faster than in the light. In yellow and red light, the plant can assimilate carbon dioxide very well, but the plant does not develop normally—it behaves as if it were growing in the dark. For normal development a tree needs, besides yellow and red light, the blue, violet, and ultraviolet rays of the sun. Those rays are not needed for photosynthesis, and their action on the growth is that of retardation. The blue end of the spectrum is needed by a tree for formative purposes.

When a tree is bent by some mechanical force, such as the wind, its normal growth is disturbed. On the upward side of the tree, the newly formed cells of the sapwood are stretched; on the lower side, they are compressed. This distortion of the wood structure, due to pressure, is often noticed in our conifers. Where a pressure is applied, there is formed so-called compression wood, which lowers the quality of lumber manufactured from such wood.

In a temperate climate, trees show an annual periodicity of growth. The annual shoot completes its growth early in the season, say at the end of June. By that time, in many forest trees, all cell division for the next year's growth is completed in the bud. This means that the next year's growth pattern of a tree is determined almost a year before—all microscopic flower buds are set; all microscopic leaf buds are formed. The next season the growth takes place mostly by elongation of the bud cells prefabricated in the previous year. Growth in diameter takes place throughout the summer by division and enlargement of cambium cells.

A long time before cold weather sets in, the tree has already completed its seasonal growth; it prepares for the winter. Evergreen trees retain their foliage for winter, but deciduous trees act differently. They remove much of the nutrient material from the leaves; then a peculiar physiological process (abscission) of the leafstalks causes the leaves to drop. The tree is in a deep rest now and can withstand a great deal of cold. An unusual warm spell in late winter or early spring, however, may cause buds to open—subsequent cold may kill them. Sometimes a northern tree transplanted in the South might open its buds too early in the spring and suffer from a later frost.

Reproduction is possible when the tree reaches its physical maturity. The sexual reproduction of trees is basically similar to that of animals. In plants, reproduction manifests itself by the appearance of male and female flowers, which may be borne either on separate trees, as in cottonwood, or on the same tree, as in pine, or even combined into a perfect flower, as in the magnolia.

Pollen of the male flower fertilizes the ovule of a female flower, which then develops into the seed. The whole process of reproduction involves setting the flower buds, development of the male and female flowers, pollination, and development of the seed and fruit. Each process depends on internal as well as external conditions.

In annual plants, the reproductive stage means subsequent death; the plant dies as soon as the seed is matured. In trees, production of seed is continued for many years. In a tree there is a delicate balance between vegetative growth and reproduction. If a tree grows too fast, it will not produce much fruit or seed. The reproductive stage is generally reached when a tree begins to slow down its most vigorous height growth.

The accumulation of carbohydrates is conducive to the flowering, while the abundance of the minerals, especially nitrogen, promotes growth at the expense of reproduction. The proper balance between organic and mineral nutrition and the possible formation of flowering hormones occurs in the tree only after a certain stage of maturity has been reached. After that, a tree begins to produce seed, but not necessarily every year. Seed bearing is a taxing process. Much material and much energy are required for it. Many trees have periodicity of seed years, and the intervals between the good seed years vary in the different trees. Again, this periodicity apparently depends on a definite combination of nutritional and external factors. As the flower buds are set during the previous summer, the weather conditions of the last year have a lot to do with the flowering. Dry, warm weather generally is favorable for setting flower buds. Weather conditions prevailing during pollination and the development of pollen grains are also of importance. A great deal of light is needed for flowering. Trees grown in the open produce flowers and seed in profusion and much earlier than trees that are grown in the shade. Abundant sunshine at the time of setting flowering buds also contributes to the seed crop the next year.

The effect of photoperiod, or day length, discovered in 1920 by W. W. Garner and H. A. Allard of the United States Department of Agriculture, is of great importance in flowering of trees. Some trees flower only when the days are short, while others bloom when the days are long. A northern tree that was growing under the long-day conditions may not bloom if moved to the South, because the summer days of the new home are too short for it. If, say, a street lamp provides that extra needed light, a northern tree may burst into bloom even in a short-day country.

Certain chemical substances, such as ethylene, are known to break the dormancy of plants. If your lilac bush unexpectedly bursts into bloom earlier than usual, it might be because you had burned some fallen leaves or clippings nearby and the smoke supplied enough ethylene to awaken the dormant flower buds.

Sexual reproduction of trees plays an important part in the development of the diversity of our trees. By combining characters of the pollen parent with those of the seed parent, new combinations are formed, some of which may be very valuable. But sexual reproduction is not absolutely necessary for trees; many of them can be reproduced by vegetative means—cuttings, grafting, and budding.

Old age comes to trees, as to all other living organisms. The span of life of a tree is specific. Gray birch is old at 40. The sugar maple lives longer, up to 500 years. Some oaks may live 1,500 years, junipers 2,000 years. Some of the giant sequoias are believed to be about 4,000 years old. Old trees are like old people—the infirmities of age are upon them. They have difficulty with respiration (its rate in old plants is much lower than in young plants); the annual shoots are not so vigorous as they once were, and the weakening cambium activity is reflected in the formation of fewer and fewer wood cells. Hence, the annual rings become narrower. As the rate of growth of the tree decreases, dead branches appear in ever-increasing numbers. The recuperative capacity of an old tree is impaired, and its wounds do not heal over so easily as before. The leaves become smaller; their moisture content decreases; the tree finds it more and more difficult to provide water for its vital functions; the inflow of food to the growing points drops; and the growth hormones probably cannot be transported in large enough quantity to the places where they are needed.

Causes of death of a tree may be numerous and are often difficult to diagnose. When a tree is broken by snowfall or uprooted by wind or killed by fire, the cause of death is evident. But often the cause is rather obscure. Sometimes lack of water may cause death of the tree, and again trees weakened by drought may fall prey to an insect or fungus attack.

Fire is an archenemy of trees. Its direct effect on trees is obvious enough. But there is also an indirect effect: Heat may injure patches of succulent inner bark of the tree trunk. Fermentation may easily start in these places and attract insects. The smoke of a fire contains some physiologically active gases—ethylene, for example, or acetylene. The gases may cause the opening of the dormant buds prematurely, thus exposing them to frost damage and contributing to the general weakening of the tree.

When a tree dies, its death almost always can be traced to some external cause—cold, fire, drought, insects, fungi, or malnutrition. Some of these causes are beyond our control. Others can be prevented. By taking good care of the tree, one can prolong its life. The tree should be well provided with water and light and be well nourished, or at least not deprived of nutritive substances. A healthy tree will resist attacks of insects and diseases; it will develop a large crown and a strong root system; and it will withstand the action of the wind.

If a tree is treated as a living organism, with an understanding of its vital functions, it will be a constant source of profit and pleasure to men.

THE NEST IN THE CAVE

BY DONALD CULROSS PEATTIE

Donald Culross Peattie (1898–1964) was born in Chicago, educated there and at Harvard, and spent three years as a botanist in the U. S. Department of Agriculture. Thereafter he was a writer, of poetry, of fiction, and of books about the natural world. In 1935 his An Almanac for Moderns *brought him honors and fame and it stands today as a modern classic. That same year he wrote* Singing in the Wilderness, *a lyric and very personal account of Audubon's early years. In 1950 he published* A Natural History of Trees of Eastern and Central America, *followed three years later by* A Natural History of Western Trees, *which combined his scientific knowledge and his lyric gift with words in one of the most eloquent and authoritative studies ever written of America's woodlands. Illness curtailed his writing in his later years, but the many books of his early and middle period were all notable for Peattie's unique combination of scientific knowledge and colorful, poetic way with the English language. This selection is a chapter from* Singing in the Wilderness, *and I have chosen it because it tells as much about Peattie as it does about Audubon and is representative of his colorful, very personal writing, at its best.*

(*Singing in the Wilderness: A Salute to John James Audubon,* by Donald Culross Peattie; G. P. Putnam's Sons, 1935.)

At this point comes over me the longing to rediscover the America that awaited that ardent French boy. Much is altered, more is gone, and at each spring sign I see or hear, I wonder if he knew it thus. Apart from the tragedy of extinction, there are pulsations in the plant and animal census. It seems to me, for instance, that there were never so many grackles as this spring. Grackles, I know, are the comedy notes; they are not to be encouraged, but the airs would be lonelier without their gabbling and mockery and the sweet squeak and gurgle as of an old mill wheel in a stream. And so much is gone from the woods! When Audubon came, the roar of the passenger pigeons' wings, the harsh call of the Carolina parrot, the drumming of the ivory-billed woodpecker were commonplaces. So too were the tawny hide of the "painter" and the frayed bark of a tree where a young buck had rubbed his horns. It is easy to impoverish a land, sometimes impossible to restore it, and "we do not always know," as an old negro said to me once, "when we are well off until we are poorly."

I have been out to gather a faggot for the fire, and I saw that to every tree spring was coming in a pale green wave, save to the hickories. The borers have got into the shagbarks, and by the look of things their dynasty is ended. It is true, of course, that they are uncouth; they are rigid, scraggly, and their bark is rags. Their leaves, if you like, were always late and dropped early, and if you don't like to work over your nuts, thin-shelled pecans will suit you better. But something is going with the hickories, a thick shell, a brown stain, a grain to turn the blade of an ax, a crude straightness whose place will not be taken by trees like my young elms and ashes.

The morning air was quite glittering with bird song. I heard the first chewinks of the year, and song-sparrows were practicing all their different tunes. The bluebird throated his warm warble. And from the edge of the prairies the meadowlarks sang out clear and loud, all wistfulness gone from their voices. On the edge of the slough I stopped, very still in my tracks, to watch two diminutive greenish birds at war in a thorn-apple tree. I was not conscious that there was anything else living close beside me except a slim brown bush just out of reach, and I watched the birds, puzzled for an instant over their identity, when suddenly they both told it to me. A tiny crest of red fury was erected upon each head, proclaiming the ruby-crowned kinglet. They teetered and swung at each other, scolding on a note as high and thin as an insect's. It was laughable to see such display of gallantry in the two smallest cock birds in all the woods.

I laughed, and the low brown bush plucked itself out of the marsh, and with dangling legs and outstretched neck became a bittern that departed, uttering its disgusted cry of "Faugh! Faugh!"

As I began to break up the black fingers of a dead oak for my fireplace, I heard the bittern from the next long slough entice me with that contented thumping for which it is called "stake-driver." I sometimes fancy that the bittern likes to be followed about; he could get away a great deal sooner if he really wanted to, but he stands there close beside you, posing with his long neck straight in the air, his eyes on the tip of his bill and his bill pointing straight toward his Creator. The general opinion, says Audubon, is that the bittern so behaves from sheer stupidity, but he protests that he never met a stupid bird.

Of the class of birds called waders, none but flamingos and ibises strike me as pretty. There is not a singing voice in the lot of them; their legs are gangling, their manners are disgusting, and they dwell in mud and fens where strange smells arise and there is no footing for humans. They are the last birds to which the amateur takes a liking, these coots and rails and herons, snipe and curlew. You may begin with the thrushes and hummingbirds, if you are a home-keeping sort of person owning eaves, vines and a garden, or with the ducks, if you are a man and an angler and Nimrod. There are some lucky enough to dwell by the ocean, and to know where the gannets weave sea thrift into their nests, to have heard the "whish!" of the puffin diving and even the sweet nightly conversation, in their burrows beneath the sod on the cliff's edge, of the petrels come in from mid-ocean to nest in sociable colonies. But however you reach the waders, it is a long way round. They are perhaps the final test of the love of birds, for one who loves them must be attuned even as Thoreau, the man who "saw beauty in ashes." When you come to love them—I do not say it is possible always to like them—you have got to the last wilderness, you are in the depths of the woods, and ankle-deep in the lost and midmost slough.

I pushed through the door with my bristling faggot, and made the fire. The first crooked blue finger of smoke stole out into the room and brought with it, as odors will, the nostalgia of old happiness that nothing seems to dim. For me there are just two kinds of dwelling—those, like the cabins of our ancestors, where there is always a whiff of woodsmoke, and those others, today a majority, whence it is banished.

I sat down in an easy chair, putting off work, and closed my eyes. I could hear two trains; one, the farther away, blew the long call of warning, softened by distance, that speed and death were on the rails—a glittering train with a name of its own, setting a record pace for a neighboring city that was still so far away that in Europe it would have lain in another land. I could imagine its proud crest of smoke rolled out upon the morning over the black ploughed land. The other train was a freight, and it plodded windily not so very far away, across the prairie beyond the woods; presently it stopped, with a long shuffle, and called a signal at some siding where the frogs would be piping tranquilly from the marsh bisected with the embankment. The engineer—(and where do you see such fine American faces as at the window of a locomotive cab?)—would be leaning out and hearing them, not thinking about them, but about the two white rails ahead, the connected million miles of steel that spiderwebs the continent. There is nothing like a train whistle for taking you everywhere. It makes you homesick for California, or Florida, or Wisconsin or Virginia. Homesick even for home, so far away will it bear you, all in a blast.

So I fell to dreaming on my country, the past and the present indistinguishable. Ox-teams and covered wagons lumbering down a bank between sallows to a ford of the Platte; men going west for gold that most of them would never find. Farmers getting into their Fords in a green twilight, their children hugging their own ribs with excitement, to go to the movies in the town and see people rich as they are rich only on the screen, in cumulative magnificence under the concentrated Kliegs. The Puritan Fathers, writing home about the fertility of New England, the wonderful climate, God's hand over them. The subdivision; lonely pavements and street signs, "Broadway," and "Rosemount Boulevard"; God's hand over advertising men. Black men and women let up out of the slaver's hold, to look at the palmetto-lined shore they shall inherit. Daniel Boone, blazing death among the antlers and the wigwams of Kentucky. Young men digging today, to put the forests back; billions for relief in a country that could not slay the bison fast enough, that feasted on the tongues and left the carcasses to rot.

This is the land to which came other men, but not Jean Jacques Audubon. Nothing ever really happened to him except birds, for he took nothing else seriously. Even his love affair, his marriage and his home were as those of the birds—a mating for life, a nesting here and there, a foraging by God's grace, a wide roaming and a sure return.

The America to which Audubon came is the bittern and the kinglet, the flamingo and the flicker. I had just myself returned from France and was enjoying my first American spring in many years; I could feel a little what the American forest must have seemed like to that rare company of naturalists who came to these shores, André Michaux, Peter Kalm, Alexander Wilson, Mark Catesby, Alexander Garden, John Clayton, Constantine Rafinesque. The dilemma of an American naturalist in Europe, however delightful his sojourn there, is that there is nothing left for him to find. Every least weed is known and atomized into varieties, encrusted with synonymy, haunted with folklore. The avifauna, though so lovable, is pared down to an attenuation of the great north Asiatic natural faunal province. From tropical Africa, cut off by the Sahara, little may reach it, and that little is hunted. In this our New World, the Linnaean explorers were enchanted with whole new families. And, to feel what they felt, we should very nearly have to stand in the forests of Mars, and hear new cries and see incredible plumage.

The first bird that fell to the gun of Alexander Wilson, nine years before Audubon's coming, as he tramped, a narrow-chested little weaver, from the Chesapeake to Philadelphia, was the redheaded woodpecker, "the most beautiful bird in the world," he wrote home. The wild turkey, the burrowing owl, the whip-poor-will, the cardinal —in the Old World there is nothing like these. The family of the mocking-birds is wholly American, with its catbirds and thrashers. Ours only are the hummingbirds, the vireos, and the gorgeous, black-dashed, whistling *Icteridae*—orioles and meadowlarks, bobolinks and grackles and redwinged blackbirds. The tanagers are ours, the phoebe and pewee; the two families of warblers keep each to its own side of the Atlantic, and though they are like enough in their habits, they sing to different tunes.

It is the annual wave of migrants from the tropics that gives our bird life its distinction. Its points of resemblance to that of Europe are greatest among our modest permanent residents and the arctic visitants of winter. It was winter still when Jean Jacques Audubon was first installed at his father's estate of Mill Grove on Perkioming Creek that flows down to the Schuylkill River. And I suppose that the icy tinkle of the tree sparrows was the best of bird music around the fine old stone farm house, in the leafless woods of Fatland Ford, a neighboring estate, and all beyond, to Valley Forge, and Gray's Ferry twenty-five miles away where Alexander Wilson was teaching bovine Pennsylvania German youngsters English with a Paisley accent.

As Audubon remembered the circumstances of his coming to America, or as he wished to believe, he had journeyed to our shores as a young gentleman come into his rightful estates—somewhat prematurely at eighteen and with his father still alive to keep a sharp eye on him. Indeed, his father's letters show that the practical Captain did not intend to make an idler of his son; he had sent him to America in the fond hope that he could make a business man of him, and his letter of introduction to Miers Fisher was a request to place the boy in the hands of a respectable American family with sound commercial connections, where he could learn the language and ways of trade.

Friend Fisher, absolutely honest with himself as with the Captain, saw no reason to let the attractive and highly connected young man go any further than his own home. He had a finger in any number of instructive businesses; of English he could teach the boy the godly "thee" and "thy" of the Quakers, and as for the lad's morals, he was sure he had every qualification for guarding them. He opposed fishing, dancing, hunting, violin playing, skating, cards, birds' nesting, skylarking, and youthful high spirits. The boy drank nothing but milk or water, and there remained only the daughters of Eve to fend off. His own daughter offered a solid bulwark against temptation. In short, Friend Fisher had young Audubon's future all arranged for him, from the moment that he fetched him in his carriage from Morristown, where the boy had lain ill with fever in the care of two excellent Quaker ladies.

But when he got his strength back, Jean Jacques saw how the wind was blowing. He took an unreasoning dislike to the gray-clad maiden so frankly put in his way, and fleeing the rule of the meeting house over his habits, he removed himself body and baggage to Mill Grove. Two Quakers of a more liberal persuasion, Friend Thomas and his wife, were his care-takers and his informal retainers. For the first time in his life he was his own master, or at least the leading strings in his father's hands stretched all the way across the Atlantic. He was the squire of broad acres, he had a gun and a dog and a horse and a house of his own. And the birds of America were already on the wing to him from the Orinoco and the Windward Islands, the pampas and the everglades.

The airs of March were icy under the first glitter of the sun; the snow still lingered on the north side of the house and the mill; the roar of the swollen yellow brook was redoubled between its steep clay banks, when Audubon found the cave with the quaint, mysterious little nest fixed in it.

He had no notion who were the owners of this home so cleverly fashioned out of mud and finest moss, but he had a true naturalist's premonition that the little architects would return to it. This was no fragile summer cottage destined to hold a cup of snow and blow to pieces in the next spring's winds; some race of birds faithful of heart and habit had built in the cave, and already his own heart went out to them. His curiosity, his zeal, were all alert for the vanguard of the unknown tribes that would surely come. He went up to his house and got his books and crayons, his papers and his gun, and removed them bodily to the cave. Thenceforward it should be his retreat, and every day he came there and lingered, standing in the mouth of the cave where the pale sunlight could lie upon him, looking south across the faintly budding maples to a wide fan of sky whence they would come.

On April 10, 1804, the phoebes returned to their nest. And in that moment was born the *Ornithological Biography*. Born, too, in Audubon's mind was that intense curiosity hedged about with significant doubts that is scientific investigation. It was an age, we have to remind ourselves, when the migration of birds was not only scarce understood, but widely disbelieved. Men still followed Pliny, who thought that the swallow skimming over the pond hibernated beneath the water like a frog. Barrington, writing to Gilbert White, maintained that British birds would certainly never leave Britain for foreign shores, but fell into a torpor in winter and hid themselves in belfries, caves, and hollow trees.

But Audubon, watching the phoebes repair their home, asked himself by what means a man could be sure that these same little masons found their way over the sea and jungle to one particular spot, for he was convinced that in those tiny gray heads memory and instinct kept the imprint of the great and the small, the continent and the cave. That such a thing should be was nearly miraculous; he would have to find some way of proving it.

So, he says, "I fixed a light silver thread on the leg of each, loose enough not to hurt the part, but so fastened that no exertions of theirs could remove it." His method was so simple that no one else had thought of it. It is astonishing that it did not occur to Gilbert White, who records the finding of a swan bearing on its neck a collar with the arms of the King of Denmark. Alexander Wilson at Gray's Ferry was trying to establish a chain of correspondents, such that not a titmouse or a wren should wing northward but he would know of it. But Audubon was the unconscious founder of the Bird Banding Society that a hundred years later would plot the marvelous course of the plover and the airy track of the bobolink.

Returning from the cave, when the woods were white with bloodroot and the mourning doves were crying contentment in the newborn softness of the weather, he was told, as he pulled off his boots by the fire, that a gentleman had been to call upon him. A Mr. Bakewell, his housekeeper said, the gentleman who had just bought Fatland Ford.

"Oh, yes, the Englishman." Jean Jacques scowled as he dragged the other boot off his foot. "Well, if he comes again, thee shall tell him I am not at home."

"I doubt he will come again, unless thee return his call."

"Little fear that the son of Captain Jean Audubon will pay homage to an Englishman," said the young cock, slipping his feet comfortably into slippers. "Has thee dressed the partridges?"

And he went into the dining-room with the high appetite of youth, the satisfaction of a naturalist who has set discovery afoot, and the obliviousness of one who has not heard the light tap of destiny upon his door.

BIG STORM

BY MARJORIE KINNAN RAWLINGS

Marjorie Kinnan Rawlings (1896–1953) was born in Washington, D.C., educated at the University of Wisconsin, worked in Kentucky and New York, but found her lasting interest in the Florida back country. She settled at Cross Creek, Florida, in 1928, and spent the rest of her life there, managing an orange grove and learning the ways of the country and its people. Her sense of nature and knowledge of the outdoors were in the very grain of her novels, and never more so than in her now classic The Yearling, *from which the following selection is taken. It won for her the Pulitzer Prize in 1939 and made Jody Baxter and his pet fawn a part of American folklore.*

(*The Yearling*, by Marjorie Kinnan Rawlings; Charles Scribner's Sons, 1938.)

The first week in September was as parched and dry as old bones. Only the weeds grew. There was a tension in the heat. The dogs were snappish. The snakes were crawling, dog days being past, and their shedding and their blindness ended. Penny killed a rattler under the grape arbor that measured seven feet in length. He had seen the coffee-weed shaking as though an alligator were passing through and had followed. The rattler, he said, was after the quail, to fill his long belly on his way to his winter quarters. He dried the great hide on the smoke-house wall and then hung it on the front-room wall beside the fireplace.

He said, "I like to look at it. I know there's one o' the boogers'll not harm nobody."

The heat was the worst of the whole summer, yet there was a vague change, as though the vegetation sensed the passing of one season and the coming of another. The golden-rod and asters and the deer-tongue thrived on the dryness. The pokeberries ripened and the birds fed on them along the fenrows. All the creatures, Penny said, were hard put to it for food. The spring and summer berries, the brier-berries, the huckleberries, the blueberries and chokeberries and the wild gooseberries, were long since gone. The wild plum and the mayhaw had had no fruit for bird or beast for many a month. The 'coons and foxes had stripped the wild grape-vines.

The fall fruits were not yet ripe, papaw and gallberry and persimmon. The mast of the pines, the acorns of the oaks, the berries of the palmetto, would not be ready until the first frost. The deer were feeding on the tender growth, bud of sweet bay and of myrtle, sprigs of wire-grass, tips of arrowroot in the ponds and prairies, and succulent lily stems and pads. The type of food kept them in the low, wet places, the swamps, the prairies and the bay-heads. They seldom crossed Baxter's Island. They were hard to hunt in the boggy places. In a month, Penny was able only to bring down one yearling buck. Its spike horns were still in the velvet. They felt like a coarse rough wool. Shreds hung, where the yearling had rubbed them against saplings, to ease the itch of growth and hurry their hardening. Ma Baxter ate them boiled, saying they tasted like marrow. Penny and Jody had no taste for them. They could see too plainly the big eyes under the new horns.

The bears, too, were in the low places. They were feeding for the most on palmetto buds, ripping out the hearts ruthlessly. The palm hammock around Sweetwater Spring looked as though a hurricane had swept through it. The low-growing palmettos were slashed into ribbons, the sweet cream-colored cores eaten below the level of the ground. Even some of the tall palms looked as though struck by lightning, where a less lazy bear or a hungrier one had scaled the trunk and torn out the bud. The palmettos, Penny said, would die.

They were like all living things. They could not live with the heart gone. One low palm had been only shredded from the outside. The heart was intact. Penny cut out the smooth cylinder with his hunting knife to carry home to cook. The Baxters liked swamp cabbage as well as the bears.

"But when them scapers runs short o' palmeeters," Penny said, "hit's look out for the shoats. You kin look to see the bears climbin' into the lot most ary night now. And your friend Flag here, you best keep him with you faithful, especial at night. I'll stand up to your Ma, do she quarrel about it."

"Ain't Flag gittin' too big for a bear to bother?"

"A bear'll kill ary creetur cain't out-run him. Why, on the prairie one year, a bear killed my bull, was nigh as big as he was. Hit made him a meal for a week. He come back to it 'til there wasn't nothin' left o' the bull but the beller, and that was gone, too."

Ma Baxter's complaint was at lack of rain. Her rain barrels were empty. All her washing must be done at the sink-hole. The clothes were looking dingy.

She said, "Clothes washes easier, anyways, on a cloudy day. My Ma allus said, 'Soft weather, soft clothes.'"

She needed rain-water, too, to clabber the milk. The milk turned rankly sour in the heat but would not clabber. In hot weather, she always depended on a few drops of rain-water to clabber it, and at every shower would send Jody to a hickory tree to catch some, for rain-water dripped from a hickory was best for the purpose.

The Baxters watched the quartering of the September moon anxiously. Penny called his wife and son when the first quarter appeared. The silver crescent was almost perpendicular. He was jubilant.

"We'll git rain soon, shore," he told them. "If the moon was straight acrost, hit'd push the water out and we'd not git none. But look at it. Hit'll rain to where you kin hang your clothes right on the line and the Lord'll wash 'em."

He was a good prophet. Three days later every sign was of rain. Passing by Juniper Springs from a hunt, he and Jody heard the alligators bellowing. Bats flew in the daytime. Frogs caah-caah-caahed steadily at night. The Dominick rooster crowed in the middle of the day. The jay-birds bunched and flew back and forth together, screaming as one. Ground rattlers crawled across the clearing in the hot sunny afternoon. On the fourth day a flock of white sea-birds flew over. Penny shaded his eyes against the sun and watched after them uneasily.

He said to Jody, "Now them ocean jessies don't belong to be crossin' Floridy. I don't like it. Hit means bad weather, and when I say bad, I mean bad."

Jody felt a lift of spirit like the sea-birds. He loved storm. It swept in magnificently and shut the family inside in a great coziness. Work was impossible and they sat about together and the rain drummed on the hand-hewn shingles. His mother was good-natured and made him syrup candy, and Penny told tales.

He said, "I hope it's a pure hurricane."

Penny turned on him sharply.

"Don't you wish sich as that. A hurricane flattens the crops and drowns the pore sailors and takes the oranges offen the trees. And down south, why, boy, hit tears down houses and cold-out kills people."

Jody said meekly, "I won't wish it agin. But wind and rain is fine."

"All right. Wind and rain. That's another thing."

The sun set strangely that night. The sunset was not red, but green. After the sun was gone, the west turned gray. The east filled with a light the color of young corn. Penny shook his head.

"I don't like it. Hit looks mighty boogerish."

In the night, a gust of wind moved through and slammed both doors. The fawn came to Jody's bed and poked its muzzle against his face. He took it up on the bed with him. The morning, however, was clear, but the east was the color of blood. Penny spent the morning repairing the roof of the smoke-house. He brought drinking water twice from the sink-hole, filling all available buckets. In the late morning, the sky turned gray and remained so. There was no air stirring.

Jody asked, "Is it a hurricane comin'?"

"I don't think. But somethin's comin', ain't natural."

In mid-afternoon the skies turned so black that the chickens went to roost. Jody drove in Trixie and the calf and Penny milked early. He turned old Caesar into the lot and put a forkful of the last remaining hay in his manger.

Penny said, "Git the eggs outen the nests. I'm goin' to the house. Hurry now, else you'll git ketched."

The hens were not laying and there were only three eggs in the lot nests. Jody climbed into the corn-crib where the old Barred Rock was laying. The left-over husks rustled under his feet. The dry, sweet-scented air was close and thick. He felt stifled. There were two eggs in the nest and he put all five inside his shirt and started for the house. He had not felt the hurry that had infected his father. Suddenly, in the false twilight stillness, he took alarm. A great roaring sounded in the distance. All the bears in the scrub, meeting at the river, might make such a roaring. It was wind. He heard it come closer from the northeast as plainly as though it came on vast webbed feet, brushing the tree-tops in its passing. It seemed to leap the corn-field in one gust. It struck the yard trees with a hissing, and the mulberries bent their boughs to the ground, and the chinaberry creaked in its brittleness. It passed over him with a rustle like the wings of many geese, high-flying. The pines whistled. The rain followed.

The wind had been high overhead. The rain was a solid wall, from sky to earth. Jody struck it flat, as though he had dived against it from a great height. It hurled him back and threw him off his balance. A second wind seemed now to reach long muscular fingers through the wall of rain and scoop up everything in its path. It reached down his shirt and into his mouth and eyes and ears and tried to strangle him. He dared not drop the eggs in his shirt. He kept one arm cupped under them and put the other over his face and scuttled into the yard. The fawn was waiting, quivering. Its tail hung wet and flat and its ears drooped. It ran to him and tried to find shelter behind him. He ran around the house and to the back door. The fawn bounded close behind him. The kitchen door was latched. The wind and rain blew so hard against it that he could not swing it open. He beat on the thick pine. For a moment he thought he was unheard in the tumult and that he and the fawn would be left outside to drown, like biddies. Then Penny lifted the latch from the inside and pushed the door open into the storm. Jody and the fawn darted inside. Jody stood gasping. He wiped the water from his eyes. The fawn blinked.

Penny said, "Who was it, now, wishin' for sich as this?"

Jody said, "Did I git my wish this quick allus, I'd wish mighty keerful."

Ma Baxter said, "Go change them wet clothes right away now. Couldn't you of shut up that fawn before you come in?"

"There wasn't no time, Ma. He was wet and skeert."

"Well—long as he don't do no mischief. Now don't put on your good breeches. You got a pair there, full o' holes as a cast-net, but they'll hold together in the house."

Penny said after him, "Don't he look like a wet yearlin' crane. All he needs is tail feathers. My, ain't he growed since spring."

She said, "I think he'll be right nice-lookin', do them freckles fade and that hair ever lay flat and them bones git covered with meat."

"A few more changes," he agreed innocently, "and he'll turn out handsome as the Baxters, thank the Lord."

She looked at him belligerently.

"And mebbe, handsome as the Alverses," he added.

"That makes more sense. You better change your tune."

"I got no idee o' startin' a ruckus, sweetheart, and you and me penned up together by no storm."

She chuckled with him. Jody, overhearing from his bedroom, could not tell whether they were making fun of him, or whether there was indeed hope for his appearance.

He said to Flag, "You think I'm purty, anyways, don't you?"

Flag butted him. He took it for assurance and they ambled back to the kitchen.

Penny said, "Well, hit's a three-day nor'easter. A might early, but I've seed change o' season this early, many a year."

"How kin you tell it'll be three days, Pa?"

"I'd not sign no papers on it, but generally the first September storm be a three-day nor'easter. The whole country changes. I reckon, one way or t'other, the world. I've heerd Oliver Hutto tell o' September storm as fur off as China."

Ma Baxter asked, "Why ain't he come to see us this time? Grandma shocks my modesty, but I do like Oliver."

"I reckon mebbe he's had enough o' the Forresters for a whiles and jest ain't travelin' this road."

"They'll not fight without he acts quarrelsome, will they? The fiddle cain't play without the bow."

"I'm feered the Forresters, leastwise Lem, 'll romp on him ary time they come up with him. Until they git the gal business settled."

"Sich doin's! Nobody acted that-a-way when I were a gal."

"No," Penny said, "I was the only one wanted you."

She lifted the broom in pretended threat.

"But sugar," he said, "the rest jest wasn't smart as me."

There was a lull in the fierce beating wind. A pitiful whine sounded at the door. Penny went to it. Rip had found adequate shelter, but old Julia stood drenched and shivering. Or perhaps she had found shelter, too, but longed for a comfort that was more than dryness. Penny let her in.

Ma Baxter said, "Now let in Trixie and old Caesar, and you'll have things about to suit you."

Penny said to Julia, "Jealous o' leetle ol' Flag, eh? Now you've been a Baxter longer'n Flag. You jest come dry yourself."

She wagged her slow tail and licked his hand. Jody was warmed by his father's inclusion of the fawn in the family. Flag Baxter—

Ma Baxter said, "How you men kin take on over a dumb creetur, I cain't see. Callin' a dog by your own name— And that fawn, sleepin' right in the bed with Jody."

Jody said, "He don't seem like a creetur to me, Ma. He seems jest like another boy."

"Well, it's your bed. Long as he don't bring fleas or lice or ticks or nothin' into it."

He was indignant.

"Look at him, Ma. Lookit that sleekity coat. Smell him, Ma."

"I don't want to smell him."

"But he smells sweet."

"Jest like a rose, I s'pose. Well, to my notion, wet fur's wet fur."

"Now I like the smell o' wet fur," Penny said. "I mind me one time, on a long hunt, I had me no coat and the weather turned cold. It was over about Salt Springs, at the head o' the run. My, it was cold. And we shot a bear, and I dressed out the skin nice, and I slept under it, with the fur side out. And in the night come a cold drizzly rain, and I poked my nose out from under, and I smelt that wet fur. Now the other fellers, Noey Ginright and Bert Harper and Milt Revells, they said I purely stunk, but I puttened my head back under the bearskin and I was warm as a squirrel in a holler tree, and that wet bear-hide smelt better to me than yellow jessamine."

The rain drummed on the roof. The wind whistled under the eaves. Old Julia stretched out on the floor near the fawn. The storm was as cozy as Jody had hoped for. He made up his mind privately that he would wish for another in a week or two. Now and then Penny peered out of the window into the dark.

"Hit's a toad-strangler of a rain," he said.

Supper was generous. There were cowpeas and smoked venison pie and biscuit pudding. Anything that was remotely an occasion stirred Ma Baxter to extra cooking, as though her imagination could speak only by the use of flour and shortening. She fed Flag a bit of pudding with her own fingers. Jody, with a secret gratitude, helped her wash and wipe the supper dishes. Penny went to bed shortly after, for his strength did not hold out, but not to sleep. A candle burned in the bedroom and Ma Baxter brought her piecing, and Jody lay across the foot of the bed. The rain hissed against the window.

He said, "Pa, tell me a tale."

Penny said, "I've told you all the tales I know."

"No, you ain't. You allus got another."

"Well, the only one comes to me I ain't told, ain't rightly a tale. I ever tell you about the dog I had when I first come to the island? The dog could cold-out study?"

Jody wriggled closer up the counterpane.

"Tell me."

"Well, sir, the dog was part fox-hound and part blood-hound and part jest dog. He had long sorrowful ears, nigh about dragged the ground, and he was so bow-legged he couldn't walk a sweet pertater bed. He had distant kind o' eyes, lookin' off some'eres, and them distracted eyes near about caused me to trade him off. Well, I hunted him a whiles, and it begun to come to me, he didn't act like no other dog I'd ever seed. He'd leave a cat-trail or a fox-trail right in the middle, and go lay down. The first time-two he done it, I figgered I jest didn't have me no dog a-tall.

"Well, sir, it begun to come to me, he knowed what he was doin'. Jody boy, go fetch me my pipe."

The interruption was exasperating. Jody tingled. He scrambled for the pipe and tobacco.

"All right now, son. You set on the floor or on a chair and keep offen the bed. Ary time I say 'trail' or 'track' you jiggle the bed to where I think the slats is busted. That's better—

"Well, sir, I was obliged to set down with that dog my own-self, to see what 'twas he was doin'. Now you know how a wild-cat or a fox'll fool most dogs? He'll double back on his own tracks. Yes sir, he'll double back on his own tracks. He'll git a good start on the dogs and he'll light out and put a heap o' distance between 'em. Then what do he do? He turns right back over his own trail. He cuts as far back as he's daresome to do, listenin' all the while for the dogs. Then he cuts off at another angle, so a picture o' his trail'd look like a big V, like the ducks makes flyin'. Well, the dogs follers the trail he made in the first place, extry strong on account of him havin' been over it twicet, and then they come to a place where they jest ain't no more trail. They nose around and they nose around and they complain, and when they jest cain't figger no sense to it, they turns back agin, back-trackin'. 'Course, they picks up then the turn-off where the fox or cat cut off in another direction. But all that time is wasted, and nine to one the cat or fox has made an out of it and got plumb away. Well, what do you figger this lop-eared dog o' mine done?"

"Tell me."

"He figgered it out, that's what he done. He figgered out about when 'twas time for the creetur to double back—and he'd slip back along the trail and lay down and wait. And when Mister Fox or Mister Cat come slippin' back, there was old Dandy waitin' to pop out on him.

"Now sometimes he'd make his cut-off too fur back, and did he hang them long ears when he guessed it wrong! But mostly speakin', he studied it out right, and he ketched me more wild-cats and more foxes than ary dog I've had, before or since."

He puffed his pipe. Ma Baxter moved her rocker closer to the candle. It was depressing to have the tale end so soon.

"What else did old Dandy do, Pa?"

"Well, one day he met his match."

"A cat or a fox?"

"Neither one. A big ol' buck, was as smart a deer as he was smart a dog. He was a buck with a twisted antler. Each year it growed in twisted. Now a deer don't generally double back on his tracks. But now and agin this old buck'd do it. And that was jest to this sly ol' dog's likin'. But this is where he wasn't smart enough. The buck'd do jest the opposite to whatever the dog figgered he'd do. One time he'd double back. Next time he'd keep on runnin'. He'd change his ways ever' whip-stitch. That went on, year in, year out, the dog and the buck tryin' to out-smart each other."

"Which was the smartest, Pa. How'd it end?"

"You shore you want the answer?"

He hesitated. He wanted the droopy-eared dog to out-smart the buck, and yet he wanted the buck to get away.

"Yes. I got to know. I got to know the answer."

"Well, hit's got a answer but no endin'. Old Dandy never come up with him."

He sighed with relief. That was a proper tale. When he thought of it again, he could picture the dog trailing the buck perpetually.

He said, "Tell another tale like that un, Pa. A tale has got a answer but no endin'."

"Now boy, they ain't many tales like that in the world. You best be content with that un."

Ma Baxter said, "I ain't much for dogs, but they was a dog oncet I takened a notion to. It was a bitch and she had the purtiest coat. I said to the feller owned her, 'When she finds pups,' says I, 'I'd like one.' He said, 'You're welcome, but 'twon't do, for you got no way o' huntin' it'—I wasn't yit married to your Pa—'and a hound'll die,' he said, 'if it ain't hunted.' 'Is she a hound?' says I, and he said, 'Yessum.' And I said, 'Then I shore don't want one, for a hound'll suck eggs.' "

Jody waited eagerly for the rest of the tale, then understood that was all there was to it. It was like all his mother's tales. They were like hunts where nothing happened. He went back in his thoughts to the dog that could out-smart wild-cats and foxes, but never caught the buck.

He said, "I'll bet Flag'll be smart when he grows up."

Penny said, "What'll you do, do somebody else's dogs take out after him?"

His throat constricted.

"I'll kill ary dog or ary man comes here, huntin' him. Nobody ain't likely to come, is they?"

Penny said gently, "We'll spread the word, so folks'll be keerful. He's not likely to roam far, no-how."

Jody decided to keep his gun always loaded, against marauders. He slept that night with Flag on the bed beside him. The wind shook the windowpanes all night and he slept uneasily, dreaming of clever dogs that ran the fawn mercilessly through the rain.

In the morning he found Penny dressed as for winter, in his heavy coat and with a shawl over his head. He was preparing to go out into the storm to milk Trixie, the only chore that was entirely necessary for the time being. There was no lessening of the torrential downpour.

Ma Baxter said, "Now you be peert and git back in here or you'll die o' the pneumony."

Jody said, "Leave me go," but Penny said, "The wind'd blow you away, boy."

It seemed to him, watching the small bones of his father leaning against the tumultuous air, that there was little to choose between them in bulk and sturdiness. Penny came in again, drenched and breathless, the milk in the gourd spotted by the rain.

He said, "Hit's a mercy I toted water yestiddy."

The day continued as stormy as it had begun. The rain fell in sheets and the wind whipped it in under the eaves, so that Ma Baxter set pans and gourds to catch it. The rain barrels outside were overflowing and the rain from the roof gurgled into their fullness. Old Julia and the fawn had to be turned out by force. They were both back at the kitchen door in a brief time, wet and shivering. This time Rip was with them, whining. Ma Baxter protested, but Penny admitted the three. Jody dried them all with the crocus sack rug from in front of the hearth.

Penny said, "We're about due for a lull."

The lull did not come. Now and then there seemed to be a few moments when the wind and rain were less intense and Penny rose hopefully from his chair and peered outside. But he had no sooner decided that he would risk going out to cut wood and see to the chickens, than the deluge came again, as violent as before. In the late afternoon he went again to milk Trixie, to feed and water Caesar, and to feed the chickens, huddled and frightened and unable to scratch for their living. Ma Baxter made him change his wet clothes immediately. They steamed and dried by the hearth with the sweet, musty smell of wet cloth.

Supper was not so ample. Penny was not inclined to tales. The dogs were allowed to sleep in the house and the family went to bed early. Darkness had come at an unseemly hour and it was impossible to tell the time. Jody awakened at what would ordinarily have been an hour before daylight. The world was dark and the rain was still falling, the wind still blowing.

Penny said, "We'll git a break this mornin'. Hit's a three-day nor'easter a'right, but sich a rain. I'll be proud to see the sun."

The sun did not appear. There was no morning break. In mid-afternoon there came the lull that Penny had expected the day before. But it was a gray lull, the roof dripping, the trees soaked, the earth sodden. The chickens came out from their huddle for a few forlorn moments and scratched half-heartedly.

Penny said, "We'll git a change o' wind now, and all be clare and fine."

The change of wind came. The gray sky turned green. The wind roared in from a distance, as before. When it came, it was not from the northeast but from the southeast, and it brought more rain.

Penny said, "I've never seed sich a thing."

The rain was more torrential than before. It poured down as though Juniper Creek and Silver Glen Run and Lake George and the St. John's River had all emptied over the scrub at once. The wind was no fiercer than before, but it was gusty. And there was no end to it. It blew and rained and blew and rained and blew and rained.

Penny said, "This must be the way the Lord made the blasted ocean."

Ma Baxter said, "Hush. You'll be punished."

"Cain't be no worse punished, woman. The 'taters'll be rotted and the corn flat and the hay ruint, and the cane."

The yard was afloat. Jody looked out of the window and saw two drowned biddies floating about with upturned bellies.

Penny said, "I've seed things in my time, but I've never seed a thing like this."

Jody offered to go to the sink-hole for drinking water.

Penny said, "Hit'll be nothin' but rain-water, and riled to boot."

They drank rain-water from a pan under the northwest corner of the house. It had a faintly woody taste from the cypress shingles. Jody did the evening chores. He went out of the kitchen door with the milk gourd into a strange world. It was a lost and desolate world, like the beginning of time, or the end of it. The vegetation was beaten flat. A river ran down the road, so that a flat-bottomed boat could have gone down it clear to Silver Glen. The familiar pines were like trees at the bottom of the sea, washed across not with mere rain, but with tides and currents. It seemed to him that he might swim to the top of the rain. The water was knee-deep in the lot, which lay at a lower level than the house. Trixie had broken down the bars that separated her from the calf and had taken it with her to a high corner. They stood huddled together. The calf had taken most of the milk and he was able only to draw a quart or so from the drained udders. The passage between the stalls and the corn-crib was a sluiceway. He meant to gather the dry husks for extra feed for Trixie, but the water swept through so discouragingly that he decided to let her make out until morning with the hay from the loft. It was a good thing, he thought, that the new crop of hay would soon be ready. There was little left. He did not know whether to try to separate the over-grown calf from the cow again. There was no place to put it where it would be dry. Yet the Baxters needed the milk as badly. He decided to wait and ask his father, coming back again if necessary. He fought his way outside and plodded to the house. The rain blinded him. The clearing seemed alien and unfriendly. He was glad to push open the door and to be again inside the house. The kitchen seemed safe and intimate. He made his report on conditions.

Penny said, "Best leave the calf stay with its mammy, a time like this. We kin make out without milk 'til mornin'. Hit'll shorely be clare by then."

Morning brought no abatement. Penny paced up and down the kitchen.

He said, "My daddy told of a storm in the '50's was mighty bad, but I don't reckon all Floridy history has had sich a rain."

The days passed with no change. Ma Baxter usually left the weather in Penny's hands, but now she cried, and sat rocking with her hands folded. On the fifth day, Penny and Jody made a rush to the pea-field to pull enough cow-peas for a meal or two. The peas were flattened. They pulled up the whole vines with their backs to the rain and wind. They stopped at the smoke-house for a piece of pickled meat from the bear Buck Forrester had shot on his last night with them. Penny remembered that his wife was short of cooking grease. They tipped the can that held the golden bear grease and filled a stone crock. They laid the meat over the top to protect it and rushed for the house.

The cow-peas were already moulding on the outside, but the peas inside were still firm and good. Supper was again a feast. There was the wild honey to fall back on, and Ma Baxter made a pudding sweetened with its rich flavor, tasting faintly of wood and smoke.

Penny said, "Don't seem possible it'll not clare by mornin', but if so be 'tain't, Jody, you and me had best git out in it and pull as many peas as we kin manage."

Ma Baxter said, "But how'll I keep 'em?"

"Cook 'em, woman, and warm 'em ever' day, if need be."

The morning of the sixth day was exactly like the others. Since they would be drenched in any case, Penny and Jody stripped to their breeches and went to the field with sacks. They worked until noon in the downpour, pulling the slippery pods from the bushes. They came in for a hurried dinner and went back again without troubling to change their clothes. They covered most of the field. The hay, Penny said, was a total loss, but they would do what they could to save the peas. Some of the pods were mature. They spent the evening and late into the night shelling the peas, sticky and mouldering. Ma Baxter built up a slow fire on the hearth and spread out the peas close to the heat to dry. Jody was awakened several times in the night by the sound of some one going out to the kitchen to replenish the fire.

The morning of the seventh day might have been the morning of the first. The gusty wind whipped around the house as though it had always blown and always would blow. The sound of the rain on the roof and in the rain-barrels was now so familiar that it was not noticed. At daylight, a limb of the chinaberry crashed to the ground. The Baxters sat silently at breakfast.

Penny said, "Well, Job takened worse punishment than this. Leastways, none of us ain't got risin's."

Ma Baxter snapped, "Find the good in it, that's right."

"They ain't no good in it. Lest it is to remind a man to be humble, for there's nary thing on earth he kin call his own."

After breakfast he took Jody to the cornfield. The corn had been broken on the stalks before the storm. The stalks were beaten to the ground but the ears were unharmed. They gathered them and brought them too into the warm dry refuge of the kitchen.

Ma Baxter said, "I ain't got the peas dried yit. How'll I dry all this?"

Penny did not answer but went to the front room and kindled a fire on the hearth. Jody went outside to bring in more wood. The wood was soaked through, but when the fat-wood was heated a little while it would burn. Penny strewed the ears of corn on the floor.

He said to Jody, "Now your job be to keep changin' it, so's it'll all git a mite o' the heat."

Ma Baxter said, "How's the cane?"

"Hit's flat."

"What you reckon has happened to the 'taters?"

He shook his head. In the late afternoon he went to the sweet potato field and dug enough for supper. They were beginning to rot. By trimming, some were usable. Again, supper seemed lavish, because of the sweet potatoes.

Penny said, "If they ain't no change by mornin', we jest as good to quit fightin' and lay down and die."

Jody had never heard his father speak so disconsolately. It froze him through. Flag was showing the effect of short rations. His ribs and backbone were visible. He bleated often. Penny had given up all attempt to milk the cow, for the sake of the calf.

In the middle of the night Jody awakened and thought he heard his father about. It seemed to him the rain was falling less violently. He was asleep again before he could be certain. He awakened on the morning of the eighth day. Something was different. There was silence instead of tumult. The rain had stopped. The long winds were still. A light the color of pomegranate blossoms sifted through the gray, wet atmosphere. Penny flung all the doors and windows wide open.

"'Tain't much of a world to go out to," he said, "but let's all go out and be thankful there's a world at all."

The dogs pushed past him and bounded out side by side. Penny smiled.

"Dogged if 'tain't like goin' outen the Ark," he said. "The animals two by two— Ory, come go out with me."

Jody jumped about and leaped down the steps with the fawn.

"We're the two deer," he called.

Ma Baxter looked across the fields and began to cry again. But the air, Jody felt, was cool and sweet and gracious. The fawn shared his feeling and bounded over the yard-gate with swift twinkling heels. The world was devastated with the flood, but it was indeed, as Penny kept reminding his wife, the only world they had.

"A PROMISE LAND"

BY ELIZABETH MADOX ROBERTS

Elizabeth Madox Roberts (1886–1941) was born in Kentucky and made that area and its history her special province as a writer. Both poet and novelist, her poetic skills helped shape her prose style. All her novels have a special quality, a sense of time and place as they have shaped people. This selection is from her novel The Great Meadow, *which tells of the beginnings of settlement in Kentucky, but tells it in terms of insistently human people.*

(*The Great Meadow*, by Elizabeth Madox Roberts; The Viking Press, 1930.)

One day, at nightfall, while Diony milked the cows at the gap, she knew by some slight uneasiness in the herd that a stranger had come to the plantation. Betty ran toward the house to learn who had walked in from the creek road, but presently she came running back to tell, for she could not leave Diony unknowing. Berk Jarvis had come bringing a stranger.

"What manner of kind is he?" Diony asked, taking forward the business of milking, her hands getting milk.

"A hunter," Betty said. "I never in all my time saw such a man as he is. I was beside myself as soon as I saw such a kind."

"A hunter is no monstrous sight to see. A hunter wouldn't fright me outen my wits now."

"This-here hunter is a different kind from e'er other you ever laid eyes on. Hit's outside my power to describe what sort he is."

Diony turned the stream of milk into the piggin with a swift free hand, thinking of hunters, and remembering that Berk Jarvis was such. He had a delight in his skill with a rifle and in his long journeys, for he had been back into Fincastle more than once. Each young man wanted to go farther than the rest. Now Diony was impatient to see this indescribable hunter Betty reported of, but the milk stream must flow in its accustomed flood. Betty moved lightly before the gap, minding away the calves.

"Do Berk Jarvis and this hunter that is a wonder to tell of, do they aim to take a night with us?" Diony asked.

Betty thought that they did. She lingered over her words, modifying all that she said with her continual astonishment. "He looks like nobody you ever before saw in life," she said.

"Tell me what he is. Say more about how he looks," Diony begged of her. The milk flowed slowly. The stream could not be slighted. Diony had a fine pride in her milking.

"I never had talk with him myself," Betty said. "But I think, apter than not, he looks like what he does because he's been all the way into the wilderness. He's been all the way to Kentuck. I never in my time saw 'eer other that's got the look he's got."

When the milk had ceased its flow, Diony put it swiftly in the dairy-house and went to the table where the evening meal was set. The two guests were in their places when, with Betty, she slipped lightly into her place. The stranger was past description strange. The supper moved swiftly, food taking the first place in the minds of all, but presently she was aware that the stranger Berk had brought had been into far regions beyond the mountains, had been to the country of Kentuck. He made no offer to speak, but when he was addressed he gave a courteous reply. Sally Tolliver sat at the farther end of the table eating her bit of food, making herself blank and dull before the dull wall, scarcely making a shape when she arose to find more bread for the platter. She had been into the far wilderness of Fincastle. She would not speak of what she had seen there, and Polly, who knew her story, was as unwilling to speak of it. Diony turned from her dull shadow and viewed the stranger again, for he gathered a brightness about himself. His body was thin and his face was gaunt and clean-shaven. He would snatch quick glances at one or another of those at the board without moving his head, sending his eyes about on quick missions. His clothes were of fresh woolsey from some farmhouse. Diony thought that he might be old, but she could gather no more of him.

Thomas Hall brought his guests to the new house with ceremony as soon as the meal was done. All crossed the dog alley slowly, Betty staying her steps, suppressed and faintly amused, wanting Diony to share her put-by mirth. The old guest was given a chair near the center of the hearth circle, and Thomas Hall sat in his accustomed place with Polly at his right hand. Diony sat beside Betty and Reuben on the bench which was fitted along the wall to the left of the fireplace, and Sam walked about the room or sat, as his eagerness would allow. The young guest, Berk Jarvis, sat on a stool near to the bench, and he took pride in the stranger as in one he had brought from a far place who would tell stories of strange wonders, for he gave a hint of what would follow.

Diony could see the old man more clearly now, the fog of surprise being gone a little way from her sight. He was far past middle age. His face was quick but ghostly under its weather marks and stains. He spread his lean strong hands along his thighs and looked from one face to another as if he scarcely knew the ways of houses and the uses of hearthsides although these had once been his knowledge, as if he slightly feared now the gentleness of women. Presently he was talking, slowly at first, Diony scarcely able to attend the meaning of what he said, being as yet surprised with the meanings his person yielded. He weighed each speech with care, making each phrase with pains, as is the way with men who have lived alone and have made decisions without the use of words or speeches. His voice was a sharp cutting-tool, placed guardedly to fall beneath a roof, carefully brought to lie low beneath rafters.

He bowed with courtesy whenever Polly spoke, or whenever Diony. His words were given with dignity, as if the silence of the unbroken forest and the cane had purged some ancient speech and refurbished its repose. Thomas took a delight in this speech regardless of what it reported of the wilderness, as if the words were more to him than the substance they conveyed, but the young men gave more heed to the cargo than to the conveyance. Diony saw her father's pleasure in the old hunter's words with a rush of love and pity, and her mind went swiftly to the letters in the desk under the shelf of books, to the books then. Only a little while had passed since the ceremonious entry from the supper room. The old hunter was clarified now, had stood forth, clearly seen and comprehended.

"Recruit the fire, Diony. Fling on another piece. We'll hear more of the Ken-tuck-ee. More, sir, more," Thomas called out.

Diony and Sam set the sticks together in the embers and moved swiftly back. The old man laid one thin hand along his thigh and spoke.

"Yea, it is a good land, the most extraordinary that ever I saw. Meadow and woodland as far as eye can behold. Beauteous tracts in a great scope, miles. A fine river makes a bound to it on the north, and another fine river flows far to the west, another boundary. To the east is a boundary of rugged mountains. And set above the mountains is a great cliff that stands across the way. Yea, you would know you had come to the country of Caintuck when you saw that place. A cliff wall makes a steep barrier across your path beyond any man's strength to climb. But high up in the mountains, cut in the cliff, is a gate. I was in and out of it for years to peer out the land and to spy its wonders. I walked far there. All the fore part of one year and on until summer came I hunted beyond the Chenoa River."

"The Author of Nature has point-blank made a promise land," Thomas said. "A place fitted to nurture a fine race, a land of promise."

"The undergrowth pea-vine, cane, nettle, all mingled with every rich weed. Its timber a fair sight to see. Honey-locust, black walnut, sugar tree, hickory, ironwood, hoopwood, mulberry, ash, elm. Oak a-plenty. I saw ash trees fifty feet high. There's a bird there, yea, a marvel. A woodcock that's a wonder to hear of."

"Hear what he tells about the trees. Pea-vine under foot. Ash trees fifty feet high. Hit's a wonder," Sam's voice cried out and another voice joined him, one flowing after another.

"If it's wonders you desire I'll name a great wonder. At Big Bone Creek by the upper salt licks I saw a greater marvel. There you'd see the bones of some monstrous beasts on the ground. The joints of the spine bone make camp stools to rest a man, and a tooth weighs five pounds to lift. It's a wonder of the earth."

"Are these beasts all dead now?"

"All dead that I saw, but it would be a most fearful thing to meet one alive. I saw a jaw tooth over four pounds in weight. I saw a rib bone eleven feet long, or such a matter. A skull bone six feet across the forehead. Tusks or horns five feet in measure."

"Such a beast to walk the earth! I'd be afeared to meet one in the dark of a night."

"And all might not be dead. The live ones might come down through the cane."

"Hear what he says. He's a mind to speak again."

"In another place are the caves, if it's wonders you crave to hear. There's a country under the earth. Men live there, it's said, under the ground, under limestone rock. Miles, you can go, and keep yourself darkling, always under the earth. It's said there are races of men there, houses and cities, citizens of the caves, dwellers of the cave lands to the west. I never saw this marvel for myself, but I had report of it."

"Oh, I'd want to go there."

"And game everywhere in plenty, he says."

"Let him tell about the game. He's about to speak. Listen."

"Buffalo, bears, elk, pigeon, waterfowls, beavers, otters, turkeys. You could never hunt your fill. Around the salt licks the bears trample one another under and you can kill as fast as you can load your weapon and fire. The pigeons black the air with their wings and their flights are like a thunder in the sky."

"A man could live off the beasts. Could kill his food with his rifle."

"But a land of blood, the redmen say. No redman can live there. He would hear the footsteps of his fathers of a night, bones that walk in the dark. It's a fearful land to a redman, a forfended place. He would hear the ghosts of the Alleghewi, the old race that lived there before his time, a lost race, the redmen say, now all out of the earth."

"Oh, I wouldn't go there. I wouldn't," a frightened voice cried, Betty crying with it, "I wouldn't go."

"Hearken now. Let him tell. Hearken."

"A redskin told me this, and told me the words that make the meaning of the name, Kentuck. Ken-tak-ee—Meadow Lands, he said. I recollect we talked a night beside a fire not far from the Big Bone Lick. Ken-tak-ee, he said, was the name of the whole place, Meadow Lands. A fearful country. Every road a place where a battle has been.

The land there is thick with broken battle-axes and under the ground run the bones of many men. A dark country. No redman lives there."

"I wouldn't go. I wouldn't."

"I aim to go, myself. Ne'er a thing could hold me," Sam said. "I'll explore the caves and see the bones of the beasts."

"I'd want a fine farm in the open country," Reuben said. "Six hundred acres would content me there."

"A safe place, though. A block-house near at hand."

"Quit, boys. Hearken. He's a mind to speak again."

"In the past summer season of the year, in June, a mighty man of valor, James Harrod, and thirty men, made a town in the caneland, the beginnings of a nation. I came to this place and I saw men felling trees and building houses. James Harrod and his thirty. Then Boone comes by to tell all Lord Dunmore is about to make a war on the redskins in the upper Ohio Valley, and all come back across the mountains to help fight Lord Dunmore's battles. But Harrod and his men will go back to the town they have begun in the cane."

"A new world has begun then, in that place. Hit's hard to see what mought come there."

"Tell more, sir, about the old race, those gone and forgotten out of the earth, that once lived there, and what relics they left." Diony asked this, wondering what it would be like to belong to such a nation.

"I saw a great stone wall, a fortified place, built, I surmise, by the Alleghewi, upwards of three hundred feet long. Sixty feet high, it was, some of the stones five hundred pounds weight. On the top of the wall you could see the stones the warriors carried there for weapons, stones to throw down on the enemy, piled high."

"I'd aim to go there, to that place," Sam said.

Diony looked across the hearth from one to another, but her quick look caught the look of Berk Jarvis, and they looked together, back and forth, his eyes bright and his head lifted as if he were about to speak. His long arms were bent, his wrists resting on his knees, his large hands loosely knotted together. Then some voice spoke.

"A long way to go," one said, "a long way."

"A long way, but the reward is more than the labor. Canelands the like never before seen on the map of the world. Or beyond the cane, tall trees, not too thick for beauty, a land of beauty, a garden place."

"But a weary road through the wilderness," Polly said then. "No path under foot, no trace to guide where you'd set your next step. Savages to kill you and get your skulp maybe. Hit may be a fair place . . . No way to send back what you couldn't carry. Hit'll ever be the case for years to come."

"But the country is like paradise. Rich cane. Trees all blowth in the spring-o'-the-year. Like paradise it is, so beautiful and good."

"Hit's said there's a woodcock there. Tell, please, about the bird you named a while ago, sir."

"A wonder, this is. Let him tell now."

"A woodcock there and its beak is pure ivory. I saw this witness for myself. Yea, I saw a woodcock with a beak that is like a jewel stone."

Diony looked across toward Berk Jarvis, her head suddenly lifted, her eyes bright, and all her inner part leaping. He smiled a delayed smile and looked happily back, and the look said to her, "I would go there, any chance I had, I, Berk Jarvis," and her look replied, "I would go, I, Diony, would go to see the ivory-beaked woodcock."

"Could you name the seven rivers that flow there?" Reuben asked.

The old man sat quiet while he searched his mind for all seven of the fair rivers of this wilderness before he replied. When he had gathered all these strands of water into a thread of memory he answered, speaking softly, putting his speech with care.

"There is first the Tenn-ess-ee, the farthest water. Then, moving hitherward, you would come to the Shawnee River, and this has been called—it is a pity—has been sometimes called the Cumberland. There is one next called the Muddy River. I saw its mouth where it pours into the Ohio but I never explored its whole course. It is a fine stream, its yellow silt to show what a great scope of land it washes. Next comes the Pigeon River, not so great in size as the Shawnee, but a fine water with many meanders and many creeks to drain a great content of land. A wonder of pigeons come to roost along its course, until they dark the sky with their flights . . . I recall then the most lovely river of all . . ."

He sank into a reverie as he contemplated this stream, letting his thought slip with its winding course among high cliffs and tree-grown hills, and Diony, having heard report of it, knew what name he would say when he took back his dreaming mind from its curving course and consented to speak again. He looked quietly into the embers and presently he spoke, naming the river softly as one might name a lover.

"Chenoa. It's called Chenoa, or some say Cuttawa, or Millewakane. Among all the rivers of the world there is no river it would give you greater content to see. I saw it in the spring-o'-the-year when the redbud brush was in flower, a blowth over the whole face of the rock-cliff, and wild plum. The river runs through a gorge gouted out through the rock, and the walls of the river stand like walls of laid stone to wind with the flow of the stream. Beyond on the level above, is a rolling land like a garden, canelands and groves of woodland . . ."

"The other rivers," Reuben said, drawing him back to the task of naming all. "Could you name the rest, sir?"

"Oh, wait," Diony cried out, "wait. Don't name another yet. This river, tell more of how it was, please, tell more."

"The Chenoa. Wild plum in flower in the spring-o'-the-year. Mile after mile, and a high cliff both sides set like stones in the wall of a fine ruin. Chenoa. You'd read about the Rhine as a fair stream, high stones and shaped cliffs the like you might never see again on the earth . . . But the Chenoa is a fine stream, lovely to see, the shapes on the stones to make a power on the mind . . ."

"It must be a great content to a man to go into a new country and name there the rivers with names he would fancy . . ." "To name a river and write it on a map." Sam and Berk spoke these fancies, echoing the one upon the other. They made an interval in which the old man dreamed quietly of the far-off water he had named with affection. He spoke at last, beginning softly, passing to the remaining of the seven streams.

"The Great Salt Lick comes next and it has a wonder of salt licks in its valleys. Close to its course are spread the bones of the great beasts. Then last, nearest the mountains, is the Chatteraway, running down from above."

The old narrator fell into a reverie then, having given report of his travels, having spent his vigor in recounting, and he made as if he would gladly rest now. But he arose to bow with a strange grace, a deep, slow courtesy which belonged to some remote life he had known beyond his knowledge of the wilderness, when Polly arose from her chair. He stood as one offering homage until she moved away from the fireside.

"I'll lay me down to sleep now," Thomas Hall said. "We'll go all." Being requested, he gave the old narrator a pile of skins by the kitchen fire, and left him to sleep there. All went quickly to their places.

SHAME TO WASTE A BOY

BY ROBERT RUARK

Robert Ruark (1915–1965) was born in Wilmington, North Carolina, grew up knowing intimately the Carolina woodlands and waters, and was educated at the University of North Carolina. He became a newspaperman, columnist, big game hunter and traveler, and he wrote a dozen books including two novels about violent life in modern Africa. But perhaps the best book he ever wrote was The Old Man and the Boy, *the first of two memoirs about his boyhood and his outdoorsman grandfather. This selection is from that book, which tells about days afield with "the Old Man" and is full of well-remembered sights, sounds, and smells as well as the elusive emotions of boyhood.*

(*The Old Man and the Boy*, by Robert Ruark; Henry Holt and Company, 1957.)

It was awful cold when the Old Man hit me a lick in the ribs with his elbow and said, "Get up, boy, and fix that fire." The stars were still up, frosty in the sky, and a wind was whistling round the corners of the tent. You could see the fire flicker just a mite against the black background of the swamp. Mister Howard was still snoring on his side of the pine-needle-canvas bed, and I remember that his mustache was riffling, like marsh grass in the wind. Over in Tom and Pete's tent you could hear two breeds of snores. One was squeaky, and the other sounded like a bull caught in a bob-wire fence. I crawled out from under the covers, shivering, and jumped into my hunting boots, which were stiff and very cold. Everything else I owned I'd slept in.

The fire was pretty feeble. It had simmered down into gray ash, which was swirling loosely in the morning breeze. There was just a little red eye blinking underneath the fine talcumy ashes. After kicking some of the ashes aside with my boot, I put a couple of lightwood knots on top of the little chunk of glowing coal, and then I dragged some live-oak logs over the top of the lightwood and waited for her to catch. She caught, and the tiny teeth of flame opened wide to eat the oak. In five minutes I had a blaze going, and I was practically in it. It was mean cold that morning.

When the Old Man saw the fire dancing, he woke up Mister Howard and reached for his pipe first and his boots next. Then he reached for the bottle and poured himself a dram in a tin cup. He shuddered some when the dram went down.

"I heartily disapprove of drinking in the morning," he said. "Except some mornings. It takes a man past sixty to know whether he can handle his liquor good enough to take a nip in the morning. Howard?"

"I'm past sixty too," Mister Howard said. "Pass the jug."

Tom and Pete were coming out of the other tent, digging their knuckles into sleepy eyes. Pete went down to the branch and fetched a bucket of water, and everybody washed their faces out of the bucket. Then Pete went to the fire and slapped some ham into the pan and some eggs into the skillet, set some bread to toasting, and put the coffee pot on. Breakfast didn't take long. We had things to do that day.

After the second cup of coffee—I can still taste that coffee, with the condensed milk sweet and curdled on the top and the coffee itself tasting of branch water and wood smoke—we got up and started sorting out the guns.

"This is a buckshot day," the Old Man said, squinting down the barrel of his pump gun. "I think we better get us a deer today. Need meat in the camp, and maybe we can blood the boy. Tom, Pete, you all drive the branch. Howard, we'll put the boy on a stand where a buck is apt to amble by, and then you and I will kind of drift around according to where the noise seems headed. One, t'other of us ought to get a buck. This crick is populous with deer."

The Old Man paused to light his pipe, and then he turned around and pointed the stem at me.

"You, boy," he said. "By this time you know a lot about guns, but you don't know a lot about guns and deer together. Many a man loses his wits when he sees a big ol' buck bust out of the bushes with a rockin' chair on his head. Trained hunters shoot each other. They get overexcited and just bang away into the bushes. *Mind* what I say. A deer ain't a deer unless it's got horns on its head and you can see all of it at once. We don't shoot does and we don't shoot spike bucks and we don't shoot each other. There ain't no sense to shootin' a doe or a young'un. One buck can service hundreds of does, and one doe will breed you a mess of deer. If you shoot a young'un, you haven't got much meat, and no horns at all, and you've kept him from breedin' to make more deer for you to shoot. If you shoot a man, they'll likely hang you, and if the man is me I will be awful gol-damned annoyed and come back to ha'nt you. You mind that gun, and don't pull a trigger until you can see what it is and *where* it is. *Mind*, I say."

Tom and Pete picked up their pump guns and loaded them. They pushed the load lever down so there'd be no shell in the chamber, but only in the magazine. The Old Man looked at my little gun and said, "Don't bother to load it until you get on the stand. You ain't likely to see anything to shoot for an hour or so."

Tom and Pete went over to where we had the dogs tethered on a line strung between two trees, and he unleashed the two hounds, Bell and Blue. Bell was black-and-tan and all hound. Blue was a kind of a sort of dog. He had some plain hound, some Walker hound, and some bulldog and a little beagle and a smidgen of pointer in him. He was ticked blue and brown and black and yellow and white. He looked as if somebody spilled the eggs on the checkered tablecloth. But he was a mighty dandy deer dog, or so they said. Old Sam Watts, across the street, used to say there wasn't no use trying to tell Blue anything, because Blue had done forgot more than you knew and just got annoyed when you tried to tell him his business.

Tom snapped a short lead on Blue, and Pete snapped another one on Bell. They shouldered their guns and headed up the branch, against the wind. We let 'em walk, while the Old Man and Mister Howard puttered around, like old people and most women will. Drives a boy crazy. What I wanted to do was go and shoot myself a deer. *Now.*

After about ten minutes the Old Man picked up his gun and said, "Let's go." We walked about half a mile down the swamp's edge. The light had come now, lemon-colored, and the fox squirrels were beginning to chase each other through the gum trees. We spied one old possum in a persimmon tree, hunched into a ball and making out like nobody knew he was there. We heard a turkey gobble away over yonder somewheres, and we could hear the doves beginning to moan—*oooh—oohoo—oooooh.*

All the little birds started to squeak and chirp and twitter at each other. The dew was staunchly stiff on the grass and on the sparkleberry and gallberry bushes. It was still cold, but getting warmer, and breakfast had settled down real sturdy in my stomach. Rabbits jumped out from under our feet. We stepped smack onto a covey of quail just working its way out of the swamp, and they like to have scared me to death when they busted up under our feet. There was a lot going on in that swamp that morning.

We turned into the branch finally, and came up to a track that the Old Man said was a deer run. He looked around and spied a stump off to one side, hidden by a tangle of dead brush. From the stump you could see clear for about fifty yards in a sort of accidental arena.

"Go sit on that stump, boy," the Old Man said. "You'll hear the dogs after a while, and if a deer comes down this branch he'll probably bust out there, where that trail comes into the open, because there ain't any other way he can cross it without leaving the swamp. Don't let the dogs fool you into not paying attention. When you hear 'em a mile away, the chances are that deer will be right in your lap. Sometimes they travel as much as two miles ahead of the dogs, just slipping along, not running; just slipping and sneaking on their little old quiet toes. And stay still. A deer'll run right over you if you stay still and the smell is away from him. But if you wink an eye, he can see it two hundred yards off, and will go the other way."

I sat down on the stump. The Old Man and Mister Howard went off, and I could hear them chatting quietly as they disappeared. I looked all around me. Nothing much was going on now, except a couple of he-squirrels were having a whale of a fight over my head, racing across branches and snarling squirrel cuss words at each other. A chickadee was standing on its head in a bush and making chickadee noises. A redheaded woodpecker was trying to cut a live-oak trunk in half with his bill. A rain crow—a kind of cuckoo, it is—was making dismal noises off behind me in the swamp, and a big old yellow-hammer was swooping and dipping from tree to tree.

There were some robins hopping around on a patch of burnt ground, making conversation with each other. Crows were cawing, and two doves looped in to sit in a tree and chuckle at each other. A towhee was scratching and making more noise than a herd of turkeys, and some catbirds were meowing in the low bush while a big, sassy old mocker was imitating them kind of sarcastically. Anybody who says woods are quiet is crazy. You learn to listen. The Tower of Babel was a study period alongside of woods in the early morning.

It is wonderful to smell the morning. Anybody who's been around the woods knows that morning smells one way, high noon another, dusk still another, and night most different of all, if only because the skunks smell louder at night. Morning smells fresh and flowery and little-breezy, and dewy and spanking new. Noon smells hot and a little dusty and sort of sleepy, when the breeze has died and the heads begin to droop and anything with any sense goes off into the shade to take a nap. Dusk smells scary. It is getting colder and everybody is going home tired for the day, and you can smell the turpentine scars on the trees and the burnt-off ground and the bruised ferns and the rising wind. You can hear the folding-up, I'm-finished-for-the-day sounds all around, including the colored boys whistling to prove they ain't scared when they drive the cows home. And in the night you can smell the fire and the warm blankets and the coffee a-boil, and you can even smell the stars. I know that sounds silly, but on a cool, clear, frosty night the stars have a smell, or so it seems when you are young and acutely conscious of everything bigger than a chigger.

This was as nice a smelling morning as I can remember. It smelled like it was going to work into a real fine-smelling day. The sun was up pretty high now and was beginning to warm the world. The dew was starting to dry, because the grass wasn't clear wet any more but just had little drops on top, like a kid with a runny nose. I sat on the stump for about a half-hour, and then I heard the dogs start, a mile or more down the swamp. Bell picked up the trail first, and she sounded as if church had opened for business. Then Blue came in behind her, loud as an organ, their two voices blending—fading sometimes, getting stronger, changing direction always.

Maybe you never heard a hound in the woods on a frosty fall morning, with the breeze light, the sun heating up in the sky, and the "aweful" expectancy that something big was going to happen to you. There aren't many things like it. When the baying gets closer and still closer to you, you feel as if maybe you're going to explode if something doesn't happen quick. And when the direction changes and the dogs begin to fade, you feel so sick you want to throw up.

But Bell and Blue held the scent firmly now, and the belling was clear and steady. The deer was moving steady and straight, not trying to circle and fool the dogs, but honestly running. And the noise was coming straight down the branch, with me on the other end of it.

The dogs had come so close that you could hear them panting between their bays, and once or twice one of them quit sounding and broke into a yip-yap of barks. I thought I could hear a little tippety-tappety noise ahead of them, in between the belling and the barking, like mice running through paper or a rabbit hopping through dry leaves. I kept my eyes pinned onto where the deer path opened into the clearing. The dogs were so close that I could hear them crash.

All of a sudden there was a flash of brown and two does, flop-eared, with two half-grown fawns skipped out of the brush, stopped dead in front of me, looked me smack in the face, and then gave a tremendous leap that carried them halfway across the clearing. They bounced again, white tails carried high, and disappeared into the branch behind me. As I turned to watch them go there was another crash ahead and the buck tore through the clearing like a race horse. He wasn't jumping. This boy was running like the wind, with his horns laid back against his spine and his ears pinned by the breeze he was making. The dogs were right behind him. He had held back to tease the dogs into letting his family get a start, and now that they were out of the way he was pouring on the coal and heading for home.

I had a gun with me and the gun was loaded. I suppose it would have fired if the thought had occurred to me to pull the trigger. The thought never occurred. I just watched that big buck deer run, with my mouth open and my eyes popped out of my head.

The dogs tore out of the bush behind the buck, baying out their brains and covering the ground in leaps. Old Blue looked at me as he flashed past and curled his lip. He looked as if he were saying, "This is man's work, and what is a boy doing here, spoiling my labor?" Then he dived into the bush behind the buck.

I sat there on the stump and began to shake and tremble. About five minutes later there was one shot, a quarter-mile down the swamp. I sat on the stump. In about half an hour Tom and Pete came up to my clearing.

"What happened to the buck?" Pete said. "Didn't he come past here? I thought I was going to run him right over you."

"He came past, all right," I said, feeling sick-mean, "but I never shot. I never even thought about it until he was gone. I reckon you all ain't ever going to take me along any more." My lip was shaking and now I *was* about to cry.

Tom walked over and hit me on top of the head with the flat of his hand. "Happens to everybody," he said. "Grown men and boys, both, they all get buck fever. Got to do it once before you get over it. Forget it. I seen Pete here shoot five times at a buck big as a horse last year, and missed him with all five."

There were some footsteps in the branch where the deer had disappeared, and in a minute Mister Howard and the Old Man came out, with the dogs leashed and panting.

"Missed him clean," the Old Man said cheerfully. "Had one whack at him no farther'n thirty yards and missed him slick as a whistle. That's the way it is, but there's always tomorrow. Let's us go shoot some squirrels for the pot, and we'll rest the dogs and try again this evenin'. You *see* him, boy?"

"I *saw* him," I said. "And I ain't ever going to *forget* him."

We went back to camp and tied up the hounds. We unleashed the fice dog, Jackie, the little sort of yellow fox terrier kind of nothing dog with prick ears and a sharp fox's face and a thick tail that curved up over his back. I was going with Pete to shoot some squirrels while the old gentlemen policed up the camp, rested, took a couple of drinks, and started to prepare lunch. It was pretty late in the morning for squirrel hunting, but this swamp wasn't hunted much. While I had been on the deer stand that morning the swamp was alive with them—mostly big fox squirrels, huge old fellers with a lot of black on their gray-and-white hides.

"See you don't get squirrel fever," the Old Man hollered over his shoulder as Pete and I went down to the swamp. "Else we'll all starve to death. I'm about fresh out of ham and eggs."

"Don't pay no 'tention to him, son," Pete told me. "He's a great kidder."

"Hell with him," I said. "He missed the deer, didn't he? At least *I* didn't miss him."

"That's right," Pete agreed genially. "You got to shoot at 'em to miss 'em."

I looked quick and sharp at Pete. He didn't seem to be teasing me. A cigarette was hanging off the corner of his lip, and his lean, brown, Injun-looking face was completely straight. Then we heard Jackie, yip-yapping in a querulous bark, as if somebody had just insulted him by calling him a dog.

"Jackie done treed hissel a squirrel," Pete said. "Advantage of a dog like Jackie is that when the squirrels all come down to the ground to feed, ol' Jackie rousts 'em up and makes 'em head for the trees. Then he makes so much noise he keeps the squirrel interested while we go up and wallop away at him. Takes two men to hunt squirrels this way. Jackie barks. I go around to the other side of the tree. Squirrel sees me and moves. That's when you shoot him, when he slides around on your side. Gimme your gun."

"Why?" I asked. "What'll I use to shoot the—"

"*Mine,*" Pete answered. "You ain't going to stand there and tell me you're gonna use a shotgun on a squirrel? Anybody can hit a pore little squirrel with a shotgun. Besides, shotgun shells cost a nickel apiece."

I noticed Pete's gun for the first time. He had left his pump gun in camp and had a little bolt-action .22. He took my shotgun from me and handed me the .22 and a handful of cartridges.

"'Nother thing you ought to know," Pete said as we walked up to the tree, a big blue gum under which Jackie seemed to be going mad, "is that when you're hunting for the pot you don't belong to make much more noise with guns than is necessary. You go booming off a shotgun, blim-blam, and you spook everything in the neighborhood. A .22 don't make no more noise than a stick crackin', and agin the wind you can't hear it more'n a hundred yards or thereabouts.

Best meat gun in the world, a straight-shootin' .22, because it don't make no noise and don't spoil the meat. Look up yonder, on the fourth fork. There's your dinner. A big ol' fox squirrel, near-about black all over."

The squirrel was pasted to the side of the tree. Pete walked around, and the squirrel moved with him. When Pete was on the other side, making quite a lot of noise, the squirrel shifted back around to my side. He was peeping at Pete, but his shoulders and back and hind legs were on my side. I raised the little .22 and plugged him between the shoulders. He came down like a sack of rocks. Jackie made a dash for him, grabbed him by the back, shook him once and broke his spine, and sort of spit him out on the ground. The squirrel was dang near as big as Jackie.

Pete and I hunted squirrels for an hour or so, and altogether we shot ten. Pete said that was enough for five people for a couple of meals, and there wasn't no sense to shootin' if the meat had to spoil. "We'll have us some venison by tomorrow, anyways," he said. "One of us is bound to git one. You shot real nice with that little bitty gun," he said. "She'll go where you hold her, won't she?"

I felt pretty good when we went into camp and the Old Man, Mister Howard, and Tom looked up inquiringly. Pete and I started dragging fox squirrels out of our hunting coats, and the ten of them made quite a sizable pile.

"Who shot the squirrels?" the Old Man asked genially. "The dog?"

"Sure," Pete grinned. "Dog's so good we've taught him to shoot, too. We jest set down on a log, give Jackie the gun, and sent him off into the branch on his lonesome. We're planning to teach him to skin 'em and cook 'em, right after lunch. This is the best dog I ever see. Got more sense than people."

"Got more sense than *some* people," the Old Man grunted. "Come and git it, boy, and after lunch you and Jackie can skin the squirrels."

The lunch was a lunch I loved then and still love, which is why I'm never going to be called one of those epicures. This was a country hunting lunch, Carolina style. We had Vienna sausages and sardines, rat cheese, gingersnaps and dill pickles and oysterettes and canned salmon, all cold except the coffee that went with it, and that was hot enough to scald clean down to your shoes. It sounds horrible, but I don't know anything that tastes so good together as Vienna sausages and sardines and rat cheese and gingersnaps. Especially if you've been up since before dawn and walked ten miles in the fresh air.

After lunch we stretched out in the shade and took a little nap. Along about two I woke up, and so did Pete and Tom, and the three of us started to skin the squirrels. It's not much trouble, if you know how. Pete and I skinned 'em and Tom cleaned and dressed 'em. I'd pick up a squirrel by the head, and Pete would take his hind feet. We'd stretch him tight, and Pete would slit him down the stomach and along the legs as far as the feet. Then he'd shuck him like an ear of corn, pulling the hide toward the head until it hung over his head like a cape and the squirrel was naked. Then he'd just chop off the head, skin and all, and toss the carcass to Tom.

Tom made a particular point about cutting the little castor glands. Squirrel with the musk glands out is as tasty as any meat I know, but unless you take out those glands an old he-squirrel is as musky as a billy goat, and tastes like a billy goat smells. Tom cut up the carcasses and washed them clean, and I proceeded to bury the heads, hides, and guts.

The whole job didn't take forty-five minutes with the three of us working. We put the pieces of clean red meat in a covered pot, and then woke up the Old Man and Mister Howard. We were going deer hunting again.

The dogs had rested too; they had had half a can of salmon each and about three hours' snooze. It was beginning to cool off when Tom and Pete put Blue and Bell on walking leashes and we struck off for another part of the swamp, which made a Y from the main swamp and had a lot of water in it. It was a cool swamp, and Tom and Pete figured that the deer would be lying up there from the heat of the day, and about ready to start stirring out to feed a little around dusk.

I was in the process of trying to think about just how long forever was when the hounds started to holler real close. They seemed to be coming straight down the crick off to my right, and the crick's banks were very open and clear, apart from some sparkleberry and gallberry bushes. The *whoo-whooing* got louder and louder. The dogs started to growl and bark, just letting off a *woo-woo* once in a while, and I could hear a steady swishing in the bushes.

Then I could see what made the swishing. It was a buck, a big one. He was running steadily and seriously through the low bush.

He had horns—my Lord, but did he have horns! It looked to me like he had a dead tree lashed to his head. I slipped off the safety catch and didn't move. The buck came straight at me, the dogs going crazy behind him.

The buck came down the water's edge, and when he got to about fifty yards I stood up and threw the gun up to my face. He kept coming and I let him come. At about twenty-five yards he suddenly saw me, snorted, and leaped to his left as if somebody had unsnapped a spring in him. I forgot he was a deer. I shot at him as you'd lead a duck or a quail on a quartering shot—plenty of lead ahead of his shoulder.

I pulled the trigger—for some odd reason shooting the choke barrel—right in the middle of a spring that had him six feet off the ground and must have been wound up to send him twenty yards, into the bush and out of my life. The gun said *boom!* but I didn't hear it. The gun kicked out but I didn't feel it. All I saw was that this monster came down out of the sky like I'd shot me an airplane. He came down flat, turning completely over and landing on his back, and he never wiggled.

The dogs came up ferociously and started to grab him, but they had sense and knew he didn't need any extra grabbing. I'd grabbed him real good, with about three ounces of No. 1 buckshot in a choke barrel. I had busted his shoulder and busted his neck and dead-centered his heart. I had let him get so close that you could practically pick the wads out of his shoulder. This was *my* buck. Nobody else had shot at him. Nobody else had seen him but me. Nobody had advised or helped. This monster was mine.

And monster was right. He was huge, they told me later, for a Carolina whitetail. He had fourteen points on his rack, and must have weighed nearly 150 pounds undressed. He was beautiful gold on his top and dazzling white on his underneath, and his little black hoofs were clean. The circular tufts of hair on his legs, where the scent glands are, were bright russet and stiff and spiky. His horns were as clean as if they'd been scrubbed with a wire brush, gnarled and evenly forked and the color of planking on a good boat that's just been holy-stoned to where the decks sparkle.

I had him all to myself as he lay there in the aromatic, crushed fern—all by myself, like a boy alone in a big cathedral of oaks and cypress in a vast swamp where the doves made sobbing sounds and the late birds walked and talked in the sparkleberry bush. The dogs came up and lay down. Old Blue laid his muzzle on the big buck's back. Bell came over and licked my face and wagged her tail, like she was saying, "You did real good, boy." Then she lay down and put her face right on the deer's rump.

This was our deer, and no damn bear or anything else was going to take it away from us. We were a team, all right, me and Bell and Blue.

I couldn't know then that I was going to grow up and shoot elephants and lions and rhinos and things. All I knew then was that I was the richest boy in the world as I sat there in the crushed ferns and stroked the silky hide of my first buck deer, patting his horns and smelling how sweet he smelled and admiring how pretty he looked. I cried a little bit inside about how lovely he was and how I felt about him. I guess that was just reaction, like being sick twenty-five years later when I shot my first African buffalo.

I was still patting him and patting the dogs when Tom and Pete came up one way and the Old Man and Mister Howard came up from another way. What a wonderful thing it was, when you are a kid, to have four huge, grown men—everything is bigger when you are a boy—come roaring up out of the woods to see you sitting by your first big triumph. "Smug" is a word I learned a lot later. Smug was modest for what I felt then.

"Well," the Old Man said, trying not to grin.

"Well," Mister Howard said.

"Boy done shot hisself a horse with horns," Pete said, as proud for me as if I had just learned how to make bootleg liquor.

"Shot him pretty good, too," Tom said. "Deer musta been standing still, boy musta been asleep, woke up, and shot him in self-defense."

"Was not, either," I started off to say, and then saw that all four men were laughing.

They had already checked the sharp scars where the buck had jumped, and they knew I had shot him on the fly. Then Pete turned the buck over and cut open his belly. He tore out the paunch and ripped it open. It was full of green stuff and awful smelly gunk. All four men let out a whoop and grabbed me. Pete held the paunch and the other men stuck my head right into—blood, guts, green gunk, and all. It smelled worse than anything I ever smelled. I was bloody and full of partly digested deer fodder from my head to my belt.

"That," the Old Man said as I swabbed the awful mess off me and dived away to stick my head in the crick, "makes you a grown man. You have been blooded, boy, and any time you miss a deer from now on we cut off your shirt tail. It's a very good buck, son," he said softly, "one of which you can be very, very proud."

Tom and Pete cut a long sapling, made slits in the deer's legs behind the cartilage of his knees, stuck the sapling through the slits, and slung the deer up on their backs. They were sweating him through the swamp when suddenly the Old Man turned to Mister Howard and said, "Howard, if you feel up to it, we might just as well go get *our* deer and lug him into camp. He ain't but a quarter-mile over yonder, and I don't want the wildcats working on him in that tree."

"What deer?" I demanded. "You didn't shoot this afternoon, and you missed the one you—"

The Old Man grinned and made a show of lighting his pipe. "I didn't miss him, son," he said. "I just didn't want to give you an inferiority complex on your first deer. If you hadn't of shot this one—and he's a lot better'n mine—I was just going to leave him in the tree and say nothing about him at all. Shame to waste a deer; but it's a shame to waste a boy, too."

I reckon that's when I quit being a man. I just opened my mouth and bawled. Nobody laughed at me, either.

The Watery Places

Man is not an aquatic animal, but from the time we stand in youthful wonder beside a spring brook in spate until we sit in old age and watch the endless roll of the sea we feel a strong kinship with the waters of this earth. The cool, sweet waters slake our thirst and nourish our fields. The great rivers are the living arteries of our land. The lakes and ponds temper the climate and shape the landscape and all its life. The oceans are forever shaping continents, breathing the mists that make our rain.

It was the little streams, grown big with April, that carved our valleys. The silt they carried down from the hilltops became rich meadows and fertile delta lands. Grass followed in their wake, and trees, to make a hospitable land. When men first traveled, they followed such streams, first along their banks, then upon their swirling currents. They followed flowing water to the oceans, and in due time embarked upon the ocean itself. Their first towns were river towns. Their first cities faced the sea.

Man's ancient ancestors emerged from the water, and man still has brine flowing in his veins. Each spring his pulse quickens when the trickling inland waters waken and creep down the hillsides. Swamps ooze with their slow drainage. Ponds brim over at the edge. Rivers test their banks. The very earth is sodden underfoot, reminder of long forgotten ages. And man, reaching back in his long racial memory, knows that he is seeing the ooze and flow not of one spring alone but of the very springtime of the earth, when the land rose out of the primeval waters long, long ago.

H.B.

WATER

BY WILLIAM C. ACKERMAN, E. A. COLMAN AND HAROLD O. OGROSKY

This selection, about the endless water cycle—from ocean to sky to land and back to the ocean—was written by a team of scientists in the United States Department of Agriculture and appeared originally in that department's yearbook for 1955, a volume titled Water. *At the time it was written, William C. Ackerman, a graduate of the University of Wisconsin, was head of the watershed hydrology section of the Agricultural Research Service; E. A. Colman, who received his doctorate from the University of California, was chief of the division of Watershed Management of the California Forest and Range Experiment Station of the Forest Service; and Harold O. Ogrosky, a graduate of the University of Minnesota, was staff hydrologist of the Soil Conservation Service.*

(*Water: The Yearbook of Agriculture,* 1955. Government publication.)

The unending circulation of the earth's moisture and water is called the water cycle. It is a gigantic system operating in and on the land and oceans of the earth and in the atmosphere that surrounds the earth.

The cycle has no beginning or ending, but because our discussion must start someplace, we can think of it as beginning with the waters of the oceans, which cover about three-fourths of the earth's surface.

Water from the surface of the oceans is evaporated into the atmosphere.

That moisture in turn is lifted and is eventually condensed and falls back to the earth's surface as precipitation.

The part of the precipitation that falls as rain, hail, dew, snow, or sleet on the land is of particular concern to man and agriculture.

Some of the precipitation, after wetting the foliage and ground, runs off over the surface to the streams. It is the water that sometimes causes erosion and is the main contributor to floods. Of the precipitation that soaks into the ground, some is available for growing plants and for evaporation. Some reaches the deeper zones and slowly percolates through springs and seeps to maintain the streams during dry periods. The streams in turn eventually lead back to the oceans, where the water originated. It is because of this never-ending circulation that the process has become known as the water cycle, or hydrologic cycle.

About 80,000 cubic miles of water are evaporated each year from the oceans. About 15,000 cubic miles are evaporated from the lakes and land surfaces of the continents. Total evaporation is equaled by total precipitation, of which about 24,000 cubic miles fall on the land surfaces—equivalent to a depth of 475 feet over all of Texas.

Circulation of the earth's atmosphere and moisture can be thought of as starting in the belt around the Equator. Because more of the sun's energy is received near the Equator than farther north or south, greater heating occurs there and the result is greater evaporation and a tendency for the air to rise. The warm, moist air flows outward from the Equator at high altitudes and because of the earth's rotation moves in a generally northeasterly direction in the Northern Hemisphere. By the time this air reaches about 30° North, which is about the latitude of New Orleans, it has lost enough heat so that it tends to sink. That downward-moving air generally divides at the earth's surface; a part of it moves southwesterly, as the trade winds do, back toward the Equator, and a part moves northeasterly across the Temperate Zone.

Far to the north, near the North Pole, another circulation pattern is in operation. There a mass of cold air builds up and flows outward in a southwesterly direction. The polar air becomes warm in its southwesterly movement, and at about 60° latitude, which is well up in Canada, it becomes warmed sufficiently to rise and flow back toward the Pole. From time to time outbreaks of this cold polar air move out across the Temperate Zone. They are an important factor in causing our general rains.

If the earth's surface were entirely covered by water, the general circulation we just described would be regular and would occur in belts around the earth. The presence of large land masses changes this regular pattern, however, because the heating effect from the sun is different over land than over water. For example, in the winter the land masses cool more rapidly and are partly covered with snow, which reflects much of the sun's heat rather than absorbing it. The polar front therefore moves far to the south over the continents in winter. The result is the formation of cells of cold, high air pressure over the land masses, and cells of warm, low air pressure over the oceans. In the summer that situation is reversed.

The three broad storm types or conditions that operate within these general movements to bring us precipitation are the cyclonic; the convectional, or thunderstorm, type; and the orographic or mountain type.

The cyclonic type, or low-pressure-area type, is the familiar storm type that produces general rains over wide areas. The storms are particularly prevalent during winter.

Cyclonic storms are atmospheric waves, formed along the polar front by the interaction of the cold polar air masses and the warm tropical air masses. The waves move generally from west to east in our latitude, following the general circulation pattern. An essential element of the cyclone is the warm-air sector on the south side of the revolving low-pressure system. The warm sector is made up of air originating in the tropical regions and contains the moisture, which undergoes change through lifting to become precipitation. This warm, moist air generally moves in a northeasterly direction and, being lighter than the existing cool air which it meets, rides up and over the wedge of cool, heavy air. The boundary plane between these air masses of differing temperature is referred to as the warm front. The result of lifting causes condensation and a broad belt of low-intensity precipitation.

To the northwest of the warm-air sector is a charge of fast-moving polar air, which moves through the warm air as a cold and heavy wedge. The leading face of this cold air is referred to as the cold front, and along it warm air is also lifted to cause precipitation.

Since the cold front moves more rapidly and is steeper, it usually results in intense precipitation, but for a short duration.

As a cyclonic storm passes a certain area in moving from west to east, precipitation usually starts with a slow, cool rain—or snow—as precipitation from the warm front falls through the underlying cool air. A period of warm and showery weather follows, as the warm sector moves across the area. The warm phase of the storm is ended by the rapid passage of the cold front, frequently with a hard shower and the beginning of a period of cold weather.

The convectional type of storm, or thunderstorm, is a second and familiar type. It ordinarily results in the most intense rainfall and occurs over rather small areas.

Thunderstorms occur throughout the country, but are most frequent in the southern part and in summer. Convectional storms are formed when, because of uneven heating, the air over a locality becomes warmer than the surrounding air. The areas of excessive heating may be over a city, whose streets and roofs are warmer than the surrounding countryside. The difference between hot, bare fields and cool woods or the difference between land and lakes produces this effect. Whatever the cause, where air receives additional heating it becomes light and therefore rises. The ascending warm air expands and cools as it rises. And if sufficient moisture is present and the cooling process proceeds sufficiently, precipitation is formed.

The preceding discussion of cyclonic and convectional storm types describes how warm, moist air was lifted and cooled to the precipitation point by a process of circulation. In the first instance, warm air was lifted over heavier cold air; in the second instance uneven heating caused air to rise.

The orographic, or mountain type is the third familiar storm type that causes precipitation. A mountain range can act as the wedge or barrier over which warm, moist air is lifted and cooled to the point where precipitation occurs. Here the warm-air movement may be related either to the general circulation within the atmosphere or to the circulation about a storm center.

The best example of orographic precipitation in this country is along the West Coast Ranges in Washington, Oregon, and California. Moist air, flowing in from the Pacific, is lifted in its general eastward movement, and a zone of normally heavy rainfall results. Orographic precipitation is generally of a low intensity, but because the mountains are fixed in one location, the resulting precipitation falls on the same general location and the annual rainfall is high. That is in contrast to the precipitation from storms that are free to move and occur in many different locations.

Variations of the three basic storm types occur, and their effects sometimes may be combined. For example, thunderstorms are more commonplace in the mountains where some preliminary orographic lifting has taken place and has increased the instability of the air and the likelihood that thunderstorms will form. Frequently the rainfall resulting from cyclonic storms is accentuated by the orographic lifting of a mountain. Another example of combination of storm types is the occurrence of thunderstorms in the unstable warm sector or with the passage of a cold front in a cyclonic storm.

Thus far we have dealt with the moisture sources, atmospheric circulation, and some of the more important processes by which moist air is lifted. When the lifting and cooling process proceeds to the point of atmospheric condensation, then small droplets are formed. The condensation takes place on dust particles in the air. As droplets, the moisture is in the form of a cloud or fog, and may remain suspended if there is any upward movement of the air to support it. In fact, it is commonplace for droplets to reevaporate without producing any precipitation. Under a number of conditions, however, the droplets will grow to sufficient size and weight to fall. The increase in size is thought to occur in two main ways. The first is in clouds, which are a mixture of ice and water particles, cooled below the freezing point. Because of differences in vapor pressure, the water droplets evaporate while condensation takes place on the ice particles. The process continues until the particles can no longer be supported by the updraft of air. They may collide when they fall and combine then to form even larger drops. Another condition under which raindrops form is when warm and cold droplets are mixed within a cloud. Again, by differences in vapor pressure, the warm droplets evaporate, and the cold ones grow in size and weight.

When raindrops are frozen while falling through cold air (as may happen below a warm front) sleet or ice pellets are formed. They differ from hail, which occurs almost exclusively in violent thunderstorms. Hailstones are composed of layers built up as a result of repeated ascents and descents or in dropping through a turbulent air mass; the stone grows larger each time a layer of moisture is condensed and then frozen on its surface. Snow—the other common form of precipitation—represents crystals and combination of crystals as flakes, which are formed when condensation takes place below freezing temperatures.

Water is delivered to the land in many forms—such as rain, hail, snow, and sleet. Its subsequent movement depends on its form of delivery and on the character of the plants, soil, and underlying material receiving it. What happens to water after its delivery to the land determines to a significant degree the severity of floods and erosion, the quantity and quality of water supplies, and the production of crops.

Vegetation will interpose leaves, branches, and litter as barriers to rain and snow, so that only a part of the precipitation reaches the soil beneath without interference. Vegetation thus affects both the quantity and distribution of precipitation that reaches the soil surface. Rain and snow are affected differently in some respects by vegetation. Part of each passes through the canopy of vegetation without being caught, but if the canopy is dense the larger part strikes leaves or branches.

Of the part thus intercepted some spills from drip points, some flows to the ground along stems, and some is held and later evaporates. Rain wets the surface it strikes. It can form only a thin water layer before it starts flowing toward the ground.

Snow may wet the surfaces it strikes, but whether it does or not, it can pile to a considerable thickness upon them. A good deal more snow than rain can thus be held by vegetation. Snow is released from vegetation by sliding—often triggered by wind—and by melt. Often in forests there is abundant evidence of both, visible in peaked snow ridges around tree crowns and snow pitted by water drops beneath them.

The quantity of precipitation intercepted by vegetation and then evaporated varies, depending on the kind and size of storm and the kind of vegetation. It represents, however, a fairly constant percentage of annual precipitation under the same vegetation conditions. In various places where it has been measured, interception loss is generally between 5 and 15 percent of the annual rainfall.

Water losses caused by interception can be reduced by thinning or changing the vegetation, so as to lessen the volume of the canopy. If the thinning or other change does not lower seriously the soil protection provided by the vegetation, some additional water may thus be delivered to the ground without damaging consequences.

In the Rocky Mountains of Colorado, for example, snow accumulation on the ground was increased the equivalent of 2 inches of water by removal of all merchantable timber from a forest of lodgepole pine. No adverse effects—such as overland water flow or erosion—followed the cutting, because summer rains were light and winter storms brought only snow. But interception loss cannot always be reduced with impunity. Some loss of this kind is inevitable if the soil is to be protected from the impact of rain.

Rain that reaches the soil surface is wholly or partly absorbed by the soil in the process of infiltration. How much of it enters the soil depends upon the rate of rainfall and the receptiveness or infiltration rate of the soil. When the rainfall rate exceeds the infiltration rate, the excess rain becomes surface flow, which runs off quickly to streams. Surface flow is undesirable because it may erode the soil and also because it often produces damagingly rapid and high flows in streams during storms.

Erosion of cultivated land is the result of water delivered to the soil at a rate higher than the infiltration rate of the soil. Because of the damaging consequences of surface-flowing water, many land management practices are designed to induce as high an infiltration rate as possible.

Infiltration rate is determined by a combination of factors—some natural to the soil, some the result of activities related to land use. Infiltration rate is naturally greater in sandy soil than in clay. Ordinarily the finer the soil texture, the lower the rate of infiltration. But the effect of texture is modified greatly by the aggregation, or arrangement, of the soil particles and by soil structure beneath the surface.

The effects of structure upon infiltration rate show themselves near the soil surface and down through the profile. A surface soil that is well supplied with organic matter is ordinarily far more receptive to water than a soil consisting mainly of mineral material. Maintenance of an organic-reinforced open structure is one of the objectives of stubble-mulching and other farming practices that mix plant residues into the soil. The plowsole, a layer of compacted soil common in some long-cultivated fields, impedes downward waterflow and thus reduces infiltration at the surface.

Water from snowmelt is not different from water supplied by rain, after it has entered the soil. It is different, however, in the way it is delivered to the soil. Water draining from the base of a snow blanket flows to the soil surface; it does not have the impact force of raindrops. Bare soil, therefore, is not damaged by snowmelt delivered to its surface. Snow cover frequently protects the soil from freezing and therefore maintains a higher infiltration rate. Except for this, the effects of land treatment and soil are the same on the infiltration of snow water and rain.

Snow is singularly subject to change as it lies on the ground. To some extent man can control the quantity, time, and rate of water release from the snow pack to the soil. Snow drifts before the wind while it is being laid upon the ground and later before it packs. Drifting is caused by windbreaks, which produce a local drop in wind velocity. They collect snow some distance to leeward and a lesser distance to windward. That is why snow fences are used along roads in snowy lands. Erected parallel to the roads, they reduce the amount of snow on the roads by causing part of it to pile up near the fences.

An exploratory investigation in Utah demonstrated the possibility of retarding snowmelt in windswept mountain lands by causing snow to drift. Snow fences were built at right angles to the prevailing direction of winter winds. The snow accumulating in the lee of the fences was deeper than that in undrifted places nearby. When all the undrifted snow had melted, within the drifts there remained 15 inches of water as snow. The drifts released their water to the soil over a longer period than did the undrifted snow, and thus contributed water to the soil and to the streams later in the spring and summer. Thus, where wind drifts the snow, it may be possible to reduce the high spring flow of streams and to increase lower flows later in the year.

Snow lying on the ground is subject to melting and sublimation, which is the transformation from a solid to a vapor. Melt rate is influenced by the amount of heat reaching the snow. The source of the heat is the sun. But besides heat received directly from the sun, snow also receives heat from the soil beneath, from heated objects such as trees, above, and from warm air that passes over it. If snow on the ground is shaded by trees or other cover, some of the sun's heat is intercepted, and the snow melts more slowly than if it is fully exposed to the sun. At first glance this suggests that a dense forest would be more desirable than an open one to prolong the melting of snow. But the matter is not so simple. More snow is intercepted by the crowns, and, generally, less snow accumulates on the ground as forest density increases. Probably for maximum control over water yield from snow, some condition less than a full forest cover is needed. The condition desired is one in which the greatest delivery of snow to the ground is coupled with the greatest amount of shade. Obviously such a condition represents a compromise between increasing snow accumulation and decreasing shade found as the forest is cut more and more heavily.

Water evaporates from the snowpack, and the solid ice crystals themselves sublime. Whenever the vapor pressure of the air above the snow is less than that at the snow surface, water evaporates from the snow. When the dewpoint is below the freezing temperature, water condenses on the snow. Thus as snow lies on the ground it may lose water to the air or receive water from it. Evaporative loss of water from snow varies from place to place and from season to season. Near the Rocky Mountain crest in Colorado, for example, 0.24 inch of water was lost from the snowpack in an open space during the winter, and 1.99 inch during the melting period in spring. In the Sierra Nevada of California, by way of contrast, evaporative losses in a large forest opening totaled 0.75 inch from December to March and 0.69 inch from April to May.

Water that has entered the soil either increases the moisture content of the soil or drains through it. If the soil is dry, the water entering wets successively deeper layers to field capacity, which is the moisture content to which each layer must be raised before water can drain through it. When the entire profile has been wet to field capacity, the additional water entering the soil drains into the underground, later emerging in springs and seeping into streams, or adding to subsurface supplies in valleys.

Water draining through the soil feeds streams longer and more evenly than water flowing over the soil. Hence for crop production of all kinds and for maximum control over water yield, the best land-use practices are those that induce the most water to enter the soil.

Water held within the soil after drainage has ceased can be transpired by plants or lost by evaporation. Plants cannot utilize all water stored in the soil; they can dry the soil only to the wilting point, a moisture content at which the force holding water to the soil particles equals the maximum water-absorbing force of plant roots. Just as clay soils can hold more water at field capacity than sands, so also is the wilting point of a clay higher than that of a sand. Both the upper and lower limits of the available moisture range, between wilting point and field capacity, are determined primarily by soil texture. Little can be done by cultural practices to increase this range.

Evaporation can dry soil below the wilting point. In the process the soil dries from the surface downward, for all soil water lost by evaporation must rise to the soil surface and pass through it. Ordinarily evaporation dries the soil most within the surface foot. But given sufficient time without water additions, soil may dry many feet deep by this process alone.

Evaporation and transpiration together take a toll of soil water in response to a number of conditions. If the soil surface is free of plants and thickly covered with an insulating layer of litter, evaporative loss will be much less than if the vegetation-free soil is bare. A deep soil loses less water under a cover of shallow-rooted plants than under plants whose roots reach to the full depth of the soil. Deep soils fully permeated with roots lose more water than shallow soils similarly permeated. Where a water table exists within or a short distance below the root zone, the lower soil layers may not dry perceptibly, although large quantities of water may be withdrawn from the standing water.

Evapotranspiration can be reduced in various ways. Protective mulches can be laid on the soil surface to reduce evaporation. Weeds can be removed from cropped lands by cultivation or killed by other means. Vegetation can be thinned, and, under some climatic conditions, evapotranspiration can be reduced as a consequence. Shallow-rooted plants can be grown on deep soil previously occupied by plants with deep roots. There are, however, limitations to how far evaporative losses can be reduced. It is obviously not desirable to reduce the density of plant cover so much that the soil is insufficiently protected against storm runoff and erosion. Production of certain crops requires water use. And if the dry season is long and severe, changing the plant cover may have little effect upon water loss.

Perhaps the most important point to make regarding evapotranspiration is that it is a natural process that occurs wherever there is vegetation. While evapotranspiration and other evaporative water losses can sometimes be reduced by treatments given the soil and its cover, they cannot be eliminated.

Water that infiltrates into the soil is known as subsurface water. It may be evaporated from the soil; it may be absorbed by the plant roots and then transpired; or it may percolate downward to groundwater reservoirs. Subsurface water occurs in a zone between the ground surface and the lower limits of porous, water-bearing rock formations. This zone is designated as the zone of rock fracture, and is subdivided into the zone of aeration and the zone of saturation.

The zone of aeration is divided into three belts—the belt of soil water, the intermediate belt, and the capillary fringe. The belts vary in depth and are not sharply defined by physical changes in the soil. Generally a gradual transition exists from one belt to another. In considering the movement of water through the soil profile, however, it is desirable to delineate zones or belts that have different effects on the subsurface movement of water.

The upper belt, or belt of soil water, consists of the topsoil and subsoil from which water is returned to the atmosphere by evaporation from the soil and transpiration of plants. As water passes through the surface and enters the belt, it is acted upon by gravity and molecular attraction. Gravity tends to pull the water downward. Molecular attraction tends to hold the water in a thin film over the particles and in the very minute spaces between the soil particles. Only when sufficient water has entered this belt to satisfy the storage requirements due to molecular attraction does water start to percolate downward under the force of gravity. Water in this belt is of particular importance to agriculture because it furnishes the supply for all vegetative growth. Water passing downward from the belt is beyond the reach of plant roots and is no longer available to support plant growth. The depth of the belt of soil water varies with the soil type and the vegetation and may vary in depth from a few feet to 50 feet.

Water passing through the belt of soil water enters the intermediate belt and continues its movement downward by gravitational action. Like the belt of soil water, the intermediate belt holds suspended water by molecular attraction. In this belt, however, suspended water can be considered dead storage since it is not available for use. In the hydrologic cycle, this belt serves only to provide a passage for water from the belt of soil water to the capillary fringe. The intermediate belt may vary in thickness from zero to several hundred feet; the thickness has a significant effect on the time it takes water to pass through the belt.

The capillary fringe lies immediately below the intermediate belt and above the zone of saturation. It contains water that is held above the zone of saturation by capillary force. The amount of water held and the thickness of the capillary fringe depend on the type of material in which the capillary fringe is located. In silty material it may extend 2 feet or more above the zone of saturation. In a coarse, gravelly material it may extend less than an inch. As in the intermediate zone, water is stored in the capillary fringe. In the hydrologic cycle, however, it also provides a passage for water being moved by gravity from the surface to the zone of saturation.

The zone of saturation, or ground water, forms a huge natural reservoir that feeds springs, streams, and wells. Water moving by gravity through the belts of the zone of aeration enters the upper surface of the zone of saturation, which is referred to as the water table. All the pores and spaces in this zone are filled with water. The depth of the zone depends on the local geology. It may include loose, unconsolidated deposits of sand and gravel, as well as porous rock formations such as sandstone and limestone. Its lower limit is that point where the rock formation becomes so dense that water cannot penetrate it. The zone may vary in depth from a few feet to hundreds of feet, and instances are known where porous rock has been found at depths of more than a mile.

The zone of saturation is extremely important, because it provides the supply for all our wells and the normal, relatively uniform flow of our streams. It acts much the same as a surface reservoir, receiving water during wet periods, which raises the water table on the upper surface of the zone as water drains into it from above. It can thus store huge supplies of water which, because of the slowness of movement through the zone, is discharged at a relatively uniform rate.

The action of gravity tends to make the surface of the zone of saturation or the water table a level surface. As the movement of water is relatively slow through the soil and rock formations, however, the frequent additions and withdrawals do not usually permit the water table to become a level surface.

During periods of low flow, the level of the water surface in a stream may drop below the level of the water table. Ground water will then seep into the stream and the level of the water table will dip toward the stream in the direction of ground-water flow. When the stream is flowing for periods at a level above the water table, seepage will take place in the opposite direction and tend to raise the water table. Because of the constant changes resulting from increased supply to ground water or the increased demand from ground water, the level of the water table is constantly changing.

Geologic formations also cause variations in the water table. Where impervious layers of material occur, it is possible to have two or more water tables at different elevations or to have water confined below an impervious layer under hydrostatic pressure, which is pressure caused by the weight of water above. Sufficient pressure occasionally occurs to cause the water to rise in a well above the land surface, creating a flowing or artesian well.

Many varying conditions occur as a result of different geologic formations, but in the hydrologic cycle the principal functions of the ground water zones are as follows:

1. Zone of aeration—receives and holds water for plant use in the belt of soil water and allows the downward movement of excess water.

2. Zone of saturation—receives and stores, and provides a natural regulated discharge of water to wells, springs, and streams.

Runoff occurs when precipitation that does not have an opportunity to infiltrate into the soil flows across the land surface; eventually most of it enters stream channels which carry it to the ocean. A part of the precipitation that infiltrates the soil percolates downward to the water table and also enters stream channels through springs or seeps. Broadly speaking, runoff is composed of water from both surface flow and seepage flow. It is an extremely important segment of the hydrologic cycle, since, on the average, about 20 percent of all precipitation is carried to the ocean by streams and rivers.

Much of our agricultural and industrial development is directly concerned with this water. Irrigation, waterpower developments, domestic and industrial water supply, water transportation, and sewage disposal depend more or less on streamflow. In order to utilize this resource to the fullest extent and also to avoid disastrous effects during periods of high flow, it is necessary to understand the factors which affect the volume and rate of flow so that estimates can be made that will assure sound future development.

The amount and the rate of precipitation affect the volume and peak flow of a stream. Although man as yet has no positive control over precipitation, estimates of water yield can be made to permit proper allowances in developments utilizing streamflow. Similarly, temperature may influence runoff. During periods of low temperatures, precipitation may accumulate in northern areas in the form of snow. Rapid temperature rises, particularly when the soil is frozen, often result in exceedingly high surface runoff.

The physical characteristics of a watershed indicate what might be expected in the way of the total volume and the peak rate of runoff. A relatively impervious, steeply sloping watershed may shed most of the precipitation falling on it, but a watershed with good permeable soil that is properly protected may permit a high percentage of the precipitation to be infiltrated into the soil.

In the first instance, high volumes and peak rates of flow would be expected, while in the latter case the peak flow would be considerably less, although the volume produced over a long period would not be reduced significantly. Steep slopes produce high peak rates of runoff but have little effect on the volume of runoff. A good vegetative cover and a well-maintained soil can materially reduce the rate at which water reaches the stream channels. It not only retards surface flow, but also increases the volume passing through the soil and entering the stream as seepage flow.

Lakes, ponds, swamps, and reservoirs also act to level off peak rates of flow in the stream reaches below. Generally, there is but little loss of flow to ground water in natural lakes and swamps since they usually exist because there is little or no percolation into the soil.

Among the many other factors that affect runoff in varying degrees are barometric pressure, which can affect the flow of springs and artesian wells; seepage from stream channels; and evaporation from streams. The degree to which such factors must be considered depends on the particular problem being studied. No two streams or watersheds are alike. Each has its own characteristics.

Although the amount of water with which we are concerned in the hydrologic cycle remains essentially constant, its distribution and occurrence are continually changing. Water is a rather unique natural resource, since it may be utilized to the fullest extent by man, processed by Nature, and returned to man through the never-ending hydrologic cycle.

THE YEAR AT HIGH TIDE

BY HENRY BESTON

Henry Beston (1888 —) wrote a classic book, The Outermost House, *which was a landmark in outdoor writing when it was published in 1928. It was a peculiarly sterile period, between the romanticists and the realists, and Beston broke with the fashion of the day to spend a year on the Great Beach of Cape Cod, to live alone, to think, to see, to write. His book reached back to the Thoreau tradition in many ways, and it still stands as a remarkable example of such writing. The selection here is from Chapter IX, the next to last chapter of the book, which deals with summer.*

(*The Outermost House,* by Henry Beston; Doubleday, Doran & Company, 1928.)

Had I room in this book, I should like to write a whole chapter on the sense of smell, for all my life long I have had of that sense an individual enjoyment. To my mind, we live too completely by the eye. I like a good smell—the smell of a freshly plowed field on a warm morning after a night of April rain, the clovelike aroma of our wild Cape Cod pinks, the good reek of hot salt grass and low tide blowing from these meadows late on summer afternoons.

What a stench modern civilization breathes, and how have we ever learned to endure that foul blue air? In the Seventeenth Century, the air about a city must have been much the same air as overhung a large village; today the town atmosphere is to be endured only by the new synthetic man.

Our whole English tradition neglects smell. In English, the nose is still something of an indelicate organ, and I am not so sure that its use is not regarded as somewhat sensual. Our literary pictures, our poetic landscapes are things to hang on the mind's wall, things for the eye. French letters are more indulgent to the nose; one can scarcely read ten lines of any French verse without encountering the omnipresent, the inevitable *parfum*. And here the French are right, for though the eye is the human master sense and chief aesthetic gate, the creation of a mood or of a moment of earth poetry is a rite for which other senses may be properly invoked. Of all such appeals to sensory recollection, none are more powerful, none open a wider door in the brain than an appeal to the nose. It is a sense that every lover of the elemental world ought to use, and, using, enjoy. We ought to keep all senses vibrant and alive. Had we done so, we should never have built a civilization which outrages them, which so outrages them, indeed, that a vicious circle has been established and the dull sense grown duller.

One reason for my love of this great beach is that, living here, I dwell in a world that has a good natural smell, that is full of keen, vivid and interesting savours and fragrances. I have them at their best, perhaps, when hot days are dulled with a warm rain. So well do I know them, indeed, that were I blindfolded and led about the summer beach, I think I could tell on what part of it I was at any moment standing. At the ocean's very edge the air is almost always cool—cold even—and delicately moist with surf spray and the endless dissolution of the innumerable bubbles of the foam slides; the wet sand slope beneath exhales a cool savour of mingling beach and sea, and the innermost breakers push ahead of them puffs of this fragrant air. It is a singular experience to walk this brim of ocean when the wind is blowing almost directly down the beach, but now veering a point toward the dunes, now a point toward the sea. For twenty feet a humid and tropical exhalation of hot, wet sand encircles one, and from this one steps, as through a door, into as many yards of mid-September. In a point of time, one goes from Central America to Maine.

Atop the broad eight-foot back of the bar, inland forty feet or so from the edge of low tide, other odors wait. Here have the tides strewn a moist tableland with lumpy tangles, wisps, and matted festoons of ocean vegetation—with common sea grass, with rockweed olive-green and rockweed olive-brown, with the crushed and wrinkled green leaves of sea lettuce, with edible, purple-red dulse and bleached sea moss, with slimy and gelatinous cords seven and eight feet long. In the hot noontide they lie, slowly, slowly withering—for their very substance is water—and sending an odor of ocean and vegetation into the burning air. I like this good natural savour. Sometimes a dead, surf-trapped fish, sometimes a dead skate curling up in the heat, adds to this odor of vegetation a faint, fishy rankness, but the smell is not earth corruption, and the scavengers of the beach soon enough remove the cause.

Beyond the bar and the tidal runnel farther in, the flat region I call the upper beach runs back to the shadeless bastion of the dunes. In summer this beach is rarely covered by the tides. Here lies a hot and pleasant odor of sand. I find myself an angle of shade slanting off from a pass of wreckage still embedded in a dune, take up a handful of the dry, bright sand, sift it slowly through my fingers, and note how the heat brings out the fine, sharp, stony smell of it. There is weed here, too, well buried in the dry sand—flotsam of last year's high, full-moon tides. In the shadowless glare, the topmost fronds and heart-shaped air sacs have ripened to an odd iodine orange and a blackish iodine brown. Overwhelmed thus by sand and heat, the aroma of this foliage has dissolved; only a shower will summon it again from these crisping, strangely colored leaves.

Cool breath of eastern ocean, the aroma of beach vegetation in the sun, the hot, pungent exhalation of fine sand—these mingled are the midsummer savour of the beach.

In my open, treeless world, the year is at flood tide. All day long and all night long, for four days and five days, the southwest wind blows across the Cape with the tireless constancy of a planetary river. The sun, descending the altar of the year, pauses ritually on the steps of the summer months, the disk of flame overflowing. On hot days the beach is tremulous with rising, visible heat bent seaward by the wind; a blue haze hangs inland over the moors and the great marsh blotting out pictorial individualities and reducing the landscape to a mass. Dune days are sometimes hotter than village days, for the naked glare of sand reflects the heat; dune nights are always cooler. On its sun-trodden sand, between the marsh wind and the coolness of ocean, the Fo'castle has been as comfortable as a ship at sea.

The duneland air burns with the smell of sand, ocean and sun. On the tops of the hills, the grass stands at its tallest and greenest, its new straw-green seed plumes rising through a dead crop of last year's withered spears. On some leaves there is already a tiny spot of orange wither at the very tip, and thin lines of wither descending on either edge. Grasses in the salt meadows are fruiting; there are brownish and greenish-yellow patches on the levels of summer green. On the dunes, the sand lies quiescent in a tangle of grass; in naked places, it lies as if it were held down by the sun. When there has been no rain for a week or more, and the slanting flame has been heavy on the beach, the sand in my path down Fo'castle dune becomes so dry, so loose and deep, that I trudge through it as through snow.

The winter sea was a mirror in a cold, half-lighted room; the summer sea is a mirror in a room burning with light. So abundant is the light and so huge the mirror that the whole of a summer day floats reflected in the glass. Colors gather there, sunrise and twilight, cloud shadows and cloud reflections, the pewter dullness of gathering rain, the blue, burning splendor of space swept free of every cloud. Light transfixes ocean, and some warmth steals in with the light, but the waves that glint in the sun are still a tingling cold.

Now do insects inherit the warm earth. When a sluggish wind blows from the marsh on a hot day, the dunes can be tropical. The sand quivers with insect lives. On such days, "greenheads," *Tabanus costalis,* stab and buzz, sand gnats or "no-see-ums" gather in myriads on the sun-drenched south wall of the house, "flatiron flies" and minor unknowns swarm to the attack. One must remain indoors or take precarious refuge at the ocean's very edge. Thanks to the wind, the coolness, and the spray, the lower beach is usually free of insect bloodletters, though the bullying, poisonous Tabanid, in the mid-August height of his season, can be a hateful nuisance. So far, however, I have had but two of these tropical visitations. Barring an extra allowance of greenheads, the dunes are probably quite as habitable as any stretch of outermost beach. The wind, moreover, saves me from mosquitoes.

Ants have appeared, and the upper beach is pitted with their hills; I watch the tiny red-brown creatures running in and out of buried weed. Just outside each hole, the fine sand is all delicately ascrawl with the small, endless comings and goings. The whole upper beach, indeed, has become a plain of intense and minute life; there are tunnels and doors and pitways everywhere. The dune locusts that were so small in June have grown large and learned to make a sound. All up and down the dunes, sometimes swept seaward out of their course by the west wind, go various butterflies. When I turn up driftwood in the dunes, crickets race off into the grass.

On the dunes, in open places near thin grass, I find the deep, finger-round mine shafts of the dune spider. A foot below, in the cooler sand, lives the black female; dig her up, and you will find a hairy, spidery ball. During the summer months the lady does not leave her cave, but in early autumn she revisits the world and scuttles through the dune grass, black, fast, and formidable. The smaller, sand-colored male runs about everywhere. I saw one on the beach the other night, running along in cloudy moonlight, and mistook him at first for a small crab. Later the same night, I found a tiny, sand-colored dune toad at the very brim of the surf, and wondered if an appetite for beach fleas had led him there.

"June bugs," *Lachnosterna arcuta,* strike my screens with a formidable boom and linger there formidably buzzing; let me but open the door, and half a dozen are tilting at my table lamp and falling stunned upon the cloth. On mounded slopes of sand, solitary black wasps scratch themselves out a cave; across my paths move the shadows of giant dragon flies.

The straggling beach peas of the region are in bloom; the west wind blows the grass and rushes out to the rippled levels of a level sea; heat clouds hang motionless in the general haze; the great sun overflows; the year burns on.

THE ENDURING SEA

BY RACHEL CARSON

Rachel Carson (1907–1964) was born and educated in Pennsylvania. She had the training of a scientist, the genius of a poet, and the courage of a crusader. She spent sixteen years as a biologist with the United States Fish and Wildlife Service, meanwhile writing two memorable books, Under the Sea Wind *and* The Sea Around Us. *The latter book's success enabled her to spend the rest of her too-short life as a writer and she produced two more books,* The Edge of the Sea *and* Silent Spring. Silent Spring *was a major factor in the battle against indiscriminate use of chemical pesticides and made Miss Carson a national figure, a role she accepted but did not enjoy. She became a leading spokesman for conservation, suffered abuse and received high honors. Her first three books will endure as monuments to her remarkable knowledge of the seas and their vast spectrum of life, and to her unique skill as a writer who could make facts sing and truth sparkle. I have chosen to include here the final brief word she had to say about life and the ocean in* The Edge of the Sea, *in part because of its beauty and its truth, in part because it sums up Rachel Carson as a deeply sensitive person and perceptive writer.*

(*The Edge of the Sea,* by Rachel Carson; Houghton Mifflin Company, 1955.)

Now I hear the sea sounds about me; the night high tide is rising, swirling with a confused rush of waters against the rocks below my study window. Fog has come into the bay from the open sea, and it lies over water and over land's edge, seeping back into the spruces and stealing softly among the juniper and the bayberry. The restive waters, the cold wet breath of the fog, are of a world in which man is an uneasy trespasser; he punctuates the night with the compelling groan and grunt of a foghorn, sensing the power and menace of the sea.

Hearing the rising tide, I think how it is pressing also against other shores I know—rising on a southern beach where there is no fog, but a moon edging all the waves with silver and touching the wet sands with lambent sheen, and on a still more distant shore sending its streaming currents against the moonlit pinnacles and the dark caves of the coral rock.

Then in my thoughts these shores, so different in their nature and in the inhabitants they support, are made one by the unifying touch of the sea. For the differences I sense in this particular instant of time that is mine are but the differences of a moment, determined by our place in the stream of time and in the long rhythms of the sea. Once this rocky coast beneath me was a plain of sand; then the sea rose and found a new shore line. And again in some shadowy future the surf will have ground these rocks to sand and will have returned the coast to its earlier state. And so in my mind's eye these coastal forms merge and blend in a shifting, kaleidoscopic pattern in which there is no finality, no ultimate and fixed reality—earth becoming fluid as the sea itself.

On all these shores there are echoes of past and future; of the flow of time, obliterating yet containing all that has gone before; of the sea's eternal rhythms—the tides, the beat of surf, the pressing rivers of the currents—shaping, changing, dominating; of the stream of life, flowing as inexorably as any ocean current, from past to unknown future. For as the shore configuration changes in the flow of time, the pattern of life changes, never static, never quite the same from year to year. Whenever the sea builds a new coast, waves of living creatures surge against it, seeking a foothold, establishing their colonies. And so we come to perceive life as a force as tangible as one of the physical realities of the sea, a force strong and purposeful, as incapable of being crushed or diverted from its ends as the rising tide.

Contemplating the teeming life of the shore, we have an uneasy sense of the communication of some universal truth that lies just beyond our grasp. What is the message signaled by the hordes of diatoms, flashing their microscopic lights in the night sea? What truth is expressed by the legions of the barnacles, whitening the rocks with their habitations, each small creature within finding the necessities of its existence in the sweep of the surf? And what is the meaning of so tiny a being as the transparent wisp of protoplasm that is a sea lace, existing for some reason inscrutable to us—a reason that demands its presence by the trillion amid the rocks and weeds of the shore? The meaning haunts and ever eludes us, and in its very pursuit we approach the ultimate mystery of life itself.

OF MARSHES AND FALL

BY PAUL L. ERRINGTON

Paul L. Errington (1902 —) was born and grew up near the Big Sioux River, a branch of the Missouri, in South Dakota. He was educated there and at the University of Wisconsin, where he was a student under Aldo Leopold. He has done extensive research on wildlife, particularly the birds and animals of the wetlands, and has written three book-length technical reports and hundreds of scientific and popular articles about it. He is now professor of zoology at Iowa State University. This selection is from Of Men and Marshes, *a book he wrote for the general reader, which is full of his knowledge and love of wildlife and profound with his understanding of the necessity for bogs and marshlands in the broad ecology.*

(*Of Men and Marshes,* by Paul L. Errington; The Macmillan Company, 1957.)

As late summer grades off into weeks of autumnal mellowness, the waterfowl migration has the appearance of a leisurely procedure. Puddle ducks cover the shallows and mud flats of the more favored marshes with thousands of loafing, sleeping, feeding bodies. In fall plumage, they look much alike from a distance, except for the long necks of the pintail drakes and the size differences of big ducks and small ducks. When diving ducks are mixed with puddle ducks, the ducks of a general brownish or grayish coloration can be hard to identify. I have often thought that I must be looking at something new or special, only to have the bird in question finally resolve itself into an ordinary green-winged teal or ringneck or pintail hen. Here and there are birds in the midst of plumage changes, with green or black or other mottlings, or, rarely, there may be a hybrid that does not fit anywhere.

Among the diving ducks, ruddies may occupy almost every pond or slough having water deep enough for them to dive in. Usually, there are ringnecks present this early in the season, along with some redheads and canvasbacks and occasionally a few white-winged scoters that seem almost as large as geese. The divers may include many bluebills or goldeneyes, their numbers varying with geography, even within a particular region.

Away off by themselves, a flock of Canada geese or mixed blues and snows may sit along the edge of a slough in some big flat pasture, extremely wary of anyone's approach on foot, yet sometimes flying directly overhead. As they fly in flock formation, their separate family groupings are still maintained. Their big bodies and slow wing beats make them seem to fly slowly, but when they sweep by, close over one's head, the illusion of slowness is lost.

The waterfowl migration before heavy frosts may not be as quiescent as it seems. There is evidence of movement in the appearance and disappearance of rarities that stand out in the general assemblages—a cinnamon teal or an old squaw duck or something else that we do not often see on Iowa or Dakota marshes. (One mild, early-fall day in South Dakota, I crouched within five yards of a European widgeon.) Or there may be noticeable changes in numbers of ducks, as when a marsh gains, overnight, several hundreds of baldpates, then, after a day or two, they are gone. Mallards outnumber the pintails for a time, or the pintails outnumber the mallards. There may be a local build-up of wood ducks until they outnumber some species we usually think of as far more commonplace on glacial marshes.

Grebes live in the sloughs with the ruddy ducks, still more reluctant than the ruddies to fly as long as they can dive. Food-rich waters are black with coots. Beaches have their shore birds of differing sizes and shapes and colors, running, wheeling in flight, standing, calling, probing. There might be dowitchers flying in a compact flock or working the mud with long bills; jacksnipes (common snipes) flushing in swift, erratic flight or flying high over the marsh; occasional big godwits and curlews, showing up conspicuously among the yellowlegs and sandpipers and killdeers; perhaps, some turnstones or stocky black-bellied plovers. I remember a distant view of what I first thought was a flock of a dozen and a half ducks, but soon knew that they were not ducks and recognized them as big shore birds. Later in the day, I saw that they were willets. They passed over me as I pushed a canoe among the central rush clumps of the marsh, and they circled and passed over me several times more, uttering the wildest of gull-like cries.

Chronically ravenous young marsh hawks hunt over marsh edges and surrounding lands and open fields. Kingfishers sit at lookout perches and fly rattling along shore. There are the crows. There are the migrating sharp-shinned and pigeon hawks from the northern forests—mostly youngsters, acting as hungry as the young marsh hawks. There are the swallows, and, on the right day at the right place, a person may sit or lie on a windy hilltop and have bank swallows flying all around. They fly against the wind, to the edge of an updraft, hover, sweep away, and beat their way back, low over the ground, again and again. At a distance, a large flock of blackbirds looks like dust; the flock turns one way, and the individual specks blacken and become distinct; it turns another way, and the whole flock disappears from view, as quickly as the closing of a shutter. Or the air over a marsh may be so full of flying blackbirds that one has trouble distinguishing other birds while the flight continues, or the blackbirds may alight in the emergent vegetation in such numbers that they weigh it down.

By mid-September to early October, most of the big and little herons may be gone, but marsh edges still have their American bitterns. The bitterns fly out of the vegetation at one's approach or they face one with head and neck pointed upward, trying to look like something else. In their approximation of invisibility through position and markings they blend into their background of vegetation, but, to me, their eyes are often a giveaway. The body could be a stick or part of a cattail stalk—then I find myself looking at eyes that are looking at me, an eye on each side of the rigidly held, upward-pointing bill. The expression I read into a bittern's eyes is one of complete distrust.

In the right places, the air and water and land edges have their white pelicans and blackish cormorants and the gulls. As a former Dakotan, I think of the clean colors of the Franklin's gull, of black and white and reddish and slaty markings; of waving flights and circling flights, of flights in great eddies, of swoops and dips, of sweet calls; of glinting wings and bodies far off, of birds sitting on water or covering new plowings or massing where the grasshoppers were thickest in stubble and mowed hayfields. I remember gulls so tame that they alighted and rode on the backs of the plow-horses. They flew about me, just out of reach, like a cloud of big butterflies.

I think of butterflies, too, and woolly-bear caterpillars and many other forms of prairie life in the fall. Skunk families search the glacial hills and marsh edges, and their droppings show the reds and yellows and serrations of grasshopper legs. There may be coyotes and jackrabbits, midges and crayfish mounds. Frogs feed on grasshoppers or sit near the water, and after a time, human eyes see little of them. Salamanders crawl toward their wintering holes. Minks leave their tracks in sand and mud, their droppings and prey remain on rocks, logs, boards, open spaces, and at the entrances of holes.

Sometimes, one sees something amusing. In a pool next to a cornfield, I saw rolling in the water an object that resembled a fur-covered basketball. The basketball spread out into a five-pointed star made up of five muskrats, each with teeth anchored to a nubbin of corn in the center. They tugged and they rolled and they whined, and, when an animal lost its hold on the corn, it would soon get back on. Finally, an enterpriser got the nubbin all to itself and whisked away, leaving the others swimming in circles. But, in a few moments, the others seemed to forget their loss and became their tending-to-own-business selves again.

My memories of marshes in fall are so loaded with nostalgia that I often find myself enjoying Iowa or Minnesota or Nebraska marshes largely to the extent that they remind me of my youth and early manhood in South Dakota. I find old copper bases of shotgun shells working out of an Iowa beach, read the "U.M.C.," "New Rival," "Referee," "Premier," along with other trademarks that long ago disappeared from hardware shelves, and visualize the distinctive colors of the cartridges as they came out of the cardboard boxes. I remember wet shells so swollen that I could not push them into the chamber of a gun, shells that would not always fire if I did get them in, the bellow and smoke of a heavy charge of black powder, the smell of a freshly fired case, the feel of a jolted shoulder, the picking up of game.

As a hunter in the old days, I was not so much a sportsman as I was a predator living off the country. It was by hunting and trapping in combination that I once made a substantial part of my living; and I did so chiefly to be able to spend more time on the marshes. The era of market hunting passed shortly before I started my own hunting, but the open seasons were still long and the bag and possession limits still large, and game remained staple diet on our marsh-side farm for many months at a stretch, as well as at my trapping camps in late fall and winter. Of the game available to us in those years, we liked most of all and naturally had most of all: ducks, ducks, ducks.

My favorite memories of fall marshes have shotguns and ducks in them—not only day-by-day killing of ducks for food, predator-like, but live ducks predominating on the water or in the air, on big marsh or small marsh or slough or open lake.

There was a fair-sized slough that possibly no human being had visited for a week or more. Its surface was covered with ducks of mixed species, divers and dabblers crowded together over acres and acres, right up to the water's edge and on the muddy shore. I made a perfect sneak for nearly a hundred yards, inching up over the ice ridge and down into the bowl of the slough until my face was concealed only by the last fringe of bulrushes. I could not see much of details until I got there, but, once there, I could almost touch ducks. The nearest were sleeping on the mud. Out on the water for a good hundred and fifty yards, ducks sat and fed. Just about every duck species that belong in South Dakota was in front of me, including—especially—canvasbacks. Canvasbacks were there by the hundreds, from ten yards or less to as far away as I could distinguish them—such special ducks, even then. I was there as a predator as well as a watcher, but I was so engrossed by the sight of the ducks that I botched the hunting. I watched and watched those dark red canvasback heads and necks sticking out among the brownish heads and necks of shovelers and gadwalls and mallards, until finally some duck saw what was upon them, and the whole gathering rose out of there so fast that I had time to line up the gun barrel on only one bird. It turned out to be one of the not-so-delectable shovelers, and I had to undress and wade fifty yards out in the muck after it.

That shoveler was my total bag for that afternoon. I told no one about the fiasco, nor did I do much talking about anything that evening. Over and over, I visualized canvasback heads, their straight lines and curves fitting in with strong necks. The dark, almost blackish, red heads of the drakes had their bright red eyes to focus attention still more. Sometimes, the more I thought of the canvasback heads, the less I could reconstruct the images of other ducks, until, with closed eyes, I could see canvasback heads as if they alone were painted distinctly against an indistinct background.

Some forty years ago, from a duck pass on the old farm, I saw flights of the now-scarce redheads during which I am sure that more redheads passed over or near me in two hours than I have seen all together in the last twenty years. Redhead flocks roaring sixty to eighty yards overhead, a half-dozen flocks abreast at times, and more and more of them coming in, all traveling in the same direction at the same speed and alighting, flock after flock, in the middle of a lake—a spectacle of magnificence that I doubt any man now living will see again on any north-central lake or perhaps anywhere in the world. I do not contend that my memories are without sadness.

The central waters of lakes also had their panoramic views of ducks other than the by-gone wonders of the canvasbacks and redheads. The divers among these other ducks were mostly bluebills and ringnecks, and they gave the appearance of black and white dots on the surface. Flights of bluebills and ringnecks would come in at any hour of day but usually toward evening, sometimes flock after flock dropping out of the sky, gliding, zigzagging, almost tumbling down to splash with outstretched feet. Or they would fly low over the water, bunched up or in spread-out formation. On a rainy or foggy day or evening, a lake might seem to be covered with bluebills and ringnecks. In stormy weather, they might either seek the quieter waters in the shelter of points or inlands or hills or wooded stretches of shore or ride the waves of the lake centers. Great rafts of mallards might likewise ride waves or huddle close to shore on stormy days or cover lake centers in calm weather. But these are not sights only of the past. We may see their equivalents involving the still-common species of ducks on lakes and marshes of today. Some of the state and federal wildlife refuges of the Dakotas still offer much the same sights of ringnecks, bluebills, mallards, pintails, ruddies, baldpates, and teals that I saw when I was young.

My choice memories of ducks are not all of panoramas. There were some stand-out sights of just a few ducks or of lone ducks—the first white-winged scoters, the first buffleheads, and the first lone wood duck that I ever saw. (The present has greatly improved over the past of my early years with respect to wood ducks, for there are undoubtedly far more wood ducks over most of the north-central region today than when I lived on the farm.) There was one oddity: it was the size of a small goose, and had a goose-like bill, green head, white breast, and other markings suggesting hybridization between an American goldeneye and I could not make up my mind what else.

The frosts of the Indian summer nights leave thicker and thicker ice on the ponds in the mornings. In shaded, quiet places, the ice may not melt all day. Where a muskrat swims, there may be a swirl of bubbles and pieces of broken ice film, or the animal travels submerged, breaking the ice film only where it surfaces. One evening, needles form a crystalline lacework on the lake-side rocks, the water's edge becomes still and films over, and the lake also, except where the ducks sit. During the night, the new ice film thickens, cracking now and then, with water oozing from the cracks to freeze in turn.

By morning, the coots are gone—all that can fly—and so are the grebes and most of the ducks that do not like ice. There may still be many bluebills and ringnecks out in the remaining open water if the freeze-up is not too hard. Muskrats sit beside open holes. New lodges and feed houses appear over the marshes. Faint, muddy prints of both muskrats and minks mark the new ice. Lake shore ice, in particular, may have a little blood, some bits of vegetation, fish scales or skin about the rocks and openings where minks and muskrats feed. Crows sit out on the ice, pecking and cawing.

With the first freeze-up, mallards typically appear by thousands. They cover the remnants of open water or sit on the ice. If the ice melts again in a day or two, the waterfowl population may not be so much different from before except for the departure of the coots and the mild-weather ducks and for the greater proportions of mallards. More of the ducks have brighter plumage in late fall: the green heads of the mallard ducks have greener, the cinnamon of the heads of the greenwing drakes stands out and so do the white throats and brown necks of the pintail drakes. The drakes of what are locally known as the "northern spoonbills" do not look like the same species as the brownish shovelers of early fall.

Mallards may be in no hurry to leave as long as they have access to cornfields and a safe place to sit between feedings. They may still be on the larger lakes by early winter.

One December, I had a trapping camp on a large island in a lake. Through the Christmas holidays, the weather remained mild, though the lakes and marshes were frozen enough to permit my walking on the ice in the morning, if not during the rest of the day. I have two outstanding memories of that month.

A loon sat in the smaller open spots and fished and called, day and night. In its grayish winter plumage, it blended into its background or flashed its whiter underparts as it stood up beating its wings, or it sank beneath the water and came up again. Sometimes it would swim from one open spot to another beneath the ice.

The other memory is of mallards. An open area of twenty or thirty acres, situated less than a quarter-mile from camp, was packed with the mallards, a danger-tempered group that knew about all that mallards needed to know to live. For weeks, most of them did not leave to feed in the cornfields before dark. At all times of night, their quacking and restless flying could be heard—every few minutes punctuated by a roar as hundreds or thousands got up, to alight again. Minks dragged over the ice the bodies of the lead-poisoned or crippled birds that sat or lay about the outskirts of the flock, but the main group lived with security from predatory enemies, including myself.

On a north-central marsh or lake, the final encroachment of ice may leave the remaining water crowded with ailing ducks and coots and with the indubitably functional goldeneyes and mergansers to which hanging about the last open water is a way of their lives. Birds that I enjoy watching are the little hooded mergansers and buffleheads, with their neat bodies and dark and white contrasts. The big, almost mallard-like American and red-breasted mergansers usually do not permit a close approach. They may circle, fly away, then return almost to drop into the water, then fly away again. Sometimes, a long-necked and long-billed western grebe is among the last occupants. Out at the South Dakota farm, we found one floundering on the ice and tried to help it take wing but nearly got speared doing so.

The migratory users of a water hole may come and go before one even sees them there. While out on the central ice of a marsh studying the "sign" about a strip of open water next to a muskrat lodge, I found myself staring at enormous bird droppings and white contour feathers stuck to the ice. Later, I saw the undoubted source of the droppings and feathers, but on another marsh—a flock of six whistling swans, here too staying about as far from shore as they could. They flew low over the central ice and rushes, rising as they approached shore until high over the big cottonwoods, then leveled off in a straight-away cruising flight.

If the real, tight freeze-up comes in fair weather, we may have one great phalanx of mallards after another going by, hundreds of yards overhead. This may be the "northern flight" so long anticipated by the hunting public, and hunters in new hunting clothes may line the hilltops and lake shores—and go home without ducks. It has now become an annual cycle, the blown-up daydreams of the northern flight, when the dubbiest dubs expect to bag their legal limits almost without trying, and the disappointing reality of the actual hunting. The ducks do not want to be shot during the northern flight any more than at any other time, and, unless they are innocents making their first acquaintance with modern man and his firearms, they may not get shot, any more than the ducks preceding them.

Mass movements of ducks in late fall need not be a disappointment to people who are not too preoccupied with shooting or bringing home game. Spectacles of clear skies full of ducks can be among the most imposing in Nature, the glinting of light on white wings and breasts far off to the side, and dark strings and bunches of flying birds to be seen in all directions, even those so distant that the position of a flock may be lost before it is much more than discovered. Add frost to the air, and the person with a capacity for enjoying rare sights may watch and watch and be glad that he lives.

Nor need one always wait until the onset of winter to see the big, high flights—they may sometimes be seen on the mildest of sunny fall days, if one looks for them, away up there, where even buckshot cannot reach. Let those who wish to see things try lying on a lake-side hill, scanning the sky for migrating ducks, geese, hawks, and now and then something more unusual, like a flock of sandhill cranes.

The northern flight may conform most closely to popular ideas when freeze-up comes with a storm. Even then, a hunter has to know how to hunt and how to shoot, if he is to bag ducks, and his opportunities may be variable. If visibility is poor for the ducks, it is also poor for the hunters, and, if the weather is bad enough, the ducks may go right on through, high up and out of range or out of sight—unless bewildered or desperate for rest, food, or water. During a blizzard, mallards may continue to pour into a strategic water hole despite gun fire from the edges, but that is not the kind of hunting that I care for. I always had a notion that ducks should be left alone under such circumstances and that human hunters have no business groping around in a snowstorm among patches of open water and thin ice out in the center of a marsh or lake, good hunting or not.

Let autumn be ended appropriately with a snowstorm, with a vague moving whiteness turning gray as night approaches, with snow settling down or streaking or swirling in aerial eddies, and the water birds—the healthy and the doomed—sitting on or about the open water. Then, a hardening of the slush, and the birds that can fly disappear into the enveloping snow; the other birds sit or walk or freeze into the slush. To the minks belong the surface as well as the edge of marsh and lake now. The night is a good night for them as they drag booty to their retreats ashore, but that is quite natural and proper. Minks have to eat, too.

DOWN THE OHIO

BY TIMOTHY FLINT

Timothy Flint (1780–1840) was a native New Englander, a Harvard graduate, who became a preacher and was sent to the Mississippi Valley as a missionary by the Missionary Society of Connecticut in 1815. He spent the rest of his life in that frontier area, preaching, teaching, traveling and participating in the life of that time and place. This selection is from his book Recollections of the Last Ten Years, *published in 1826, and describes his first trip west, down the Ohio River. His* Recollections *is one of the earliest and best accounts of the look of that country and the ways of life there, certainly one of the very first written by a well-educated man.*

(*Recollections of the Last Ten Years,* by Timothy Flint, published in 1826.)

Our first river voyage commenced in the early part of November, on a beautiful autumnal afternoon. We had waited a considerable time for the rising of the river, for as yet no boat of any considerable draught of water was able to descend. We had become impatient of remaining here (Pittsburgh, Pennsylvania), and embarked in a very small flat-boat, laden with factory cottons and cutlery. The owner was from Dorchester in Massachusetts, and probably his whole capital was embarked on this bottom. He was as little experienced in this mode of navigation as we were. Our notions of what we had to expect on this voyage were formed from contemplating the gentle and equable current of this beautiful river, and resulted in the persuasion, that the whole trip would be an excursion of pleasure and entire safety. Hundreds of emigrants from the eastern country commence this descent equally inexperienced.

About one o'clock in the afternoon we began to float down the Allegany, and in a few moments we were moving on the broad bosom of the Ohio, at the point of junction nearly a mile in width. The autumns of every part of our country are beautiful, but those of the western country are preeminently so. Nothing resulting from beauty of sky, temperature of air, and charm of scenery, can surpass what was now above us and around us. The bright sun, the mild blue sky, a bland feeling of the atmosphere, the variegated foliage of the huge sycamores which line the banks of the Ohio, their leaves turning red and yellow, and finely contrasting with the brilliant white of their branches, the unruffled stream, which reflected in its bosom the beautiful surrounding nature,—all things conspired to give us very high anticipations from being wafted down "la belle riviere." We were congratulating each other, that this was indeed worth all the toils and privations, we had endured in arriving at the Ohio. But, alas for human calculations! While we were noticing every object on the banks with such intense interest, while the owner was seated amidst his goods and wares, indulging probably in golden dreams of easy, certain, and great profits, while one of the company that you know of, was completely given up to reverie, at which you have so often smiled, —on a sudden the roar of the river admonished us that we were near a ripple. We had with us that famous book "The Navigator," as it is called. The boat began to exchange its gentle and imperceptible advance for a furious progress. Soon after, it gave a violent bounce against a rock on one side, which threatened to capsize it. On recovering her level, she immediately bounced on the opposite side, and that in its turn was keeled up. Instead of running to the oar, we ran to look in the "Navigator." The owner was pale. The children shrieked. The hard ware came tumbling upon us from the shelves, and Mrs. F. was almost literally buried amidst locks, latches, knives, and pieces of domestic cotton. The gentle river had not intended in this first alarm to swallow us up, but only to give us timely warning, that too much tranquillity and enjoyment are not to be expected here. We floated off from this ripple, which bore the ominous name of "Dead Man's," into the smooth water, with no other injury than the chaotic state of our lading. But from that moment, adieu to our poetic dreams of floating down the beautiful river in such perfect safety. We were continually running to the "Navigator," astonished to find how full the river was of chutes and ripples.

It was now the middle of November. The weather up to this time had been, with the exception of a couple of days of fog and rain, delightful. The sky has a milder and lighter azure than that of the northern states. The wide, clean sand-bars stretching for miles together, and now and then a flock of wild geese, swans, or sand-hill cranes, and pelicans [sic], stalking along on them; the infinite varieties of form of the towering bluffs; the new tribes of shrubs and plants on the shores; the exuberant fertility of the soil, evidencing itself in the natural as well as cultivated vegetation, in the height and size of the corn, of itself alone a matter of astonishment to an inhabitant of the northern states, in the thrifty aspect of the young orchards, literally bending under their fruit, the surprising size and rankness of the weeds, and, in the enclosures where cultivation had been for a while suspended, the matted abundance of every kind of vegetation that ensued,—all these circumstances united to give a novelty and freshness to the scenery. The bottom forests everywhere display the huge sycamore, the king of the western forest, in all places an interesting tree, but particularly so here, and in autumn, when you see its white and long branches among its red and yellow fading leaves. You may add, that in all the trees that have been stripped of their leaves, you see them crowned with verdant tufts of the viscous or mistletoe, with its beautiful white berries, and their trunks entwined with grapevines, some of them in size not much short of the human body. To add to this union of pleasant circumstances, there is a delightful temperature of the air, more easily felt than described. In New England, when the sky was partially covered with fleecy clouds, and the wind blew very gently from the southwest, I have sometimes had the same sensations from the temperature there. A slight degree of languor ensues; and the irritability that is caused by the rougher and more bracing air of the north, and which is more favourable to physical strength and activity than enjoyment, gives place to a tranquillity highly propitious to meditation. There is something, too, in the gentle and almost imperceptible motion, as you sit on the deck of the boat, and see the trees apparently moving by you, and new groups of scenery still opening upon your eye, together with the view of these ancient and magnificent forests, which the axe has not yet despoiled, the broad and beautiful river, the earth and the sky, which render such a trip at this season the very element of poetry. Let him that has within him the "bona indoles," the poetic mania, as yet unwhipt of justice, not think to sail down the Ohio under such circumstances, without venting to the genius of the river, the rocks and the woods, the swans, and perchance his distant beloved, his dolorous notes. . . .

Accordingly, in the same keel-boat which brought us from Cincinnati, we moved in September to St. Charles. The tenth of that month, 1816, we saw the mouth of the Missouri, the largest tributary stream in the world. It strikes the upper Mississippi, which is a broad, placid stream, a mile in width, nearly at right angles. It pours along a narrow, but deep, rapid, and turbid current, white with the amount of marly clay, with which it is charged. It is impossible to contemplate, without interest, a river which rises in vast and nameless mountains, and runs at one time through deep forests, and then through grassy plains, between three and four thousand miles, before it arrives here. My family ascended to St. Charles in the boat, and I went up by land.

Having crossed a deep bottom of two miles in width, I came out upon the first prairie of any great size or beauty that I had seen. It was Sabbath, and a fine September morning. Every object was brilliant with a bright sun, and wet with a shower that had fallen the preceding evening. The first time a stranger comes in view of this prairie, take it all in all, the most beautiful that I have ever seen, a scene strikes him that will never be forgotten. The noble border of wood, that with its broad curve skirts this prairie, has features peculiar to the Missouri bottom, and distinct from that of the Mississippi. I observed the cotton trees to be immensely tall, rising like Corinthian columns, enwrapped with a luxuriant wreathing of ivy, and the bignonia radicans, with its splendid, trumpet-shaped flowers, displayed them glittering in the sun, quite on the summits of the trees. The prairie itself was a most glorious spectacle. Such a sea of verdure, in one direction extending beyond the reach of the eye, and presenting millions of flowers of every scent and hue, seemed an immense flower-garden. The air was soft and mild. The smoke streamed aloft from the houses and cabins, which indented the prairie, just in the edge of the wood. The best view of this prairie is from the "Mamelles," which bound it on the west.

There are evident indications, that these mighty rivers, the Missouri and the upper Mississippi, once united at the foot of the Mamelles. These are a succession of regular, cone-shaped bluffs, which the French,—who are remarkable for giving names significant of the fancied resemblance of the thing,—have supposed to resemble the object whose name they bear. From the declivity of these beautiful eminences to the present union of the rivers, is, by their meanders, twenty-five miles. The prairie extends from them more than half this distance towards the junction. To the right, the Missouri converges toward the Mississippi, by an easy curve, the limits of which are marked by the Missouri bluffs, which form a blue and indented outline, over the tops of the grand forest bottoms. You can trace these bluffs to the point of union. To the left, your eye catches the much broader curve of the upper Mississippi, which presents a regular section of an immense circle. Your eye follows this curve forty miles. In the whole of this distance, the opposite, or Illinois shore, is marked with a noble and bold outline, over which hovers a blue and smoky mist. The perfect smoothness of the basin enclosed between the two rivers, a carpet of verdure diversified with the most beautiful flowers, and the great extent of the curve, give the perpendicular bluffs that bound the basin, the aspect of mountains. This curve presents an unbroken blue outline, except in one point, and through that chasm is seen the Illinois, whose cliffs are just discovered fading away in the distance, at the east.

Between such magnificent outlines, from the foot of the Mamelles, the prairie, in ascending towards the north, has a width of five miles, and is seventy miles in length. On the Mississippi side, the prairie touches the river for most of this distance. The aspect of the whole surface is so smooth, so level, and the verdure so delightful, that the eye reposes upon it. Houses at eight miles distance over this plain, seem just at your feet. A few spreading trees planted by hand, are dotted here and there upon the surface. Two fine islands of woodland, of a circular form, diversify the view. Large flocks of cattle and horses are seen grazing together. It is often the case that a flock of wild deer is seen bounding over the plain. In the autumn, immense flocks of pelicans (possibly white pelicans), sand-bills, cranes (sand-hill cranes), geese, swans, ducks, and all kinds of aquatic fowls, are seen hovering over it. The soil is of the easiest culture and the most exuberant productiveness. The farms are laid out in parallelograms. At the foot of the Mamelles are clumps of hazel bushes, pawpaws, wild grapes, and prairie plums, in abundance. The grass is thick and tall. Corn and wheat grow in the greatest perfection. When I first saw this charming scene, "Here," said I to my companion who guided me, "here shall be my farm, and here I will end my days!" In effect, take it all in all, I have not seen, before nor since, a landscape which united, in an equal degree, the grand, the beautiful, and fertile. It is not necessary in seeing it to be very young or very romantic, in order to have dreams steal over the mind, of spending an Arcadian life in these remote plains, which just begin to be vexed with the plough, far removed from the haunts of wealth and fashion, in the midst of rustic plenty, and of this beautiful nature.

THE ISLAND

BY JOHN GRAVES

John Graves (1920 —) was born in Texas, educated at Rice Institute and Columbia University, served in the Marine Corps in World War II. Since the war he has been a teacher, a writer and, as he says, a wanderer. Most of his writing has been fiction, for which he has won several awards. He is now teaching at Texas Christian University. This selection is from Goodbye to a River, *his nonfiction book about a canoe trip he made down the Brazos River, a dachshund pup his only companion, to renew memories and know the river again before a projected government dam destroyed its meaning. It is one of the richest narratives I know, and though it somewhat reminds me of Thoreau's* A Week on the Concord *it is uniquely John Graves, every word, memory and emotion.*

(*Goodbye to a River*, by John Graves; Alfred A. Knopf, Inc., 1960.)

There was an island, long and slim, built up of the variegated Brazos chert gravel, which, when wet and shining, looks like the jewels in a storybook treasure chest. Its top was padded with white sand and bordered by big willows and small cottonwoods. Toward the blunt upper end, where spring's drouth-breaking floods had worked to most effect, lay a bare-swept sandy plain, and the few trees along the shoreline there were bent downstream at steep angles. Against stubs and stumps down the length of the island the same force had laid up tangled jams of driftwood—ash and cedar, elm and oak, good fuel. Here and there where silt had accumulated, Bermuda grass or weeds bristled in patches.

Because I liked the look of it, I stopped there in the middle of a quiet bright afternoon and made a solid camp on flat gravel under willows, eight feet above the water but only a few nearly vertical steps from the canoe. I was tired and my gear needed tending, and it looked like the kind of place I'd been waiting for to spend a couple of nights and to loaf through a little of what the abstractly alliterative military schedules used to call "matériel maintenance." Islands are special, anyhow, as children know with a leaping instinct, and when they lie in public domain you can have a fine sense of temporary ownership about them that's hard to get on shores, inside or outside of fences.

By the time I'd finished setting up and hauling my chattels from the canoe—all of them, since they all needed cleaning or fixing—it was nearly evening. The stronger of the channels flanking the island ran on the side where I was camped; I walked up the narrow beach and put out a catfish line just below where the water dropped out of a rapids, tying a rock to the line's end and throwing it straight out so that when the line came taut the rock dropped gurgling and anchored the line in a long bow across the head of the deep run, back to a willow stub beside me. Trotlines from shore to shore get you more fish and bigger ones, but they're also more labor. After I'd finished with the line I worked along the beach, spin-casting bootlessly for bass. Four Canada geese came diagonally over the river, low, calling, and in a moment I heard a clamor at the head of the island, shielded from me by the island's duned fringe and by willows. I climbed up through them to look. At least 200 more honkers took off screaming from the sand bar at the upper end of the bare plain. The passenger ran barking after them. Calling him back, I squatted beside a drift pile, and in the rose half-light of dusk watched through the field glass as they came wheeling in again, timid but liking the place as I had liked it, and settled by tens and twenties at the bar and in the shallows above it where the two channels split.

Nine skeptics, maybe the ones that had seen me at first and raised the alarm, circled complaining for a time before they flew on elsewhere. Black against water that held the west's reflected red, the others stalked about till their alertness had softened, then began to drink and cavort, lunging at one another, leaping into the air with their wings spread and circling two by two in a kind of dance.

Old John Magnificence was with me:

> What call'st thou solitude, is not the Earth
> With various living creatures, and the Aire
> Replenisht, and all these at thy command
> To come and play before thee? . . .

He was. I used to be suspicious of the kind of writing where characters are smitten by correct quotations at appropriate moments. I still am, but not as much. Things do pop out clearly in your head, alone, when the upper layers of your mind are unmisted by much talk with other men. Odd bits and scraps and thoughts and phrases from all your life and all your reading keep boiling up to view like grains of rice in a pot on the fire. Sometimes they even make sense. . . .

I thought of the shotgun at my camp a hundred yards below, but it would have been useless if I'd had it; they were a long way from any cover. And for that matter there was about them something of the feel that the bald eagle had had for me in the mountain country. I'd been a hunter most of my life, except for two or three years after the war. Young, I'd made two-hour crawls on my belly through standing swamp water for the mere hope of a shot at a goose, nearly always frustrated. Just now, though, it seemed to matter little that these were safe out of range. Watching the red-and-black shadow show of their awkward powerful play was enough, and listening to their occasional arrogant horn shouts. I squatted there watching until nearly dark, then backed down quietly to the beach and went to camp.

Supper was a young squirrel who had nevertheless achieved an elder's stringiness, roasted in foil on the embers, and a potato baked in the same way. I'd been going lazy on the cooking lately, mostly because I had little appetite, and that little most generally for things I'd have disliked in town—bouillon, or coffee thickly sweet with honey, or the stewed mixed fruit that made my breakfasts. From such sparse eating and from exercise I'd lost weight—maybe twelve or fifteen pounds since Possum Kingdom, to judge from the slack in my waistband. I ate the potato and chewed a little on the squirrel and gave the rest of it to the pup.

Hearing the geese honk still from time to time, I knew it would have been easy enough, on that moonless night, to ease up the defiladed beach near them and sneak across the sand on my stomach for a sniping shot. All it would take was patience. But I was years past being tempted by that kind of dirtiness; the contradictory set of rules that one works out for killing, if he keeps on killing past a certain age, usually makes an unreasonable distinction between ways that are honorable and ways that aren't, and for me night pot shots weren't. . . . And I didn't think I needed anything as big as a goose.

Someone else's rules were less strict, or maybe his need was greater; when I'd put a couple of heavy chunks of elm on the fire and sat watching them, sniffing the faintly urinal sharpness of their burning, two rapid shots sounded far off down the river and a minute later geese were calling confusedly in the sky. Stacked alongside my own abstention it angered me a little, but on the other hand it was none of my right business.

From brief yards away, in a cottonwood, a barred owl cut loose with flourishes: *Who, who, whoo, whoo, whah, whah, hah,* HAH, HAH, WHO ALL!

Then, an afterthought, he said: YOU ALL!

Certain it meant specifically him, the passenger barked back once almost under his breath, growled a little with an angry ridge of short hair dark along his spine, and sought my lap.

Elm stinks, wherefore literal farmers give it a grosser name, but it makes fine lasting coals. That morning I was up before dawn to blow away the ashes from the orange-velvet embers underneath, and to build more fire on them with twigs and leaves and brittle sticks of dead cottonwood. I huddled over it in the cold, still, graying darkness and watched coffee water seethe at the edges of a little charred pot licked by flame, and heard the horned owl stop that deceptively gentle five-noted comment he casts on the night. The geese at the island's head began to talk among themselves, then to call as they rose to go to pastures and peanut fields, and night-flushed bobwhites started whistling *where-you? where-you?* to one another somewhere above the steep dirt river bank. Drinking coffee with honey in it and canned milk, smoking a pipe that had the sweetness pipes only have in cold quiet air, I felt good if a little scratchy-eyed, having gone to sleep the night before struck with the romance of stars and firelight, with the flaps open and only the blanket over me, to wake at two thirty chilled through.

On top of the food box alligator-skin corrugations of frost had formed, and with the first touch of the sun the willows began to whisper as frozen leaves loosed their hold and fell side-slipping down through the others that were still green. Titmice called, and flickers and a redbird, and for a moment, on a twig four feet from my face, a chittering kinglet jumped around alternately hiding and flashing the scarlet of its crown. . . . I sat and listened and watched while the world woke up, and drank three cups of the syrupy coffee, better I thought than any I'd ever tasted, and smoked two pipes.

You run a risk of thinking yourself an ascetic when you enjoy, with that intensity, the austere facts of fire and coffee and tobacco and the sound and feel of country places. You aren't though. In a way you're more of a sensualist than a fat man washing down sauerbraten and dumplings with heavy beer while a German band plays and a plump blonde kneads his thigh. . . . You've shucked off the gross delights, and those you have left are few, sharp, and strong. But they're sensory. Even Thoreau, if I remember right a passage or so on cornbread, was guilty, though mainly he was a real ascetic.

Real ones shouldn't care. They ought to be able to live on paté and sweet peaches and roast suckling pig or alternatively on cheese and garlic in a windmill or the scraps that housewives have thrown in begging bowls. Groceries and shelter should matter only as fuel and frame for life, and life as energy for thought or beyond-communion or (Old Man Goodnight has to fit somewhere, and a fraught executive or two I've known, and maybe Davis Birdsong hurling his bulldozer against the tough cedar brush in a torn shirt and denim pants, coughing yellow flu sputum while the December rain pelts him, not caring) for action.

But I hadn't set up as an ascetic, anyhow. I sat for a long time savoring the privilege of being there, and didn't overlay the taste of the coffee with any other food. A big red-brown butterfly sat spread on the cottonwood log my ax was stuck in, warming itself in the sun. I watched until it flew stiffly away, then got up and followed, for no good reason except that the time seemed to have come to stir and I wanted a closer look at the island than I'd gotten the evening before.

It was shaped like an attenuated teardrop or the cross section of an airplane's wing, maybe three quarters of a mile long and 100 yards or so wide at its upper, thicker end. Its foundation everywhere appeared to be a heavy deposit of the multicolored gravel, and its flat top except for a few high dunes of the padding sand was eight or ten feet above the present level of the river. All around, it dropped off steeply, in spots directly to the water, in others to beaches, and toward the pointed tail the willows and weeds stood rank. I rooted about there and found nothing but coon tracks and a few birds still sleepy and cold on their roosts, but, emerging among cockleburs above a beach by the other channel, scared four ducks off a quiet eddy. I'd left the gun in the tent; shots from here and there under the wide sky's bowl reminded me that busier hunters than I were finding game.

Let them. I considered that maybe in the evening I'd crouch under a bush at the island's upper end and put out sheets of notepaper on the off chance that more geese would come, and the off-off chance that if they did they'd feel brotherly toward notepaper. You can interest them sometimes in newspapers.

And maybe I wouldn't.

The shores on either side of the river from the island were dirt and steep, twenty feet high, surmounted by pecans and oaks with the bare sky of fields or pastures beyond. They seemed separate from the island; it was big enough, with a strong enough channel on either side, to seem to have a kind of being of its own distinct from that of the banks—a sand and willow and cottonwood and driftwood biome—though in dry times doubtless there would be only one channel and no island, but just a great bar spreading out below the right bank.

Jays, killdeers, wrens, cardinals, woodpeckers . . . With minute and amateurish interest, I found atop a scoop in the base of a big, drifted, scorched tree trunk five little piles of fox dung, a big owl's puke ball full of hair and rat skulls, and three fresher piles of what had to be coon droppings, brown and small, shaped like a dog's or a human's.

Why, intrigued ignorance asked, did wild things so often choose to stool on rocks, stumps, and other elevations?

Commonsense replied: Maybe for the view.

On the flat beach at the head of the island the night's geese had laid down a texture of crisscrossed toe-prints. Elsewhere, in dry sand, I found little pointed diggings an inch in diameter and four to five inches deep, much like those an armadillo makes in grassland but with no tracks beside them. A bird? A land-foraging crawfish? Another puzzle for my ignorance, underlined now by the clear note of the unknown sad-whistling bird from a willow a few steps from me. He wouldn't show himself, and when I eased closer said irascibly: *Heap, heap!* and fluttered out the other side. . . .

The trouble was, I *was* ignorant. Even in that country where I belonged, my ken of natural things didn't include a little bird that went *heap-heap* and

———, ———,

and a few moronic holes in the sand. Or a million other matters worth the kenning.

I grew up in a city near there—more or less a city, anyhow, a kind of spreading imposition on the prairies—that was waked from a dozing cow-town background by a standard boom after the First World War and is still, civic-souled friends tell me, bowling right along. It was a good enough place, not too big then, and a mile or so away from where I lived, along a few side streets and across a boulevard and a golf course, lay woods and pastures and a blessed river valley where the stagnant Trinity writhed beneath big oaks. In retrospect, it seems we spent more time there than we did on pavements, though maybe it's merely that remembrance of that part is sharper. There were rabbits and squirrels to hunt, and doves and quail and armadillos and foxes and skunks. A few deer ran the woods, and one year, during a drouth to the west, big wolves. Now it's mostly subdivisions, and even then it lay fallow because it was someone's real-estate investment. The fact that caretakers were likely to converge on us blaspheming at the sound of a shot or a shout, scattering us to brush, only made the hunting and the fishing a bit saltier. I knew one fellow who kept a permanent camp there in a sumac thicket, with a log squat-down hut and a fireplace and all kinds of food and utensils hidden in tin-lined holes in the ground, and none of the caretakers ever found it. Probably they worried less than we thought; there weren't many of us.

I had the Brazos, too, and South Texas, where relatives lived, and my adults for the most part were good people who took me along on country expeditions when they could. In terms of the outdoors, I and the others like me weren't badly cheated as such cheatings go nowadays, but we were cheated nevertheless. We learned quite a lot, but not enough. Instead of learning to move into country, as I think underneath we wanted, we learned mostly how to move onto it in the old crass Anglo-Saxon way, in search of edible or sometimes just mortal quarry. We did a lot of killing, as kids will, and without ever being told that it was our flat duty, if duty exists, to know all there was to know about the creatures we killed.

Hunting and fishing are the old old entry points into nature for men, and not bad ones either, but as standardly practiced these days, for the climactic ejaculation of city tensions, they don't go very deep. They aren't thoughtful; they hold themselves too straitly to their purpose. Even for my quail-hunting uncles in South Texas, good men, good friends to me, all smaller birds of hedge and grass were "chee-chees," vermin, confusers of dogs' noses. . . . And if, with kids' instinctive thrustingness, we picked up a store of knowledge about small things that lived under logs and how the oriole builds its nest, there was no one around to consolidate it for us. Our knowledge, if considerable, remained random.

This age, of course, is unlikely to start breeding people who have the organic kinship to nature that the Comanches had, or even someone like Mr. Charlie Goodnight. For them every bush, every bird's cheep, every cloud bank had not only utilitarian but mystical meaning; it was all an extension of their sensory systems, an antenna as rawly receptive as a snail's. Even if their natural world still existed, which it doesn't, you'd have to snub the whole world of present men to get into it that way.

Nor does it help to be born in the country. As often as not these days, countrymen know as little as we others do about those things. They come principally of the old hardheaded tradition that moved onto the country instead of into it. For every Charles Goodnight there were several dozen Ezra Shermans, a disproportion that has bred itself down through the generations. Your standard country lore about animals—about the nasal love life of the possum, or the fabled hoop snake—is picturesque rather than accurate, anthropocentric rather than understanding.

But Charlie Goodnight and the Ezra Shermans and their children and grandchildren all combined have burned out and chopped out and plowed out and grazed out and killed out a good part of that natural world they knew, or didn't know, and we occupy ourselves mainly, it sometimes seems, in finishing the job. The rosy preindustrial time is past when the humanism of a man like Thoreau (*was* it humanism?) could still theorize in terms of extant human beings. The terms of today's human beings are air conditioners and suburbs and water impoundments overlaying whole countrysides, and the hell with nature except maybe in a cross-sectional park here and there. In our time quietness and sun and leaves and bird song and all the multitudinous lore of the natural world have to come second or third, because whether we wanted to be born there or not, we were all born into the prickly machine-humming place that man has hung for himself above that natural world.

Where, tell me, is the terror and wonder of an elephant, now that they can be studied placid in every zoo, and any office-dwelling sport with a recent lucky break on the market can buy himself one to shoot through telescopic sights with a cartridge whose ballistics hold a good fileful of recorded science's findings? With a box gushing refrigerated air (or warmed, seasonally depending) into a sealed house and another box flashing loud bright images into jaded heads, who gives a rat's damn for things that go bump in the night? With possible death by blast or radiation staring at us like a buzzard, why should we sweat ourselves over where the Eskimo curlew went?

The wonder is that a few people do still sweat themselves, that the tracks of short varmints on a beach still have an audience. A few among the audience still know something, too. If they didn't, one wouldn't have to feel so cheated, not knowing as much. . . . Really knowing, I mean—from childhood up and continuously, with all of it a flavor in you . . . Not just being able to make a little seem a lot; there is enough of that around. I can give you as much book data about the home life of the yellowbreasted chat as the next man can. Nor do I mean vague mystic feelings of unity with Comanche and Neanderthal as one wanders the depleted land, gun at the ready, a part of the long flow of man's hunting compulsion. I mean *knowing.*

So that what one does in time, arriving a bit late at an awareness of the swindling he got—from no one, from the times—is to make up the shortage as best he may, to try to tie it all together for himself by reading and adult poking. But adult poking is never worth a quarter as much as kid poking, not in those real terms. There's never the time for that whole interest later, or ever quite the pure and subcutaneous receptiveness, either.

I mean, too—obviously—if you care. I know that the whicker of a plover in the September sky doesn't touch all other men in their bowels as it touches me, and that men whom it doesn't touch at all can be good men. But it touches me. And I care about knowing what it is, and—if I can—why.

Disgruntled from caring, I went to run my throwline. Coon's fresh tracks along the beach overlaid my own of the evening before; one had played with the end of the line and had rolled the jar of blood bait around on the sand trying to get inside it. The passenger followed some of the tracks into a drift tangle but lost interest, not knowing what he was trailing, robbed by long generations of show-breeding of the push that would have made him care. . . . In my fingers the line tugged with more than the pulse of the current, but when I started softly hand-over-handing it in, it gave a couple of stiff jerks and went slacker, and I knew that something on it in a final frenzy had finished the job of twisting loose. They roll and roll and roll, and despite swivels at last work the staging into a tight snark against whose solidity they can tear themselves free. Whatever it had been, channel or yellow or blue, it had left a chunk of its lip on the second hook, and two hooks beyond that was a one-pounder which I removed, respectful toward the sharp septic fin spines.

In the old days, we'd taken the better ones before they rolled loose by running the lines every hour or so during the night, a sleepless process and in summer a mosquito-chewed one. Once in Hood County, Hale and I and black Bill Briggs had gotten a twenty-five-pounder, and after an argument with Bill, who wanted to try to eat it, we sold it to a bridge-side café for a dime a pound. Another time on the Guadalupe to the south—but this is supposed to be about the Brazos. . . .

Tethering the little catfish to the chain stringer by the canoe, I got a rod and went down to the sharp tail of the island to cast a plug into green deep eddies I'd seen there while exploring. Without wind, the sun was almost hot now. From a willow a jay resented me with a two-note muted rasp like a boy blowing in and out on a harmonica with stuck reeds, and in an almost bare tree on the high river bank a flock of bobolinks fed and bubbled and called, resting on their way south.

Cast and retrieve, shallow and deep, across current and down and up, and no sign of bass . . The sun's laziness got into me and I wandered up the lesser channel, casting only occasionally into holes without the expectation of fish. Then, on a long flow-dimpled bar, something came down over my consciousness like black pain, and I dropped the rod and squatted, shaking my head to drive the blackness back. It receded a little, I waddled without rising to the bar's edge and scooped cold water over my head. After four or five big throbs it went away, and I sat down half in the water and thought about it. It didn't take much study. My stomach was giving a lecture about it, loud. What it amounted to was that I was about half starved.

I picked up the rod, went back to camp, stirred the fire, and put on a pot of water into which I dumped enough dried lima beans for four men, salt, an onion, and a big chunk of bacon. Considering, I went down to the stringer and skinned and gutted the little catfish and carried him up and threw him in the pot, too. While it boiled, I bathed in the river, frigid in contrast to the air, sloshed out the canoe and sponged it down, and washed underclothes and socks. In shorts, feeling fine now but so hungry it hurt, I sat by the fire and sharpened knives and the ax for the additional hour the beans need to cook soft in the middle. Fishing out the skeleton of the disintegrated catfish, and using the biggest spoon I had, I ate the whole mess from the pot almost without stopping, and mopped up its juices with cold biscuit bread.

Then I wiped my chin and lay back against the cottonwood log with my elbows hanging over it behind and my toes digging into the sand, and considered that asceticism, most certainly, was for those who were built for it. Some were. Some weren't. I hadn't seen God in the black headache on the sand bar and I didn't want to try to any more, that way. . . . Starving myself hadn't had much to do with spirituality, anyhow, but only with the absence of company.

Philosophically equilibrated, I rolled down into the sand and went to sleep for two or three hours, waking into a perfect blue-and-yellow afternoon loud with the full-throat chant of the redbird.

Wood . . . I went roaming with the honed ax among the piles of drift, searching out solid timber. Bleached and unbarked as much of it is, you have a hard time seeing what it may be, but a two-lick notch with the ax usually bares its grain enough to name it. Cottonwood and willow slice soft and white before the first blow, and unless you're hard up you move on to try your luck on another piece; they're not serious fuel:

> The fire devoureth both the ends of it, and the midst of it is burnt. Is it meet for any work?

But the river is prodigal of its trees, and better stuff is usually near.

If food is to sit in the fire's smoke as it cooks, any of the elms will give it a bad taste, though they last and give good heat. Cedar's oil eats up its wood in no time, and stinks food, too, but the tinge of it on the air after supper is worth smelling if you want to cut a stick or so of it just for that. Rockhard bodark—Osage orange if you want; bois d'arc if you're etymological—sears a savory crust on meat and burns a long time, if you don't mind losing a flake out of your ax's edge when you hit it wrong. For that matter, not much of it grows close enough to the river to become drift. Nor does much mesquite —a pasture tree and the only thing a conscientious Mexican cook will barbecue kid over. Ash is all right but, as dry drift anyhow, burns fast. The white oaks are prime, the red oaks less so, and one of the finest of aromatic fuels is a twisted, wave-grained branch of live oak, common in the limestone country farther down the river.

Maybe, though, the nutwoods are best and sweetest, kind to food and long in their burning. In the third tangle I nicked a huge branch of walnut, purple-brown an inch inside its sapwood's whitened skin. It rots slowly; this piece was sound enough for furniture making—straight-grained enough, too, for that matter. I chopped it into long pieces. The swing and the chocking bite of the ax were pleasant; the pup chased chips as they flew, and I kept cutting until I had twice as many billets as I would need. Then I stacked them for later hauling and went to camp to use up the afternoon puttering with broken tent loops and ripped tarps and sprung hinges on boxes, throwing sticks for the passenger, looking in a book for the differences among small streaked finches, airing my bed, sweeping with a willow branch the sandy gravel all through a camp I'd leave the next day. . . .

I lack much zeal for camping, these years. I can still read old Kephart with pleasure: nearly half a century later hardly anyone else has come anywhere near him for information and good sense. But there's detachment in my pleasure now. I no longer see myself choosing a shingle tree and felling it and splitting out the shakes for my own roof, though if I did want to he would tell me how. . . . Nor have I passion for canoeing, as such; both it and the camping are just ways to get somewhere I want to be, and to stay there for a time. I can't describe the cross-bow rudder stroke or stay serene in crashing rapids. I carry unconcentrated food in uncompact boxes. I forget to grease my boots and suffer from clammy feet. I slight hygiene, and will finger a boiled minnow from the coffee with equanimity, and sleep with my dog. My tent in comparison to the aluminum-framed, tight-snapping ones available is a ragged parallelogrammatic disaster.

Nevertheless, when camping for a time is the way of one's life, one tries to improve his style. One resolves on changes for future trips—a tiny and exactly fitted cook box; a contour-cut tarp over the canoe hooking to catches beneath the gunwales; no peaches in the mixed dried fruit. . . . One experiments and invents, and ends up, for instance, with a perfect aluminum-foil-reflector for baking that agreeable, lumpy, biscuit-mixed bread that the Mexicans call "*pan ranchero*" and the northwoods writers "bannock" and other people undoubtedly other names.

One way or the other, it all generally turns out to be work. Late that afternoon, carrying abrasive armloads of the walnut from where I'd chopped it to camp, I got as though from the air the answer to a question that used to come into my mind in libraries, reading about the old ones and the Indians. I used to wonder why, knowing Indians were around, the old ones would let themselves be surprised so often and so easily. Nearly all the ancient massacres resulted from such surprise.

The answer, simple on the island, was that the old ones were laboring their tails off at the manifold tasks of the primitive life, hewing and hauling and planting and plowing and breaking and fixing. They didn't have time to be wary. Piped water and steam heat and tractors might have let them be alert, just as I'd been among the stacked tomes of the Southwest Collection.

It was a good day, work and all. At evening I sat astraddle the bow of the canoe on the beach, putting new line on the spinning reel, when three big honkers came flying up the river slowly, low searchers like the first ones of the evening before. The gun was at hand. Even though they veered separating, as I reached for it, they still passed close, and it needed only a three-foot lead on the front one's head to bring him splashing solidly, relaxed, dead, into the channel. I trotted downstream abreast of him as he drifted and finally teased him ashore with a long crooked piece of cottonwood.

Till then I'd had the visceral bite of the old excitement in me, the gladness of clean shooting, the fulfillment of quarry sought and taken. But when I got him ashore and hefted the warm, handsome eight or nine pounds of him, and ran my fingers against the grain up through the hot thick down of his neck, the just-as-old balancing regret came into it. A goose is a lot of bird to kill. Maybe size shouldn't matter, but it seems to. With something that big and that trimly perfect and, somehow, that meaningful, you wonder about the right of the thing. . . .

For a while after the war I did no shooting at all, and thought I probably wouldn't do any more. I even chiseled out a little niche for that idea, half Hindu and tangled with the kind of reverence for life that Schweitzer preaches. But then one day in fall beside a stock tank in a mesquite pasture a friend wanted me to try the heft of a little engraved L. C. Smith, and when I'd finished trying it I'd dropped ten doves with sixteen shots and the niche didn't exist any longer.

Reverence for life in that sense seems to me to be like asceticism or celibacy: you need to be built for it. I no longer kill anything inedible that doesn't threaten me or mine, and I never cared anything about big-game hunting. Possibly I'll give up shooting again and for good one of these years, but I believe the killing itself can be reverent. To see and kill and pluck and gut and cook and eat a wild creature, all with some knowledge and the pleasure that knowledge gives, implies a closeness to the creature that is to me more honorable than the candle-lit consumption of rare prime steaks from a steer bludgeoned to death in a packing-house chute while tranquilizers course his veins. And if there's a difference in nobility between a Canada goose and a fat whitefaced ox (there is), how does one work out the quantities?

Though I threw the skin and head and guts into the river to keep them away from the pup, an eddy drifted them into shore and he found them and ate a good bit before I caught him at it. The two big slabs of breast hissed beautifully in foil on the fire after dark. When they were done I hung them up for a time uncovered in the sweet walnut smoke and then ate nearly all of one of them. The other would make sandwiches at noon for two or three days, tucked inside chunks of biscuit bread. Despite his harsh appetizers, the passenger gobbled the drumsticks and organs I'd half roasted for him, and when I unrolled the sleeping bag inside the tent he fought to be first into it.

Later, in half-sleep, I heard a rattle of dirty metal dishes beside the fire. I shot the flashlight's beam out there and a sage, masked face stared at me, indignant. Foreseeing sport, I hauled the pup up for a look. He blinked, warm and full, and dug in his toes against ejection into the cold air, and when I let him go he burrowed all the way down beside my feet, not a practical dog and not ashamed of it, either. The coon went away.

Later still, the goosefeathers began their emetic work and I woke to the rhythmic *wump, wump, wump* that in dogs precedes a heave. Though the account of it may lack wide interest, later it seemed to me that there had been heroic co-ordination in the way I came out of sleep and grabbed him, holding his jaws shut with one hand while I fought to find the bag's zipper with the other, then fought to find and loose the zipper of the tent, too, and hurled him out into the night by his nose. He stayed there for a while, and when I was sure he'd finished I let him back in, low-eared and shivering, but I preferred his unhappiness to what might have been.

It came to me then who it was that had slept with a dog for his health. Leopold Bloom's father. The dog's name had been . . . Athos! Old Man Bloom had slept with Athos to cure his aches and pains.

One can get pretty literary on islands.

WHITE OAK AND BLUE HERON

BY LEONARD HALL

Leonard Hall (1899 —) is a native Missourian who has made the Ozark country his own as farmer, naturalist, photographer and lecturer. He lives on and actively farms Possum Trot Farm near Caledonia, Missouri, and for the past twenty years has written an outdoor column, first for the St. Louis Post-Dispatch, *currently for the St. Louis* Globe-Democrat. *In 1959 he won the Thomas Stokes Award for the year's best conservation writing in America. His book,* Stars Upstream, *about a series of trips he and his wife, Virginia, made down the beautiful Ozark stream, the Current River, was instrumental in establishing the Ozark National Scenic Riverway which made the Current River America's first national river. This selection is taken from that book.*

(*Stars Upstream*, by Leonard Hall; University of Chicago Press, 1958.)

Our camp below the mouth of Grassy Creek was such a pleasant spot that we lazed over breakfast and afterward took our time packing the gear and stowing it aboard the canoe. Thus it was nine o'clock or later when we were ready to resume the downstream journey. The river, which had been quite dingy when we left Round Spring yesterday, was clearing rapidly—as it always does unless the rains upstream have been torrential. The deep pool in front of our gravel bar had all but returned to its normal blue-green color, and I judged that the bass should start striking some time during the day. So when everything was packed, we rigged Ginnie's fly rod and tucked it into the bow of the canoe beside her. Then I whistled Tiger into his small compartment just aft of the bow seat, and we were afloat once more.

There is plenty of fast water on this stretch of river, and the first bit to challenge us below our campsite was Randolph Chute. This is a long, swift rapid that goes foaming for a half-mile down a rocky bank where the channel is generously strewn with boulders and sunken logs. It is also one of the finest stretches of bass water on the river. The problem in negotiating Randolph, however, lies not so much in running the Chute itself as in getting lined out and into it in the first place. As you approach it, the river makes a sharp left turn out of a swift, deep pool and plunges into a gravel run that is narrowed to three or four feet of negotiable channel by some wicked snags which have lodged in it. At its lower end, this run piles full force into a rocky bluff beneath overhanging trees, makes another ninety-degree turn to the right, and goes tumbling down Randolph Chute proper.

Two good paddlers in an empty canoe might manage to run this rough water above the Chute if they hit it just right. With our heavy load including not only the camp gear but my movie and still cameras, the challenge was decidedly not worth the risk. But there was still the problem of how to step out, swing the canoe down through the upper rapid on its stern-rope, straighten it out at the head of the chute where the rushing water is more than waist deep, and then scramble aboard. Somehow I managed it, and then, with Ginnie holding the bow downstream with her paddle, I climbed over the stern and we went shooting down Randolph with waves breaking over the bow. In these tight spots we always expect Tiger to become as excited as we are, but he never does. His faith in us seems complete—plus which, although I doubt he thinks about this, he can swim like an otter in any kind of water.

Randolph Chute and the long pool below it are named for the Ozark family which has lived here since Current River valley was settled back in 1836. The Randolph farm lies in a big bend in the river and is a good one, as mountain farms go. Its proprietor for many years was Will Randolph, who was not only a farmer but also the neighborhood blacksmith, carpenter, cabinetmaker, and all-round artisan. He lived in a frame house of considerable size, set on the "second bench" above the bend in the river and safely out of reach of high water. Not far from the house and log barns was the blacksmith shop which, even after the old man was well along in his eighties and had retired, was still an interesting place. Inside and outside the shop could be found all the oddments of four generations of primitive mountain living: wheel hubs and the wide iron tires of log wagons, an ox yoke or two, a bull-tongued plow, wheat cradles, and the rest.

Even after Will Randolph had stopped blacksmithing, his neighbors still came to use the shop and the tools—many of them handfashioned—that hung above the carpenter benches and the anvil and forge. A hundred yards or so away from the shop, standing on a knoll, was a huge white-oak tree. This had been used, in pre-Civil War days, as a "fur press." At that time a storekeeper and trader named Deatheridge lived nearby (the name is still a common one in the neighborhood), and he took most of his currency in the form of pelts and furs. Once every so often these were baled up for transportation to the distant city. A deep notch had been chopped into the trunk of the oak tree near the ground, and in this was thrust the butt end of a long pole. Under this pole the folded skins were piled, and then weight was applied to the free end. Thus the skins were compressed tightly and could be bound into bales for shipment.

Old man Randolph is long gone, and it has been some years since we have pulled in at the rough landing on the east side of the river and climbed the hill to the farmhouse. Across the river from the farm, however, lies a forested area that contained, until very recently, some of the largest virgin white-oak trees in the country. This tract was part of a large acreage originally owned by a cooperage company which manufactured white-oak barrel staves, chiefly for the ageing of Bourbon whiskey. In the steep hollows running down to the river and in the deeper alluvial soils found in the valley, the white oaks grew to giant size. But the terrain was so rough that the area had not been logged.

During World War II the holdings of the cooperage company, which totaled some 80,000 acres and constituted probably the largest stand of virgin white oak remaining in America, were purchased by one of the distillery combines. The distillers set up the area as a "perpetual tree farm," advertised widely what splendid conservationists they were, and employed a topnotch forester to supervise the harvest of the big oaks on a sustained-yield basis. What this actually meant was cutting the individual trees as they passed maturity and began to deteriorate. But one day the distillers decided to fill a need for cash by liquidating some of their assets rather than going into the public market for money. In a little more than two years they cut every white oak large enough for barrel staves on the entire 80,000 acre tract.

This story seems an example of the all too frequent attitude of American industry toward natural resources; yet the outcome in this case was not a total disaster. The stand of white oak was mature, which means that many of the trees had reached an age of 200 years or more. But a white oak must be at least 14 inches at breast height to make a stave tree; and even after these were harvested, there were a great many trees left. Some of these were smaller white oaks, but there were also extensive stands of pine seedlings, some pine of larger size, and other species of hardwoods such as scarlet and black oak, hickory, and sour gum. A large part of the acreage was eventually acquired by a young businessman, Leo Drey of St. Louis, who has accumulated something like 130,000 acres of timber land in a long-range forestry project and is today perhaps the largest individual landowner in the Ozark highland.

Through an agreement made with the distillery people at the time they were harvesting the big oaks, a small area was left uncut on the bank of Current River at Randolph Hole. Here are some of the largest white oaks as well as splendid specimens of the other oaks, hickory, and gum; and these will be preserved so that future generations may know what our forests looked like before they were despoiled by the lumberman.

As our canoe drifted along close to the bank opposite the stand of big trees, I noticed a mud slide coming down into the river and paddled to shore to see what had made it. We climbed the bank and the first thing we found was a huge freshly cut cottonwood tree, the work of a family of beavers. Sap still oozed from the trunk, and many insects fed on it. The task of cutting the smaller branches from the tree had just started, and these were evidently being pulled into the river, then floated downstream and across to bank dens on the far side.

It has been almost twenty-five years since the first planting of a family of beavers was made on the headwaters of Current River, some forty miles above the place where we found this colony. For a long time it was difficult to tell whether they had established themselves or not, for beavers are notable travelers and move long distances during the warm months. But finally, after an absence of more than a hundred years, there is no mistaking that the beaver has returned to the Ozarks. Today we find these interesting engineers of the animal world well-established along the entire Current River watershed and on most other Ozark streams.

Unlike beavers that live in areas with sluggish streams which can be easily dammed, most of our beavers are bank dwellers. Here and there along the Current in backwaters and eddies that we call "bays," one may find the beginnings of a dam. But the sudden, violent floods that roll down our Ozark rivers make dam building an unprofitable occupation and, in any case, I doubt that big dams which create extensive ponds are necessary for the beavers in our latitude. It seems probable that in a cold climate where the ice freezes a foot or more thick, beavers must have a pond a dozen feet or so in depth in which to store their supply of willow, cottonwood, or other species that provide the succulent bark for their winter food. Here in the Ozarks with mild winter temperatures and swift-running spring-fed streams, ice is not a factor, and the animals can come and go from their bank burrows all winter long. They will, it is true, cut and store a supply of limbs; yet they will hardly ever experience more than a day or two at a time when the water is not open.

Throughout Missouri as a whole the beaver has already increased to the point where a trapping season has been opened. The fur business with the exception of mink, however, is in such a bad state that few beavers are taken. Wildlife biologists have lately developed a theory that normal cyclic variations in furbearer populations can be avoided and a high plateau of abundance maintained year after year simply by taking what they call a "maximum sustained harvest" each year.

As far as we know, the beaver population is not cyclic. My feeling about the other furbearers is that cyclic variations in population have many causes and may occur regardless of the harvest and that numbers depend in final analysis on the carrying capacity of the habitat for the species. In the case of the beaver, there is certainly plenty of room along our hundreds of miles of streams. The food supply is at least fair, and carrying capacity may depend chiefly on stream stability which, in turn, depends on the condition of the watershed. Since the state of the Ozark watersheds is gradually improving, the number of beavers can be expected to increase for some time to come.

Not far below the Randolph place we encountered another stretch of rough water—this one a long, swift chute filled with a tangle of sunken logs—which several of the river guides had told us they managed to negotiate in their John-boats with powerful outboard motors. Here there was no chance of wading to let the canoe down by rope; but fortunately the river split into two channels around an island. The smaller channel shoaled out in several places until we had to walk and drag the boat over the shallows, but at least we didn't swamp it.

Below this rapid the river makes two great oxbows, once again boxing the compass completely. Around one of the oxbows is a stretch of fast and rocky water that has always seemed to us one of the most beautiful on Current River. The left bank is low with sycamores and willows growing to the water's edge, and on the right the forested mountain climbs steeply to a height of several hundred feet. In times of low water this is not an easy stretch to run, for countless boulders lie just beneath the surface. On this day, however, the stream was flush, and we needed only to watch out for a few big rocks. I held the canoe back as much as possible, Ginnie dropped her fly over against the bank, and it wasn't long until our supper was on the stringer—a fine pair of twelve-inch smallmouth.

Once more, as the day slipped by, we found the bird life interesting. Just opposite the shady spot where we stopped for luncheon was a clay bank perhaps twenty feet high, and we saw that this was full of small holes. We watched these with our binoculars and soon discovered not only a colony of bank swallows but also the nesting holes of two pairs of kingfishers. The bank swallows are somewhat drab in comparison with the brightly colored barn and cliff swallows. Yet they are graceful on the wing, and we would sometimes see them fly directly into the tiny openings of their nests. If they checked speed at all as they came in, it was impossible to tell it.

Bank swallows and kingfishers are almost the only American birds that nest in holes in the ground which they themselves excavate, and so it is not unnatural to find them together. The kingfisher is, of course, twice as large as the barn swallow and is a bird of entirely different habit. Yet the two get along amicably and are often found side by side in the same clay or sand bank. In the environs of civilization where angling is an artificial sport depending on "planted" fish, the kingfisher is likely to be persecuted as a potential enemy of the game species. The truth is that he lives on minnows and other shallow-water fish that are pests to the angler. He also, however, includes in his diet crayfish, frogs, and many noxious insects which he takes when the fishing is poor. He is, moreover, an individualist and as interesting to watch as any bird along the stream. From our observation, each pair or family of kingfishers has its own hunting territory from which any intruder is promptly driven away.

When you think of the tremendous skill exercised by the kingfisher in his angling, it is impossible not to have considerable respect for this cheerful and aggressive fellow with his bright blue coat, belt and crest, white collar, oversized head, and huge bill. Incidentally, this is one American bird in which the female has more decorative coloring than the male, for Mrs. Kingfisher sports a sort of reddish waistcoat. I think not even the eagle has keener eyesight than the kingfisher, which can drop unerringly from a perch fifty feet above the water and come up with a wriggling minnow clutched securely in its bill.

There is a legend about the kingfisher, which is called the Halcyon in Europe, that is worth recounting. It seems that Alcyone, the daughter of Aeolus, grieving for her husband who had been shipwrecked, threw herself into the sea, where she was changed by the gods into a kingfisher, called Halcyon by the Latins. Pliny says: "The Halcyons lay their eggs and sit about mid-winter when the daies be short; and the time whiles they are broodie is called the halcyon daies; for during that season the sea is calm and navigable." The belief was that the seven days preceding the winter solstice were used for building the nest and the days immediately following for laying and hatching the eggs. These were called the "halcyon days," and even now in the Mediterranean countries they are a time of picnics and outings along the sea beaches, on quiet streams, or in the woods and fields.

Many representatives of the heron family are found along the Ozark rivers in summer, and most of these we will glimpse in a float of two or three days. Probably the one oftenest seen is the eastern green heron, which goes by the less dignified names of Fly-up-the-creek or shitepoke. This rather small heron with short legs seems clumsy and befuddled when you put him to flight and he goes flapping up to make a precarious landing on a willow branch. Yet the impression is soon changed if you watch this fellow at his fishing; for he has an eagle eye and is expert at the art of spearing minnows, frogs, salamanders, and similar food with his long, sharp bill.

The eastern green heron generally appears blue or black from a distance but, close up, is quite distinctively marked with blue-green back and crest and brown underparts. The bird has the interesting habit of "freezing" when flushed from the water to a perch in the willows, probably in an effort to escape observation. Of all the herons, I believe that only the eastern green and the bitterns build solitary nests; the rest preferring to gather in colonies during the breeding season.

The great blue heron, which stands four feet tall and has a six foot wing spread, is certainly the most spectacular of our herons. We have never discovered the nest of the great blue on Current River; yet we are quite sure he hatches his young here, since we often see the big birds in family groups in late summer. Earlier in the summer, each pair seems to claim a territory, very much like the osprey which we have already described. As we float downstream, one of the great blue herons will often precede us, flapping ahead of the canoe for an hour or more. When he reaches the end of his "beat," however, we will always see him crossing overhead on his return journey.

The little blue heron is not normally a denizen of the Ozark streams. Yet the young of this species, which keep the white plumage of infancy until they are two years old, have the odd habit of wandering far afield in late summer and autumn. Often we see whole families of them along Current River, and only occasionally are they accompanied by the adult birds. If one were not familiar with their coloration, he might easily mistake the young little blue herons for either the American or snowy egret. Neither of these latter nests along the Ozark rivers; yet both appear here in autumn, perhaps having traveled all the way from the Gulf. Distinguishing the birds is not difficult if one remembers that the American egret is quite large with yellow bill and dark legs and feet; the snowy is small with black bill and legs and bright yellow feet; and the immature little blue heron is of medium size with dark bill, legs, and feet and very often a slightly bluish cast to at least a few of its feathers.

Three other herons are seen occasionally along the Current, these being the American and least bitterns and the black-crowned night heron. I consider it doubtful that any of them nests along the stream. There is, however, one more large wading bird that we sometimes see in autumn. This is the immature wood ibis, which, like some of the herons, is a great traveler after the breeding season is over and the young are on the wing. The wood ibis is our only true stork. He stands four feet tall, has a wing spread of nearly six feet, is white with black wing patches, and has an odd bald head. Unlike the herons, he flies with neck outstretched and alternately flaps and sails. Sadly, this interesting bird which was once plentiful in Florida and along the Gulf Coast is today threatened with extinction because of the destruction of nesting rookeries through drainage and heavy logging of the last stands of cypress in the South.

On this second day of our journey from Round Spring to the Junction, we pulled in rather late to camp on a tiny gravel bar above the mouth of Brushy Creek. Here a towering bluff across from us shut off the setting sun so that twilight came early. We went for a swim which, in the 75-degree water, was refreshing; but we didn't linger long, because the heat of the September day had died with the coming of dusk.

Thereafter we doubly enjoyed the evening toddy while the bass browned in the skillet and I pitched the tent and got in the duffle bags and other gear. After supper the moon came up over the trees down river to compete with the light of our campfire. But it had been a fairly strenuous day, and not long after we had finished the second cup of coffee, washed the dishes, and made everything ready for the night, we were glad to seek the comfort of our bedrolls. For once, Tiger was as tired as we were and slept the whole night through.

GREAT RIVER: PROLOGUE

BY PAUL HORGAN

Paul Horgan (1903 —) was born in Buffalo, New York, but went to New Mexico as a student at the New Mexico Military Institute. There he laid the groundwork for an interest in the Southwest that led him back there in 1926 and has kept him there, with Roswell as his base, ever since. He has won many honors as a writer, first of fiction, then of history, particularly the history of the Southwest. His two-volume study of the Rio Grande, one of the Rivers of America *series, was awarded the Pulitzer Prize in history in 1954. This selection from the prologue of that work shows Horgan's poetic reach and his unique approach to nature and to history in its big terms.*

(*Great River: The Rio Grande in North American History,* by Paul Horgan; Rinehart & Company, 1954.)

Creation: Space.

Abstract movement.

The elements at large.

Over warm seas the air is heavy with moisture. Endlessly the vast delicate act of evaporation occurs. The seas yield their essence to the air. Sometimes it is invisible, ascending into the upper atmosphere. Sometimes it makes a shimmer in the calm light that proceeds universally from the sun. The upper heavens carry dust—sea dust of salt evaporated from ocean spray, and other dust lingering from volcanic eruption, and the lost dust of shooting stars that wear themselves out against the atmosphere through which they fly, and dust blown up from earth by the wind. Invisibly the volume of sea moisture and dust is taken toward the land by prevailing winds; and as it passes over the coast, a new condition arises—the wind-borne mass reflects earth temperatures, that change with the earth-forms inland from the sea. Moving rapidly, huge currents of air carrying their sea burdens repeat tremendously in their unseen movement the profile of the land forms over which they pass. When land sweeps up into a mountain, the laden air mass rolling upon it must rise and correspond in shape.

And suddenly that shape is made visible; for colder air above the mountain causes moisture to condense upon the motes of dust in the warm air wafted from over the sea; and directly in response to the presence and inert power of the mountain, clouds appear. The two volumes, invisible warm air, immovable cold mountain—continue to meet and repeat their joint creation of cloud. Looking from afar calm and eternal, clouds enclose forces of heat and cold, wind and inert matter that conflict immensely. In such continuing turbulence, cloud motes collide, cling together, and in the act condense a new particle of moisture. Heavier, it falls from cold air through warmer. Colliding with other drops, it grows. As the drops, colder than the earth, warmer than the cloud they left, fall free of cloud bottom into clear air, it is raining.

Rain and snow fall to the earth, where much runs away on the surface; but roots below ground and the dense nerve system of grasses and the preservative cover of forest floors detain the runoff, so that much sky moisture goes underground to storage, even through rock, for rock is not solid, and through its pores and cracks and sockets precipitation is saved. The storage fills; and nearing capacity, some of its water reappears at ground level as springs which find upward release through the pores of the earth just as originally it found entry. A flowing spring makes its own channel in which to run away. So does the melt from snow clinging to the highest mountain peaks. So does the sudden, brief sheet of storm water. Seeking always to go lower, the running water of the land struggles to fulfill its blind purpose—to find a way over, around or through earth's fantastic obstacles back to the element which gave it origin, the sea.

In this cycle a huge and exquisite balance is preserved. Whatever the amount of its element the sea gives up to the atmosphere by evaporation, the sea regains exactly the same amount from the water which falls upon the earth and flows back to its source.

This is the work, and the law, of rivers.

Gazetteer: Out of a vast interaction between ocean, sky and land, the Rio Grande rises on the concave eastern face of the Continental Divide in southern Colorado. There are three main sources, about two and a half miles high, amidst the Cordilleran ice fields. Flowing from the west, the river proper is joined by two confluents—Spring Creek from the north, and the South Fork. The river in its journey winds eastward across southern Colorado, turns southward to continue across the whole length of New Mexico which it cuts down the center, turns southeastward on reaching Mexico and with one immense aberration from this course—the Big Bend—runs on as the boundary between Texas and Mexico, ending at the Gulf of Mexico.

In all its career the Rio Grande knows several typical kinds of landscape, some of which are repeated along its great length. It springs from tremendous mountains, and intermittently mountains accompany it for three fourths of its course. It often lies hidden and inaccessible in canyons, whether they cleave through mountains or wide level plains. From such forbidding obscurities it emerges again and again into pastoral valleys of bounty and grace. These are narrow, at the most only a few miles wide; and at the least, a bare few hundred yards. In such fertile passages all is green, and the shade of cottonwoods and willows is blue and cool, and there is reward for life in water and field. But always visible on either side are reaches of desert, and beyond stand mountains that limit the river's world. Again, desert closes against the river, and the gritty wastelands crumble into its very banks, and nothing lives but creatures of the dry and hot; and nothing grows but desert plants of thirsty pod, or wooden stem, or spiny defense. But at last the river comes to the coastal plain where an ancient sea floor reaching deep inland is overlaid by ancient river deposits. After turbulence in mountains, bafflement in canyons, and exhaustion in deserts, the river finds peaceful delivery into the sea, winding its last miles slowly through marshy bends, having come nearly one thousand nine hundred miles from mountains nearly three miles high. After the Mississippi-Missouri system, it is the longest river in the United States.

Along its way the Rio Grande receives few tributaries for so long a river. Some are sporadic in flow. Reading downstream, the major tributaries below those of the source are Rock Creek, Alamosa Creek, Trinchera Creek and the Conejos River in Colorado; in New Mexico, the Red River, the Chama River, and four great draws that are generally dry except in storm when they pour wild volumes of silt into the main channel—Galisteo Creek, the Jemez River, Rio Puerco and Rio Salado; and in Texas and Mexico, the Rio Conchos (which renews the river as it is about to die in the desert), the Pecos River, the Devil's River, (another) Rio Salado and Rio San Juan. The river commonly does not carry a great volume of water, and in some places, year after year, it barely flows, and in one or two it is sometimes dry. Local storms will make it rush for a few hours; but soon it is down to its poor level again. Even at its high sources the precipitation averages only five inches year-round. At its mouth, the rainfall averages in summer between twenty and thirty inches, but there the river is old and done, and needs no new water. In January, at the source the surface temperature is fourteen degrees on the average, and in July fifty degrees. At the mouth in the same months the averages read fifty and sixty-eight. In the mountainous north the river is clear and sparkling, in the colors of obsidian, with rippling folds of current like the markings of a trout. Once among the pastoral valleys and the desert bench terraces that yield silt, the river is ever after the color of the earth that it drags so heavily in its shallow flow.

Falling from so high to the sea, and going so far to do it, the river with each of its successive zones encounters a new climate. Winter crowns the source mountains almost the whole year round, in the longest season of cold in the United States. The headwaters are free of frost only three months out of the year, from mid-June to mid-September. Where the river carves its way through the mesas of northern New Mexico the seasons are temperate. Entering the Texas desert, the river finds perennial warmth that rises in summer to blasting heat. At the end, the channel wanders under the heavy moist air of the tropics, mild in winter, violently hot in summer.

Cycle: Landscape is often seen as static; but it never is static. From its first rock in the sky to its last embrace by the estuary at the sea, the river has been surrounded by forces and elements constantly moving and dynamic, interacting to produce its life and character. It has taken ocean and sky; the bearing of the winds and the vagary of temperature; altitude and tilt of the earth's crust; underground waters and the spill of valleys and the impermeable texture of deserts; the cover of plants and the uses of animals; the power of gravity and the perishability of rock; the thirst of things that grow; and the need of the sea to create the Rio Grande.

The main physical circumstances of the Rio Grande are timeless. They assume meaning only in terms of people who came to the river.

THE CANYON

BY JOHN W. POWELL

John Wesley Powell (1834–1902) was born in the Genesee Valley of western New York but grew up and was educated in Wisconsin and Illinois. A Civil War soldier, at the age of twenty-eight he lost his right arm in the battle of Shiloh. After the war he became a geologist, entered government service and led a series of notable expeditions for the Geological Survey. In 1885 he was appointed Director of that bureau. He will always be remembered for his exploration of the Grand Canyon of the Colorado. The voyage he made through it with a party of ten men in 1869 remains one of those incredible feats that mark the history of the West. Powell's party started the voyage at Green River, Wyoming, went down the Green River to the Colorado and down the Colorado to the mouth of the Virgin River, about fifty miles above the present site of Boulder Dam. This selection is from Powell's official report, The Exploration of the Colorado River, *published in 1875, and tells of the voyage through the Grand Canyon itself. The Powell party was the first, and for many years the only one, to traverse the Canyon. It is worth noting that of the ten men who started the trip, six completed it, one-armed Powell among those six.*

(*The Exploration of the Colorado River,* by John Wesley Powell; an official government document, published in 1875.)

August 13. We are now ready to start on our way down the Great Unknown. Our boats, tied to a common stake, are chafing each other, as they are tossed by the fretful river. They ride high and buoyant, for their loads are lighter than we could desire. We have but a month's rations remaining. The flour has been resifted through the mosquito-net sieve; the spoiled bacon has been dried, and the worst of it boiled; the few pounds of dried apples have been spread in the sun, and reshrunken to their normal bulk; the sugar has all melted, and gone on its way down the river; but we have a large sack of coffee. The lightening of the boats has this advantage; they will ride the waves better, and we shall have but little to carry when we make a portage.

We are three quarters of a mile in the depths of the earth, and the great river shrinks into insignificance, as it dashes its angry waves against the walls and cliffs, that rise to the world above; they are but puny ripples, and we but pigmies, running up and down the sands, or lost among the boulders.

We have an unknown distance yet to run; an unknown river yet to explore. What falls there are, we know not; what rocks beset the channel we know not; what walls rise over the river, we know not. Ah, well! we may conjecture many things. The men talk as cheerfully as ever; jests are bandied about freely this morning; but to me the cheer is somber and the jests are ghastly.

With some eagerness, and some anxiety, and some misgiving, we enter the canyon below, and are carried along by the swift water through walls which rise from its very edge. They have the same structure as we noticed yesterday—tiers of irregular shelves below, and, above these, steep slopes to the foot of marble cliffs. We run six miles in a little more than half an hour, and emerge into a more open portion of the canyon, where high hills and ledges of rock intervene between the river and the distant walls. Just at the head of this open place the river runs across a dike; that is, a fissure in the rocks, open to depths below, has been filled with eruptive matter, and this, on cooling, was harder than the rocks through which the crevice was made, and, when these were washed away, the harder volcanic matter remained as a wall, and the river has cut a gateway through it several hundred feet high, and as many wide. As it crosses the wall, there is a fall below, and a bad rapid, filled with boulders of trap; so we stop to make a portage. Then we go, gliding by hills and ledges, with distant walls in view; sweeping past sharp angles of rock; stopping at a few points to examine rapids, which we find can be run, until we have made another five miles, when we land for dinner.

Then we let down with lines, over a long rapid, and start again. Once more the walls close in, and we find ourselves in a narrow gorge, the water again filling the channel, and very swift. With great care, and constant watchfulness, we proceed, making about four miles this afternoon, and camp in a cave.

August 14. At daybreak we walk down the bank of the river, on a little sandy beach, to take a view of a new feature in the canyon. Heretofore, hard rocks have given us bad river; soft rocks, smooth water; and a series of rocks harder than any we have experienced sets in. The river enters the granite!

We can see but a little way into the granite gorge, but it looks threatening.

After breakfast we enter on the waves. At the very introduction, it inspires awe. The canyon is narrower than we have ever before seen it; the water is swifter; there are but few broken rocks in the channel; but the walls are set, on either side, with pinnacles and crags; and sharp, angular buttresses, bristling with wind and wave-polished spires, extend far out into the river.

Ledges of rocks jut into the stream, their tops sometimes just below the surface, sometimes rising few or many feet above; and island ledges, and island pinnacles, and island towers break the swift course of the stream into chutes, and eddies, and whirlpools. We soon reach a place where a creek comes in from the left, and just below, the channel is choked with boulders, which have washed down this lateral canyon and formed a dam, over which there is a fall of thirty or forty feet; but on the boulders we can get foothold, and we make a portage.

Three more such dams are found. Over one we make a portage; at the other two we find chutes, through which we can run.

As we proceed, the granite rises higher, until nearly a thousand feet of the lower part of the walls are composed of this rock.

About eleven o'clock we hear a great roar ahead, and approach it very cautiously. The sound grows louder and louder as we run, and at last we find ourselves above a long, broken fall, with ledges and pinnacles of rock obstructing the river. There is a descent of, perhaps, seventy-five or eighty feet in a third of a mile, and the rushing waters break into great waves on the rocks, and lash themselves into a mad, white foam. We can land just above, but there is no foothold on either side by which we can make a portage. It is nearly a thousand feet to the top of the granite, so it will be impossible to carry our boats around, though we can climb to the summit up a side gulch, and, passing along a mile or two, can descend to the river. This we find on examination; but such a portage would be impracticable for us, and we must run the rapid, or abandon the river. There is no hesitation. We step into our boats, push off and away we go, first on smooth but swift water, then we strike a glassy wave, and ride to its top, down again into the trough, up again on a higher wave, and down and up on waves higher and still higher, until we strike one just as it curls back, and a breaker rolls over our little boat. Still, on we speed, shooting past projecting rocks, till the little boat is caught in a whirlpool, and spun around several times. At last we pull out again into the stream, and now the other boats have passed us. The open compartment of the "Emma Dean" is filled with water, and every breaker rolls over us. Hurled back from a rock, now on this side, now on that, we are carried into an eddy, in which we struggle for a few minutes, and are then out again, the breakers still rolling over us. Our boat is unmanageable, but she cannot sink, and we drift down another hundred yards, through breakers; how, we scarcely know. We find the other boats have turned into an eddy at the foot of the fall, and are waiting to catch us as we come, for the men have seen that our boat is swamped. They push out as we come near, and pull us in against the wall. We bail our boat, and on we go again.

The walls, now, are more than a mile in height—a vertical distance difficult to appreciate. Stand on the south steps of the Treasury building, in Washington, and look down Pennsylvania Avenue to the Capitol Park, and measure this distance overhead, and imagine cliffs to extend to that altitude, and you will understand what I mean; or, stand at Canal Street, in New York, and look up Broadway to Grace Church, and you have about the distance; or, stand at Lake Street bridge in Chicago, and look down to the Central Depot, and you have it again.

A thousand feet of this is up through granite crags, then steep slopes and perpendicular cliffs rise, one above another, to the summit. The gorge is black and narrow below, red and gray and flaring above, with crags and angular projections on the walls, which, cut in many places by side canyons, seem to be a vast wilderness of rocks. Down in these grand, gloomy depths we glide, ever listening, for the mad waters keep up their roar; ever watching, ever peering ahead, for the narrow canyon is winding, and the river is closed in so that we can see but a few hundred yards, and what there may be below we know not; but we listen for falls, and watch for rocks, or stop now and then, in the bay of a recess, to admire the gigantic scenery. And ever, as we go, there is some new pinnacle or tower, some crag or peak, some distant view of the upper plateau, some strange-shaped rock, or some deep, narrow side canyon. Then we come to another broken fall, which appears more difficult than the one we ran this morning.

A small creek comes in on the right, and the first fall of the water is over boulders, which have been carried down by this lateral stream. We land at its mouth, and stop for an hour or two to examine the fall. It seems possible to let down with lines, at least a part of the way, from point to point, along the right-hand wall. So we make a portage over the first rocks, and find footing on some boulders below. Then we let down one of the boats to the end of her line, when she reaches a corner of the projecting rock, to which one of the men clings, and steadies her, while I examine an eddy below. I think we can pass the other boats down by us, and catch them in the eddy. This is soon done and the men in the boats in the eddy pull us to their side. On the shore of this little eddy there is about two feet of gravel beach above the water. Standing on this beach, some of the men take the line of the little boat and let it drift down against another projecting angle. Here is a little shelf, on which a man from my boat climbs, and a shorter line is passed to him, and he fastens the boat to the side of the cliff. Then the second one is let down, bringing the line of the third. When the second boat is tied up, the two men standing on the beach above spring into the last boat, which is pulled up alongside of ours. Then we let down the boats, for twenty-five or thirty yards, by walking along the shelf, landing them again in the mouth of a side canyon. Just below this there is another pile of boulders, over which we make another portage. From the foot of these rocks we can climb to another shelf, forty or fifty feet above the water.

On this bench, we camp for the night. We find a few sticks, which have lodged in the rocks. It is raining hard, and we have no shelter, but kindle a fire and have our supper. We sit on the rocks all night, wrapped in our ponchos, getting what sleep we can.

August 15. This morning we find we can let down for three or four hundred yards, and it is managed in this way: We pass along the wall, by climbing from projecting point to point, sometimes near the water's edge, at other places, fifty or sixty feet above, and hold the boat with a line, while two men remain aboard, and prevent her from being dashed against the rocks, and keep the line from getting caught on the wall. In two hours we have brought them all down, as far as it is possible, in this way. A few yards below, the river strikes with great violence against a projecting rock, and our boats are pulled up in a little bay above. We must now manage to pull out of this, and clear the point below. The little boat is held by the bow obliquely up the stream. We jump in, and pull out only a few strokes, and sweep clear of the dangerous rock. The other boats follow in the same manner, and the rapid is passed.

It is not easy to describe the labor of such navigation. We must prevent the waves from dashing the boats against the cliffs. Sometimes, where the river is swift, we must put a bight of rope about a rock, to prevent her being snatched from us by a wave; but where the plunge is too great, or the chute too swift, we must let her leap, and catch her below, or the undertow will drag her under the falling water, and she sinks. Where we wish to run her out a little way from shore, through a channel between rocks, we first throw in little sticks of driftwood, and watch their course, to see where we must steer, so that she will pass the channel in safety. And so we hold, and let go, and pull, and lift, and ward, among rocks, around rocks, and over rocks.

And now we go on through this solemn, mysterious way. The river is very deep, the canyon very narrow, and still obstructed, so that there is no steady flow of the stream; but the waters wheel, and roll, and boil, and we are scarcely able to determine where we can go. Now, the boat is carried to the right, perhaps close to the wall; again, she is shot into the stream, and perhaps is dragged over to the other side, where, caught in a whirlpool, she spins about. We can neither land nor run as we please. The boats are entirely unmanageable; no order in their running can be preserved; now one, now another, is ahead, each crew laboring for its own preservation. In such a place we come to another rapid. Two of the boats run it perforce. One succeeds in landing, but there is no foothold by which to make a portage, and she is pushed out again into the stream. The next minute a great reflex wave fills the open compartment; she is water-logged, and drifts unmanageable. Breaker after breaker rolls over her, and one capsizes her. The men are thrown out; but they cling to the boat, and she drifts down some distance, alongside of us, and we are able to catch her. She is soon bailed out, and the men are aboard once more; but the oars are lost, so a pair from the "Emma Dean" is spared. Then for two miles we find smooth water.

Clouds are playing in the canyon today. Sometimes they roll down in great masses, filling the gorge with gloom; sometimes they hang above, from wall to wall, and cover the canyon with a roof of impending storm; and we can peer long distances up and down this canyon corridor, with its cloud roof overhead, its walls of black granite, and its river bright with the sheen of broken waters. Then, a gust of wind sweeps down a side gulch, and, making a rift in the clouds, reveals the blue heavens, and a stream of sunlight pours in. Then, the clouds drift away into the distance, and hang around crags, and peaks, and pinnacles, and towers, and walls, and cover them with a mantle, that lifts from time to time, and sets them all in sharp relief. Then, baby clouds creep out of side canyons, glide around points, and creep back again, into more distant gorges. Then, clouds, set in strata, across the canyon, with intervening vista views, to cliffs and rocks beyond. The clouds are children of the heavens, and when they play among the rocks, they lift them to the region above.

It rains! Rapidly little rills are formed above, and these soon grow into brooks, and the brooks grow into creeks, and tumble over the walls in innumerable cascades, adding their wild music to the roar of the river. When the rain ceases, the rills, brooks, and creeks run dry. The waters that fall, during a rain, on these steep rocks, are gathered at once into the river; they could scarcely be poured in more suddenly, if some vast spout ran from the clouds to the stream itself. When a storm bursts over the canyon, a side gulch is dangerous, for a sudden flood may come, and the inpouring waters will raise the river, so as to hide the rocks before your eyes.

Early in the afternoon, we discover a stream, entering from the north, a clear, beautiful creek, coming down through a gorgeous red canyon. We land, and camp on a sand beach, above its mouth, under a great, overspreading tree, with willow-shaped leaves. . . .

August 24. The canyon is wider today. The walls rise to a vertical height of nearly three thousand feet. In many places the river runs under a cliff, in great curves, forming amphitheaters, half dome-shaped.

Though the river is rapid, we meet with no serious obstructions, and run twenty miles. It is curious how anxious we are to make up our reckoning every time we stop, now that our diet is confined to plenty of coffee, very little spoiled flour, and very few dried apples. It has come to be a race for a dinner. Still, we make such fine progress, all hands are in good cheer, but not a moment of daylight is lost.

August 25. We make twelve miles this morning, when we come to monuments of lava, standing in the river; low rocks, mostly, but some of them shafts more than a hundred feet high. Going on down, three or four miles, we find them increasing in number. Great quantities of cooled lava and many cinder cones are seen on either side; and then we come to an abrupt cataract. Just over the fall, on the right wall, a cinder cone, or extinct volcano, with a well-defined crater, stands on the very brink of the canyon. This, doubtless, is the one we saw two or three days ago. From this volcano vast floods of lava have been poured down into the river, and a stream of the molten rock has run up the canyon, three or four miles, and down, we know not how far. Just where it poured over the canyon wall is the fall. The whole north side, as far as we can see, is lined with the black basalt, and high up on the opposite wall are patches of the same material, resting on the benches, and filling old alcoves and caves, giving to the wall a spotted appearance.

The rocks are broken in two, along a line which here crosses the river, and the beds, which we have seen coming down the canyon for the last thirty miles, have dropped 800 feet, on the lower side of the line, forming what geologists call a fault. The volcanic cone stands directly over the fissure thus formed. On the side of the river opposite, mammoth springs burst out of this crevice, one or two hundred feet above the river, pouring in a stream quite equal in volume to the Colorado Chiquito.

This stream seems to be loaded with carbonate of lime, and the water, evaporating, leaves an incrustation on the rocks; and this process has been continued for a long time, for extensive deposits are noticed, in which are basins, with bubbling springs. The water is salty.

We have to make a portage here, which is completed in about three hours, and on we go.

We have no difficulty as we float along, and I am able to observe the wonderful phenomena connected with this flood of lava. The canyon was doubtless filled to a height of twelve or fifteen hundred feet, perhaps by more than one flood. This would dam the water back; and in cutting through this great lava bed, a new channel has been formed, sometimes on one side, sometimes on the other. The cooled lava, being of firmer texture than the rocks of which the walls are composed, remains in some places; in others a narrow channel has been cut, leaving a line of basalt on either side. It is possible that the lava cooled faster on the sides against the walls, and that the centre ran out; but of this we can only conjecture. There are other places, where almost the whole of the lava is gone, patches of it only being seen where it has caught on the walls. As we float down, we can see that it ran out into side canyons. In some places this basalt has a fine, columnar structure, often in concentric prisms, and masses of these concentric columns have coalesced. In some places, when the flow occurred, the canyon was probably at about the same depth as it is now, for we can see where the basalt has rolled out on the sands, and, what seems curious to me, the sands are not melted or metamorphosed to any appreciable extent. In places the bed of the river is of sandstone or limestone, in other places of lava, showing that it has all been cut out again where the sandstones and limestones appear; but there is a little yet left where the bed is of lava.

What a conflict of water and fire there must have been here! Just imagine a river of molten rock, running down into a river of melted snow. What a seething and boiling of the waters; what clouds of steam rolled into the heavens!

Thirty-five miles today. Hurrah!

August 26. The canyon walls are steadily becoming higher as we advance. They are still bold, and nearly vertical up to the terrace. We still see evidence of the eruption discovered yesterday, but the thickness of the basalt is decreasing, as we go down the stream; yet it has been reinforced at points by streams that have come down from volcanoes standing on the terrace above, but which we cannot see from the river below.

Since we left the Colorado Chiquito, we have seen no evidences that the tribe of Indians inhabiting the plateaus on either side ever come down to the river; but about eleven o'clock today we discover an Indian garden, at the foot of the wall on the right, just where a little stream, with a narrow flood plain, comes down through a side canyon. Along the valley, the Indians have planted corn, using the water which burst out in springs at the foot of the cliff, for irrigation. The corn is looking quite well, but is not sufficiently advanced to give us roasting ears; but there are some nice, green squashes. We carry ten or a dozen of these on board our boats, and hurriedly leave, not willing to be caught in the robbery, yet excusing ourselves by pleading our great want. We run down a short distance, to where we feel certain no Indians can follow; and what a kettle of squash sauce we make! True, we have no salt with which to season it, but it makes a fine addition to our unleavened bread and coffee. Never was fruit so sweet as these stolen squashes.

After dinner we push on again, making fine time, finding many rapids, but none so bad that we cannot run them with safety, and when we stop, just at dusk, and foot up our reckoning, we find we have run thirty-five miles again.

What a supper we make! unleavened bread, green squash sauce, and strong coffee. We have been for a few days on half rations, but we have no stint of roast squash.

A few days like this, and we are out of prison.

August 27. This morning the river takes a more southerly direction. The dip of the rocks is to the north, and we are rapidly running into lower formations. Unless our course changes, we shall very soon run again into the granite. This gives us some anxiety. Now and then the river turns to the west, and excites hopes that are soon destroyed by another turn to the south. About nine o'clock we come to the dreaded rock. It is with no little misgiving that we see the river enter these black, hard walls. At its very entrance we have to make a portage; then we have to let down with lines past some ugly rocks. Then we run a mile or two farther, and then the rapids below can be seen.

About eleven o'clock we come to a place in the river where it seems much worse than any we have yet met in all its course. A little creek comes down from the left. We land first on the right, and clamber up over the granite pinnacles for a mile or two, but can see no way by which we can let down, and to run it would be sure destruction. After dinner we cross to examine it on the left. High above the river we can walk along on the top of the granite, which is broken off at the edge, and set with crags and pinnacles, so that it is very difficult to get a view of the river at all. In my eagerness to reach a point where I can see the roaring fall below, I go too far on the wall, and can neither advance nor retreat. I stand with one foot on a little projecting rock, and cling with my hand fixed in a little crevice. Finding I am caught here, suspended 400 feet above the river, into which I should fall if my footing fails, I call for help. The men come, and pass me a line, but I cannot let go of the rock long enough to take hold of it. Then they bring two or three of the largest oars. All this takes time which seems very precious to me; but at last they arrive. The blade of one of the oars is pushed into a little crevice in the rock beyond me, in such a manner that they can hold me pressed against the wall. Then another is fixed in such a way that I can step on it, and thus I am extricated.

Still another hour is spent in examining the river from this side, but no good view of it is obtained, so now we return to the side that was first examined, and the afternoon is spent in clambering among the crags and pinnacles, and carefully scanning the river again. We find that the lateral streams have washed boulders into the river, so as to form a dam, over which the water makes a broken fall of eighteen or twenty feet; then there is a rapid, beset with rocks, for two or three hundred yards, while, on the other side, points of the wall project into the river. Then there is a second fall below; how great, we cannot tell. Then there is a rapid, filled with huge rocks, for one or two hundred yards. At the bottom of it, from the right wall, a great rock projects quite halfway across the river. It has a sloping surface extending upstream, and the water, coming down with all the momentum gained in the falls and rapids above, rolls up this inclined plane many feet, and tumbles over to the left. I decide that it is possible to let down over the first fall, then run near the right cliff to a point just above the second, where we can pull out into a little chute, and, having run over that in safety, we must pull with all our power across the stream, to avoid the great rock below. On my return to the boat, I announce to the men that we are to run it in the morning. Then we cross the river, and go into camp for the night on some rocks, in the mouth of the little side canyon.

After supper Captain Howland asks to have a talk with me. We walk up the little creek a short distance, and I soon find that his object is to remonstrate against my determination to proceed. He thinks that we had better abandon the river here. Talking with him, I learn that his brother, William Dunn, and himself have determined to go no farther in the boats. So we return to camp. Nothing is said to the other men.

For the last two days, our course has not been plotted. I sit down and do this now, for the purpose of finding where we are by dead reckoning. It is a clear night, and I take out the sextant to make observation for latitude, and find that the astronomic determination agrees very nearly with that of the plot—quite as closely as might be expected, from a meridian observation on a planet. In a direct line, we must be about forty-five miles from the mouth of the Rio Virgen. If we can reach that point, we know that there are settlements up that river about twenty miles. This forty-five miles, in a direct line, will probably be eighty or ninety in the meandering line of the river. But then we know that there is comparatively open country for many miles above the mouth of the Virgen, which is our point of destination.

As soon as I determine all this, I spread my plot on the sand, and wake Howland, who is sleeping down by the river, and show him where I suppose we are, and where several Mormon settlements are situated.

We have another short talk about the morrow, and he lies down again; but for me there is no sleep. All night long, I pace up and down a little path, on a few yards of sand beach, along by the river. Is it wise to go on? I go to the boats again, to look at our rations. I feel satisfied that we can get over the danger immediately before us; what there may be below I know not. From our outlook yesterday, on the cliffs, the canyon seemed to make another great bend to the south, and this, from our experience heretofore, means more and higher granite walls. I am not sure that we can climb out of the canyon here, and, when at the top of the wall, I know enough of the country to be certain that it is a desert of rock and sand, between this and the nearest Mormon town, which, on the most direct line, must be seventy-five miles away. True, the late rains have been favorable to us, should we go out, for the probabilities are that we shall find water still standing in holes, and, at one time, I almost conclude to leave the river. But for years I have been contemplating this trip. To leave the exploration unfinished, to say that there is a part of the canyon which I cannot explore, having already almost accomplished it, is more than I am willing to acknowledge, and I determine to go on.

I wake my brother, and tell him of Howland's determination, and he promises to stay with me; then I call up Hawkins, the cook, and he makes a like promise; then Sumner, and Bradley, and Hall, and they all agree to go on.

August 28. At last daylight comes, and we have breakfast, without a word being said about the future. The meal is as solemn as a funeral. After breakfast, I ask the three men if they still think it best to leave us. The elder Howland thinks it is, and Dunn agrees with him. The younger Howland tries to persuade them to go on with the party, failing in which, he decides to go with his brother.

Then we cross the river. The small boat is very much disabled, and unseaworthy. With the loss of hands, consequent on the departure of the three men, we shall not be able to run all of the boats, so I decide to leave my "Emma Dean."

Two rifles and a shotgun are given to the men who are going out. I ask them to help themselves to the rations, and take what they think to be a fair share. This they refuse to do, saying they have no fear but that they can get something to eat; but Billy, the cook, has a pan of biscuits prepared for dinner, and these he leaves on a rock.

Before starting, we take our barometers, fossils, the minerals, and some ammunition from the boat, and leave them on the rocks. We are going over this place as light as possible. The three men help us lift our boats over a rock twenty-five or thirty feet high, and let them down again over the first fall, and now we are all ready to start. The last thing before leaving, I write a letter to my wife, and give it to Howland. Sumner gives him his watch, directing that it be sent to his sister, should he not be heard from again. The records of the expedition have been kept in duplicate. One set of these is given to Howland, and now we are ready. For the last time, they entreat us not to go on, and tell us that it is madness to set out in this place; that we can never get safely through it; and, further, that the river turns again to the south into the granite, and a few miles of such rapids and falls will exhaust our entire stock of rations, and then it will be too late to climb out. Some tears are shed; it is rather a solemn parting; each party thinks the other is taking the dangerous course.

My old boat left, I go on board of the "Maid of the Canon." The three men climb a crag, that overhangs the river, to watch us off. The "Maid of the Canon" pushes out. We glide rapidly along the foot of the wall, just grazing one great rock, then pull out a little into the chute of the second fall, and plunge over it. The open compartment is filled when we strike the first wave below, but we cut through it, and then the men pull with all their power toward the left wall, and swing clear of the dangerous rock below all right. We are scarcely a minute in running it, and find that, although it looked bad from above, we have passed many places that were worse.

The other boat follows without more difficulty. We land at the first practicable point below and fire our guns, as a signal to the men above that we have come over in safety. Here we remain a couple of hours, hoping that they will take the small boat and follow us. We are behind a curve in the canyon, and cannot see up to where we left them, and so we wait until their coming seems hopeless, and push on.

And now we have a succession of rapids and falls until noon, all of which we run in safety. Just after dinner we come to another bad place. A little stream comes in from the left, and below there is a fall, and still below another fall. Above, the river tumbles down, over and among the rocks, in whirlpools and great waves, and the waters are lashed into mad, white foam. We run along the left, above this, and soon see that we cannot get down on this side, but it seems possible to let down on the other. We pull upstream again, for two or three hundred yards, and cross. Now there is a bed of basalt on this northern side of the canyon, with a bold escarpment, that seems to be a hundred feet high. We can climb it, and walk along its summit to a point where we are just at the head of the fall. Here the basalt is broken down again, so it seems to us, and I direct the men to take a line to the top of the cliff, and let the boats down along the wall. One man remains in the boat, to keep her clear of the rocks, and prevent her line from being caught on the projecting angles. I climb the cliff, and pass along to a point just over the fall, and descend by broken rocks, and find that the break of the fall is above the break of the wall, so that we cannot land; and that still below the river is very bad, and that there is no possibility of a portage. Without waiting further to examine and determine what shall be done, I hasten back to the top of the cliff, to stop the boats from coming down. When I arrive, I find the men have let one of them down to the head of the fall. She is in swift water, and they are not able to pull her back; nor are they able to go on with the line, as it is not long enough to reach the higher part of the cliff, which is just before them; so they take a bight around a crag. I send two men back for the other line. The boat is in very swift water, and Bradley is standing in the open compartment, holding out his oar to prevent her from striking against the foot of the cliff. Now she shoots out into the stream, and up as far as the line will permit, and then, wheeling, drives headlong against the rock, then out and back again, now straining on the line, now striking against the rock. As soon as the second line is brought, we pass it down to him, but his attention is all taken up with his own situation, and he does not see that we are passing the line to him. I stand on a projecting rock, waving my hat to gain his attention, for my voice is drowned by the roaring of the falls. Just at this moment, I see him take his knife from its sheath, and step forward to cut the line. He has evidently decided that it is better to go over with the boat as it is, than to wait for her to be broken to pieces. As he leans over, the boat sheers again into the stream, the stem-post breaks away, and she is loose. With perfect composure Bradley seizes the great scull oar, places it in the stern rowlock, and pulls with all his power (and he is an athlete) to turn the bow of the boat downstream, for he wishes to go bow down, rather than to drift broadside on. One, two strokes he makes, and a third just as she goes over, and the boat is fairly turned, and she goes down almost beyond our sight, though we are more than a hundred feet above the river. Then she comes up again, on a great wave, and down and up, then around behind some great rocks, and is lost in the mad, white foam below. We stand frozen with fear, for we see no boat. Bradley is gone, so it seems. But now, away below, we see something coming out of the waves. It is evidently a boat. A moment more, and we see Bradley standing on deck, swinging his hat to show that he is all right. But he is in a whirlpool. We have the stem-post of his boat attached to the line. How badly she may be disabled we know not. I direct Sumner and Powell to pass along the cliff, and see if they can reach him from below. Rhodes, Hall, and myself run to the other boat, jump aboard, and put out, and away we go over the falls. A wave rolls over us, and our boat is unmanageable. Another great wave strikes us, the boat rolls over, and tumbles and tosses, I know not how. All I know is that Bradley is picking us up. We soon have all right again, and row to the cliff, and wait until Sumner and Powell can come. After a difficult climb they reach us. We run two or three miles farther, and turn again to the northwest, continuing until night, when we have run out of the granite once more.

August 29. We start very early this morning. The river still continues swift, but we have no serious difficulty, and at twelve o'clock emerge from the Grand Canyon of the Colorado.

We are in a valley now, and low mountains are seen in the distance, coming to the river below. We recognize this as the Grand Wash.

A few years ago, a party of Mormons set out from St. George, Utah, taking with them a boat, and came down to the mouth of the Grand Wash, where they divided, a portion of the party crossing the river to explore the San Francisco Mountains. Three men—Hamblin, Miller, and Crosby—taking the boat, went on down the river to Callville, landing a few miles below the mouth of the Rio Virgen. We have their manuscript journal with us, and so the stream is comparatively well known.

Tonight we camp on the left bank, in a mesquite thicket.

The relief from danger, and the joy of success, are great. When he who has been chained by wounds to a hospital cot, until his canvas tent seems like a dungeon cell, until the groans of those who lie about, tortured with probe and knife, are piled up, a weight of horror on his ears that he cannot throw off, cannot forget, and until the stench of festering wounds and anaesthetic drugs has filled the air with its loathsome burthen, at last goes out into the open field, what a world he sees! How beautiful the sky; how bright the sunshine; what "floods of delirious music" pour from the throats of birds; how sweet the fragrance of earth, and tree, and blossom! The first hour of convalescent freedom seems rich recompense for all—pain, gloom, terror.

Something like this are the feelings we experience tonight. Ever before us has been an unknown danger, heavier than immediate peril. Every waking hour passed in the Grand Canyon has been one of toil. We have watched with deep solicitude the steady disappearance of our scant supply of rations, and from time to time have seen the river snatch a portion of the little left, while we were ahungered. And danger and toil were endured in those gloomy depths, where ofttimes the clouds hid the sky by day, and but a narrow zone of stars could be seen at night. Only during the few hours of deep sleep, consequent on hard labor, has the roar of the waters been hushed. Now the danger is over; now the toil has ceased; now the gloom has disappeared;

now the firmament is bounded only by the horizon; and what a vast expanse of constellations can be seen!

The river rolls by us in silent majesty; the quiet of the camp is sweet; our joy is almost ecstasy. We sit till long after midnight, talking of the Grand Canyon, talking of home.

WIND AND WEATHER

BY WYMAN RICHARDSON

Wyman Richardson (1896–1953) lived two separate, distinguished careers, one as a noted Boston physician and teacher in Harvard Medical School, the other as Cape Cod naturalist and writer. Son of a noted surgeon, he was born at Marion, Massachusetts, and grew up knowing and loving the outdoors. Duck hunting with his uncle, Frank Benson, and other veteran gunners, he came to know Cape Cod intimately. Just out of Harvard, he served with honor in World War I, then returned to Harvard for his medical education. After many years of medical practice and teaching, ill health forced him to retire. He returned to the Cape, renewed an earlier interest in writing, and produced a series of informal, richly perceptive essays. A volume of them was collected and published two years after his death. This selection, from that book, The House on Nauset Marsh, *shows why Dr. Richardson is remembered as the voice of Nauset and the Outer Cape, which he loved, knew so well, and understood so profoundly.*

(*The House on Nauset Marsh*, by Wyman Richardson; W. W. Norton & Company, Inc., 1955.)

My eldest son, Wyman Jr., considers me a very good long-range prophet—"long" taken to mean a prophecy covering the next day's weather. Whenever I make such a forecast, he makes plans for exactly the opposite condition, and claims to find me very reliable in this respect.

Be that as it may, in our doings at the Farm House we do not need to know the next day's weather. We may lie awake planning what we will do on our forecasted weather, but should it turn out differently, our plans can easily be shifted. It is, however, very important, when we plan our expeditions, to know what the weather is going to do in the next four to six hours. At this I claim to be an expert, in Eastham, anyway.

Here on the Nauset Marsh, our short-range forecasts depend on a knowledge of local weather habits, observation of wind and cloud changes—the "trend," as we call it—and the set to a small barometer in the corner of the living room which, though it records about eight tenths of an inch too high, rises and falls as does any other barometer, sometimes with great celerity.

In winter it is fairly easy. The weather tends to go in cycles. With a high glass, the day will dawn clear. There is either a flat calm, or there are light and variable airs. Visibility is good. Objects stand out in sharp profile. Even the wires on the poles on the East Orleans headland can be seen with the naked eye. Sounds seem to be magnified. Hermie Dill's banging on a tire rim comes sharply across the bay below the hill, and the whistle of the up-freight sounds complainingly clear, even from South Wellfleet. As the surf begins to make up, its ceaseless roar seems to come from close aboard the house.

Shortly the sun's brilliance becomes slightly dulled. An almost invisible "smur" thickens; a light air comes in from the east, and the barometer starts to drop. Such a day, known as a "weather-breeder" on Cape Cod, means a real easterly is in the offing.

While in bed, I can tell by the sound which direction the wind is blowing from—that is, if it has any force. An easterly or northeasterly makes only a loud rushing noise. There is very little banging of this and that, and the windows do not rattle. A nor'wester roars steadily through the cedar at the southwest corner of the house. It roars hard and it roars loud, but it has a clean sound, and when I try to take a sip of water from the glass by my bed, I bump my nose on a skim of ice. A summer sou'wester—that horrid hot blast—rattles and shakes, bangs and batters, blows through the window and screens, covers sheets and table with dirt, and makes life miserable. This is the "smoky sou'wester," the thinnest wind there is. A good, solid southeaster, on the other hand, smacks the windows with pelting rain, while their loud rattling interferes with sleep. A southeaster drives water through all the windows, but especially the upstairs south window, and loosens the plaster on the living room ceiling.

Let me tell you of a December nor'wester.

The previous day's northeast gale, splashing rain and slush into our faces, drove the tide way over the marsh and flooded our cover just as the ducks started to fly. We came home wet, cold, tired, and discouraged, with very little to show for our efforts. But during the night, the wind backed into the northwest. From time to time, between our dreams, the steady roar from the cedars proclaimed its presence, as did also the cold toes and the cold nose.

The alarms, two of them just for safety, start their clatter at four-fifteen. The wise one, who has slept in his woolly underwear, builds a quick fire in the fireplace, before which he bundles up for the coming ordeal. A quick breakfast of coffee, bacon, and eggs is prepared on the oil stove. The coal stove is also started, to keep the pump from freezing. Come to think of it, better trip the pump anyway; the thermometer outside the kitchen window records eighteen degrees.

Then comes the stumbling walk down the hill, burdened with gun, shells, water (which will freeze), and lunch (which will also freeze). The wind blows stark from the northwest, so strong that to look into it numbs the face and makes the eyes water. Anticipatory excitement is tempered by a real feeling of fear. Can we make it, and get back safely? Already a red dawn begins to show, and fast-scurrying, purple clouds become salmon-tinted. Quickly we stow away our gear and push off into the dark water.

It is a simple trip down the marsh—that is, if the tide is either up or down. But beware of the half tide. Under such conditions, it takes long experience, real knowledge, and a considerable amount of luck to find your way out to the Main Channel through the winding run from the Salt Pond Creek. Otherwise, it's a fair wind, and only your left arm gets tired trying to keep your gunning float from yawing.

Likely it's Byzoon Cove you are headed for, a spot little appreciated by the rank and file. Incidentally, a "byzoon" is the ideal duck day: the wind from the nor'west, at thirty-two miles per hour; the temperature 28.5 degrees Fahrenheit, and four-minute snow squalls every twenty minutes. Many neophytes make the mistake of calling all-out gales or storms, especially those from the northwest, byzoons. This is greatly to be deplored, as such storms lead to much suffering and usually to little game.

Byzoon Cove is the place to be, in a typical byzoon. It is one of the few places on the Nauset Marsh where one can shoot black ducks on a lee shore. This is much to be desired, as otherwise, if there is a fly of birds, many shots will be lost when you are in the boat to retrieve your game.

Daylight comes. Your shooting is highly inaccurate. Why shouldn't it be, you say, when you are facing into a gale of wind, when you are bundled up to the ears, and when your fingers even inside your mittens are so numb you cannot tell thumb from forefinger? Still and all, you have accumulated several days' supply of dinner. Many ducks have come sliding in on stiff wings. When really close, the light streak about the face looks almost white. How could you miss such an easy shot? Did you allow for windage?

Comes lunch time. The cold chicken is really cold, so cold it has to be thawed in the mouth before it can be eaten. The water bottle is half frozen, but not broken. Fortunately, one does not need much water under such conditions. The thermos bottle of once hot coffee is almost more than cold hands can deal with and turns out only a lukewarm brew.

Meanwhile, ice is forming all the time. The decoys' heads get so iced that they capsize. Slur begins to change to cake ice. You wonder about the upper channels. Are they getting plugged? The day wanes; as the sun drops, the cold increases. And all of a sudden, the thought of the cozy Farm House becomes irresistible.

Then starts the long fight home against the ebb. You watch a clamshell on the bottom, where the tide runs strong by Pull Devil Corner. You see it first just forward of the forward oar post. You pull and pull, and then you see it amidships. Pull, pull some more, and finally it disappears astern. After a long, long while you get under the lee of the hill and coast back to the boathouse.

Finally the last, long, weary trudge up the hill, the "clumpf" of boots on the platform, the breaking of guns to make sure that they are unloaded, and, as the door is opened, that indescribable, delicious Farm House smell. The house seems warm at first. But no sooner are outer layers peeled than it becomes apparent that it is not warm. There is ice in the water pitcher. Before long, however, fires are roaring and warming drinks forthcoming. It wasn't so bad, after all, down there on the marsh.

I make no apologies for shooting ducks, and no excuses. Nature, in many respects, seems very cruel. I remember watching a garter snake trying to swallow a wood frog. The snake had the frog by one leg, and the frog was trying to hop away by means of the other. My sympathies were with the frog, but I did not interfere. It seemed to me that the snake had as much right on his side as did the frog on his. (As it happened, the frog won out.) Man is an omnivorous animal, and, to satisfy his carnivorous needs, destroys countless other animals. I get a primitive satisfaction in hunting and fishing—supplying food by my own efforts.

So it is that Farm House Rule 1 reads that anything shot must be eaten. (A later amendment excepted rats, mice and fur-bearing animals.) Consequently, especially when a boy, I came to eat many strange things, including hawk, gull, grebe, night heron, and crow. If properly prepared, they are all good, except crow.

A nor'wester is a fighting man's wind. It blows clean and strong. It knows the rules and plays the game. It may lick you in a fair fight, but at least you know what you are dealing with.

Not so one of those cussed sou'westers. It's the sneakiest wind there is. Suppose you are out sailing a light boat. With some pride, by leaning way out to windward, you go through the strongest puff with full sail, only to capsize to windward as the breeze suddenly quits.

It's a fussy wind, a complaining wind. It shrieks through the screens one minute, and heaves a subsiding sigh the next. It's a humid wind. It cakes the salt shakers, and mildews the sails. It's a lasting wind. It's a horrid wind.

For days on end, sometimes for nearly two weeks, the canoe will stay land-bound. Each day, more and more scud clouds make up, the haze thickens, and you think a good rain will clear things up. But not so. This is just one of the sou'wester's tricks. It makes you think it is bringing on a good rain that will freshen the crops and fill the well, but just as it becomes darkest, a sudden ray of sunshine streaks across the southern sky, and the next moment it is hazy and hot again.

About all a sou'wester is good for, here at the Farm House, is fishing off the beach. One must admit that a good fresh southwest breeze will carry an eel a long way out to sea—not that it matters much, but it does make you feel that your fishing has somehow become more important, if not more dignified. Trouble is, these sou'westers frequently blow so hard that they blow the sand. Have you ever been on the Nauset Beach when the sand was blowing? Well, you don't want to be.

We go fishing with bare feet and bare legs, and the sand stings us like a thousand biting ants. We perforce take to the water, where we become thoroughly soaked by underestimating the "swooshers." There may be an easterly swell, even in a southwester. You learn to figure the big seas. They pile up higher and higher, pound down, not far from your feet, and sweep up the rise with a regularity that is easily dealt with. But beware the swoosher. It does not look like much. It is not a high wave, and frequently follows docilely the path of its bigger brother. But it carries a lot of power. Without noise or fuss it comes welling up the rise and, catching you completely off guard, soaks you from fore to aft, mostly aft.

If you figured on supper on the beach and dumped a basket of food, extra clothing, and extra reel there, better leave it. Neither food, nor clothing, nor reel will ever be any good again. Unless you have a gizzard, you cannot use the food, your great-grandchildren will still find sand in their inherited clothing, and the reel will squeak and grind forever after.

Smoky sou'westers are most frequent in July and August. If you plan on coming down to the Farm House, better wait until September. Even then, you may not escape.

October is a wonderful month at Eastham. Summers are cool, for here the Cape is only four miles wide and most breezes (except the sou'wester) come across the water. But when night temperatures consistently go well below the water temperatures—as they do in late September and after—we have warmer weather than further inland, where the land at night cools sharply. The Cape has, therefore, a late fall.

One day in October, my son Fred and I decided to see if we could get some meat for dinner, the quota for the crew being two black ducks. We left the house in the very early dawn, with the temperature at thirty-six degrees. There was not a breath of air. The hollows were filled with "river damp," and, to the east, looked like tiny lakes. As we descended the hill, it got noticeably colder and the steel of our gun barrels became too cold for the bare hand.

When we pushed out of the Salt Pond Creek, the stars were shining brightly, and we could just make out the cupola of the Town Hall to the west. Three minutes later, we rowed into what seemed like a dense fog, yet the stars still shone brightly, and the top of our hill was clearly visible. It was a curious sensation. We could not make out any of the landmarks, or perhaps better, "marsh" marks. We could neither find First Hummock nor Uncle Heeman's Creek. Yet all the while the upper shore line was visible.

By compass bearing we got to the easterly 'Tween Channels Hummock, where we made a good set. But as the sun rose (according to our watches), the river damp thickened until we became immersed in a really dense fog—dense overhead, that is, as well as below. We wondered why this was, and concluded that the rising sun was causing an upward movement of the mist. Unidentified fowl would suddenly loom over our decoys, and as suddenly disappear. Sometimes we fired a futile shot; sometimes we were too late even for that. A gull or two would silently glide overhead in ghostly dimness.

Not until nearly an hour and a half after sunrise did the sun's warmth absorb the fog. Suddenly all was clear. It was not like a sea fog rolling away or gradually lifting; one moment we were in complete isolation, with a two-hundred-foot limit of visibility, and the next moment we could see a ship, hull down, six or seven miles out to sea.

By hook or by crook, we did get our two ducks in spite of the flat calm—a calm so complete that Fred blew a smoke ring clear across the channel. At ten o'clock we gave up and lazed back up the channel, the now hot rays of the sun making us devoutly wish we had forgotten about heavy woollies. On our way back over the flat, we picked up a half basket of scallops which had suddenly appeared in the bay below our hill, and proudly we struggled up to the house, with a royal meal in the making.

Unless it be a question of beach fishing, a "dry northeaster" is one of our best winds. Come with us to the Cape in late March or early April and you will likely run into one.

This is a wonderful time of year to stay at the Farm House. There are no activities possible which require a huge amount of thought and effort, such as duck shooting or bass fishing. The only fishing at this time is flounder fishing. Though the flounders may run large (my wife caught one of four-and-one-fourth pounds), it is ordinarily very cold sport, and the fun is tempered by the thought of filleting.

There comes a morning in late March when the brightness of the rising sun, shining through the south window, wakes you at six-thirty. The floor is cold; the house is cold. You build a quick fire in the fireplace, having remembered to get the logs and kindling ready the night before. Your first weather observation comes only after you have fully, but not too warmly, dressed before the fire. The thermometer reads thirty-eight degrees, the wind is fresh from the northeast, the sky is clear, and the air is full of the finest champagne.

The thing to do on such a day is to walk down the beach to the Inlet and back. At ten o'clock you start off, full of energy, blowing all the dust-laden, worry-burdened city air out of your system, and replacing it with the clean, fresh, salt-tangy breeze from the sea.

First you skirt the Cedar Bank. So high it is, that you can see the whole marsh laid out before you. You will find six Canada geese on the Minister's Flat, the old gander standing erect, neck outstretched, only occasionally taking time out to find some succulent root. You will find black ducks, mostly in pairs, darker blobs on the dark sedge which has been cropped short by the winter's ice. You will see whistlers (goldeneyes) fly up the channel, stop, turn, and light with unbelievable suddenness, and, if the wind is not too strong, you may hear the musical winnowing of the cock whistler's wings.

Further along, by Clam Diggers Headquarters, you will find a flock of about twenty-five buffleheads, those tiny fast-flying ducks, the male with a pie-shaped piece of white transecting his lovely iridescent purple head. In the pines by Little Creek you will start out eight or ten hardy night herons which have spent the winter there, unless that fierce marauder, the great horned owl, has cleaned them out. By the marsh shore, you skirt the cliff, atop which is perched the Nauset Coast Guard Station, and start your walk down the beach.

It is best to go down the beach on the inside—that is, on the marsh side—just why, I do not know. You may see various kinds of fowl on the way down, and surely many black ducks. Horned larks will fly past in loose flocks, uttering their curious thin little note. ("Pippy birds," we used to call them.) If you are lucky, you will see, on the top of a Coast Guard telephone pole, a snowy owl. As you approach fairly close, his neckless head appears to turn around and around, while his baleful brassy eye glares menacingly at you.

When you get to the Inlet Run, a deep pool that comes up to a sandy beach will tempt you, and you may take a swim—or more accurately, a dip—and dry off in the lee of a high dune, where the wind has undercut a "hen bank."

Finally you reach the Inlet, where a fast ebb is boiling out through a deep channel. Further out, where the channel shoals, the current meets the surge of oncoming seas carried by the force of the fresh northeast breeze. From bar to bar, across the mouth, all is a smother of white, and only the experienced eye can tell where the channel runs. Better not count on the Nauset Marsh for a safe landfall. Only hardy lobstermen in powerful motorboats regularly go in and out, and very few of them.

Then comes the turn back on the outer beach, the Great Beach, that stretches from the tip of Monomoy to Race Point at Provincetown. As you gaze north and south, the beach gives you a feeling of infinity; it seems as if it must go on and on as it disappears into the haze of breaking surf. Not so the horizon, sharp and clear, broken only by the lumpiness of the sea. It seems shaped like the edge of a saucer, and appears to curve comfortingly back to land.

The sting of the breeze off the sea gives you fresh energy, as first you try walking the soft sand at the top of the rise, and then the wet sand at the bottom, where you have to be nimble to avoid a wetting. Stunning white gannets, their black wing tips hardly visible, glide to windward over wave crest and into trough with almost no effort. A curious seal pops his dog-like head out of the water at forty yards and, reappearing every hundred yards or so, follows you along all the way to the Coast Guard Station. And if you are lucky, you will hear a sweet, soft whistle, and if you look sharp, you will see a light-colored stone suddenly start to run on twinkling feet. It's a piping plover, whose cheery note and beady black eye tender you a wary welcome.

It is a long walk up the beach, but the invigorating air has sustained you. Now comes the hard part. You have left the beach at the Coast Guard cut-through, and again have reached the pines at Little Creek, where the night herons were, known to us as the "Quawkery." Better stop for ten minutes' rest and look over the marsh with the glasses. You *might* see a European widgeon, and you will very likely see eight or ten of the big pond sheldrake, or goosanders, for they seem to like the region of Little Creek.

It is hard to heave your bulk off the mossy sand at the Quawkery and start the last lap back. No skirting the Cedar Bank now. It is a straight course to the Farm House. You pass the shallow pond and for the twenty-first time put the glasses on the dark object on the further shore, and discover it to be a stump. Then down by the pond-hole back of the barn, where once we saw a pair of wood ducks, and once a single scaup, and often a black duck or two. And so up the last long hill to the weather-beaten Farm House, which looks as if it had been standing there for centuries.

For a moment, we stand on the platform and look south off across the marsh. The low hills in front of us are a warm brown. Through the dip between our hill and the Cedar Bank we see the marsh whose wide channels and bays are today almost a robin's-egg blue, contrasting with the dark brown of the winter sedge. Further out is the thin line of dunes along which we have just walked, the wind-swept hollows, white where the sun strikes, dark in shadow, both encircled by the yellow-green of the surrounding beach grass. And still further out, except where hidden by the highest dunes, stretches a gentian-blue ocean which seems to sparkle and dance.

Our legs are weary and we tumble gratefully into our chairs. It is not such a long walk, perhaps seven or eight miles. But a mile on that beach is a very long mile indeed. Right now, unless something about dinner needs doing, we are content to sit in our chairs, or perhaps on the edge of the platform, and watch the marsh and the sea; watch that marsh hawk as he hangs on an updraft over the hill, motionless, as if suspended by an invisible wire, and casts a sharp eye for motion in the grass below; watch the gulls, soaring higher and higher, apparently just for the fun of it, for frequently they come back to the point from which they started; watch a white cloud as it drifts across a clear blue sky; or just watch.

Yes, come down to the Farm House in late March or early April, and hope for a dry northeaster. It will blow all the musty cobwebs from your mind, clear your lungs, and put a zip into your blood which will carry you through many a weary day.

We were at the Farm House on September 21st, 1938, the day of the "first hurricane." We left the house about half past four in the afternoon on a mushroom hunt. The wind was then blowing out of the southeast, and freshening. It is a Farm House rule that a breeze which hangs to the southeast and freshens in the later afternoon, or after sunset, bodes ill.

We found a few mushrooms, and, besides, the breeze became so strong that it blew the ones we had found out of the colanders we had taken along to put them in. So we eased home from the Cedar Bank before the wind. The old folks stopped at the house, but Marg and Char, then ten and thirteen years old and delighted with the feel of it, went romping off to leeward. Suddenly I began to have some qualms.

"If you can't get back, stop at the Riches'!" we called out.

By now it was blowing really pert, still straight from the southeast, and dark clouds were getting heavier as they raced past overhead. We went down to the boathouse, my wife and I, to see if all was snug. I remember thinking, as I peeked around the corner of the boathouse, that I would hate to be out shooting in such a wind, and wondered if two of us could row against it. I noted two winter yellowlegs, unable to make straight to windward, taking long tacks, finally giving up and lighting on the edge of the Salt Pond Creek.

When we got back to the house, we were relieved to find the children safely ensconced. I went out to shut the barn door, for I thought the wind might shift to the southwest, and blow nearly directly into the barn. Somehow, with the door open, it seemed too much like a huge spinnaker set in a gale of wind. The barn might take off for the Coast Guard Station. I got the door shut all right and stepped out from the corner. The next thing I knew, I was flat on my face. Then I realized we were up against something unusual. I admit a weight of two-hundred-and-twenty pounds, and I do not easily blow over.

In the house there was a continuous roar of sound, and heavy spats of rain slammed at the windows. At six o'clock there was a sudden and complete lull, with blue sky above. You, as well as the house, seemed to feel it necessary to brace against the wind, and the tendency was to fall over to windward. Twenty minutes later, the clouds shut down, and the wind slatted into the southwest, hauling later to the west-southwest. It blew harder, if anything, and started the frames of one of the south doors and of the south bedroom window. I had to spike them down.

But we were snug and didn't really think much of it. I thought I was bold when I recorded in the log an estimated wind velocity of seventy-five miles per hour at the peak. We went to bed happy and serene, with no worries.

The next day, we still did not think much about it. To be sure, they came over from the new house, which is dependent on electricity for its modern gadgets, to get some pump water. Later, they came with perishable food to put in our ice box, and rather diffidently asked if they might use our privy. We were, of course, delighted to accommodate, and sent them back with a couple of our kerosene lamps. It was not until the following day that we realized the impact of the storm.

All this came to me the other day when Tom, who delivers ice for us, seemed much puzzled.

"I can't understand these hurricanes," says he. "Here one hit Florida, and then turned right 'round and hit it again. Sometimes, when I try to think too much, I get be-wildered." And then, after a long pause, "Sometimes I think it's better not to think too much."

I agree.

A POND IN HIS LIFE

BY JOHN K. TERRES

John K. Terres (1905 —) was born in Philadelphia, grew up in the woods and fields of southern New Jersey, was educated at Pennsylvania State Teachers College and Cornell. For a time he was a field biologist for the U. S. Department of Agriculture and for some years he was editor of Audubon Magazine. *Currently he is a free-lance writer and editor of outdoor books. Eight years of outdoor observation went into* The Wonders I See, *published in 1960, the book from which this selection is taken, and the book is a selection and distillation of the entries into Mr. Terres' outdoor journals during those years.*

(*The Wonders I See*, by John K. Terres; J. B. Lippincott Company, 1960.)

April 2. Shu Swamp, Mill Neck, Long Island, New York. Cloudy and cool; temperature in the forties.

To find the earliest signs of spring, I go to a swamp, a marsh, or a pond. It is in the waterways and in the wet protected places that the first life of the awakening year appears. In Shu Swamp today I saw the first rusty blackbirds of the year and heard their singing; I saw the first red flowering of the swamp maple trees; painted turtles sunning along the banks of Beaver Dam Pond, and the first active spiders, salamanders, and centipedes in the brown leaves and rotting logs of the swamp woods. A farmer friend of mine knew this secret of where to find early life. It was not in the upland fields and meadows that were still frozen or covered with snow. And so he brought a pond to his farm, and this is his story.

Early one April morning in 1941, Bob Coles, a farmer of western New York State, was startled at his breakfast table by a strange tumult of wild voices. He parted the neat white window curtains at the kitchen window and looked out on his newly built farm pond. In the gray morning light he saw something that wrung a shout from him and brought his wife running to the window. A flock of fifty wild mallards and ten Canada geese were swimming about in the shallow upper end of the pond. It was the first time Bob Coles had seen waterfowl on his farm in his lifetime.

He told me about it afterwards and I shall never forget the glow in his eyes and the excitement in his voice. If he had discovered oil on his farm he couldn't have been more exultant. He was smiling when he spoke: "I'm beginning to realize what you fellows meant when you said I'd get more out of this pond than water for my cattle!"

Bob Coles' story goes back to 1939 when he asked the Soil Conservation Service to help him put soil-conserving practices to work on his eighty-acre farm. I was the biologist called upon to assist a forester, an engineer, and a crop specialist with the conservation plan. We knew from giving practical aid to thousands of farmers that our recommendations would prevent large losses of good farm soil, and that we could help restore a crop of songbirds and other wild creatures to his eroded land. We were to find that every erosion control practice we put into effect would benefit wildlife.

The farm lay in a little upland valley. It was rectangular, bounded on the south by a dusty country road, and on the north, east and west by other farms. The cropland sloped steeply southward from a grazed woodland bare of undergrowth, and a property line hedgerow, to a small white farmhouse and barn near the road. The crop fields were eroded—soil had been washing away with every rain. Bob Coles had been cultivating his land up and down the slope, unconsciously inviting the rainfall, and with it, the topsoil, to leave the farm as quickly as possible. To the east of the house, a long trough-shaped pasture extended from the north to the south boundary of the farm. A brushy watercourse ran the length of the pasture, but it dwindled to shallow pools in late summer. The steep pasture slopes were only sparsely covered with grass. In some places, bare soil was exposed where erosion had worn the thin sod away. The pasture was overgrazed—it needed fertilizer, and a rest.

We planned strip-cropping to protect Bob Coles' sloping fields of cultivated land. The strips of crops would cover the hillsides from top to bottom in horizontal bands, each clean-tilled crop strip alternating with a hay strip. Thus rainfall would be kept from racing down the slope, taking a pilfered burden of good farm soil on the first stage of a journey to the sea. Bird life would be benefited too. On this strip-cropped land we were to find the bird population rising to twice that of adjacent cropland not in strips. Along one of the strip edges crossing half the width of the farm, we planned a low-growing contour hedge. The shrubbery would not only help prevent erosion. It would attract the thicket-dwelling catbirds, thrashers, and other insect-eating birds into open cropland where they could feed on insects and carry them to their young.

Bob Coles' pasture would be improved by fertilization to thicken the sod. And by fencing it into smaller units and rotating grazing, the overcropped grasses would be given a chance to rest and grow vigorous again. On the hill above the cropland, a new fence would separate woodland from pasture to protect the woods from grazing. Within a few years, if left undisturbed, the large barren areas under the big sugar maples and basswoods would thicken with new generations of forest trees and shrubs. And with their return would come the birds of the woodland understory. The forest soil would no longer be packed hard by the dairy herd roving there for a few spears of grass, and a normal population of insect-eating mice and shrews would again burrow their myriad tunnels under the deepening leaf litter. Gradually the hard-packed soil would loosen and absorb the rainfall that had been running out of the woods and spilling over the cropland below. And on another part of Bob Coles' farm there would be a small pond, perhaps more striking in its attractiveness to wildlife than any other development in our conservation plan.

There was an excellent site for the pond in the lower end of the brushy pasture. The stream bed was choked with cut-grass, sedges, and willows. Water flowed there only part of the year, but the supply was sufficient to maintain the pond. The land was wet and unproductive, and lay like a narrow valley at the foot of the steep pasture slopes. It would not have been good economy to build a pond on productive farmland anyway. Our engineer designed a small pond, with an emergency flood capacity, that would do triple service. Not only would it hold back floodwaters from the valley farms below, but it would supply drinking water for livestock and serve as a wildlife refuge.

The earthen dam was completed in 1940 and backed the waters of the sluggish stream two to six feet deep over an acre and a half of pasture bottomland. Cattle were kept away from the pond—excluded by a barbed-wire fence strung at least fifty feet from the edge of the water. They drank of the pond waters piped to a trough below the dam. Bob Coles sowed grass on the raw banks and on the dam. A grass sod would prevent the waves from cutting into the dam, and from washing soil from the pond banks. Farther up on the pond slopes he planted trees and shrubs that would provide food and cover for wildlife and keep silt from moving down into the water. Within a few years those trees and shrubs would be tall enough to cast cooling shade on the pond that would lessen evaporation on hot summer days. That was all the planting that was done, but that year saw the beginning of a remarkable transformation.

The pond had been completed only a few weeks when it attracted the first wild visitors. In the late summer of 1940, muskrats came and built a dome-shaped lodge among the cattails at the upper end of the pond. In the following spring, the wild geese and mallards came noisily to rest there for the first time. After the waterfowl had left, a pair of Virginia rails slipped into the little marsh at the shallow end of the pond. We heard their peculiar grunting and chuckling calls long before we saw them. No one knows when the spotted sandpipers first came, but one spring day we saw them. A pair stayed all that first summer, teetering and crying plaintively along the edge of the waters over which bank swallows and rough-winged swallows now came skimming. Red-winged blackbirds had always nested in the cattails of the old watercourse, but two years after the pond was built they had doubled from five to ten pairs. Cattle no longer disturbed their nesting. Three pairs of Savannah sparrows appeared within the fenced sedge meadow, and song sparrows grew from two to four pairs. Meadowlarks and bobolinks nested in the tall grasses now protected from cattle by the fence. In the years before, those grasses had been grazed down to their roots. On the pastured side of the fence, the killdeers, which prefer the short grass and open cultivated land, still flew in the faces of cattle that stepped too near their eggs.

In the summer of 1941, the first water plants arrived in the pond. Perhaps they were always there, growing unnoticed in the stagnant and dying pools of the old watercourse. Bob Coles thought the wildfowl had brought them on their feet. Perhaps they were washed down the streambed from farther up the valley. There were not many that first year—a few floating clusters of the little round-leaved duckweed, *Lemna,* and submerged clumps of bushy pondweed and water purslane. Bulrushes, sedges, and cut-grass came to the shallows at the pond edge, and on the banks there suddenly appeared a dense growth of barnyard millet, smartweed, stonecrop, wild mint, grasses and shrub willows. And so a few fence-posts and barbed wire that kept out cattle wrought their magic. Wildlife nesting cover and food plants came to pond waters and banks because hooves could no longer trample the herbs and grasses. The pond waters stayed clear and unspoiled, and the cattle themselves were less exposed to internal parasites and the dreaded anthrax. Their drinking water was safer in the trough. It could not be contaminated by bovine feet and dung.

Wildflowers, too, came to the fenced pond. Long-stemmed purple violets and yellow marsh marigolds brightened the borders of the pond in spring. And in summer, spiky sweet-smelling orchids—ladies' tresses and habernarias flowered there and flaming cardinal flowers, sky-blue lobelias, white-tufted cotton grass, and pink willow herb. And one day we discovered that this little pasture-marsh might once have been a swamp forest. In the sedge meadow we found several aged stumps covered with sphagnum and haircap mosses, cinnamon ferns, and a dwarfed swamp plant called purple-twisted stalk.

With the coming of the water plants, animal life swarmed in the pond. Thousands of dragonfly nymphs crawled up the stems of the sedges and cut-grasses. The big-winged adults emerged, leaving their dried pupal husks still clinging to the plants. Bob Coles called the nymphs "perch bugs," and said they were excellent bait for fish. The dense mats of bushy pondweed harbored the greatest abundance of water animals. Here we saw diving beetles, giant water bugs, pond snails, water boatmen, mites, back-swimmers, and water scorpions. And always on the quiet pond surface, the little whirligig beetles spun in dizzy gyrations.

Perhaps the most impressive part of the developing pond community was the population of frogs. Both pickerel and leopard frogs were there in thousands. If one walked in the sedges near the shore line they skipped across the shallows like stones thrown by small boys, diving in hordes to the safer depths of the pond. One day a pair of bitterns arrived with a little green heron. I think they knew of the frogs that swarmed there before we did. And when the first snows of 1941 fell, eight muskrat lodges had been built in the cattails at the head of the pond.

Bob Coles became a happier man. His soil seldom muddied the valley creek below. The ungrazed woodland, poised above the cropland, was gaining the absorptive capacity of a huge sponge. Strip-cropping, contour cultivation, and denser pasture grasses held topsoil and moisture on the land. A million tiny ridges wrinkled the cultivated slopes where the plow and the cultivator had flung them up. Like tiny barriers, each fought a delaying action against gravity, each checked the rainfall from the swift scouring flight that may wear the productive soil away in one or two generations. Rainfall was given pause; it was delayed and detoured; it had more time to soak down into crop roots. And the farm crops responded to the increased moisture, for more corn, wheat, hay, and pasture were produced on each acre of land.

The Coles farm became more habitable for a greater variety of wildlife than before. With the coming of soil-conserving practices, birds came back to bird-lean acres throughout the farm. On cropland they doubled their forces against insects that eat farm crops. Within the once-grazed woodland, birds, forest mice, shrews, and small game animals made a startling comeback. The farm pond was a refuge for more than twenty species of birds, more kinds than in any comparable area on the farm. And the pond even gave Bob Coles fire protection, with a large quantity of water available if a fire occurred.

The muskrats became a thriving colony from which the neighboring farm boys trapped a few each year. The wild ducks and geese came each fall and spring, for Bob Coles allowed no shooting on the pond. The pied-billed grebes came and nested again, and Wilson's snipe stopped in spring to probe the wet borders of the little marsh. The pond was stocked with fish and, in summer, kingfishers and great blue herons came with the bitterns to enjoy the open fishing rights. Bob Coles wanted them to have their share. The second year of the pond, a pair of mallards stayed and nested in the sedge meadow. That was a crowning development, far beyond the expectation of this kindly farmer. He was beginning to reap a new product of the land—one that brought joy with every season. He had sown a crop of birds and the harvest was rich and unfailing. If you ask him, he will tell you that he owes it all to an acre of water and a roll of barbed wire.

I remember the last time I saw Bob Coles. It was just a few weeks before I left to go into the Army. We were standing near his barn watching a flock of Canada geese resting on the pond. "You'll come back," he said prophetically. "Just like those fellows down there that return to me every year." He turned to me with a smile. "Tell them something for me. . . ."

"Tell who, *what?*" I asked in surprise.

"Tell *anybody* that if they want to get a new interest in life—just build themselves a farm pond!"

LA SALLE ON THE MISSISSIPPI

BY HENRI DE TONTI

Henri de Tonti (1650–1704) was born in or near Paris, son of the man who originated and gave his name to "tontine insurance." Henri lost his right hand in an Italian naval campaign and thereafter wore a metal hand, an effective close-combat weapon among the Indians when he came to America with explorer Sieur de la Salle in 1678. He was La Salle's lieutenant on the exploring expedition down the Mississippi in 1682, which was the basis for French claim to the whole Mississippi Valley. Tonti made several later trips down the Mississippi, started several settlements in its valley, and died, probably of yellow fever, near present-day Mobile, Alabama. This selection is from Tonti's account of the first trip down the Mississippi, and was written at the time or soon after, 1682 or 1683.

(*Account of La Salle's Expedition on the Mississippi*, by Henri de Tonti, c. 1683.)

When we came to Lake Frontenac, M. de la Salle went forward, and I waited for his boat at the village of Texagon. When it arrived there I embarked for the Illinois. At the Miamis River I assembled some Frenchmen and savages for the voyage of discovery, and M. de la Salle joined us in October. We went in canoes to the River Chicagou, where there is a portage which joins that of the Illinois. The rivers being frozen, we made sledges and dragged our baggage thirty leagues below the village of Illinois where, finding the navigation open, we arrived at the end of January at the great River Mississippi. The distance from Chicagou was estimated at 140 leagues. We descended the river and found, six leagues below, on the right, a great river, which comes from the west, on which there are numerous nations. We slept at its mouth.

The next day we went on to the village of Tamarous, six leagues off to the left. There was no one there, all the people being at their winter quarters in the woods. We made marks to inform the savages that we had passed, and continued our route as far as the River Ouabache, which is eighty leagues from that of Illinois. It comes from the east, and is more than 500 leagues in length. It is by this river that the Iroquois advance to make war against the nations of the south. Continuing our voyage about sixty leagues, we came to a place that was named Fort Prudhomme, because one of our men lost himself there when out hunting, and was nine days without food. As they were looking for him they fell in with two Chikasas savages, whose village was three days' journey inland. They have 2,000 warriors, the greatest number of whom have flat heads, which is considered a beauty among them, the women taking pains to flatten the heads of their children, by means of a cushion which they put on the forehead and bind with a band, which they also fasten to the cradle, and thus make their heads take this form. When they grow up their faces are as big as a large soup plate. All the nations on the seacoast have the same custom.

M. de la Salle sent back one of them with presents to his village, so that if they had taken Prudhomme they might send him back, but we found him on the tenth day, and as the Chikasas did not return we continued our journey as far as the village of Cappa, fifty leagues off. We arrived there in foggy weather, and as we heard the sound of the tambour, we crossed over to the other side of the river where, in less than half an hour, we made a fort. . . . It must be remarked that these villages, the first of which is Osotonoy, are six leagues to the right descending the river and are commonly called Akancas. The first three villages are situated on the great river, Mississippi. They have cabins made with the bark of cedar; they have no other worship than the adoration of all sorts of animals. Their country is very beautiful, having abundance of peach, plum and apple trees, and vines flourish there; buffaloes, deer, stags, bears, turkeys, are very numerous. They have even domestic fowls. They have very little snow during the winter, and the ice is not thicker than a dollar. They gave us guides to conduct us to their allies, the Taencas, six leagues distant.

The first day we began to see and kill alligators, which are numerous and from 15 to 20 feet long. When we arrived opposite to the village of Taencas, M. de la Salle desired me to go to it and inform the chief of his arrival. I went with our guides, and we had to carry a bark canoe for ten arpens, and to launch it on a small lake in which their village was placed. I was surprised to find their cabins made of mud and covered with cane mats. The cabin of the chief was 40 feet square, the wall 10 feet high, a foot thick, and the roof, which was of a dome shape, about 15 feet high. I was not less surprised when, on entering, I saw the chief seated on a camp bed, with three of his wives at his side, surrounded by more than 60 old men, clothed in white cloaks, which were made by the women out of the bark of the mulberry tree, and are tolerably well worked. . . .

When I was in his cabin the chief told me with a smiling countenance the pleasure he felt at the arrival of the French. I saw that one of his wives wore a pearl necklace. I presented her with ten yards of blue glass beads in exchange for it. She made some difficulty but the chief having told her to let me have it, she did so. . . .

We left on the 22nd of March and slept on an island ten leagues off. The next day we saw a canoe, and M. de la Salle ordered me to chase it, which I did, and as I was just on the point of taking it, more than 100 men appeared on the banks of the river to defend their people. M. de la Salle shouted out to me to come back, which I did. We went on and encamped opposite them. Afterwards, M. de la Salle expressing a wish to meet them peaceably, I offered to carry them the calumet, and embarking went to them. At first they joined their hands, as a sign that they wished to be friends; I, who had but one hand, told our men to do the same thing.

I made the chief among them cross over to M. de la Salle, who accompanied them to their village, three leagues inland, and passed the night there with some of his men. The next day he returned with the chief of the village where he had slept, who was a brother of the great chief of the Natches; he conducted us to his brother's village, situated on the hillside, near the river, at six leagues' distance. We were well received there. This nation counts more than 300 warriors. Here the men cultivate the ground, hunt, and fish, as well as the Taencas, and their manners are the same. We departed thence on Good Friday and after a voyage of 20 leagues, encamped at the mouth of a large river, which runs from the west. We continued our journey, and crossed a great canal, which went towards the sea on the right. Thirty leagues further on we saw some fishermen on the bank of the river, and sent to reconnoitre them. It was the village of the Quinipissas, who let fly their arrows upon our men, who retired in consequence. Twelve leagues from this village, on the left, is that of the Tangibaos. Scarcely eight days before this village had been totally destroyed. Dead bodies were lying on one another, and the cabins were burnt. We proceeded on our course, and after sailing 40 leagues, arrived at the sea on the 7th of April, 1682.

M. de la Salle sent canoes to inspect the channels; some of them went to the channel on the right hand, some to the left, and M. de la Salle chose the center. In the evening each made his report, that is to say, that the channels were very fine, wide and deep. We encamped on the right bank; we erected the arms of the King, and returned several times to inspect the channels. The same report was made. The river is 800 leagues long, without rapids, 400 from the country of the Scioux, and 400 from the mouth of the Illinois river to the sea. The banks are almost uninhabitable, on account of the spring floods. The woods are all those of a boggy district, the country one of canes and briars and of trees torn up by the roots; but a league or two from the river, the most beautiful country in the world, prairies, woods of mulberry trees, vines, and fruits that we were not acquainted with. The savages gather the Indian corn twice in the year. In the lower part of the river, which might be settled, the river makes a bend N. and S., and in many places every now and then is joined by streams on the right and left. The river is only navigable (for large vessels?) as far as the village of the Natches, for above that place the river winds too much; but this does not prevent the navigation of the river from the confluence of the Ouabache and the Mississippi as far as the sea. There are but few beavers, but to make amends there are a large number of buffaloes, bears, large wolves, stags and hinds in abundance, and some lead mines which yield two-thirds of ore to one of refuse. As these savages are sedentary and have some habits of subordination, they might be obliged to make silk in order to procure necessaries for themselves; bringing them from France the eggs of silkworms, for the forests are full of mulberry trees. This would be a valuable trade.

As for the country of Illinois, the river runs 100 leagues from the Fort St. Louis, to where it falls into the Mississippi. Thus it may be said to contain some of the finest lands ever seen. The climate is the same as that of Paris, though in the 40th degree of latitude. The savages there are active and brave, but extremely lazy, except in war, when they think nothing of seeking their enemies at a distance of 500 or 600 leagues from their own country. This constantly occurs in the country of the Iroquois whom, at my instigation, they continually harass. Not a year passes in which they do not take a number of prisoners and scalps. A few pieces of pure copper, whose origin we have not sought, are found in the river of the Illinois country. Polygamy prevails in this nation, and is one of the great hindrances to the introduction of Christianity, as well as the fact of their having no form of worship of their own. The nations lower down would be more easily converted, because they adore the sun, which is their divinity. This is all that I am able to relate of those parts.

HIGH WATER ON THE MISSISSIPPI

BY MARK TWAIN

Mark Twain (Samuel Langhorne Clemens—1835–1910) was born and grew up on the Mississippi River in Missouri. Printer, river pilot, author and lecturer, he was one of our literary giants. Outdoor America, and especially the river he knew so well, was in the very fabric of his most enduring books, as it was in the fabric of the man, though he spent many years and did his best writing in Connecticut. The Big River is the background for Tom Sawyer *and* Huckleberry Finn, *and it is the theme, of course, of* Life on the Mississippi, *from which this selection is taken. No one ever wrote about the river with more intimate knowledge or better understanding than Mark Twain had, and he wrote this book at the height of his powers, immediately before* The Adventures of Huckleberry Finn.

(*Life on the Mississippi*, by Mark Twain, 1883.)

The face of the water, in time, became a wonderful book—a book that was a dead language to the uneducated passenger, but which told its mind to me without reserve, delivering its most cherished secrets as if it uttered them with a voice. And it was not a book to be read once and thrown aside, for it had a new story to be told every day. Throughout the long twelve hundred miles there was never a page that was void of interest, never one that you could leave unread without loss, never one that you would want to skip, thinking you could find higher enjoyment in some other thing. There never was so wonderful a book written by man; never one whose interest was so absorbing, so unflagging, so sparklingly renewed with every re-perusal. The passenger who could not read it was charmed with a peculiar sort of faint dimple on its surface (on the rare occasions when he did not overlook it altogether); but to the pilot that was an *italicized* passage; indeed, it was more than that, it was a legend of the largest capitals, with a string of shooting exclamation-points at the end of it, for it meant that a wreck or a rock was buried there that could tear the life out of the strongest vessel that ever floated. It is the faintest and simplest expression the water ever makes, and the most hideous to a pilot's eye. In truth, the passenger who could not read this book saw nothing but all manner of pretty pictures in it, painted by the sun and shaded by the clouds, whereas to the trained eye these were not pictures at all, but the grimmest and most dead-earnest of reading-matter.

Now when I had mastered the language of this water, and had come to know every trifling feature that bordered the great river as familiarly as I knew the letters of the alphabet, I had made a valuable acquisition. But I had lost something, too. I had lost something which could never be restored to me while I lived. All the grace, the beauty, the poetry, had gone out of the majestic river! I still kept in mind a certain wonderful sunset which I witnessed when steamboating was new to me. A broad expanse of the river was turned to blood; in the middle distance the red hue brightened into gold, through which a solitary log came floating, black and conspicuous; in one place a long, slanting mark lay sparkling upon the water; in another place the surface was broken by boiling, tumbling rings, that were as many-tinted as an opal; where the ruddy flush was faintest, was a smooth spot that was covered with graceful circles and radiating lines, ever so delicately traced; the shore on our left was densely wooded, and the somber shadow that fell from this forest was broken in one place by a long, ruffled trail that shone like silver; and high above the forest wall a clean-stemmed dead tree waved a single leafy bough that glowed like a flame in the unobstructed splendor that was flowing from the sun. There were graceful curves, reflected images, woody heights, soft distances; and over the whole scene, far and near, the dissolving lights drifted steadily, enriching it every passing second with new marvels of coloring.

I stood like one bewitched. I drank it in, in speechless rapture. The world was new to me, and I had never seen anything like this at home. But as I have said, a day came when I began to cease from noting the glories and the charms which the moon and the sun and the twilight wrought upon the river's face; another day came when I ceased altogether to note them. Then, if that sunset scene had been repeated, I should have looked upon it without rapture, and should have commented upon it, inwardly, after this fashion: "This sun means that we are going to have wind tomorrow; that floating log means that the river is rising, small thanks to it; that slanting mark on the water refers to a bluff reef which is going to kill somebody's steamboat one of these nights, if it keeps on stretching out like that; those tumbling 'boils' show a dissolving bar and a changing channel there; the lines and circles in the slick water over yonder are a warning that that troublesome place is shoaling up dangerously; that silver streak in the shadow of the forest is the 'break' from a new snag, and he has located himself in the very best place he could have found to fish for steamboats; that tall dead tree, with a single living branch, is not going to last long, and then how is a body ever going to get through this blind place at night without that friendly old landmark?" . . .

The next few months showed me strange things. . . . We met a great rise coming down the river. The whole vast face of the stream was black with drifting dead logs, broken boughs, and great trees that had caved in and been washed away. It required the nicest steering to pick one's way through this rushing raft, even in the daytime, when crossing from point to point, and at night the difficulty was mightily increased; every now and then a huge log, lying deep in the water, would suddenly appear right under our bows, coming head-on; no use to try to avoid it then; we could only stop the engines, and one wheel would walk over that log from one end to the other, keeping up a thundering racket and careening the boat in a way that was very uncomfortable to passengers. Now and then we would hit one of those sunken logs a rattling bang, dead in the center, with a full head of steam, and it would stun the boat as if she had hit a continent. Sometimes this log would lodge and stay right across our nose, and back the Mississippi up before it; we would have to do a little crawfishing then, to get away from the obstruction. We often hit *white* logs in the dark, for we could not see them until we were right on them, but a black log is a pretty distinct object at night. A white snag is an ugly customer when the daylight is gone.

Of course, on the great rise, down came a swarm of prodigious timber-rafts from the headwaters of the Mississippi, coal-barges from Pittsburgh, little trading-scows from everywhere, and broadhorns from "Posey County," Indiana, freighted with "fruit and furniture" —the usual term for describing it, though in plain English the freight thus aggrandized was hoop-poles and pumpkins. Pilots bore a mortal hatred of these craft, and it was returned with usury. The law required all such helpless traders to keep a light burning, but it was a law that was often broken. All of a sudden, on a murky night, a light would pop up, right under our bows, almost, and an agonized voice, with the backwoods "whang" to it, would wail out:

"Whar'n the —— you goin' to! Cain't you see nothin', you dash-blasted, aig-suckin', sheep-stealin', one-eyed son of a stuffed monkey!"

As I have said, the big rise brought a new world under my vision. By the time the river was over its banks we had forsaken our old paths and were hourly climbing over bars that had stood ten feet out of the water before; we were shaving stumpy shores, like that at the foot of Madrid Bend, which I had always seen avoided before; we were clattering through chutes like that of 82, where the opening at the foot was an unbroken wall of timber till our nose was almost at the very spot. Some of these chutes were utter solitudes. The dense, untouched forest overhung both banks of the crooked little crack, and one could believe that human creatures had never intruded there before. The swinging grape-vines, the grassy nooks and vistas glimpsed as we swept by, the flowering creepers waving their red blossoms from the tops of dead trunks, and all the spendthrift richness of the forest foliage, were wasted and thrown away there. The chutes were lovely places to steer in; they were deep, except at the head; the current was gentle; under the "points" the water was absolutely dead, and the invisible banks so bluff that where the tender willow thickets projected you could bury your boat's broadside in them as you tore along, and then you seemed fairly to fly. . . .

The water cuts the alluvial banks of the "lower" river into deep horseshoe curves; so deep, indeed, that in some places if you were to get ashore at one extremity of the horseshoe and walk across the neck, half or three-quarters of a mile, you could sit down and rest a couple of hours while your steamer was coming around the long elbow at a speed of ten miles an hour to take you on board again. When the river is rising fast, some scoundrel whose plantation is back in the country, and therefore of inferior value, has only to watch his chance, cut a little gutter across the narrow neck of land some dark night, and turn the water into it, and in a wonderfully short time a miracle has happened: to wit, the whole Mississippi has taken possession of that little ditch, and placed the countryman's plantation on its bank (quadrupling its value), and that other party's formerly valuable plantation finds itself away out yonder on a big island; the old watercourse around it will soon shoal up, boats cannot approach within ten miles of it, and down goes its value to a fourth of its former worth. Watches are kept on those narrow necks at needful times, and if a man happens to be caught cutting a ditch across them, the chances are all against his ever having another opportunity to cut a ditch. . . .

When the water begins to flow through one of those ditches I have been speaking of, it is time for the people thereabouts to move. The water cleaves the banks away like a knife. By the time the ditch has become twelve or fifteen feet wide, the calamity is as good as accomplished, for no power on earth can stop it now. When the width has reached a hundred yards, the banks begin to peel off in slices half an acre wide. The current flowing around the bend traveled formerly only five miles an hour; now it is tremendously increased by the shortening of the distance. I was on board the first boat that tried to go through the cut-off at American Bend, but we did not get through. It was toward midnight, and a wild night it was—thunder, lightning, and torrents of rain. It was estimated that the current was making about fifteen or twenty miles an hour; twelve or thirteen was the best our boat could do, even in tolerably slack water, therefore perhaps we were foolish to try the cut-off. However, Mr. Brown was ambitious, and he kept on trying. The eddy running up the bank, under the "point," was about as swift as the current out in the middle; so we would go flying up the shore like a lightning express-train, get on a big head of steam, and "stand by for a surge" when we struck the current that was whirling by the point. But all our preparations were useless. The instant that current hit us it spun us around like a top, the water deluged the forecastle, and the boat careened so far over that one could hardly keep his feet. The next instant we were away down the river, clawing with might and main to keep out of the woods. We tried the experiment four times. I stood on the forecastle companionway to see. It was astonishing to observe how suddenly the boat would spin around and turn tail the moment she emerged from the eddy and the current struck her nose. The sounding concussion and the quivering would have been about the same if she had come full speed against a sand-bank. Under the lightning flashes one could see the plantation cabins and the goodly acres tumble into the river, and the crash they made was not a bad effort at thunder. Once, when we spun around, we only missed a house about twenty feet that had a light burning in the window, and in the same instant that house went overboard. Nobody could stay on our forecastle; the water swept across it in a torrent every time we plunged athwart the current. At the end of the fourth effort we brought up in the woods two miles below the cut-off; all the country there was overflowed, of course. A day or two later the cut-off was three-quarters of a mile wide, and boats passed up through it without much difficulty, and so saved ten miles. . . .

We noticed that above Dubuque the water of the Mississippi was olive-green—rich and beautiful and semitransparent, with the sun on it. Of course the water was nowhere as clear or of as fine a complexion as it is in some other seasons of the year; for now it was at flood stage, and therefore dimmed and blurred by the mud manufactured from caving banks.

The majestic bluffs that overlook the river, along through this region, charm one with the grace and variety of their forms, and the soft beauty of their adornment. The steep, verdant slope, whose base is at the water's edge, is topped by a lofty rampart of broken, turreted rocks, which are exquisitely rich and mellow in color—mainly dark browns and dull greens, but splashed with other tints. And then you have the shining river, winding here and there and yonder, its sweep interrupted at intervals by clusters of wooded islands threaded by silver channels; and you have glimpses of distant villages, asleep upon capes; and of stealthy rafts slipping along in the shade of the forest walls; and of white steamers vanishing around remote points. And it is all as tranquil and reposeful as dreamland, and has nothing this-worldly about it—nothing to hang a fret or a worry upon.

Until the unholy train comes tearing along—which it presently does, ripping the solitude to rags and tatters with its devil's war-whoop and the roar and thunder of its rushing wheels—and straightaway you are back in this world, and with one of its frets ready to hand for your entertainment: for you remember that this is the very road whose stock always goes down when you buy it, and always goes up again as soon as you sell it. It makes me shudder to this day, to remember that I once came near not getting rid of my stock at all. It must be an awful thing to have a railroad left on your hands.

ICE FISHING

BY HENRY VAN DYKE

Henry van Dyke (1852–1933) was born in Germantown, Pennsylvania, educated at Princeton and in Germany. Preacher, professor, diplomat, poet, author and fisherman, he was a remarkably gifted and versatile man. He wrote about a broad variety of topics—religion, philosophy, literature, the outdoors—but among the most popular of his many books were three volumes of outdoor essays, Little Rivers, Fisherman's Luck, *and* Days Off. *His outdoor writing sometimes verged on the sentimental, and he was inclined to moralize; but he was a thoroughgoing outdoorsman with a joy of life that he was able to communicate to his readers. Fishing was his enduring recreation, and he wrote about it with verve and intimate knowledge. He also had a sense of humor, which often saved an essay that might have become precious. The selection I have chosen here is from* Fisherman's Luck.

(*Fisherman's Luck,* by Henry van Dyke; Charles Scribner's Sons, 1899.)

That wise man and accomplished scholar, Sir Henry Wooton, the friend of Izaak Walton and ambassador of King James I. to the republic of Venice, was accustomed to say that "he would rather live five May months than forty Decembers." The reason for this preference was no secret to those who knew him. It had nothing to do with British or Venetian politics. It was simply because December, with all its domestic joys, is practically a dead month in the angler's calendar.

His occupation is gone. The better sort of fish are out of season. The trout are lean and haggard: it is no trick to catch them and no treat to eat them. The salmon, all except the silly kelts, have run out to sea, and the place of their habitation no man knoweth. There is nothing for the angler to do but wait for the return of spring, and meanwhile encourage and sustain his patience with such small consolations as a friendly Providence may put within his reach.

Some solace may be found, on a day of crisp, wintry weather, in the childish diversion of catching pickerel through the ice. This method of taking fish is practiced on a large scale and with elaborate machinery by men who supply the market. I speak not of their commercial enterprise and its gross equipage, but of ice-fishing in its more sportive and desultory form, as it is pursued by country boys and the incorrigible village idler.

You choose for this pastime a pond where the ice is not too thick, lest the labor of cutting through should be discouraging; nor too thin, lest the chance of breaking in should be embarrassing. You then chop out, with almost any kind of a hatchet or a pick, a number of holes in the ice, making each one six or eight inches in diameter, and placing them about five or six feet apart. If you happen to know the course of a current flowing through the pond, or the location of a shoal frequented by minnows, you will do well to keep near it. Over each hole you set a small contrivance called a "tilt-up." It consists of two sticks fastened in the middle, at right angles to each other. The stronger of the two is laid across the opening in the ice. The other is thus balanced above the aperture, with a baited hook and line attached to one end, while the other is adorned with a little flag. For choice, I would have the flags red. They look gayer, and I imagine they are more lucky.

When you have thus baited and set your tilt-ups,—twenty or thirty of them,—you may put on your skates and amuse yourself by gliding to and fro on the smooth surface of the ice, cutting figures of eight and grapevines and diamond twists, while you wait for the pickerel to begin their part of the performance. They will let you know when they are ready.

A fish, swimming around in the dim depths under the ice, sees one of your baits, fancies it, and takes it in. The moment he tries to run away with it, he tilts the little red flag into the air and waves it backward and forward. "Be quick!" he signals all unconsciously: "here I am; come and pull me up!"

When two or three flags are fluttering at the same moment, far apart on the pond, you must skate with speed and haul in your lines promptly.

How hard it is, sometimes, to decide which one you will take first! That flag in the middle of the pond has been waving for at least a minute; but the other, in the corner of the bay, is tiltup and down more violently: it must be a larger fish. Great Dragon! there's another red signal flying, away over by the point! You hesitate, you make a few strokes in one direction, then you whirl around and dart the other way. Meanwhile one of the tilt-ups, constructed with too short a cross-stick, has been pulled to one side, and disappears in the hole. One pickerel in the pond carries a flag. Another tilt-up ceases to move and falls flat upon the ice. The bait has been stolen. You dash desperately towards the third flag and pull in the only fish that is left,—probably the smallest of them all!

A surplus of opportunities does not insure the best luck.

A room with seven doors—like the famous apartment in Washington's headquarters at Newburgh—is an invitation to bewilderment. I would rather see one fair opening in life than be confused by three dazzling chances.

There is a good story about fishing through the ice which formed part of the stock-in-conversation of that ingenious woodsman, Martin Moody, Esquire, of Big Tupper Lake. "'T was a blame cold day," he said, "and the lines friz up stiffer'n a fence-wire, jus' as I pulled 'em in, and my fingers got so dum' frosted I couldn't bait the hooks. But the fish was thicker and hungrier 'n flies in June. So I jus' took a piece of bait and held it over one o' the holes. Every time a fish jumped up to get it, I'd kick him out on the ice. I tell ye, sir, I kicked out more 'n four hundred pounds of pick'rel that morning. Yaas, 't was a big lot, I 'low, but then 't was a cold day! I jus' stacked 'em up solid, like cordwood."

Let us now leave this frigid subject! Ice fishing is but a chilling and unsatisfactory imitation of real sport. The angler will soon turn from it with satiety, and seek better consolation for the winter of his discontent in the entertainment of fishing in books.

The Plains and Deserts

There are only two dimensions to the plains, time and distance, but they add up to forever. Thin the grass and cut the rainfall in half and the plains become the desert, which has still a third dimension, patience. The plains persist. The desert waits.

Sky above, grass underfoot, and everywhere the horizon—that is the plains. Trees, like all strangers there, cling to the few watercourses, to sustenance and reassurance. Few besides the hawk, the buffalo, the coyote, and the plainsman, tall in the saddle, were ever at home on the plains, and even they were transients. It is a land of infinity, where an ant outranks a man and a grass seed is of more enduring importance. Time and distance, stretching from the Big Muddy to the Rockies, from the Gulf into

Canada—the grass of forever, the sun, the wind, the blizzard, the incredible gentleness of spring—the plains.

There is a completion to the plains, but the desert is unfinished business, waiting for time to catch up. Its mountains are still stark, its soil still rocks and sand, its plants prisoners of drouth, its animals fugitives from the killing sun. Waiting, all of them, from stark mountain to thorny cholla, for the blessing of rain. Man lives here only on the desert's harsh terms, even as the cactus, even as the Gila monster. And all who live in the desert partake of its own dimension, which is patience. Time lags, and this is still a land awaiting completion, not by man, but by time itself.

H.B.

CACTUS COUNTRY

BY MARY AUSTIN

Mary Austin (1868–1934) was born and educated in Illinois but spent most of her life in the desert country of the Southwest. She was a keen observer and wise interpreter of the life of the Southwest in all its forms, including the native Indians. Her many books included studies of the Indians, of the land and its plants and animals, of the complexity of existence and the conflict of the primitive and the modern. She was both poet and philosopher and, though I doubt that she ever used the term, ecologist. Her books about the desert country are among the best ever written. This selection is a chapter from The Land of Journeys' Ending, *a particularly perceptive book about the Southwest before The Bomb and the restless surge of population made its quiet towns and villages into teeming cities with suburbs as populous as the vanished prairie-dog towns.*

(*The Land of Journeys' Ending,* by Mary Austin; D. Appleton-Century, 1924.)

Not all the country that the cactus takes, belongs to it. That gypsy of the tribe, the prickly-pear, goes as far east and north on the great plains as the Spanish adventurers ever went, perhaps farther. It goes

as a rarity into Old World gardens, runs wild and thrives wherever there are sun and sand to bring its particular virtues into play. For the virtue of all cacti is that they represent the ultimate adaptations of vegetative life on its way up from its primordial home in the sea shallows, to the farthest, driest land. The prickly-pears—*Opuntia* is their family name, and the connection is a large one—run to arid wastes as gypsies do to the wilds, not because there the environment is the only one which will tolerate them, but because it is the one in which all the cactus tribe find themselves fulfilled, triumphant.

Here, in the country below the Mogollon Rim, the business of plants in making this a livable world, goes on all open to the light, not covered and confused by the multiplicity of its manifestations, as in the lush, well-rained-on lands. Here, in this veritable corner of southwestern Arizona, it has traveled the perfect round, from the filmed protoplasmic cell, by all the paths of plant complexity, to the high simplicity of the great king cactus, the sahuaro.

Going west by the Old Trails Road, you do not begin to find sahuaro until you are well down toward the black hills of Tucson, and it is not at its best this side of the toad-like heap of volcanic trap which turns the river out of its course, called Tummomoc. Here it rises to a height of twenty-five or thirty feet, erect, columnar, dull green, and deeply fluted, the outer ridges of the flutings set with rows of lateral spines that inclose it as in a delicate grayish web. Between the ridges the sahuaro has a texture like well-surfaced leather, giving back the light like spears, that, seen from a rapidly moving car, make a continuous vertical flicker in the landscape. Marching together against the rose-and-vermillion evening, they have a stately look, like the pillars of ruined temples.

For the first hundred years or so the sahuaro preserves the outline of its virgin intention to be straight, but in the case of wounding, or perhaps in seasons of excess, it puts forth without calculation immense columnar branches like the arms of candelabra, curving to bring their tips parallel to the axis of the main stem, which they reproduce as if from their own roots.

The range of the sahuaro is restricted. Beginning with isolated specimens about the San Pedro River, it spreads south and west, but the true sahuaro forests are not reached until the gate of Papagueria is past, or the flats of Salt River. A small plantation of them has crossed the Colorado River and established itself in California. South they pass into Sonora as far as Altar, and approach almost to the gulf shore, where they are replaced by the still more majestic *sowesa.*

The leafless, compact outline of the sahuaro, its erect habit and indurated surfaces give it a secret look. Surmounting the crest of one of these denuded desert ranges, or marching up nearly vertical slopes without haste or stooping, or pushing its way imperturbably toward the sun from the midst of cat-claw and mesquite and palo-verde, it has the effect of being forever outside the community of desert life. Yet such is the succulence of its seedlings, that few of them would survive the first two or three seasons without the shelter of the spiny undergrowth. Once the recurved spines have spread and stiffened across the smooth, infolded intervals, the sahuaro is reasonably safe, even from the hard-mouthed cattle of the desert ranges. In very dry years, small rodents will gnaw into the flutings as far up as they can creep between the spines. High up out of reach of all marauders, the woodpecker drills his holes in the pulpy outer mass; but against these the sahuaro protects itself by surrounding its wounds with pockets of woody fiber woven to the shape of the woodpecker's burrow.

Indians of that country will often remove these pocket linings before the fiber has hardened, and make use of them for household containers, or you may find them kicking about the sand, hard as oak-knots, long after the sahuaro that wove them has sloughed off its outer layer in decay. For the woodpecker never penetrates to the sahuaro core, inclosed as it is in a tube of woody, semi-detached ribs which remain standing long after the spongy masses that fill and surround it have completely desiccated, slowly fraying outward from the top as the ribs part, until at last the Papago carries them away to roof his house or his family tomb.

In the vast *abras* of southern Arizona, there is no woody growth capable of furnishing the woodpecker with the cool, dark home in which he brings up his broods. In a single unbranched sahuaro near Casa Grande, this year, I counted seventeen woodpecker holes, ranged up and down like the little openings of the old cliff-dwellers' caves. Frequently the vacated apartments of the sahuaro skyscraper will be occupied by the pygmy owl, who may have made a meal of the eggs or young birds before he established his own family there. Everywhere, from the sahuaro towers, little blue-headed hawks may be seen perching, or, from the vantage of their height, launching swift predatory flights. But when in the crotch of some three-hundred-year-old specimen the fierce red-tail has made his nest, you will find all that neighborhood vacant of bird life.

It is not easy to take the life of a sahuaro, even when, just to see the tiny wavering flame run up the ridges, you set a match to the rows of oily spines. Even uprooted, as it may be in torrential rains, the prostrate column has unmeasured powers of living on its stored waters, and making an upward turn of its growing tip. One such I found at the back of Indian Oasis, toward Topohua, which had turned and budded after what must have been several seasons of overthrow.

If the column is by any accident broken, lateral branches start from the wound and curve upward toward the sun. Successive dry years constrict its columnar girth, as successive wet ones swell it, tracing in the undulations of the vertical outline, a record of three or four centuries of rains. Around Tucson there must be sahuaros that could tell what sort of weather it was the year Father Kino came to the founding of San Xavier, and at Salt River I made my siesta under one that could have given a better guess than any of our archaeologists at what became of the ancient civilizations of Casa Grande and Los Muertos.

For I suppose the sahuaro harvest, and the ceremonial making of sahuaro wine to be the oldest food festival of the cactus country. In the excavations of the buried cities of the Great-house culture, buried before the queen was born whose jewels opened the portals of the West, they found little brown jars hermetically sealed with clay, after the fashion in which Papago housewives preserve sahuaro syrup at Cobabi and Quitovaquita.

From the Month of Cold Touching Mildly to the Inner Bone Month of the winter, the flutings of sahuaro stems are folded deep. With the first of the rains they begin to expand, until, if the season is propitious, the smooth leathery surfaces are tight as drums. In May, on the blunt crowns, on the quarter most exposed to the sun, buds appear like clusters of green figs, close-packed as if in a platter. About this time red-tailed hawks, in their shelterless nests in the tallest crotches, will be hatching their young, and the quail in pairs going house-hunting in and out of the *garamboyas*. Within a week or two the green fig-shaped buds open, one by one, in filmy white-rayed circles, deep-yellow hearted, the haunt of innumerable flies. By the latter part of June or July the delicate corollas are replaced by fig-shaped fruits that as they curl open when fully ripe, revealing the full-seeded, crimson pulp, have the effect of a second vivid flowering.

Just before the fruits burst, the Pima and Papago women turn out by villages to harvest them with long hooks made of a sahuaro rib and a cross-piece of acacia twig. Often, to save labor, they will peel the fruit as they collect it; returning at night with their great jars and baskets overflowing with the luscious juicy pulp. For this, and for all that I have written of the sahuaro festival in Papagueria, it is counted a crime to destroy a sahuaro.

There is a singular charm of the sahuaro forest, a charm of elegance, as the wind, moving like royalty across the well-shaped intervals, receives the courtesies of ironwood and ocotillo and palo-verde. It begins with the upright next-of-blood, with a stately rocking of the tall pillars on their roots, and a soft *ss-ss-ss* of the wind along their spiny ridges. Suddenly the bright blossom-tips of the ocotillo take flight like flights of scarlet birds, as the long wands bow and recover in the movement of the wind, and after an appreciable interval the thin-leaved ironwood rustles and wrestles with it, loth to let it go, until it drops with almost a sullen note to the stiff whisper of the palo-verde, while the creosote fairly casts its forehead to the ground.

The ocotillo is not a true cactus, but belongs rather by nature of its adaptation to the fellowship of the mesquite and that leafless thorny shrub often found in its neighborhood, called *corona de Jesús*. It does not store moisture as the cactus does, but remains in the long seasons between the rains in a state of complete aridivation, putting forth miraculously after the first showers, at the ends of its branches, crowded panicles of bloom like the bloody tips of spears. The gray, thorny wands of the ocotillo, growing from ten to fifteen feet, brought together in a lovely vase form by the central stem, a few inches from the ground, are leafless for all but a brief season, when perhaps the first sign of spring is the flush of green creeping up their swaying lengths, in the shape of thin, blunt emerald leaves. After the leaves fall away, the petiole which supports them becomes a spine, for the sake of which the stems of ocotillo are used for chicken-fences and corrals, thick-set in the ground, from which, as the spring comes around, they take heart of life, growing delicately green and scarlet-tipped again.

Ocotillo and sahuaro are to be found growing together on gravelly slopes of the *abras*, and with them the bisnaga or barrel-cactus, which the stranger frequently mistakes for a young sahuaro. It has the same fluted, branchless, columnar habit, but the bisnaga is a darker green, its spines frequently reddish, its circumference larger, and its height seldom equal to the height of a man. It may also be distinguished from the other cacti by having the axis of its growth, like the pointer of a dial, angling directly toward the sun. It is only when the observer finds several bisnagas growing together that the uniform slant begins to appear something more than an accident.

Now it is discovered that there is a crumpling of the surfaces toward the downthrow, and a half-turn of the flutings around the axis of growth, as if the plants had all been pulled by an irresistible force, out of their intention to grow symmetrically plump and upright. It seems probable that this disturbance of the barrel-shaped bulk is due to the more rapid evaporation of the side next to the sun; for the bisnaga is nothing, really, but a huge capsule of vegetable pulp, distended by the water which it collects and carries with the utmost parsimony from rain to rain. When the rains cease, it has been known to subsist on its own stores for a dozen years. Anywhere along the flood basins you are likely to see plump specimens of bisnaga uprooted from the rain-softened soil by their own weight, going on comfortably with their life processes while lying on one side. Also you will find here and there globose individuals, having gray fibrous scars in place of the fruit-bearing crown, which has been sliced off by some thirsty traveler. One stroke of the machete, and a little maceration of the white pulp with a stick or the bare hands, will provide in a few minutes a pint or more of cool, slightly insipid drink. Or if the machete is lacking, the spines may be burned off and the barrel broken open with a stone.

There are scores of variations of the bisnaga type, "niggerhead," "fish-hook," and "cushion" cacti, running to fat button shapes or short thickened cylinders, widely distributed through the Southwest. Rendered inconspicuous in the landscape by webs of grayish spines, they prick themselves on the attention by burning, brilliant bloom. But after the great sahuaro, it is only the opuntias that successfully modify the desert scene. Of these there are two general types, the flat-branched prickly-pears, and the round-jointed chollas. If I called the prickly-pear the gypsy of its tribe, it was not without recollecting that the gypsies have their queen in *Opuntia santa rita,* with its coin-shaped disks of red and electric blue, touched in the spring with a delicate silver sheen. *Santa rita* is, however, too shy a grower to compete, as a feature of the landscape, with the chollas, which have a tree-like form and a social habit.

Among the chollas, the unaccustomed eye will distinguish the "old-man," having a silvery-haired appearance from the sheaths of its dense covering of spines, from the deer-horn type, slender-jointed, sparsely spined, and with a tendency of the stems to take the general tone of its red or yellowish bloom. Both the old-man and the horned cholla have the habit of propagating by dropped joints, and the same facilities for distribution by hooking their easily detachable sections to passing animals. But it is only the silver-haired varieties, *Opuntia fulgida* and *Opuntia Bigelovii,* sowing themselves across the mesas in thick droves like sheep, that give character to the country below the Rim.

Chollas will grow, in favored localities, as high as a horse, but a peculiar sheep-like outline is achieved by the habit of the fruiting stems. The fruits, bright lemon yellow after inconspicuous bloom, are produced on the topmost boughs, but after setting, remain in place several years, during which a slow movement of the shaggy whitish branches takes place, to bring the fruiting joints closest to the ground on which they are finally cast. A plantation of cholla, which will sometimes cover acres, any plant of which might have sprung from the dropped joints of a single individual, is called a chollital, place of the cholla, one of the expressive native terms which I mean to spell hereafter as it is pronounced, choyital.

Between Tucson and Phoenix, south of the paved road, there is a vast cactus garden that I can never pass without crossing my fingers against its spell. Often in the midst of other employments I am seized with such a fierce backward motion of my mind toward it as must have beset Thoreau for his Walden when he had left it for the town. So that if I should disappear some day unaccountably from my accustomed places, leaving no trace, you might find me there in some such state as you read about in monkish tales, when one walked in the woods for an hour and found that centuries had passed. Look for me beyond the last spur of Santa Catalina, where there is a one-armed sahuaro having a hawk's nest in the crotch. Beyond that there is a plantation of thistle poppies on the tops of whose dusty green stems have perched whole flocks of white, wind-ruffled doves, always about to take flight and yet never freed. Then small droves of *Opuntia Bigelovii,* like lambs feeding with their tails between their legs; here and there a bisnaga, dial pointed above its moving shadow; silvery flocks of cholla, now and then a sahuaro pushing aside the acacia under which its youth survived, or a stiff, purple-flowered ironwood, and droves and droves of cholla leading down to the dry arroyo, from which at intervals arise green cages full of golden palo-verde flowers.

Inside the choyital, where ancient black trap overlaps the sand, there will be islands of needle-grass, preferred by the reddish-stemmed *Opuntia* which is called, from the manner of its branching, "stag-horn," and dense, globose clumps of *Opuntia arbuscula.* But far down the sandy middle strip, stooping low, you can see the sand thick sown with detached joints, awaiting with a breathless effect of suspense, the rain that brings the chance to root and grow.

There is an extraordinary feeling of intimacy about the choyital, where practically all the life goes on below the level of the observer's eye. The opuntias are seldom man-high, and the scant grass lends no cover to the intense activity of insect and small rodent life. Only the infrequent sahuaro lifts a bird-flight out of reach, and the wide-searching light pours unstinted around its meager shade.

In this country the chollas are the favorite nesting-places of birds. Early in April, before the sun renders the thin screen of spines inadequate, the thrush and the mocking-bird and the mourning-dove rear their broods on shallow platforms of twigs in the antlered tops of *Opuntia tetracantha,* and the cactus-wren weaves her thick balls of needle-grass in the spiniest depths of the "old-man" cholla. But this excess of safety has its dire results, for at the entrance of the long tunnel leading to the nest, the pygmy owl sits watching like a cat, and now and then one comes upon pitiful fragments of nestlings impaled on the cactus spines in their first, clumsy, tumbling flight.

It is the cast joints of cholla which the kangaroo-rat drags about its runways, in mazes in which the coyote would hesitate to set its paw. The road-runner is also credited with using them to fence in a snake it has marked for its prey. Understand that I am familiar enough with the road-runner to believe anything I am told about it, but my observation would lead me to conclude that this fencing in of the prey would take place only after the snake's back is broken with a driving stroke of the long bill, and would have as its object the protection of the quarry from other marauders. Once I saw this sleek cock of the choyital kill a small striped snake by alternately skimming about it in circles until the victim coiled, and then striking at the moveless rings, once, and away again, until, with the snake's back broken in two places, a blow on the head stilled the wriggling length. Usually, however, you will see this *corredor del camino* catching lizards or picking up black pinacate-beetles such as you find in great numbers at certain seasons, standing on their heads in the sand.

Around the outskirts of the cactus gardens, the conical hills of the farmer-ants arise out of circular cleared spaces not more than a yard or two in diameter, though farther north I have seen them as much as twenty or thirty feet. After the first rains, around these clearings, spring up downy carpets of inch-high "Indian wheat," like hoar-frost, whose full-seeded heads are harvested by the ants the moment they are matured. Ripening underground, the husks expand, each one in its tiny ball of fluff, which is carried up and deposited by the farmers in a white, webby ring around the hill, where it lies until the wind carries it away. Warm days toward the end of April, when the heads are bursting in the hidden storehouses, you can see the white ring widen visibly, while the particles of fluff seem to boil out of the ant-heap of their own force.

Days like this there is a sense of concentration of life in the choyital that is only partly accounted for by the movement of bird and insect life, intensified as it is by the withdrawal of the circling ranges behind successive veils of light and heat. By mid-morning the small furred folk are asleep in their stopped earths, the singing-birds retreat to their nests, the hawks rest in the shadows of the sahuaros, wings adroop, but the choyital does not sleep. Life gathers full at the brim of the cup, where any drop might overfill it, and there stays. When the drop falls, the arrested cycle of life triumphant begins again.

Here in the choyital we reach the full diapason of the adaptive rhythms of the spirit of vegetating life. If the word spirit has too much color for you, say the complex of energy: whatever it is we begin to know as the protoplasmic speck in ancient water-borders, shallow enough to be penetrated by the light of the sun and constant enough to keep the dawn-plant perpetually bathed in the sustaining flood. Perhaps the earliest adaptive motion of the undifferentiated vegetative mass was the specialization of its surfaces to produce organs of anchorage to hold it well within the favoring conditions. Then, as the unstable seas forced upon it the necessity of maintaining itself alive under conditions of intermittent ebb, it learned the rhythm of the tides, holding its breath from ebb to flow. It possessed the marshes, it crept up the rivers, it ventured on dry land. What had been a colloidal mass of vegetable protoplasm was root and stem and frond.

It grew by nodes and internodes, to rhythms established by the seasonal rains. But all its precious reproductive processes were still accomplished in the element from which it rose. Up grew the spore-producing stem, waxing great, with waving fronds; and down upon the water-film of the swamp and river-border, it cast the prothallium in a wafer of green, on whose under surfaces were developed the two essential elements of production. Thus the Vegetative Spirit preserved itself through the medium of two generations, the stem- and spore-producing generation, in which what we now know as pollen, could reach the pistil only in the presence of a thin film of water. Along the wet edges of fern-beds may still be seen the mechanisms by which the ancient vegetable world accomplished its double necessity of surviving on land and reproducing in water, in fleets of minute irregular leaf-surfaces afloat in the water-borders.

But before any conquest of the progressively drying earth could be made, some method must be found by which the second reproductive generation could be supplied with moisture by the mechanism already invented by the stem-generation, drawing it up as a sap. Thus it gradually came about that the prothallium, instead of being dropped upon the desiccating earth, was retained in place at the tip of the growing stem, and the marriage of the reproductive elements was trusted to the wind.

Look well, then, on that green film which you find floating on the wet fern-borders, for it became the rose! All the lovely intricacies of flowers and the lusciousness of fruit are but so many phases of the adaptations by which the parent generation maintains the reproductive generation on its own stem. Last and loveliest is the filmy-petaled, heavy-pollened cactus-flower.

It is only by keeping these things in mind that you will get anything more than a poet's or a painter's notion of plant life in the arid regions. For there is no such thing as a desert science of botany, no special desert way of flowering and bearing fruit. There are only highly specialized adaptations of the stem- and leaf-bearing generation, by which the reproductive generation is supplied, under conditions of extreme aridity, with the necessary water-supply. The journey's end of such successive adaptations is found in the sahuaro.

It is probable that the country below the Rim has not changed much since little *Eohippus* ran about there on his toes. Since there are no fossils of arid-region plants, it seems more than likely that previous to the Pleistocene times, since which our southwestern desert has undergone no essential modification, there were no such types. They have, in fact, evolved there in the places where we find them, out of ceaseless operation of the vegetable complexes in contact with desert conditions. Of the moisture-loving plant forms, only such types survive there as are able to compress their flowering and fruiting processes into the curtailed seasons of quick rains. But out of some forgotten ancestry, there have sprung tribes of plants that survived not by hurrying their processes but by holding them through rainless periods, in arrested states, similar to those in which the great bears pass the winter's snows. On this type are the creosote, the mesquite, the cat-claw, the smoke-bush, and palo-verde. By varnishing its leaves, or dispensing with leaves; by reducing its branches to stubs and thorns, each in its own fashion establishes an equilibrium between its necessities and the water-supply. For so much water there is so much growth; and then no growth at all for indefinite periods, prolonged sometimes over several seasons. By this suspension of the functions of growth, the whole life-cycle has been indefinitely extended in shrubs like the mesquite and the creosote. I have reason to believe that the mesquite in the neighborhood of Death Valley has lived at least four centuries, and as far as our knowledge goes, the creosote is immortal. Times when I have had to destroy one of these ancients, to prop my tent or cook my food, I have wished that I knew some such propitiatory rite for the appeasement of its spirit as the Navajos taught me to use before and after the killing of a bear.

To appreciate a creosote plantation, one must be able to think of the individual shrub as having its tail waving about in the sun and wind, and its intelligence underground. Then the wide spacing of the growing crowns is explained by the necessary horizontal spread of the root system in search of the thin envelope of moisture around the loose particles of the gravelly soil. In the rainy season the roots drink by means of minute hairs that are cast off when the last drop has been absorbed, after which the soul of the creosote sits and waits.

Plants of this type will run successfully through the average rainfall from century to century, but for growths of a shorter life-cycle and a more exigent bloom, it has been important, possibly more important in the early Pleistocene than now, to meet conditions of great irregularity in the water-supply with water-storage. For this the yuccas and agaves developed in their pithy stems and the thickened bases of their bayonet-pointed leaves, storage-capacity that enables them to send up, with magical rapidity, great spikes of waxen bloom to grace the rainless years. The obvious difference between yucca and agave is that the yucca produces its blossom crown from a lateral bud, and may go on doing so for indefinite periods, but the agave blooms from the central stem, and, blooming, dies. The great *Agave Americana,* called the century-plant, is a visitor across our southern border, and out of its stored energies,—which by no means run the hundred years with which it is popularly credited,—it throws up, in the course of days, a flowering stalk three or four times the height of a man, bearing seven thousand flowers, in whose fragrance the whole life of the agave is exhaled.

It is the yellow-flowered *Agave Palmeri,* taken just before the expanding growth begins, while the leaf bases are still packed with the sugary substance of the flowering bud, that is the mescal of the Southwestern tribes. Anywhere about the three-thousand- or four-thousand-foot levels of the mountains of southern Arizona you may come upon the pits where the mescal is roasted, or even surprise a group of Indians feasting on the nutritious but not very attractive mass. When I calculate the seasons through which, drop by drop, the agave has collected the material for its stately bloom, eating mescal is to me a good deal like eating a baby.

The long central stem of the yuccas enables them to make much more of a figure in the landscape, particularly the one known as "Joshua-tree," whose weird stalking forms can be found farthest afield in pure desertness, or the sotol (*Dasylirion Wheelerii*), whose dense plumes of long rapier-like, saw-edged leaves and tall pyramids of delicate racemes, are visible like companies of bandoliers far across the mesas. This sort holds its dried flower stalk aloft long after the fruit has been eaten and scattered by the birds; even on into the next season's bloom. There is a humbler variety which goes everywhere, like the prickly-pear, and, under the name of amole, furnishes those who know enough not to despise its narrow, yellowish, pointed leaf varieties, with an excellent fiber, and, from its roots, a substitute for soap. But the final, most successful experiment of the Vegetative Spirit on its way up from the sea-borders to the driest of dry lands, is the great sahuaro, *Carnegea gigantea.*

In the economy of the sahuaro, branch and twig have been reduced to spines, the green of its leaves absorbed into its skin. The need of woody fiber has been perfectly met by the stiff but strong hollow cylinder of semi-detached ribs that hold the stem erect, and its storage capacity rendered elastic by the fluted surfaces, swelling and contracting to the rhythm of evaporation and the intake of the thirsty roots. After successive wet seasons, new flutings are let into the surfaces, like gores in a skirt; or, after shortage, taken up with the neatness of long experience. By such mechanisms, the cactus-plant surpasses the stone-crops, the "hen-and-chickens," the "live-forevers," of other arid regions, so that until some plant is found able to make water out of the gaseous constituents in the air, we may conclude that here in the great sahuaro, the Vegetative Spirit comes to rest. Here it has met and surmounted all the conditions that for our cycle, menace, on this planet, the vegetative type. Passing, I salute it in the name of the exhaustless Powers of Life.

MINATAREE VILLAGE

BY GEORGE CATLIN

George Catlin (1796–1872) grew up with firsthand stories of Indian life; his mother, as a child, had been an Indian captive. He studied law, practiced for a time in his native Pennsylvania, but was more interested in painting so quit the law to become a portrait painter. He painted many prominent people in Philadelphia and Washington, Dolley Madison among them. Then, in his early thirties, he decided to dedicate his life to "rescuing from oblivion the looks and customs of the vanishing races of native man in America," and began years of travel and life among the Indians of the West. Between 1829 and 1838 he painted portraits of more than six hundred noted Indians, meanwhile collecting Indian costumes and artifacts. His pictures are probably the most complete record we have of the Indians before they were transformed by the white man's ways. His writing was almost entirely about his own experiences and is marked, sometimes marred, by his vanity, though pride in his accomplishment certainly was justified. He had the artist's eye for detail, and he wrote clearly and vividly. This selection is from the two-volume edition of North American Indians, *which he subtitled, "Being Letters and Notes on Their Manners, Customs and Conditions, Written During Eight Years' Travel Amongst the Wildest Tribes of Indians in North America, 1832–1839."*

(*North American Indians,* by George Catlin; published by the author in London, 1880.)

Ba'tiste, Bogard and I . . . started on a visit to the upper town of the Minatarees, which is half a mile or more distant, and on the other bank of the Knife River, which we crossed in the following manner:—The old chief, having learned that we were to cross the river, gave directions to one of the women of his numerous household, who took upon her head a skin-canoe (more familiarly called in this country, a bull-boat), made in the form of a large tub, of a buffalo's skin, stretched on a frame of willow boughs, which she carried to the water's edge; and placing it in the water, made signs for the three of us to get into it. When we were in, and seated flat on its bottom, with scarce room in any way to adjust our legs and our feet (as we sat necessarily facing each other), she stepped before the boat, and pulling it along, waded towards the deeper water, with her back towards us, carefully with the other hand attending to her dress, which seemed to be but a light slip, and floating upon the surface until the water was above her waist, when it was instantly turned off, over her head, and thrown ashore; and she boldly plunged forward, swimming and drawing the boat with one hand, which she did with apparent ease. In this manner we were conveyed to the middle of the stream, where we were soon surrounded by a dozen or more beautiful girls, from twelve to fifteen and eighteen years of age, who were at that time bathing on the opposite shore.

They all swam in a bold and graceful manner, and as confidently as so many otters or beavers; and gathering around us, with their long black hair floating about on the water, whilst their faces were glowing with jokes and fun, which they were cracking about us, and which we could not understand.

In the midst of this delightful little aquatic group, we three sat in our little skin-bound tub (like the "three wise men of Gotham, who went to sea in a bowl," etc.), floating along down the current, losing sight, and all thoughts, of the shore, which was equi-distant from us on either side; whilst we were amusing ourselves with the playfulness of these dear little creatures who were floating about under the clear blue water, catching their hands on to the sides of our boat; occasionally raising one-half of their bodies out of the water, and sinking again, like so many mermaids.

In the midst of this bewildering and tantalizing entertainment, in which poor Ba'tiste and Bogard, as well as myself, were all taking infinite pleasure, and which we supposed was all intended for our special amusement; we found ourselves suddenly in the delightful dilemma of floating down the current in the middle of the river; and of being turned round and round to the excessive amusement of the villagers, who were laughing at us from the shore, as well as these little tyros, whose delicate hands were besetting our tub on all sides; and for an escape from whom, or for fending off, we had neither an oar, or anything else, that we could wield in self-defence, or for self-preservation. In this awkward predicament, our feelings of excessive admiration were immediately changed, to those of exceeding vexation, as we now learned that they had peremptorily discharged from her occupation our fair conductress, who had undertaken to ferry us safely across the river; and had also ingeniously laid their plans, of which we had been ignorant until the present moment, to extort from us in this way, some little evidences of our liberality, which, in fact, it was impossible to refuse them, after so liberal and bewitching an exhibition on their part, as well as from the imperative obligation which the awkwardness of our situation had laid us under. I had some awls in my pockets, which I presented to them, and also a few strings of beautiful beads, which I placed over their delicate necks as they raised them out of the water by the side of our boat; after which they all joined in conducting our craft to the shore, by swimming by the sides of and behind it, pushing it along in the direction where they designed to land it, until the water became so shallow, that their feet were upon the bottom, when they waded along with great coyness, dragging us towards the shore, as long as their bodies, in a crouching position, could possibly be half concealed under the water, when they gave our boat a last push for the shore, and raising a loud and exulting laugh, plunged back again into the river; leaving us the only alternative of sitting still where we were, or of stepping out into the water a half leg deep, and of wading to the shore, which we at once did, and soon escaped from the view of our little tormentors, and the numerous lookers-on, on our way to the upper village.

Here I was politely treated by the Yellow Moccasin, quite an old man, who seemed to be the chief of this band or family, constituting their little community of thirty or forty lodges, averaging, perhaps, twenty persons to each. I was feasted in this man's lodge and afterwards invited to accompany him and several others to a beautiful prairie, a mile or so above the village, where the young men and young women of this town, and many from the village below, had assembled for their amusements; the chief of which seemed to be that of racing their horses. In the midst of these scenes, after I had been for some time a looker-on, and had felt some considerable degree of sympathy for a fine-looking young fellow whose horse had been twice beaten on the course, and whose losses had been considerable; for which his sister, a very modest and pretty girl, was most piteously howling and crying. I selected and brought forward an ordinary-looking pony, that was evidently too fat and too sleek to run against his fine-limbed little horse that had disappointed his high hopes; and I began to comment extravagantly upon its muscle, etc., when I discovered him evidently cheering up with the hope of getting me and my pony on to the turf with him; for which he soon made me a proposition; and I, having lauded the limbs of my little nag too much to "back out," agreed to run a short race with him of half a mile, for three yards of scarlet cloth, a knife, and half a dozen strings of beads, which I was willing to stake against a handsome pair of leggings, which he was wearing at the time. The greatest imaginable excitement was now raised amongst the crowd by this arrangement; to see a white man preparing to run with an Indian jockey, and that with a scrub of a pony, in whose powers of running no Indian had the least confidence. Yet there was no one in the crowd who dared to take up several other little bets I was willing to tender (merely for their amusement, and for their final exultation); owing, undoubtedly, to the bold and confident manner in which I had ventured on the merits of this little horse, which the tribe had all overlooked; and needs must have some *medicine* about it.

So far was this panic carried that even my champion was ready to withdraw; but his friends encouraged him at length and we galloped our horses off to the other end of the course, where we were to start; and where we were accompanied by a number of horsemen, who were to witness the "set off." Some considerable delay here took place, from a condition, which was then named to me and which I had not observed before, that in all the races of this day, every rider had to run entirely denuded and ride a naked horse! Here I was completely balked, and having no one by me to interpret a word, I was quite at a loss to decide what was best to do. I found, however, that remonstrance was of little avail; and as I had volunteered in this thing to gratify and flatter them, I thought it best not positively to displease them in this; so I laid off my clothes, and straddled the naked back of my round and glossy little pony, by the side of my competitor, who was also mounted and stripped to the skin, and panting with a restless anxiety for the start.

Reader! did you ever imagine that in the *middle of a man's life* there could be a thought or a feeling so *new* to him, as to throw him instantly back to infancy; with a new world and a new genius before him—started afresh, to navigate and breathe the elements of naked and untasted liberty, which clothe him in their cool and silken robes that float about him; and wafting their life-inspiring folds to his inmost lungs? If you have never been inspired with such a feeling, and have been in the habit of believing that you have thought of and imagined a little of everything, try for a moment to disrobe your mind and your body, and help me through feelings to which I cannot give utterance. Imagine yourselves as I was, with my trembling little horse beneath me, and the cool atmosphere that was floating about and ready more closely and familiarly to embrace me, as it did the next moment, when we "were off," and struggling for the goal and the prize.

Though my little Pegasus seemed to dart through the clouds, and I to be wafted on the wings of Mercury, yet my red adversary was leaving me too far behind for further competition; and I wheeled to the left, making a circuit of the prairie, and came in at the starting point, much to the satisfaction and exultation of the jockeys, but greatly to the murmuring disappointment of the women and children, who had assembled in a dense throng to witness the "coming out" of the "white medicine-man." I clothed myself instantly and came back, acknowledging my defeat and the superior skill of my competitor, as well as the wonderful muscle of his little charger, which pleased him much; and his sister's lamentations were soon turned to joy, by the receipt of a beautiful scarlet robe and a profusion of vari-colored beads, which were speedily paraded on her copper-colored neck.

After I had seen enough of these amusements, I succeeded with some difficulty in pulling Ba'tiste and Bogard from amongst the groups of women and girls, where they seemed to be successfully ingratiating themselves; and we trudged back to the little village of earth-covered lodges, which were hemmed in and almost obscured from the eye by the fields of corn and luxuriant growth of wild sunflowers, and other vegetable productions of the soil, whose spontaneous growth had reared their heads in such profusion as to appear like a dense and formidable forest.

We loitered about this little village awhile, looking into most of its lodges and tracing its winding avenues, after which we recrossed the river and wended our way back again to headquarters, from where we had started in the morning. This day's ramble showed to us all the inhabitants of this little tribe, except a portion of their warriors who are out on a war-excursion against the Riccarees. . . .

The Minatarees . . . are a bold, daring and warlike tribe, quite different in these respects from their neighbors, the Mandans, carrying war continually in their enemies' country, thereby exposing their lives and continually diminishing the number of their warriors to that degree that I find two or three women to a man, through the tribe. They are bold and fearless in the chase also, and in their eager pursuits of the bison, or buffaloes, their feats are such as to excite the astonishment and admiration of all who behold them. Of these scenes I have witnessed many since I came into this country, and amongst them all nothing have I seen to compare with one to which I was an eyewitness a few mornings since, and well worthy of being described.

The Minatarees, as well as the Mandans, had suffered for some months past for want of meat and had indulged in the most alarming fears that the herds of buffaloes were migrating so far off from them that there was great danger of their actual starvation, when it was suddenly announced through the village one morning at an early hour that a herd of buffaloes was in sight, when an hundred or more young men mounted their horses with weapons in hand and steered their course to the prairies. The chief informed me that one of his horses was in readiness for me at the door of his wigwam, and that I had better go and see the curious affair. I accepted his polite offer, and mounting his steed galloped off with the hunters to the prairies where we soon descried at a distance a fine herd of buffaloes grazing, when a halt and a council were ordered and the mode of attack was agreed upon. I had armed myself with my pencil and sketch-book only, and consequently took my position generally in the rear, where I could see and appreciate every maneuvre.

The plan of attack, which in this country is familiarly called a "surround," was explicitly agreed upon and the hunters who were all mounted on their "buffalo horses" and armed with bows and arrows or long lances, divided into two columns, taking opposite directions, and drew themselves gradually around the herd at a mile or more distance from them, thus forming a circle of horsemen at equal distances apart who gradually closed in upon them with a moderate pace, at a given signal. The unsuspecting herd at length "got the wind" of the approaching enemy and fled in a mass in the greatest confusion. To the point where they were aiming to cross the line, the horsemen were seen at full speed, gathering and forming in a column, brandishing their weapons and yelling in the most frightful manner, by which means they turned the black and rushing mass which moved off in an opposite direction where they were again met and foiled in a similar manner, and wheeled back in utter confusion; by which time the horsemen had closed in from all directions, forming a continuous line around them, whilst the poor affrighted animals were eddying about in a crowded and confused mass, hooking and climbing upon each other; when the work of death commenced. I had rode up in the rear and occupied an elevated position at a few rods distance. . . .

In this grand turmoil a cloud of dust was soon raised, which in part obscured the throng where the hunters were galloping their horses around and driving the whizzing arrows or their long lances to the hearts of these noble animals; which in many instances, becoming infuriated with deadly wounds in their sides, erected their shaggy manes over their blood-shot eyes and furiously plunged forward at the sides of their assailants' horses, sometimes goring them to death and putting their dismounted riders to flight for their lives; sometimes their dense crowd was opened and the blinded horsemen, too intent on their prey amidst the cloud of dust, were hemmed and wedged in amidst the crowding beasts, over whose backs they were obliged to leap for security, leaving their horses to the fate that might await them in the results of this wild and desperate war. Many were the bulls that turned upon their assailants and met them with desperate resistance; and many were the warriors who were dismounted and saved themselves by the superior muscles of their legs; some who were closely pursued by the bulls wheeled suddenly around and snatching the part of a buffalo robe from around their waists, threw it over the horns and eyes of the infuriated beast, and darting by its side drove the arrow or the lance to its heart. Others dashed off upon the prairies by the side of the affrighted animals which had escaped from the throng, and closely escorting them for a few rods, brought down their hearts' blood in streams, and their huge carcasses upon the green and enamelled turf. . . .

The scene after the battle was over was novel and curious in the extreme; the hunters were moving about amongst the dead and dying animals, leading their horses by their halters, and claiming their victims by their private marks upon their arrows, which they were drawing from the wounds in the animals' sides.

Amongst the poor affrighted creatures that had occasionally dashed through the ranks of their enemy, and sought safety in flight upon the prairie (and in some instances, had undoubtedly gained it), I saw them stand awhile, looking back, when they turned and, as if bent on their own destruction, retraced their steps and mingled themselves and their deaths with those of the dying throng. Others had fled to a distance upon the prairies, and for want of company, of friends or of foes, had stood and grazed on till the battle-scene was over; seemingly taking pains to stay and hold their lives in readiness for their destroyers, until the general destruction was over, when they fell easy victims to their weapons—making the slaughter complete.

After this scene, and after arrows had been claimed and recovered, a general council was held, when all hands were seated on the ground, and a few pipes smoked; after which, all mounted their horses and rode back to the village.

A deputation of several warriors was sent to the chief, who explained to him what had been their success; and the same intelligence was communicated by little squads to every family in the village; and preparations were made at once for securing the meat. For this purpose, some hundreds of women and children, to whose lots fall all the drudgeries of Indian life, started out upon the trail which led them to the battle-field, where they spent the day in skinning the animals, and cutting up the meat, which was mostly brought into the villages on their backs, as they tugged and sweated under their enormous and cruel loads.

I rode out to see this curious scene. . . . Amidst the throng of women and children that had been assembled, and all of whom seemed busily at work, were many superannuated and disabled nags, which they had brought out to assist in carrying in the meat; and at least one thousand semi-loup dogs, and whelps, whose keen appetites and sagacity had brought them out to claim their shares of this abundant and sumptuous supply.

I stayed and inspected this curious group for an hour or more, during which time I was almost continually amused by the clamorous contentions that arose, and generally ended, in desperate combats; both amongst the dogs and women, who seemed alike tenacious of their local and recently acquired rights, and disposed to settle their claims by "tooth and nail"—by manual and brute force.

When I had seen enough of this I rode to the top of a beautiful prairie bluff, a mile or two from the scene, where I was exceedingly amused by overlooking the route that lay between this and the village, which was over the undulating green fields for several miles that lay beneath me; over which there seemed a continual string of women, dogs and horses, for the rest of the day, passing and repassing as they were busily bearing home their heavy burthens to their village, and in their miniature appearance, which the distance gave them, not unlike a busy community of ants as they are sometimes seen, sacking and transporting the treasures of a cupboard, or the sweets of a sugar bowl.

THE SETTLEMENT OF GRASSLANDS

BY EVERETT E. EDWARDS

Everett E. Edwards, a native of Minnesota and a graduate of Carleton College and Harvard University, has been researching and writing about the history of agriculture since 1927. When this selection was first published, in the Agriculture Department yearbook for 1948, he was senior agricultural historian in the Bureau of Agricultural Economics, U. S. Department of Agriculture.

(*Grass: The Yearbook of Agriculture,* 1948. Government publication.)

The agricultural settlement of the United States took nearly three centuries and involved two processes—horizontal movements of pioneer conditions across the continent and vertical movements of improvements within every community.

Quickenings and some lags occurred within the two processes. Old and new systems of farming and crop rotations might exist side by side for a considerable time. Grassland generally tended to be the marginal part of every farm, and its integration into a farming system was slow. To the average farmer, grass was only grass. While some kinds were eventually recognized as better than others for livestock, the general recognition of the place of the various grasses and forage plants in rotations, soil improvement, and animal nutrition came slowly and relatively late.

In considering the place of grasses in the farming of the Thirteen English Colonies that became the United States, we should recall two basic background situations. One is the state of the farming that was familiar to the folk who colonized the North Atlantic seaboard. The second is the state of the forage resources that they found where they settled.

Another point: In the history of grasslands settlement in the United States, several factors make careful historical delineations and generalizations difficult. Grass was generally such a taken-for-granted item that it was not commented upon in historical records unless something went amiss with the supply. In the records also, and especially in the seventeenth and eighteenth centuries, the terminology used for grasses was vague and overlapping—a grass might be known by one name in one part of the country and by quite a different one in another; or two distinct grasses might be known by the same name in different localities.

Although agriculturists have long recognized the prime importance of an abundant supply of nutritious forage plants for the successful raising of livestock, the early colonists of the seventeenth century were not keenly cognizant of this fact. They came from an England whose agriculture was primitive. Arable and pasture land were still regarded as permanently separate. The introduction of a rotation of crops, founded on the field cultivation of roots and clover usually attributed to Sir Richard Weston, did not take place until after the first settlements in America were made, and popularization of improved methods of farming and of better livestock was still more than a century and a half away.

The vegetation of North America at the time of European colonization was strikingly deficient in forage plants suitable for livestock. The American Indians had made phenomenal progress in the domestication and development of economic plants, but they had used these for human food. They had no herbivorous domestic animals and had, therefore, no occasion to give attention to forage plants.

The first pastures in the English Colonies were the natural openings or clearings in the lowlands along the banks of streams and the woods where the underbrush had been burned by the Indians for hunting. In these places the colonists found two native forage plants, the wild-rye and the broom-straw. The first was common along the Atlantic coast from Virginia northward, and the second was dominant in the Middle Colonies and in parts of New England.

These grasses grew high and thick and the early commentators wrote enthusiastically about them. The cattle ate them freely during the summer, but shortly came the realization that it was practically impossible to make enough hay of these grasses to carry the cattle through the winter. The fact was that the proportion of roughage to nutrient made them of little value as hay.

The attention the early settlers gave to the coarse reeds and sedges of the fresh- and salt-water marshes emphasizes the lack of good pasture and hay in the first half of the seventeenth century. If droughts reduced the forage, whole herds might be lost. Sometimes cattle were slaughtered to keep them from starvation, and there was always this danger as long as the livestock had to depend on native grasses.

It was not long, however, before the grasses of England appeared in the Colonies. On shipboard the animals were fed the forage provided for them, and when they were landed the ships were cleared of litter and manure. The grasses thus introduced spread rapidly and in a few generations came to be regarded as indigenous. In 1665 English grass, a term which regularly included bluegrass and white clover, was noted in a report on Rhode Island. In 1679, a visitor on Long Island saw fields of clover in bloom "which diffused a sweet odor in the air for a great distance."

Long before this time some of the seeding was intentional. In 1685 William Penn described an experiment in sowing English grass and noted that one of his colonists had sowed "great and small clover." As the seed used for these intentional sowings was unwinnowed chaff from hay stacks, the resulting pastures included an abundance of Old World weeds.

In view of the state of knowledge concerning livestock husbandry and the scarcity of labor, the first colonists turned their livestock loose on the unoccupied lands adjacent to their holdings as a matter of course and depended on the natural vegetation to carry them at all seasons. The realization that the rigorous winters of the more northern latitudes dictated shelters and supplies of fodder came slowly. As a system of mixed farming prevailed in all the earliest settlements, the protection of growing crops from the depredations of livestock was a prime necessity. Enclosures or fences of some kind were obviously needed, but fencing would have taken more labor than could be spared from clearing land, providing shelter, and cultivating crops. Out of this situation emerged several forms or stages of range husbandry which, generally speaking, were repeated again and again during the course of the American westward movement.

In New England and in the localities developed by New Englanders in New York and northern New Jersey, the method of community settlement made possible a system of common pasturage. The duties of the community cowherd who went through the village street every morning sounding his horn and gathering the livestock were set forth repeatedly in the ancient town records.

If the farmers of the community had enough sheep to justify segregation they were handled separately by a shepherd during the grazing season. Swine were especially troublesome and became the subject of more legislation than any other single agricultural matter. Circumstances soon compelled the registering of livestock brands and earmarks with the town authorities.

The Dutch of New Netherland had common pastures, and the practice was recognized legally when the colony was taken over by the English. In the Middle Colonies, where settlements were made by individuals without group cooperation at first, each farmer had to handle his own livestock. Farther south the same situation prevailed.

In the Southern Colonies the abundance of open range, even though poorly provided with grasses, discouraged the planting of artificial grasses. The straw of wheat, rice, and other small grains was used for roughage, and Virginia farmers sometimes pastured growing wheat. The soils of the Coastal Plain would have needed special fertilization for the growing of the ordinary meadow and pasture grasses and the extreme heat of the summers would also have hindered their extensive introduction.

On the frontier of the Southern Colonies a range-cattle industry developed—which was an eighteenth-century counterpart of the later industry on the Great Plains. Even at the close of the seventeenth century, herds of wild cattle and horses ranged on the western edge of the Virginia settlements. These animals were hunted by the planters, driven into pens, and branded as needed. Cattle raisers, learning from the fur traders about the rich pea-vine pastures of the uplands, pushed into the Piedmont. Sometimes they drove their herds from range to range; sometimes they established permanent ranges around the cowpens that they erected. The cattle were marketed in Charleston and later even driven to Baltimore, Philadelphia, or New York. Sometimes the cattle were sold to Delaware farmers for fattening. By the middle of the eighteenth century the outbreak of diseases necessitated colonial regulation of the cattle drives.

By the eighteenth century the problem of adequate pasturage on farms became accentuated. The supply of grasses in the woods and unenclosed meadows did not keep pace with the increase in livestock.

Pehr Kalm, the famous Swedish botanist who visited the Colonies in the middle of the century, noted that the pastures of the older settlements in Pennsylvania and New Jersey were failing because they were overstocked and the annual grasses could not ripen and reseed themselves. Because of the persistence of the practice of burning the woods, the timber forage declined. The lands, worn out from overtillage and then abandoned to a weed fallow, made poor pasture. Perhaps half of the average farm was a vast pasture largely overrun with sour grass, briers, and bushes. The farmers continued to cut their hay chiefly from the natural meadows and the marshes. Large quantities of coarse hay, chiefly Carex, were gathered, but as the livestock numbers increased the sources became increasingly unreliable.

Some time before 1750 the German farmers of Pennsylvania began to irrigate natural meadows. The streams flowing through the meadows were diverted along the hillsides and the water distributed by lateral ditches over the lowlands. The procedure often took much labor, but the increased hay crops apparently justified the expense. Farms with a large acreage capable of irrigation were highly valued. A few localities in New England also developed what was called "watered meadows." In the years 1745 to 1760 many of the salt marshes along the Delaware River were drained with dikes and tide gates and the land seeded to grain and then to clover or other English grasses.

A step of significance for the livestock industry was the creation of so-called artificial meadows. The seeding of tilled uplands with tame grasses as a substitute for weed fallow provided the farm stock with a very necessary and better supply of forage. The procedure was an important step forward in crop management.

In the eighteenth century such sowings increased, and selected seed began to be substituted for haymow sweepings. In 1749 Kalm saw fields of red clover near New York, and a decade later another observer found Pennsylvania farmers sowing clover seed "after they have harrowed in their wheat to make the crop stronger." The culture of clover, however, did not become widespread until after the American Revolution. By the beginning of the nineteenth century the advantage of using cultivated grasses on uplands as the source of hay had won recognition, and there was less reliance on natural meadows in the older and more settled parts of the country. Even the Pennsylvania-German farmers no longer valued irrigated meadows.

Timothy was the first grass cultivated in America to attract much attention. It was supposedly found growing near Portsmouth, in New Hampshire, about 1700 by a man named John Herd, and as its cultivation spread through New England it came to be known appropriately as Herd's grass. Seed was taken to New York, Maryland, Virginia, and North Carolina by one Timothy Hanson, and there the plant was called timothy. Although long assumed to be indigenous in America, it is now recognized as an Old World plant that grew naturally in England, where it was called catstail grass. The cultivation of timothy spread through New England and the Middle Colonies during the eighteenth century. Its dominance as a hay plant in the United States today is a tribute to the shrewdness of the colonists who first recognized its value.

Different kinds of grasses had been tried in the Colonial South.

In 1635 the prospective settlers of Maryland were urged to bring a "good store of Claver grasse seede, to make good meadow."

In 1735 the settlers at Frederica, in Georgia, planted lucerne, and a few years later Eliza Lucas began experimental plantings of it in South Carolina. George Washington tried lucerne at Mount Vernon in the 1760's but the soil was not suitable.

Thomas Jefferson, in his *Notes on the State of Virginia,* published in 1785, stated: "Our grasses are Lucerne, St. Foin, Burnet, Timothy, ray (rye), and orchard grass; red, white and yellow clover; greensward, blue grass, and crab grass." The fact that Jefferson listed these grasses does not mean, however, that they were widely cultivated even in Virginia.

Before the American Revolution the growing scarcity of open range led some of the more enterprising planters of Maryland and Virginia to introduce timothy and clover and to give attention to watered meadows. But even in the 1790's foreign travelers noted the backwardness of the meadow in these States as compared with those to the north. In the Carolinas and Georgia even less attention was paid to artificial pastures and meadows. No wild grass was mowed for hay. The livestock shifted for themselves at all seasons.

The data of the first agricultural census delineate the Northeastern States as the main hay-producing area in 1839. Except where wheat dominated in western New York and Pennsylvania, hay was the staple. To the west of Ohio the cultivation of grasses and clover was still unimportant, and the hay harvested was largely native grasses. In the older settled East increased use was being made of clover and of gypsum, lime, and manure.

The growth of towns and cities necessitated stage, livery, and private stables. Until the advent of the motor-car and truck in the twentieth century, these stables were an ever-growing market for hay. As early as 1837 Essex County, in Massachusetts, supplied more than a thousand tons to the Boston market, and the average price was about $16 a ton.

In the older communities of the Atlantic seaboard, market opportunities influenced the management of grasslands increasingly as the nineteenth century progressed. Localities that could specialize in beef fattening or dairying improved their upland mowing lands by sowing clover and other grasses and even permanent meadows might be manured occasionally. Arable fields were regularly laid down to grass after two or three grain crops and then mowed or pastured for several years.

The pasturage afforded by the natural openings west of the Alleghenies was richer than that of the Atlantic seaboard. The wild-rye and Andropogons grew more luxuriantly. The first settlers also found bluegrass and white clover, and their presence there in advance of settlement gave rise to the belief that they were indigenous. The cane along the banks of the rivers was used as forage for livestock. There were also two indigenous species, buffalo grass and buffalo clover, which were unknown east of the Alleghenies. The first of these was a coarse grass with a broad leaf. It belonged to the same family as the famous buffalo grass of the Great Plains. The latter was a native clover.

The pioneer farmers who began to push westward across the Alleghenies during and following the American Revolution were confronted with the same task of carving out farms from the heavy timber just as their ancestors had done in the Atlantic Coastal Plain. Although the natural openings or treeless meadows were more numerous and extensive west of the Alleghenies, they were neglected except for pasturage. Nearly two centuries of the woodland farming had developed techniques which the pioneers did not abandon until confronted with the true prairies of Illinois. The farm seekers had come to select their soils on the basis of the kind of forest growth that covered them. It was reasonable to believe that land which grew only grass was not valuable.

In the Ohio River Valley the natural openings became the starting point of another extensive range-cattle industry. As early as 1805 George and Felix Renick of Ohio drove a herd of range cattle overland to Baltimore, where they cleared a profit of more than $30 a head. Their success led to other similar drives, and shortly the marketing of range cattle in the East became the main source of cash income for many western farmers of that time. The cattle were started eastward in the early spring. Each night the herds were halted at drove stands, where food and shelter were provided for both the drivers and their charges.

By 1840 the farmers of the Ohio Valley had taken on the fattening of their own cattle with corn, and this development became concentrated in a zone bounded on the north by the 40° parallel and on the south by the 36° parallel. The Scioto Valley and the bluegrass region of Kentucky were centers of corn feeding, and many of the leaders in the enterprise were former Virginians who had known of similar methods on the banks of the Potomac in the days of Washington. Eventually these feeders reached out to the prairies of Illinois, Iowa, and Missouri for additional stock. In the absence of large-scale refrigeration, the eastern cattle drives continued until the coming of railroads.

By 1840 the westward movement was confronted with the true prairies of what came to be known as the Middle West. Many of the small prairies of Ohio and Indiana adjacent to rivers and timber had already been occupied, and the prairies of Stark County, Ohio, had become a leading wheat center. The oak openings and the small prairies of Michigan, Indiana, Wisconsin, Illinois, and Missouri then were being settled.

But the pioneers hesitated on the edge of the large prairies with their seemingly endless expanse of thick grass. There was a sense of vastness about them that seemed overpowering, an impression of a greatness that could not be subdued. Indeed, some contended that they would not be brought under cultivation for centuries.

There were many reasons for this hesitation on the edge of the prairies.

There was the lore of woodland farming that associated certain types of soil with specific stands of timber. Besides, forests were of great importance in the pioneer economy. They sheltered the game that constituted a chief source of meat, and they supplied logs for cabins, stock shelters, fuel, fences, furniture, and tools. They offered protection from winds and storms that open prairies did not give.

In addition to the lack of timber, the prairies did not provide a proper water supply until wells were dug. In some places the land of the prairies was low and swampy and needed to be drained before cultivation. Fever and ague attacked the settlers who tried these parts.

Another reason for avoiding the prairies was the desire to be near the watercourses that provided avenues of transportation. Trails into the prairies were practically impassable in the spring because of the deep mud.

It was soon demonstrated that the cast-iron plows brought from the East would not scour when used to break the prairie sod. Large plows with wooden moldboards plated with iron strips would turn furrows, but it took as many as six yoke of oxen to pull them. The process of prairie breaking cost less per acre than woodland in terms of manual labor but far more in terms of animal power.

Necessity eventually forced the conquest of the prairies. By the 1840's the land east of the Mississippi River that provided the favorite combination of timber and small clearings was occupied by settlers or held by speculators. Latecomers had to try the prairies or go farther west.

The development of the steel plow provided a satisfactory means of turning over the sod. The building of railroads across the prairie region connected the farmers with better markets and brought them fuel and building material. The advent of the reaper pointed to the day when the farmers would prefer the open, level prairies with their glaciated soils for extensive grain production.

As the cost of timber for the traditional types of fences became almost prohibitive, resort was made to sod fences, smooth wire, and Osage-orange hedges, but the problem of fences on the prairies remained essentially unsolved until the invention of barbed wire in 1874—a simple thing, but one of great significance.

The problems of prairie settlement were not peculiar to the Middle West. They were much accentuated on the Great Plains, where the uncertainties of rainfall were an additional factor. Similar problems arose on the pampas of Argentina, the grassy steppes of Siberia, and even on the grasslands of North Manchuria when the Chinese migrated there this century.

The systematic occupation of semi-arid California was begun by the Spaniards in 1769. To this end they used three institutions—the presidio or military establishment, the pueblo or colonial settlement, and the mission. Of these the last became by far the most significant agriculturally. Although the friars introduced the crops and fruits and irrigation practices of their Mediterranean homeland, the natural grasses and related vegetation were sufficient to support cattle raising as the dominant occupation during the Spanish-Mexican period, 1769–1848, and even into the 1860's, when droughts ended it as a distinctive industry.

Migratory sheep raising recovered from the droughts, reached its peak in 1874, and then began to decline. Except in isolated areas livestock husbandry became a subsidiary part of the specialized agriculture which came to dominate the California scene.

By 1850 the westward-moving frontier of agricultural settlement had reached the eastern edge of the Great Plains, where it halted for nearly two decades. Mounted on horses, the Plains Indians were a much more effective barrier to the advance of the white men than the native population to the eastward had been. For two and a half centuries the Plains Indians maintained themselves against the Spaniards, English, French, Mexicans, Texans, and Americans despite missionaries, whiskey, diseases, gunpowder, and lead.

Besides, it was generally believed that this region was unfit for white settlement. The geographers of the day pictured large portions of it as the Great American Desert. In addition, the rush to the gold fields in 1849 and the years immediately following made California a great objective of those moving west. The Great Plains and the Rocky Mountain region became merely a long, tedious, and hazardous roadway to the Pacific coast. The basic reason, however, for the halt of the frontier at approximately the eastern edge of the Great Plains was that it, by virtue of its climate, challenged the accepted methods of agricultural conquest.

The vegetation of the Great Plains was strikingly different from that of the United States to the eastward. The level land from the ninety-eighth meridian westward was practically treeless. The characteristic natural vegetation was grass and desert shrub, ranged according to the rainfall in generally north-to-south belts. In the low plains, like the prairies to the eastward, the grass was tall, luxuriant, and deep-rooted. To the west, on the high plains, the grass was short but the surface sodded. Farther west the grass grew in tufts or bunches because the rainfall was too scanty to support continuous growth. In the arid intermountain region beyond, creosote bush was characteristic in the south, sagebrush in the north, and greasewood in the salt-desert areas.

The main short grasses were the grama, galleta, buffalo, and mesquite. Although not continuous, the grama grass extended through Colorado, New Mexico, Arizona, and Utah, especially in the higher valleys and plateaus. The galleta grass was found in New Mexico, Arizona, and Utah. The buffalo grass thrived from the Panhandle of Texas to South Dakota. Mesquite grass grew where there was summer rainfall in western Texas, southern New Mexico, and Arizona.

Largely because of its natural vegetation the Great Plains became the scene of a range-cattle industry which far exceeded in scale and results any of its predecessors in American history. The building of the Union Pacific Railroad brought hunters who supplied the construction crews with buffalo meat, and its completion in 1869 let in additional throngs which eliminated the buffalo and left the grasses of the plains unused.

During the years of the Civil War a vast reserve of range cattle had grown up on the Texas plains. The growth of population in the East and the advance of the railroads into the Great Plains provided both a market and a means for shipping these cattle. This combination of circumstances enabled the range-cattle industry to dominate the Great Plains from the late sixties to the late eighties. A less-publicized but comparably important cattle business overflowed from the interior of the Oregon Country during 1875–85.

Starting from their breeding grounds in lower Texas, great herds of cattle were driven northward to Abilene and other shipping points in Kansas. Later, herds were pushed into Nebraska, the Dakotas, and

Montana, first to provide meat for Indian reservations and military posts and later to raise cattle for eastern markets. Incident to this business, trial-and-error experimentation developed standard procedures for trail management, the round-ups, and so on, which contributed so much romance and color to American history through western stories, movies, and folklore. The grass supply of the vast range of the Great Plains seemed unlimited, and the region was regarded as a permanent paradise for cattlemen.

About 1880 the boom element began to enter this cattle industry. Companies financed chiefly with outside, generally European, capital entered the business. The number of cattle increased rapidly, and soon the range was fully stocked. The land was still largely public domain, unfenced and unclaimed, except for extralegal holdings of the ranchers. Without regulated grazing, the supply of tall grass was soon exhausted, leaving only buffalo grass and grama grass, and shortly these also were threatened in many places.

The lack of adequate provision for winter feed spelled widespread and terrific disaster when the unusually severe winter of 1886–87 came. The decreased grass supply of the summer range, due to the prolonged drought of 1886–95, brought further losses to the cattle companies, and the inroads of homesteaders on the range contributed other difficulties. Because of these circumstances, large-scale cattle ranching was gradually replaced by smaller operations.

The range-cattle industry eventually found farming invading its domain from both the east and west. The railroads had made the development of the industry possible; they also brought in homesteaders and other land seekers who disrupted the range and forced the cattlemen to shift to a ranch basis. The uncertainties of the business, especially the water supply and the problem of winter forage, had long since demonstrated the value of permanent headquarters.

With the decline of gold production in California, the miners turned eastward to the unoccupied valleys and mountain ranges. Their rush into the region of Colorado laid the basis for permanent settlement there. The corresponding occupation of Nevada, Arizona, New Mexico, western Montana, Idaho, and eastern Washington took place during the decade of the Civil War. The need for food supplies for the mining camps led to the beginning of agriculture in the favored parts of the intermountain valleys.

The farmers from the East who pushed into the Great Plains brought with them the eastern ways of farming, but the fact that this was a region with less than 20 inches of rainfall a year foredoomed them to failure except in favored localities and years. In the end the farmers had to develop new methods and crops adapted to the region. In some places irrigation was the permanent solution. In others dry farming became important for the first time in the United States, and as a method it also had to pass through stages of adaptation and experimentation as regards tillage methods, machinery, crops, and rotations.

As long as the grass of the public domain was the main reliance for the grazing of stock, whether cattle, sheep, or horses, no thought was given by their owners to range conservation. The prevailing principle was first come, first served. Besides, the stockmen were unaware of the rudiments of forage growth and requirements of plants. Shortly the indigenous forage plants were being gnawed to the roots and so weakened that they gave place to worthless weeds and annuals or even only dust heaps. The shrubs along the streams were devoured and the meadows dried out, thus giving freshets a chance to tear gashes in the sod and soil. This destruction, which took place both on the open plains and in the intermountain ranges, was accentuated in periods of drought.

The inevitable disasters resulting from the unbridled competition of the stockmen for the grass of the public domain were anticipated in the 1870's by Maj. J. W. Powell and a few other scientists.

Powell strongly urged classification of the remaining public lands and development of a scientific system of survey and disposal for each of the classes defined. The Public Land Commission, authorized by Congress in 1879, investigated the whole land system and proposed general reforms.

In the early 1880's there was a marked quickening of public interest in the conservation of the Nation's remaining natural resources. The attempts to reform the land system during President Cleveland's first administration met with only temporary success. The Federal Government remained committed to the principle of homesteads adopted in 1862 as the main means of developing the West. To this end various supplementary acts, which by their nature acknowledged that the homestead policy was not suitable for the region to which it applied, were passed. Even in 1916, when the

Stock-Raising Homestead Act was enacted, Congress clung to the homestead principle at the same time that it belatedly acknowledged the destiny of much of the land in the West.

Not until the end of the nineteenth century was the necessity for regulating grazing on the public domain generally conceded by stockmen. At a national meeting in Denver in 1898 two divergent proposals were considered. One called for the ceding of the remaining public lands to the States, and this idea continued to have its advocates as late as President Hoover's administration, when it was embraced as the official objective of the executive branch of the Government. The other proposal at Denver urged that the Federal Government lease the public lands for grazing. Being better able to adjust to varying conditions, the sheep interests opposed all suggestions, but many of the cattlemen ultimately favored some form of control similar to that which the Forest Service was gradually working out for the management of the grazing ranges within the national forests. By this system stockmen were issued annual permits to graze a specified number of livestock on a range deemed big enough to support them.

The ultimate solution of the problem was provided by the Taylor Grazing Act of 1934, which undertook "To stop injury to the public grazing lands by preventing overgrazing and soil deterioration; to provide for their orderly use, improvement, and development; to stabilize the livestock industry dependent upon the public range. . . ." To effect these ends, 142,000,000 acres of the public lands were to be organized into grazing districts under the control of the Department of the Interior. It was also given broad powers to develop water power, to carry on soil-erosion control, and to provide for the disposal of land not needed for the grazing districts.

The history of grasslands settlement in the United States reveals definite patterns of utilization that were largely determined by the relationship between the supply of grassland and population.

In most newly settled communities the livestock were turned loose to graze on such grasses and other palatable vegetation as they could find in the natural clearings and woods. While in this stage, the owners of the livestock might be engaged in clearing their first fields for corn and garden crops, but there was nothing even approximating systematic crop farming. Communities settled by group action might hire one or more herders to watch their livestock.

The second stage emerged when the keeping of large numbers of stock by semi-herding methods was combined with the production of crops. In this stage, and sometimes also in the first, the crops rather than the livestock were enclosed with fences of some sort.

The third stage began to develop when the grass on the range became scarce, and the raising of livestock had to be integrated with general farming. With the introduction of this stage, the first steps toward systematic animal husbandry were taken. In some communities, especially in plantation districts and other staple-producing areas, the raising of stock became subordinate to the production of staples and was continued largely for domestic needs. In other communities, notably in the Corn Belt as it moved westward to its present location, livestock continued to have an important place and most of the crops were marketed in the form of animals ready for slaughter. Cattle also gained a dominant place in communities that specialized in dairying.

In this third stage consideration had to be given to grassland, regardless of what the livestock were kept for, because they had to have pasture of some sort during the grazing season and hay for the winter. The farmers might depend on enclosed natural grassland, either clear or cut-over, for considerable time. In the end, however, they had to integrate the grassland with the rest of the farming system. They might try to improve the natural meadows by cursory seeding to tame grasses, by manuring, or even by irrigation.

The nature of the open-range stage of grassland utilization ultimately necessitated not only community but colony-wide and Statewide regulations of various sorts. The depredations of wild animals and Indians led to the hiring of herders and similar safeguards. Most communities also burned the range in order to get a seemingly luxuriant spring growth of grass, regardless of injuries to the soil. The supply of grass also led to regulations as to who could utilize the range. To facilitate identification and to thwart stealing, extensive legislation concerning branding and earmarks became necessary. In the early development of farming communities the relatively small acreage in crops led to the requirement that the crops rather than the range be fenced, but as communities became well settled this practice was usually reversed. Even in the colonial period, this situation with regard to fencing resulted in fence wars.

The limitations and failures of the grass supply led to range wars between ranchers or groups of ranchers and also between cattlemen and sheepmen. Incident to such clashes, associations were formed which, among other things, divided the range into zones of priority for the various herds. Each rancher had to give attention to the water supply needed for his herds. A group of buildings to use as headquarters for the range operations was also necessary. Probably the earliest record in United States history of such headquarters is a court judgment on the Eastern Shore of Virginia in 1634 which refers to the "cowpens" of that time. Except in the southern latitudes, the problem of winter feed shortly pressed for attention. At first this was usually met by making hay of the natural grass. Later fields of tame grasses, legumes, or fodder plants were developed for the purpose. In the end the operations were shifted from the open range on the public domain to ranches on privately owned land. In other words, the range industry became a ranch industry.

Sooner or later individuals who wished to develop farms invaded the domain of the range industry. The result was friction and conflict until one or the other way of life prevailed. The interests of the rancher and the nester clashed inevitably not only along the Atlantic coast in the seventeenth century but in the Great Plains as late as the early twentieth century. Ultimately the issue was usually resolved according to the economic returns from the land. Farming of some sort prevailed in the humid regions and also in semi-arid regions where irrigation and dryland methods could be used. In the semi-arid regions ranching as the most profitable occupation continued on private holdings and on public grazing districts where geographical factors gave it the necessary advantage.

SEA OF GRASS

BY PETER FARB

Peter Farb (1929 —) was born in New York City, educated at Vanderbilt University and Columbia. After brief experience as a magazine editor and advertising writer, he became a full-time writer about the natural sciences. His scientific background includes entomology and biology, but his interest and research have reached out to include all phases of the ecological picture as well as America's prehistory and American Indian culture. He is one of the best informed and most talented of our younger naturalists and he writes with a keen sense of the whole spectrum of interrelated life. This selection is from his Face of North America, *one of the most comprehensive books for the general reader about this continent, its climate, vegetation, soil, geology and natural life, all presented with an acute sense of the big spans of time.*

(*Face of North America; the Natural History of a Continent,* by Peter Farb; Harper & Row, 1963.)

As one approaches the western limit of the eastern forests, the dense green blanket becomes increasingly threadbare. For this is a disputed borderland, in which the trees are victorious over the grasses only in sheltered low places and along streams. These woods are sparse by eastern standards; from an airplane, even in midsummer, it is possible to see down through the canopy of leaves to the forest floor. Elsewhere the grasses are the conquerors; rippled by the wind, their long blades appear to be waves that engulf the lingering forests.

The grasses that have wrenched the land from the forests do not possess the bulk, strength, or longevity of trees. But they are the meek that inherit the soil. No other family of higher plants lives under such a wide range of conditions as the grasses; the number of individual grass plants on the continent is probably much greater than that of any other group of higher plants. These humble growths live in the polar regions and on mountain tops; they endure the dry conditions of deserts, and the constant immersion of marshes and tidal flats. They are efficient and uncomplicated mechanisms for survival and dispersal. A grass stem is constructed of solid joints, from each of which arises a single leaf consisting of a sheath that fits around the stem like a split tube. The flowers are minute, attracting little attention either from human beings or from insects. Since they are wind-pollinated, they need neither fragrance nor inviting colors. Their seeds, too, are minute specks that are carried far by the wind.

Between the Mackenzie River of Canada and the highlands of northern Mexico, there is a vast inland sea of grasses, more than 3000 miles long, bordered on the east and the west by forests. As one travels westward from the Mississippi River, the elevation of the land gradually but persistently rises. So gradual is the upward tilt that in western Kansas one seems to be standing on level land, but this is an illusion; actually it is an upward slope that will gain another 1500 feet before it meets the Rockies. And just as steadily as the land rises toward the west, the rainfall decreases. This is not so obvious in Iowa nor in eastern Kansas, but even here, by degrees, the green of the plants takes on a lighter cast, and more bare soil becomes visible between the growths. Then, between the 98th and 100th meridians, there is an abrupt change. This is the boundary between an agriculture where a farmer can depend on the weather and one where he must keep an anxious eye peeled toward the clouds; for here the winds coming over the Rockies have had nearly all the moisture squeezed out of them, and have not yet accumulated a new supply from the Great Lakes and the Gulf of Mexico.

As a result of this decrease in humidity, the grassland falls into two main subdivisions, with a transition zone between. From Ohio to eastern Oklahoma is the tall-grass prairie, where the native grasses once grew higher than the height of a tall man. Such tall grasses once mantled the whole central heartland of the continent, regardless of differences in soil and topography. These diverse lands had in common a flora of waving grasses dotted with colorful flowers. In this sea of grass during the millennia, deep roots had built a sod so dense that in turning it the homesteaders broke their plows. The characteristic native grasses of the prairie are big and little bluestem and Indian grass; nowadays most of the land they covered makes up the corn belt. To the west of the prairie is a transition zone where grasses do not grow so high, nor as a continuous carpet. June grass, wheat grass, and little bluestem grow in clumps, the spaces between the clumps being filled with an abundance of wildflowers; this is the great winter wheat region. Farther still to the west, in the rain shadow of the Rockies, grow the short grasses of the high plains: grama, needle grass, buffalo grass; today this is an extensive grazing area.

The contrast between the grassland zones is best seen in a drive from east to west across Kansas. At the Missouri border, on the east, the elevation is about 3000 feet below that of the Colorado border on the west; Kansas, in other words, is like a vast tabletop raised toward the west. The eastern portion of the state is rolling and well covered with trees; west of Wichita, around the Great Bend of the Arkansas River, the trees thin out. The westernmost part of Kansas, which is wholly within the short-grass zone, is level and practically treeless. The decrease in the size of plants, owing to the lessened rainfall, is best illustrated as one moves westward by the sunflower, the state flower of Kansas. In the eastern part of the state, sunflowers light up the roadsides from stalks eight feet high. Westward they shrink, not just in the height of their stems, but also in the diameter of their yellow-bordered disks. Finally, at the parched Colorado border, they grow as little wildflowers that one has to stoop down to examine.

Kansas is wheat country, and wheat is a grass—like corn, rye, barley, and oats. From Kansas southward, winter wheat is grown. The seed is sown in the fall and germinates before frost; thus it has a head start and ripens several months ahead of the wheat planted in the spring. Spring wheat is grown north of Kansas, where the climate is too severe for the young plants to survive the winter. Wheat was one of the first plants cultivated by man; ancient kernels discovered in Iraq reveal that there has been little appreciable change in this crop for the last 7000 years. Wheat and the other grains, owing to their remarkable nutritional qualities, have been the cornerstone of many civilizations around the globe. The grain of a cereal is composed of a thin shell that covers the embryo and a food supply for the nourishment of the young plant. This food supply contains carbohydrates, proteins, fats, minerals, and vitamins; that is why a cereal grain comes closer than any other plant to providing an adequate diet.

A corner of northern Kansas was covered by the glaciers; so was almost all of the rich farmland of Iowa. Yet here none of the earmarks of glaciation familiar in the northeastern states are to be seen. There are no boulders that require being piled endlessly into stone fences; there are few glacier-cut valleys. Although moraines are abundant throughout Iowa, Illinois, and Indiana, they are quite unlike those of New England. Whereas the New England glaciers were able to carry huge boulders southward, the rock material carried by the glaciers that descended upon the prairies was made up of fine particles that spread out as a veneer.

Although corn is grown in every mainland state, the tall-grass prairie is the true corn belt; in Iowa one passes for mile after mile through fields of towering deep-green stalks. No other plant, even among the grasses, has a seed-bearing organ quite like the ear of corn. It consists of a specialized flower cluster, enclosed in a husk, which when mature bears several hundred naked seeds. The threads known as cornsilks, which extend beyond the tip of the husk, catch the fine grains of pollen. Each pollen grain develops into a tube that sometimes travels more than ten inches down the silk thread before it reaches the ovary; each ovary in an ear has its own thread and must be fertilized individually in order to produce a kernel. With the aid of man, corn is a most efficient mechanism for producing food; but it would die out if left on its own, because it has no method of seed dispersal. The ear of corn drops to the ground and a hundred seedlings may emerge, growing so closely together that in the competition for water and soil space, all of them die.

Corn originated in the New World and was unknown in Europe until Columbus found it growing in Cuba. The Mound Builders of the Mississippi Valley, the Cliff Dwellers of the Southwest, the Aztecs of Mexico, and the Mayas of Central America all relied almost exclusively on corn. No longer having to hunt and fish for their food, they were given ample time by the abundance of corn to build extremely advanced civilizations, which excelled in mathematics, astronomy, engineering, and art. The oldest fossil remains of corn in North America, which were found in Mexico, date back less than about 5000 years. Much of the development of corn has come within the past three decades, with the widespread use of hybrid corn; today, more than 95 per cent of the corn grown in North America is hybrid. Nevertheless, the idea of crossing varieties to obtain a superior hybrid one was known to the American Indians, who planted rows of different kinds of corn close together, thus effecting cross-pollination. When pollen from different varieties fertilizes an ear, the result is often a varicolored ear, as may be seen in the Indian corn often sold for Halloween and Thanksgiving decorations.

In numerous places throughout the eastern grasslands, trees grow perfectly well when planted by man, even though few trees were found growing naturally by the pioneers. Many theories have been offered to explain why certain places become prairie while others support trees. One of these is that the sod formed by the tall grasses is almost impenetrable to invading plants. A dense network of roots extends many feet down, completely occupying the upper layers of the soil. Many of the grasses may live twenty years or more, and even when they die the soil occupied by their roots is quickly taken over by neighboring grasses. It is nearly impossible for a seedling tree to invade such a soil.

Another theory is that the prevalence of prairie fires in the past favored the growth of grasses over that of trees. A grass fire removes only one year's growth, leaving the roots relatively undisturbed; but when a tree is burned, the growth of decades is destroyed. Within a year or two after a fire, the perennial grasses are flooding the burned area with an abundance of seeds; trees and shrubs, on the other hand, require many years before they reach seed-bearing age. The sharp decrease in fires since this land was settled seems to be tipping the balance in favor of trees and shrubs. The grasslands are at present undergoing an invasion by mesquite and other shrubs, which have spread from their former locations along stream channels into the grassland.

There are still remnants of native prairie that were overlooked by the plow, and that manage to endure as scattered islands surrounded by a growth of alien crops. Only three cultivated plants have been able to gain access to the virgin prairie: asparagus, timothy, and bluegrass. But none of these invaders makes much headway, and they would be promptly eliminated were there not a yearly renewal of their seeds from neighboring cultivated fields. A striking illustration of the endurance of the prairie is seen in railroad and highway rights of way, and along fencerows. These little strips of unbroken prairie have survived as closed communities, although they are bombarded year after year by the seeds of numerous weeds.

The grassland appears almost as monotonous as a placid sea. But its apparent calm is an illusion, for these lands are the scene of a battle each year in which no species is completely victorious, none wholly vanquished. Because the grasses are long-lived, because they reproduce by seeds as well as vegetative growth, and because they all find a hospitable environment in the prairies, there is a continual struggle for light, water, and nutrients. The plant is crowded not only by its neighboring competitors but by its offspring as well.

The result of this competition through the ages has been the development of many compromises among the plants. The root systems of various species grow at different levels in the soil. Each species, as it attempts to enlarge its holdings, meets the opposition of other entrenched species. The struggle for dominance is demonstrated by two major plants of the tall-grass prairie. Big bluestem is able to occupy the good soils and the moist lower slopes, and to exclude its smaller rival, the little bluestem. The little bluestem is only about half the height of its larger relative; but its root system is more efficient for gathering water, and its smaller leaf surface further reduces the total amount of water it needs in order to grow. As a result, little bluestem is dominant on the drier uplands. The ranges of the two grasses overlap on the middle slopes, where there is much jockeying for position. It is only there that they come into conflict; otherwise each fits a niche the other grass is unable to occupy.

Despite the renewal of warfare underground each spring, an undisturbed grassland is a stabilized community. Not by design, but through compromise, each species aids its competitors, and receives benefits in return. The taller plants protect the lower ones from the heat of the sun; the little grasses, in turn, reduce the loss of water from the soil by mulching it with their own prostrate forms. The wildflowers of the prairies are in direct competition with the perennial grasses, but they have made numerous adjustments to ensure their places in the sun. Violet, ground plum, wood sorrel, and cat's paw all flower and produce seeds quickly, before they are overshadowed by the grasses. During the rest of the summer, these low plants grow in the subdued light of the understory; they present little competition to the summer grasses, but they are protected from being dried out by the winds and sun.

Other wildflowers, such as the hawkweed, stake out a territory by growing a tight rosette of leaves that shades a portion of the soil. But the shade cast by the rosette cannot long suppress the vigorous grasses; so as these grow taller, the hawkweed's stem grows taller along with them, keeping the rosette in the sun. Other species vary the method by developing a tall stem before their leaves or blossoms unfold, thus first assuring themselves of access to the sunlight. The autumn flowers manage to survive alongside the spring flowers by making few demands upon the prairie community until it is time for them to blossom; by then, most of the spring-flowering plants have withered away. All of these methods ensure that the grassland soil is utilized to the maximum, thus creating a greater bastion against invasion by newcomers.

Conditions for life in the grasslands differ greatly from those in a forest. A forest-dwelling animal can easily find shelter under the canopy of leaves, but the inhabitants of the grasslands require speed, strength, or the ability to burrow into the ground. To gather the food of the forest, an animal must either be agile like the squirrels, have wings like the birds, or remain small like the insects. The grassland mammals, on the other hand, find an abundance of food, rich in nutrients, only by bending down to nibble it; thus the grasslands are traditionally the home of large grazing mammals.

When European man arrived in the grasslands, bison were its chief inhabitants. Perhaps 60 million bison inhabited North America, living primarily in the grasslands, but in the eastern forests as well; as late as the eighteenth century they roamed in Florida and reached the Atlantic shore in Georgia, the Carolinas, and Chesapeake Bay. Early naturalists who had journeyed into the grasslands described great congregations of bison that extended, tightly packed, as far as the eye could see. The trampling of huge herds cut trails across the continent, which were followed by the pioneers heading west. Many of the railroad routes were laid along beds first leveled by the bison, and the Europeans sweeping westward followed portage paths and passages through the mountains pioneered by the bison.

The heavy tread of the bison trampled the grasses and compacted the soil, creating bare areas in which weeds could gain entrance to the sod. The herds of bison thus were potentially able to destroy the very habitat on which their lives depended. But other animals in the grassland community counteracted the damage done to the soil by the trampling hoofs. Gophers and ground squirrels dug numerous burrows, opening the soil again, allowing air and moisture to penetrate. It has been estimated that in some places the soil-inhabiting rodents of the grassland gave the soil the equivalent of a plowing every twenty years. But these little animals likewise potentially could destroy the habitat. In North Dakota and Manitoba, the heaviest consumer of grass is not the bison, or the pronghorn, or any of the insects; it is a small mole which in places is so abundant that every square foot of soil has several runways. Some species of these meadow mice may populate grasslands in excess of 50 mice per acre. The checks on their population are disease, starvation, and predators. Hawks and owls, snakes and coyotes all take a great annual toll of these little rodents.

In their intimate association with each other, the plants and animals of the grassland had woven a tight but elastic web. In years in which the supply of grasses was reduced by drought, the grazing animals were weakened and fell prey to coyotes; their decline relieved the pressure on the grass, and during the next wet year it recovered. In a year when the grass supply was ample, the rodents multiplied rapidly, whereupon the coyotes switched over to a rodent diet, relieving the pressure on the grazers. With abundant food, the grazers were free from the threat of starvation; since the coyotes were busy with the rodents, the size of the herds increased. When drought returned, the grazers once again went into decline, making more food available for the predators. The balance of life in the grassland can thus be visualized as one that swayed rhythmically, that altered from year to year, but under natural conditions never broke down.

However, as soon as any one strand in the grassland web is broken, the entire web begins to unravel. Extermination of large numbers of bison at the end of the last century caused the grasses to suffer, for the droppings of the huge beasts had served them as a natural fertilizer. Extermination campaigns against hawks and owls caused a corresponding increase in the rodents on which these birds had preyed. The reverberations of a decreased population of birds of prey echoed through the grasslands: as inroads were made on the grass by the multiplying rodents, the grazers suffered from a lessened food supply, and other kinds of predators increased. In places where the prairie grasses suffered from damage by the rodents, wind and water stripped the unprotected soil and deposited it on other areas, smothering the grass.

Driving hour after hour through the prairie today, one catches but a faint glimpse of its former splendor. By 1920, only a few score bison remained in the United States. Since then, many herds, numbering thousands of animals, have been built up at wildlife refuges. In some of these refuges, the grassland is coming back also. At the National Bison Range near Moiese, Montana, for example, there are nearly 500 bison. The original buffalo grass does not grow there, but wheat grass and other native grasses are abundant. Predators such as prairie falcons, horned owls, goshawks, coyotes, and bobcats have moved into the refuge. Gradually, helped by the hand of man, the web of grassland life is being rewoven.

The grassland has produced animals that rely on speed and endurance for safety and to find water and winter forage. Sight also is of survival value in the open spaces of the grassland, and many of the animal inhabitants accordingly possess keen vision. The herd instinct which causes animals to congregate in large groups, and which is much more noticeable in grassland species than in those of forests, is likewise believed to be an aid to survival.

Typical of the grassland dwellers of the continent is the American antelope or pronghorn. (It is not a member of the antelope family of the Old World, and is more properly called simply a pronghorn. Its horns are hollow, like those of goats, although it sheds them as deer do.) It lives solely in the grassland and most particularly in the western short-grass plains. It is well suited for this environment. It possesses remarkable powers of sight, and can spot danger at tremendous distances; by nature it is as wary as a deer. It is the swiftest runner of all mammals on the continent. These provisions for safety are combined with a most efficient signal system that enables it to warn other members of the herd, even when they are a great distance away. The signal is a white patch on the pronghorn's rump; when the animal becomes frightened, its muscles contract so that the white hairs rise and the patch flashes in the sun like a tin pan. In addition, the animal possesses a gland that throws off a musky warning odor at the same time that the white patch is flashed.

Prairie dogs also rely on sight and the herd instinct for protection in the grassland. The prairie dog's real nature is concealed by two inaccurate names. It is not a dog; rather, it is related to the squirrel. Nor does it usually inhabit the prairies, but rather the short-grass plains. Before the plains were settled, prairie-dog towns in many places stretched as far as the eye could see. One group of Texas prairie-dog towns was estimated, probably with some exaggeration, to cover 25,000 square miles, and to have a total population of 400 million animals. But the settlers declared war on the little rodents, and today they have largely disappeared from the Great Plains, except in the national parks and other refuges. The towns that one finds today cover only tens of acres.

The sun-baked soil and sparse grass of a prairie-dog town are dotted with mounds constructed by the animals. The plump, cinnamon-colored rodents sit on their haunches and bark at visitors and one another; they are constantly going and coming, chasing and playing games with each other. A complex pattern of social behavior has developed in these towns. Most mammals are content to live in family groups or small herds, perhaps combining into larger herds at migration time; but the prairie dogs reach a height of sociability. There are complex rules of town government which the young prairie dogs must learn. There are rules to protect the town against attack by predators, and rules to prevent overcrowding of the population.

The landscape of the town is altered to suit the needs of the animals. Any tall grass that happens to grow within the town limits is uprooted, achieving two benefits: predators have less cover by which to infiltrate the town; and the growth of weeds, whose abundant seeds are a source of food, is encouraged. The burrows are intricate pieces of engineering, not simply holes in the ground. There may be upwards of twenty entrances to the acre; each one is in the middle of a mound of soil a foot or two high and about four or five feet across. The digging is usually undertaken immediately after a rain, when the earth is soft and can be easily worked, for the prairie dog's only tools are the long digging claws on its front feet. The elevation of the burrow usually prevents it from being flooded during cloudbursts and also serves as a lookout platform. The rodents have much to be wary about. Destruction comes from the air in the shape of hawks and eagles, on the ground from coyotes, foxes, bobcats, badgers, and ferrets.

The burrow entrance leads into a precipitous tunnel, sometimes descending to a depth of fourteen feet. Then it turns at a right angle, continues horizontally for a distance, and gradually rises. Short branches fork off from this main route. One of them is a grass-lined nest. Another is a flood hatch located at the end of the rise, within a few inches of the surface. When water overtops the mound and pours into the burrow, the prairie dog scrambles to this underground flood hatch. There it is safe, because the inrushing water produces an air pocket in this highest part of the burrow. The flood hatch is the reason why so few prairie dogs are drowned, even though their towns may be inundated completely for several hours.

Each town is divided into numerous "precincts," and animals inhabiting one precinct are unwelcome in another. Occasionally an animal is seen to jump to its hind legs and raise its forefeet into the air, so abruptly that it sometimes falls over backward. At that time it gives a loud yip, a territorial warning to another prairie dog not to trespass upon that precinct. No territorial yip goes unanswered; there are immediate replies from neighboring mounds, and one after another the animals near by jerk themselves into the air and give their loud call. The spread of territorial yips through a town is somewhat like the spread of coughing in a theater; one does not know from exactly which direction the next outburst will come.

Prairie dogs belonging to the same precinct maintain friendly relations and use each other's burrows. They groom each other's fur, and they are constantly at play. Whenever one prairie dog on a patrol along the precinct border sees another, it will scurry alongside and rub noses. That is their means of identifying a fellow member of the precinct; if the animal is an outsider it will not rub noses, but instead run off at the approach of the other.

The imminence of danger produces a call quite unlike that of the territorial yip. One kind of call is merely a warning; upon hearing it, all the prairie dogs of the surrounding precincts immediately stop feeding and sit up alert. A higher-pitched call of alarm causes them all to plunge hurriedly into their burrows. In this way, predators are usually detected long before they reach the town limits. The eyes of prairie dogs are particularly well adapted to spotting any predators in the air; they are placed so high on the head that they are the first part of the animal's body to emerge when it crawls out of its burrow. Most predators leave the town hungry. It is only a lucky hawk that catches an ailing or slow animal far from its burrow. Black-footed ferrets, which can race through the burrows, and badgers, which can dig the prairie dogs out, are more serious threats.

Prairie dogs are comparatively slow breeders; nevertheless, they have developed a remedy for overpopulation. In late spring, after the birth of the young, the adults begin to forage in the suburbs, outside the limits of the town. At first they return every night to their precinct, but gradually they spend more and more time away from it. A few individuals become pioneers, starting new villages miles from the old towns; others find a neighboring precinct that is underpopulated, and appropriate a portion of it. It is during this temporary breakup of the precinct system that expansions and re-adjustments of territory are made; and thus some precincts come to resemble gerrymandered voting districts. By summer the boundaries are again fixed, and the young of the year have learned, from re-prisals taken on them while wandering, just where the boundaries are.

The mounds of the prairie dogs are welcome disruptions of the monotony of the high plains. A traveler coming toward the Rockies from the east is made aware by numerous subtle changes that he has crossed into the high plains. In the vicinity of the 100th meridian —the line of longitude that passes through eastern North Dakota down to western Texas—the colors of the landscape change from muted greens to brown. East of the meridian the annual rainfall is more than twenty inches a year; to the west it is less than twenty.

At approximately the 100th meridian the border of the high plains is also marked by a low, east-facing escarpment. In some places the escarpment forms a quite definite belt of hills or ridges; elsewhere it is absent. It can be clearly seen in southern Canada. In North Dakota, if one looks to the west from a point about 50 miles east of the Missouri River, one can make out a range of low hills between 300 and 400 feet high, which form the edge of the high plains. Pronounced escarpments are found throughout almost the whole length of South Dakota. In southern Kansas they appear as the rugged Red Hills, which swing westward into Oklahoma and then southward into Texas. In many places the escarpment can be recognized as a belt a few miles wide in which considerable erosion has taken place.

To the west of the escarpment, the high plains are as flat as any land surface can ever be. The origins of the high plains go back millions of years, to an uplift of the Rocky Mountains and the ensuing reduction in rainfall to the east. Before the uplift of the Rockies captured the moisture in the winds, the region was one of extensive forests. The surface of the high plains today consists of an overlying mantle of debris brought down from the Rockies by streams. A moist climate like that of the northeastern states is characterized by stream erosion, the taking away of rock materials by water; a dry climate, on the other hand, is usually characterized by stream deposits or building up of the land. A debris-laden stream rushing down from the Rockies is slowed as it reaches the plains, and the debris is deposited as an alluvial fan. The formation of an alluvial fan is due to the dwindling of the river as it rushes out of the mountain. There is rapid evaporation on the hot plains; much water is absorbed by the dry, porous soil; there is little rainfall to keep the river flowing. As the river gradually diminishes in size and volume, it spreads its load of debris at the base of the mountains.

Such deposits gradually fill in the bed of the stream itself; the stream overflows either to the right or to the left, finds a new channel, and repeats the process of deposition there. Since all of the streams issuing from the Rockies build alluvial fans, the result has been that the fans have eventually merged and spread away from the base of the mountains. Through the course of time, the process has laid down a single gentle, sloping plain. The escarpment of the high plains at the 100th meridian marks approximately the farthest eastward extension of this apron of debris from the eroding Rockies.

There are many parts of the high plains, such as the Staked Plains of western Texas and New Mexico, that have been virtually untouched by stream erosion. Instead, they are subject to erosion by wind. The faster the wind blows, the more soil it carries away with it. The particles may be transported only a few feet, or they may travel for hundreds of miles. When the wind dies down, the load of soil is dropped. Anyone driving through the plains in the spring cannot escape the sight of the wind at work. The air is hazy and yellow with countless motes of soil; little clouds of it seem to rise out of the earth. Every year nearly four million acres of agricultural land, on an average, suffer damage from blowing. During the dust bowl years of the 1930's, a total of about eighteen million acres was turned into desert by the winds. Huge clouds of plains dust billowed over New York City and darkened the skies over the city of Washington; throughout the plains themselves, street lights had to be turned on at noon.

Great as the dust storms have been in recent decades, they do not approach in magnitude those that occurred following the retreat of the glaciers. Everywhere in the plains can be seen thick deposits of loess, the name given by geologists to wind-deposited dust. The outwash from the glaciers consisted of immeasurable quantities of powdered rock which, once they had dried, were easily picked up and carried in swirling clouds by the wind. Once aloft, the lighter particles traveled immense distances; there are even loess deposits on the slopes of the Rockies, at altitudes above 10,000 feet. Some of these deposits, more than a hundred feet deep, are revealed where the Missouri and other rivers have cut through them; around Sioux City, Iowa, are towering loess cliffs that bear testimony to the power of the winds and the abundance of dust.

The most violent of all wind phenomena, the tornado, has its greatest occurrence in the plains. Oklahoma, Kansas, Nebraska, and southern Iowa form the heart of the tornado belt; next in frequency are Arkansas, northern Texas, western Missouri, and a long, narrow belt across the deep south from Mississippi to Georgia. Tornadoes may occur practically anywhere in the eastern two thirds of the United States; they almost never occur west of the Rockies. More than 900 tornadoes strike the United States every year, the majority of them in the plains.

A tornado bears a superficial resemblance to the dust devil, a spinning funnel of soil which rarely reaches more than a few hundred feet into the air, and which is often seen on the plains. But there is a great difference between the two. A dust devil is a whirlpool of air created by the heating effects of the sun. It begins at the level of the ground, and occurs only during the day. A tornado, on the other hand, is a funnel of whirling air that begins in the atmosphere and may occur during day or night. No one knows exactly how a tornado is born; one expert asserts that at least 26 weather conditions must coincide before a tornado can develop. A major requirement is that extremely hot air must meet cold air; this condition frequently occurs in the plains and prairies, where hot air from the Gulf of Mexico collides with air that has been cooled by its passage over the Rockies. When the two air masses meet, they try to pass each other, with the result that the air begins to whirl upward, just as water does when it is stirred rapidly.

Only when the tip of the funnel reaches the ground does the tornado cut its long swath of destruction. Its color turns brown, black, or white from the soil or snow it has picked up. No tornado ever measures more than 1300 feet in width where it touches the ground; more often it is not much wider than a city street. Each tornado packs a terrifying punch as a result of the pressure at its edge and the suction in its center. An ordinary fifty-mile-an-hour windstorm can uproot trees; some tornadoes exert pressures a hundred times greater than that. So great is the force exerted by a tornado that it has been known to lift a railroad locomotive off its tracks. Its life is brief; ordinarily it breaks up suddenly and disappears less than three hours after it has first formed.

There are, however, extensive areas in the plains where erosion by water also has occurred, producing the bizarre landscape known as a "badland." This is an area where streams have dug so deeply into soft rock that only pinnacles remain. The badlands are trapped in an endless cycle: since erosion there is very rapid, plants have little chance to become established; because there are few plants to pin down the land, erosion continues to take place rapidly. Badlands originate as a high plateau through which a river flows, leaving bluffs on both sides of its channel. As the river meanders along its course, the zone of bluffs retreats farther from the stream; the tributary streams flowing to join the large mainstream keep pace by likewise cutting deeply into the plateau. The result is a landscape dissected by a maze of channels and gullies.

The most dramatic example of this type of scenery in North America exists at the Badlands National Monument in southwestern South Dakota. There the White River has cut a deep valley into the soft, easily eroded rock of what were once gently rolling hills. The cliffs of the White River have now retreated until in some places they are miles away from the channel. The flat land that today exists between the river and the cliffs was once badland also; but it has been eroded down to a plain as its materials were carried away by the river. The erosional remnants between the gullies have taken on an innumerable variety of strange shapes. There are razor-sharp ridges, complex canyons, knobs and spires.

The badlands of South Dakota are an almost barren world. It has been estimated that about 60 per cent of the land included in the Monument is devoid of vegetation. There are, however, a few trees that manage to survive in this tortured land, usually along the courses of streams. The deep green of scattered small groves of juniper relieves the harshness of the landscape. Peppering the ravines are other trees: cottonwood, elm, boxelder, chokecherry. A remarkable variety of birds can be seen at the Monument, feeding on the seeds of wildflowers and grasses and the fruits of trees and shrubs. From the east come the robin, the black-capped chickadee, the white-breasted nuthatch, the northern cliff swallow, and the goldfinch. In the South Dakota badlands they meet representatives of the western fauna; the western vesper sparrow, the western lark sparrow, the canyon wren, and many others.

It is the life of the past that most often intrigues visitors to the Badlands National Monument. As the sediments poured down from the Rockies, tens of millions of years ago, to form the original upland, numerous kinds of animals were buried. These overlying sediments have now been removed by erosion, uncovering extensive fossil beds. From these fossils it is possible to reconstruct a picture of what the life of the badlands was like some 40 million years ago. This land was once flat, with many swamps, shallow lakes, and sluggish streams. The vegetation was luxuriant and supported many grazing animals, such as horses, camels, and rhinoceroses, as well as rats, mice, squirrels, and rabbits. These animals provided food for predators: tigers, wild dogs, eagles, and owls. This community of the Dakota swamps was utterly obliterated by the mantle of sediments, as much as 2000 feet thick, that poured over it.

The badlands were nearly level in the past, and ultimately they will be level again. Every breeze and each raindrop dislodges additional particles of rock; the spires and pinnacles are continually being undercut and toppled; gullies are incessantly merging to produce flat land. In time, the fissured hillsides will be reduced to gentle mounds, which will become covered with grass. These mats of vegetation will retard erosion and the badlands will become stabilized, as have many other areas of the high plains. This step in the development of the badlands can already be seen in places. Grass, mostly the grama and needle-and-thread of the high plains, extends to the very wall of the badlands. Eventually the sea of grass will engulf the badlands and the landscape will again stretch unbroken to the horizon.

THE PRAIRIES

BY JOSIAH GREGG

Josiah Gregg (1806–1850) was born in Tennessee, grew up in Illinois and Missouri, and had a better-than-average education. Somehow he picked up enough knowledge of medicine and surgery to be called Dr. Gregg, though he never practiced. In 1831 he accompanied a trader's caravan from Independence, Missouri, to Santa Fe, hoping to improve his health. He not only recovered health but decided to become a trader himself and for nine years traveled the Santa Fe Trail as a trader. He kept copious notes and journals and in 1843 wrote a book from them about the Trail and the trade. He took his manuscript to New York where he met John Bigelow, later co-editor with William Cullen Bryant of the New York Evening Post. *Bigelow helped revise the manuscript and found a publisher. The book,* Commerce of the Prairies, *was an immediate success. Gregg returned to the West, served with Doniphan in the Mexican War, made one more Trail trip to Santa Fe in 1849, and went to California. There he died of hunger and exposure during an exploring trip in the winter of 1850. He had a keen eye, encyclopedic interests, and a wide range of knowledge. His book has become a classic in its field. This selection is from its geographic section. I have often wondered whether Gregg or Bigelow was responsible for the somewhat purple patches of writing, illustrated here when the subject is flowers. I suspect Bigelow. Gregg was a factual, practical man.*

(*Commerce of the Prairies*, by Josiah Gregg; New York, 1844; Arthur H. Clark Company, Cleveland, 1905.)

In many of the rich bottoms from the Canadian to Red River, for a distance of one or two hundred miles west of the frontier, is found the celebrated *bois-d'arc* (literally, *bow-wood*), usually corrupted in pronunciation to *bowdark*. It was so named by the French on account of its peculiar fitness for *bows*. This tree is sometimes found with a trunk two or three feet in diameter, but, being much branched, is rarely over forty or fifty feet high. The leaves are large, and it bears a fruit a little resembling the orange in general appearance, though rougher and larger, being four or five inches in diameter; but it is not used for food. The wood is of a beautiful light orange color, and, though coarse, is susceptible of polish. It is one of the hardest, firmest and most durable of timbers, and is much used by wagon-makers and mill-wrights, as well as by the wild Indians, who make bows of the younger growths.

On the Arkansas and especially its southern tributaries as far west as the Verdigris, and up those of Red River nearly to the False Wachita, the bottoms are mostly covered with cane. And scattered over all the south to about the same distance westward, the sassafras abounds, which grows here in every kind of soil and locality.

The celebrated *Cross Timbers* . . . extend from the Brazos, or perhaps from the Colorado of Texas, across the sources of Trinity, traversing Red River above the False Wachita, and thence west of north, to the Red fork of the Arkansas, if not further. It is a rough hilly range of country, and, though not mountainous, may perhaps be considered a prolongation of that chain of low mountains which pass to the northward of Bexar and Austin City in Texas.

The Cross Timbers vary in width from five to thirty miles, and entirely cut off the communication betwixt the interior prairies and those of the great plains. They may be considered as the "fringe" of the great prairies, being a continuous brushy strip, composed of various kinds of undergrowth; such as black-jacks, post-oaks, and in some places hickory, elm, etc., intermixed with a very diminutive dwarf oak, called by the hunters "shin-oak." Most of the timber appears to be kept small by the continual inroads of the "burning prairies;" for, being killed almost annually, it is constantly replaced by cions of undergrowth, so that it becomes more and more dense every reproduction. In some places, however, the oaks are of considerable size, and able to withstand the conflagrations. The under-wood is so matted in many places with grape-vines, green-briars, etc., as to form almost impenetrable "roughs," which served as hiding places for wild beasts, as well as wild Indians; and would, in savage warfare, prove almost as formidable as the hammocks of Florida. . . .

The region of the Cross Timbers is generally well-watered; and is interspersed with romantic and fertile tracts. The bottoms of the tributaries of Red River, even for some distance west of the Cross Timbers (perhaps almost to the U. S. boundary), are mostly very fertile, and timbered with narrow stripes of elm, hackberry, walnut, hickory, mulberry, bur-oak and other rich growths. . . .

With regard to fruits, the Prairies are of course not very plentifully supplied. West of the border, however, for nearly two hundred miles, they are covered, in many places, with the wild strawberry; and the groves lining the streams frequently abound in grapes, plums, persimmons, mulberries, paccans, hackberries, and other "sylvan luxuries." The high prairies beyond, however, are very bare of fruits. The prickly pear may be found over most of the dry plains; but this is neither very palatable nor wholesome, though often eaten by travelers for want of other fruits. Upon the branches of the Canadian, North Fork, and Cimarron, there are, in places, considerable quantities of excellent plums, grapes, chokecherries, gooseberries, and currants—of the latter there are three kinds, black, red, and white. About the ravines and marshy grounds (particularly towards the east) there are different kinds of small onions, with which the traveler may season his fresh meats. On the plains, also, I have met with a species resembling garlic in flavor.

But the flowers are among the most interesting products of the frontier prairies. These gay meadows wear their most fanciful piebald robes from the earliest spring till divested of them by the hoary frosts of autumn. When again winter has fled, but before the grassy green appears, or other vegetation has ventured to peep above the earth, they are bespeckled in many places with a species of erythronium, a pretty lilaceous little flower, which springs from the ground already developed, between a pair of lanceolate leaves, and is soon after in full bloom. But the floriferous region extends only about two hundred miles beyond the border: the high plains are nearly as destitute of flowers as they are of fruits.

The *climate* of most parts of the Prairies is no doubt healthy in the extreme; for a purer atmosphere is hardly to be found. But the cold rains of the "wet season" and the colder snows of winter, with the annoying winds that prevail at nearly all times, often render it very unpleasant. It can hardly be said, it is true, that the Prairies have their regular "dry and rainy seasons;" yet the summers are often so droughty, that, unless some change should be effected in nature's functions, cultivators would generally find it necessary, no doubt, to resort to irrigation. That portion, however, which is conterminous with our western border, and to the distance of nearly two hundred miles westward, in every respect resembles the adjacent States of Missouri and Arkansas in climate. The south is a little disposed to chills and fevers; but the northern portion is as healthy as the most salubrious uplands of Missouri.

MAN AND NATURE

BY GEORGE BIRD GRINNELL

George Bird Grinnell (1849–1938), by his long life and extensive writing, formed one of our rare links with the frontier past and the untamed Indians. He accompanied Custer's Black Hills expedition of 1874 as official naturalist, and the next year was a member of the Ludlow expedition to Yellowstone National Park. He was one of the first of America's insistent conservationists. He had firsthand knowledge of the Indians, particularly those of the West, and wrote many books about them, their way of life, their customs, their beliefs. This selection, from The Story of the Indian, *deals with the Indian's attitude toward and relationship with nature.*

(*The Story of the Indian,* by George Bird Grinnell; D. Appleton & Company, 1895.)

Like the wild bird and the beast, like the cloud and the forest tree, the primitive savage is a part of nature. He is in it and of it. He studies it all through his life. He can read its language. It is the one thing that he knows. He is an observer. Nothing escapes his eye. The signs of the clouds, the blowing of the winds, the movements of birds and animals—all tell him some story. It is by observing these signs, reading them, and acting on them that he procures his food, that he saves himself from his enemies, that he lives his life.

But though a keen observer, the Indian is not a reasoner. He is quick to notice the connection between two events, but often he does not know what that connection is. He constantly mistakes effect for cause, *post hoc* for *propter hoc*. If the wind blows and the waves begin to roll on the surface of the lake, he says that the rolling of the wave causes the blowing of the breeze. The natural phenomena which we understand so little, he does not understand at all. In his attempts to assign causes for them, he gives explanations which are grotesque. The moon wanes because it is sick, and at last it dies and a new one is created; or it grows small because mice are gnawing at its edges, nibbling it away. He hears a grouse rise from the ground with a roar of wings, and concludes that the roar of the thunder must be made by a bird much larger; or he sees an unknown bird rise from the ground, and just as it flies the thunder rolls, hence this bird causes the thunder and is the thunder bird.

To him the sun, moon and stars are persons. The animals, trees and mountains are powers and intelligences. The raven foretells events to come, the wolves talk to him of matters which are happening at a distance. If he is unhappy and prays fervently for help, some animal may take pity on him and assist him by its miraculous power. He understands his own weakness and realizes the strength of the forces of nature. He realizes, too, their incomprehensibility. To him they are mysteries.

The Indian's life is full of things that he does not understand—of the mysterious, of the superhuman. These mysteries he greatly fears, and he prays without ceasing that he may be delivered from the unknown perils which threaten him on every hand. He has a wholesome dread of material dangers, of enemies on the warpath, of bears in the mountains; but far more than these he fears the mysterious powers that surround him—powers which are unseen until they strike, which leave no tracks upon the ground, the smoke of whose fires cannot be seen rising through the clear air. He fears the burning arrow shot by the thunder; the unseen under-water animals which may seize him, as he is crossing stream or lake, and drag him beneath the waves; the invisible darts of evil spirits which cause disease not to be cured by any medicine of roots or herbs; the ghost, terrible not for what it may do, but only because it is a ghost. Against such dangers he feels that he has no defence. So it is that he prays to the sun, the moon, the stars, the mountains, the ghosts, the above-people, and the under-water people. For pity and for protection he appeals to everything in nature that his imagination indues with a power greater than his own.

In an Indian camp it is not the average man that has communication with the other and unseen world. All pray, it is true, but to most of these prayers no answer is vouchsafed. It is only now and then that visions and communications from the supernatural world come to men and women. Those who are thus specially favored are not, so far as we can tell from their histories, particularly deserving. The help that they receive they owe not so much to any good works that they have performed, or to any merit of their own, as to the kindness of heart of the supernatural powers . . . The practice of dreaming for power, an act of penance and self-sacrifice which, when carried out, often secured the pity and help of the supernatural powers . . . seems to have been well-nigh universal among the Indians.

The powers influencing the Indian's life may be either malignant or beneficent, but by far the greater number seem to be well disposed and helpful. Stories about this latter class are much more numerous than those of hurtful powers, and it seems that usually these supernatural beings are easily moved by prayer and accessible to pity. On the other hand, a man who fails to show respect to these forces is likely to die. On the west side of the Rocky Mountains, there is a mountain sheep skull grown into a great pine tree trunk. This is a sacred object, reverenced by all. Once, however, a Nez Percé laughed at his companions because they had offered presents to this skull, and to show that he did not believe in it he shot at it with his gun. The next day as he was traveling along his rifle, accidentally discharged, killed him.

The depths of the water shelter a horde of mysterious inhabitants. Some of them are people, but quite different from those who live on the prairie. Others are animals similar to those which we have on land, while others are monsters. The under-water people use the water fowl—the swans, geese and pelicans—for their dogs; that is, for their beasts of burden. Small water birds are used as messengers by the supernatural powers. The Dakotas and Cheyennes tell us that the under-water monsters have long horns and are covered with hair. The Cheyennes say that they lay eggs, and that any human being who eats one of these eggs, shortly becomes himself one of these water monsters.

With some prairie tribes there seems in early times to have been a tendency to explain the advent of any animal new to them by concluding that it was an under-water animal that had taken to living on the land. Thus, by some, the first white men were thought to be under-water people, just as by others they were believed to be spirits or mysteries. The Piegans tell with much detail how the first horses came up out of a lake. The story which was told me by Almost-a-Dog, and since by other old people, is this:

A long time ago a Piegan warrior's dream told him about a lake far away, where there were some large animals, which were harmless and which he could catch, tame, and use to pack on, like dogs. And, because they were very large and could carry a heavy load, they would be better to use than dogs, on which the people then carried their packs. "Go to this lake," said his dream, "and take with you a rope, so that you can catch these animals."

So the man took a long rope of bull's hide, and went to the shore of the lake, and dug a hole in the sand there, and hid in it. While he watched, he saw many animals come down to the lake to drink. Deer came down and coyotes and elk and buffalo. They all came and drank. After a while, the wind began to blow and the waves to rise and roll upon the beach, saying *sh-h-h-h sh-h-h-h*. At last came a band of large animals, unlike any that the man had ever seen before. They were big like an elk, and had small ears and long tails hanging down. Some were white, and some black, and some red and spotted. The young ones were smaller. When they came down to the water's edge and stopped to drink, his dream said to the man, "Throw your rope and catch one." So the man threw his rope, and caught one of the largest of the animals. It struggled and pulled and dragged the man about, and he was not strong enough to hold it, and at length it pulled the rope out of his hand, and the whole band ran into the lake and under the water and were not seen again. The man went back to camp feeling very sad.

He prayed for help to his dream, which said, "Four times you may try to catch these animals. If in four times trying you do not get them, you will never see them again." Then the man made a sacrifice, and prayed to the Sun and to Old Man, and his dream spoke to him in his sleep, and told him that he was not strong enough to catch a big one, that he ought to try to catch one of the young—that he could hold it. The man went again to the shores of the big lake, and again dug a hole in the sand and lay hidden there. He saw all the animals come down to drink—the deer, the wolves, the elk, and the buffalo. At last the wind began to rise and the waves to roll and say *sh-h-h-h, sh-h-h-h* upon the shore. Then came the band of strange animals to drink at the lake. Again the man threw his rope, and this time he caught one of the young and was able to hold it. He caught all of the young ones out of the band and took them to camp. After they had been there, the mares—the mothers of these colts—came trotting into camp; their udders were full of milk. After them came all the others of the band.

At first the people were afraid of these new animals and would not go near them, but the man who had caught them told everybody that they were harmless. After a time they became tame, so that they did not have to be tied up, but followed the camp about as it moved from place to place. Then the people began to put packs on them, and they called them *po-no-kah'mi-ta*, that is, elk-dog, because they are big and shaped like an elk, and carry a pack like a dog. That is how the Piku'ni got their horses.

If the under-world is peopled with mysterious and terrible inhabitants, not less strange and powerful are those who dwell in the regions of the upper air. There lives the thunder, that fearful one, who strikes without warning, whose bolt shatters the lofty crag, blasts the tallest pine, and fells the strongest animal, a moment before active and full of life. There are the winds, the ghosts, and many other persons, whom sometimes we feel, but never see.

As has been said, the thunder is usually regarded as a great bird, but this appears to have relation merely to the sound that it produces. Often the thunder is described as a person, sometimes as a dreadful man with threatening eyes, or again, young and handsome. Sometimes it is a monster, birdlike only in that it has wings and the power of flight. Thunder is terrible and must be prayed to, and besides this, he brings rain which makes the crops to grow and the berries large and sweet, and for this reason, too, he must be prayed to. The rainstorm and the thunder are scarcely separated in the Indian's mind. Sometimes, when the thunder appears most dangerous, it can be frightened away. A friend of mine was once on the prairie in a very severe storm. The hair of his head and the mane of his horse stood straight out. The thunder was crashing all around him and kept drawing nearer and nearer. The man was very much frightened and did not know what to do, but at length in despair he began to shoot his gun at the thunder, loading as fast as he could, and firing in the direction of the sound. Soon after he began to do this, the thunder commenced to move away and at last ceased altogether.

Some tribes believe that a bitter hostility exists between the thunder birds and the under-water monsters, the birds attacking these last when they see them, and striving to carry them off.

The Rev. J. O. Dorsey tells of a Winnebago Indian, who was said to have been an eye-witness of such a conflict, and who was called on by each of the combatants for assistance in the fight, each promising to reward him for his aid. The man was naturally very much afraid, and was doubtful what part he should take in the combat, but at length he determined to assist the thunder bird and shot an arrow into the water monster. This terminated the fight in favor of the aerial power, which then flew away with its foe. But the wounded under-water monster called back to the man, "Yes, it is true that you may become great, but your relations must die." And it was so. The man did become great, but his relations died. Sometimes, however, arrows shot by man will not injure an under-water animal. It pays no attention to the arrows. . . .

The winter storms of snow and cold are ruled by a person sometimes called the Coldmaker. He is white, not as the white man is white, but rather like the snow, and is clad in white, and rides a white horse. He brings the storm, riding in the midst of it, and some people have the power to call him and bring on a snowstorm.

The wind does not often take material shape and is seldom seen, yet in some cases it speaks to people. Also it is sometimes made a messenger by the ruler. Various causes are assigned for the blowing of the wind, and one of these—told me years ago by an old Blood Indian, who knew the men to whom this happened—is perhaps worth repeating:

A good many years ago the camp was moving from the north down through this country (along Milk River and the headwaters of the Marias). When they got down here they ran out of *l'herbe* and moved up toward the mountains to gather some, and there they saw the Windmaker.

There were three young men who went out to gather *l'herbe*. They went up on the foothills, and as they were going along they saw, down below them in a valley, a strange animal. It was small—the size of a white man's cow, blue-roan in color, and had a very long tail. They stood looking down at it, and said to each other, "What kind of an animal is that?" None of them had ever seen anything like it.

At length, while it was walking about grazing, it raised its head and looked toward them, and they saw that it had very long ears. When it looked toward them, it moved its ears backward and forward two or three times, and at once there came two or three terrible gusts of wind. It turned, and started to trot off toward the mountains, and they followed it. It threw its ears backward and forward, and gusts of wind kept coming. They chased it, and it ran into a piece of timber, in which there was a lake. Here the men separated, one going around the timber on either side of the lake, while the third followed the animal.

When the two men had gone around the timber and came to the further edge of the lake, the wind died down very suddenly. They stood there, waiting and looking for the animal. The man who had followed it saw the tracks going into the lake, and signed to the others to come to him. They, too, saw where it had gone into the water, but although they went all around the lake, they could not see any tracks where it had come out. They waited till dark, but it did not come out of the lake, so they went back to their camp and told the medicine man what they had seen.

Before that the people had never known what it was that made the wind blow, but now, when they had seen this animal, the medicine man decided that it caused the wind, and they called it Windmaker.

The beliefs in animals are as numerous as the tribes—almost as the individuals of the tribes . . . The Dakotas believe that the bear and the wolf exert evil influences, and cause disease and death, while the Pawnees regard them as friendly and helpful. Besides the reverence felt for the buffalo, there are believed to exist certain mysterious buffalo which cannot be killed and have great power.

The Pawnee Indians have a special belief about a little animal which they call ground dog, and which, from their description, I believe to be the black-footed ferret (*Putorius nigripes*). This animal, being nocturnal in habit and, spending most of its time in burrows underground, is seldom seen. The Pawnees believe that if this animal sits up and looks at a man, working its jaws, as if chewing, the entrails of that man will at once be cut to pieces and he will die.

A considerable proportion of the "medicine" performances in any camp have to do with healing. While the Indians are skillful in curing simple ailments and in surgery of a certain kind, there are many more serious diseases which they do not at all comprehend, and for such they have no medical treatment. Such diseases they believe to be caused by evil spirits, which must be driven away by the dream power of the doctor, who relies for help on this power and not on any curative agents. The treatment consists of burning sweet-smelling vegetation to purify the air, of singing and praying to invoke the help of the power, of rattling and making alarming sounds to frighten away the evil spirits, and of sucking and brushing off the skin of the patient to remove the mechanical causes of the disease. The different operations of this healing process have often been described. Usually such treatment gives no relief and the patient dies, but in wounds or other injuries these doctors have success which oftentimes is very remarkable. . . .

A small party of Piegans were camped at Fort Brule, at the mouth of the Marias River, when, one morning about daylight, a war party of enemies rushed upon them. The gates of the fort were barred, so some of the women put up their travois against the stockade and climbed over the walls for shelter, while some dug pits in the ground outside the stockade. A very heavy fight began. Two women and one man were killed just outside the stockade by a lance in the hands of a Cree.

There was another camp of Piegans not far off, and when the fight began one of the Indians ran from Fort Brule and told these others that the Crees were attacking them. A party of warriors hurried down, and when they reached the fort, the Crees began to retreat. The Piegans followed them, and the two parties took their stand on a ridge, the Crees on one side and the Piegans on the other. A Piegan named White Bear was trying to get closer to the enemy, and a Cree crept up close to him and shot him through the body, the ball entering at the kidneys and coming out at the shoulders. His companions dragged the man to camp. He was still breathing when they got him to camp. Soon after he died.

There was an old woman in the camp, a very powerful doctor, and when she saw that the man was dead, she took her buffalo robe and painted it on the head and on the back and down the sides. She covered the body with the painted robe, and then asked for a dish of yellow clay and some water. When these were brought to her, she untied from White Bear's neck the skin of a little mole that he used to carry about, and put this skin in the dish of yellow clay. Then she began to sing her medicine song, and went up to the dead man and caught him by the little finger and shook him and said, "Wake up." At this time the lodge was crowded full, and many stood about looking under the lodge skins, which were raised. The woman would shake the robe on which lay the man, and say, "Wake up; you are wanted to smoke." After she had done this four times, the fourth time she did it, this man moved. When he moved, the old woman asked that the pipe be lighted. This was done and the pipe handed to her, and after taking a small smoke and making a prayer to the ghosts, she said to the young man, "Wake up," and at the same time pulled the robe off him. White Bear staggered to his feet and reached out his hand to take the pipe, but the old woman kept backing away from him, till she came to where stood the dish of yellow chalk with the skin in it. There the man took the pipe and began to smoke, and the blood poured from both the bullet holes. He sat down beside the dish that had the mole in it, and finally lay down and smoked, and when he smoked he blew the smoke toward the mole and the yellow clay. When he had finished smoking he covered the mole skin over with a piece of buckskin, and then after a minute or two took the skin off, and the mole was there alive, scratching and digging in the yellow clay. He lay down beside it, and the mole left the dish, ran over onto his body, went to the bullet hole, put his head in it, and began to pull out clots of blood. After it had done this at one hole, it ran to the other and did the same thing, and when it had done that it went back to the dish and remained there, and White Bear again covered it with the piece of buckskin. Then he took it off, and when he did so, there was nothing there but the stuffed skin. After he had sung a song, White Bear made a speech, saying that he had been dead, but now he had come to life, and that after four nights he would be well. The fourth day he was able to go about.

A few days after he was able to get about, White Bear started out as leader of a war party against the Pend d'Oreilles. One day as they were marching along, he said to his fellows, "I am going ahead to see what I can discover." A war party of the enemy saw him coming, and lay in ambush for him in a ravine. As he was walking along with folded arms, they fired on him, and a ball went through his wrist and through his body. His party was not far behind, and when they heard the shooting, they rushed up and drove off the enemy and saved their leader. When the fight was over White Bear said, "I am badly hurt. We will have to go back."

They started back, and when they reached the camp White Bear was nearly dead. They thought he was going to die. The same doctoring was gone through with that had been performed a few days before, and with the same result. White Bear was cured. . . .

Other stories are told in which the skin of a weasel and a skunk became alive and worked similar cures, and the list might be indefinitely prolonged.

If a white man saw such things as this happen he could not explain them, and would be likely to consider them the work of the devil, or at least of some supernatural power. The Indians cannot explain them either; and believing the evidence before their eyes, they also believe that these things are done by the dream, or the secret helper, of the person who exercises the power.

All these things which we speak of as medicine the Indian calls mysterious, and when he calls them mysterious this only means that they are beyond his power to account for, that they are inexplicable. We say that the Indian calls whisky "medicine water." He really calls it mysterious water—that is, water which acts in a way that he cannot understand, making him dizzy, happy, drunk. In the same way some tribes call the horse "medicine dog" and the gun "medicine iron." He whom we call a medicine man may be a doctor, a healer of diseases; or if he is a juggler, a worker of magic, he is a mystery man. All Indian languages have words which are the equivalents of our word medicine, something with curative properties; but the Indian's translation of "medicine," used in the sense of magical or supernatural, would be mysterious, inexplicable, unaccountable.

The word "medicine," as we use it in this connection, is from the French word for doctor. The early trappers saw the possessors of this supernatural power use it in healing, and called the man who employed it a *médecin* or doctor. From calling the doctor *médecin,* it was an easy transition to call his power by the same name, and the similarity in sound of the English and French words made the term readily adopted by English-speaking people. The term "medicine man" originally meant doctor or healer, but one who effected his cures by supernatural power. So at last "medicine" came to mean this power, and "medicine man" the person who controlled this power, and the notion of curing or healing became in a measure lost.

THE CONTEMPLATIVE TOAD

BY JOSEPH WOOD KRUTCH

Joseph Wood Krutch (1893 —) was fifty-five years old before he wrote his first book that dealt with nature, and it was a book about Thoreau, not nature direct. The next year, 1949, he wrote The Twelve Seasons, *about the Connecticut countryside where he then lived, and since then he has been observing and writing about the natural world almost continuously. In 1951 he moved to Arizona, became a desert dweller, and wrote his first book about that area,* The Desert Year, *from which this selection is taken. His earlier career was devoted primarily to literature and the drama, as critic and teacher, in which field he also wrote many books. His books about nature, of which* The Desert Year *is a good example, are full of keen observation, intense curiosity, and astute insight. Not as cantankerous as Thoreau, he still likes to raise the embarrassing question, toss it in the teeth of the experts, and draw his own conclusions. This piece about the desert spadefoot toad is a good example.*

(*The Desert Year*, by Joseph Wood Krutch; William Sloane Associates, 1952.)

Those toads which surprised me by coming from nowhere after our first big rain and who sang their hallelujah chorus on every side have surprised me again. They have disappeared as mysteriously as they came. The desert floor and the desert air are as toadless as ever. Obviously, they are creatures as moderate as all amphibia should be, and one night of revelry was enough.

The next evening I did, to be sure, hear a few scattered voices, like those of stubborn guests who won't go home when a party is over. But all the rest had lapsed into silence and retired into invisibility. More than a month has passed, and despite one more rain as heavy as that which summoned them forth, not one has made himself heard. Nevertheless, I have a very good way of knowing that I did not dream the night they took over.

Forty-eight hours afterward, the largest of my puddles was swarming with tadpoles quite unaware of the fact that fate had assigned them an impossible situation. One more day of hot sun and the puddle was only a damp spot in the sand, covered at its very center with a mass of what had once been potential toads. Obviously the tadpoles had drawn closer and closer together as the puddle shrank, much as a human community might have concentrated itself as the waters of some rising flood drove all its members to the last remaining area of high ground. And they had been overwhelmed at last by the suffocating air, as human beings might have been by relentless water.

But how on earth do any ever survive to carry on the population which is obviously in quite a flourishing state? This puddle was an unusually large one. So far as I know, there was no other larger (and there is certainly no permanent water) within a mile or two of its position. I took it for granted that the tadpoles of this particular species must turn into toads in a remarkably brief period. But however brief it might be, it was obviously not brief enough to be covered by my puddle's duration. These toads, it would appear, ought to have become extinct in this region long ago. Obviously, they haven't.

Before long, I found that my ignorance was ceasing to be a pleasure. The first thing I discovered was that I need not have determined —as originally I did—to preserve it for a while; it has turned out to be not easy to dispel. My confidence that of course someone could answer all my questions was faith misplaced. No one, it now appears, knows very much more about my toads than I do.

Fortunately, I had captured one of the two-inch adults and I kept him prisoner until I could consult Wright and Wright's authoritative check list of American toads and frogs. It was easy enough to identify him as the Sonoran spadefoot (*Scaphiopus couchii*) who inhabits Arizona, Utah, Mexico, and parts of Texas. He has an eastern relative, not especially uncommon but seldom recognized by the layman. Like all the spadefoots, he is a great digger with his hind legs and he is conveniently distinguished from all the Bufos (the genus to which the common garden toad belongs) by the fact that the contracted pupil of his eye is vertical like a cat's, not round or horizontal like that of the Bufos.

There is, then, no trouble about naming him, but the available information does not go much beyond that. He is believed to mate only once a year and always after a summer rain. At other periods he has been accidentally dug up out of the earth. But in what sort of pool does he successfully raise his family? How much time does he remain buried? Does he come out to eat occasionally during the almost year-long period when he is rarely if ever seen? Finally, how does he like the extraordinary existence which he seems to lead? On these questions, the books cover their silence with the air of not having the space to go in for that sort of thing. Queried face to face, the authorities shrug their shoulders: "Wish I knew."

Now, this situation offers a splendid opportunity for the favorite employment of the amateur in any field—namely, expert-baiting . . . But if one *were* going to bait the biologists (which of course I am not), the line of attack would go something like this: Biologists spend too much time in laboratories—which is a highly reputable occupation—and too little observing creatures who are not specimens but free citizens of their own world. The odor which clings to these scientists is too seldom that of the open air, too often that biologist's odor or sanctity, formaldehyde. They learn an enormous number of the things which can be learned in a laboratory, especially the things which can be learned by dissecting preserved corpses, but comparatively few of the things which it would take a much longer time to find out in the field.

If, for example, you should want to know just what is the difference between a toad and a frog and if, perhaps, you have some vague sort of idea that one spends more time in the water than the other, or that toads are the kind that have (and give) warts, you will promptly be set right. "A toad is a tailless amphibian having a divided sternum, the cartilaginous element of one side overlapping the other; a frog is a tailless amphibian whose sternum is otherwise." Better yet, if all you want is a name, you will either get it or (most improbably unless you have been traveling in some very remote place) you will become famous in very limited circles as the discoverer of a new species, which may even be called Somethingorother smithii after you. But if you want to know more than a name, you may very easily run into difficulty. There are thousands of creatures, some of them quite common in well-frequented places, which are Nomen et praeterea nihil.

Names are important, of course, and it is worth while to make a good deal of fuss over them because otherwise two observers would not know whether or not they were talking about the same creature, and endless confusion would result. But it is a great pity that all information—and, too often, all curiosity—should stop with what is really only a preparation for learning something. Any biologist whose field of interest includes the amphibia would recognize my toad at a glance. Even a rank amateur like myself can, thanks to the care with which keys to the species have been worked out, find his name without difficulty. He is even rather readily distinguished from a very similar species common in the same region and called *Scaphiopus hammondii.* But very little is known about the lives of either of them.

At least since the time of Thoreau, amateurs of natural history have been grumbling about this state of affairs. Thoreau himself, when he got hold of a large and costly monograph on the turtle, was outraged to find that in the whole volume not one word was said about how any turtle conducted his life. Since Thoreau's time, a great deal has been discovered and published concerning the sort of thing which he wanted to know about his fellow creatures. But a century after my time others will probably be complaining, as I am now complaining (mildly) a century after Thoreau's.

This is partly because the distinguishing of species is a relatively easy as well as a rather gratifyingly esoteric business. Any young beginner in academic circles who demonstrates to his colleagues that the members of an accepted species can be divided into two slightly different species gets a very conspicuous good mark against his name. In many cases he even helps along a colleague who, a decade later, will again reduce the two species to one, and get an equally good mark against his. Usually, when further study of a carefully named creature is taken up, the next thing to be investigated is the details of his anatomy—simply because that also can be done in a laboratory and from thoroughly dead specimens. Moreover, since most college teachers have been trained in this sort of thing, the introductory college course almost invariably begins not with the observation of some living creature—and it is certainly only because they were once alive that the dead ones are interesting—but with the dissection of a preserved but still smelly earthworm or frog. It is as though the subject of the course were not, as the catalogues maintain, *bio*logy but rather *thanato*logy instead.

Since I am, by trade, a Professor myself, it hardly becomes me to indulge in contemptuous remarks about "the professors," but a certain amount of it is almost obligatory in a book of this sort. Having discharged the obligation, I shall conclude with one concession and one admission. The concession is that the most important reason why there are so many gaps in the available life histories of even the commoner animals is less the perversity of professors than the fact that there are an awful lot of these common creatures and that actually to follow their lives from day to day is a very difficult, time-consuming task. The admission is that, despite my special interest, the definitive monograph on the life history of *Scaphiopus couchii* will not be written by me.

Certain face-saving things I have, however, undertaken to do. Before disappearing among the bound volumes of *Copeia* and the other technical journals in the library of the University of Arizona, I rescued about a score of the tadpoles from the pool to which a careless Mother Nature had unkindly consigned them. Only later did I discover in Wright and Wright that these tadpoles, unlike other tadpoles of my acquaintance, are carnivorous. Perhaps by preference they are. But mine got such green algae as I could lay hands on, plus wheat germ, now so favorably known as a health food. They ate both eagerly, and they not only thrived but beat by four days an official record—transforming themselves into toads in eleven instead of the official minimum of fifteen days.

The first sign of leg buds had appeared in seven days. Forty-eight hours later those legs were functioning, and two days after that the toads left the water. This all but incredible speed of transformation, so fast indeed that one could all but see the body completely reshaping itself while, in the little insides, the vital organs were at the same time changing over from a water- to an air-breathing mechanism, is obviously the explanation of a part of the mystery. These toads can breed in the desert because instead of requiring water, as most frog and toad tadpoles do, for a period running from three months to two years, they require it for only the short time that at least some rain pools must last.

Mine climbed out of the water into which I had put them, still carrying behind them tails of scarcely reduced size. In the course of twenty-four hours those tails shrank to stubs, like the tail remnant of a fox-terrier, and only rarely, perhaps only by accident, did the toads ever get back even briefly into the water I kept available. Yet, rapid as the transformation was it was not rapid enough to permit the survival of those I had left where nature put them. *Scaphiopus couchii* doesn't ask for much. But like exceptionally modest men, he sometimes doesn't get even the little he thinks he could do with.

The technical journals didn't yield much. Seven or eight years ago, a biologist living in Tucson had noted the sudden appearance and sudden disappearance of my friend the Sonoran spadefoot fifteen or twenty miles from where I observed him—about two weeks earlier in the season and under exactly the same conditions. But he did not raise any tadpoles and I have no local check on the time I established for transformation. Most of the other references were from somewhat less arid parts of *Scaphiopus*' range and they offered little more than guesses that he breeds but once a year—in midsummer—and that he spends most of the rest of his time buried in the sand. . . .

Meanwhile the toadlets to whom I, not nature, played the tender mother have been leading artificial but perhaps not unpleasant lives. In the rough world they would, I presume, have been compelled before now to take refuge underground, at least from time to time. But since I do not know just how soon they would be prepared to endure such desiccation and since I was anxious not to lose them, they have been protected against all rigors. The sand on the bottom of the box to which they have been confined has been slightly sprinkled daily. Theirs is a world where it showers pleasantly every afternoon and where food appears at regular intervals rather than when some luckless bug happens to wander by. They have been given such small insects as I could find, plus bits of meat—waved in front of them on the end of a toothpick—which the more up-and-coming have learned to take, though the stubborner or the stupider will have none of it. They have grown prodigiously and it is worth noting just how high the percentage of viability is under favorable conditions. Of the seventeen original tadpoles, not one failed to become a toad. Of the four toads I kept, only one failed to survive for at least the two months I tended them all in their box. Obviously, were nature as kind as I, the earth would soon be knee-deep in toads.

Most of them I released to make their own way in the world, taking care only to place them in what looked to me like a good place for creatures of their kind. I have decided to keep indefinitely only one—partly to reduce the trouble of feeding, partly because he or she is to change his status from that of a specimen to that of a pet and it is a bad plan to spread affection too thin. I have bestowed a name —Ina, in honor of the road near which the original puddle collected —and thus I have determined that, whatever anatomy may say, my toad is, by human convention, a she.

All her brothers and sisters had the habit of digging little resting pits for themselves in the damp sand, and once or twice an individual buried himself completely. After their numbers had been reduced, a favorite refuge for those who remained was the narrow crevice between the sand and the edge of a water saucer in which they exhibited otherwise little interest. The daily shower usually brought them out, but most of the time they just sat.

At the present moment Ina is, as usual, resting—though I don't know from what—in a little cup which her body exactly fits. Her body long ago assumed perfectly the shape of a toad, which is a shape not without dignity and charm if one is broad-minded enough to accept it. She measures well over an inch from the tip of her nose to the place where her tail would be had she cared to keep it. And since the tadpole from which she developed was only one-fifth of an inch, exclusive of tail, I calculate that she has increased her weight one hundred and twenty-five fold; which is as though a human baby were to reach eight hundred pounds in a similar period.

Last night she had raw spareribs for dinner and seemed to find it a tasty dish. But of course I don't know what effect an unusual and probably unusually plentiful diet, as well as other artificial conditions, have had upon her growth. Indeed, I know very little about what her history would have been had she been leading the normal life of her species. And that, of course, is the trouble with laboratory specimens, to say nothing of pets like Ina.

Had I so much as aspired clumsily to science, I should have divided my seventeen baby toads into groups, tried to find out how soon each could endure a given degree of desiccation, what they would do if food was denied them, etc., etc. Even then, to be sure, it would still have been no satisfactory substitute for an attempt to live with the toads in the field, at least as far as that is humanly possible. Going to an opposite extreme, I made a pet of Ina; I am probably over-solicitous of her comfort; and letting science go hang, I grumble mildly at "the professors" for not having found out for me what I am not taking the trouble to learn even as well as I might.

OÑATE GOES EAST

BY DON JUAN DE OÑATE

Don Juan de Oñate (c.1555–1616c.) was a Spanish explorer and Governor of New Mexico from 1595 to 1608. He founded Santa Fe in 1605. In 1601 he led an expedition to the northeast and penetrated as far as modern Kansas, possibly reaching the site of present-day Wichita. It was one of the great Spanish explorations of that unknown area, though it led to no settlement or actual conquest. The account of the expedition, though signed by Oñate, was written either by an unknown and unhonored secretary, or possibly by Gaspar de Villagrá, who is known to have written other accounts of Oñate's travels. Whoever it was, he had the good sense and ability to describe the country and its natural history in more than usual detail. This selection is from the Oñate report to his superiors and deals with the period from late June into October, 1601.

(*True Account of the Expedition of Oñate Toward the East—1601*, by Don Juan de Oñate.)

The most necessary things having been arranged for the journey, with the supply of provisions, arms, ammunition, and other requisite military stores, with more than seventy picked men for the expedition, all very well equipped, more than seven hundred horses and mules, six mule carts, and two carts drawn by oxen conveying four pieces of artillery, and with servants to carry the necessary baggage, the journey was begun this year of 1601, the said adelantado, Don Juan de Oñate, governor and captain-general, going as commander, with Vicente de Caldivar Mendoca as his maese de campo and sargento mayor, and two religious of the order of our father San Francisco, Fray Francisco de Velasco, priest, and Fray Pedro de Vergara, lay brother. For reasons which prevented all the people from setting out together, it was necessary that some should go out ahead of the others to a convenient place where all should unite. The first left this camp of San Gabriel on the 23d of the month of June, eve of the Most Blessed Precursor, San Juan Bautista, and having travelled for days they reached the post or pueblo which is called Galisteo, which is one of these first settlements.

There the greater part of the men came together in five or six days, and from there they commenced to march toward the east; and although at two leagues from this post there arose the difficulty of a large mountain which it was feared the carts could not ascend, our Lord was pleased to overcome it by opening a road through which they passed very easily. Having travelled five days we all came to a river in an opening, with peaceful waters, covered with shady groves of trees, some bearing fruits, and with very good fish. Having reached the river on the eve of the learned and seraphic San Buenaventura, we named it San Buenaventura River [now the Pecos].

Next day we continued through some extensive plains with very abundant pasturage to another river which they call River of the Bagres [now the Gallinas] and justly so, because of the many catfish which it contains. After the horses had rested we continued our journey, always going east, and in three days arrived at another river, which we named Magdalena [now the Canadian], having reached it on her day. Although at first it did not appear promising, we having seen it at a point where it flowed sluggishly among some rocks, and as its banks were not inviting at this point, yet next day and on the other days during which we travelled along it we found it to be so verdant, pleasant, and so covered with vines and other fruits on all sides that we clearly saw that it was one of the best rivers which we had seen in all the Indies. Here some Indians of the nation called Apache came out with signs of peace. The governor and the other men who were with him made them so many presents that they felt compelled, in view of the small number who had come at the first to see us, to return, and in a little while to come back to our camp with men, women and children, who ratified [the actions of the others] by raising their hands to the sun, which is the ceremony they use as a sign of friendship, and brought to us some small black and yellow fruit of the size of small tomatoes, which is plentiful on all that river. It was as healthful as it was pleasant to taste, for although eaten freely it injured no one.

We took joyous leave and, enjoying the great improvement in the land which we saw each day, we travelled on, following the course of this river, although upon entering the plains which they call Cibola or Cebolo we encountered some openings of rocks half detached, which are those which the mountains of this land give off. They caused the carts trouble, but with the great diligence of the good soldiers who were in charge of them they passed this difficult threshold very well and came out at some very extensive and pleasant plains, where scarcely any mountains like those passed could be seen.

Learning from the guide whom we were taking with us that all the country was now level, we began to travel with greater rapidity and with pleasure occasioned by the coming of the maese de campo with the rest of the men who remained behind. And like good soldiers, desirous of serving God our Lord and his Majesty, they were undismayed by the absence of four or five cowardly soldiers, who, frightened by military service as by a nightmare, turned their backs, just when the hopes of seeing grander things were becoming brighter. For these the country promised, since each day, as we descended, it seemed warmer, and it doubtless was warmer than the settlements from whence we had started.

At times it became necessary for us to depart from the main river in order to find a road for the carts; and although we feared the lack of watering places for the cattle, there are so many in this country that throughout the journey at distances of three or four leagues there was always sufficient water for the cattle and for the men; and in many places there were springs of very good water and groves of trees.

In some places we came across camps of people of the Apache nation, who are the ones who possess these plains, and who, having neither fixed place nor site of their own, go from place to place with the cattle always following them. We were not disturbed by them at all, although we were in their land, nor did any Indian become impertinent. We therefore passed on, always close to the river, and although on one day we might be delayed in our journey by a very heavy rain, such as are very common in those plains, on the following day and thereafter we journeyed on, sometimes crossing the river at very good fords.

Each day the land through which we were travelling became better, and the luxury of an abundance of fish from the river greatly alleviated the hardships of the journey. And the fruits gave no less pleasure, particularly the plums, of a hundred thousand different kinds, as mellow and good as those which grow in the choicest orchards of our land. They are so good that although eaten by thousands they never injured anybody. The trees were small, but their fruit was more plentiful than their leaves, and they were so abundant that in more than one hundred and fifty leagues, hardly a day passed without seeing groves of them, and also of grapevines such that although they hid the view in many places they produced sweet and delicious grapes. . . .

Proceeding on the day of the Glorious Levite and Martyr, San Lorenzo, God was pleased that we should begin to see those most monstrous cattle called cibola. Although they were very fleet of foot, on this day four or five of the bulls were killed, which caused great rejoicing. On the following day, continuing our journey, we now saw great droves of bulls and cows, and from there on the multitude which we saw was so great that it might be considered a falsehood by one who had not seen them, for, according to the judgment of all of us who were in any army, nearly every day and wherever we went as many cattle came out as are to be found in the largest ranches of New Spain; and they were so tame that nearly always, unless they were chased or frightened, they remained quiet and did not flee. The flesh of these cattle is very good, and very much better than that of our cows. In general they are very fat, especially the cows, and almost all have a great deal of tallow. By experience we noted that they do not become angry like our cattle, and are never dangerous.

All these cattle are of one color, namely brown, and it was a great marvel to see a white bull in such a multitude. Their form is so frightful that one can only infer that they are a mixture of different animals. The bulls and the cows alike are humped, the curvature extending the whole length of the back and even over the shoulders. And although the entire body is covered with wool, on the hump, from the middle of the body to the head, the breast, and the fore-legs, to just above the knee, the wool is much thicker, and so fine and soft that it could be spun and woven like that of the Castilian sheep. It is a very savage animal, and is incomparably larger than our cattle, although it looks small because of its short legs. Its hide is of the thickness of that of our cattle, and the native Indians are so expert in dressing the hides that they convert them into clothing. This river is thickly covered on all sides with these cattle and with another not less wonderful, consisting of deer which are as large as large horses. They travel in droves of two and three hundred and their deformity causes one to wonder whether they are deer or some other animal [possibly wapiti, or American elk].

Having travelled to reach this place one hundred and eleven leagues, it became necessary to leave the river, as there appeared ahead some sand dunes [Antelope Hills]; and turning from the east to the north, we travelled up a small stream until we discovered the great plains covered with innumerable cattle. We found constantly better roads and better land, such that the carts could travel without hindrance or difficulty, and although we encountered some large ravines and broken hills, nowhere were there any over which the carts had to pass, as the land was in general level and very easy to traverse. We continued in this direction for some days, along two small streams [Beaver Creek (North Fork) and Cimarron River] which flowed toward the east, like the one previously mentioned. We wandered from the direction we had been following, though it did not frighten us much, as the land was so level that daily the men became lost in it by separating themselves for but a short distance from us, as a result of which it was necessary to reconnoitre the country from some of the stopping places. Therefore the camp continued its march by the most direct route possible.

In order to further insure our safety, the governor and adelantado decided to send ahead the maese de campo with some companions, and, with the lucky star which even guides him, in a short time he returned, having found many signs of people, and a country full of pasture lands, which was the matter of deepest concern, since they had been lacking for several days, as there had been none for many leagues, for the fields there were covered with flowers of a thousand different kinds, so thick that they choked the pasture. The cattle of this territory must eat these flowers far better than ours are wont to do, because wherever they were there were multitudes of cattle. Great was the joy felt by all at this good news, because it was what they were hoping for. With the forethought and diligence of the maese de campo, which, like a good soldier, he always displayed in matters of war, he had his people prepared and ordered for whatever might happen; and all together we continued our journey and route and reached a small river, carrying little water but so grown with timber that its banks resembled thickly wooded mountains. Here we found many walnut trees loaded with nuts which were nearly as good as those of our country, the trees being taller and having more abundant foliage, and the land being so grown with pasture that it could scarcely be seen. Having slept one night in this pleasant spot, we went on next day three leagues from this point to where flowed a river carrying more water than the last one, and with many fish and larger groves, both of walnuts and of oak, and other valuable timbers. The land was better than that which we had hitherto seen, so good indeed that all said that they never had seen any better in their lives. The cattle were innumerable, and of all kinds of game there was a great abundance—Castilian partridges, turkeys, deer, and hares. . . .

[Indians then] guided us to a river [the Arkansas] seven leagues from this place, with wonderful banks, and, although level, so densely wooded that the trees formed thick and wide groves. Here we found a small fruit the size of the wild pear or yellow sapodilla, of very good flavor. The river contained an abundance of very good fish, and although at some points it had good fords, in other parts it was extremely deep and vessels could sail on it with ease. It flowed due east, and its waters were fresh and pleasant to taste. Here the land was fertile and much better than that which we had passed. The pastures were so good that in many places the grass was high enough to conceal a horse. . . .

We set out from this place the next day, and, leaving the river and passing through some pleasant plains, after having travelled four leagues we began to see people who appeared upon some elevations of a hill. Although hostile to this nation they came on, inviting us to battle and war, shouting and throwing dirt into the air, which is the sign used in all this region to proclaim cruel war. Three or four hundred people awaited us in peace, and by the signs which one side was able to make to the other we were assured of friendship. Peace being made, some of these people came to us, and throwing among us some beads which they wore about their necks, proclaimed themselves our friends. They invited us to their houses, but as it was already late it was not possible to go that day, and it became necessary to go to the banks of a large river called the Rio de San Francisco, whose banks in these parts were most beautiful to look upon and were covered with mulberry trees and other trees bearing fruit of very fine flavor. Many people constantly came and went to see us, bringing ears of maize, which were the first we had seen in this good country, and some round loaves of bread, as large as shields and three or four fingers thick, made of the same maize. . . .

We remained here for one day in this pleasant spot surrounded on all sides by fields of maize and crops of the Indians. The stalks of the maize were as high as that of New Spain and in many places even higher. The land was so rich that, having harvested the maize, a new growth of a span in height had sprung up over a large portion of the same ground, without any cultivation or labor other than the removal of the weeds and the making of holes where they planted the maize. There were many beans, some gourds, and, between the fields, some plum trees. The crops were not irrigated but dependent on the rains, which, as we noted, must be very regular in that land, because in the month of October it rained as it does in August in New Spain. It was thought certain that it had a warm climate, for the people we saw went about naked, although they wore skins. Like the other settled Indians they utilize cattle in large numbers. It is incredible how many there are in that land.

JOURNEY TO THE ARKANSAS

BY FRANCIS PARKMAN

Francis Parkman (1823–1893) was born in Boston and educated at Harvard where he also studied law "for the mental training it offered," though he never practiced. Most of his vacation time was spent exploring the woods and wildernesses of New England, on foot or in a canoe. He seemed to know early that he would be a historian, and immediately after college he went to St. Louis and spent some months traveling from there into the frontier country along the Oregon Trail, living with Indians and trappers and learning at firsthand ways of life that vanished only a few years later. It was his only major expedition, for the rigors of it broke his uncertain health. During a long convalescence he dictated an account of the trip, his first book, published in 1849 as The California and Oregon Trail, *a title later shortened to* The Oregon Trail. *The rest of his life was plagued by physical and mental illness and by partial blindness, but he wrote some of the most vigorous and authoritative history of the nineteenth century. His collected work runs to twenty volumes. He had both a keen narrative sense and a high respect for original source material, using it as none had used it before him. But his* The Oregon Trail, *from which this selection is taken, remains a classic example of the firsthand account of frontier life, with all his youthful vigor and sense of discovery.*

(*The Oregon Trail*, by Francis Parkman; first published in 1849.)

On the day of my arrival at Fort Laramie, Shaw and I were lounging on two buffalo-robes in the large apartment hospitably assigned to us; Henry Chatillon also was present, busy about the harness and weapons, which had been brought into the room, and two or three Indians were crouching on the floor, eyeing us with their fixed, unwavering gaze.

"I have been well off here," said Shaw, "in all respects but one; there is no good *shongsasha* to be had for love or money."

I gave him a small leather bag containing some of excellent quality, which I had brought from the Black Hills. "Now, Henry," said he, "hand me Papin's chopping-board, or give it to that Indian, and let him cut the mixture; they understand it better than any white man."

The Indian, without saying a word, mixed the bark and the tobacco in due proportions, filled the pipe, and lighted it. This done, my companion and I proceeded to deliberate on our future course of proceeding; first, however, Shaw acquainted me with some incidents which had occurred at the fort during my absence.

About a week before, four men had arrived from beyond the mountains: Sublette, Reddick, and two others. Just before reaching the fort, they had met a large party of Indians, chiefly young men. All of them belonged to the village of our old friend Smoke, who, with his whole band of adherents, professed the greatest friendship for the whites. The travellers therefore approached and began to converse without the least suspicion. Suddenly, however, their bridles were seized, and they were ordered to dismount. Instead of complying, they lashed their horses, and broke away from the Indians.

As they galloped off, they heard a yell behind them, with a burst of derisive laughter, and the reports of several guns. None of them were hurt, though Reddick's bridle-rein was cut by a bullet within an inch of his hand. After this taste of Indian manners, they felt for the moment no disposition to encounter farther risks. They intended to pursue the route southward along the foot of the mountains to Bent's Fort; and as our plans coincided with theirs, they proposed to join forces. Finding, however, that I did not return, they grew impatient of inaction, forgot their late danger, and set out without us, promising to wait our arrival at Bent's Fort. From thence we were to make the long journey to the settlements in company, as the path was not a little dangerous, being infested by hostile Pawnees and Camanches.

We expected, on reaching Bent's Fort, to find there still another reinforcement. A young Kentuckian had come out to the mountains with Russel's party of California emigrants. One of his chief objects, as he gave out, was to kill an Indian; an exploit which he afterwards succeeded in achieving, much to the jeopardy of ourselves, and others who had to pass through the country of the dead Pawnee's enraged relatives. Having become disgusted with his emigrant associates, he left them, and had some time before set out with a party of companions for the head of the Arkansas. He left us a letter, to say that he would wait until we arrived at Bent's Fort, and accompany us thence to the settlements. When, however, he came to the fort, he found there a party of forty men about to make the homeward journey, and wisely preferred to avail himself of so strong an escort. Sublette and his companions also joined this company; so that on reaching Bent's Fort, some six weeks after, we found ourselves deserted by our allies and thrown once more upon our own resources.

On the fourth of August, early in the afternoon, we bade a final adieu to the hospitable gateway of Fort Laramie. Again Shaw and I were riding side by side on the prairie. For the first fifty miles we had companions with us: Troché, a trapper, and Rouville, a nondescript in the employ of the Fur Company, who were going to join the trader Bisonette at his encampment near the head of Horse Creek. We rode only six or eight miles that afternoon before we came to a little brook traversing the barren prairie. All along its course grew copses of young wild-cherry trees, loaded with ripe fruit, and almost concealing the gliding thread of water with their dense growth. Here we encamped; and being too indolent to pitch our tent, we flung our saddles on the ground, spread a pair of buffalo-robes, lay down upon them, and began to smoke.

Meanwhile Deslauriers busied himself with his frying-pan, and Raymond stood guard over the band of grazing horses. Deslauriers had an active assistant in Rouville, who professed great skill in the culinary art, and, seizing upon a fork, began to lend his aid in cooking supper. Indeed, according to his own belief, Rouville was a man of universal knowledge, and he lost no opportunity to display his manifold accomplishments. He had been a circus-rider at St. Louis, and once he rode round Fort Laramie on his head, to the utter bewilderment of the Indians. He was also noted as the wit of the fort; and as he had considerable humor and abundant vivacity, he contributed more that night to the liveliness of the camp than all the rest of the party put together. At one instant he would kneel by Deslauriers, instructing him in the true method of frying antelope-steaks, then he would come and seat himself at our side, dilating upon the correct fashion of braiding up a horse's tail, telling apocryphal stories how he had killed a buffalo bull with a knife, having first cut off his tail when at full speed, or relating whimsical anecdotes of the *bourgeois* Papin. At last he snatched up a volume of Shakespeare that was lying on the grass, and halted and stumbled through a line or two to prove that he could read. He went gamboling about the camp, chattering like some frolicsome ape; and whatever he was doing at one moment, the presumption was a sure one that he would not be doing it the next. His companion Troché sat silently on the grass, not speaking a word, but keeping a vigilant eye on a very ugly little Utah squaw, of whom he was extremely jealous.

On the next day we travelled farther, crossing the wide sterile basin called "Goché's Hole." Towards night we became involved among ravines; and being unable to find water, our journey was protracted to a very late hour. On the next morning we had to pass a long line of bluffs, whose raw sides, wrought upon by rains and storms, were of a ghastly whiteness most oppressive to the sight. As we ascended a gap in these hills, the way was marked by huge footprints, like those of a human giant. They were the tracks of the grizzly bear, of which we had also seen abundance on the day before.

Immediately after this we were crossing a barren plain, spreading in long and gentle undulations to the horizon. Though the sun was bright, there was a light haze in the atmosphere. The distant hills assumed strange, distorted forms in the mirage, and the edge of the horizon was continually changing its aspect. Shaw and I were riding together, and Henry Chatillon was a few rods before us, when he stopped his horse suddenly, and turning round with the peculiar earnest expression which he always wore when excited, called us to come forward. We galloped to his side. Henry pointed towards a black speck on the gray swell of the prairie, apparently about a mile off. "It must be a bear," said he; "come, now we shall all have some sport. Better fun to fight him than to fight an old buffalo bull; grizzly bear so strong and smart."

So we all galloped forward together, prepared for a hard fight; for these bears, though clumsy in appearance, are incredibly fierce and active. The swell of the prairie concealed the black object from our view. Immediately after it appeared again. But now it seemed very near to us; and as we looked at it in astonishment, it suddenly separated into two parts, each of which took wing and flew away. We stopped our horses and looked at Henry, whose face exhibited a curious mixture of mirth and mortification. His eye had been so completely deceived by the peculiar atmosphere that he had mistaken two large crows at the distance of fifty rods for a grizzly bear a mile off. To the journey's end Henry never heard the last of the grizzly bear with wings.

In the afternoon we came to the foot of a considerable hill. As we ascended it, Rouville began to ask questions concerning our condition and prospects at home, and Shaw was edifying him with an account of an imaginary wife and child, to which he listened with implicit faith. Reaching the top of the hill, we saw the windings of Horse Creek on the plains below us, and a little on the left we could distinguish the camp of Bisonette among the trees and copses along the course of the stream. Rouville's face assumed just then a ludicrously blank expression. We inquired what was the matter; when it appeared that Bisonette had sent him from this place to Fort Laramie with the sole object of bringing back a supply of tobacco. Our rattle-brain friend, from the time of his reaching the fort up to the present moment, had entirely forgotten the object of his journey, and had ridden a dangerous hundred miles for nothing. Descending to Horse Creek, we forded it, and on the opposite bank a solitary Indian sat on horseback under a tree. He said nothing, but turned and led the way towards the camp.

Bisonette had made choice of an admirable position. The stream, with its thick growth of trees, enclosed on three sides a wide green meadow, where about forty Dahcotah lodges were pitched in a circle, and beyond them a few lodges of the friendly Shiennes. Bisonette himself lived in the Indian manner. Riding up to his lodge, we found him seated at the head of it, surrounded by various appliances of comfort not common on the prairie. His squaw was near him, and rosy children were scrambling about in printed calico gowns; Paul Dorion, also, with his leathery face and old white capote, was seated in the lodge, together with Antoine Le Rouge, a half-breed Pawnee, Sibille, a trader, and several other white men.

"It will do you no harm," said Bisonette, "to stay here with us for a day or two, before you start for the Pueblo."

We accepted the invitation, and pitched our tent on a rising ground above the camp and close to the trees. Bisonette soon invited us to a feast, and we suffered abundance of the same sort of attention from his Indian associates. The reader may possibly recollect that when I joined the Indian village, beyond the Black Hills, I found that a few families were absent, having declined to pass the mountains along with the rest. The Indians in Bisonette's camp consisted of these very families, and many of them came to me that evening to inquire after their relatives and friends. They were not a little mortified to learn that while they, from their own timidity and indolence, were almost in a starving condition, the rest of the village had provided their lodges for the next season, laid in a great stock of provisions, and were living in abundance. Bisonette's companions had been sustaining themselves for some time on wild cherries, which the squaws pounded, stones and all, and spread on buffalo-robes to dry in the sun; they were then eaten without farther preparation, or used as an ingredient in various delectable compounds.

On the next day, the camp was in commotion with a new arrival. A single Indian had come with his family from the Arkansas. As he passed among the lodges, he put on an expression of unusual dignity and importance, and gave out that he had brought great news to tell the whites. Soon after the squaws had pitched his lodge, he sent his little son to invite all the white men and all the more distinguished Indians to a feast. The guests arrived and sat wedged together, shoulder to shoulder, within the hot and suffocating lodge. The Stabber, for that was our entertainer's name, had killed an old buffalo bull on his way. This veteran's boiled tripe, tougher than leather, formed the main item of the repast. For the rest, it consisted of wild cherries and grease boiled together in a large copper kettle. The feast was distributed, and for a moment all was silent, strenuous exertion; then each guest, though with one or two exceptions, turned his wooden dish bottom upwards to prove that he had done full justice to his entertainer's hospitality.

The Stabber next produced his chopping-board, on which he prepared the mixture for smoking, and filled several pipes, which circulated among the company. This done, he seated himself upright on his couch, and began with much gesticulation to tell his story. I will not repeat his childish jargon. It was so entangled, like the greater part of an Indian's stories, with absurd and contradictory details, that it was almost impossible to disengage from it a single particle of truth. All that we could gather was the following:—

He had been on the Arkansas, and there he had seen six great war-parties of whites. He had never believed before that the whole world contained half so many white men. They all had large horses, long knives, and short rifles, and some of them were dressed alike in the most splendid war-dresses he had ever seen. From this account it was clear that bodies of dragoons and perhaps also of volunteer cavalry had passed up the Arkansas. The Stabber had also seen a great many of the white lodges of the Meneaska, drawn by their long-horned buffalo. These could be nothing else than covered ox-wagons, used, no doubt, in transporting stores for the troops. Soon after seeing this, our host had met an Indian who had lately come from among the Camanches, who had told him that all the Mexicans had gone out to a great buffalo hunt; that the Americans had hid themselves in a ravine; and that when the Mexicans had shot away all their arrows, the Americans fired their guns, raised their war-whoop, rushed out, and killed them all. We could only infer from this, that war had been declared with Mexico, and a battle fought in which the Americans were victorious. When, some weeks after, we arrived at the Pueblo, we heard of General Kearney's march up the Arkansas, and of General Taylor's victories at Matamoras.

As the sun was setting that evening a crowd gathered on the plain by the side of our tent, to try the speed of their horses. These were of every shape, size, and color. Some came from California, some from the States, some from among the mountains, and some from the wild bands of the prairie. They were of every hue, white, black, red, and gray, or mottled and clouded with a strange variety of colors. They all had a wild and startled look, very different from the sober aspect of a well-bred city steed. Those most noted for swiftness and spirit were decorated with eagle feathers dangling from their manes and tails. Fifty or sixty Dahcotah were present, wrapped from head to foot in their heavy robes of whitened hide. There were also a considerable number of the Shiennes, many of whom wore gaudy Mexican ponchos, swathed around their shoulders, but leaving the right arm bare. Mingled among the crowd of Indians was a number of Canadians, chiefly in the employ of Bisonette,—men whose home is the wilderness, and who love the camp-fire better than the domestic hearth. They are contented and happy in the midst of hardship, privation, and danger. Their cheerfulness and gayety is irrepressible, and no people on earth understand better how "to daff the world aside and bid it pass." Besides these, were two or three half-breeds, a race of rather extraordinary composition, being according to the common saying half Indian, half white man, and half devil.

Antoine Le Rouge was the most conspicuous among them, with his loose trousers and fluttering calico shirt. A handkerchief was bound round his head to confine his black snaky hair, and his small eyes twinkled beneath it with a mischievous lustre. He had a fine cream-colored horse, whose speed he must needs try along with the rest. So he threw off the rude high-peaked saddle, and substituting a piece of buffalo-robe, leaped lightly into his seat. The space was cleared, the word was given, and he and his Indian rival darted out like lightning from among the crowd, each stretching forward over his horse's neck and plying his heavy Indian whip with might and main. A moment, and both were lost in the gloom; but Antoine soon came riding back victorious, exultingly patting the neck of his quivering and panting horse.

About midnight, as I lay asleep, wrapped in a buffalo-robe on the ground by the side of our cart, Raymond came and woke me. Something, he said, was going forward which I would like to see. Looking down into the camp, I saw on the farther side of it a great number of Indians gathered about a fire, the bright glare of which made them visible through the thick darkness; while from the midst proceeded a loud, measured chant which would have killed Paganini outright, broken occasionally by a burst of sharp yells. I gathered the robe around me, for the night was cold, and walked down to the spot. The dark throng of Indians was so dense that they almost intercepted the light of the flame. As I was pushing among them with little ceremony, a chief interposed himself, and I was given to understand that a white man must not approach the scene of their solemnities too closely. By passing round to the other side where there was a little opening in the crowd, I could see clearly what was going forward, without intruding my unhallowed presence into the inner circle.

The society of the "Strong Hearts" were engaged in one of their dances. The "Strong Hearts" are a warlike association, comprising men of both the Dahcotah and Shienne nations, and entirely composed, or supposed to be so, of young braves of the highest mettle. Its fundamental principle is the admirable one of never retreating from any enterprise once begun. All these Indian associations have a tutelary spirit. That of the Strong Hearts is embodied in the fox, an animal which white men would hardly have selected for a similar purpose, though his subtle character agrees well enough with an Indian's notions of what is honorable in warfare. The dancers were circling round and round the fire, each figure brightly illumined at one moment by the yellow light, and at the next drawn in blackest shadow as it passed between the flame and the spectator. They would imitate with the most ludicrous exactness the motions and voice of their sly patron the fox. Then a startling yell would be given. Many other warriors would leap into the ring, and with faces upturned towards the starless sky, they would all stamp, and whoop, and brandish their weapons like so many frantic devils.

We remained here till the next afternoon. My companion and I with our three attendants then set out for the Pueblo, a distance of three hundred miles, and we supposed the journey would occupy about a fortnight. During this time we all hoped that we might not meet a single human being, for should we encounter any, they would in all probability be enemies, in whose eyes our rifles would be our only passports.

For the first two days nothing worth mentioning took place. On the third morning, however, an untoward incident occurred. We were encamped by the side of a little brook in an extensive hollow of the plain. Deslauriers was up long before daylight, and before he began to prepare breakfast he turned loose all the horses, as in duty bound. There was a cold mist clinging close to the ground, and by the time the rest of us were awake the animals were invisible. It was only after a long and anxious search that we could discover by their tracks the direction they had taken. They had all set off for Fort Laramie, following the guidance of a mutinous old mule, and though many of them were hobbled, they travelled three miles before they could be overtaken and driven back.

For two or three days, we were passing over an arid desert. The only vegetation was a few tufts of short grass, dried and shrivelled by the heat. There was abundance of strange insects and reptiles. Huge crickets, black and bottle green, and wingless grasshoppers of the most extravagant dimensions, were tumbling about our horses' feet, and lizards without number darting like lightning among the tufts of grass. The most curious animal, however, was that commonly called the horned-frog. I caught one of them and consigned him to the care of Deslauriers, who tied him up in a moccasin. About a month after this, I examined the prisoner's condition, and finding him still lively and active, I provided him with a cage of buffalo-hide, which was hung up in the cart. In this manner he arrived safely at the settlements. From thence he travelled the whole way to Boston, packed closely in a trunk, being regaled with fresh air regularly every night. When he reached his destination he was deposited under a glass case, where he sat for some months in great tranquillity, alternately dilating and contracting his white throat to the admiration of his visitors. At length, one morning about the middle of winter, he gave up the ghost, and he now occupies a bottle of alcohol in the Agassiz Museum. His death was attributed to starvation, a very probable conclusion, since for six months he had taken no food whatever, though the sympathy of his juvenile admirers had tempted his palate with a great variety of delicacies.

We found also animals of a somewhat larger growth. The number of prairie-dogs was astounding. Frequently the hard and dry plain was thickly covered, for miles together, with the little mounds which they make at the mouth of their burrows, and small squeaking voices yelped at us, as we passed along. The noses of the inhabitants were just visible at the mouth of their holes, but no sooner was their curiosity satisfied than they would instantly vanish. Some of the bolder dogs—though in fact they are no dogs at all, but little marmots rather smaller than a rabbit—would sit yelping at us on the top of their mounds, jerking their tails emphatically with every shrill cry they uttered. As the danger drew nearer they would wheel about, toss their heels into the air, and dive in a twinkling into their burrows.

Towards sunset, and especially if rain was threatening, the whole community made their appearance above ground. We saw them gathered in large knots around the burrow of some favorite citizen. There they would all sit erect, their tails spread out on the ground, and their paws hanging down before their white breasts, chattering and squeaking with the utmost vivacity upon some topic of common interest, while the proprietor of the burrow sat on the top of his mound, looking down with a complacent countenance on the enjoyment of his guests. Meanwhile, others ran about from burrow to burrow, as if on some errand of the last importance to their subterranean commonwealth. The snakes are apparently the prairie-dog's worst enemies; at least I think too well of the latter to suppose that they associate on friendly terms with these slimy intruders, which may be seen at all times basking among their holes, into which they always retreat when disturbed. Small owls, with wise and grave countenances, also make their abode with the prairie-dogs, though on what terms they live together I could never ascertain.

On the fifth day after leaving Bisonette's camp, we saw, late in the afternoon, what we supposed to be a considerable stream, but on approaching it, we found to our mortification nothing but a dry bed of sand, into which the water had sunk and disappeared. We separated, some riding in one direction and some in another, along its course. Still we found no traces of water, not even so much as a wet spot in the sand. The old cotton-wood trees that grew along the bank, lamentably abused by lightning and tempest, were withering with the drought, and on the dead limbs, at the summit of the tallest, half a dozen crows were hoarsely cawing, like birds of evil omen. We had no alternative but to keep on. There was no water nearer than the South Fork of the Platte, about ten miles distant. We moved forward, angry and silent, over a desert as flat as the outspread ocean.

The sky had been obscured since the morning by thin mists and vapors, but now vast piles of clouds were gathered together in the west. They rose to a great height above the horizon, and looking up at them I distinguished one mass darker than the rest, and of a peculiar conical form. I happened to look again, and still could see it as before. At some moments it was dimly visible, at others its outline was sharp and distinct; but while the clouds around it were shifting, changing, and dissolving away, it still towered aloft in the midst of them, fixed and immovable. It must, thought I, be the summit of a mountain; and yet its height staggered me. My conclusion was right, however. It was Long's Peak, once believed to be one of the highest of the Rocky Mountain chain, though more recent discoveries have proved the contrary. The thickening gloom soon hid it from view, and we never saw it again, for on the following day, and for some time after, the air was so full of mist that the view of distant objects was entirely cut off.

It grew very late. Turning from our direct course, we made for the river at its nearest point, though in the utter darkness it was not easy to direct our way with much precision. Raymond rode on one side and Henry on the other. We heard each of them shouting that he had come upon a deep ravine. We steered at random between Scylla and Charybdis, and soon after became, as it seemed, inextricably involved with deep chasms all around us, while the darkness was such that we could not see a rod in any direction. We partially extricated ourselves by scrambling, cart and all, through a shallow ravine. We came next to a steep descent, down which we plunged without well knowing what was at the bottom. There was a great cracking of sticks and dry twigs. Over our heads were certain large shadowy objects; and in front something like the faint gleaming of a dark sheet of water. Raymond ran his horse against a tree; Henry alighted, and feeling on the ground, declared that there was grass enough for the horses. Before taking off his saddle, each man led his own horses down to the water in the best way he could. Then picketing two or three of the evil-disposed, we turned the rest loose, and lay down among the dry sticks to sleep.

In the morning we found ourselves close to the South Fork of the Platte, on a spot surrounded by bushes and rank grass. Compensating ourselves with a hearty breakfast for the ill-fare of the previous night, we set forward again on our journey. When only two or three rods from the camp, I saw Shaw stop his mule, level his gun, and fire at some object in the grass. Deslauriers next jumped forward, and began to dance about, belaboring the unseen enemy with a whip. Then he stooped down, and drew out of the grass by the neck an enormous rattlesnake, with his head completely shattered by Shaw's bullet. As Deslauriers held him out at arm's length with an exulting grin, his tail, which still kept slowly writhing about, almost touched the ground; and his body in the largest part was as thick as a stout man's arm. He had fourteen rattles, but the end of his tail was blunted, as if he could once have boasted of many more.

From this time till we reached the Pueblo, we killed at least four or five of these snakes every day, as they lay coiled and rattling on the hot sand. Shaw was the St. Patrick of the party, and whenever he killed a snake he pulled off his tail and stored it away in his bullet-pouch, which was soon crammed with an edifying collection of rattles, great and small. Deslauriers with his whip also came in for a share of praise. A day or two after this, he triumphantly produced a small snake about a span and a half long, with one infant rattle at the end of his tail.

We forded the South Fork of the Platte. On its farther bank were the traces of a very large camp of Arapahoes. The ashes of some three hundred fires were visible among the scattered trees, together with the remains of sweating lodges, and all the other appurtenances of a permanent camp. The place, however, had been for some months deserted. A few miles farther on we found more recent signs of Indians; the trail of two or three lodges, which had evidently passed the day before; every footprint was perfectly distinct in the dry, dusty soil. We noticed in particular the track of one moccasin, upon the sole of which its economical proprietor had placed a large patch. These signs gave us but little uneasiness, as the number of the warriors scarcely exceeded that of our own party.

At noon we rested under the walls of a large fort, built in these solitudes some years since by M. St. Vrain. It was now abandoned and fast falling to ruin. The walls of unbaked bricks were cracked from top to bottom. Our horses recoiled in terror from the neglected entrance, where the heavy gates were torn from their hinges and flung down. The area within was overgrown with weeds, and the long ranges of apartments once occupied by the motley concourse of traders, Canadians, and squaws, were now miserably dilapidated. Twelve miles farther on, near the spot where we encamped, were the remains of another fort, standing in melancholy desertion and neglect.

Early on the following morning we made a startling discovery. We passed close by a large deserted encampment of Arapahoes. There were about fifty fires still smouldering on the ground, and it was evident from numerous signs that the Indians must have left the place within two hours of our reaching it. Their trail crossed our own, at right angles, and led in the direction of a line of hills, half a mile on our left. There were women and children in the party, which would have greatly diminished the danger of encountering them. Henry Chatillon examined the encampment and the trail with a very professional and business-like air.

"Supposing we had met them, Henry?" said I.

"Why," said he, "we hold out our hands to them, and give them all we've got; they take away everything, and then I believe they no kill us. Perhaps," added he, looking up with a quiet, unchanged face, "perhaps we no let them rob us. Maybe before they come near, we have a chance to get into a ravine, or under the bank of the river; then, you know, we fight them."

About noon on that day we reached Cherry Creek. Here was a great abundance of wild cherries, plums, gooseberries, and currants. The stream, however, like most of the others which we passed, was dried up with the heat, and we had to dig holes in the sand to find water for ourselves and our horses. Two days after, we left the banks of the creek, which we had been following for some time, and began to cross the high dividing ridge which separates the waters of the Platte from those of the Arkansas.

The scenery was altogether changed. In place of the burning plains, we passed through rough and savage glens, and among hills crowned with a dreary growth of pines. We encamped among these solitudes on the night of the sixteenth of August. A tempest was threatening. The sun went down among volumes of jet-black cloud, edged with a bloody red. But in spite of these portentous signs, we neglected to put up the tent, and, being extremely fatigued, lay down on the ground and fell asleep. The storm broke about midnight, and we pitched the tent amid darkness and confusion. In the morning all was fair again, and Pike's Peak, white with snow, was towering above the wilderness afar off.

We pushed through an extensive tract of pine woods. Large black-squirrels were leaping among the branches. From the farther edge of this forest we saw the prairie again, hollowed out before us into a vast basin, and about a mile in front we could discern a little black speck moving upon its surface. It could be nothing but a buffalo.

Henry primed his rifle afresh and galloped forward. To the left of the animal was a low rocky mound, of which Henry availed himself in making his approach. After a short time we heard the faint report of the rifle. The bull, mortally wounded from a distance of nearly three hundred yards, ran wildly round and round in a circle. Shaw and I then galloped forward, and passing him as he ran, foaming with rage and pain, discharged our pistols into his side. Once or twice he rushed furiously upon us, but his strength was rapidly exhausted. Down he fell on his knees. For one instant he glared up at his enemies, with burning eyes, through his black tangled mane, and then rolled over on his side. Though gaunt and thin, he was larger and heavier than the largest ox. Foam and blood flowed together from his nostrils as he lay bellowing and pawing the ground, tearing up grass and earth with his hoofs. His sides rose and fell like a vast pair of bellows, the blood spouting up in jets from the bullet-holes. Suddenly his glaring eyes became like a lifeless jelly. He lay motionless on the ground. Henry stooped over him, and, making an incision with his knife, pronounced the meat too rank and tough for use; so, disappointed in our hopes of an addition to our stock of provisions, we rode away and left the carcass to the wolves.

In the afternoon we saw the mountains rising like a gigantic wall at no great distance on our right. *"Des sauvages! des sauvages!"* exclaimed Deslauriers, looking round with a frightened face, and pointing with his whip towards the foot of the mountains. In fact, we could see at a distance a number of little black specks, like horsemen in rapid motion. Henry Chatillon, with Shaw and myself, galloped towards them to reconnoitre, when to our amusement, we saw the supposed Arapahoes resolved into the black tops of some pine-trees which grew along a ravine. The summits of these pines, just visible above the verge of the prairie, and seeming to move as we ourselves were advancing, looked exactly like a line of horsemen.

We encamped among ravines and hollows, through which a little brook was foaming angrily. Before sunrise in the morning the snow-covered mountains were beautifully tinged with a delicate rose-color. A noble spectacle awaited us as we moved forward. Six or eight miles on our right, Pike's Peak and his giant brethren rose out of the level prairie, as if springing from the bed of the ocean. From their summits down to the plain below they were involved in a mantle of clouds, in restless motion, as if urged by strong winds. For one instant some snowy peak, towering in awful solitude, would be disclosed to view. As the clouds broke along the mountain, we could see the dreary forests, the tremendous precipices, the white patches of snow, the gulfs and chasms as black as night, all revealed for an instant, and then disappearing from the view.

On the day after, we had left the mountains at some distance. A black cloud descended upon them, and a tremendous explosion of thunder followed, reverberating among the precipices. In a few moments everything grew black, and the rain poured down like a cataract. We got under an old cotton-wood tree, which stood by the side of a stream, and waited there till the rage of the torrent had passed.

The clouds opened at the point where they first had gathered, and the whole sublime congregation of mountains was bathed at once in warm sunshine. They seemed more like some vision of eastern romance than like a reality of that wilderness; all were melted together into a soft delicious blue, as voluptuous as the sky of Naples or the transparent sea that washes the sunny cliffs of Capri. On the left the sky was still of an inky blackness; but two concentric rainbows stood in bright relief against it, while far in front the ragged clouds still streamed before the wind, and the retreating thunder muttered angrily.

Through that afternoon and the next morning we were passing down the banks of the stream, called "Boiling Spring Creek," from the boiling spring whose waters flow into it. When we stopped at noon, we were within six or eight miles of the Pueblo. Setting out again, we found by the fresh tracks that a horseman had just been out to reconnoitre us; he had circled half round the camp, and then galloped back at full speed for the Pueblo. What made him so shy of us we could not conceive. After an hour's ride we reached the edge of a hill, from which a welcome sight greeted us. The Arkansas ran along the valley below, among woods and groves, and closely nestled in the midst of wide corn-fields and green meadows, where cattle were grazing, rose the low mud walls of the Pueblo.

DAKOTA PLAINS

BY THEODORE ROOSEVELT

Theodore Roosevelt (1858–1919) was born in New York City, educated at Harvard, and first planned a career in the law. Instead, he turned to history and writing and at the age of twenty-four wrote a history of the War of 1812. In 1883 he bought a ranch in Dakota Territory and for several years spent much of his time there, partly for the adventure and experience, partly for his health. Out of that period came his intense interest in the outdoors and conservation. He entered New York politics partly by chance, and the story of his rise to the Presidency is history. As President, he gave conservation his full support, made it a matter of national importance, and left a public legacy of national forests and wilderness areas. He also fired a bitter barrage at the romantic nature writers of the time and did much to put an end to the worst of the anthropomorphic nonsense. Though not a trained naturalist, he was interested in everything alive and was a keen observer and good reporter. He continued to write most of his life, and most of his books show his rich awareness of nature. This selection is from one of his early books, Hunting Trips of a Ranchman, *which deals with his experiences in Dakota. Written when he was only twenty-six, it is full of youth and enthusiasm, but it is also vivid and accurate. It presents a splendid picture of the Dakota plains as they were in the 1880s.*

(*Hunting Trips of a Ranchman,* by Theodore Roosevelt; Charles Scribner's Sons, 1885.)

I started in the very earliest morning, when the intense brilliancy of the stars had just begun to pale before the first streak of dawn. By the time I had left the river-bottom land and struck off up the valley of a winding creek, which led through the Bad Lands, the eastern sky was growing rosy; and soon the buttes and cliffs were lit up by the level rays of the cloudless summer sun. The air was fresh and sweet, and odorous with the sweet scents of the springtime that was but barely passed; the dew lay heavy, in glittering drops, on the leaves and the blades of grass, whose vivid green, at this season, for a short time brightens the desolate and sterile-looking wastes of the lonely Western plains. The rose-bushes were all in bloom, and their pink blossoms clustered in every point and bend of the stream; and the sweet, sad songs of the hermit-thrushes rose from the thickets, while the meadow-larks perched boldly in sight as they uttered their louder and more cheerful music. The round-up had passed by our ranch, and all the cattle with our brands—the Maltese cross and cut dewlap, or the elk-horn and triangle—had been turned loose; they had not yet worked away from the river, and I rode by long strings of them, walking in single file off to the hills, or standing in groups to look at me as I passed.

Leaving the creek, I struck off through a region of scoria buttes, the ground rising into rounded hills, through whose grassy covering the red volcanic rock showed in places, while boulder-like fragments of it were scattered all through the valleys between. There were a few clumps of bushes here and there, and near one of them were two magpies, who lit on an old buffalo skull, bleached white by sun and snow. . . .

After passing the last line of low, rounded scoria buttes, the horse stepped out on the border of the great, seemingly endless stretches of rolling or nearly level prairie, over which I had planned to travel and hunt for the next two or three days. . . . Nowhere, not even at sea, does a man feel more lonely than when riding over the far-reaching, seemingly never-ending plains; and after a man has lived a little while on or near them, their very vastness and loneliness and their melancholy monotony have a strong fascination for him. The landscape seems always the same, and after the traveller has plodded on for miles and miles he gets to feel as if the distance were indeed boundless. As far as the eye can see there is no break; either the prairie stretches out into perfectly level flats, or else there are gentle, rolling slopes, whose crests mark the divides between the drainage systems of the different creeks; and when one of these is ascended, immediately another precisely like it takes its place in the distance, and so roll succeeds roll in a succession as interminable as that of the waves of the ocean. Nowhere else does one seem so far off from all mankind; the plains stretch out in deathlike and measureless expanse, and as he journeys over them they will for many miles be lacking in all signs of life. Although he could see so far, yet all objects on the outermost verge of the horizon, even though within the ken of his vision, look unreal and strange; for there is no shade to take away from the bright glare, and at a little distance things seem to shimmer and dance in the hot rays of the sun. The ground is scorched to a dull brown, and against its monotonous expanse any objects stand out with a prominence that makes it difficult to judge of the distance at which they are. A mile off one can see, through the strange shimmering haze, the shadowy white outlines of something that looms vaguely up till it looks as large as the canvas top of a prairie wagon; but as the horseman comes nearer it shrinks and dwindles and takes clearer form, until at last it changes into the ghastly staring skull of some mighty buffalo, long dead and gone to join the rest of his vanished race. . . .

The sun was just setting when we crossed the final ridge and came in sight of as singular a bit of country as I have ever seen. The cowboys, as we afterward found, had christened the place "Medicine Buttes." In plains dialect, I may explain, "Medicine" has been adopted from the Indians, among whom it means anything supernatural or very unusual. It is used in the sense of "magic" or "out of the common."

Over an irregular tract of gently rolling sandy hills, perhaps about three-quarters of a mile square, were scattered several hundred detached and isolated buttes or cliffs of sandstone, each butte from fifteen to fifty feet high, and from thirty to a couple of hundred feet across. Some of them rose as sharp peaks or ridges, or as connected chains, but much the greater number had flat tops like little table-lands. The sides were perfectly perpendicular, and were cut and channelled by the weather into extraordinary forms: caves, columns, battlements, spires, flying buttresses were mingled in the strangest confusion. Many of the caves were worn clear through the buttes, and they were at every height in the sides, while ledges ran across the faces, and shoulders and columns jutted out from the corners. On the tops and at the bases of most of the cliffs grew pine-trees, some of considerable height, and the sand gave everything a clean, white look.

Altogether, it was as fantastically beautiful a place as I have ever seen; it seemed impossible that the hand of man should not have had something to do with its formation. There was a spring of clear cold water a few hundred yards off, with good feed for the horses around it, and we made our camp at the foot of one of the largest buttes, building a roaring pine-log fire in an angle of the face of the cliff, while our beds were under the pine-trees. It was the time of the full moon, and the early part of the night was clear. The fire leaped up the side of the cliff, the red light bringing out into lurid and ghastly relief the bold corners and strange-looking escarpments of the rock, while against it the stiff limbs of the pines stood out like rigid bars of iron. Walking off out of sight of the circle of firelight, among the tall crags, the place seemed almost as unreal as if we had been in fairyland. The flood of clear moonlight turned the white faces of the cliffs and the ground between them into shining silver, against which the pines showed dark and somber, while the intensely black shadows of the buttes took on forms that were grimly fantastic. Every cave or cranny in the crags looked so black that it seemed almost to be thrown out from the surface, and when the branches of the trees moved, the bright moonlight danced on the ground as if it were a sheet of molten metal. Neither in shape nor in color did our surroundings seem to belong to the dull gray world through which we had been travelling all day.

DUST STORM

BY GEORGE MIKSCH SUTTON

George Miksch Sutton (1898 —) was born in West Virginia, educated at Texas Christian University, Bethany College, the University of Pittsburgh, and Cornell University. An ornithologist, he has painted birds and written about them in many books and his research trips have taken him to arctic Canada as well as other out-of-the-way places. This selection, which is about dust storms rather than birds, is from Discovery, *a volume of firsthand experiences of a group of outstanding naturalists.*

(*Discovery: Great Moments in the Lives of Outstanding Naturalists*, edited by John K. Terres; J. B. Lippincott Company, 1961.)

The Dust Bowl, as I experienced it while studying the birds of the Oklahoma Panhandle in 1936 and 1937, was an appalling place. It was not a desert in any ordinary sense, though desert it certainly was. Even in midsummer it had a bleak, wintry appearance. The glare of its smooth dust drifts was like the glare of snow. The telegraph poles that lined its highways, the small, colorless houses, the half-buried farm machinery and toppling fences, the blasted cottonwood and hackberry trees—these seemed utterly unreal on a warm, bright morning in June. Seen through the dust that blew nine days out of every ten, they called to mind a setting for some gruesome crime. They loomed against the dun void like sandstone grotesqueries carved by the wind.

Dust was everywhere. It was on every twig, every blade of grass, every strand of wire. It was in the plumage of the horned larks that flitted along the roads. It was in the hair of the half-starved jack rabbits and prairie dogs. It was the unfamiliar bloom on the tiger beetle's emerald wings. It softened even the bull snake's bold color pattern, clinging tenaciously to the skin between the velvety scales.

Dust was part of every dawn and every sunset. Especially was it part of every noon, for especially at noon did the wind blow. It settled reluctantly when the blast subsided; but the instant a zephyr stirred, it was up again. With every step a man took through the dead weeds a pungent cloud ascended. Let him touch a twig, and there was a puff of gray. Rains occasionally drenched the parched waste, and pools formed; but with the passing of the clouds the sun appeared, the wind rose, and lo! a thick veil of dust shut the new-formed pools from sight.

I drove across the Dust Bowl eight times between 1932 and 1937. I experienced what was called "bad local dust" in the stretch from Guymon to Boise City, Oklahoma, six times of the eight. The inhabitants of Cimarron and Texas counties—the westernmost counties of the Oklahoma Panhandle—had become so accustomed to this local dust that they paid little attention to it as a rule. Nobody talked about it. It was taken for granted, along with sunlight and air.

Occasionally, however, there swept down from the north a vast cloud of dust that was not local. It may have been Kansas dust, or Colorado dust, or dust from one of the Prairie Provinces of Canada. Such clouds moved slowly. Not often were they accompanied by a gale. But they were inexorable. They turned day to night. Death was in them. These storms were called "black dust storms" by the cattlemen who lived in the valley of the Cimarron. It was such a black storm that caught me at about six o'clock on the evening of May 21, 1937, while I was watching a bird among the mesas near Kenton, Oklahoma, a few miles east of the New Mexico state line.

That had been a pleasant day, calm, bright, not unusually warm. Our party of four—John B. Semple, Karl Haller, Leo Luttringer, Jr., and I—had been out all morning, studying, photographing, and collecting birds for scientific study. At noon we had returned to the little hotel at Kenton.

Since my catch was not large, I had finished my drawing and preparation of bird specimens by five o'clock in the afternoon, somewhat earlier than usual. Realizing that I had a few hours of daylight at my disposal, I decided to go after a canyon wren, a species that had thus far eluded us. Taking my shotgun and specimen basket, I started for my automobile.

"How about giving me a lift to that mesa just east of town, Doc?" called Luttringer, our photographer. "I want to get some good shots of this country before we leave. The light's perfect this evening."

"Sure!" I replied.

I deposited Leo and his big Graflex at the foot of his mesa and drove slowly on. It was a windless evening, a trifle warmer than it had been, I thought, but not disagreeably so. I enjoyed the prospect of a leisurely walk. I loved this mesa country. The fragrance of the pinons and junipers always did me good, and the mysteriousness of the arid canyons fascinated me.

Within twenty minutes I reached an eminence from which I frequently had surveyed the broad flood plain of the Cimarron. Pulling the car to the right of the road, I stopped to listen. Sure enough, on the rise just to the north, and not very far away, a canyon wren was singing. The very bird I was after! How clear and bold was that cascade of notes! With my mind's eye I could see the small performer perched on the top of a boulder, the feathers of his white throat lifting and quivering.

I locked the car; then, glancing at it as I usually did before leaving it, I noted that the right rear tire had lost most of its air. It was not flat, but it was down. It would have to be changed.

Unlocking the car, I started to drag out the jack and wrench. Then, impulsively, I shoved them back and relocked the door. I'll not change it now, I thought. I'd better go after the wren while I know where it is. That tire's been having slow leaks anyway. If I get the wren right off, I'll be back long before dark.

I swung away, crossed the fence, and within a quarter of an hour had reached the base of the vast, tablelike slab of rock which crowned the hill. From the side of the slab gigantic boulders had broken away.

Back of these opened low caverns, some of them large enough to furnish the cattle a shelter in winter.

In this rough and shadowy world lived the wren I had heard. In and out of the crevices, under and behind the boulders, through the darkest, most remote parts of the caverns, now at the brow of the rock rim above me, now in a fissure at my very feet, the little bird flitted and ran. Part of the time he scolded me, using his harshest voice. Then, after a period of complete silence, during which I had no notion of his whereabouts, he emerged, mouselike, from his hiding place, looked at me with glittering eyes, lifted his head, opened his slender bill, and sang as if he rated me, of all possible enemies, the least considerable. I with my great blunderbuss of a gun! I with my clumsy feet, picking my way about *his* rocks! I could have shot at him several times, but I didn't. His temerity, the ripple of echoes that his song roused, the way he scuttled about—up and down, this way and that, as if he never in his life had tripped on anything—all this must have cast some kind of spell over me.

I watched the little bird as he lifted his head to sing. I saw him clearly, for he was perched at the very edge of the rock above me. All was blue-bright back of him, the blue brightness of the sky. He sang two notes of his descending scale, two bold, ringing notes, then stopped. Stopped as if he had been stricken. Stopped, faced about, crouched, turned his head to one side as if following with his eyes the towering of a prairie falcon, and darted into a crevice.

No falcon appeared. So far as I could see there was nothing for the wren to fear. Then why this strange behavior, this abrupt breaking off of song? Had the little bird seen a speck in the upper air, some point of black too far away for me to descry? At once it dawned on me that the evening chorus of the mockingbirds and lark sparrows too had ceased, that the world had grown unaccountably silent.

I looked once more for the wren. He had disappeared. Above the spot at which he had sung, and sharp against the sky, was the bright edge of a thick cloud. That this was an unusual cloud I sensed immediately. It looked solid, like a grayish yellow wall hung with smoke. That it was slowly rising I perceived in an instant, for more and more of it showed above the rock.

To see more clearly I ran back a little and clambered up out of the cavern. Before me was such a scene as I had never beheld before: a vast brown cloud, the only cloud in the sky, stretching as far to the east and as far to the west as the eye could see, so dense and so low-hanging that it had completely obliterated the northern horizon. Its uppermost borders, which were eerily bright, were the grayish yellow wall I had first seen.

Slowly and gracefully the cloud bank moved, upward with the rolling effect of smoke from a great conflagration, and forward. I watched it spellbound. The beauty, the ineffable serenity, the horrible majesty of the thing! No wonder all the birds had ceased from their singing. As the wall advanced, it shut out more of the world to the north. Now even the purple dome of the Black Mesa was going. The last glimpse I had of the mighty mountain made me think of Napoleon and his final look at the Kremlin as it stood there unscathed in the midst of burning Moscow.

Suddenly, with a feeling of impotence that fairly buckled my knees under me, I realized that this opaque mass bearing down upon me had nothing to do with rain. That it was dust! That shelter in the caverns along the side of the hill would be no shelter at all from this! I looked once more at the advancing cloud, then back toward the highway. The storm would catch me long before I could reach the car.

I ran across the rock-strewn slope, memorizing certain details of what I saw before me. I perceived that if I made a certain low ridge, I could crawl along that ridge back to the highway no matter how thick the storm. Out of breath, I turned to face my pursuer, noting that it no longer seemed brown, but was white instead. Its edges were feather-soft. Behind and below the fluffiness of these nearest wisps was a darkness sullen and menacing.

I reached the little ridge. The highway was not far off. Terrified though I was, I now felt that I could not lose my way. I glanced at the car, remembering . . . the tire.

When I turned once more to look at the dust, it was upon me. No sky was visible now anywhere to the north. The vague blueness above me was plumed with gray and white. A mass of dust with the fluid appearance of muddy water slipped along the ground a little in advance of the high cloud, running between the trees and boulders like a wave about to break. There was no breaking of this queer wave. No ripple, no splash, no foam. Forward it slipped, always keeping just a little ahead of the cloud itself.

I saw the wave of dust flow about my shoes. I saw it grow deeper, shutting my knees from sight. Its thickness and its unexpected coldness struck new terror. Running headlong, I reached the fence along the north side of the highway. The wave was winning. Running again, I crossed the highway, grasped a strand of barbed wire, and sank to my knees.

By this time the light was going, for the wave was engulfing me. The wind was not as fierce as I had expected it to be. It was strong, but not fierce. And it was cold. With it rose a hissing moan. I looked toward the south, toward the only light that remained. That light was weird, unearthly, reddish in cast. In an instant it was gone—as if a huge curtain had dropped; as if a vast lid had suddenly been clapped on the world. "Awful! Awful!" I seemed to be saying, almost aloud. "Being buried alive must be like this. Drowning must be like this—drowning at the bottom of the sea!"

Just as the light had gone, a bird had fluttered past me. It had flown close enough for me to identify it as a mockingbird. It had careened off downwind as if in a wild dream. That bird was the last thing I clearly saw for a long time. Its image, black against the lurid light in the south, was to linger in my mind for years. It, too, drowning! It, too, at the bottom of the sea!

With my hand upon the friendly fence I breathed hard, thankful that I knew exactly where I was. For a moment I wondered if I could possibly survive. It was so dark that I could not see my hand or handkerchief no matter how close I held them to my face. My eyes did not pain me. I knew I had not been blinded. No, the light had simply gone. There was no light anywhere. The evening that had been so serenely bright had turned to utter darkness—the darkness of the tomb.

I realized that the dust was not choking me. I could feel dust on my lips and against my tongue and teeth, but I was not suffocating. I was surprised that breathing was as easy as it was. I kept my eyes shut and my face turned away from the blast.

With the passing of the first thick wave, the wind grew stronger and a trifle cooler. The complete darkness must have lasted twenty minutes. Then I thought I saw a dull red glow off to the north. Looking at my handkerchief again I could barely see it when I held it a few inches from my eyes. The worst was probably over.

I followed the fence to the car, holding my eyes shut most of the time. Fitting the key into the lock at last, I opened the door, turned on the lights, found a flashlight. The tire was down, flat.

Fearing that my companions might have started in search of me, wondering what fate had befallen Leo Luttringer, and feeling that it would be much better in every way to be at Kenton for the duration of the storm, I changed tires. It was a laborious, anything but pleasant job.

The headlights of the car penetrated the dust only a few feet, but I managed to turn around, to keep to the highway, to get back to the small bridge where I had let Leo out. There I stopped, blew the horn, and shouted as loudly as I could, shouted and blew the horn again. No response.

I drove on. So thick was the dust that I might have missed Kenton had it not been for a light at the very edge of the street near the one and only filling station. That light made me think of a photographer's darkroom.

Friends at the hotel laughed when they saw me. Though alarmed they had sensed full well the futility of starting after me, for no one knew where I had gone. "Where were you when it struck?" they asked, almost in a chorus. "What did you do, get under something? Did you notice the way the cattle stood, looking up at the cloud? Did you notice the way the birds all stopped singing?"

I told them of the wren, of the race back to the highway, of changing the tire. Everybody in the place had some observation to make, some tale to tell. It was all so absorbing that I actually forgot about Leo.

Then all at once I remembered. "Say, where's Leo? Isn't he back yet?"

They, too, had momentarily forgotten. My question brought a look of concern to every face. Somebody went to the front door for a glance at the storm. It had abated, but the dust was still so thick that it was impossible to see across the street.

I thought of the way the storm had caught me. Of the awful darkness that had shut down. Of Leo trying to make his way down a steep slope, along an unfamiliar ridge, among the pathless junipers. "We ought to go after him," I said. "A fellow might get lost in this and wander around all night. He's on that first mesa to the east. Leo doesn't know this country anything like as well as I do."

I started for the car. Pard Collins stepped forward. "Guess you don't mind if I go with you," he said. Collins was an oldtimer in the Black Mesa country, one of that country's real pioneers. He had seen many a dust storm and knew a bad one when he saw it.

We had turned the car and started eastward when the form of a man loomed directly ahead of us in the middle of the street. In the form's hand was a squarish object, a box with a handle. It was Leo and the Graflex.

Leo was almost in tears. Not because there was dust in his eyes. Not because he might have lost his life or broken his leg. Not because he had got his hands and knees full of sandburrs and cactus spines—but because he had not taken his movie camera with him to the mesa.

"Doc," he almost shouted at me. "Think of it, Doc! There I was with that terrible thing coming right at me. Why, it would have been a world-beater! It would have been worth real money! There I sat on that mesa looking at it for twenty minutes before I realized what it was. I thought it was just a low cloud. Honest, Doc, just a cloud! I could have come back and got my movie outfit and got a record of the thing from start to finish! I'm just sick about it!" He held his hand to his stomach. "Honest, Doc, it gives me an empty feeling right here to think of missing a chance like that. I'll never have it again, never as long as I live. Never!"

Leo had got down from the mesa before the storm struck. Running for Kenton he had stumbled into a deserted house at the east edge of town just as the darkness shut down. Inside the hotel once more, where we could really see him, he looked like a mummy with glittering glass eyes. His hair reminded me of the ruff of a great anthropoid ape that had wallowed in dust. His whole person was gray—his face, his hands, his clothes. His mustache was a trifle muddy. He laughed hilariously, saying that he had never seen me looking so funny. I laughed at Leo. We all laughed. We were a very happy party now that we were reunited.

Some of the darkness was now the darkness of night, for it must have been well past nine o'clock. After Leo and I had taken off our shirts and given ourselves a thorough washing, we all went to the kitchen. Supper had been ready at six o'clock, but with the coming of the storm, plates had been put over all the food and the meal forgotten.

We turned out the light so as to watch the electricity playing about the base of the big iron stove. Pard Collins told us he had seen such sparks shooting out from the horns of cattle and the ears of horses. "It's a bad storm, this storm is," he declared. "It's like the black storm we had in April a few years back. I don't know but maybe it's even some worse."

It was good to see my friends, all safe about me. We were hungry as bears. There was an unwonted sparkle in the eyes that turned my way now and then during supper.

The wind continued most of the night, but when morning came all was calm. A thick gray haze shut out the horizon, gave the Black Mesa a ghostly dimness, softened the outline of the nearer hills and ridges. The sun did not appear at its accustomed hour. Finally we saw it, halfway on its climb to the zenith. It was not the golden sun we had been seeing. Nor was it red, as we had thought it might be. It was white, silvery white, and about it shone a faintly opalescent halo.

The above account was written in 1937. On February 16, 1955, in the little cemetery in Kenton, they buried Pard Collins. The afternoon of the funeral I stood in the kitchen of the Collins home, the building that had once been the town's only hostelry, looking with a feeling of indescribable affection and loneliness at the stove about which we had seen the sparks playing on that memorable evening so long before. Pard Collins's widow, Pearl Collins, a fragile, beautiful woman, smiled as I spoke of the way we had all watched that stove, wondering what would happen next. Wesley Collins, Pard's fine man of a son, was there, smiling too. Pard's little grandson was there, his hand in Wesley's. Of the four of us, only the lad was not smiling. He did not have the black storm and the sparks to remember. I realized as I stood there near the old stove that I would never forget Pard Collins and the way he had offered to help me find my friend Leo in the storm.

The Mountains

There's something about a mountain that engraves itself upon a man's emotions. Any mountain does it, whether it is the old and weathered uplift of the Berkshires, the more rugged upthrust of the Alleghenies, the singular oak-clad Ozarks, or the majestic Rockies and the Sierra. Mountains are barriers. Mountains are adventure. Mountains are the dwelling place of the gods.

Approaching the mountains, one senses the presence of great forces, forces beyond easy comprehension. Even as wrinkles on the earth's old forehead, they are stupendous. Man is inconsequential in their presence; yet in their presence man rises to a kind of magnificence of his own. Who can stand in the presence of a mountain and remain unchanged?

We rationalize our mountains. We love them for their cool air, their pines and spruces, their white-water streams. We go to them to find change, or isolation, or grandeur. And yet it is what happens to us, inside, it is the emotional and even the spiritual surge, that draws us back to the mountains again and again. It was not altogether a matter of mysticism that prompted the ancients to the belief that their gods dwelt in the high places of this earth. Those gods, by whatever name we call them, still dwell there, and we would from time to time draw near to them, that we may know them, and ourselves, more intimately.

H.B.

OLYMPIC MOUNTAINS

BY WILLIAM O. DOUGLAS

William O. Douglas (1898 —) was born in Minnesota and grew up in Washington State where he spent much of his youth exploring the remote mountain areas on foot and on horseback. After almost fifteen years as a teacher and lawyer, he was appointed a Justice of the United States Supreme Court in 1939. But he has continued an inveterate explorer of remote places, an able naturalist with special interest in botany, and an insistent advocate of conservation. He has written many books about the outdoors and the life community there. His two volumes My Wilderness: The Pacific West *and* My Wilderness: East to Katahdin *are among the most comprehensive accounts that have been written of the principal natural areas in the United States. This selection, a chapter from* My Wilderness: The Pacific West, *is a good example of his intimate knowledge of nature observed at first hand, of his understanding of the problems of ecology and conservation, and of his vigorous, clean-cut way of writing. Justice Douglas probably has explored more remote areas in America than any other outdoor writer alive today.*

(*My Wilderness: The Pacific West,* by William O. Douglas; Doubleday & Company, Inc., 1960.)

The Olympics—that loom up from Puget Sound as jagged peaks against the western sky—are low, as mountains go. Of the twenty-odd major peaks there is none over 8000 feet. Only six are over 7000 feet, Mount Olympus rising 7954 feet. Yet no American range has more interesting features. The rain forests near the base are botanical wonders. Above them are alpine meadows and peaks that offer challenges. At least fifty living glaciers flank these peaks, three on Mount Olympus being two miles or more in length.

The work of the ice age is evident on every hand. Great cirques mark the heads of most valleys. Deep blue lakes lie above moraines. The peaks are highly polished. There are few rounded domes, most of the peaks being sharp and pointed. Many ridges are razor-edged.

The Olympics are sandstone, shale, and lava. During four successive periods—each separated by millions of years—the site of this range was covered by the sea. Each period of inundation was followed by an uplift. The first three uplifts were reduced by erosions to nearly sea level. The fourth uplift was also followed by erosion, which removed thousands of feet of sediment, leaving stubs of mountains. Once again parts of the area were inundated. Then came the great geologic period of mountain building—between one and eleven million years ago. That was the date of the fifth uplift of the Olympics, which took place when the Alps, Cascades, and Himalaya were being created.

Peaks that have come and gone four times should halt a man in his steps.

The rivers that run off the western slopes of the Olympics are among our shortest. The Quillayute, Hoh, and Quinault are not much more than fifty miles long, and their water is as clean as the rain and snow that feed them, save for the glacial "flour" that at times discolors them. Their run to the Pacific is through land as close to the jungle as the Temperate Zone has created. The west and south watersheds have rainfall that averages in the lower reaches about twelve inches a month. Higher up there has sometimes been twenty inches a month. The result is a mass of vegetation so thick that the newcomer will think it impenetrable.

Salmon and steelhead run these streams in the Fall and Winter, cutthroat trout in the Summer. The Quinault Indians use canoes, hewn by hand out of cedar logs. Memories of my hours with them on fast waters, fishing for cutthroat, are bright. There are pools where one can hold a canoe for several casts with a fly. But in most places the water of the Quinault is too swift for that. One cast at the point of a log, one on the edge of white water below a swirl, one in an opening left by vine maple that partially covers flat water, one where a graceful red alder touches a pool. One cast, a wait of a split second while the fly drifts and the canoe shoots on. Almost before the fly can be retrieved the canoe is above another spot. The timing must be perfect, the cast must bring the fly down softly, the reprieve must be quick. This is exquisite fishing. Chances are won or lost in a split second.

The miles run off in rapid fashion in these fast waters; the cinema of white, roaring whirlpools, boulders barely missed, fast runs under alder, swirling eddies around logs make me lose all sense of time. Strange as it may seem, there is no letdown, no sense of frustration if I return empty handed. A morning on one of those fast streams brings joy and excitement enough.

One who runs these rivers has the sense of being primitive man pitted against the elements. His skills, his endurance are all that count. There is no community to underwrite his errors, to make up for his mistakes. All that matters is his skill, and his alone.

A rowboat takes one down leisurely. By August the water is down and spits of white sand, ideal for sun bathing, are exposed. The woods by then are fairly dry; red alders offer shade and thick ferns make a restful bed for an afternoon siesta.

The slow drift by boat offers a deep solitude, unbroken except for the sound of rushing water, the splash of a muskrat, or the song of a water ouzel. The wilderness presses in on all sides and shuts out the world of man. The roar of civilization is left behind. I like to hold the boat against the side of the pool and watch the river life go by. Hellgrammites and periwinkles are in the gravel. A crayfish moves cautiously. A frog is spread out as if relaxed. Swarms of small fish, hatched on nearby spawning grounds, race by. Some of these fingerlings are steelhead who stay in the river two winters before moving to the sea. Fullgrown cutthroat are deep in the pool—poised, alert, intent. A salmon weighing thirty pounds or more—probably a jack—heads upstream. A stray steelhead streaks across the pool.

There are swifts along the river and hummingbirds too. The western belted kingfisher is busy. A little flycatcher with grayish body and yellow belly calls "swit-zo, swit-zo" from the alders. The chickadee calls over and over from the brush. The brilliant western tanager, high in the alders, shouts "petik, petik."

By June the elk are in alpine meadows. There are deer where there is browse; and these black-tailed deer love the river bottoms. The bear are numerous. I remember one bright August day when August Slathar had the oars, holding the middle of the Bogachiel on a long, slow drift in flat water as I whipped the river with a fly. As we rounded a bend, we saw a large black bear on the next point, a couple of hundred yards distant. Augie gave me a knowing look and pointed the boat directly to the animal. The wind was right and, as fortune would have it, the rear end of the bear was pointed our way. He had flipped a big fish from the water and was leisurely engaged in eating it. When the boat was within three feet of the bear, I reached over and gave it a slap on the back, shouting, "What are you doing here?"

It was seconds before the message reached the bear's brain. Meanwhile his sympathetic nervous system went into operation. His rear legs visibly stiffened; his back seemed to freeze. Then the danger signal reached consciousness and the animal was off through the dense brush, not once looking behind.

Winter fishing on these streams offers different rewards. Rain brings the water level up as much as eleven feet. The pools are still there, although there are few old landmarks to identify them.

The sooty or blue grouse have come down from the mountains. The loons have arrived from the north. So have the Oregon juncos. Geese and ducks are in migration, and if one is lucky he'll see a veritable armada of whistling swan flying south in a single line that is several city blocks long. If one looks closely, he may see a pygmy owl sitting on an old snag.

The days are dark, foggy, and cold. Ice forms on the ferrules of the fishing rod. The chill in the air strikes into the marrow. These are the days when the steelhead come upstream. They have good cover under the flood waters.

Sandy Balcom—best of all steelheaders—is my mentor. We try to hold a boat above a pool and to fish it according to its peculiar hydraulics. We try to cast so that the current at the head of the pool will take the bait in a long arc to the far end. The theory is that a steelhead lies in wait there for food that the river brings down. Frequently the theory works. The strike may be a ferocious taking, or it may be only the gentlest of touches. Once the hook is set, a battle royal begins, and numb fingers are forgotten. The fish may circle the pool several times, breaking water and shaking its head to get rid of the hook. Before long it heads downstream and makes the reel fairly sing.

Not all winter days are alike. Once there was no rain for a month and the temperature was so low that no snow was melting. Sandy Balcom and I had to drag our boat over gravel from pool to pool. The sun was out, the day bright. The low water made every steelhead unusually wary. Our dream of hooking 25-pound steelheads—about the largest in these streams—vanished. By noon we were ready to settle for much less. By mid-afternoon we would have been happy with cutthroat. By late afternoon we had about given up hope. We had drifted twelve miles without a strike. When we came to an old, abandoned farm, we beached the boat and walked downstream to fish two pools shaded by a western hemlock and heavily guarded by thick stands of salal. Before we made the first cast a dark cloud drifted in from the Pacific, shutting out the sun. In less than three minutes Sandy and I were each playing steelheads—twins that weighed six pounds each.

As we dressed the fish, the silence of this wilderness closed in. Though we were only a mile or so from my fishing lodge, the distance from civilization seemed great. The trees and brush formed a tangled jungle on each side of the river and towered over us. The river was our one path home. Now a cold, soft rain began to fall and the dense woods set up a dripping that would last for days.

The lower reaches of the Olympics have many small bogs, ponds, or lakes a few acres in size, formed in the glacial period. Some are true sphagnum bogs. James Lake has not quite reached that stage, though it is on its way. It is only a mile or so from my fishing lodge and has supplied me with an interesting listening point. The short walk there is an experience. I always go cross-country under the dark canopy of western hemlock and spruce. There is a tangle of brush, ferns, and down timber. I climb over logs that are eight feet or more in diameter and make my way through thick salal brush. James Lake is a small target—only a few acres in size and easy to miss. I wait some minutes before stepping out of the jungle, so as not to disturb any animals that may be there. This is a quiet alcove to approach reverently. It is a sanctuary where voices above a whisper seem almost sacrilegious. Here I remember Thoreau's words, "I enter a swamp as a sacred place." A hemlock fell decades ago and now lies partly above the water. Its bark is gone, and its wood, worn by weather into long grooves, is decorated with moss and lichens. Beside it grow swamp laurel, Labrador tea, and northern cranberry. It is here I like to stretch out on a summer day. A biologist lying on my log will see life without end in the shallow, darkish water. A botanist, too, will find adventure here.

The bog myrtle and crabapple get their feet wet along the shore line. So does the cascara. The Douglas spirea flourishes here. The surrounding woods, made up mostly of western hemlock and red cedar, put up a thick green wall around this placid lake. Its waters are dark blue against a somber green setting. Lily pads show white and yellow blossoms throughout the season. There are gentians, northern starflowers and violets along the edges of the log. The far shore shows cotton grass. A wood duck (green head, red chest, and buff-colored sides) lands to cruise the opposite shore. A colony of muskrat is busy. A doe steps into the open, her big ears flicking. A bumblebee breaks the silence; a Virginia rail makes an excited call. To my left there is the sound of a stick quickly cracked. The noise is as sharp as a rifle shot. A huge bear, dark brown in color, comes to the edge of the lake. He does not see me nor pick up my scent. He sits down on a log, his back to me, and starts scooping off salmonberries. He has nearly had his fill when I raise myself slightly and cough. The echo comes back from the opposite shore, but not before the doe has lifted her head and stiffened. The wood duck, too, takes notice by changing its direction and picking up speed. A muskrat crossing a nearby log freezes in his tracks. A frog jumps off the lily pad. The bear jumps as if hit by buckshot and bolts into the woods. He crashes through thick stands of brush, putting everything out of the way. He does not stop running for several hundred yards, while the noise of his hurried exit fills the place.

James Lake changes with the seasons. Summer finds it low. The fall rains raise its level. The first snows on the high slopes of the Olympics cause the elk to start down. By late October they are in the woods around James Lake. One who lies on my log at dawn or dusk at that time can count herds up to sixty that come there to browse and to drink.

When I paddle a canoe through the north country of Minnesota or fish the high lakes of Oregon or Washington, those waters seem permanent and enduring. But James Lake teaches the lesson that lakes, too, must pass. Like other life, lakes are in transition. They gradually fill up, form sphagnum and peat bogs, collect all the debris that rains wash in and that vegetable growth produces. Before long they are dry and reclaimed by the forests.

Another hold the Olympics have on me comes from the rain forests. Of the several rain forests the one to my liking is on the Hoh River. The zone that lies in the Hoh Valley below 1000 feet is as interesting and unique as any segment of our forests the nation over.

One who comes from the ocean front passes through a spruce-cedar climax forest. This lies below the 1000-foot level and is made up of the Sitka spruce, red cedar, and western hemlock. The rain forest is farther inland. Each rain forest has a bottom carved out by a glacier. The valley is not a mile wide in places and runs on average fourteen miles in length within park boundaries. The stream gradients are very gradual. Yet in spite of this and the heavy rainfall, the valley floors—consisting of glacial till and water-deposited sands and gravel—are well drained, little standing water being in evidence even after the heaviest rain.

Sitka spruce is dominant in the rain forest, some of them 300 feet high and over ten feet in diameter. Western hemlock, which rises up to 200 feet high, comes next among the conifers, and the red cedar last. Douglas fir is here too. Douglas fir, which occasionally reaches 300 feet, is what the foresters call a pioneer species. It comes in whenever the mineral soil is bared, as after a heavy windfall or fire. Since Douglas fir cannot reproduce in shade, the western hemlock and red cedar eventually take over. That process, continued indefinitely, would eliminate the Douglas fir from the Pacific Northwest forests. Something, however, is always happening that clears the thick woods and opens them up. When that occurs, Douglas fir manages to hold its own.

The Sitka spruce dominate the rain forest today. The branches and leaves of these high trees form a roof that lets in only shafts of sunlight. The understory is big leaf maple, vine maple, devil's club.

Down logs are covered with a thick carpet of mosses. Sometimes they are so completely covered by moss and so heavy with young growth that they look like a low hedge. The trees are hung with mosses, liverworts, and lichens that cover the trunks and even the crowns. These are the epiphytes that have no connection with the soil. They get their nutrients from rain water, windborne particles, and the decaying bark of their host. They are not parasites but rather hitch-hikers of the rain forest. Underfoot are bracken and other ferns, the bead-ruby with glossy leaves, wood sorrel, wild strawberries, red huckleberries, Oregon grape, and fragrant bed-straw. There are snails and millipedes in the moss. Some lichens are coral colored with brilliant red tips. Some are shaped like cups and painted orange.

Due to the extreme wetness of the forest, the down logs are ancient relics. Decomposition is so slow that some have lain there for 400 years. They often have tiny rows of Sitka spruce on them, seedlings not more than a few inches high. The seeds that fall on the damp ground, heavy with moss, ferns, and grass, have little chance for survival. Those that land on the old log have head room to grow and lesser competition. This old log will be a nurse to the seedlings for many years. In time they will send their roots down and around the nurse log to the ground. For some years the new trees will appear to be standing on stilts. But in time—perhaps several hundred years later—the nurse log will have decomposed, much of it being absorbed by the new trees. Then the roots will enlarge and fill up the space left by the nurse log. Those that travel the forest on that future day will see giants where I saw seedlings. Not knowing about the old nurse log, they may wonder why it is that these new trees are swollen, distorted, and heavily buttressed at the base. And they may also wonder why the trees stand in a row, giving a colonnade effect.

Loggers often claim that overage trees and down trees are wasted and should be removed. That is a false premise in the Olympics. For in the true rain forest these rotting logs are the best seed ground available.

Thanks to the elk, the forest floor is fairly free of thick underbrush; one can see for some distance.

On a rainy day the force of the storm is broken by the treetops. Only a slight drizzle comes through. After a hard rain the trees will drip for days. On a bright day the shafts of sunlight fill the rain forest with a soft green light that is restful to the eyes. Rain or shine, this forest has a quiet that is deep and profound. A winter wren sings high overhead. Though few birds are seen in the rain forest, many breed there—ruffed grouse, jays, tanagers, grosbeaks, finches, siskins, juncos, warblers, and song sparrows. A snowshoe rabbit runs underfoot. A Douglas squirrel sounds the alarm. Every noise is soft and muted. The quiet and the light induce a mood of reverence. This is not a place to run, to shout. This is a cathedral, draped in mosses and lichens and made of gigantic trees. The trees alone are enough to bring humility to man. The western hemlock is over twenty-five feet in girth, Douglas fir over fifty feet, and Sitka spruce over forty feet. These are virgin trees in a virgin forest. They would have disappeared by now if the logging interests had had their way. There are some who see in them no more than so many board feet. But they are among the great wonders of creation. Kellogg bluegrass and the delicate trefoil foam flower flourish near the trail in the rain forest. The trailing raspberry with its starry five-petaled white flowers is bright. The showy miner's lettuce, with white petals, makes a thick stand. The waxen white wintergreen and the rose-colored Oregon oxalis sorrel are almost hidden in the litter of the forest floor. The snowberry—later to have white fruit—shows pink flowers. Everywhere stands the graceful vanilla leaf, its slender cluster of white flowers high on a single stem rising above one leaf divided into three broad leaflets.

There are fungi in every forest and every field. But I never feel their presence so vividly as I do in the rain forest. Here are molds, mildew, mushrooms, shelf fungus, rust, to mention only a few. Thousands of others work unseen in the vegetation that makes a soft, thick carpet underfoot. Some produce spores that fill the air and cause people to suffer from allergies. But all of them perform functions crucially essential to forests and fields.

Forest humus is not a mass of plant remains but a living mass of fungi. The genera alone run into the thousands. Bacteria predominate in soil rich in nutrients, cultivated, and fertilized. Fungi are more active in the forests and in compact, poor soils. They are present even in nearly pure silicious sands.

Since the fungi have no chlorophyll, they lack the means of manufacturing their own food. They must, therefore, be parasites and live on other living things, or be saprophytes, or scavengers, and live on dead organic matter. They do one or the other, most of them being saprophytic. The latter have a far wider range of food than the parasites.

Parasites do not live on vegetation alone. Some live on microscopic animals, insects, worms, fluke eggs, and the larvae of mosquitoes.

While some saprophytes are scavengers of vegetable matter, others consume carcasses of animals, some live on animal excrement, and so on. Each supply of organic material seems to have its special saprophyte.

Dozens of strains of fungi have been shown to be capable of inhibiting the growth of bacteria and of producing a variety of antibiotic substances. Some fungi destroy other fungi that are parasitic, and bacteria as well.

Soil-inhabiting fungi produce organic acids which dissolve inorganic soil elements such as calcium, magnesium, and phosphorus and make them available for food. Sometimes this food, produced by the fungi, is used by them. Most of it, however, is used by green plants. The decomposed materials, not eaten by the fungi or used by green plants, are left as humus. Humus is resistant to rapid attack by micro-organisms and forms a cohesive part of the soil system. These soil fungi—whether in forests or fields—are, therefore, highly important to soil fertility.

The logs at my feet in the Olympics have been collecting spores of fungi from the time the trees fell. Only those spores which can use this particular wood will flourish on this down timber. Some fungi feed on hardwoods, some on conifers, some on leaves. Each has its special diet. One set of fungi may cause the primary decay in the logs; another set may come in later and attack the remains. Some fungi, such as the coral mushroom, are parasitic on the roots of trees. Poking my foot into the litter of the forest floor, I turn up a small colony of mushrooms, *Agaricus subrutilescens*. These tender morsels, low to the ground and shaped like a Japanese parasol, are delicious when broiled in butter. They are one of many mushrooms that flourish in the dark, damp wood of the rain forest. And when we pick them it has no more effect on the mushroom plant than picking fruit from a tree. What we pick is the fruit. The plant is a vast network of threads so fine that they are not visible to the naked eye until they are twisted into strands. These threads produce enzymes which digest food particles outside the threads. When the digested material is in solution, and only then, is it absorbed by the plant. The spores from this dainty mushroom at my feet will spread; but the plant will produce mushrooms over and over again. If I can only mark this spot, I will find, on my return after more warm rains, a new crop from the old plant.

I learned in the Olympics an important lesson in ecology. The lesson is that wilderness areas are essential to our long-time welfare and well-being as a nation. The wilderness area is the norm. In the areas where man has introduced crops, sprays, fertilizers, the ecological balance has been upset. At times the result may be harmful. DDT can make milk from cows dangerous to humans. Certain fruit sprays kill bees that are essential to pollenization. At other times the remedy used by man merely helps nature in her corrective process. Yet the wilderness stands as the true "control" plot for all experimentation in the animal and vegetable worlds. Only through knowledge of the norm can an appraisal of the abnormal or diseased be made. The "control" plot, where vegetable and animal growth continues undisturbed, is as essential to successful diagnosis and management of soil conditions as normal individuals are to the practice of medicine.

That is, I think, what Thoreau meant when he wrote, "In wildness is the preservation of the world." Farming, for example, imports plants, animals, and fertilizers. It eliminates native flora and fauna and even some of the unseen fungi and bacteria that have built the soil. All this is necessary for human existence. But will it stabilize the soil or will we end with sterile land and ugly gullies? No one knows. Nature got stability by encouraging great diversity. We do not yet know whether we can do the same through man-made substitutes.

No species should ever be eliminated, for man in his wisdom does not yet know the full wonders and details of the cosmic scheme.

On one side lichens, fungi, insects, bacteria, mammals, birds, and on the other the trees, ferns, and underbrush are interlocked or combined into a community in this Olympic forest. It is a community of competition and of interdependence. It is a series of food chains too intricate for man to comprehend in all its ramifications.

The rain forests are so radiant with soft green light, so filled with endless wonders that I hate to leave them. Yet when I reach the high ridges and meadows of the Olympics I hate to leave them also.

There are many paths that lead to the summits. My favorite is

Graves Creek, one of the tributaries of the Quinault. From road's end it is only twelve miles to the Enchanted Valley, and in that distance one gains only a few hundred feet in elevation. The trail is fine for horses, and there are lush meadows at the head of the canyon where they can graze. Yet one should take this trip only on foot.

That is the way Daniel B. Beard, of the Park Service, Elon Gilbert, and I reached the Enchanted Valley. Dan was born to the woods and is a naturalist of distinction. To Elon any stretch of woods is a sanctuary. So as we hiked we had keen, observing, understanding eyes absorbing even the minutiae.

This is ground to explore closely. Even when travel is slow it would take repeated journeys to see only a part of the wonders. There are small streams every quarter mile or so, and their water seems sweeter to the taste than any I know. After the rain forest proper has been left behind, the ground is still thick with moss. Big-leafed maples now appear in open orchards, every bit of them from trunk to crown hung with thick mats of bright green moss. On the river flats the red alder grows in spectacular stands. They seldom stand straight; yet, unlike trees in wind-blown areas, they do not lean one way. They are gracefully arranged to make every grove an artistic creation. And the higher one goes the lighter the bark, until in some places it seems that this is a bit of the birch forests of the northland transplanted.

The western hemlock marches most of the way to the Enchanted Valley. And its cones—the smallest of any of our western conifers—literally cover sections of the trail, making the underfooting soft and springy.

If the fireweed is at its peak in the lower valley, the trail along Graves Creek is almost certain to be lined for miles and miles with the Siberian miner's lettuce. The dainty pinkish flowers stand gracefully on slender stalks growing out of two broad basal leaves. The plant is succulent, as good as lettuce. The trefoil foam flower, with tiny white lacelike flowers, is second in abundance. Occasional stands of the monkey flower show bright yellow. Cinquefoil shows an even deeper yellow. Delicate white hawkweeds grow in the damper places. The tiny American speedwell adds touches of blue. Purple self-heal (whose juices the Indians mixed with grease to make an ointment) are common. Bleeding hearts are abundant. The low bunchberry dogwood is nearly gone. The bloom of the oxalis has passed, but its shamrock-shaped leaves cover the shaded ground. The vanilla leaf is in seed. Some blackberries are still in bloom. The thimbleberries are beginning to ripen, and the red huckleberry too.

Along the river bank are water ouzels, flitting from rock to rock looking for beetles in the moss and periwinkles in the water. Somewhere high in the trees is the tiny western winter wren, who serenades the traveler all the way to the Enchanted Valley.

The eastern canyon wall at Enchanted Valley is almost sheer. It is an imposing precipice, adorned by rugged escarpments and ledges without number. This wall spouts several dozen waterfalls in July. Some will last all Summer, for they are fed by large pockets of perpetual snow. These waterfalls that drop 2000 feet or so fill the deep, narrow valley with music that can be heard above the murmur of Graves Creek. This eastern wall is a spectacle at the close of day. The sun leaves the bottom of the canyon early and sends a shadow up the eastern wall, turning it into a sundial. And in the morning the shadow creeps slowly downward on the opposite wall. Morning or night is the time to watch this steep eastern wall for mountain goat. Though the cliffs seem sheer, there are pockets of meadows among them. Here the goats feed, though it may take field glasses to detect them.

At the head of this canyon is Anderson Peak (7365 feet), which shows Hanging Glacier on its south slopes. This glacier used to move downward until it hung over the edge of the canyon wall. Then it would break into huge ice blocks with a roar that would fill the Enchanted Valley. These Olympic glaciers, like others of the Pacific Northwest, are the habitat of the snow or ice worms—species of the genus *Mesenchytraeus*. They are black and an inch long. Their activity picks up with the melting snow. But they die when removed and exposed to normal temperature. The birds of the Olympics feast on them. Hanging Glacier these days is receding. It is an invitation to those who have crampons, rope, and ice axes. One crosses it when he climbs Anderson Peak. But there is a trail that swings west and south of Anderson and climbs the western wall above the Enchanted Valley and takes one to Hart Lake and La Crosse Lake—two alpine gems of the Olympics.

At about 4000 feet the western hemlock is supplanted by the

mountain hemlock, every cone of which is a miniature tree, perfectly formed. Now the Pacific silver fir and the peaked alpine fir take over. Mountain ash begins to appear, along with a few Alaska yellow cedars. The Hart Lake trail is mostly in shade all the way to the top, except where it crosses alpine meadows. In July the elderberry bush is in bloom at these altitudes. The pioneer violet shows dainty yellow flowers. A few queencup bead-lily are beginning to show their dainty white petals between two glossy leaves. In open areas the tiny purple alpine speedwell is in bloom. Shooting stars show purplish pink in shady spots. The Alaska spirea is much in evidence. Mountain dandelions are on display. Marsh marigolds—white petals with yellow centers—seem to be rushing into bloom on warm hillsides. A few clumps of squaw grass show their creamy white blossoms. Some delicate western pasqueflowers, whose dainty plumes appear in August, are beginning to bloom in mid-July. A tiny alpine buttercup is gay. The alpine meadows have just been rid of their thick snow blankets. The alpine fir has hardly yet recovered from the great weight that was on it for months. Sedges that will grow eighteen inches high are beginning to reach upward. Lupine is not yet in bloom. Only a few blossoms of the low-bush blueberry and the thickly matted white-flowered cassiope are out. False hellebore is fresh and thick but yet to blossom. The alpine meadows are on the edge of a great awakening that will transform them. What gives them their greatest distinction this day is the avalanche lily. This delicate flower with white petals and yellow centers comes up on the very edge of snowbanks and follows the snow as it retreats. Mid-July, Dan Beard, Elon Gilbert, and I found acres of them on the high slopes along the trail to Hart Lake. We sat in the shade of mountain hemlock, admiring them. Three bull elk in turn watched us and then stepped behind a clump of alpine fir and hurriedly crossed several snow fields. A Pacific varied thrush called over and over again. A ruffed grouse set up his drumming in the thick forest below us.

The snow fields on these high Olympic ridges will not be gone until August first. Shortly Fall will set in. There will be five feet of snow or more in the Enchanted Valley before many months pass. On the high ridge where we sit the drifts will be many times that deep. In the short interval between now and then the canyon walls of the Enchanted Valley will be ablaze with colors.

Life comes quickly and passes quickly on these Olympic ridges. Those who have the urge to turn their backs on cities and seek the glories of high alpine meadows have only a few precious weeks for their adventure.

CROSSING THE SIERRA IN WINTER

BY JOHN CHARLES FRÉMONT

John Charles Frémont (1813–1890) was a remarkable and controversial figure in American history—Army engineer, Civil War general, explorer, United States Senator, Presidential candidate, Governor of Arizona Territory. His major writings consist of his reports of various government expeditions he led. Virtually all these explorations were guided by trappers and frontiersmen who had previously explored the areas, but in most instances Frémont's reports were the first extensive reports published. He is sometimes credited with opening the Oregon Trail, though it was traveled by many others before Frémont. His report of a journey through the Great Salt Lake area in Utah is said to have persuaded Brigham Young to choose it as a haven for the Mormons, though trappers and traders were long familiar with the area and had written about it before Frémont saw it. This selection, taken from the Frémont report of an expedition made in 1842–45, is an account of what has been called the first crossing of the Sierra Nevada under winter conditions, though Jedediah Smith led a small party of trappers across the snowbound Sierra almost twenty years earlier. Frémont's account, however, remains vividly accurate and dramatically detailed.

(Report of the Exploring Expedition to the Rocky Mountains in the Year 1842, and to Oregon and North California

in 1843–44, by John Charles Frémont; official government report, 1845.)

November 18, 1843. [At the Dalles] . . . . Carson had removed the camp a little nearer to the hills, where the animals had better grass. We found everything in good order, and arrived just in time to partake of an excellent roast of California beef. . . .

The camp was now occupied in making the necessary preparations for our homeward journey, which, though homeward, contemplated a new route, and a great circuit to the south and southeast, and the exploration of the Great Basin between the Rocky Mountains and the Sierra Nevada. Three principal objects were indicated, by report or by maps, as being on this route, the character or existence of which I wished to ascertain, and which I assumed as landmarks, or leading points, on the projected line of return. The first of these points was the Klamath lake, on the tableland between the head of Fall River, which comes to the Columbia, and the Sacramento, which goes to the Bay of San Francisco; and from which lake a river of the same name makes its way westwardly direct to the ocean. This lake and river are often called Klamath. . . . The position of this lake, on the line of inland communication between Oregon and California; its proximity to the demarcation boundary of latitude 42°; its imputed double character of lake, or meadow, according to the season of the year; and the hostile and warlike character attributed to the Indians about it—all made it a desirable object to visit and examine. From this lake our course was intended to be about southeast, to a reported lake called Mary's, at some days' journey in the Great Basin; and thence, still on southeast, to the reputed Buenaventura River [nonexistent], which has had a place in so many maps, and countenanced the belief of the existence of a great river flowing from the Rocky Mountains to the Bay of San Francisco. From the Buenaventura the next point was intended to be in that section of the Rocky Mountains which includes the heads of Arkansas River, and of the opposite waters of the California Gulf; and thence down the Arkansas to Bent's Fort, and home.

This was our projected line of return—a great part of it absolutely new to geographical, botanical, and geological science—and the subject of reports in relation to lakes, rivers, deserts, and savages hardly above the condition of mere wild animals, which inflamed desire to know what this terra incognita really contained. It was a serious enterprise, at the commencement of winter, to undertake the traverse of such a region, and with a party consisting only of twenty-five persons, and they of many nations—American, French, German, Canadian, Indian, and colored—and most of them young, several being under twenty-one years of age.

All knew that a strange country was to be explored, and dangers and hardships to be encountered; but no one blenched at the prospect. On the contrary, courage and confidence animated the whole party. Cheerfulness, readiness, subordination, prompt obedience, characterized all; nor did any extremity of peril and privation, to which we were afterward exposed, ever belie, or derogate from, the fine spirit of this brave and generous commencement. . . .

January 31st [1844]. We took our way over a gently rising ground, the dividing ridge being tolerably low; and traveling easily along a broad trail, in twelve or fourteen miles reached the upper part of the pass, when it began to snow heavily, with very cold weather. The Indians had only the usual scanty covering, and appeared to suffer greatly from the cold. All left us except our guide. Half-hidden by the storm, the mountains looked dreary; and as night began to approach, the guide showed great reluctance to go forward. I placed him between two rifles, for the way began to be difficult. Traveling a little farther, we struck a ravine, which the Indian said would conduct us to the river; and as the poor fellow suffered greatly, shivering in the snow which fell upon his naked skin, I would not detain him any longer, and he ran off to the mountain, where, he said, there was a hut near by. He had kept the blue and scarlet cloths I had given him tightly rolled up, preferring rather to endure the cold than to get them wet.

In the course of the afternoon, one of the men had a foot frostbitten; and about dark we had the satisfaction of reaching the bottoms of a stream timbered with large trees, among which we found a sheltered camp. We saw an abundance of such grass as the season afforded for the animals. We saw before us, in descending from the pass, a great continuous range, along which stretched the valley of the river, the lower parts steep, and dark with pines, while, above, it was hidden in clouds of snow. This we felt instantly satisfied was the central ridge of the Sierra Nevada, the great California Mountain, which only now intervened between us and the waters of the bay. We had made a forced march of twenty-six miles, and three mules had given out on the road. Up to this point, with the exception of two stolen by Indians, we had lost none of the horses which had been brought from the Columbia River, and a number of these were still strong and in tolerably good order. We had now sixty-seven animals in the band.

We had scarcely lighted our fires when the camp was crowded with nearly naked [Washoe] Indians; some of them were furnished with long nets in addition to bows, and appeared to have been out on the sage hills to hunt rabbits. These nets were, perhaps, thirty to forty feet long, kept upright in the ground by slight sticks at intervals, and were made from a kind of wild hemp, very much resembling, in manufacture, those common among the Indians of the Sacramento Valley. They came among us without any fear, and scattered themselves about the fires, mainly occupied in gratifying their astonishment. I was struck by the singular appearance of a row of about a dozen, who were sitting on their haunches perched on a log near one of the fires, with their quick sharp eyes following every motion.

We gathered together a few of the most intelligent of the Indians, and held this evening an interesting council. I explained to them my intentions. I told them that we had come from a very far country, having been traveling now nearly a year, and that we were desirous simply to go across the mountain into the country of the other whites. There were two who appeared particularly intelligent—one, a somewhat old man. He told me that before the snows fell, it was six sleeps to the place where the whites lived, but that now it was impossible to cross the mountain on account of the deep snow; and showing us, as the others had done, that it was over our heads, he urged us strongly to follow the course of the river, which he said would conduct us to a lake in which there were many large fish. There, he said, were many people; there was no snow on the ground, and we might remain there until the spring.

From their descriptions we were enabled to judge that we had encamped on the upper water of the Salmon Trout River [near the present Markleeville, California]. It is hardly necessary to say that our communication was only by signs, as we understood nothing of their language; but they spoke, notwithstanding, rapidly and vehemently, explaining what they considered the folly of our intentions, and urging us to go down to the lake. Tah-ve, a word signifying "snow," we very soon learned to know, from its frequent repetition. I told him that the men and the horses were strong, and that we would break a road through the snow; and spreading before him our bales of scarlet cloth, and trinkets, showed him what we would give for a guide. It was necessary to obtain one, if possible; for I had determined here to attempt the passage of the mountain. . . .

The snow, which had intermitted in the evening, commenced falling again in the course of the night, and it snowed steadily all day. In the morning I acquainted the men with my decision, and explained to them that necessity required us to make a great effort to clear the mountains. I reminded them of the beautiful valley of the Sacramento, with which they were familiar from the descriptions of Carson, who had been there some fifteen years ago, and who, in our late privations, had delighted us in speaking of its rich pastures and abounding game, and drew a vivid contrast between its summer climate, less than a hundred miles distant, and the falling snow around us. I informed them (and long experience had given them confidence in my observations and good instruments) that almost directly west, and only about seventy miles distant, was the great farming establishment of Captain Sutter—a gentleman who had formerly lived in Missouri, and, emigrating to this country, had become the possessor of a principality. I assured them that from the heights of the mountain before us we should doubtless see the valley of the Sacramento River, and with one effort place ourselves again in the midst of plenty.

The people received this decision with the cheerful obedience which had always characterized them; and the day was immediately devoted to the preparations necessary to enable us to carry it into effect. Leggings, moccasins, clothing—all were put into the best state to resist the cold. Our guide was not neglected. Extremity of suffering might make him desert; we therefore did the best we could for him. Leggings, moccasins, some articles of clothing, and a large green blanket, in addition to the blue and scarlet cloth, were lavished upon him, and to his great and evident contentment. He arrayed himself in all his colors, and, clad in green, blue, and scarlet, he made a gay-looking Indian and, with his various presents, was probably richer and better clothed than any of his tribe had ever been before.

I have already said that our provisions were very low; we had neither tallow nor grease of any kind remaining, and the want of salt became one of our greatest privations. The poor dog which had been found in the Bear River Valley, and which had been a compagnon de voyage ever since, had now become fat, and the mess to which it belonged requested permission to kill it. Leave was granted. Spread out on the snow, the meat looked very good, and it made a strengthening meal for the greater part of the camp. Indians brought in two or three rabbits during the day, which were purchased from them. . . .

February 2d. It had ceased snowing, and this morning the lower air was clear and frosty; and six or seven thousand feet above, the peaks of the Sierra now and then appeared among the rolling clouds, which were rapidly dispersing before the sun. Our Indian shook his head as he pointed to the icy pinnacles shooting high up into the sky, and seeming almost immediately above us. Crossing the river on the ice, and leaving it immediately, we commenced the ascent of the mountain along the valley of a tributary stream. The people were unusually silent; for every man knew that our enterprise was hazardous, and the issue doubtful.

The snow deepened rapidly, and it soon became necessary to break a road. For this service, a party of ten was formed, mounted on the strongest horses; each man in succession opening the road on foot, or on horseback, until himself and his horse became fatigued, when he stepped aside; and, the remaining number passing ahead, he took his station in the rear. Leaving this stream, and pursuing a very direct course, we passed over an intervening ridge to the river we had left.

On the way we passed two low huts entirely covered with snow, which might very easily have escaped observation. A family was living in each; and the only trail I saw in the neighborhood was from the door hole to a nut-pine tree near, which supplied them with food and fuel. We found two similar huts on the creek where we next arrived; and, traveling a little higher up, encamped on its banks in about four feet depth of snow. Carson found near an open hillside, where the wind and the sun had melted the snow, leaving exposed sufficient bunch grass for the animals tonight. . . .

February 4th. I went ahead early with two or three men, each with a led horse, to break the road. We were obliged to abandon the hollow entirely, and work along the mountainside, which was very steep, and the snow covered with an icy crust. We cut a footing as we advanced, and trampled a road through for the animals; but occasionally one plunged outside the trail, and slid along the field to the bottom, a hundred yards below. . . .

Toward a pass which the guide indicated here we attempted in the afternoon to force a road; but after a laborious plunging through two or three hundred yards, our best horses gave out, entirely refusing to make any further effort; and, for the time, we were brought to a stand. The guide informed us that we were entering the deep snow, and here began the difficulties of the mountain; and to him, and almost to all, our enterprise seemed hopeless. I returned a short distance back, to the break in the hollow, where I met Mr. Fitzpatrick.

The camp had been all the day occupied in endeavoring to ascend the hill, but only the best horses had succeeded, the animals, generally, not having sufficient strength to bring themselves up without the packs; and all the line of road between this and the springs was strewed with camp stores and equipage, and horses floundering in snow. . . .

Tonight we had no shelter, but we made a large fire around the trunk of one of the huge pines; and covering the snow with small boughs, on which we spread our blankets, soon made ourselves comfortable. The night was very bright and clear, and though the thermometer was only down to 10°, a strong wind which sprang up at sundown made it intensely cold, and this was one of the bitterest nights during the journey.

Two Indians joined our party here; and one of them, an old man, immediately began to harangue us, saying that ourselves and animals would perish in the snow, and that if we would go back, he would show us another and a better way across the mountain. He spoke in a very loud voice, and there was a singular repetition of phrases and arrangement of words which rendered his speech striking and not unmusical.

We had now begun to understand some words, and, with the aid of signs, easily comprehended the old man's simple ideas. "Rock upon rock—rock upon rock—snow upon snow—snow upon snow," said he; "even if you get over the snow, you will not be able to get down from the mountains." He made us the sign of precipices, and showed us how the feet of the horses would slip, and throw them off from the narrow trails which led along their sides.

Our Chinook, who comprehended even more readily than ourselves, and believed our situation hopeless, covered his head with his blanket and began to weep and lament. "I wanted to see the whites," said he; "I came away from my own people to see the whites, and I wouldn't care to die among them; but here"—and he looked around into the cold night and gloomy forest, and, drawing his blanket over his head, began again to lament. Seated around the tree, the fire illuminating the rocks and the tall bolls of the pines round about, and the old Indian haranguing, we presented a group of very serious faces. . . .

February 6th. Accompanied by Mr. Fitzpatrick, I set out today, with a reconnoitering party, on snowshoes. We marched all in single file, trampling the snow as heavily as we could. Crossing the open basin, in a march of about ten miles we reached the top of one of the peaks, to the left of the pass indicated by our guide.

Far below us, dimmed by the distance, was a large snowless valley, bounded on the western side, at the distance of about a hundred miles, by a low range of mountains, which Carson recognized with delight as the mountains bordering the coast. "There," said he, "is the little mountain—it is fifteen years ago since I saw it; but I am just as sure as if I had seen it yesterday." Between us, then, and this low coast range, was the valley of the Sacramento; and no one who had not accompanied us through the incidents of our life for the last few months could realize the delight with which at last we looked down upon it. At the distance of apparently thirty miles beyond us were distinguished spots of prairie; and a dark line, which could be traced with the glass, was imagined to be the course of the river; but we were evidently at a great height above the valley, and between us and the plains extended miles of snowy fields, and broken ridges of pine-covered mountains. . . .

With one party drawing sleighs loaded with baggage, I advanced today about four miles along the trail, and encamped at the first grassy spot where we expected to bring our horses. Mr. Fitzpatrick, with another party, remained behind, to form an intermediate station between us and the animals.

February 8th. The night had been extremely cold but perfectly still and beautifully clear. Before the sun appeared this morning the thermometer was 3° below zero; 1° higher, when his rays struck the lofty peaks; and 0° when they reached our camp. Scenery and weather combined must render these mountains beautiful in summer; the purity and deep-blue color of the sky are singularly beautiful; the days are sunny and bright, and even warm in the noon hours; and if we could be free from the many anxieties that oppress us, even now we would be delighted here; but our provisions are getting fearfully scant. . . . We continued on for a mile and a half, and encamped at the foot of a long hill on this side of the open bottom. . . . Elevation of the camp, by the boiling-point, is seven thousand nine hundred and twenty feet.

February 9th. During the night the weather changed, the wind rising to a gale, and commencing to snow before daylight; before morning the trail was covered. We remained quiet in camp all day, in the course of which the weather improved. Four sleighs arrived toward evening, with the bedding of the men. We suffer much from the want of salt; and all the men are becoming weak from insufficient food.

February 10th. . . . The wind kept the air filled with snow during the day; the sky was very dark in the southwest, though elsewhere very clear. The forest here has a noble appearance: the tall cedar is abundant; its greatest height being one hundred and thirty feet, and circumference twenty, three or four feet above the ground; and here I see for the first time the white pine, of which there are some magnificent trees. . . .

The elevation of the camp, by the boiling-point, is eight thousand and fifty feet. We are now one thousand feet above the level of the South Pass in the Rocky Mountains; and still we are not done ascending. The top of a flat ridge near was bare of snow, and very well sprinkled with bunch grass, sufficient to pasture the animals two or three days, and this was to be their main point of support. . . .

Putting on our snowshoes, we spent the afternoon in exploring a road ahead. The glare of the snow, combined with the great fatigue, had rendered many of the people nearly blind; but we were fortunate in having some black silk handkerchiefs, which, worn as veils, very much relieved the eyes.

February 11th. High wind continued, and our trail this morning was nearly invisible—here and there indicated by a little ridge of snow. Our situation became tiresome and dreary, requiring a strong exercise of patience and resolution.

In the evening I received a message from Mr. Fitzpatrick, acquainting me with the utter failure of his attempt to get our mules and horses over the snow—the half-hidden trail had proved entirely too slight to support them, and they had broken through, and were plunging about or lying half-buried in snow. He was occupied in endeavoring to get them back to his camp, and in the meantime sent to me for further instructions. I wrote to him to send the animals immediately back to their old pastures; and, after having made mauls and shovels, turn in all the strength of his party to open and beat a road through the snow, strengthening it with branches and boughs of the pines.

February 12th. We made mauls, and worked hard at our end of the road all the day. The wind was high, but the sun bright, and the snow thawing. We worked down the face of the hill, to meet the people at the other end. Toward sundown it began to grow cold, and we shouldered our mauls, and trudged back to camp.

February 13th. We continued to labor on the road, and in the course of the day had the satisfaction to see the people working down the face of the opposite hill, about three miles distant. During the morning we had the pleasure of a visit from Mr. Fitzpatrick, with the information that all was going on well. A party of Indians had passed on snowshoes, who said they were going to the western side of the mountain after fish. This was an indication that the salmon were coming up the streams; and we could hardly restrain our impatience as we thought of them, and worked with increased vigor.

The meat train did not arrive this evening, and I gave Godey leave to kill our little dog (Klamath), which he prepared in Indian fashion—scorching off the hair, and washing the skin with soap and snow, and then cutting it up into pieces, which were laid on the snow. Shortly afterward the sleigh arrived with a supply of horse meat; and we had tonight an extraordinary dinner—pea soup, mule, and dog.

February 14th. With Mr. Preuss [Charles Preuss, cartographer], I ascended today the highest peak near us, from which we had a beautiful view of a mountain lake at our feet, about fifteen miles in length, and so entirely surrounded by mountains that we could not discover an outlet. We had taken with us a glass; but though we enjoyed an extended view, the valley was half hidden in mist, as when we had seen it before. Snow could be distinguished on the higher parts of the coast mountains; eastward, as far as the eye could extend, it ranged over a terrible mass of broken snowy mountains, fading off blue in the distance. . . .

February 16th. We had succeeded in getting our animals safely to the first grassy hill. . . .

We started again early in the morning. The creek acquired a regular breadth of about twenty feet, and we soon began to hear the rushing of the water below the icy surface, over which we traveled to avoid the snow; a few miles below we broke through where the water was several feet deep, and halted to make a fire and dry our clothes. We continued a few miles farther, walking being very laborious without snowshoes.

I was now perfectly satisfied that we had struck the stream on which Mr. Sutter lived; and, turning about, made a hard push and reached the camp at dark. Here we had the pleasure to find all the remaining animals, fifty-seven in number, safely arrived at the grassy hill near the camp; and here, also, we were agreeably surprised with the sight of an abundance of salt. Some of the horse guard had gone to a neighboring hut for pine nuts, and discovered unexpectedly a large cake of very white, fine-grained salt, which the Indians told them they had brought from the other side of the mountain; they used it to eat with their pine nuts, and readily sold it for goods.

On the 19th, the people were occupied in making a road and bringing up the baggage; and, on the afternoon of the next day, February 20, 1844, we encamped with the animals and all the material of the camp, on the summit of the pass in the dividing ridge, one thousand miles by our traveled road from the Dalles of the Columbia. The people, who had not yet been to this point, climbed the neighboring peak to enjoy a look at the valley.

The temperature of boiling water gave for the elevation of the encampment nine thousand three hundred and thirty-eight feet above the sea [Carson Pass, actual elevation, 8,635 feet]. This was two thousand feet higher than the South Pass in the Rocky Mountains, and several peaks in view rose several thousand feet still higher. . . .

February 21st. We now considered ourselves victorious over the mountain; having only the descent before us, and the valley under our eyes, we felt strong hope that we should force our way down. But this was a case in which the descent was not facile. Still deep fields of snow lay between, and there was a large intervening space of rough-looking mountains, through which we had yet to wind our way.

Carson roused me this morning with an early fire, and we were all up long before day, in order to pass the snow fields before the sun should render the crust soft. We enjoyed this morning a scene at sunrise, which even here was unusually glorious and beautiful. Immediately above the eastern mountains was repeated a cloud-formed mass of purple ranges, bordered with bright yellow-gold; the peaks shot up into a narrow line of crimson cloud, above which the air was filled with a greenish orange; and over all was the singular beauty of the blue sky. . . .

Shortly afterward we heard the roll of thunder, and looking toward the valley, found it all enveloped in a thunderstorm. For us, as connected with the idea of summer, it had a singular charm; and we watched its progress with excited feelings until nearly sunset, when the sky cleared off brightly, and we saw a shining line of water directing its course toward another, a broader and larger sheet. We knew that these could be no other than the Sacramento and the Bay of San Francisco; but, after our long wandering in rugged mountains, where so frequently we had met with disappointments, and where the crossing of every ridge displayed some unknown lake or river, we were yet almost afraid to believe that we were at last to escape into the genial country of which we had heard so many glowing descriptions, and dreaded again to find some vast interior lake, whose bitter waters would bring us disappointment. On the southern shore of what appeared to be the bay could be traced the gleaming line where entered another large stream. . . .

We had the satisfaction to know that at least there were people below. Fires were lit up in the valley just at night, appearing to be in answer to ours; and these signs of life renewed, in some measure, the gaiety of the camp. They appeared so near that we judged them to be among the timber of some of the neighboring ridges; but, having them constantly in view day after day, and night after night, we afterward found them to be fires that had been kindled by the Indians among the tulares, on the shore of the bay, eighty miles distant.

Among the very few plants that appeared here was the common blue flax. Tonight a mule was killed for food. . . .

February 23d. This was our most difficult day: we were forced off the ridges by the quantity of snow among the timber, and obliged to take to the mountainsides, where, occasionally, rocks and a southern exposure afforded us a chance to scramble along. But these were steep, and slippery with snow and ice; and the tough evergreens of the mountain impeded our way, tore our skins, and exhausted our patience. Some of us had the misfortune to wear moccasins with parfleche soles, so slippery that we could not keep our feet, and generally crawled across the snow beds.

Axes and mauls were necessary today to make a road through the snow. Going ahead with Carson to reconnoiter the road, we reached in the afternoon the river which made the outlet of the lake. Carson sprang over, clear across a place where the stream was compressed among rocks, but the parfleche sole of my moccasin glanced from the icy rock, and precipitated me into the river. It was some few seconds before I could recover myself in the current, and Carson, thinking me hurt, jumped in after me, and we both had an icy bath. We tried to search awhile for my gun, which had been lost in the fall, but the cold drove us out; and making a large fire on the bank, after we had partially dried ourselves we went back to meet the camp. We afterward found that the gun had been slung under the ice which lined the banks of the creek. . . .

February 24th. . . . We continued down the south face of the mountain; our road leading over dry ground, we were able to avoid the snow almost entirely. In the course of the morning we struck a footpath, which we were generally able to keep; and the ground was soft to our animals' feet, being sandy or covered with mold. Green grass began to make its appearance, and occasionally we passed a hill scatteringly covered with it. . . .

The opposite mountainside was very steep and continuous—unbroken by ravines, and covered with pines and snow; while on the side we were traveling, innumerable rivulets poured down from the ridge. Continuing on, we halted a moment at one of these rivulets, to admire some beautiful evergreen trees, resembling live oak, which shaded the little stream. They were forty to fifty feet high, and two in diameter, with a uniform tufted top; and the summer green of their beautiful foliage, with the singing birds, and the sweet summer wind which was whirling about the dry oak leaves, nearly intoxicated us with delight; and we hurried on, filled with excitement, to escape entirely from the horrid region of inhospitable snow to the perpetual spring of the Sacramento.

When we had traveled about ten miles, the valley opened a little to an oak and pine bottom, through which ran rivulets closely bordered with rushes, on which our half-starved horses fell with avidity; and here we made our encampment. Here the roaring torrent has already become a river [South Fork of the American River], and we had descended to an elevation of three thousand eight hundred and sixty-four feet. . . . Another horse was killed tonight, for food.

February 25th. Believing that the difficulties of the road were passed, and leaving Mr. Fitzpatrick to follow slowly, as the condition of the animals required, I started ahead this morning with a party of eight, consisting (with myself) of Mr. Preuss and Mr. Talbot, Carson, Derosier, Towns, Proue, and Jacob. We took with us some of the best animals, and my intention was to proceed as rapidly as possible to the house of Mr. Sutter, and return to meet the party with a supply of provisions and fresh animals. . . .

The forest was imposing today in the magnificence of the trees; some of the pines, bearing large cones, were ten feet in diameter; cedars also abounded, and we measured one twenty-eight and one-half feet in circumference four feet from the ground.

UP THE NORTH PLATTE

BY WASHINGTON IRVING

Washington Irving (1783–1859), a native New Yorker, trained for the law but soon turned to writing. Best remembered as the creator of Diedrich Knickerbocker, Rip Van Winkle, and Ichabod Crane, and the author of sentimental books about England and Spain, he also wrote three books about the American West. The first, A Tour of the Prairies, *was a report of a trip to the Pawnee and Osage country after seventeen years abroad. Its success led him to two hack jobs,* Astoria, *a flattering account of John Jacob Astor's venture into the far western fur trade, and* The Adventures of Captain Bonneville, U.S.A., *a glorified account of Bonneville's wanderings in the western mountain country. Bonneville, a native of France but a graduate of West Point, served without distinction in various frontier Army posts until 1830 when he got financial backing for an expedition to the Rockies ostensibly to explore, actually to engage in the fur trade. He made no discoveries, failed in the fur trade, returned to the Army and served without distinction in the Mexican War. Irving's book is based on Bonneville's journals. I have included a selection from it for its flavor and its moderately accurate descriptions. Irving's mannered prose tends to magnify Bonneville's imaginative romanticism and create an aura of heroics over what was really a rather fumbling fiasco of an expedition.*

(*The Adventures of Captain Bonneville, U.S.A., in the Rocky Mountains and the Far West*, by Washington Irving; G. P. Putnam, 1849.)

From the middle to the end of May, Captain Bonneville pursued a western course over the vast undulating plains, destitute of tree or shrub, rendered miry by occasional rain, and cut up by deep water-courses where they had to dig roads for their wagons down the soft crumbling banks, and to throw bridges across the streams. The weather had attained the summer heat; the thermometer standing about fifty-seven degrees in the morning, early, but rising to about ninety degrees at noon. The incessant breezes, however, which sweep these vast plains, render the heats endurable. Game was scanty, and they had to eke out their scanty fare with wild roots and vegetables, such as the Indian potato, the wild onion, and the prairie tomato, and they met with quantities of "red root," from which the hunters make a very palatable beverage. The only human being that crossed their path was a Kansas warrior, returning from some solitary expedition of bravado or revenge, bearing a Pawnee scalp as a trophy.

The country gradually rose as they proceeded westward, and their route took them over high ridges, commanding wide and beautiful prospects. The vast plain was studded on the west with innumerable hills of conical shape, such as are seen north of the Arkansas River. These hills have their summits apparently cut off about the same elevation, so as to leave flat surfaces at top. It is conjectured by some that the whole country may originally have been of the altitude of these tabular hills, but through some process of nature may have sunk to its present level; these insulated eminences being protected by broad foundations of solid rock.

Captain Bonneville mentions another geological phenomenon north of Red River, where the surface of the earth, in considerable tracts of country, is covered with broad slabs of sandstone, having the form and position of grave-stones, and looking as if they had been forced up by some subterranean agitation. "The resemblance," says he, "which these very remarkable spots have in many places to old churchyards is curious in the extreme. One might almost fancy himself among the tombs of the pre-Adamites."

On the 2d of June they arrived on the main stream of the Nebraska or Platte River; twenty-five miles below the head of the Great Island. The low banks of this river gave it an appearance of great width. Captain Bonneville measured it in one place, and found it twenty-two hundred yards from bank to bank. Its depth was from three to six feet, the bottom full of quicksands. The Nebraska is studded with islands covered with that species of poplar called the cotton-wood tree. Keeping up along the course of this river for several days, they were obliged, from the scarcity of game, to put themselves upon short allowance, and occasionally to kill a steer. They bore their daily labors and privations, however, with great good humor, taking their tone, in all probability, from the buoyant spirit of their leader. "If the weather was inclement," says the captain, "we watched the clouds, and hoped for a sight of the blue sky and the merry sun. If food was scanty, we regaled ourselves with the hope of soon falling in with herds of buffalo, and having nothing to do but slay and eat." We doubt whether the genial captain is not describing the cheeriness of his own breast, which gave a cheery aspect to everything around him.

There certainly were evidences, however, that the country was not always equally destitute of game. At one place they observed a field decorated with buffalo skulls, arranged in circles, curves, and other mathematical figures, as if for some mystic rite or ceremony. They were almost innumerable, and seemed to have been a vast hectacomb offered up in thanksgiving to the Great Spirit for some signal success in the chase.

On the 11th of June they came to the fork of the Nebraska, where it divides itself into two equal and beautiful streams. One of these branches rises up in the west-southwest, near the headwaters of the Arkansas. Up the course of this branch, as Captain Bonneville was well aware, lay the route to the Comanche and Kioway Indians, and to the northern Mexican settlements; of the other branch he knew nothing. Its sources might lie among the wild and inaccessible cliffs, and tumble and foam down rugged defiles and over craggy precipices; but its direction was in the true course, and up this stream he determined to prosecute his route to the Rocky Mountains. Finding it impossible, from quicksands and other dangerous impediments, to cross the river in this neighborhood, he kept up along the south fork for two days, merely seeking a safe fording place. At length he encamped, caused the bodies of the wagons to be dislodged from the wheels, covered with buffalo hides, and besmeared with a compound of tallow and ashes; thus forming rude boats. In these they ferried their effects across the stream, which was six hundred yards wide, with a swift and strong current. Three men were in each boat, to manage it; others waded across, pushing the barks before them. Thus all crossed in safety. A march of nine miles took them over high rolling prairies to the north fork; their eyes being regaled with the welcome sight of herds of buffalo at a distance, some careering the plain, others grazing and reposing in the natural meadows.

Skirting along the north fork for a day or two, excessively annoyed by musquitoes and buffalo gnats, they reached, in the evening of the 17th, a small but beautiful grove, from which issued the confused notes of singing birds, the first they had heard since crossing the boundary of Missouri. After so many days of weary travelling through a naked, monotonous and silent country, it was delightful once more to hear the song of the bird, and to behold the verdure of the grove. It was a beautiful sunset, and the sight of the glowing rays, mantling the tree-tops and rustling branches, gladdened every heart. They pitched their camp in the grove, kindled their fires, partook merrily of their rude fare, and resigned themselves to the sweetest sleep they had enjoyed since their outset upon the prairies.

The country now became rugged and broken. High bluffs advanced upon the river, and forced the travellers occasionally to leave its banks and wind their course into the interior. In one of the wild and solitary passes they were startled by the trail of four or five pedestrians, whom they supposed to be spies from some predatory camp of either Arickara or Crow Indians. This obliged them to redouble their vigilance at night, and to keep especial watch upon their horses. In these rugged and elevated regions they began to see the black-tailed deer, a species larger than the ordinary kind, and chiefly found in rocky and mountainous countries. They had reached also a great buffalo range; Captain Bonneville ascended a high bluff, commanding an extensive view of the surrounding plains. As far as his eye could reach, the country seemed absolutely blackened by innumerable herds. No language, he says, could convey an adequate idea of the vast living mass thus presented to his eye. He remarked that the bulls and cows generally congregated in separate herds.

Opposite to the camp at this place was a singular phenomenon, which is among the curiosities of the country. It is called the chimney. The lower part is a conical mound, rising out of the naked plain; from the summit shoots up a shaft or column, about one hundred and twenty feet in height, from which it derives its name. The height of the whole, according to Captain Bonneville, is a hundred and seventy-five yards. It is composed of indurated clay, with alternate layers of red and white sandstone, and may be seen at the distance of upward of thirty miles.

On the 21st they encamped amid high and beetling bluffs of indurated clay and sandstone, bearing the resemblance of towers, castles, churches and fortified cities. At a distance it was scarcely possible to persuade one's self that the works of art were not mingled with these fantastic freaks of nature. They have received the name of Scott's Bluffs from a melancholy circumstance. A number of years since, a party were descending the upper part of the river in canoes, when their frail barks were overturned and all their powder spoiled. Their rifles being thus rendered useless, they were unable to procure food by hunting and had to depend upon roots and wild fruits for subsistence. After suffering extremely from hunger, they arrived at Laramie's Fork, a small tributary of the north branch of the Nebraska, about sixty miles above the cliffs just mentioned. Here one of the party, by the name of Scott, was taken ill; and his companions came to a halt, until he should recover health and strength sufficient to proceed. While they were searching round in quest of edible roots they discovered a fresh trail of white men, who had evidently but recently preceded them. What was to be done? By a forced march they might overtake this party, and thus be able to reach the settlements in safety. Should they linger they might all perish of famine and exhaustion. Scott, however, was incapable of moving; they were too feeble to aid him forward, and dreaded that such a clog would prevent their coming up with the advance party. They determined, therefore, to abandon him to his fate. Accordingly, under pretence of seeking food, they deserted him and hastened forward upon the trail. They succeeded in overtaking the party of which they were in quest, but concealed their faithless desertion of Scott; alleging that he had died of disease.

On the ensuing summer, these very individuals visiting these parts in company with others, came suddenly upon the bleached bones and grinning skull of a human skeleton, which, by certain signs they recognized for the remains of Scott. This was sixty long miles from the place where they had abandoned him; and it appeared that the wretched man had crawled that immense distance before death put an end to his miseries. The wild and picturesque bluffs in the neighborhood of his lonely grave have ever since borne his name.

Amid this wild and striking scenery, Captain Bonneville, for the first time, beheld flocks of the ahsahto or bighorn, an animal which frequents these cliffs in great numbers. They accord with the nature of such scenery, and add much to its romantic effect; bounding like goats from crag to crag, often trooping along the lofty shelves of the mountains, under the guidance of some venerable patriarch, with horns twisted lower than his muzzle, and sometimes peering over the edge of a precipice so high that they appear scarce bigger than crows; indeed, it seems a pleasure to them to seek the most rugged and frightful situations, doubtless from a feeling of security.

This animal is commonly called the mountain sheep, and is often confused with another animal, the "woolly sheep," found more to the northward, about the country of the Flatheads. The latter likewise inhabits cliffs in summer, but descends into the valleys in the winter. It has white wool, like a sheep, mingled with a thin growth of long hair; but it has short legs, a deep belly, and a beard like a goat. Its horns are about five inches long, slightly curved backward, black as jet, and beautifully polished. Its hoofs are of the same color. This animal is by no means as active as the bighorn, it does not bound as much, but sits a good deal upon its haunches. It is not so plentiful either; rarely more than two or three are seen at a time. Its wool alone gives it a resemblance to the sheep; it is more properly of the goat genus. The flesh is said to have a musty flavor; some have thought the fleece might be valuable, as it is said to be as fine as that of the goat of Cashmere, but it is not to be procured in sufficient quantities.

The ahsahto, argali, or bighorn, on the contrary, has short hair like a deer, and resembles it in shape, but has the head and horns of a sheep, and its flesh is said to be delicious mutton. The Indians consider it more sweet than any other kind of venison. It abounds in the Rocky Mountains, from the fiftieth degree of north latitude quite down to California; generally in the highest regions capable of vegetation; sometimes it ventures into the valleys, but on the least alarm, regains its favorite cliffs and precipices, where it is perilous, if not impossible for the hunter to follow. . . .

On the 26th of May, the travellers encamped at Laramie's Fork, a clear and beautiful stream, rising in the west-southwest, maintaining an average width of twenty yards, and winding through broad meadows abounding in currants and gooseberries, and adorned with groves and clumps of trees. . . .

For some days past Captain Bonneville had been made sensible of the great elevation of country into which he was gradually ascending, by the effect of the dryness and rarefaction of the atmosphere upon his wagons. The woodwork shrunk; the paint boxes of the wheels were continually working out, and it was necessary to support the spokes by stout props to prevent their falling asunder. The travellers were now entering one of those great steppes of the Far West where the prevalent aridity of the atmosphere renders the country unfit for cultivation. In these regions there is a fresh sweet growth of grass in the spring, but it is scanty and short, and parches up in the course of the summer, so that there is none for the hunters to set fire to in the autumn. It is a common observation that "above the forks of the Platte the grass does not burn." All attempts at agriculture and gardening in the neighborhood of Fort William have been attended with very little success. The grain and vegetables raised there have been scanty in quantity and poor in quality. The great elevation of these plains, and the dryness of the atmosphere, will tend to retain these immense regions in a state of pristine wildness.

In the course of a day or two more, the travellers entered that wild and broken tract of the Crow country called the Black Hills, and here their journey became toilsome in the extreme. Rugged steeps and deep ravines incessantly obstructed their progress, so that a great part of the day was spent in the painful toil of digging through the banks, filling up the ravines, forcing the wagons up the most forbidding ascents, or swinging them with ropes down the face of dangerous precipices. The shoes of their horses were worn out, and their feet injured by the rugged and stony roads. The travellers were annoyed also by frequent but brief storms, which would come hurrying over the hills, or through the mountain defiles, rage with great fury for a short time, and then pass off, leaving everything calm and serene again. . . .

Everything around bore traces of some fearful convulsion of nature in times long past. Hitherto the various strata of rock had exhibited a gentle elevation toward the southwest, but here everything appeared to have been subverted, and thrown out of place. In many places there were heavy beds of white sandstone resting upon red. Immense strata of rocks jutted up into crags and cliffs; and sometimes formed perpendicular walls and overhanging precipices. An air of sterility prevailed over these savage wastes. The valleys were destitute of herbage, and scantily clothed with a stunted species of wormwood, generally known among traders and trappers by the name of sage. . . .

Though the thermometer at mid-day ranged from eighty to ninety, and even sometimes rose to ninety-three degrees, yet occasional spots of snow were to be seen on the tops of the low mountains, among which the travellers were journeying, proofs of the great elevation of the whole region. . . .

On the 12th of July Captain Bonneville abandoned the main stream of the Nebraska, which was continually shouldered by rugged promontories, and making a bend to the southwest, for a couple of days, part of the time over plains of loose sand, encamped on the 14th on the banks of the Sweet Water, a stream about twenty yards in breadth, and four or five feet deep, flowing between low banks over a sandy soil, and forming one of the forks or upper branches of the Nebraska. Up this stream they now shaped their course for several successive days. . . .

It was on the 20th of July that Captain Bonneville first came in sight of the grand region of his hopes and anticipations, the Rocky Mountains. He had been making a bend to the south, to avoid some obstacles along the river, and had attained a high, rocky ridge, when a magnificent prospect burst upon his sight. To the west rose the Wind River Mountains, with their bleached and snowy summits towering into the clouds. These stretched far to the north-northwest, until they melted away into what appeared to be faint clouds, but which the experienced eyes of the veteran hunters of the party recognized for the rugged mountains of the Yellowstone; at the feet of which extended the wild Crow country: a perilous, though profitable region for the trapper. . . .

The Wind River Mountains are notorious in hunters' and trappers' stories: their rugged defiles, and the rough tracts about their neighborhood, having been the lurking places for the predatory hordes of the mountains, and scenes of rough encounter with Crows and Blackfeet. It was to the west of these mountains, in the valley of the Seeds-ke-dee Agie, or Green River, that Captain Bonneville intended to make a halt, for the purpose of giving repose to his people and his horses, after their weary journeying; and of collecting information as to his future course. This Green River Valley, and its immediate neighborhood, as we have already observed, formed the main point of rendezvous, for the present year, of the rival fur companies, and the motley populace, civilized and savage, connected with them. Several days of rugged travel, however, yet remained for the captain and his men before they should encamp in this desired resting-place.

MOUNTAIN WINTER

BY DAVID LAVENDER

David Lavender (1910 —), a native Coloradan, was educated at Princeton and Stanford with the idea of becoming a lawyer. Instead, he became a writer and a teacher after various jobs in a Colorado mine, in advertising, and as a ranchman. Deeply steeped in western history, he has written both fiction and nonfiction about the mountain men and the fur trade. His knowledge of the men of that period gives his books both validity and vitality. His Land of Giants *was a volume in the* Mainstream of America *series.* Bent's Fort, *from which this selection is taken, shows how Lavender combines the setting, the men, and the problems of the trappers in one brief narrative that summarizes both time and place. He now lives in California and is head of the English Department of the Thatcher School.*

(*Bent's Fort*, by David Lavender; Doubleday & Company, Inc., 1954.)

Lying along the north-south axis in central Colorado are four huge, mountain-cupped bowls. Grass-filled, gently rolling, almost treeless, they derive from their circling whale-backed peaks an austerity that makes the word "lovely" too gentle for describing them. The southernmost is called San Luis Valley; the others by the mountain name of park—North, Middle and South parks, the latter the famed Bayou Salade of the fur hunters.

It was in North Park, called Park Kyack by the French fur trappers, that Sylvestre Pratte fell seriously ill in the fall of 1827, perhaps of the same disease that had troubled him previously in Santa Fe. After an anxious time of rude nursing, he died. Solemnly the trappers buried him and then took counsel among themselves. The result was a serious decision for Pratte's clerk and second-in-command.

The men were uneasy about their status. They had been out for some time now, had already caught about three hundred pounds of beaver. Some among them thought that in order to secure their wages they should seize the fur, together with personal property belonging to Sylvestre—his rifle, pistol, gloves, the cloth he had brought along for Indian trade, his seventeen traps, seven mules, eight horses. Then what? Should the party disintegrate into competitive groups, trying to beat each other to the best streams during what remained of the fall season? Should they return to Taos and face the winter with whatever they had managed to garner and hope for a new *bourgeois* to sign them up in the spring?

Wiser heads said no. It was better to stick together.

But suppose the winter-long effort ended in failure? Who, then, would guarantee their wages?

They turned to Ceran (St. Vrain), a veteran of twenty-five. Would he assume command—and responsibility?

The safe thing was to refuse. Keeping the men out through the winter would cost six or seven thousand dollars in wages. If the trip failed to net that amount, what was to prevent the St. Louis executors of Pratte's estate from disclaiming the account on the grounds that the expedition could have, and should have, disbanded after Sylvestre's death? Yet Ceran returned the trust which his men held for him. They were good hunters. They would stick to their jobs and the venture might pull through. He decided to take the chance.

Trapping as they went, the party moved along the sources of the North Platte toward the present Colorado-Wyoming border. By now they were shaken into trail shape. On a pack horse each man carried the furs he had caught, his buffalo bed robes, and a heavy skin sack (which could be boiled and eaten in emergency) loaded with six five-pound traps costing from twelve to sixteen dollars in St. Louis, the traps' three-pound chains, spare springs, and tools for repair. On the rider's own mount was a "possible sack" bulky with powder, galena lead, flints, tobacco, sewing materials, occasionally a book or two, and dressed deerskin for replacing his moccasins, which wore out rapidly. About his person hung a skinning knife, whetstone, pipe case, awl holder, perhaps a tomahawk, scent container, bullet pouch, and a powder carrier of black buffalo horn scraped as thin as isinglass and stoppered with a wooden plug. Always in hand was his gun—generally a heavy one, eleven to twelve pounds, with a forty-inch barrel, .50-caliber, firing a half-ounce slug with impact enough to drop a grizzly or buffalo. A man loved his gun, named it (Ceran called his Silver Heels), and had it rebored again and again to repair damage from water and dust, until it looked as huge as a tunnel. His wiping stick was carried in the bore and served, in addition to its intended function, as a rest on which the hunter could lean the ponderous muzzle when he knelt to take aim. In spite of affection for the gun, however, the men were not above using bows and arrows; the weapons conserved ammunition, gave no telltale report, and in the sightless night could be aimed by hunch better than a rifle.

Down to his shoulders hung the hunter's long hair, covered with a felt hat or perhaps the hood of a capote. He liked wool clothing, for it would not shrink as it dried and wake him, when he dozed beside the fire, by agonizingly squeezing his limbs. But wool soon wore out, and he then clad himself in leather, burdensomely heavy to wear, fringed on the seams with the familiar thongs which were partly decorative but mostly utilitarian, to let rain drip off the garment rather than soak in, and to furnish material for mending. Further waterproofing was added by wiping butcher and eating knives on the garments until they were black and shiny with grease. Upper garments might be of the pull-over type or cut like a coat, the buttonless edges folded over and cinched into place with a belt. No underclothing was worn, just a breechclout. "Trousers" were often nothing more than Indian-style, thigh-length leggings, the lower parts perhaps made of non-shrinkable strips of blanket. In extreme cold a Hudson's Bay blanket or a buffalo robe was draped Indian-wise over the entire costume.

Much of the hunter's life was spent in water. In the evening twilight he waded cautiously upstream, searching out good sets for his traps. These he placed under water in the beaver's natural runway, chaining each trap in such fashion that the caught animal would be drowned before it could reach land and gnaw off its paw. Over each set he bent a twig baited with the evil-smelling castoreum. The next dawn he examined his line, often having to reach deep to retrieve his prey, skinned the corpses, and packed the hides back to camp. There they were "grained" (the clinging bits of flesh removed) on slant-topped wooden blocks and then stretched on oval willow frames to dry, a process sometimes hastened by burning punky wood in a pit beneath them. In big-company brigades the handling of the skins was the work of the camp tenders; free trappers did it themselves. In either case, there was little leisure. A thirty-man company could skim the cream off a circle of considerable radius during a single night, and therefore camp sites were moved every day or so.

When setting their traps the men split into twos and threes. Some individualists worked singly and jealously—Old Bill Williams for one, and evidently Tom Smith also, at least on Ceran's 1827–28 expedition. Indians found this habit an invitation to attack from ambush, and St. Vrain's party had already had a skirmish or two along the North Platte. A frontier maxim rightly held that the best Indian fighter was the one who avoided the most battles. Ceran was worried. When Tom Smith kept brazenly exposing himself, the captain rode out to the stream one day to tell him for God's sake to quit taking so many chances. As they were arguing about it, a discharge came from the brush—a gun, according to some accounts; an arrow, according to others. Probably it was a gun, because whatever struck Tom just below the knee had power enough to break both leg bones.

Ceran flopped down to meet a charge, but the shot had been a typical skulking strike from ambush with no follow-up. He looked for Tom. The man had tried to jump to his rifle leaning against a nearby tree, but his leg had caved in. Now he was writhing on the ground.

They got him back to camp, choked down some of his cursing with a bolt of Taos Lightning, and cut away the legging. Splintered ends of the bones protruded through the flesh. The men glanced sideways at each other. They had seen enough mangled beaver limbs to know that Tom's lower leg would never be any good again. So had Tom.

"Cut it off," he said.

Amputating a beaver's leg and a man's are two different things. The group stood there hang-handed. Tom roared for Basil, the cook, to bring him a sharp knife. Reluctantly it was produced, and with his own hands Tom began slicing at the body flesh. His snarls brought the watchers out of their trance for such accessories as they had—water, horsehair or perhaps buffalo sinews for ligatures, a tourniquet, more whiskey. The bone was a problem. Some stories have it that the camp possessed a keyhole saw which was pressed into service; others say that teeth were filed into a knife blade. But perhaps, if both tibia and fibula were shattered badly enough, no saw was necessary. At any rate, before the job was completed, Tom slid toward unconsciousness. Milton Sublette took the knife and finished.

There had been preparations to stop the gush of blood by searing the stump with a hot iron. But the sight of the glowing bar had made Tom bellow protest. Well, they thought, it wouldn't matter much what they did. Humor him along. Abandoning the projected searing, they tied up the arteries as best they could, wrapped the stump in a dirty shirt, and swaddled Tom in a buffalo robe. After promising not to abandon him until they were sure he was dead (as young Jim Bridger, green to the trade, had abandoned Old Hugh Glass after Hugh was mangled by a grizzly), they went on about their work. Poor old Tom. He was as strident as a bull elk, as obstreperous a drunk as ever cleaned out a Taos fandango. But he was a gone beaver now.

The weather was icy, the night a knife-edged glitter under the frozen stars. The cold seeped into Tom's bed. Perhaps that was what coagulated the blood. When Ceran and big Milton Sublette came the next morning to look at his corpse, the bleeding had ceased and Tom was perky enough to curse them soundly. Amazed, they stayed in camp another day, waiting for him to get his dying over with. When he strengthened instead, they stitched him up in a wrapper and a sugar-loaf hat made from red flannel trade cloth. Then they slung a litter tandem between two horses and loaded him in. Ceran appointed two men as his special attendants, and on they went. After all, business was business.

They turned west from the North Platte across the Park Mountains, their horses floundering in the soft, still snow as they searched for openings through thick forests of spruce and among the most gigantic aspen trees on the continent. The rough going grew rougher when they dropped down through dense scrub oak into the narrow valley of the Little Snake, aptly named from its looping progress along the present Colorado-Wyoming border. The willows were thick, the hillsides rocky. In sleety weather the litter horses lost their footing. Down the bank they rolled. Out of the tangle flew Smith, to land sitting in an ice-scummed pool. His nurses called for help. This time he was killed for certain. But no, there he sat in his red wrapper, his red hat askew and dripping as he bawled out his opinion of matters in general. The men began to laugh, and gradually Tom did too.

Leaving the Little Snake where it swung south toward the huge valley of the Yampa, the party struck across southern Wyoming into the valley of the Green. There winter caught them—cruel, merciless, snow-heaped, the most rigorous, St. Vrain later wrote Bernard Pratte, that he had ever experienced. Either now or perhaps a little earlier Tom discovered that the bone ends left protruding by his shrinking flesh were loose. He had Sublette pull them out with a bullet mold used as pincers. Further cure was applied by a band of Ute Indians who moved in to share winter quarters with the trappers. Men, women, children—the whole howling, chanting, singing lot—chewed up roots and spat them on the stump. Obviously it was the proper remedy, for the flesh healed, and as Tom lay snugly in one of the lodges he began whittling out a wooden substitute. From now on he would be Peg-Leg Smith, growing in time beyond the cramped confines of reality into a myth of the nation's youth. Youth propping itself against frontier bars, unstrapping a wooden leg, and with its very symbol of defeat pounding its assailants into submission. Youth picking up, one summer in the desert, gold nuggets whose source could never be located again, and by the failure preserving the dream that took men west—everyman's dream of a lost Peg-Leg mine, never quite found and so never pinching down and growing thin with truth. Tomorrow, always tomorrow, it would be there, gloriously waiting. . . .

Time did not lie heavy. There were clothes to mend with awls for needles and sinews for thread, and fur-lined moccasins to make—unless a man could pick up a squaw to attend to these domestic matters for him. He ate when hungry, slept when he was tired, regardless of the hour. A pot of herb-flavored meat boiled continuously on the fire, and also one of tea or coffee as long as such luxuries lasted. *Boudins* (intestines filled with minced tenderloin) sizzled on wooden spits; marrow bones roasted; tongues steamed in the coals. It was a greasy, all-meat diet, perhaps seasoned with a dash of gunpowder, and was supposed to "make a man shed rain like an otter and stand cold like a polar bear."

Endless yarns were spun, not just for entertainment but for the sharing of knowledge; there, in what mountain man Osborne Russell called Rocky Mountain College, young Bill Bent picked up bits of professional lore that would serve him well in the years to come. (Not all the education was pragmatic, however; Joe Meek learned to read from copies of Shakespeare and the Bible in a winter camp, and later named a half-breed daughter Helen Mar after a heroine in Jane Porter's *Scottish Chiefs.*) Hunting was a necessity, of course, and often possible only by means of improvised snowshoes. When there was stock, it required continual care. When streams froze tight, water holes had to be chopped for them (animals suffered more from thirst than from hunger during mountain winters); and when the grass was covered too deep for pawing, cottonwood branches had to be cut. Both horses and mules fared well on the juicy bark, though too much of it reputedly caused hair to fall out; and it was said that a winter camp's location could be recognized for years afterward by the numbers of peeled, whitened sticks lying around.

Blizzards did not roar endlessly. During clear, sparkling days there was much movement. As forage and game became depleted, the men searched out a fresh camp site. Hunters would spy the tracks or fires of another outfit and go over for a visit. Wandering Indians, insatiably curious, would roam from camp to camp, spreading news as they went. The whites also ranged far. Over on Idaho's Portneuf River, Peter Skene Ogden noted in his journal that on December 20, 1827, two Americans, probably from Smith's, Sublette's and Jackson's company, dropped by with word of Ogden's associates. A few days later more American trappers, these led by Samuel Tulloch, came by the Portneuf. When Tulloch wanted to buy snowshoes from Ogden, the Britisher refused lest the Americans use them to go to a camp near the Great Salt Lake and return with trappers and whiskey.

A terrible winter, Ogden says again and again. January and February were particularly bad. . . .

With the coming of spring . . . Ceran St. Vrain's New Mexicans found only mediocre trapping. Worried perhaps by the thought of how Bernard Pratte would react to the poor showing, Ceran decided not to reduce profits still more by waiting to sell his pelts for cheap mountain prices at the Bear Lake rendezvous. In late April he headed his men eastward, intending to go to St. Louis. Along the way he changed his mind. The cause, so he and his engagés later declared at

Taos, was a large war party of Indians whose traces the brigade intersected on the Platte. Outnumbered and short of ammunition, the group concluded that wisdom dictated a retreat to Taos.

There is a certain convenience in the reasoning. Those men were used to dodging Indians when they wished, and it may be that the threat served mostly to make the green fields of Taos look still greener. After all, the town was by now home to many of them, and Ceran could write Sylvestre's father about the misfortunes rather than tell Bernard face to face. Whatever their real motives, they swung abruptly south along the tawny base of the Colorado foothills, reached Taos on May 23, 1828.

There Ceran sold 1636 pounds of beaver for $5708.50. This was less than the pelts would have brought in St. Louis, and even when Sylvestre Pratte's personal property was tossed into the pot, the gross returns came to only $6393.75. This money Ceran distributed to his men with meticulous honesty, drawing on some of his own share of the proceeds in order to complete the payments due them. When the returns reached Bernard Pratte, his clerks toted up the columns and found that "expenses made for going for biver" reached $6915.41½. Thus one amputated leg and a rough winter had resulted in a net loss of more than $500. There was trouble about it. Pratte sent agents to Taos to check up. Their testimony, however, evidently convinced the company that Ceran had acted properly if not profitably. His stewardship was honored and he received the full $1910.02½ due him for approximately nine months' labor. The salary of a top-ranking trader on the Missouri was $1000 a year, and the average laborer there earned $130 for a "wintering"—that is, for ten to eleven months' service.

FIRST ACROSS THE CONTINENT: THE LEWIS AND CLARK EXPEDITION

The Lewis and Clark expedition of 1804–06 was one of the great explorations of all history and its report is a classic. The expedition itself was the first crossing of the continent north of Mexico by a party of white men and, aside from its epochal political and economic consequences, the incredible journey was a constant discovery of land and life never before seen or described by literate men. In this sense the report was the first and a fundamentally basic natural history report of the western half of this continent.

The first report, published in 1814, was edited by Nicholas Biddle from journals kept by Meriwether Lewis and William Clark as well as other members of the company. Other versions based on this first one followed, but not until this century did anyone go back to the original journals, which are in the archives of the American Philosophical Society in Philadelphia. Then, in 1904–05, Reuben Gold Thwaites edited *Original Journals of the Lewis and Clark Expedition,* in eight volumes. Finally, in 1953, Bernard DeVoto edited a condensed version of the Thwaites edition for the general reader. The selections I have included here are from the Thwaites edition but may also be found in the DeVoto volume.

For convenience and to give individual credit, I have chosen two segments of the *Journals,* the first written by William Clark, the second by Meriwether Lewis. I have put the Clark entries first because they precede the Lewis entries chronologically. The two men, though remarkably well fitted for joint command, were quite different in personality, temperament and training, as well as in style of writing. Each in his own way was an accurate observer and vivid, factual reporter. And both were aware of their unique opportunity to see and describe country and wildlife in a vast, virgin area never before seen by men equipped to study and write about it.

(*Original Journals of the Lewis and Clark Expedition*, edited by Reuben Gold Thwaites; eight volumes, published by Dodd, Mead & Company, 1904–05.)

TO THE GREAT FALLS

BY WILLIAM CLARK

William Clark (1770–1838), younger brother of George Rogers Clark, was born in Virginia but went to Kentucky with his parents when he was fifteen. He had little formal education but grew up with skills as outdoorsman and surveyor and with the inborn quality of leadership. After ten years' soldiering in frontier Indian country he retired to Kentucky, only to be summoned by Meriwether Lewis to join the expedition to the Pacific. Nominally second in command, Clark was in fact co-leader and proved more daring and resourceful than Lewis. On the expedition's successful return, Clark was named Superintendent of Indian Affairs for Louisiana Territory, and after Lewis' tragic death in 1809 Clark was named Governor. He spent the rest of his life working for peace on the frontier and justice for the Indians. The selections from the Journals *included here are a part of Clark's record of the outbound trip near the Great Falls in the heart of present-day Montana. It is likely that Clark used Lewis' notes as the basis for his technical description of the bighorn sheep, though Clark was a thoroughly competent observer himself. Clark spelled by ear, capitalized at random and punctuated at whim, and I have followed the printed text except where an added letter would make an obscure word understandable.*

May 25th Satturday 1805

I walked on shore and killed a female *Ibi* or big horn animal in my absence Drewyer & Bratten killed two others, this animal is a species peculiar to this upper part of the Missouri, the head and horns of the male which Drewyer killed today weighed 27 lbs. it was somewhat larger than the mail of the Common Deer; the body reather thicker deeper and not so long in proportion to it's hight as the common Deer; the head and horns of the male are remarkably large compared with the other parts of the animal; the whole form is much more delicate than that of the common goat, and there is a greater disparity in the size of the mail and female than between those of either the deer or the goat. The bone above the eye is remarkably prominant; the head nostrils and division of the upper lip are precisely in form like the sheep. their legs resemble the sheep more than any other animal with which I am acquainted tho' they are more delicately formed, like the sheep they stand farward in the knee and the lower joint of the fore leg is smallest where it joins the knee, the hoof is black and large in perpotion, is divided, very open and roundly pointed at the toe; like the sheep; is much hollowed and Sharp on the under edge like the Scotch goat, has two small hoofs behind each foot below the ankle as the goat Sheep and Deer have, the belley, iner side of the legs, and the extremity of the rump and buttock's for about two inches ½ around the but of the tail, are white, as is also the tail except just at its extremity on the upper side which is of a dark brown.

the tail is about 3 inches in length covered with short hair, or at least not longer than that of the body; the outer part of the animal are of a dusky brown or reather a lead coloured light brown; the animal is now Sheding its winter coat which is thick not quite as long as that of the Deer and appears to be inter mixt with a considerable quantity of fine fur which lies next to the Skin and concealed by the coarcer hair; the shape of the hair itself is cylindric as that of the Antilope is, but is smaller, shorter and not compressed or flatened as that of the deers winter coat is. I believe this animal only sheds its hair once a year. it has Eight fore teeth in the under jaw and no canine teeth. The *Horns* are large at their base, and occupy the crown of the head almost entirely, they are compressed, bent backwards and lunated; the surface swelling into wavey rings which incircleing the horn continue to succeed each other from the base to the extremity and becomeing less elivated and more distant as they receed from the head. The horn for about two thirds of its length is filled with a porus bone which is united with the frontal bone the horns of the *female* are small, but are also compressed and bent backwards and incircled with a succession of wavy rings. the horn is of a light brown colour; when Dressed it is almost white extreamly transparent and very elastic. this horn is used by the natives in constructing their bows; I have no doubt of it's elegance and usefullness in hair combs, and might probably answer as maney valuable purpoces to civilized man, as it does to the native indians, who form their water cups, spoons and platters of it. the females have already brought forth their young, indeed from the size of the young, I suppose that they produce them early in March. they have from one to two at birth. they feed on grass, but principally on the arramatic herbs which grow on the clifts and inaxcessable heights which they frequent most commonly, and the places they generally collect to lodge in the cranies or cevices of the rocks in the face of inaccessable precepices, where the Wolf nor Bear can reach them, and where indeed man himself would in maney instances find a similar deficiency; yet those animals bound from rock to rock and stand apparently in the most careless manner on the Side of precipices of maney hundred feet. they are very shy and quick of both sent and sight.

In my walk of this day I saw mountts on either side of the river at no great distance, those mountains appeared to be detached, and not ranges as laid down by the *Minetarrees*, I also think I saw a range of high Mounts, at a great distance to the S S W. but am not certain as the horozon was not clear enough to view it with certainty. The appearance of salts, and bitumun still continue. we saw a *polecat* to day being the first which we have seen for some time past. The Air of this quarter is pure and helthy. the water of the Missouri tasted not quite so muddy as it is below, not withstanding the last rains has raised the river a little it is less muddy than it was before the rain.

June 5th Wednesday 1805

Some little rain & snow last night the mountains to our S.E. covered with snow this morning air verry cold & raining a little, we saw 8 buffalow opposit, the made 2 attempts to cross the water being so swift they could not, about the time we were setting out *three* white bear approached our camp we killed the three & eate part of one & set out & proceeded on N. 20 degrees W 11 miles struck the river at maney places in this distance to a ridge on the N. Side from the top of which I could plainly see a mountain to the South & W covered with Snow at a long distance, The mountain opposit to us to the S.E. is also covered with snow this morning. a high ridge from those mountains approached the river on the S E side forming some cliffs of hard dark Stone. From the ridge at which place I struck the river last, I could discover that the river ran west of south a long distance, and had a strong rapid current, as this river continued its width depth & rapidity and the course west of south, going up further would be useless, I deturmined to return, marked my name in a tree N. side near the ridge where the little river brakes thro'

June 10th Monday 1805

we drew up our large Perogue into the middle of a small Island in the North fork and covered her with bushes after makeing her fast to the trees, branded several trees to prevent the Indians injureing her, Sahcahgagwea our Indian woman verry sick I blead her, we deturmined to assend the South fork, and Capt Lewis selects 4 men George Drewyer, Gibson, J. Fields & Gutrich to accompany him & deturmine to set out in the morning. The after noon or night cloudy some rain, river riseing a little.

June 14th Friday, 1805

a fine morning the Indian woman complaining all night & excessively bad this morning. her case is somewhat dangerous. two men with the Tooth ake 2 with Tumers, & one man with a Tumor & a slight fever passed the camp Capt Lewis made the 1st night at which he had left part of two bear their skins &c. three men with Tumers went on shore and stayed out all night one of them killed 2 buffalow, a part of which we made use of for brackfast, the current excessively rapid more so as we assend we find great dificuelty in getting the Perogue & canoes up in safety, canoes take in water frequently, at 4 oClock this evening Jo: Fields returned from Capt. Lewis with a letter for me, Capt. Lewis dates his letter from the Great Falls of the Missouri, which Fields informs me is about 20 miles in advance & about 10 miles above the place I left the river the time I was up last week.

June the 15th Satturday 1805

we set out at the usial time and proceeded on with great dificuelty as the river is more rapid we can hear the falls this morning verry distinctly. our Indian woman sick & low spirited I gave her the bark & apply it externaely to her region which revived her much. the current excessively rapid and dificuelt to assend great numbers of dangerous places, and the fatigue which we have to encounter is incretiable the men in the water from morning untill night hauling the cord & boats walking on sharp rocks and round slippery stones which alternately cut their feet & throw them down, notwith standing all this dificuelty they go with great chearfulness, aded to those dificuelties the rattle snakes inumerable & require great caution to prevent being bitten.

June 18th Tuesday 1805

this evening, one man A. Willard going for a load of meat at 170 yards distance on an Island was attact by a white bear and verry near being caught, prosued within 40 yards of the camp where I was with one man I collected 3 others of the party and prosued the bear (who had prosued my track from a buffalow I had killed on the island at about 300 yards distance and chanced to meet Willard) for fear of his attacking one man Colter at the lower point of the Island. before we had got down the bear had allarmed the man and prosued him into the water at our approach he retreated, and we relieved the man in the water, I saw the bear but the bushes was so thick I could not shoot him and it was nearly dark.

June 20th Thursday 1805

I direct stakes to be cut to stick up in the prairies to show the way for the party to transport the baggage &c. &c. we set out early on the portage, soon after we set out it began to rain and continued a short time we proceeded on thro' a tolerable level plain, and found the hollow of a Deep riveen to obstruct our rout as it could not be passed with canos & baggage for some distance above the place we struck it. I examined it for some time and finding it late determined to strike the river & take its Course & distance to camp which I accordingly did the wind hard from the S.W. a fair after noon, the river on both sides cut with raveens some of which it passes thro steep clifts into the river, the country above the falls & up the Medison river is level, with low banks, a chain of mountains to the west some part of which particler those to the N W & S W are covered with snow and appear verry high. I saw a rattle snake in an open plain 2 miles from any creek or woodd. When I arrived at camp found all well with quantities of meet . . .

Dureing the time of my being on the Plains and above the falls I as also all my party repeatedly heard a nois which proceeded from a Direction a little N. of West, a loud noise and resembling precisely the discharge of a piece of ordinance of 6 pounds at the distance of 5 or six miles. I was informed of it several times by the men J: Fields particularly before I paid any attention to it, thinking it was thunder most probably which they had mistaken. at length walking in the plains yesterday near the most extreem S.E. bend of the River above the falls I heard this nois very distinctly it was perfectly calm clear and not a cloud to be seen, I halted and listened attentively about two hour dureing which time I heard two other discharges, and took the direction of the sound with my pocket compass which was as nearly West from me as I could estimate from the sound. I have no doubt but if I had leasure I could find from whence it issued. I have thought it probable that it might be caused by running water in some of the caverns of those emence mountains, on the principal of the blowing caverns; but in such case the sounds would be periodical and regular, which is not the case with this, being sometimes heard once only and at other times several discharges in quick succession. it is heard also at different times of the day and night. I am at a great loss to account for this Phenomenon, I well recollect hereing the Minitarees say that those Rocky mountains make a great noise, but they could not tell me the cause, neither could they inform me of any remarkable substance or situation in these mountains which would autherise a conjecture of a probable cause of this noise.

UP JEFFERSON'S RIVER

BY MERIWETHER LEWIS

Meriwether Lewis (1774–1809) was born, grew up and was educated in rural Virginia. He dreamed from boyhood of exploring an overland route to the Pacific and when only eighteen asked Thomas Jefferson, then Secretary of State, to authorize such a trip. Jefferson refused and Lewis spent five years in the Army before Jefferson, newly elected President, chose him as his private secretary. Even before the Louisiana Purchase, Jefferson planned the expedition Lewis had earlier suggested. Congress agreed. Lewis was sent to Philadelphia for special training in botany, zoology and celestial navigation, and named to head the expedition. At Jefferson's suggestion, Lewis chose William Clark as his "companion officer," and the two of them made history. On their return, Jefferson appointed Lewis Governor of Louisiana Territory. Only three years later Lewis died under mysterious circumstances in a backwoods inn on the Natchez Trace in Tennessee on his way to Washington to untangle a red-tape snarl. No one yet knows whether it was murder or suicide. The selection from the Journals *I have included here is from Lewis' entries covering that part of the outbound trip when the party was in what is now the Montana-Idaho boundary area. Though well-read and much better educated than Clark, Lewis was erratic in spelling and used few capitals. I have kept to the original text almost entirely, even to his misspelling of well-known names.*

Sunday, July 28th, 1805

Both Captain C. and myself corrisponded in opinion with rispect to the impropriety of calling either of these streams the Missouri and accordingly agreed to name them after the President of the United States and the Secretaries of the Treasury and state having previously named one river in honour of the Secretaries of War and Navy. In pursuance of this resolution we called the S.W. fork, that which we meant to ascend, Jefferson's River in honor of that ullustrious personage Thomas Jefferson (the author of our enterprise.) The Middle fork we called Madison's River in honor of James Madison, and the S.E. Fork we called Gallitin's River in honor of Albert Gallitin. the two first are 90 yards wide and the last is 70 yards. all of them run with great velocity and throw out large bodies of water. Gallitin's River is reather more rapid than either of the others, is not quite as deep but from all appearances may be navigated to a considerable distance. Capt. C. who came down Madison's river yesterday and has also seen Jefferson's some distance thinks Madison's reather the most rapid, but it is not as much so by any means as Gallitin's. the beds of all these streams are formed of smooth pebble and gravel, and their waters perfectly transparent; in short they are three noble streams. there is timber enough here to support an establishment, provided it be erected with brick or stone either of which would be much cheaper than wood as all the materials for such a work are immediately at the spot. there are several small sand-bars along the shores at no great distance of pure sand and the earth appears as if it would make good brick. I had all our baggage spread out to dry this morning; and the day proving warm, I had a small bower or booth erected for the comfort of Capt. C. our leather lodge when exposed to the sun is excessively hot . . . in the evening about 4 O'Ck the wind blew hard from the South West and after some little time brought on a Cloud attended with thunder and Lightning from which we had a fine refreshing shower which cooled the air considerably; the showers continued with short intervals untill after dark. in the evening the hunters all returned they had killed 8 deer and 2 Elk, some of the deer were in excellent order. . . .

Tuesday, July 30th, 1805

Capt. Clark being much better this morning and having completed my observations we reloaded our canoes and set out, ascending Jeffersons river. Sharbono, his woman two invalleds and myself walked through the bottom on the Lard. side of the river about 4½ miles when we struck it again at the place the woman informed us she was taken prisoner. here we halted untill Capt. Clark arrived which was not until after one P.M. the water being strong and the river extremely crooked. we dined and again proceeded on; as the river now passed through the woods the invalleds got on board together with Sharbono and the Indian woman. I passed the river and continued my walk on the Stard. side. saw a vast number of beaver in many large dams which they had maid. I directed my course to the high plain to the right which I gained after some time with much difficulty and wading many beaver dams to my waist in mud and water. I would willingly have joined the canoes but the brush was so thick, the river crooked and bottoms intercepted in such manner by the beaver dams, that I found it uceless to attempt to find them, and therefore proceeded on up the river in order to intersept it where it came near the plain and would be more collected into one channel.

at length about sunset I arrived at the river only about six miles from my calculation on a direct line from the place I had left the canoes but I thought they were still below me. I found the river was divided where I reached it by an Island and was therefor fearful that they might pass without my seeing them, and went down to the lower point of the large island; here I discovered a small island, close under the shore on which I was; I passed the narrow channel to the small island and examined the gravely bar along the edge of the river for the tracks of the men, knowing that from the appearance of the river at this place if they had passed they would have used the cord on the side where I was. I saw no tracks and was then fully convinced that they were below me. I fired my gun and hallooed but could hear nothing of them. by this time it was getting nearly dark and a duck lit on the shore in about 40 steps of me and I killed it; having now secured my supper I looked out for a suitable place to amuse myself in combating the musquetos for the ballance of the evening. I found a parsel of drift wood at the head of the little island on which I was and immediately set it on fire and collected some willow brush to lye on. I cooked my duck which I found very good and after eating it layed down and should have had a comfortable nights lodge but for the musquetoes which infested me all night. late at night I was awakened by the nois of some animal running over the stoney bar on which I lay but did not see it; from the weight with which it ran I supposed it to be either an Elk or a brown bear.

Wednesday, July 31st, 1805

This morning I waited at my camp very impatiently for the arrival of Capt. Clark and party; I observed by my watch that it was 7 A.M. and they had not come in sight. I now became very uneasy and determined to wait until 8 and if they did not arrive by that time to proceed on up the river taking it as a fact that they had passed my camp some miles last evening. just as I set out to pursue my plan I discovered Sharbono walking up shore some distance below me and waited untill he arrived. I now learnt that the canoes were behind, they arrived shortly after. their detention had been caused by the rapidity of the water and the circuitous rout of the river. they halted and breakfasted after which we all set out again and I continued my walk on the Stard. shore. the river now becomes more collected the islands tho' numerous ar generally small. the river continues rapid and is from 90 to 120 yds. wide has a considerable quantity of timber in its bottoms. toward evening the bottoms became much narrower and the timber much more scant. . . .

August 1st, 1805

At half after 8 A.M. we halted for breakfast and as had been previously agreed on between Capt. Clark and myself I set out with 2 men in quest of the Snake Indians. the men I took were the two interpreters Drewyer and Sharbono and Sergt. Gass. the rout we took lay over a rough high range of mountains on the North side of the river. the river enetered these mountains a few miles above where we left it. . . .

The mountains are extremely bare of timber and our rout lay through the steep valleys exposed to the heat of the sun without shade and scarcely a breath of air; and to add to my fatigue in this walk of about 11 miles I had taken a doze of glauber salts in the morning in consequence of a slight desentary with which I had been afflicted for several days; being weakened by the disorder and the opperation of the medecine I found myself almost exhausted before we reached the river. I felt my sperits much revived on our near approach to the river at the sight of a herd of Elk of which Drewyer and myself killed two. we then hurried to the river and allayed our thirst. I ordered two of the men to skin the Elk and bring the meat to the river while myself and the other prepared a fire and cooked some of the meat for our dinner. we made a comfortable meal of the Elk and left the ballance of the meat on the bank of the river for the party with Capt. Clark. this supply was no doubt acceptable to them as they had had no fresh meat for two days except one beaver Game being very scarce and shy. we had seen a few deer and some goats but had not been fortunate enough to kill any of them. after dinner we resumed our march and encamped about 6 M. above on the Stard. side of the river.

Shortly after I left Capt. Clark this morning he proceeded on and passed through the mountains; they formed tremendious clifts of ragged and nearly perpendicular rocks; the lower part of this rock is of the black grannite before mentioned and the upper part a light coloured freestone. these clifts continue for 9 miles and approach the river very closely on either side. he found the current very strong. Capt. C killed a big horn on these clifts which himself and party dined on. after passing this range of mountains he entered this beautiful valley in which we also were. just at the upper side of the mountain there is a bad rappid. here the toe line of our canoe broke in the shoot of the rapids and swung on the rocks and had very nearly overset.

Friday, August 2ed, 1805

We resumed our march this morning at sunrise. finding that the river still boar south I determined to pass it if possible in order to shorten our rout; this we effected by wading the river about 5 miles above our encampment of the last evening. we found the current very rapid waist deep and about 90 yds. wide. bottom smooth pebble with a small mixture of coarse gravel. this is the first time I ever dared to wade the river, tho' there are many places between this and the forks where I presume it might be attempted with equal success. The valley along which we passed today, and through which the river winds it's meandering course is from 6 to 8 miles wide and consists of a beatifull level plain with but little timber and that confined to the verge of the river; the land is tolerably fertile, and is either black or dark yellow loam, covered with grass from 9 inches to 2 feet high. the plain ascends gradually on either side of the river to the bases of two ranges of high mountains. the tops of these mountains are yet covered partially with snow, while we in the valley are nearly suffocated with the intense heat of the mid-day sun; the nights are so cold that two blankets are not more than sufficient covering . . .

Saturday, August 3rd, 1805

Set out early this morning, or before sunrise; still continued our march through the level valley on the lard. side of the river. the valley much as yesterday only reather wider; I think it is 12 Miles wide, tho' the plains near the mountains rise higher and are more broken with some scattering pine near the mountain. in the leveler parts of the plain and river bottoms which are very extensive there is no timber except a scant proportion of cottonwood near the river. The Mountains continue high on either side of the valley and are but scantily supplyed with timber; small pine appears to be the prevalent growth; it is of the pitch kind, with a short leaf. at 11 A.M. Drewyer killed a doe and we halted 2 hours and breakfasted, and then continued our rout till night without halting. . . .

Capt. Clark set out this morning as usual. he walked on shore a small distance this morning and killed a deer. in the course of his walk he saw a track which he supposed to be that of an Indian from the circumstance of the large toes turning inward. he pursued the track and found that the person had ascended a point of a hill from which his camp of the last evening was visible; this circumstance also confirmed the belief of its being an Indian who had thus discovered them and ran off. They found the river as usual much crowded with islands, the currant more rapid & much more shallow than usual. in many places they were obliged to double man the canoes and drag them over the stone and gravel. this morning they passed a small creek on Stard. at the entrance of which Reubin Fields killed a large Panther. we called the creek after that animal Panther Creek. they also passed a handsome little stream on Lard. which is form of several springs which rise in the bottoms and along the base of the mountains with some little rivulets from the melting snows. in the evening they passed a very bad rappid where the bed of the river is formed entrely of solid rock and encamped on an island just above. the men wer compelled to be a great proportion of their time in the water today; they have had a severe days labour and are much fortiegued.

Tuesday, August 6th, 1805

about five miles above the forks I heard the hooping of the party to my left and changed my rout towards them; on my arrival found that they had taken the rapid fork and learnt from Capt. Clark that he had not found the note which I left for him at that place and the reasons which had induced him to ascend this stream. it was easiest & more in our direction, and apd. to contain as much water. he had however previously to my comeing up with him, met Drewyer who informed him of the state of the two rivers and was on his return. One of their canoes had just overset and all the baggage wet, the medicine box among other articles and several articles lost a shot pouch and horn among with all the implements for one rifle lost and never recovered.

I walked down to the point where I waited their return. on their arrival found that two other canoes had filled with water and wet their cargoes completely. Whitehouse had been thrown out of one of these canoes as she swing in a rapid current and the canoe had rubbed him and pressed him to the bottom as she passed over him and had the water been inches shallower must inevitably have crushed him to death. our parched meal, corn, Indian presents and a great part of our most valuable stores were wet and much damaged on this ocasion. to examine, dry and arrange our stores was the first object; we therefore passed over to the lard. side opposite the entrance of the rapid fork where there was a large gravly bar that answered our purposes; wood was also convenient and plenty. here we fixed our camp, and unloaded all our canoes and opened and exposed to dry such articles as had been wet. a part of the load of each canoe consisted of the leaden canestirs of powder which were not in least injured, tho' some of them had remained upwards of an hour under water. about 20 lbs. of powder which we had in a tight Keg or at least one we thought sufficiently so got wet and entirely spoiled. this would have been the case with the other had it not been for the expedient which I had fallen on of securing the powder by means of the lead having the latter formed into canesters which were filled with the necessary proportion of powder to discharge the lead when used, and those canesters well secured with corks and wax. in this country the air is so pure and dry that any vessel however well seasoned the timber may be will give way or shrink unless it is kept full of some liquid. we found that three deer skins which we had left at a considerable height on a tree were taken off which we supposed had been done by a panther. we sent out some men to hunt this evening they killed 3 deer and four Elk which gave us plentifull supply of meat once more.

Shannon had been dispatched up the rapid fork this morning to hunt, by Capt. Clark before he met with Drewyer or learnt his mistake in the rivers. when he returned he sent Drewyer in surch of him, but he rejoined us this evening and reported that he had been several miles up the river and could find nothing of him. we had the trumpet sounded and fired several guns but he did not join us this evening. I am fearful he is lost again. this is the same man who was separated from us 15 days as we came up the Missouri and subsisted 9 days of that time on grapes only. . . .

NEW ENGLAND'S MOUNTAINS

BY BETTY FLANDERS THOMSON

Betty Flanders Thomson was born and grew up in Ohio, got her interest in the outdoors, primarily in botany, there. Her education at Mount Holyoke College, in Holyoke, Massachusetts, however, acquainted her with New England and its countryside and she remained to become an Associate Professor of Botany at Connecticut College. In her own words, she has spent much time "poking around the back roads by car, just looking, more or less in the capacity of 'inspector of snowstorms.'" Obviously she has done more than just look, for in The Changing Face of New England *she incorporated a wealth of intimate knowledge about New England's geography, geology, and ecology. This selection, taken from that book, shows her understanding of the vast span of geologic time as well as her broad knowledge of the interrelated natural sciences.*

(*The Changing Face of New England,* by Betty Flanders Thomson; The Macmillan Company, 1958.)

New England's hills and mountains are of very ancient lineage. The geological convulsions that gave rise to their original ancestors took place a long time ago even in terms of geological ages. What we see today are merely the exposed roots of mountains whose upper bulk has long since been stripped away by erosion through an almost inconceivably long reach of time. The shifting and heaving of the earth that went into the making of the ancestral mountains and the great pressures that acted on what then were basement layers have folded and broken all but the youngest rocks almost beyond deciphering. The general course of events is not too hard to understand, but when it comes to ancient details, a geologist may prefer to talk of other things, and he sends his students to the newer Rockies, where the workings of the earth seem by contrast clear and simple.

Whatever the one-time alpine scenery of New England, a large part of its surface was subsequently eroded almost to flatness. There have been minor ups and downs of the earth's crust meanwhile, but no real mountain making has gone on for several aeons. The present roughness of the country has been wrought not by upheavals of the earth, but rather by the less dramatic forces of erosion acting on a relatively stable land.

The uplands of New England fall rather clearly into two categories according to their erosional history. The higher peaks that qualify as mountains in this part of the world are remnants of the primordial alps that were never quite smoothed away by moving water or ice. Some of them survive because they are made of especially resistant rocks. Others lie on inland watersheds that the headwater streams have not yet had time to level off. The lower hills that form a large expanse of rolling upland are the knobs and ridges left between the many valleys that have been carved into a once flat land surface. The old, smooth plain can still be seen with only a small effort of imagination wherever there is a wide view across the low hills. Then it is apparent that all the hilltops for long distances around rise to about the same height; and a line connecting their crests makes an even skyline that represents the one-time level land surface.

The higher mountains of New England fall into several quite different groups. Whether or not one extends the term "mountain" to include the Berkshires is a matter of definition. Their official name is the Berkshire Hills. This little rough plateau land is a clearly bounded entity, its eastern side rising abruptly from the Connecticut Valley, its western dropping sharply into the Hoosic and Housatonic Valleys. The northern part of the Berkshires is really the trailing end of Vermont's Green Mountains; their southern end tapers off into the hills of northwestern Connecticut.

The two thousand foot elevation of the Berkshires is not an impressive altitude in an automobile in summertime. But a traveler crossing over it during the changing seasons of spring and fall finds the weather and the state of the vegetation quite different on the hills of West Cummington from what he left half an hour ago in the valley at Northampton. In April, for example, when crocuses are out and tree buds bursting in the valley, the hills are still locked in wintry snow and ice. Not only is the year-round climate colder on the upland, but the growing season—the time between spring and autumn frosts—is substantially shorter. Botanists figure that for plants, a thousand feet up is the equivalent of six hundred miles or more north; indeed, fields and forests high in the Berkshires have a quite northern aspect compared to that of the nearby valleys.

In colonial times these modest hills that we find so charming today were a serious hindrance to pioneer settlement, so much so that they were long called the "Berkshire Barrier." The first white men who crossed them, traveling on foot and on horseback from Westfield in 1694, reported that "the greatest part of our road this day was a hideous howling wilderness" beset with "hideous high mountains." This was clearly a sentiment of the days before the romantic age revolutionized our attitudes toward scenery.

Pioneer settlers finally pushed into the Berkshires in the 1720's along the old trail followed by the present road from Westfield to Great Barrington. Once settlement began, the hill country developed rapidly. It reached its vigorous heyday about the time of the Revolution and continued for several decades in this happy state. During that time the entire primeval forest was either removed or at least drastically altered by clearing for farms, logging for sawmills and tanneries, and making charcoal to feed the local iron foundries. Then around the time of the Civil War the great rural decline that affected so much of New England's hill country struck hard at the Berkshires; and here, too, the forest has since come back.

The flavor of the changing times can still be sensed in contrasts of the present day. To see it, visit first the boyhood home of William Cullen Bryant. He was born at Cummington in 1794, the son of a frontier doctor. The house has been preserved, a substantial dwelling that still looks out over open, rolling fields. Though the countryside is quieter now, one can easily in imagination picture it checkered with many small, flourishing farms, and reconstruct the village as a busy little place with a surprisingly large number of small industries, from harness makers to textile mills and spool factories.

Then go to Buckland and search out Mary Lyon's birthplace. When she set out on the path that finally led her to the founding of Mount Holyoke Female Seminary in 1837, she came down from a simple but comfortable farm home in a well populated rural district. There were many neighboring houses in sight here and there across the open fields. Today you follow a back road up into the lonely, wooded hills, and find at journey's end only a cellar hole in a small clearing, the spot marked by a bronze plaque on one of the ever-present boulders.

Only those versed in geography or geology remember that the Taconics are a separate range of mountains. They stretch in a long, narrow belt along the line where New York State adjoins Vermont and Massachusetts, sweeping sharply up on the west side of the great limestone valleys of the Housatonic and the Hoosic and the marble vales of the Batten Kill and Otter Creek in Vermont. The range is studded with monadnocks, highest among them Graylock, Equinox, and Dorset, all rising to about 3,500 feet. This is a modest altitude, but it has its full dramatic value in contrast with the broad, deep valleys from which the mountains rise. Mount Graylock is an imposing mass when seen from the six hundred foot valley floor only a few miles away.

The Green Mountains virtually *are* Vermont. These ridges with their parallel valleys that run the length of the state are the last remnant, the very core, of an ancient up-fold of the earth's crust. In the southern part of this venerable wrinkle, thousands of feet of overlying rock have been stripped away, and the ridge of the mountain crest exposes pre-Cambrian rock. This is the oldest kind on the face of the earth, so old that no surely recognizable fossil of even the lowliest of once-living creatures has been found in it.

Much of the rock that forms the Green Mountains consists of gneiss, a hard and resistant type, rather like granite, that has been sheared and compressed in such a way that it has taken on a banded structure. The bands were once straight and level, and their present contorted pattern is evidence of the intense bending and folding the rocks have undergone in their long history. In the Green Mountains folding has been so strong that in some places, especially toward the north, the folds of rock have broken and toppled over on their sides. Since then the upper layers have been pushed westward for as much as fifty miles, overriding the younger layers of the former surface like a giant sledge. Where banded or layered rocks are exposed in a cross-sectional view, one can see for himself their folded and crushed nature and imagine the intricate processes that have gone on through the long mists of geological time.

Across the river in New Hampshire lie the White Mountains. Their tallest peaks form the Presidential Range, where Mount Washington rises 6,290 feet above sea level, the highest point east of the Rockies and north of the Smokies. The White Mountains lie in clumps and clusters that lack the clearly elongated ridge and valley pattern so common in eastern America. In the broader sense they include several groups that straggle eastward for a hundred and fifty miles to Mount Katahdin, a 5,200-foot monadnock outlier in northern Maine. All of these mountains are geologically related, although several groups among them have their own names, like the Blue Mountains and Boundary Mountains.

West of Katahdin and north of Moosehead Lake lies a large expanse of rolling plateau land that stands some 1,100 to 1,250 feet high, covered with a forest of spruce and hardwoods and strewn with lakes and bogs. So few people travel this remote wilderness that its great extent is not commonly realized. Then in extreme eastern Maine the plateau falls away to a lowland formed by the upper valleys of the Penobscot, the Aroostook, and the Saint John Rivers. Except for the potato region, this is still a forest country, and in spite of more than a century's lumbering, the whole area still answers quite well to Thoreau's description of it in "The Maine Woods."

The White Mountains proper, in New Hampshire, are New England's most mountainous mountains. They were born long ago when a tremendous mass of molten rock welled up from deep within the earth and eventually solidified into a dome of tough, resistant granite. The thousands of feet of softer rock that originally overlay the granite have long since been worn away. The peaks we know were sculptured from the remaining hard core by streams whose drainage pattern still radiates from the center of the mass. Rock structure here has little influence on topography, except in a few places such as the Flume Gorge, where a mountain stream has cut deep down along a sheet of softer basalt that strikes through the general granite.

When the climatic changes began that in time produced the continental ice sheet, small glaciers formed in the highest mountain valleys, especially on the east side of the Presidential Range. These became large enough and lasted long enough to gouge their valley heads into steep, amphitheaterlike glacial cirques. Perhaps the most familiar one is the head of Tuckerman's Ravine, where in the chilly shadows snow lies late in spring, to the joy of ardent skiers. Other ravines and "gulfs" originated in the same way. Lower down, the rivers of ice scoured their sharp, narrow valleys into rounded troughs with broad, smooth bottoms like that of Crawford Notch. All these features are rudimentary but classic examples of true alpine geology.

The separate valley glaciers had no more than begun their work and had scarcely nibbled into the mountain mass when they were swallowed up in the advancing continental ice sheet. Eventually the ice flowed over even the highest peaks, scraping and smoothing the contours of the solid granite. In spite of the extreme weathering that takes place on the heights, stray erratic boulders dropped by the glacier remain almost on the very crests as tokens of the passing ice.

The glacier, when it finally melted, left behind its usual mantle of bouldery till. This still remains on the lower slopes, but higher up little but the larger boulders has withstood the wash of running water, and soil becomes increasingly scarce. Farther down, the broader valleys among the mountains are spread with a layer of glacial till that makes a soil more or less adequate for farming, especially in the spots that once were occupied by temporary post-glacial lakes. Such relatively level areas among the mountains are locally known as "intervales." No very serious farming is attempted in the higher valleys, but some of the intervale meadows still produce a passable crop of hay.

The vegetation that covers the mountains is neatly zoned according to the altitude and exposure where it grows. A journey up Mount Washington takes one through several different kinds of forest zone and finally, at the top, out into the open above timberline.

The feet and lower slopes of the mountain are clothed with a forest of hardwoods—beech, maple, birch, and others—mixed with red spruce and balsam. Farther up, some of the hardwood species begin to drop out, leaving white birch and mountain ash relatively more important. As the cold and the wind increase, black spruce appears, first as vigorous, symmetrical trees, then more and more showing the effects of the struggle with the elements. At first the trees are merely stunted because of their extremely slow growth in the cool air and stone-bound mountain soil. Then as the force of the wind becomes increasingly a factor to be reckoned with, the trees become increasingly deformed, although in sheltered hollows or in the lee of rocks or ridges, needles and twigs are normally formed and thrifty in their growth.

The shearing effect of the wind can be seen everywhere. A few upright trees stream away from the prevailing wind in a flag form. Other venturesome stalks rising above the general surface may survive for a few years; but eventually they succumb to the fury of a severe winter, leaving their bleached skeletons as monuments to foolhardiness. Plants that cannot grow upward will then grow horizontally. The windshorn spruce sends out a multitude of low ground-hugging branches that develop into a tough, impenetrable tangle firm enough to support a man walking over the top. The smoothly pruned contours of the matted thickets show just where the edge of the wind rushes past, and where the winter snow collects in sheltered and sheltering drifts or is swept clean away by the scouring blast.

Still higher, where not even deformed and stunted spruce can survive, dwarf shrubby species of birch and alpine willows appear. These also grow in a dense mat, never more than knee-high, and commonly reaching scarcely to the shoetops.

At last you come out above even the dwarf trees onto true alpine tundra at the top of the world. On a clear day there is nothing to break the view for a thousand miles or more except the earth's own curvature. To stand as high as the peak of Mount Washington you would have to go to Mount Mitchell in North Carolina or the Black Hills of South Dakota. The wind blows in a steady torrent, and much of the time it carries wisps and drifts of cloud through your streaming hair. When you take shelter from the wind's whistle, you can hear the songs of distant hermit thrushes and white-throated sparrows floating up from the forest far below.

All around the earth falls away in a rolling sea of gray rock slabs and boulders. Loose soil has long ago been washed or blown from the exposed places and filtered down into the crevices, leaving the mountain top covered with a rough, cobbled pavement of giant stones.

Here on the tundra in the nooks where anything at all can grow, the most abundant plants are grassy-looking little sedges. More picturesque are the evergreen mats or cushions of species that grow in the far North, as their scientific descriptive names of *lapponicum* or *groenlandicum* reveal. So far as plants are concerned, a trip to the top of Mount Washington is the equivalent of a journey of hundreds of miles, as far north as Labrador or the Arctic Barrens.

Alpine flowers, the rarer the better, have always held a fascination for lowland dwellers. Specimens of all of these have been collected, identified, and cherished by countless amateur botanists through the years. They are indeed charmers, neat little mounds or doilies of small, dark leaves, usually evergreen, thickly studded in June and July with flowers of the most fetching forms and colors. There is the Lapland rosebay, *Rhododendron lapponicum,* like small red-purple azaleas. There are *Diapensia lapponicum* and the smaller mountain sandwort, *Arenaria groenlandica,* each one a cushion of dainty white flowers. Tiniest of all is the minute alpine azalea, *Loiseluria procumbens,* with bright pink blossoms scarcely a quarter of an inch across. Less prettily colorful but equally exotic as northern tundra plants are crowberries, mountain cranberries, and prostrate dwarf willows. There are many others. Some of them grow on other high peaks in New England and the Adirondacks, but to see them all in their northern lowland homes one would have to cross hundreds of miles of intervening forest where not a one of them is to be found.

People familiar with our western mountains are not likely to be impressed with the mountainous character of five or six thousand foot peaks. Even a novice, provided he is strong enough in lung and limb, can climb any of the trails on Mount Washington. Then, too, the whole region has been swarming with tourists almost since it was first settled in the 1770's. The most sedentary of travelers can reach the top of the highest peak, taking his choice of auto road or cog railway. Yet Mount Washington has taken far more lives than any other mountain in America, and those who have worked both here and in the Antarctic say that the top of this little mountain has the worst weather in the world.

Consider for a moment what the place is like. Winds of hurricane force occur here in every month of the year, in winter on an average of four days a week. Two-hundred-mile winds blow occasionally, and the highest wind velocity ever measured, 231 miles an hour, was recorded here. In January the wind roars past at an average rate of fifty-five miles an hour. In July, even counting in the occasional still days, the wind speed averages a smart twenty-three miles an hour.

Temperatures are also severe and show strongly the effect of altitude. Not far away in Boston, winters vary around 30° F. On Mount Washington the figure is 7.1°. Whereas summer averages 72° on the coast, it is 48° on the mountain. Once the mercury fell to 49° below zero. And it usually snows sometime during every month of the year.

These are the conditions that mountain-top plants have to contend with. A man on foot must take into account not only wind and cold, but also blinding rain and mist. Here are a few more figures. It rains or snows on 57 percent of the days in an average summer, and half the mornings in July are foggy until well past sunup. The close spacing of stone marker cairns along the rocky foot trails near the summit should remind the fairweather hiker of the very real hazards of this extremely exposed place. If this is not graphic enough, there is a hair-raising little book called "Three Days on the White Mountains, being the Perilous Adventure of Dr. B. L. Ball on Mount Washington during October 25, 26 and 27, 1855."

Scientists have wondered why timberline on New England mountains should lie at about half the elevation that it does at the same latitude in the west. Probably it is the completely exposed position of the eastern peaks that accounts for the difference. There is nothing to break the force of the weather, nothing within a thousand feet of the height of Mount Washington and very little approaching that between it and the far side of the Great Plains.

Plants exposed to the eternal wind that blows here must survive not only its mechanical force and its cold and drying effects, but also the onslaught of wind-driven snow and sleet. Typical alpine plants hug the ground or lie low in pockets and crevices between the rocks. In this way they really avoid rather than endure the effect of the wind. In larger sheltered spots and hollows especially where protecting snowdrifts lie all winter, trees can grow right up to the ceiling that the wind makes. In 1940 a visiting botanist was able to find small, isolated trees growing right to the mountain top, the highest one a fir standing not more than seventy feet from the summit. All this strongly suggests that it is not so much extreme cold as wind that determines the location of timberline on our eastern mountains.

Alpine tundra above timberline closely resembles that of the Arctic. On Mount Washington alpine plants are especially abundant on the relatively level, almost lawnlike expanses long known as the Alpine Gardens. Like the arctic tundra, these are cold, wet, windy places where the soil is stony and sparse. Here the earth is well drained because of the topography, but always moist from the frequent rain and mist. Much of the area is a jumble of rock slabs, with soil enough for rooted plants only in small pockets in between. Those who have tried digging report that there is more good soil down under than is commonly believed; but overlying rocks conceal most of it and make it inaccessible for small plants.

The surface soil where small plants are rooted is in a constant state of flux. For a large part of the year it alternately freezes and thaws. This has a churning effect and makes the soil do a sort of creep movement down hill. Even level spots where soil is a little more abundant are subject to constant stirring. In addition to this kind of disturbance, high winds from time to time dislodge and blow away tufts of vegetation along with the soil they are growing in. People familiar with the high country report instances of coming back repeatedly to a favorite clump of some little flower until one year it just isn't there any more.

In spite of years of botanizing by many people on the higher mountains, little is known for certain about the relationships of the plants that grow there to their environment and to each other. Wind and cold and dampness are all obviously important, as well as the instability of the soil. But which of these factors is critical? Is it the same one for all plants? Is it merely chance that brings the various alpine species into now one and now a quite different combination? For these and many more questions there are more or less informed guesses but no well-founded answers, and some hardy mountain lover with a bent for experiment and a knowledge of plants and of measuring instruments has a wide open field for research.

The treeless area on Mount Washington is some eight miles long by two or three miles wide. There are similar but smaller places on no less than twenty-five of New Hampshire's peaks, as well as on Camel's Hump and Mount Mansfield in Vermont and Katahdin in

Maine. Most of these can be reached only on foot. Happily for those with willing spirits but weak or rebellious flesh, it is possible to journey to the tundra of Washington or Mansfield in an hour's ride in the ease and comfort of one's own automobile.

THE ORDEAL

BY STEWART EDWARD WHITE

Stewart Edward White (1873–1946) was born, grew up and was educated in Michigan where he learned to know and love the outdoors. Schooled in the law, he turned to writing instead and over a long and active career wrote many books, almost all of them with a dominant outdoor background. He was a splendid storyteller, but he knew and was meticulously accurate about his settings and the life that abounded there. His trilogy of novels about Andy Burnett, The Long Rifle, Ranchero, *and* Folded Hills, *tell the story of the mountain men of legendary memory and the early history of California, and they tell it with superb skill and remarkable knowledge of the West in the early years of the nineteenth century. This excerpt from* Folded Hills *is fiction, but it is also outdoor writing of distinction, shaped to dramatic form with such skill that it has the sense of complete truth—which it is, of course, in substance and detail. The Djo of this story is the half-Spanish son of Andy Burnett and Carmel, Andy's wife.*

(*Folded Hills,* by Stewart Edward White; Doubleday, Doran & Company, 1934.)

By the time he was ten years old Djo had acquired several accomplishments unknown to other children of California. He could shoot; he could throw a knife, not by the blade, *vaquero* fashion, but from the flat of his hand; he possessed a strange lore of woodcraft. That part of Djo's education was empirical. He accompanied Andy everywhere—Don Largo's shadow. As they rode together Andy threw off information. Days later, unexpectedly, he would catechize.

"What did you notice near the High Tenaja?"

He would listen, generally without comment, to Djo's reply.

Occasionally he would utter a brief commendation; that was a happy occasion. Occasionally he would shake his head.

"Ride up there and look again," he might command; or merely maintain a disapproving silence; and Djo was abashed.

That was the way Andy remembered, that he himself had learned, and he saw again, across the years, the leafy Pennsylvania forests and the fantastic figure of Joe Crane striding ahead, and almost he could hear once more the slow drawl of the mountain man:

"In Injun country quakin' asp's yore best fire. It ain't got no smoke nor smell. . . ."

These things were delightful to Djo, and in his growing proficiencies Andy took a vast satisfaction; but to the people of the ranch they seemed entirely useless. On his tenth birthday Djo killed a buck with the old Boone gun, which was much taller than he was, and which he had to rest over Andy's shoulder to make the shot. Both he and Andy were inordinately proud of this feat, though nobody else saw any sense or glory in it. Why anyone should climb a high mountain to shoot an animal that was not much good anyway, when there was beef to be had for the roping, was beyond Californian conception.

At the conclusion of the festivities celebrating Djo's twelfth birthday Andy summoned his son to appear before him. He surveyed the youngster with a newly appraising eye. He saw a handsome boy, dressed in the Californian costume of the period. Except for Andy's straight frowning brows, his gray-blue steady eyes, and the determined set of his jaws, his appearance was Spanish. Certain features, considered singly in isolation, were almost effeminate. For example, the long upcurled black lashes, in arresting contrast to the eyes. His body was straight, with a hint of whalebone supple strength in its slenderness. He would stand perhaps three or four inches above five feet. Andy's heart swelled with pride and affection; but no hint of this illumined his face.

Djo stood patiently and respectfully at attention.

"You are twelve years old today," Andy broke silence at last. He spoke in English, so Djo knew this for a real conference, man to man. "Back in the Indian country they used to say that a boy stopped being a child when he was twelve years old. They let him do a lot of grown-up things, by himself, that he couldn't do before. Let him play men's games. Look here, Djo; suppose suddenly you found yourself over yonder in the mountains, without anything, how do you think you'd make out? Could you take care of yourself?"

"Yes, sir," said Djo promptly. His father and he had often played similar games, when riding the country; but on a smaller scale.

"Now hold on," Andy checked him. "You got to think this over. Never go off half cocked. Look-a here." He held up his great hand and checked the items on his fingers. "You've got no horse; that's been stole. You've got no gun. You haven't even got any clothes. Nothing but your two hands—well, maybe you saved your knife. But that's all you've got; and," Andy added, "that's more than many a good man, white or red, was left with in a sight harder country than this."

Djo considered.

"Yes, sir," he said confidently at last.

"Want to try?"

Djo's correct posture broke in a wriggle of delight.

"It's a game!" he cried. "Let's call it Wildman!"

"Well, yes; it's a game. We'll call it Wildman; that's a good name. And if you play it you'll have to stick to the rules." Djo nodded. "Well, here they are. You know all you need to know, if you remember what I taught you. You'll have your knife. The game is to see how long you can make out. You can come home any time you want to quit. Any time at all. Just come home. Or we can fix a signal and come and get you. Things might go wrong first time, you know. All right. But while you're out you've got to do it all yourself. No help. Of any kind. From nobody. You've got to promise that, and stick to your promise."

"Yes, sir," agreed Djo happily. "When can I try?"

"Tomorrow, if you want to."

The boy's face clouded with the doubt of an afterthought.

"Will Mother permit—and Vicenta?" he asked.

"They will permit," promised Andy, "—but perhaps we'd better not say tomorrow. Say on Monday."

That Andy was able to meet his promise was only because, as *patrón,* he had authority and used it. The idea was fantastic, senseless—even dangerous. There were wild cattle, there were bear, there might even be Indians from the *tulares.* And the cold! the *pobrecito* would die of the cold! Deliberately to expose one's own son to such perils, for no reason at all, would be the act of a madman! Or an *americano,* it was added as an afterthought of loyalty; and it had always been said that *americanos* were mad. Thus Vicenta; and much more; and after her every other dweller of Folded Hills, with the one exception of Panchito, the head *vaquero.* Partly from his hard-bitten conviction that hardship is good for anybody, mostly because of Vicenta, he defended the *patrón.* When it was realized that Don Largo really meant what he said, a dozen petty conspiracies came to life.

Andy could silence the ranch people with a command. But Carmel was another affair. It took some time for him to convince her that the whole matter was not a joke. Andy was patient and gentle; but beneath the gentleness was an inflexible determination against which Carmel's protests beat in vain.

"But it is madness!" she cried. "He is an infant! He will perish!"

"He is no longer an infant. He is grown. He will not perish. He has been taught enough to care for himself, if he remembers what he is taught. And he can come home at any time."

"But he is my baby. This is a foolishness. The season of the rains is not yet past. No: this I cannot suffer. He is mine. I shall not permit."

"He is mine, also," persisted Andy steadily. "You have had him as a child; now I must have him as a man."

Carmel threw out her hands.

"But I ask it of you that you do not insist. I cannot bear it. It is a little thing to ask. You have never refused me anything that I ask."

Andy was troubled and distressed.

"Do not ask me, *querida,*" he begged. "I wish this very much."

"But why, why, why?" demanded Carmel.

"Djo is twelve. Back in my old Indian country when a boy became a man in years they tried him to see if he was a man at heart as well. I think it was a good idea."

"Djo is not an Indian. What is it you would try? Is he not strong and brave? Is he not *hidalgo?* Have you no eyes in your head to see? Must you do this madness to prove to yourself that he is your son?"

"It is not that. But Djo must prove it to himself. Yes; that is it. He must prove it to himself."

"I do not understand," wailed Carmel.

Nor did Andy himself quite understand his own obstinacy. There was some mysterious, mystic inner compulsion. Deep within him were subtleties too profound for the analysis of his simple mind, insistences born of his hard and savage training, distrusts that were racial, hopes that were a passion of love. This that to Djo was an exciting game, to Carmel a dangerous madness, had become to Andy high ordeal. He could not have explained to himself, much less to Carmel, the almost tremulous anxiety of soul with which he awaited the event. She would not have understood it if he had. Old Abel Means came nearest.

"What's the idee, boss?" asked the millwright. "Ain't there some other game you can play with the young-un that ain't so skeery for the women? Looks like you're carryin' matters a leetle fur, don't it?"

"Doggone it, Abel," burst out Andy, "I've got to *know*."

"Know what?" asked Means curiously.

"How much guts he has."

"Oh, that young-un's got guts," said Abel, "eff'n that's all you got to know."

But it was not quite all. It was something besides; though Andy himself did not know what it was.

"There you are, son." Andy reined his horse after a stiff climb. "This is pretty favorable. There's water and other things to keep you if you know enough. Scared at all?"

"What of?" demanded Djo.

"Well, there's nothing to be scared of," admitted Andy, "if you know how to take care of yourself. And you ought to: you've been well taught. And it's pretty favorable here." He looked about at the little basin, or "park." The new grass was well started; the live-oaks were brilliantly mottled with fresh leaves among the old. Birds were singing ecstatically, and the quail chirked and called and muttered and twittered, scurrying beneath the chaparral like dried leaves.

"Pretty favorable," Andy repeated. He was remembering the Rockies, in winter. "Or the desert," he said aloud.

"Sir?"

"I was thinking that after the big mountains and the desert this is pretty soft."

"May I try them some day?"

"Better try this first," said Andy dryly. He became businesslike. "Climb down," he commanded. "I'll take your horse. Strip off. Tie your clothes on the saddle. You can keep your shoes; your feet aren't hard for barefoot." Djo stood before him, a straight, brown, strong little figure. Andy's eye traveled over him with satisfaction. "Take that off," he ordered dryly.

"What, sir? The *botas*?" Djo looked up at his father with limpid eye of innocence.

"You know better. Hand it over."

Djo grinned, undid his loincloth. Andy grinned back.

"Thought you knew how to use that, didn't you?"

"Yes, sir."

"Isn't in the game. Here's your outfit." He handed Djo the long-bladed knife. "Now we're going to play fair. I'm not going to spy on you. See that big flat rock up there on the edge? We can see that from the house plain, with the glasses. We want to know you're safe. So every morning you go up there and put a pretty fair size stone on that rock. Lay 'em in a row so we can count 'em. Better see to it, for as soon as a rock is missing we'll come up after you, and the game is over. And, remember, any time you want to quit or you can't make it, come right on home. Or go sit on the rock where we can see you, and we'll come and get you. This is just a game, you know. You can always try again, if you don't make it the first time." Andy checked himself. He was becoming garrulous. This was now Djo's affair, to be carried through, one way or another, by his own inner promptings, without the aid or handicap of suggestion. He gathered up the reins.

"Good luck, son," said he.

At the edge of the chaparral he turned in his saddle. The straight naked little figure stood where he had left it, bronze in the sunlight. Andy raised his hand, palm outward, Indian fashion. He rode slowly down the mountain. It did not occur to him that the situation was fantastic; that this deliberate abandonment by its father of a child to the mercies of the wilderness was grotesque; that there might be pathos in the tiny naked figure. For the moment Andy was all Indian. The solid and actual world had vanished. He, and with him in spirit Djo, had moved apart into a mighty world of shadows, just they two, where awaited the event an enduring truth of spiritual relationship. There lay Djo's heritage, could he find it. Andy sensed it dimly as something bright and glowing and precious, that had illumined the struggle of the Dark and Bloody Ground, a guarded flame held in the high heart of the old woman, his grandmother, in a Pennsylvania farm, a living fire that quickened himself to a part in destiny. His hand tightened on the stock of the long rifle that Boone himself had borne. This was Djo's heritage. But he must find it for himself. Andy could not help him further. While these things resolved themselves in the alchemy of ordeal, he must stand apart. No one but himself understood, and he but dimly, and rather with the heart than with the mind. For an instant the lonesomeness of a complete isolation in space overcame him. He shivered slightly as though with a chill. And then a slow warmth bathed him. It was as though a companionship had drawn near. At certain crises of life this thing had come to him. He felt himself surrounded, upheld.

He gathered up the reins, touched spur, rode on down the mountain, humming half-voice. He was unconscious of the fact that he sang. The song was the Blackfoot song of prayer for the intercession of the Above People.

Djo did not come in the first day, as Vicenta volubly predicted. Nor the second; nor the third. Regularly the stones agreed upon as a signal appeared one by one on the flat rock. After Andy had determined this fact with the telescope, each in turn took a peek through that instrument. Each must see for himself. Andy moved, withdrawn in his preoccupation with the inner spiritual crisis which, it must be repeated, he did not understand. It was as though the ranch and its people were of shadow substance. In his presence they felt shadowy: his piercing abstracted gaze through them made even the least imaginative *mozo* doubt for a fleeting instant his own substantiality. This was true even of the little girl, Amata; even of Carmel herself.

"Come back," she pleaded. "You have gone so far! See, I am no longer angry. I was foolish to become angry. I do not understand wholly; but he is now a man child and you are a man, and it is yours to make him a man."

With the adaptability of her race when deeply in love, she had swung even beyond Andy's own viewpoint. Reassured by the regular appearance of the all's-well signals, her anxieties were giving way to a truly Spanish pride in Djo's prowess. She thought Andy must also be feeling both the relief and the pride. She could not understand why he did not share them with her, why he remained thus removed.

On the morning of the seventh day of this strange testing, Andy on arising did not as usual take down the telescope from its pegs on the wall.

"Today, when you have arisen, we shall ride," he told Carmel.

She parted her lips, but checked her eager question in a sudden queer illusion that her voice would not carry to the still remoteness in which his spirit poised. In silence she hurried into her riding garments, in silence she piled the dark masses of her hair, and on her head placed the woven straw riding hat with the soft sun cloth weighted with little golden apples. In silence she gulped down the chocolate. They crossed the *sala* together, and out the door into the early freshness. In the half-light just before sun-up the guardian oaks spread wide as though in sanctuary to the last dusk of dying night crouched beneath their brooding. The mourning notes of doves floated through their branches, spaced and slow and soft, like the drift downward of golden flakes. Beneath the oaks were horses waiting, in charge of Panchito; and, surrounding them, the other people of the ranch. They were all there, a notable gathering: the *vaqueros*; the women of the household; the *mozas* who washed clothes at the stream; the very Indians and *mozos* whose affair was the varied menial business of the estate; and the children big and little. Benito had trudged up from the *milpas* and grain fields in the flats below. Abel Means leaned against the trunk of an oak, chewing tobacco. None spoke. They looked.

Andy helped Carmel to the saddle, himself mounted and took the reins.

"We ride alone," he said briefly to Panchito, who prepared to follow as usual.

The assembly watched them ride away. They eyed one another furtively and quietly dispersed. Something in the occasion had awed comment. They feared to voice what was in the minds of all, for each had looked into Andy's face and seen there something he could not understand. Only Vicenta, her eyes following her mistress, crossed herself, muttering.

"*La pobrecita!* The *patrón* is mad!"

"Silence, woman!" cried Panchito harshly.

And for once Vicenta made him no reply.

Andy and Carmel rode up the mountain together, meeting the warm sunlight on its slopes. They topped the rim of the park, and Carmel uttered a joyous cry. Andy laid a restraining hand on her horse's bridle.

Djo squatted before a fire. He was naked, as Andy had left him, except that he had replaced the confiscated loincloth with the skin of some small animal. He was intent on cooking something, and various objects were scattered about on the ground near him.

After a moment Andy relinquished his grasp. The two moved slowly forward.

Djo looked up and saw them. Carmel could no longer be restrained. Her horse leaped forward. She flung herself from the saddle and clasped the little figure to her, laughing and crying at once, babbling endearments and questions, her hands caressing Djo's body in reassurance of her eyes. Andy followed at a footpace. He reined in his horse, and sat, his hands crossed on the broad saddle horn, his eyes slowly and appraisingly taking in the details of what lay before him. He said nothing, and his face was grave. Djo had stiffened in his mother's embrace. He stood at rigid attention, and his eyes met those of his father unwaveringly. Carmel felt the tension. She released Djo and rose from her knees, looking from one to the other in perplexity. And at once she felt herself set aside. It was as though she were not there; as though she had become a disembodied onlooker at this encounter.

"Why do you come, *senor padre?*" asked Djo in Spanish. "Have I then failed?"

"That we shall see," said Andy.

"I have here made me fire," commented Djo, "and I have eaten well, and I have slept warm. If you had not come so soon I would have also clothes, for today, or tomorrow at most, I would have trapped a deer. Could I have done more?"

"You have done this without help?" demanded Andy searchingly.

"Of a surety, *senor padre*. Was not that the rule?"

He looked into Andy's face, hesitated.

"One came offering me help," he said reluctantly after a time. "But that I would not accept, and I made her—" He broke off confusedly.

A cold smile crossed Andy's face without relieving its austerity.

"That, naturally, I know," said he. "The sign was plain on the trail."

"But naturally, *senor padre,*" agreed Djo. "But," he added, "surely Vicenta must not be blamed."

Andy smiled grimly. "She is not blamed," he said briefly.

He said nothing further. His eyes again swept over the details of the little camp.

Djo's face clouded with enlightenment and anxiety.

"These are from the *milpa,*" suggested Andy at last; and waited.

"But yes, *senor padre,*" cried Djo eagerly. "From the *milpa,* of a surety. But no one brought them to me; I myself took them. Is not that in the game? And I went there, not at night, which would have been too easy and, I think, not in the game, but in the daytime, while Benito and the Indians were there working, and I crept there under their very noses and took them, and I covered my trail so that they never knew." Djo chuckled boyishly, then became grave again. "If they had caught me I would have come straight to you, *senor padre,* to tell you I had failed. Was not that all right?" he asked anxiously. "I remember how you told me of stealing into the Indian villages. . . ."

Andy heard no more. For an instant in his relief from suspicion, he felt lightheaded, a little dizzy, so that he grasped the pommel of his saddle for support. And in that instant he caught for the third time in his life at a rather tremendous inner experience, a sensation as of the uplifting of austere presences outside of and beyond himself; living, actual presences that had shared and which now rejoiced. And suddenly he seemed to himself to be rushed back as on a mighty wind from the remoteness in which he had for the past week poised, and to be free once more of warm and living and human relationship. He flung himself from the saddle with a mighty shout and in his turn clasped Djo in his arms. And between the man and the boy a last thin barrier broke so that thenceforward both knew they were wholly akin.

Carmel threw her hands wide in despair.

"These Burnett!" she muttered. "Never, never shall I know them!"

But in that second she was swept into the general embrace; and strangely enough she forgot all her maternal agonizings of the past week, she even forgot Djo. Passionately she clung to Andy, sobbing.

"Oh, *querido, querido!*" she cried over and over again. "You have come back! You have come back to me! Never, never go so far from me again!"

Andy sat on a fallen oak bole while Djo made his report. Or, rather, while Djo answered his catechism.

"How did you get your fire?"

"I found a fire stone and hit upon it with the back of the knife."

"And for tinder," Andy grinned at him. "That's where that breech clout would have come in handy, eh? Did you think of that when I made you give it up?"

Djo grinned back.

"Yes, *senor padre.*"

"I thought so. Good boy. What did you use for tinder?"

"It was difficult," submitted Djo, "for this is still the season of rains, and all is green, and nothing is ripe, so there is no dry pith in any of the plants you told me. I found some dry rotted oak, but it would not take the spark I could make with my fire stone. It was not very good, not like a real flint."

"What is that yonder next that mariposa?" said Andy suddenly, pointing.

"It's a lizard," replied Djo.

Andy sighed, arose from the bole, made two strides to the mariposa, and picked up a good-sized chunk of rock, which he tossed to Djo.

"Plain sight," he commented.

Djo stared at the fragment.

"But—but there should be no flint in these mountains," he stammered.

"No," conceded Andy, "I put it there. If you'd had that you wouldn't have had much trouble making your fire, would you? Well, why didn't you see it? I put it there for you to see; in plain sight." Djo hung his head. "I'll tell you. It was because you didn't *expect* to see it. Go ahead. How did you get your fire?"

"I didn't, until the next day," confessed Djo.

"Oh!" cried Carmel. "The cold! My poor baby!"

But this was a false note; as she instantly realized, and fell silent, for she saw this was men's business, and Carmel was not devoid of common sense—or of humor.

"There's no cold—what you can call cold—in this country," Andy flung to her. "And next day?"

"While searching up the hill yonder, for a *mescal,* I came upon a cave in which were many bats. There was much droppings which were dry almost like powder, so I struck a spark in it to try. It is much better than tinder, *senor padre.* It takes the fire instantly."

"Now that I did not know!" cried Andy. "That is something worth knowing!"

Djo glowed at the approbation.

"Once I had my fire, there was no more trouble. There are here many rabbits, and quail—and other things. And, *senor padre,* if you had not come so soon I would have had a deer."

"Until then you were hungry?"

Djo made a comical face.

"I ate," he said briefly.

"But what?" cried Carmel.

"The new buds just starting in the trees," enumerated Djo, "the curl tips of ferns, some seeds of the grass—there was one place where the sun was hot where they were ripe, the berries of manzanita. They were not very good; but I was not hungry."

Carmel made a murmur of indignant protest.

"You caught your rabbits and quail with snares?" suggested Andy.

"Yes, *senor padre,* as you had showed me—at the first."

Andy grinned again.

"Loincloth would have come in handy again, wouldn't it?"

Again Djo answered the grin in acknowledgment.

"What did you use for your snares?"

"I climbed to the *puerto suelo* where I remembered we saw mares last month, and I searched until I found where hair from their tails had caught in the brush."

"*Bueno!*" cried Andy, then in English: "That shines!"

He arose from the tree trunk and began to pace back and forth.

"When I had eaten the meat of the rabbit," Djo continued, "I cut leaves of the *mescal* and pounded them with stones and scraped them with the knife until the fibers were bare and wove me a strong cord. Like this,"—he fumbled behind a rock and produced a fragment.

"I learned this from Pascal," Djo explained, "while I was making bricks."

Andy glanced at Carmel.

"It is with this that I would catch the deer," Djo continued. "I finished it yesterday, and I made a loop and laid it where the deer come to drink."

"We shall look at that," said Andy. "It is not as easy to catch a deer as a rabbit."

"No, *senor padre*," acknowledged Djo, "and it may be I have not set it well. It is not easy to bend a large enough young tree with no one to help, for I am not very heavy."

"For why do you bend a young tree?" Carmel could not restrain her curiosity. Her interest was kindling. She became aware that her menfolk looked down upon her from superior masculine heights. She chuckled to herself in appreciation.

"The loop catches the deer by a foot," Andy explained patiently, as though the thing were obvious, "but it could easily pull loose. The sapling is bent, like a spring, to lift the foot from the ground so it cannot do so. You are as heavy as a small deer," he told Djo. "Possibly a small deer might be caught—if you set the loop and the trigger properly. We will take a look. What else?"

"I also made this." Djo submitted a strip of rabbit hide, in each end of which he had tied a hard clay ball. "You hold it by the middle and whirl it about your head like a *reata,* and throw it," he explained to Carmel. "Sometimes it hits something. I am not very good with it. But it is fun. And I did kill a quail with it, and two rabbits."

"I did not teach you this," said Andy.

"No: Pascal told me. He said it was better for ducks. I have not tried it for ducks. Pascal also told me how *los indios* catch ducks with a net woven of *tules*. I was going to try that, but the *laguna* is far, and I wanted to catch my deer first, and I must place the stone each day on the flat rock, as you told me."

"With nets," repeated Andy. "Now there is something I do not know. How can that be done? To strike the ducks with the *bola,* yes, that I see. But nets? How do you do that?"

Djo explained, his manner modest, but his whole being suffused with delight.

"Why, one makes a wide net of *tules,*" said he, "and finds a narrow slough with the *tules* growing high on either side, and he sets up the net across the slough on stakes; and he makes some small bundles of *tules* and sets them afloat by the net, so that the ducks flying see them, and come down to swim with them, thinking that they are other ducks."

"Decoys," Andy supplied the English word.

"Decoys." Djo repeated the word experimentally. "One hides, very carefully, close below the net. And when there are many ducks swimming, one leaps out suddenly and some of the ducks dash against the net and fall back, and one seizes them quickly before they recover."

"Well," observed Andy, "I never heard of that!" He ruminated the idea. "It doesn't sound reasonable. Pascal told you they catch ducks that way?"

"Yes, *senor padre.*"

"We've got to try that."

"Yes, *senor padre,*" said Djo happily.

Andy prowled about restlessly. Djo waited. Carmel watched them both with bright eyes.

"Bough bed's not so bad, eh?" suggested Andy, reverting to English. "Next time put her next a rock and make your fire t'other side of your bed. You'll sleep warmer: rock reflects the heat back.—Hm? Make you any deadfalls?"

"No, *senor padre.*"

"Snares good enough, eh? Try a pit trap?"

"Yes, *senor padre,*" acknowledged Djo, with a certain reluctance which Andy could not but notice.

"It's quite a trick," the latter consoled the boy for supposed failure. "Animals are pretty noticing. It's hard to hide things from them. Takes practice." He examined his son's face keenly. "What is it, Djo? Out with it."

"It wasn't that," said Djo. "I caught a skunk," he blurted out.

Andy threw back his head with a roar of laughter; in which, after a moment, Djo joined.

"*Gato montés,*" Andy translated the word to Carmel.

Still chuckling, Andy crossed the tiny grass plot to the horses. He untied a bundle from the saddle strings.

"Here, son," he said, "here's your clothes. If Vicenta sees you with nothing on but that rabbit skin she'll have my scalp. Well, what is it?"

"My deer snare," said Djo.

"We'll ride up later and take a look."

Djo still hesitated, the bundle in his hands.

"Come along!" urged Andy.

"*Senor padre,*" began Djo, and stopped.

"Well?"

"Oh, *senor padre,* must I go back now?" pleaded Djo in a rush of words. "Cannot I stay just a little, just a few days more? I shall catch my deer, I know it. And I shall make clothes. And—and—"

"And?"

Djo eyed his father doubtfully.

"Over beyond the *puerto suelo* there lives a bear." He stopped.

Andy was eyeing him steadily.

"Well, what of it?"

Djo was embarrassed, unable to proceed.

"What do you think you can do, monkeying with a bear?" demanded Andy in English. "Don't talk foolish."

"If I catch my deer I could make a strong *reata* of rawhide," urged Djo in the more familiar Spanish, "and it might be that I could trap the bear. I have thought of it much, *senor padre.* With another *reata* and a heavy stone to help I could bend down a strong tree, and—"

"And after you have caught your bear—if you did—what would you do with him? Go up and bite his ear?" asked Andy sarcastically.

Djo flushed but stood his ground.

"I have the knife," said he. "I could stand to one side, and if I threw it just so I might—"

Andy surveyed the small figure mockingly, but with a very tender light in his eye.

"Son," he said at last, still in English, "you're a good boy and I'm proud of you. Proud of you," he repeated emphatically. "But there's one thing you've got to learn."

"Yes, *senor padre.*"

"Don't bite off more than you can chew. Now you get on those duds and come along."

Djo mounted behind his father. They rode slowly down the mountain. All three were happy, though each in a different way. Djo had had a wonderful time, and glowed with pardonable triumph that he had played the game of Wildman well enough to earn his father's praise; for Djo knew that in such matters his father's praise was worth while. Carmel's heart was singing because this prank was finished, and because Djo was safe and well; but above all because her lover had come back to her from across mysterious and terrifying spaces.

But Andy's happiness was a happiness of his whole being, for it was made of the dissolution of something that had long lain heavy in his heart. The fact that he had had no conscious knowledge of it until these past few days had not lessened its effect. Now he saw it clearly; could even put it into words. He was astonished, even a little uneasy, as though at an implication of disloyalty. But with characteristic honesty he now put it to himself bluntly.

In Djo's veins ran the blood of two races. Andy admired and loved the Californian people with whom he had cast his lot. Nevertheless, he did not want Djo like them; not even like Ramón or the stately old *hacendado*, Don Sylvestre. He wanted Djo to be an American of his own breed, the breed of mountain men; and that was something that could not be taught, but must come from the inner spirit; could not be told, but must be tested.

His mind flashed back to the old days. Before it arose a picture of Running Elk in full ceremonial costume watching gravely the initiation ceremony of which his son was part. The boy was dragging about a buffalo skull by means of a cord passed through deep slits in the muscles of his chest. This he must do until by his own leapings and plungings against the weight he could tear the cord through the flesh, and so stand free, nor must he flinch or fail. Andy recalled his own admiration, both for the boy's courage, and for Running Elk's stolid calm, for he knew Running Elk's affection for the lad. The warrior puffed at his pipe with detached indifference; but Andy particularly remembered the fine circlet of perspiration that stood out on Running Elk's brow. Now, many years after, he understood that Running Elk agonized in spirit not so much at the terrible physical torture, as Andy had thought with sympathy at the time, but with a deeper anxiety lest by failure the boy should prove his only in flesh and not in the deeper kinship of spirit. The ordeal had been long and severe, for the lad was strongly built and his muscles were tough. Even Andy, hardened as he was by the wild life, had felt a little squeamish, and would gladly have retired could he have done so without grave offense. At last the boy tore free, standing rigid with the last remnant of his strength, hand uplifted, facing the setting sun, a figure of mingled pathos and glory, the blood streaming from his breast. And even now in Andy's ears tolled the deep resonance of old Running Elk's voice:

"The Above People have given me a son!"

Andy was suddenly snatched back from the high pure cold of the Rockies to the bathing golden warmth of the California hillside. Carmel was laughing at him.

"What is it you say, *querido*, in that strange language?"

"I did not know I spoke," said he. "It was the Blackfoot language. I was just remembering."

But he would not tell her what it was. That was between himself and the Above People.

PART II. THE LIFE

Animals

Birds

Insects

Plants and Trees

Animals

First there was the germ of life, or perhaps only the idea of life that became a nucleal germ. Then there was life, and one kind of life moved about, in the water, on the land, in the air. It achieved fins, or wings, or legs. It was the animal, the living thing with a brain, the power to move about.

It was life in one broad form, the special inheritance, the mysterious treasure, eternally changing within the eternal constant. Eventually it was man, the most sentient animal we know; but it was all the other movers and doers of this world, too, man's companions and kin in this mysterious journey through time and space. It was blood, which is akin to sea water, and bones, which are elemental calcium, and flesh, which is protoplasmic. And a brain, which makes all the difference.

The squirrel in the treetop, the mouse in the meadow, the hibernating woodchuck, the bear in the remote woodland, even the fish, even the salamander—we share the earth, the water, the air. The pulse throbs, the eyes see, the nerves react, the flesh hungers and sickens and dies. There is procreation, perpetuation each of its kind. There is the urge to live, to go on living.

Give us a name—vertebrates, because we have backbones. Give us a shape—we have heads, torsos, limbs of some sort. Give us a purpose—life. We are of a kind, yet infinitely different. And in all of us that inexplicable brain, of so varied a capacity; that sentience; that capacity to move about upon this planet, to be squirrel, or bear, or salamander, or man.

H.B.

BOOM AND BUST

BY DURWARD L. ALLEN

Durward L. Allen (1910 —) was born and grew up in Indiana, educated at the University of Michigan and Michigan State University. He was a research biologist for the State of Michigan for a time, then did similar research for the U. S. Fish and Wildlife Service, eventually becoming Assistant Chief, Branch of Wildlife Research. He left government service in 1954 to accept a professorship at Purdue University. As a writer, he reminds me of the late Aldo Leopold in his trenchant style and forthright viewpoint. His Our Wildlife Legacy, *from which this selection is taken, is a far-ranging study of fundamental ecology, solidly based and full of challenge. It is also a splendid example of how scientific material can be made not only readable but provocative and important.*

(*Our Wildlife Legacy*, by Durward L. Allen; Funk and Wagnalls Company, 1954.)

In the fall of 1834, Bartholomew County in south-central Indiana was the scene of a squirrel hunt not unique in its day, but the like of which will not be seen again.

The floor of cool forests in the rich flat-lands was deep with the mast of beech, white oak, and shagbark hickory that crunched into the cushiony duff at every step. Ridges were strewn with the bounty of chestnut oaks, and everywhere timber was a-rustle with swarms of fattening gray squirrels.

More than a century of development had brought the Kentucky rifle (née Pennsylvania) to a high state of perfection, and barking a squirrel at 60 yards was largely a matter of the clear eye and steady hand.

The good men and true of Sand Creek Township considered themselves the elite of the squirrel-hunting world and did not hesitate to advertise it. The riflemen of Wayne Township denied this presumption and challenged them to a contest. The two townships agreed that each would select 50 hunters who would shoot squirrels for three days, at the end of which a grand barbecue would be held, with the losing side footing the bill.

The full details of this shooting fest are not available, but enough was recorded to give some idea of the abundance of the gray squirrel in some of its best native range. The winner of the hunt presented 900 *squirrels* at the end of the three days and the runner-up had 783!

Such abundance was not just a local occurrence. Squirrels took heavy toll of cornfields in forest openings, and in 1749 the colony of Pennsylvania paid bounties on 640,000 of them. There was a time in Ohio when county taxes were payable in squirrel scalps, and an early record mentions a gunner who killed 160 in a day—at a time when they were not especially plentiful.

Among frontier hunters the gray squirrel was known as the migratory squirrel, and with good reason. Periodically its numbers built up to a density that became intolerable to the species itself. Probably it is safe to say that the climax in this increase always occurred during a year when mast production was heavy. September and October are the season when young animals are on the move to find comfortable sites for future living, but that is different from the pervasive restlessness that seized entire populations. They would begin to travel, evidently in one direction, not stopping for lakes, streams, or anything else.

During such a movement the residents of Saginaw, Michigan, would awake, mornings, to find bedraggled black squirrels (the commonest color phase in the North) perched on every piling in the river. In a southward migration near Racine, Wisconsin, the animals were passing for two weeks, and it was a month before all had disappeared.

After a migration the woods would seem deserted of squirrels, but it did not take long for their numbers to become conspicuous again. The best evidence indicates that northern gray squirrels could be expected to migrate about every five years.

They were going nowhere, and they got nowhere. On these marches mortality was heavy from all causes, and the numbers were worn down and dissipated. Over large areas gray squirrels disappeared when dense forests were cut, but recently, here and there, the animals have become sufficiently prosperous so that a reversion to the old migratory habit has been observed.

The migrations, it seems, were a device for clearing the land of a too-numerous population and converting a million animals back into the humus of the earth. A part of the time, at least, the gray squirrel is sufficiently immune to the effects of external controls (disease, predators, etc.) so that in the course of the ages it has developed a *sociological* means of getting rid of excess numbers.

In contrast, the fox squirrel is not habitually migratory. Probably because it inhabited forest *edges* rather than extensive continuous stands of woodland, it did not build up, in depth, to mass hordes like the gray squirrel. Nevertheless it did, and does, become highly abundant periodically, and studies in the Midwest have shown what happens:

There comes a spring when a late frost, or some other climatic condition, nips the mast crop before it gets started. A food scarcity develops, and young animals are brought into competition with the abundant adults for what acorns and other nuts are still buried in the ground. Ordinarily, from early summer on they would find the oaks and hickories weighted with green mast to be had for the cutting, but now this basic supply is missing. As mentioned previously, a healthy fall population of fox squirrels should contain about two-thirds young of the year. But when numbers are high and food short the mortality of young is far greater than usual. By autumn they may compose only a quarter of the population.

The real crisis comes when a poor mast year is followed by an old howler of a winter. Ordinarily the squirrels would be well layered with belly fat, and in periods of deep snow, ice, and blizzards they would roll up in the nest and snooze it out. This winter they are thin and must have food regardless of weather. It is hard to find and hard to dig up. A diet of buds will not sustain them for long. The scabies mite (mange) is ever-present and on weakened animals it takes over. Part or all of the hair falls out and open lesions develop in the skin. Undernourishment appears also to induce a deficiency of blood sugar that gives rise to fatal seizures of shock when the animal is excited or over-exerts. Many squirrels become so weak they no longer can climb. They starve, freeze, and are easily taken by predators.

But the end is not yet. Fox squirrels usually breed in mid-winter, and in this year of sorrows bare survival is the best they can do. Only those animals come through that are in the most favorable locations. The new crop of young may be drastically reduced or entirely missing in the spring that follows.

Although this situation was first observed in Michigan, it probably is a frequent occurrence in northern squirrel ranges, and something similar has been recorded in Europe. Squirrels are the foremost game animals in Finland, and work in recent years has shown that they fluctuate radically in numbers about every five years, usually with ten years between major peaks. In a large area where they were studied, the animals died off within a couple of months in the fall of 1943. It was estimated that the drop in numbers was such that there was one animal where there had been 450 before.

Food failures have been a cause of squirrel declines in that region also, but probably of greater importance are the epizootics* that go through the population when numbers are at their maximum. Coccidiosis has been of particular importance. Shortages of fir cones, a primary food supply, appear to help induce diseases in the same manner as in Michigan.

It is a recurring picture of numbers building up to a point of instability, the downfall being brought about by one cause or another, or by a combination of causes. A dense population of animals is a precarious structure. It becomes weaker as it builds, and what triggers the collapse is, perhaps, not too important. It is highly important, however, for the sportsman to realize that a reduction from abundance is almost always inevitable.

For most purposes, one head of small game per acre is generally accepted as about the maximum population it is reasonable to ex-

* The same as an epidemic among humans.

pect as a result of good management. In fact, for a given species, one animal per acre as an annually recurring maximum would make nearly any area known for its hunting.

Although this applies to rabbits as much as to quail or other species, it is true that under exceptionally favorable conditions rabbits and hares may reach levels of abundance they are unable to maintain for long. A good example of this is what happened to the cottontail on 3,600-acre Fisher's Island (New York), which lies two miles off-shore from New London, Connecticut.

The island had excellent cover, and about 1925 several dozen rabbits were introduced. House cats were the only mammalian predators present. By 1938 the cottontails were so plentiful they were doing serious damage to shrubbery around lawns and golf courses. That winter a bounty of 20 cents per pair of ears resulted in a kill of more than 3,000 rabbits!

The bounty was removed, but another kill of 1,200 was taken the following winter. There was no evident decrease in the rabbits, and in the fall of 1940 the population was estimated by New York game biologists to be approximately 10 per acre. At that time the animals appeared to be in good condition.

During the next two years there were numerous rabbits found dead, and living animals were heavily parasitized with ticks. Another field investigation in the spring of 1943 showed that the population had declined to about one rabbit per four acres, and the animals were dying off. Remains of 119 of them were picked up, and 33 were fresh enough for examination. The dead rabbits had been carrying an average of 65 adult ticks plus an undetermined number of tick nymphs. All of them showed evidence of anemia, and many infections had resulted from the tick bites.

These ticks (of two species) had been present from the start, and under ordinary conditions they would not especially bother the host. But when rabbits became overconcentrated, conditions evidently developed which enabled the external parasites to take over and bring about a drastic reduction of the population. It was similar to the way the scabies mites got the upper hand of the Michigan fox squirrels during a winter of starvation.

These are good examples of how *density-dependent* factors operate. The more animals there are the more rapidly a disease (including such parasites as ticks and mites) can spread and the more certainty there is of a quick reduction of the population. In a year when snowshoe hares in Minnesota increased from 275 per square mile to 420 per square mile, the tick infestation rose from 2,400 to 4,900 per animal. Thus, roughly a 50 percent increase in rabbits seemed to have made possible a 100 percent increase in ticks. With ticks multiplying at twice the rate of the rabbits it is apparent that this could not go on for very long.

It has been recognized since early in the present century that about every ten years there is a spectacular boom and bust of snowshoe hare populations along the northern fringe of the United States and in Canada. The regularity of this phenomenon first became apparent in the fur returns of the Hudson's Bay Company. Skins of this northern hare have been an article of commerce with export records available since 1821.

Records of the Hudson's Bay Company have been studied repeatedly, and especially in connection with a thoroughgoing investigation of the hare cycle by Duncan A. MacLulich, then of the University of Toronto. Deriving his information from all available sources, including intensive field work, MacLulich reached some significant conclusions:

In past and current records he identified peak years for snowshoe populations in 1856, 1864, 1875, 1886, 1895, 1914, 1924, and 1934. Hare numbers in Ontario were found to vary from one per square mile at the low of the cycle to more than a thousand at the maximum. The greatest density observed was 3,400 per square mile!

From the evidence available, a theoretical ten-year sequence of year-end populations on a square mile of hare range was determined to be as follows:

4 — 12 — 36 — 108 — 324 — 1,396 — 4,188 — 288 — 18 — 2

This series shows the steady build-up to a maximum when the breeding stock reproduced in the eighth year. In the summer of that year (typically) an abrupt die-off is represented as occurring.

The decline that MacLulich observed began in 1932 in a small area of southern Ontario and progressed to the central and northern parts of the province in 1933, 1934, and 1935. A summary of reports and observations from widespread areas indicated that sick and ailing hares were common, and infections of various kinds and heavy parasitism frequently attended the dying-off. These conditions varied from one area to another, however, and no specific disease agent could be designated as particularly important. It appeared that local decimation was not always brought about by the same factor but that some lethal agent became effective when the population reached a point of topheavy abundance. "The length of the cycle is about the same each time because it depends chiefly on the time the population takes to grow from scarcity to abundance . . . and secondly on the time required for the . . . reaction."

Here, according to MacLulich's interpretation, the density factor was not only involved, but it developed with a constancy that imparted a relatively precise timing to the "bust" of populations at intervals of about a decade.

In Minnesota, during the mid-thirties, the snowshoe hare population underwent a reduction that appears to have been related to the widespread decline in Ontario. In the Lake Alexander area, R. G. Green and his associates carried on an intensive study of populations and pathology from 1931 to 1938. What they found seems to agree fairly well with the general picture of the cycle as given by MacLulich.

Earlier observations indicated a build-up in hare numbers from 1928 on and this continued to 1933, at which time the maximum density of nearly 500 to the square mile was attained. In the two years following, there were local reductions and in 1935 there began a sharp drop in numbers that extended through 1938. The low point at that time was represented by populations about 10 percent as large as the maximum.

The Minnesota work was unique and particularly significant in that it revealed the presence of "shock disease" in the declining population and showed that in this case, at least, the condition largely affected young of the year rather than adults or the entire population. This type of shock was found to be caused by a deficiency of blood sugar similar to what was identified later among Michigan fox squirrels. Hares taken in box traps, handled, or just held in pens, went into convulsions followed by a coma and death.

Whether shock disease might have been involved in the reports of "dopey" rabbits received by MacLulich in Ontario is conjectural. Why it appeared with high population density and its subsequent abatement were obscure at that time. More light has since been thrown upon it, and it is now coming to be looked upon as one of the most characteristic of density-dependent diseases.

William Rowan, for long an investigator of the cycle in Alberta, gave a graphic account of the snowshoe-hare crisis in the early forties: "In 1942 rabbits had attained a peak. They were so numerous that even within the city limits of sprawling Edmonton . . . rabbits could periodically be seen scuttling out of the way of cars right in town or chased by dogs across vacant lots.

". . . Bill Schmidt of Fawcett, Alberta, exterminated his cat on account of the surfeit of rabbits. The cat had produced a litter of kittens in the horse barn and apparently decided to rear them on rabbits. She would bring in anything up to 20 per day and deposit them all over the floor for men and horses to slither on till the situation became intolerable. When a cat can kill up to 20 rabbits daily the supply may certainly be deemed unlimited!

"In 1942 nearly six million rabbit skins were shipped to felt and hat manufacturers of the United States from Alberta's northland, a kill that was barely enough to scratch the surface of the hare population. Yet, such is the nature of the crash, that in the year that followed (1943), contracts had to be cancelled and shipments discontinued for lack of rabbits."

The snowshoe hare does not starve or migrate; disease seems to be the regular mechanism for relieving the insupportable density that it attains. In effect, it depletes the food supply and crowds its habitat to a point where the result is an outdoor slum, and pestilence of one kind or another does the deed. Physical ailments seem to spread into less favorable range where numbers are low, since the wiping out is not restricted to heavily populated areas.

While the snowshoe hare is fresh in our minds, we should mention that it forms the principal food supply for the northern lynx, and the fur records on this animal also show a ten-year cycle of ups and downs that correlates closely with that of the hare.

Although the investigator may look long, he probably will fail to find an example of a predator species that alone "controls" the numbers of a widely distributed prey species, yet here seems to be a clear case of such a prey animal bringing about periodic and drastic reductions in its principal enemy.

Concerning the close relationship between lynx and hare, Seton observed that: "Of all the Northern creatures, none are more dependent on the Rabbits than is the Canada Lynx. It lives on Rabbits, follows the Rabbits, thinks Rabbits, tastes like Rabbits, increases with them, and on their failure dies of starvation in the unrabbited woods."

In the northern portion of the Quebec Peninsula a relationship reminiscent of the hare and lynx is found between mouse-like rodents and foxes. In Ungava the species involved are chiefly the lemming and arctic fox; farther east, in Labrador, the principals are preponderantly the vole and "colored" fox. There is much overlap of range, and several other rodents enter the picture also. The colored fox includes the three phases, red, cross, and silver.

In Labrador, the take of colored foxes during a 92-year period showed a striking oscillation in periods varying from 2 to 6 years. The average length of the 23 cycles was 4 years, and 13 of the 23 were exactly of that duration. The white foxes of Ungava have a similar round of abundance and scarcity and in both cases the underlying cause is seen in a radical build-up and die-off, about every 4 years, of the rodents which form the food mainstay of the fox.

These rodents also are the principal food item of the snowy owl, which evidently builds in numbers during times of abundance and then is caught short when the voles and lemmings disappear.

But the owl, being a mobile species, drifts southward, usually about hunting season, and invades northeastern United States. It is then that every outdoor page carries photographs and speculation about the white visitors from the North and every taxidermy shop does a rush business in owl "trophies." Actually, the birds have little fear of man and it is likely that few of them last out the winter. The influx of owls, at about four-year intervals, reflects the rodent cycle of the barrens.

Practically all cycles show regional variations—the peak may be reached here this year and farther on next year; yet a rough coincidence usually can be observed. Elton has pointed out that the cycle in mouse-like rodents (and, as we have seen, in other species such as the hares) is a circumpolar phenomenon. "A similar violent fluctuation, keyed to lemmings, with different species of lemmings, but practically the same species of owls and foxes, is found in Lapland, Novaya Zemlya, Arctic Siberia, Kamchatka, Alaska, the Western Arctic and the Arctic Archipelago of Canada, and in North and East Greenland."

It seems to be true that, as one proceeds southward from the Arctic, with its stark, violent, and relatively simple relationships, into warmer regions, the tendency toward regularity in population changes is lost in a welter of cross-purpose factors and extreme variability in local conditions.

When the food situation deteriorates for an abundant arctic fox population, it appears that short-range emigration and the onset of disease are more characteristic developments than outright starvation. The carnivores seem to be particularly susceptible to diseases, such as rabies and distemper, that affect the central nervous system. Epizootics of this kind among foxes, wolves, and sled dogs are well known in the North and they occur commonly in other regions when a species becomes too plentiful.

Cowan reported a rabies-like disease as being responsible for a widespread die-off of foxes on the Mackenzie Delta in the winter of 1944–45. Red foxes (heretofore referred to as "colored") had been plentiful over the western Arctic region in the early forties and in the winter of reduction there were reports of ailing and "crazy" foxes that ran in an aimless fashion, blundering through thickets or making perfunctory attacks on trappers. Dead foxes were encountered frequently. That winter rabies was identified from an arctic fox, a wolf, and a sled dog in Northwest Territory. There were other reports of peculiar behavior on the part of wolves that entered camp and fought with dogs—which afterward sickened and died.

The increase in foxes during the forties was not restricted to the North; farther south it was continent-wide and involved several species. As elsewhere, New York had more than enough foxes, and rabies appeared in the winter of 1945–46. During the next two years there were reports of 308 and 273 rabid foxes, respectively. In 1948 the number dropped to 153. An intensive effort by State trappers hired for the job, plus a vaccination campaign for dogs, may have helped bring the epizootic under control.

Biologists freely predicted such outbreaks as this when it became evident that foxes were reaching a widespread and unprecedented high in numbers over much of the nation. Mange also was evident, as always, during the spotty regional reduction of foxes that took place in the late forties. These diseases are perennially in the offing when the carnivores become prosperous and they can be watched for with the certainty that it is only a matter of time.

Something similar happened to skunks in the Midwest, and possibly the East, from about 1938 to 1941. From a low point around 1933, the species had steadily gained in numbers and was abundant in many areas previous to 1939.

Reports from fur buyers indicated that in the late thirties skunks were declining in northern Ohio and Indiana. In the winter of 1939–40 the trend appeared unmistakably in Illinois and trappers in the southern counties of Michigan were reporting sick and dying skunks.

It so happened that skunks were being intensively studied that winter at a state wildlife experiment station near Lansing. When a disease hit the animals, it was ascertained immediately. There was abnormal fighting among skunks, and the animals wandered about in daylight acting "crazy" and irresponsible. Many died in winter dens and elsewhere.

The disease was diagnosed as a virus infection of the brain—in short, "encephalitis." Accounts of trappers indicated that this condition was widespread. In Michigan the slump lasted at least through 1942, after which it appeared that skunks again were slowly increasing.

With plenty of food, it seems, the carnivores are able to build their numbers to a point that is both uneconomic for man and unhealthy for the species concerned. Sometimes, with no evident change in food conditions, the flesh-eaters are laid low by maladies that seem always to be featured in their periods of ill fortune—rabies, distemper, encephalitis, and mange.

At other times the portent of hard times comes with a scarcity of food, which may operate directly or prepare the population for an epizootic of characteristic disease. Probably this is an oversimplification, but it provides us with a reliable working hypothesis of what to expect when Bre'r Fox appears, as Herr Hitler once did, about to sweep all before him.

Most of the types of fluctuations that occur among mammals and birds can be identified also in fish populations, and some that are new and different appear as a result of conditions under which aquatic life is renewed. A brief sampling will illustrate this, and no more than that is practical here.

In 1912, the planting of a shipment of smelt eggs in Crystal Lake, Benzie County, Michigan, inaugurated one of the most intriguing fish stories in Great Lakes history. Other plantings probably failed, but this one, after a slow start, made good with a vengeance.

It was six years before the first fish appeared. In 1918 they made a spawning run up Cold Creek from Crystal Lake. In 1923 they were found on the east shore of Lake Michigan, and a year later they had crossed to Big Bay de Noc. In 1928 nets were taking them in the Wisconsin waters of Green Bay. Steadily new horizons were invaded in the big lakes, and a few smelt even got through to Erie; but the mass abundance remained centered in Lake Michigan.

For years the smelt was looked upon by fishermen as a nuisance, and trepidation was felt for the possible effects of its burgeoning numbers on native fish. Then in 1931 Wisconsin commercial netters took, and sold, 86,000 pounds of smelt. The demand was good and the supply prodigious. Top production was reached in 1941 with a total catch for the market in Lake Michigan of more than 4¾ million pounds.

In the meantime April spawning runs up northern streams had drawn off-season tourists by the thousand. Smelt festivals became an annual vacation event. Torchlight crowds waded hip-deep in wriggling rivers of slender, green-and-silver fish. They dipped them out by the ton. The take by "sport" fishermen in the two states was more than double the commercial catch. Rolled in flour, browned crisp in deep fat, and eaten bones and all, the 7- to 9-inch, delectable, 5-cents-a-pound smelt took its rightful place on the table of the gourmet and as king of the fish fries.

It got better and better, an industry was established, and in the public eye the smelt came to symbolize inexhaustible manna. Nature, they thought, wore a waxen smile. Not so the biologist. The more the smelt prospered, the more sour-puss certain he became that it couldn't last. The little fish that went to market were riding for a fall.

In 1942 it came. Somewhere in central Lake Huron, the smelt began to die. On October 3, at Black River, a Michigan conservation officer saw them washing ashore.

The blight ran through the lakes like the flash of a powder train. Smelt died in Saginaw Bay, Georgian Bay, and the North Channel. The contagion spread through the Straits of Mackinac into Lake Michigan. By the end of November it had reached Point Aux Barques, and in February the smelt were dying in Green Bay, the center of the fishery.

It took just 4½ months for some sort of epizootic (it hasn't been spotted to this day) to wipe out perhaps 90 percent of the smelt. In 1944 a meagre 4,500 pounds were marketed. After that they began to increase again. By 1950 near-record catches were being taken.

The die-off of smelt came a year before conditions deteriorated for small game and it may be a case simply of a species that got too plentiful. On the other hand, what has occurred will occur again, and it may be that the smelt will come and go with regularity. This happens to other species of fish, and the causes are diverse.

A bottomland lake in the Illinois River Valley has exhibited cycles of four to five years in the size and abundance of black crappies, even though the poundage remained the same from year to year. At one end of the cycle the fish would be ten times as abundant, but they would be only one-tenth as large.

The reason for the fluctuation was cannibalism, and here is the way it worked: At a time when the population consisted of a few old fish, these breeders produced a large crop of young, many of which survived. In the years that followed, this generation grew and spawned, but its food requirements were so great it devoured both its own young and those of other species. No new generation of crappies could be established and the dominant brood, like the little recruit, just grew and grew. Finally the old fish reached the end of their time and died off, leaving another numerous generation of young to repeat the process.

"In this way the crappie not only produces a cycle in its own kind but imposes it on many other non-cannibalistic fish. This has a striking effect on both hook-and-line and commercial fishing. During part of the cycle . . . as many as 99 percent of the black crappies are of catchable size. This is followed by a period when there were as few as one or two percent of large fish."

Atlantic salmon in the Maritime region of Canada furnish another good example of cyclic behavior. Annual yields of these fish were studied by Huntsman from 1870 to 1930.

Of greatest interest here is the fact that figures for four regions from the Gaspé Peninsula to the Bay of Fundy were examined separately and the existence of a general 9- to 10-year cycle clearly established. In the case of St. John's River fish it was possible to determine the average period as 9.6 years. And this fluctuation of salmon *showed depressions coinciding with cyclic lows of the snow-*

shoe rabbit in the North. The rhythm was of unknown origin and in it salmon seemed to be responding to the same influence that conditions the waxing and waning of many other creatures.

The most recent comprehensive putting-together of the evidence on cycles has been carried out by Lauri Siivonen, Director of the Game-Research Institute, Helsinki, Finland.

Dr. Siivonen's basic material was the long-term and detailed records on black game and capercaillie in Finland, and he made use of the published records on all species from North America and Europe. After extensive statistical studies, he concluded that the short cycle of 3 to 4 years that had long been recognized in some far-northern species was a universal basic rhythm for cyclic birds and mammals. He found its average length to be 3⅓ years.

This analysis indicated that the 10-year fluctuation in grouse, hares, and certain carnivorous animals is an exceptionally high peak of the 3⅓-year period. It becomes most marked when the short cycle is lengthened by a year or two.

It was suggested also that major deviations from the norm were likely to appear "in connection with a period of general, great, climatic disturbances . . ."

There are other recent findings to be added to the file of cycle information. In discussing animal numbers we have given proper weight and emphasis to the matter of density. Although it probably is not the entire explanation, it undoubtedly is a key condition in cycle mechanics. Recent investigations in the realm of physiology have helped to clarify current understanding of what is commonly called "shock."

It is known to most people that there is an automatic body reaction to conditions such as anger, fear, pain, etc. Crudely stated, this involves secretions of certain ductless glands—in particular, portions of the pituitary and adrenals.

Wild animals have similar reactions that undoubtedly have survival value in stimulating the individual in the presence of danger or discomfort. It has been found, however, that when living conditions deteriorate and an animal is under constant physical harassment, its reaction mechanism becomes exhausted and shock symptoms develop.

J. J. Christian assembled information on this subject and concluded that shock was most likely to appear during the severe weather of winter following a fall population peak. At such times the number of animals in a given area undoubtedly is far beyond normal carrying capacity and a condition of acute biological squalor develops. Concentrated wintering populations would be subjected to a variety of unfavorable influences: "(1) food scarcity, (2) lack of proper cover, (3) increased muscular exertion resulting from longer food forage trips, (4) fights with other individuals . . . (5) increased exposure to cold from longer forage trips and inadequate cover, (6) fighting resulting from territorial encroachment . . . (7) utilization of inadequate foods, (8) increased exposure to predators due to lack of cover as well as migration of predators into areas of abundant food supply in the form of a peak population, and (9) nutritional deficiencies."

These are the environmental burdens that were involved in the winter of hard times described for Michigan fox squirrels. They bring on a chain of physical abnormalities that includes blood-sugar deficiency, adrenal enlargement, reduction of sugar storage in the liver, liver degeneration, diminished fat, and changes in blood chemistry.

Shock undoubtedly is the most characteristic density-dependent factor yet discovered. Christian suggested that it might be a primary cause of cyclic declines in mammals—directly or in predisposing a population to other ailments. In this case the length of a cycle would depend on the reproductive rate and the time required for a population to build back up again.

Superficially it would appear that the multiplying tensions which develop in animal concentrations have some parallel in what seems to be happening to people exposed to the complex existence of large cities. We hear much speculation about how the rapidly mounting stresses of modern living are reacting on the mental and physical health of the individual. Nervous disorders, ulcers, psychosomatic diseases appear to be on the increase—unless we are misled by the fact that they are just getting recognition. The fact that many wild animals develop the shock syndrome when there are too many of them, and frequently are killed off wholesale, might indicate that such creatures are socially less calloused than man. Nevertheless, although humans have ways of softening the impacts of their environment, the evidence suggests that this ability is far from perfect and that we, too, have reactions akin to the physical break-down that overtook the squirrels and snowshoe hares.

Undoubtedly the new understanding of shock is another important piece in the puzzle, but the picture is not yet clear. Sometimes such a collapse comes independent of any known cyclic trend. But when the ten-year peak has been reached and the slump is due, populations, great and small, are toppling. At such times susceptibility to unfavorable influences becomes striking.

If we are dealing entirely with a density phenomenon, then it should theoretically be possible, by heavy shooting, to prevent grouse or other game species from building up to the lethal peak. This is something that could best be tried on an island, and thus far it has not been done. Certainly, something would be learned from such an experiment.

But if population declines were induced entirely by crowding and habitat deterioration, that would not explain why such dissimilar creatures as the grouse and hare cycle together and how so many other pulsations, on at least a continental scale, could be so nearly in phase. Something appears to be lending an approximate coincidence to widely diverse events.

Many investigators have looked for some basic cosmic rhythm that could account for this. Sunspots were under suspicion, but the cycle in question was found to be slightly longer than the biological fluctuation. Variations in atmospheric ozone (tri-atomic oxygen) also have been considered a possibility. Nothing satisfactory has been found, but the search undoubtedly will go on.

It cannot be doubted that the earth is much affected by many kinds of radiation from the sun and outer reaches of the universe. Recently Maxwell O. Johnson, working in Hawaii, has shown that the major and minor planets have important electromagnetic influences on the sun and that these are most potent at times when two of the planets are in the same heliocentric longitude (i.e. lined up with the sun). Such formations recur at regular intervals, and the time elapsing between two similar ones is called the synodic period for the two planets in question.

Johnson found that there were cycles in rainfall corresponding to the combined effects of synodic periods of the planets. It is especially thought provoking at present (in the light of Siivonen's recent findings) that in Pacific precipitation records he identified a 3.32-year cycle "superimposed on a 10-year cycle, or six cycles in a 20-year periodicity." In records of mean annual temperature from New Haven,

Connecticut, he found that the "most probable . . . periodicity was a 20-year one with six shorter cycles . . ."

This is not to imply an explanation of the apparently regular coming and going of animal numbers, but to point out that such a phenomenon would by no means be unique. The natural world is geared to an assortment of repetitive events—night and day, summer and winter, high and low tides. They are dependable and can be foretold, but conditions accompanying them are not always the same because of variables on earth and mutually interfering cosmic influences that may appear irregular, but which may be part of a long-term symmetry of motion.

FLORA AND FAUNA OF SPANISH FLORIDA

BY WILLIAM BARTRAM

William Bartram (1739–1823) was the son of John Bartram, America's first great botanist. Growing up on the Bartram "botanical farm" on the edge of Philadelphia, he became an all-round naturalist and a major influence in the development of our native natural science, as a writer, an artist and a counselor and teacher. As a young man he tried various business ventures, first in Philadelphia, then in South Carolina; but after accompanying his father on an exploration of Florida in 1765–66 he quit business, spent four years exploring the wilderness of the Southeast, wrote his classic Travels, *and thereafter devoted himself to botany and ornithology. A skilled artist, his drawings of plant life brought him fame both here and abroad. His writing was a basic source for early books on botany and botanical materia medica. His* Travels *undoubtedly inspired books and poems by Chateaubriand, Coleridge and Wordsworth. He was adviser and teacher to Alexander Wilson, and his list of 215 native species of birds was the most nearly complete for eastern America until Wilson published his* American Ornithology. *This selection from Bartram's* Travels *describes his trip along the St. Johns River and through the nearby area of Florida in the summer of 1774.*

(Travels Through North and South Carolina, Georgia, East and West Florida, the Cherokee Country, the Extensive Ter-

ritories of the Muscogulges, or Creek Confederacy, and the Country of the Choctaws, by William Bartram; Philadelphia, 1791.)

Being desirous of continuing my travels and observations higher up the river, and having an invitation from a gentleman who was agent for, and resident at, a large plantation, the property of an English gentleman, about sixty miles higher up, I resolved to pursue my researches to that place; and having engaged in my service a young Indian, nephew to the white captain, he agreed to assist me in working my vessel up as high as a certain bluff, where I was, by agreement, to land him, on the West or Indian shore, whence he designed to go in quest of the camp of the White Trader, his relation.

Provisions and all necessaries being procured, and the morning pleasant, we went on board and stood up the river. We passed for several miles on the left, by islands of high swamp land, exceedingly fertile, their banks for a good distance from the water, much higher than the interior part, and sufficiently so to build upon, and be out of the reach of inundations. They consist of a loose black mould, with a mixture of sand, shells, and dissolved vegetables. The opposite Indian coast is a perpendicular bluff, ten or twelve feet high, consisting of a black sandy earth, mixed with a large proportion of shells, chiefly various species of fresh water cochleae and mytuli. Near the river, on this high shore, grew corypha palma, magnolia grandiflora, live oak, callicarpa, myrica cerifera, hibiscus spinifex, and the beautiful evergreen shrub called wild lime or tallow nut. This last shrub grows six or eight feet high, many erect stems spring from a root; the leaves are lanceolate and entire, two or three inches in length and one in breadth, of a deep green colour, and polished; at the foot of each leaf grows a stiff sharp thorn; the flowers are small and in clusters, of a greenish yellow colour, and sweet scented; they are succeeded by a large oval fruit, of the shape and size of an ordinary plumb, of a fine yellow colour when ripe; a soft sweet pulp covers a nut which has a thin shell, enclosing a white kernel somewhat of the consistence and taste of the sweet almond, but more oily and very much like hard tallow, which induced my father, when he first observed it, to call it the tallow-nut.

At the upper end of this bluff is a fine orange grove. Here my Indian companion requested me to set him on shore, being already tired of rowing under the fervid sun, and having for some time intimated a dislike to his situation. I readily complied with his desire, knowing the impossibility of compelling an Indian against his own inclinations, or even prevailing upon him by reasonable arguments, when labour is in the question. Before my vessel reached the shore, he sprang out of her and landed, when uttering a shrill and terrible whoop, he bounded off like a roebuck, and I lost sight of him. I at first apprehended, that as he took his gun with him, he intended to hunt for some game and return to me in the evening. The day being excessively hot and sultry, I concluded to take up my quarters here (near Manhatten) until next morning.

The Indian not returning this morning, I sat sail alone. The coasts on each side had much the same appearance as already described. The palm-trees here seem to be of a different species (royal palm) from the cabbage tree; their straight trunks are sixty, eighty, or ninety feet high, with a beautiful taper, of a bright ash colour, until within six or seven feet of the top, where it is a fine green colour, crowned with an orb of rich green plumed leaves: I have measured the stem of these plumes fifteen feet in length, besides the plume, which is nearly of the same length.

The little lake (Lake Dexter), which is an expansion of the river, now appeared in view; on the east side are extensive marshes, and on the other high forests and orange groves, and then a bay, lined with vast cypress swamps, both coasts gradually approaching each other, to the opening of the river again, which is in this place about three hundred yards wide. Evening now drawing on, I was anxious to reach some high bank of the river, where I intended to lodge; and agreeably to my wishes, I soon after discovered, on the west shore, a little promontory (now Idlewild Dock), at the turning of the river, contracting it here to about one hundred and fifty yards in width. This promontory is a peninsula, containing about three acres of high ground, and is one entire orange grove, with a few live oaks, magnolias, and palms. Upon doubling the point, I arrived at the landing, which is a circular harbour, at the foot of the bluff, the top of which is about twelve feet high; the back of it is a large cypress swamp, that spreads each way, the right wing forming the west coast of the little lake, and the left stretching up the river many miles, and encompassing a vast space of low grassy marshes. From this promontory, looking eastward across the river, I beheld a landscape of low country, unparalleled as I think; on the left is the east coast of the little lake, which I had just passed; and from the orange bluff at the lower end, the high forests begin, and increase in breadth from the shore of the lake, making a circular sweep to the right, and contain many hundred thousand acres of meadow; and this grand sweep of high forests encircles, as I apprehend, at least twenty miles of these green fields, interspersed with hommocks or islets of evergreen trees, where the sovereign magnolia and lordly palm stand conspicuous. The islets are high shelly knolls, on the sides of creeks or branches of the river, which wind about and drain off the super-abundant waters that cover these meadows during the winter season.

The evening was temperately cool and calm. The crocodiles (alligators) began to roar and appear in uncommon numbers along the shores and in the river. I fixed my camp in an open plain, near the utmost projection of the promontory, under the shelter of a large live oak, which stood on the highest part of the ground, and but a few yards from my boat. From this open, high situation, I had a free prospect of the river, which was a matter of no trivial consideration to me, having good reason to dread the subtle attacks of the alligators, who were crowding about my harbour. Having collected a good quantity of wood for the purpose of keeping up a light and smoke during the night, I began to think of preparing my supper, when, upon examining my stores, I found but a scanty provision. I thereupon determined, as the most expeditious way of supplying my necessities, to take my bob and try for some trout (large-mouthed bass). About one hundred yards above my harbour began a cove or bay of the river, out of which opened a large lagoon (Mud Lake). The mouth or entrance from the river to it was narrow, but the waters soon after spread and formed a little lake, extending into the marshes: its entrance and shores within I observed to be verged with floating lawns of the pistia and nymphea and other aquatic plants; these I knew were excellent haunts for trout.

The verges and islets of the lagoon were elegantly embellished with flowering plants and shrubs; the laughing coots with wings half spread were tripping over the little coves, and hiding themselves in the tufts of grass; young broods of the painted summer teal (wood duck), skimming the still surface of the waters, and following the watchful parent unconscious of danger, were frequently surprised by the voracious trout; and he, in turn, as often by the subtle greedy alligator. Behold him rushing forth from the flags and reeds. His enormous body swells. His plaited tail brandished high, floats upon the lake. The waters like a cataract descend from his open jaws. Clouds of smoke issue from his dilated nostrils. The earth trembles with his thunder. When immediately from the opposite coast of the lagoon, emerges from the deep his rival champion. They suddenly dart upon each other. The boiling surface of the lake marks their rapid course, and a terrific conflict commences. They now sink to the bottom folded together in horrid wreaths. The water becomes thick and discoloured. Again they rise, their jaws clap together, re-echoing through the deep surrounding forests. Again they sink, when the contest ends at the muddy bottom of the lake, and the vanquished makes a hazardous escape, hiding himself in the muddy turbulent waters and sedge on a distant shore. The proud victor exulting returns to the place of action. The shores and forests resound his dreadful roar, together with the triumphing shouts of the plaited tribes around, witnesses of the horrid combat.

My apprehensions were highly alarmed after being a spectator of so dreadful a battle. It was obvious that every delay would but tend to increase my dangers and difficulties, as the sun was near setting, and the alligators gathered around my harbour from all quarters. From these considerations I concluded to be expeditious in my trip to the lagoon, in order to take some fish. Not thinking it prudent to take my fusee (flintlock gun) with me, lest I might lose it overboard in case of a battle, which I had every reason to dread before my return, I therefore furnished myself with a club for my defence, went on board, and penetrating the first line of those which surrounded my harbour, they gave way; but being pursued by several very large ones, I kept strictly on the watch, and paddled with all my might towards the entrance of the lagoon, hoping to be sheltered there from the multitude of my assailants; but ere I had half-way reached the place, I was attacked on all sides, several endeavouring to overset the canoe. My situation now became precarious to the last degree: two very large ones attacked me closely, at the same instant, rushing terribly and belching floods of water over me. They struck their jaws together so close to my ears, as almost to stun me, and I expected every moment to be dragged out of the boat and instantly devoured. But I applied my weapons so effectually about me, though at random, that I was so successful as to beat them off a little; when, finding that they designed to renew the battle, I made for the shore, as the only means left me for my preservation; for, by keeping close to it, I should have my enemies on one side of me only, whereas I was before surrounded by them; and there was a probability, if pushed to the last extremity, of saving myself, by jumping out of the canoe on shore, as it is easy to outwalk them on land, although comparatively as swift as lightning in the water. I found this last expedient alone could fully answer my expectations, for as soon as I gained the shore, they drew off and kept aloof. This was a happy relief, as my confidence was, in some degree, recovered by it. On recollecting myself, I discovered that I had almost reached the entrance of the lagoon, and determined to venture in, if possible, to take a few fish, and then return to my harbour, while day-light continued; for I could now, with caution and resolution, make my way with safety along shore; and indeed there was no other way to regain my camp, without leaving my boat and making my retreat through the marshes and reeds, which, if I could even effect, would have been in a manner throwing myself away, for then there would have been no hopes of ever recovering my bark, and returning in safety to any settlements of men. I accordingly proceeded, and made good my entrance into the lagoon, though not without opposition from the alligators, who formed a line across the entrance, but did not pursue me into it, nor was I molested by any there, though there were some very large ones in a cove at the upper end. I soon caught more trout than I had present occasion for, and the air was too hot and sultry to admit of their being kept for many hours, even though salted or barbecued. I now prepared for my return to camp, which I succeeded in with but little trouble, by keeping close to the shore; yet I was opposed upon re-entering the river out of the lagoon, and pursued near to my landing (though not closely attacked), particularly by an old daring one, about twelve feet in length, who kept close after me; and when I stepped on shore and turned about, in order to draw up my canoe, he rushed up near my feet, and lay there for some time, looking me in the face, his head and shoulders out of water. I resolved he should pay for his temerity, and having a heavy load in my fusee, I ran to my camp, and returning with my piece, found him with his foot on the gunwale of the boat, in search of fish. On my coming up he withdrew sullenly and slowly into the water, but soon returned and placed himself in his former position, looking at me, and seeming neither fearful nor any way disturbed. I soon dispatched him by lodging the contents of my gun in his head, and then proceeded to cleanse and prepare my fish for supper; and accordingly took them out of the boat, laid them down on the sand close to the water, and began to scale them; when, raising my head, I saw before me, through the clear water, the head and shoulders of a very large alligator, moving slowly towards me. I instantly stepped back, when, with a sweep of his tail, he brushed off several of my fish. It was certainly most providential that I looked up at that instant, as the monster would probably, in less than a minute, have seized and dragged me into the river. This incredible boldness of the animal disturbed me greatly, supposing there could now be no reasonable safety for me during the night, but by keeping continually on the watch: I therefore, as soon as I had prepared the fish, proceeded to secure myself and effects in the best manner I could. In the first place, I hauled my bark upon the shore, almost clear out of the water, to prevent their oversetting or sinking her; after this, every moveable was taken out and carried to my camp, which was but a few yards off; then ranging some dry wood in such order as was the most convenient, I cleared the ground round about it, that there might be no impediment in my way, in case of an attack in the night, either from the water or the land; for I discovered by this time, that this small isthmus, from its remote situation and fruitfulness, was resorted to by bears and wolves. Having prepared myself in the best manner I could, I charged my gun, and proceeded to reconnoitre my camp and the adjacent grounds; when I discovered that the peninsula and grove, at the distance of about two hundred yards from my encampment, on the land side, were invested by a cypress swamp, covered with water, which below was joined to the shore of the little lake, and above to the marshes surrounding the lagoon; so that I was confined to an islet exceedingly circumscribed, and I found there was no other retreat for me, in case of an attack, but by either ascending one of the large oaks, or pushing off with my boat.

It was by this time dusk, and the alligators had nearly ceased their roar, when I was again alarmed by a tumultuous noise that seemed to be in my harbour, and therefore engaged my immediate attention. Returning to my camp, I found it undisturbed, and then continued on to the extreme point of the promontory, where I saw a scene, new and surprising, which at first threw my senses into such a tumult, that it was some time before I could comprehend what was the matter; however, I soon accounted for the prodigious assemblage of crocodiles at this place, which exceeded every thing of the kind I had ever heard of.

How shall I express myself so as to convey an adequate idea of it to the reader, and at the same time avoid raising suspicions of my veracity? Should I say, that the river (in this place) from shore to shore, and perhaps near half a mile above and below me, appeared to be one solid bank of fish, of various kinds (large-mouthed bass, shadines, etc.), pushing through this narrow pass of St. Juan's into the little lake, on their return down the river, and that the alligators were in such incredible numbers, and so close together from shore to shore, that it would have been easy to have walked across on their heads, had the animals been harmless? What expressions can sufficiently declare the shocking scene that for some minutes continued, whilst this mighty army of fish were forcing the pass? During this attempt, thousands, I may say hundreds of thousands, of them were caught and swallowed by the devouring alligators. I have seen an alligator take up out of the water several great fish at a time, and just squeeze them betwixt his jaws, while the tails of the great trout flapped about his eyes and lips, ere he had swallowed them. The horrid noise of their closing jaws, their plunging amidst the broken banks of fish, and rising with their prey some feet upright above the water, the floods of water and blood rushing out of their mouths, and the clouds of vapour issuing from their wide nostrils, were truly frightful. This scene continued at intervals during the night, as the fish came to the pass. After this sight, shocking and tremendous as it was, I found myself somewhat easier and more reconciled to my situation; being convinced that their extraordinary assemblage here was owing to the annual feast of fish; and that they were so well employed in their own element, that I had little occasion to fear their paying me a visit.

It being almost night, I returned to my camp, where I had left my fish broiling, and my kettle of rice stewing; and having with me oil, pepper, and salt, and excellent oranges hanging in abundance over my head (a valuable substitute for vinegar) I sat down and regaled myself cheerfully. Having finished my repast, I rekindled my fire for light, and whilst I was revising the notes of my past day's journey, I was suddenly roused with a noise behind me toward the main land. I sprang up on my feet, and listening, I distinctly heard some creature wading the water of the isthmus. I seized my gun and went cautiously from my camp, directing my steps towards the noise: when I had advanced about thirty yards, I halted behind a coppice of orange trees, and soon perceived two very large bears, which had made their way through the water, and had landed in the grove, about one hundred yards distance from me, and were advancing towards me. I waited until they were within thirty yards of me: they there began to snuff and look towards my camp: I snapped my piece, but it flashed, on which they both turned about and galloped off, plunging through the water and swamp, never halting, as I suppose, until they reached fast land, as I could hear them leaping and plunging a long time. They did not presume to return again, nor was I molested by any other creature, except being occasionally awakened by the whooping of owls, screaming of bitterns, or the wood-rats running amongst the leaves.

The wood-rat is a very curious animal. It is not half the size of the domestic rat; of a dark brown or black colour; its tail slender and shorter in proportion, and covered thinly with short hair. It is singular with respect to its ingenuity and great labour in the construction of its habitation, which is a conical pyramid about three or four feet high, constructed with dry branches, which it collects with great labour and perseverance, and piles up without any apparent order; yet they are so interwoven with one another, that it would take a bear or wild-cat some time to pull one of these castles to pieces, and allow the animals sufficient time to secure a retreat with their young.

The noise of the crocodiles kept me awake the greater part of the night; but when I arose in the morning, contrary to my expectations, there was perfect peace; very few of them to be seen, and those were asleep on the shore. Yet I was not able to suppress my fears and apprehensions of being attacked by them in future; and indeed yesterday's combat with them, notwithstanding I came off in a manner victorious, or at least made a safe retreat, had left sufficient impression on my mind to damp my courage, and it seemed too much for one of my strength, being alone in a very small boat, to encounter such collected danger. To pursue my voyage up the river, and be obliged every evening to pass such dangerous defiles, appeared to me as perilous as running the gauntlet betwixt two rows of Indians armed with knives and firebrands. I however resolved to continue my voyage one day longer, if I possibly could with safety, and then return down the river, should I find the like difficulties to oppose. Accordingly I got every thing on board, charged my gun, and set sail, cautiously, along shore. As I passed by Battle lagoon, I began to tremble and keep a good look-out; when suddenly a huge alligator rushed out of the reeds, and with a tremendous roar came up, and darted as swift as an arrow under my boat, emerging upright on my lee quarter, with open jaws, and belching water and smoke that fell upon me like rain in a hurricane. I laid soundly about his head with my club, and beat him off; and after plunging and darting about my boat, he went off on a straight line through the water, seemingly with the rapidity of lightning, and entered the cape of the lagoon. I now employed my time to the very best advantage in paddling close along shore, but could not forbear looking now and then behind me, and presently perceived one of them coming up again. The water of the river hereabouts was shoal and very clear; the monster came up with the usual roar and menaces, and passed close by the side of my boat, when I could distinctly see a young brood of alligators, to the number of one hundred or more, following after her in a long train. They kept close together in a column, without straggling off to the one side or the other; the young appeared to be of an equal size, about fifteen inches in length, almost black, with pale yellow transverse waved clouds or blotches, much like rattlesnakes in colour. I now lost sight of my enemy again.

Still keeping close along shore, on turning a point or projection of the river bank, at once I beheld a great number of hillocks or small pyramids, resembling hay-cocks, ranged like an encampment along the banks. They stood fifteen or twenty yards distant from the water, on a high marsh, about four feet perpendicular above the water. I knew them to be the nests of the crocodile, having had a description of them before; and now expected a furious and general attack, as I saw several large crocodiles swimming abreast of these buildings. These nests being so great a curiosity to me, I was determined at all events immediately to land and examine them. Accordingly, I ran my bark on shore at one of their landing-places, which was a sort of nick or little dock, from which ascended a sloping path or road up to the edge of the meadow, where their nests were; most of them were deserted, and the great thick whitish egg-shells lay broken and scattered upon the ground round about them.

The nests or hillocks are of the form of an obtuse cone, four feet high and four or five feet in diameter at their bases; they are constructed with mud, grass and herbage. At first they lay a floor of this kind of tempered mortar on the ground, upon which they deposit a layer of eggs, and upon this a stratum of mortar, seven or eight inches in thickness, and then another layer of eggs; and in this manner one stratum upon another, nearly to the top. I believe they commonly lay from one to two hundred eggs in a nest: these are hatched, I suppose, by the heat of the sun; and perhaps the vegetable substances mixed with the earth, being acted upon by the sun, may cause a small degree of fermentation, and so increase the heat in those hillocks. The ground for several acres about these nests shewed evident marks of a continual resort of alligators; the grass was every where beaten down, hardly a blade or straw was left standing; whereas, all about, at a distance, it was five or six feet high, and as thick as it could grow together. The female, as I imagine, carefully watches her own nest of eggs until they are all hatched; or perhaps while she is attending her own brood, she takes under her care and protection as many as she can get at one time, either from her own particular nest or others, but certain it is, that the young are not left to shift for themselves; for I have had frequent opportunities of seeing the female alligator leading about the shores her train of young ones, just as a hen does her brood of chickens; and she is equally assiduous and courageous in defending the young, which are under her care, and providing for their subsistence; and when she is basking upon the warm banks, with her brood around her, you may hear the young ones continually whining and barking like young puppies. I believe but few of a brood live to the years of full growth and magnitude, as the old feed on the young as long as they can make prey of them.

The alligator when full grown is a very large and terrible creature, and of prodigious strength, activity and swiftness in the water. I have seen them twenty feet in length, and some are supposed to be twenty-two or twenty-three feet. Their body is as large as that of a horse; their shape exactly resembles that of a lizard, except their tail, which is flat or cuneiform, being compressed on each side, and gradually diminishing from the abdomen to the extremity, which, with the whole body is covered with horny plates or squammae, impenetrable when on the body of the live animal, even to a rifle ball, except about their head and just behind their fore-legs or arms, where it is said they are only vulnerable. The head of a full grown one is about three feet, and the mouth opens nearly the same length; their eyes are small in proportion, and seem sunk deep in the head, by means of the prominency of the brows; the nostrils are large, inflated and prominent on the top, so that the head in the water resembles, at a distance, a great chuck of wood floating about. Only the upper jaw moves, which they raise almost perpendicular, so as to form a right angle with the lower one. In the forepart of the upper jaw, on each side, just under the nostrils, are two very large, thick, strong teeth or tusks, not very sharp, but rather the shape of a cone: these are as white as the finest polished ivory, and are not covered by any skin or lips, and always in sight, which gives the creature a frightful appearance: in the lower jaw are holes opposite to these teeth, to receive them: when they clap their jaws together it causes a surprising noise, like that which is made by forcing a heavy plank with violence upon the ground, and may be heard at a great distance.

But what is yet more surprising to a stranger, is the incredible loud and terrifying roar, which they are capable of making, especially in the spring season, their breeding time. It most resembles very heavy distant thunder, not only shaking the air and waters, but causing the earth to tremble; and when hundreds and thousands are roaring at the same time, you can scarcely be persuaded, but that the whole globe is violently and dangerously agitated.

An old champion, who is perhaps absolute sovereign of a little lake or lagoon (when fifty less than himself are obliged to content themselves with swelling and roaring in little coves round about) darts forth from the reedy coverts all at once, on the surface of the waters, in a right line; at first seemingly as rapid as lightning, but gradually more slowly until he arrives at the centre of the lake, when he stops. He now swells himself by drawing in wind and water through his mouth, which causes a loud sonorous rattling in the throat for near a minute, but it is immediately forced out again through his mouth and nostrils, with a loud noise, brandishing his tail in the air, and the vapour ascending from his nostrils like smoke. At other times, when swollen to an extent ready to burst, his head and tail lifted up, he spins or twirls around on the surface of the water. He acts his part like an Indian chief when rehearsing his feats of war; and then retiring, the exhibition is continued by others who dare to step forth, and strive to excel each other, to gain the attention of the favourite female.

Having gratified my curiosity at this general breeding-place and nursery of crocodiles, I continued my voyage up the river without being greatly disturbed by them.

NEIGHBORS OF THE NIGHT

BY MORGAN BULKELEY

Morgan Bulkeley (1913 —) was born in Hartford, Connecticut, and educated at the Hotchkiss School and Yale. In 1941 he bought a farm high in the Berkshire hills in Mount Washington, the smallest township, and one of the most rugged, in Massachusetts, where he has lived and worked since as a farmer-poet-naturalist and free-lance writer. Since 1959 he has written a weekly column, "Our Berkshires," for the Pittsfield, Massachusetts, daily Berkshire Eagle. *The following selection, about flying squirrels, appeared first in that column, and Mr. Bulkeley has added a few paragraphs of additional material to round out the story for use here.*

(From "Our Berkshires" column in the Pittsfield, Massachusetts, *Berkshire Eagle,* May 9, 1963; June 20, 1963; November 14, 1963; May 7, 1964; August 16, 1964.)

May 9, 1963

It was late to be cleaning out the birdboxes around the yard, April 28th, to be exact. Things had been delayed by a Berkshire April that bestowed only two showers and sulked in the 20s and 30s at night. Finally two bluebirds had begun housekeeping, and it was time for some spring cleaning.

At the top of a ladder we started to cast a presumed deermouse nest from a flicker box when out the door flashed a flying squirrel. In the bottom of the box were four wiggly little squirrels with eyes still closed. They were furred in gray-brown velvet above and pinkly bare beneath, being about two weeks old. The mother clung on the white-oak bark within two feet watching the depredation with large misty eyes unaccustomed to bright sunlight. We could not resist taking, as a dividend for living in the deep woods, a part of the ample nest and two little ones, knowing what gentle pets they would make.

The nest was a matted woven chilting of shredded reddish bark, perhaps grapevine strips, no red cedar being handy, with some shredded grasses, paper and cotton picked up about the yard. It filled the box with a loose, musky-scented insulation so that the little creatures destined to spend the major part of their six-year life span upon the bark were actually cradled in bark and breathed through it.

The elfin twins graced the scales at a sylph-like one ounce, not apiece but together. Their soft pelage seemed too large for them with extra folds of skin extending along both sides from wrist to ankle—like girls wearing boys' sweaters. It was difficult to envision them fullgrown when, with limbs outstretched and with flattened tail, they would present fifty square inches of gliding surface to the thin air as they slanted down it with three and one-half ounces of weight in glides up to eighty yards. Instinctively and perfectly these little Pythagoreans would measure the hypotenuses of innumerable triangles, given two sides, the ground and the trees. Their travels would all be triangles as they went about their nocturnal business, original measurers of wood and bark in the country town, inspectors of buds, berries, seeds and nuts.

If this destiny was to be, there was very presently the matter of milk. The twins let it be known with faint dry vocal sounds, like the scratchings of a grasshopper, while they heaved the barky nest-blanket in the box over the radiator. In a few days they were supping eagerly at a doll-feeding bottle, six or eight gulps (drops) of dilute Similac baby formula, which usually put them right to sleep. Such tiny stomachs meant two-hour feedings, which we simplified to 10 P.M., 2 A.M., and 6 A.M., in the wee hours.

Once there was a near-fatal accident in the protected cradle of the nest. One little one slipped his head into a grass loop and performed several turns like a bedding dog, cinching the noose and nearly strangling himself on a grass blade. On such slight filaments and cobwebs do the lives of tiny creatures depend. An attentive mother would have nipped this near-tragedy.

To confirm the doubtful spring, we had only to take the little ones in to a cupped hand. They lay contented with eyes that would not open for two more weeks, warm in dreamy oblivion, sides pulsating softly, the surest evidence of spring birth, two wholly new creatures. Somehow they had a classic air about them, as though they had been around for a long time, and would be. Maybe it was the long silver whiskers about the muzzle or the folds of extra fur drawn about them. They looked like old Romans sleeping in their togas.

Occasionally they stirred and turned, settling into the warm palm: "Like one who wraps the drapery of his couch about him, and lies down to pleasant dreams," to quote Bryant, who probably had flying squirrels in his Berkshire attic.

June 20, 1963—*Wilbur and Orville*

Anyone rash enough to adopt infant woodland creatures must be able to supply the three basics: food, warmth and shelter. Within a week the little squirrels were eating Pablum in their Similac; their box, now kept in an electric frying pan, remained at a steady eighty degrees; and we had begun to believe that home was a hollow tree.

After ten days in the new nesting cavity, when they were about twenty-five days old, their eyes opened on a world that for them would never again be dark. Instinct guided their learning; and in fact before they could see, they were storing scattered sunflower seeds in one corner of their box, strictly provision for the future since their teeth could not crack them.

Experiments have shown that hatching chicks will accept the first object that moves as their parent, which, in the laboratory, may be a ping-pong ball dragged by a string. In the case of the squirrels, it was our hands which were warm, sheltering and provided food and drink. The more progressive Orville soon advanced to a dish without losing affection.

When the squirrels were a month old in the middle of May, they began to enjoy a regular exercise period, running about the rug in a wobbly, humping gait and shunning the bare floor as if it were wet. They scrambled about sure-footedly on an oak log cut by beaver cousins, sometimes considering a four-inch jump to the floor by bobbing their heads in a vertical plane to get the range, much as an Indian would move his head from side to side to judge a bowshot through the trees. The vertical plane was instinctively their frame of reference. To execute all future glides they would perform quick, simple triangulation by this bobbing of the head.

About this time they began nibbling other foods, much preferring shelled nuts. They assumed the distinctive evening wear of maturity, soft gray brown above and full-dress white beneath, with a sharp Plimsoll line along the gliding edge. They were acquiring the speed and agility of ballet dancers, and as one of those might spin on a toe, so Orville and Wilbur frequently hung by one toenail from our clothing about which they climbed easily.

Somehow they suggested birds more than squirrels. They began a birdlike chittering and at times voiced soft musical warbles. Their tails grew to the broad plumose quality of an owl feather, and their pelage was like the plumage of a cedar waxwing.

They were becoming venturesome. One night in our absence, Orville for the first time scaled the steep walls of the box as the first Americans were scaling Everest, causing a hasty midnight search through the house, under the furniture, behind pillows, in desk pigeonholes and in the apertures of radiators. If we had considered his arboreal nature, we would have found him right away—at the highest point in the room. There he sat watching the circus below like a Wallenda on a trapeze. He was balanced restfully on a valance, wearing a jaunty swatch of cobweb on one ear, with nothing but ceiling between him and sky. This location afterward became sanctuary for both squirrels. They scrambled up the drapes as up a tree trunk and were much more at home there than on the floor.

It is said that to train a dog one must know more than the dog. Since we knew little about flight, it was clear that Orville and Wilbur were going to glide by instinct or remain grounded. The answer came while Gordon Cooper was making his twenty-two orbits around the earth.

The flying squirrels were a month old. We took them into the confusing spaciousness of outdoors, placing them upon a plank bench where they scurried back and forth uneasily. Wilbur ran to the nearest point from his master's familiar clothing, bobbed his head a few times and leaped trustingly into space, completing a four-foot glide to a trouser leg. Seeing this, the fatter Orville, who had given up the doll-feeding bottle a week earlier and considered himself something of a prodigy, did not bother to seek the shortest line. He undertook a prodigious diagonal and ended in a pratfall in the gravel. First flights for flying squirrels had been the same for generations.

Not so for man. Within the period of one lifetime human flight lengthened from Wilbur Wright's one hundred twenty feet in twelve seconds to the Russian multi-ring cosmic circus in progress that very week.

Yet, who could say surely that man was more progressive than the flying squirrel? More than one hundred years ago Melville and Hawthorne, talking late into Berkshire nights, were questioning the direction and inevitability of human achievement.

November 14, 1963—*How They Grew*

The mother flying squirrel kept us for neighbors after we adopted two of her little ones. She merely moved the remaining ones two trees away to another birdbox. If she was willing to trust us, we would trust her, so a swap was arranged in June. The mother accepted Wilbur back in exchange for Amelia. Now Orville had a sister for company in domesticity.

She was fairer fawn color and slightly larger than he, from natural diet, and becomingly shy. She tamed readily by following his lead and was soon familiar with his runways over furniture, up the curtains and down the bannisters. Nothing in the house was out of bounds except as doors were closed. The two even jumped from the top of a clock onto a porcupine fish suspended from the ceiling where they somehow swung and balanced without stabbing themselves.

Their flights and frolics in the house had to be limited to evening exercise periods in order to preserve some order. At other times they were in residence in a wire cage on the porch where they slept the day away in a stub hollowed out by a woodpecker. They emerged from the nest they had built of cattail down, dry leaves, corn silk and other vegetable fibers, well after sunset. Their acrobatic antics continued throughout the night. They eagerly accepted moths and other insects and frequently ate them held in the forepaws while hanging batlike from the top wires of the cage, forestalling stealing by the other.

Cage life seemed as interesting to them as a barn to kittens. They had a spinning wheel for carnival, and they pell-melled around the cage in imaginary wheels and figure eights, seeming to flow unerringly as quicksilver. Amelia busied herself refurbishing nests in the two stubs at her disposal, and Orville was constantly hiding or finding nuts in the floor litter. Hickory nuts and acorns were favorites, and one hollow stub was filled up and above the entrance in October when the instinct to store became overpowering.

Scientists attribute this storage impulse to photoperiodism, the lengthening or, in this case, shortening of days which directly affects so much plant, animal and insect behavior. We could see a second reason for this when we went into direct competition with deer, chipmunks, red and gray squirrels, partridges and jays in foraging for winter provender which disappeared as fast as it fell.

The flying squirrels were not without visitors. Other squirrels, several chipmunks, deer mice and chickadees envied the occupants their land of plenty. If the wild members of their own family came at night, we never saw them. When great horned or barred owls hooted in the vicinity, the two would freeze instinctively in terror or chirp angrily from the refuge of their hole. Bob-tailed flying squirrels have been seen that must have experienced near misses at the talons of these night marauders.

The docility and trust of these soft-furred, large-eyed creatures was as much a joy to behold as their quickness and agility. They jumped eagerly from the cage onto the clothing to come in for exercise periods. Orville pawed with excited chuckles at his master's collar and plunged down inside like a boy on a slippery-slide, kicking softly and finally fumbling his way out at waist or wrist. Both liked their people upright like trees and deserted any who sat down.

Amelia enjoyed tumbling in a warm pocket with an acorn. When offered Kleenex, she wadded up a large mouthful and glided off with it to a nest built in the bookshelf behind a set of Henry Thoreau, who once captured a flying squirrel in his own handkerchief, kept it a night in his room and admired its "innocent" eye and "neat, flat, fawn-colored distichous tail that was a great ornament." Doubtless Amelia equally admired the woodsy smelling pages of his journal that formed her nest cavity, else why had she chosen that set from hundreds of books?

Seldom did the squirrels bother to chuck and eat nuts in their household universe. They preferred to bury them hastily under the rug, in the pages of a magazine, in a desk pigeonhole or high behind a picture, against a time of longer nights and shorter rations. There was too much else to do. They would sometimes take time to drink from a vase of flowers or partake of an ice-cream treat, but there were still a few unexplored nooks and untried flights, and a few things left to tip over.

A bull in a china shop and a railroad through the middle of the house are nothing compared to a flying squirrel circus. Right now Orville is trying to take this pencil before the para

May 7, 1964—*How They Wintered*

We were grayer, but the flying squirrels were livelier after their first winter in the woodpecker stub on the front porch. They largely dreamed the winter away nestled in bits of wool blanket.

But they were not as inactive as many naturalists guessing in the dark have supposed. Even on nights well below zero or with snow sifting through the cage out of the northwest, they would venture out for short exercise periods. Their basement was filled with acorns, hickory nuts and hazelnuts; but they always came out to forage for more, leaving the nest hole blocked with leaves and wool to keep it warm.

Perhaps it was the need for drink that brought them out so regularly. Their water was usually frozen solid; but they gnawed it like a nut or ate snow, suggesting that in the wild, flying squirrels may not drink water all winter. If they do, it is certainly at great risk along a running brook where snow cornices can avalanche, and a little creature with wrist webbed to ankle would be swiftly swept away.

Their silky, slate coats, creamy white underneath, became swiftly dense as winter intensified, and their flat furry tails served as both scarf and muff. They were clad for winter nights, and were seldom brought indoors unless to exercise or entertain.

One night after the company had been assured that the squirrels had never bitten anyone, in they came to join the party, or to steal it. Amelia failed in an attempt to secure some blond hair for her nest behind Thoreau's works and retired to the top of a valance to wash her face. Orville, meanwhile, was struggling to hide a nut behind a picture on the wall. A guest veterinary reached up to take him and was promptly nipped on an already injured hand. He became the only member of a very exclusive society: Gored by a Bull and Bitten by a

Flying Squirrel on the same hand the same day. Ne plus ultra, even in hard-bitten Hemingway.

The way these trim little squirrels moved or glided about the room hap-hazard and helter-skelter, one might suppose, as we are wont to do with the least creatures, that they were mechanical in their reactions and without memory. All their paths and turnings seemed random response to immediate environment or base instinct. They appeared creatures of the moment.

Yet as soon as there was a human attachment, this seemed no longer true. After being out all winter where they might have become shy, the squirrels still delighted in clambering over the clothing and in and out of pockets. Orville remembered his slippery-slide down through the shirt collar and out at waist or cuff.

In the spring he made an escape flight one night before he could be returned to the cage. He was gone two days and two nights in a world full of tasty, burgeoning buds from birch sweet to cherry bitter. All calls to the dark were of no avail. We did not expect to see him again.

But the third night he was back home again in the cage. Not that he needed food and water; they were everywhere. He must have had memories of the past year, for he jumped directly to shoulder and ran down into a pocket. We were not flattered that he had returned entirely to see us. Amelia with those large, sultry eyes was waiting, and could be expecting.

August 16, 1964—*How They Flew*

The flying squirrels had known only a limited world. One year, one month and one week back, when their infant eyes first opened, it had been a cardboard carton which their adolescent explorations and escapes enlarged to the living room and later to the entire house, whereupon they were promoted to the wire cage on the porch. The progression suggested kindergarten, grade school, high school and college.

Now it was June fifteenth, commencement time, time for them to get out into a world redolent with more than a hundred aromatic flavors of bark. Preparation had been long and not entirely to the point. In fact, pampering and spoon-feeding might work against them when it came to owls and storing food for a winter on their own.

The diploma was an open cage door with a slim tree trunk leading to the ground or to the porch floor. Their instincts were so aerial and arboreal that we never did see them take to the ground without gliding.

In the dusk of that first freedom, they skipped nimbly and noisily about the porch roof, scampered in the gutters and scrambled up inside the leaders to the upper roof, returning now and then to familiar cage or shoulder. They discovered the outside of the house they knew so well inside. They clambered on the screens and accepted almonds at the bedroom window. The patter of their feet sounded like gusts of rain on the roof in the night. Next morning like trusty prisoners both were asleep in their hollow stub in the open cage.

Next evening at the usual rising time a half hour after sunset, Orville leaped from our shoulder into a large sugar maple. We heard his rustling and fumbling up through the dense foliage; then suddenly there was a swish down the whole tree. He plopped lightly but inadvertently on the ground, and we saw that with his built-in parachute he never would be hurt by falling. It was like the puppy pratfall of his first attempted flight more than a year before, and like that time he scrambled up into a pants pocket to recover composure.

Soon both squirrels were launching into glides from roof corners to the trunks of the nearest trees; then running to tops or along reaching branches, they would glide to a roof-landing with a dull thud. By the light of the June moon they could be seen describing all sorts of triangles. Sometimes the pitch would be very steep from a tall white oak to the base of a hemlock thirty yards away. Again trajectory was almost level except for a slight initial drop when they planed from the porch roof to the oak. A faint stir of disturbed air could be heard as they glided up for a silent landing on the bark beside one's shoulder.

Gradually they edged into the wild where gray squirrels looked like elephants, where aggressive red squirrels had possession of the best holes, where chipmunks by their very numbers kept the ground clean of food, and where their own wild brethren got to the best treetop food first. It was a considerable step from their luxury hotel to hardscrabble survival. And they often came back to the hotel.

After a week, Orville passed an occasional day sleeping in the trees, and by the end of June Amelia joined him. A great hollow oak near the edge of the lawn became their new abode. There they found a wild brother who could be seen cavorting with them in the half-light of evening.

In July a heavy thunderstorm sent them both back to the cage to sleep. Their new roof may have leaked. While citizens were rejoicing in the new freedom of the Civil Rights Act and others were celebrating the country's independence, these two would-be woodland denizens were still not sure that they wanted freedom at all.

A month after their emancipation sometimes one, sometimes the other, sometimes both and sometimes neither returned to sleep. After one year and ten weeks we were still not sure we had passed our test as a mother flying squirrel.

Finally all ties gave, and the squirrels were gone for good. The last time we saw them was in August dusk. They had found and slept the day away in the birdbox where they were born, starting afresh where they had begun as though the captivity of one-sixth of their lives had been the dream of a single day.

Two silvery-whiskered faces poked from the small entrance regarding us attentively in the oncoming twilight with large, luminous eyes that first opened a year before to find us the one point of trust. Now the wildlings did not offer to come, nor did we call them. Instead there seemed a sharing of freedom as they planed off into their newfound, limitless, sylvan world of bark, dusk and moonbeams.

THE DEER MOUSE

BY SALLY CARRIGHAR

Sally Carrighar was born in Cleveland, Ohio, spent much of her childhood at her grandparents' farm where, as she says, she "first learned what it is to have an intimate feeling for plants, trees, birds and animals." Summers in Canada, the Rockies, northern Michigan and the Ozarks, where she once worked as a fishing guide, added to her outdoor knowledge. After various commercial writing jobs she returned to her first love, nature, and built a groundwork of natural science by supplementing science courses with field as well as library research. Her first book was One Day on Beetle Rock, *about wildlife in California's Sequoia National Park. It was followed by a parallel book about a marsh and its wildlife. Then she went to Alaska and wrote two books about life there. She now lives in New Jersey, and her latest book is* Wild Heritage. *This selection, from* One Day on Beetle Rock, *shows her uncanny outdoor knowledge as well as her skill as a writer.*

(*One Day on Beetle Rock*, by Sally Carrighar; Alfred A. Knopf, Inc., 1945.)

The Deer Mouse was trapped by a sound. Startled as she sped about on the floor of the night, she had run beneath the edge of a stone. There now she hid in her fur, nose on her chest, feet all covered. But her ears' wide membranes stood high with alarm, twitching as though attached to the sound by threads.

She heard a whisper of something coming. Something was sweeping on thin wings between the needles of the trees; something was streaming across the hillside grasses, brushing the brittle husks of the seeds. Feet were stealing, seeking through the dry stalks, and leaping over the Mouse's stone.

Sometimes the sound sighed down. Then the Mouse would dare to turn around, trying to fit deeper into the crack between the stone and the ground. She wanted the walls of the nook to press her all over, but, however she crouched, one of her sides had no touch of shelter on it. That side yearned with a sense of lack, with a sort of skin-hunger, quite apart from its feeling of cold.

At other times the sound snapped. Then the Deer Mouse dropped flat, ready to dodge a hunter's pounce. She did not know that the enemy was less substantial, even, than she—that it was the wind, tossing twigs and rustling the grasses. Most of her experience was in matters as small as seeds and flies, the voices of mice, and the look of her clean white forepaw with its tiny claws, like pearl slivers. What could she understand of a battle of winds above a canyon?

The Deer Mouse wished to return to her mother's nest, an earthy cavern among the roots of a manzanita bush. The nestball of grass and feathers was as soft as the arching belly of a mother mouse, and behind it the roots were strong, like a mother's bones that would hold off any enemy. The Deer Mouse had grown beyond the need for cuddling, but she longed for the proof on her skin of sheltering walls. Not tonight alone, but for several days, she had been obsessed with the loveliness of crannies shaped to cover a mouse.

Shortly before midnight she could have run back to the nest quite safely, for there were signs that the real dangers had drawn away. The owls were down in the hollow, as their hooting told, but in tones too low to sound in ears of deer mice. The bears had gone up the draw and were not yet due to return. Now the coral king snake would be too cold to forage. The swirling wind carried no warning of wildcat or shrew. But the swish in the grass had more meaning for a mouse.

Finally the sound shifted farther off. The Deer Mouse left the stone and raced to the manzanita, each bound as light as if she were a woolly aster released from the wind's pressure. She entered the nest and crept upon the furry heap that was her mother and sister. Now her back and sides were pushed against the dome of fibres, giving her such solid, real assurance of being hidden that she quickly relaxed in sleepy peace.

Her vibrissae were brushed by a fourth mouse groping in. He was the brother, who had left the family several days before. The wind had brought him home. Its uneasy sounds had meant for him, too, that predators were swarming through the forest, and made him long for the security he associated with his mother's nest. But while he was fitting himself among the other mice, the earth jarred. A powerful weight had struck beside the bush. It was a great horned owl, who had seen the brother slip into the dead leaves over the roots.

The leaves were swept away and claws scraped into the soil. Then the nest jolted as the roots were pulled apart. The whole pile of mice was a-tremble with frantic little heartbeats. All the mice were ready to leap as soon as the nest was torn—that was now!

The Deer Mouse alighted beneath a pine tree and darted into the fallen needles. Around her was a fanning out of quick patters. That shriek must have meant that the owl caught one mouse, perhaps the sister, always slower, more cautious, abnormally afraid of predators. The Deer Mouse's nose was pushed into the soil, but her great black eyes looked up through the needles. Against the brightness of moon-silvered clouds she saw the owl rise and sweep away.

The needles were no firm shelter. Now the Mouse was bounding down to a log in the crease of a gully. She crept under the log's curve and waited until her panting ceased. Then she found a split in the wood where she could hide. It was a tight refuge, but after such a fright she could endure being crowded by the touch of walls. The middle of the night had come, a heavy time when deer mice liked to sleep. She let her fears fall away and closed her eyes.

Moonlight woke her. It had entered even her cramped little niche. The Mouse slipped out and down the dark side of the log. She was hungry, but the log was surrounded with glittering granite gravel. The very sight of it made her back up tighter against the wood. Not even a tuft of grass grew near, for the log lay in a cradle of sand. The Mouse prowled out and found a spot where the soil smelled tempting. Her forepaws whirled into it, scooping it towards her so fast that she was continually astride a mound, which her hind feet kicked back. Now her claws struck an acorn, split by its swelling germ. She hooked her sharp front teeth into it, gave it a mighty pull, and it came free. She ran back to the log, then, with the acorn in her mouth. There she ate it, morsel by morsel—delicious nut, succulent with new life. The Chickaree had buried it. His stores, cached around the gully, had furnished the deer mice with many a meal. They watched even his cones, and when one dried enough to open they reached between the scales with their tiny paws, drew out the seeds and carried them to their own hoard in a pine stump.

Feeling untidy now, the Mouse licked her forepaws and scrubbed the pink tip of her nose. Taking each hind foot in her forepaws, she turned it and washed it. With the hind feet she smoothed her shoulders, and she washed her sides and back. Even her striped furry tail she cleaned. A quick shake then, and all her pretty coat, white below, oak-leaf brown above, was smooth. She seemed hardly at all like a house mouse, more like a toy doe, and so similar in color that it was clear why human beings had named her a deer mouse.

She had slept, she had eaten, and she was groomed. With these needs out of the way, she became a quiet mouse, facing a great emergency, for she was homeless. As she crouched in the shadow of the log, some delicacy of pose, or soft wildness in her eyes, gave her the unreal look of fawns. She was a small, brief union of breath, pulse, and grace, yet the apparent nothingness of her, the hint that she soon would vanish, if she had not already, actually was her strength.

All mice were so hunted that some kinds had become erratic, but deer mice learned to bound ahead of the strain of attack. They lived with a lightness that served very well for poise. Always—their way was—be ready to drop the game or gnawing or nest-building, and disappear, noiseless as a blown thistle. Dig to the sprout with airy speed, before a falling leaf may warn of claws on the bough above, before the breeze flies ahead of an enemy bringing his scent. However close come the beak or teeth, then, never hoard the fright. Don't let even death be important, since it is so familiar. Try to escape if there is a chance, but if there is not, give up life quickly.

Yet the Deer Mouse was more than a fluff of a little being. She, as well as any bear or coyote, must have her established place at Beetle Rock. Among the boulders, brush, and trees must be one cranny recognized as hers. The wrecking of her mother's nest had made it necessary to find her own niche and her own life, but she was ready, anyway, to cease the play of a young mouse and become a grown one. Before her brother left, he had raced with her on the boughs of the manzanita, and she had loved that swift motion as fawns love to bound down a slope, or chickarees to leap from tree to tree. Afterwards she sometimes had run through the bush alone, whirling herself exquisitely half out of her senses, but now a different interest had stirred in her, an impulse that soft speed would not quiet.

Oh, where, now, was a cranny into which she might fit—some hole sweet and snug, with firm walls, a secret entrance, so placed that winds would not blow, nor moisture drain, into it? Lowland deer mice dug burrows, and in some other places they made nests in trees, but the Beetle Rock deer mice searched for their nooks instead of building them. The Mouse would begin at the log.

She found a knothole and started into it, eager and pleased until she discovered a scent of other mice. She turned down towards the ground. A strip of bark, loosened by beetles, hung away from the wood. The Mouse crept under and felt the space, its size and shape, not with her paws or nose but with her vibrissae, the whiskers of various lengths which she moved like fingers over an object to give her information about it. Around this pocket went the spray of her tactile hairs, quivering into every crack. At the far end she turned. The wood and bark touched her all over, as she liked, yet some instinct warned her that this could not be a permanent home.

Now she looked up the moon-spangled gully. Almost irresistible was her wish to return to the thicket above. The shadow of a cloud fell upon the gravel, and gave her the chance to go.

Back in the manzanita thicket, the Mouse slipped under the dead leaves beneath. As she pattered along, ears flattened and vibrissae down her sides, she was hidden from any searching eye, although the leaves kept whispering:

"She is *here*."

She was making her way towards one of the root-crowns, but when she reached it she found that a family of juncos lived at the center of that bush. The Mouse crept close to their cup of woven grasses, so softly that the mother bird continued to sleep. She climbed up on the rim of the nest. Most of the junco's feathers were the color of a night shadow, but the sides of her tail gleamed white, and so did her ivory beak. The Mouse touched her tactile hairs over the wings and tail, outspread to cover four nestlings. She was sniffing, too, scenting the birds' light breaths, and their flesh, delicate with the sweetness of seed-food. Once more she felt over the strong walls of the birds' home, over the mother, and the nestlings' down at the edges of her wings. Then the Mouse dropped again into the brittle, rustling leaves.

At an opening in the brush she came to a mound of the leaves, pawed together by a deer. She scrambled through them, but they all flew; nothing here was strong enough to support a nest. The next manzanita bush had been home. The Mouse sped past. A short way beyond, she came to a braid of scents left by the Weasel and her five kits when the pack of little hunters crossed the thicket. The Mouse dodged away towards the open ground under the trees.

Her home-range extended on one side as far as a spring, and on the other to the foot of an open slope. In the space between grew three pines and an ancient fir. The Mouse knew the exposed part of the trees only as circular trunks and a vague overhead thicket; trees, to her, were underground things. She had her own view, too, of the earth's surface. That was not the smooth mat of needles it looked to a human eye. Chains of small shelters led almost everywhere.

Here was this tumbleweed, only a tuft of dry twigs but a mouse could hide under it. One leap from there and she reached a fallen branch. The tiny foliage of staghorn lichen covered it. Beneath the lichen she ran to the other end, her feet spinning like the feet of a house mouse. A bound, then, to a piece of bark, and from that to a root of the fir—she must let this search for her nook take her wherever it would. Most animals looked in particular kinds of places for their home-sites, but a deer mouse's cranny was accidental, an earth pocket washed out by the rain, a stump just enough decayed, a log fallen aslant a rock.

The cloud passed; moonlight slid out upon the forest floor. Now the Mouse must go underground, down into other animals' burrows, hoping to find an abandoned one. Deer mice often did appropriate such homes, whose owners had disappeared, having suddenly, unexpectedly, no more use for the patiently dug tunnel, the nest chamber, and the storeroom filled with seeds.

She would begin with the burrows of the meadow mice, who lived in the grass near the spring. She crept into the stems, moving over a web of runners and dry fallen stalks. In it was the ground-litter of this tiny wilderness—petals of the grass flowers, seed husks, skeletons of dead insects, and living insects, sleeping or numb with cold. When she found these, the Deer Mouse stopped to nibble them up, while the wavy currents of the grass stirred above her, the sound in the moist green blades as harmless as the song of gnats.

Before she had gone far she reached one of the meadow mice's surface roads, which led to all parts of the grass patch, in a curving network, regular as a cobweb but more graceful. Underfoot was a smooth pavement, kept clear by the industrious owners. The Deer Mouse passed two at work on the roads, chewing off new shoots which might be food in some places but here were troublesome weeds. She went into each sidepath, and soon found one that ended at a burrow entrance.

Down she sped into the clean little tube, just mouse-width, now straight, now curving to pass a root, a path all dark but impossible to lose. With the smell of the soil was mixed the meadow-mouse odor, grass juice crushed into fur, and musk, and here an extra odor, that of milk. The Deer Mouse followed a branch tunnel to a nest chamber. There she found five newborn young. They cried to her with appealing squeaks; perhaps they thought her their mother. She felt all over the little mice, then returned to the main burrow.

She saw mice eating, carrying nest fibres, and sleeping, for meadow mice worked either night or day. At the opening of each tunnel she sniffed the mouse scent and everywhere found it fresh; there was no vacant home for her in the grass patch. She was not anxious, anyway, to live where a road through the stems might lead snakes or weasels direct to one's nest.

Each time she had left a burrow, she had shaken the dirt out of her fur. Now she washed all over. When she felt clean she was ready for a new exploration.

She bounded to a break in the matted fir needles, but it led to no cave, only to the emerging stalk of a snow plant. She crouched there briefly, above the roots of the tree. She knew that a crook of its largest root was sheltering a chipmunk family, parents and young, whose burrow was the cleanest of all the underground neighborhood. It had even a separate space for empty seed husks. Twice while the owners slept, the Mouse had prowled through their home, one to envy but never likely to be hers. Chance hardly would remove seven chipmunks at one time.

Meshing into the roots of the fir, too, was an underground village of digger squirrels, a labyrinth of hiding places, nests for families and single squirrels, and places for the stores of seeds packed in dry sand. Sometimes the squirrels deserted old nests, but the Deer Mouse would not investigate now. Morning was too near. The waking squirrels would not be friendly to mice.

Among these tunnels were others that the Mouse did not know. Her last search took her into one. The entrance was a well-concealed hole between stones. Beyond the Mouse crept down and down, much lower into the earth than she had been before. Finally the tunnel turned and wound beneath the tree's root-platform.

Strange and remote was the smell here, of very old soil, powdered fibres of ancient plants, and the dust of rocks. Even the roots above the tunnel smelled of the past, for the tree's food and drink came now from newer roots, pushed out into fresher humus. The Mouse knew the odor of the occupant; she had smelled it behind the lively heels of the golden-mantled squirrels. The air in the burrow was very cold, but the Mouse, delicate though she was, could hold away the chill. In fact, when the winter snows would fall, her little white feet would be running over the frosty white crystals, while the owner of this home, much larger than she, would have retreated into sleep.

The Mouse reached the nest chamber, where the squirrel lay sleeping, coiled in his fur. From here several tunnels radiated to a passageway that half circled the nest—a whole web of roads for escape. The Mouse went into a tunnel beyond and abruptly found herself in the open air. She had come out at the foot of the fir trunk, through an emergency exit disguised in the bark.

Now daylight was lifting the night away. The ground had a yellow-gray cast on it, too bright for safety. The Mouse would spend the day behind the loose bark on the gully log, not a trustworthy niche, but the best she knew. She started towards it. But why did this strange deer mouse lie on the needles, warm, alive, yet surely not sleeping? The Mouse found the hole in its skin, smelling of the poison transferred with a shrew's bite. And here came the shrew, smaller than the Mouse but with venom for her, too, in its pointed snout. The Mouse escaped the death-sleep; practice in racing had made her feet faster than the shrew's. Soon she had curled up between the bark and the log, her panting already becoming lighter, and her round eyes narrower, now but gleaming black lines, and now lost in fur.

A few times she roused, but only briefly, until late morning. Then a strange sound reached in and loosened her sleep. The wind had shifted and was driving the sand in gusts, like minute, sharp rain, against the bark. Soon real rain was dropping in coarse thuds on the log. All damp things smelled strongly of their dampness.

The Mouse pushed back against the walls of the niche. The rain was becoming a roar. A sudden thunderclap startled her to a blank. Her ears had not begun to rise again, nor her forepaws to relax, when a stream of cold water began to flow over her tail.

She climbed higher in the nook, and the water rose. She crept along to the end of the bark. A turbulent brook now entirely circled the log. The Mouse did what she must—plunged into it and spun over the top. Soon the current whirled her against a branch. She raced back upon it to the gully-side, then bounded in pelting rain up through the thicket, to the trunk of the fir and the burrow exit of the golden-mantled squirrel. In his tunnel she shook herself vigorously, made herself as flat as a turtle, and pushed into the soft soil of the wall. Here her own heat would make her dry. She fell asleep.

After the Deer Mouse woke, she slipped out into the tunnel and, perched on the sloping floor, washed and groomed her fur. No place more practical than this cranny could be found for a deer mouse's nest. But of course she could not stay; a golden-mantled squirrel would not allow his exit to be revealed by the path to a nest of mice. The squirrel already had smelled her there. She heard him coming up to drive her away, so she slipped out into the daylight.

Now sunshine fell in most places where the rain had fallen, making the earth steamy. The Deer Mouse crouched between the fir trunk and a fallen cone. Her eyes were flicking over the ground, trying to find a better shelter, when the Coyote came prowling from under the thicket. He walked towards the fir.

His scent was almost as tangible as the pierce of sharp teeth. How keen was his hunting; he was not living lightly; for him this instant might have been the storm's peak, so intense were his nerves. His nose was at the ground and his feet moved forward compactly. He was following a scent trail, perhaps of the Mouse herself.

Of course he would find her here. She had no chance to escape—yet she must make that last, desperate leap. But when the instant came that she would have jumped, the bit of buff shadow lay instead a trifle lower between the cone and the fir trunk. The Mouse had slipped into a faint, perhaps thus saving her life, for if she had sprung from her refuge the Coyote certainly would have seen her.

When her speck of consciousness drifted back, the Coyote was gone and the Mule Deer Buck had come under the tree. He stood looking across the gully, apparently also aware of the Coyote, for his feet shifted in a strained way and his head was high, his ears pointing stiffly forward. What a great, powerful creature he was—yet he shared with the Deer Mouse a fear of their common enemy.

With the Deer there, the Mouse felt more safe. He would not harm her. When he relaxed, she ran out from her hiding place and examined branches and tufts of lichen torn down by the storm. One might be large enough to give her a refuge. But while she searched, another deer came, a doe in so nervous a temper that soon the Buck's hoofs and the doe's were stomping wildly. The Mouse must leave.

As the Grouse fluttered down from one of the fir boughs, the Mouse looked up. At once she raced for the trunk. In a hole up in the tree she had seen the face of a flying squirrel, a gentle creature that she had met at night on the ground. Now the Mouse reached the hole and stopped, clinging to the bark. The squirrel turned its mellow eyes upon her. The Mouse crept over the rim of the hole and down into the nest cavity. At the bottom lay four young flying squirrels, piled together as the Mouse had slept with her family. She pushed between the fur of one and the bed of shredded cedar bark.

During the afternoon the screams of a red-tailed hawk woke the innocent creatures in the tree. There was a brief, startled stir as each tried to creep in deeper, and then they lay still. When the fearful cries came no more, the squirrels moved slightly, easing their tension, and the Deer Mouse slipped farther into her furry refuge.

The next time she opened her eyes she backed out of the squirrel's coat. Now she was sharply awake. The hole at the top of the nest cavity shone but faintly. She ran up. The night's darkness had drawn to the western horizon, but the star-brightened sky cast a soft light into the trees bordering Beetle Rock.

On a branch outside the hole the flying squirrel crouched, ready to glide to the ground. Looking like a furry leaf, with her legs and their connecting membranes spread, the squirrel dropped into an air current that took her lightly to the ground. The Deer Mouse ran down the trunk of the tree. Families of deer mice sometimes shared the nests of flying squirrels, but the Mouse still preferred to find her own niche. Besides, she had no family.

Perhaps tonight she would explore the slope above her home-range. The air was so still that no stalk or leaf stirred against another. She nibbled through the bases of several lupines so they would fall, and then ate the succulent tips. When her hunger was satisfied, she made herself dainty and neat, and bounded off into the grasses.

Near the top of the slope the grasses thinned, finally coming to an end. The Mouse continued on among the trees. Ahead she saw the speeding, white, upcurved tail of another deer mouse. He led towards some thing that was new to her—a cabin, a nook of human beings. He ran into its open door and the Deer Mouse went in, too.

The human creatures were not there. But upon everything lay their scent, the scent of predators but not of animals that preyed upon mice. The Deer Mouse did not belong to the unclean species of mice who lived in the dark corners of human homes, but she felt no terror here, only her natural wariness in a strange place. The other deer mouse had climbed at once to a shelf and was gnawing a box, apparently familiar with the cabin and not frightened. The Deer Mouse began to explore.

Everywhere she found corners, and they gave her confidence. Few were completely covered, but they were nooks that she could back into and feel the shelter-touch. The room itself had corners and there were others around the shelves, luggage, books, and many more objects, mysterious to a mouse. She liked the fact that nothing moved. Since hunters must always move to catch prey, mice's eyes were alarmed by most motions, even of leaves. Here all was pleasantly still.

The Mouse smelled and touched many curious things. While she was examining a cold metal flashlight, she seemed suddenly overwhelmed by all the strangeness and sat up, clenching a small forepaw against her breast and quivering her ears to find the other mouse. His gnawing had ceased. The Deer Mouse raced down the table-leg and towards the door, but discovered her companion eating at a pile of oats which had poured from his hole in the box and onto the floor. She stopped and tasted the oats. Delicious! Now she sat beside the other mouse, rapidly nibbling pawfuls of the new food.

Outside, sounds approached—a man and woman talking, walking towards the cabin. They entered and shut the door. The Deer Mouse zigzagged across the floor, hunting one of the room's crannies. Dimly she saw her companion's tail slipping behind a dustpan. She glided along the edge of the wall and joined him.

Now the darkness was destroyed, not gradually as when the dawn comes, but instantaneously. The man exclaimed over the spilled oats, came striding towards the mice, and lifted the dustpan away. Silent as shadows the mice moved behind an ax. The man swept up the oats and threw them into the stove, hitting the dustpan on the iron with a noise so sharp that both mice winced.

The people's voices were tremendous, and might have been frightening, but curiously were not. For all their loudness, they had no angry tones, as animals' growls did. The Mouse could hear only the higher tones, and therefore caught more of the woman's voice than the man's. Both people were getting undressed, and the mice watched. After the human beings had taken off their shoes and part of their clothes they sat on the beds, across the room from each other, still talking.

As abruptly as the light had come on, it went out. There was a creaking of springs, shrill in the Mouse's ears, when the people got into their beds. Their voices continued. The other mouse returned to the food shelves as soon as the room was dark, and the Deer Mouse followed. Now he was gnawing a new hole in the box of oats, for the man had turned the other hole to the top. The Deer Mouse helped with the gnawing. The man said:

"Do you hear something?"

Then both people were silent, and the mice, too, kept quiet. When the voices began again the mice chewed once more at the box. Soon the oats were spilling onto the shelf and the mice were eating them.

Finally the people talked no longer. First one, then the other, breathed more deeply and slowly. For the male mouse this was a sign that he could make more noise. He began to gnaw at a crack under the door. He was a little knot of energy, now flat, his mouth turned straight up as he chewed at the bottom of the door, now huddled against the crack so that nothing of him showed but his furry haunches, and now a mound that pivoted from side to side while his hind feet kept a steady grip on the floor. While he worked, he held his tail straight out, its tip upturned with eagerness. But occasionally he became tired or bored, and pattered around the cabin.

A large splinter came away and the male mouse slid out. The Deer

Mouse followed. She leapt from the still to the ground airily and ran to the base of a tree, where she crouched. The other mouse came out of a burrow hole under a stone, and bounded towards her.

Lightly she sped away from him, back down the slope and into the grasses, dodging among the stems in a bewildering way. She seemed to be trying to lose the fine small rustle that followed, yet she never ran so fast that she quite escaped. Soon she was in her home-range, leading over familiar ways.

This was like racing with her brother, only somehow more amusing. The Deer Mouse dipped under a root, up and over another root, a gasp of a little run. A pause, then as soon as the pursuing patter came close, she rippled across the gravel to the log. She slipped to the log's other end. Finally she led to one of the manzanita bushes.

Back and forth on the gnarled stalks the Mouse flew, as if she had snapped the threads of gravity. Even the lift of a bird's wing hadn't a freer motion. The other mouse raced well, too. Sometimes he would leap from behind her onto the branch above or below, and skim ahead. Then, unexpectedly, he left her, ran down the main stalk and crouched at the base of the bush, a secret place only visible from the branches above. The Deer Mouse could see him there. And he could see her, the gleaming white fur under all of her body, streaming along the boughs.

The male mouse beat on the bush with his forepaw, a spray of patters, then another quick knocking. The Deer Mouse crouched motionless and listened. The drumming was repeated. She came in along the branch. Once more he drummed. She hesitated—then sped down. With a soft brightness she drew up to the mouse. Playfully she began to nibble his ankle.

DAVY CROCKETT KILLS A BEAR

BY DAVID CROCKETT

David Crockett (1786–1836) was born in frontier Tennessee and had little education except as a woodsman and hunter. Yet he became a famed soldier, magistrate, state legislator, United States Congressman, and Texas freedom-fighter. He was one of the handful of defenders who fought to the death at the Alamo. He prided himself as a hunter, especially of bears; by his own count he killed 105 bears during one nine-month period in the Tennessee backwoods. Several autobiographical books were published under his name, but none of them resembles, either in style or content, the letters he is known to have written. A Narrative of the Life of David Crockett . . . Written by Himself, *published in 1834, is a vivid account of many things he is known to have done as well as quite a few that are undoubtedly apocryphal. This story of a bear hunt, from that book, is written in the language and with the high exaggeration typical of frontier tales of that day. Its actual author is not known.*

(A Narrative of the Life of David Crockett . . . Written by Himself, 1834.)

It was evening and I was coming along, my pack horse loaded and my dogs following. All at once Soundwell held up his head and looked about, then rubbed his nose against a bush, and opened. I knew from the way he sung out that it was an old he-bear. The other dogs buckled in, and off they went like a thundergust right up a hollow. I tied my horse and set out after the dogs. The hollow up which the bear had gone made a bend, and I knew he would follow it, so I run across to head him. The sun was down now. 'Twas growing dark mighty fast, and 'twas cold: so I buttoned my jacket fast around me and run on. I hadn't gone far when I heard the dogs tack, and then come a tearing right down the hollow. Then I heard the old bear rattling through the cane, and the dogs like lightning after him. I dashed on and felt like I had wings, my dogs made such a roaring cry. They rushed by me and I harked them on. They all broke out again in their deep tones, and the woods echoed back and back with their voices.

'Twasn't long before they overhauled him and I could hear 'em fighting not far from me. Just before I got there the old bear made a break and got loose, but the dogs kept close up, and ever once in a while they stopped him and had a fight. I tried for my life to get up but before I'd get there he'd get loose. I followed him this way for three or four miles through briars and cane, and he deviled me mightily.

Once I thought I had him. 'Twas so dark I couldn't tell him from a dog, and I started to go to him, but I found out there was a creek between us. How deep it was I didn't know, but it was too late to turn back, so I held up my rifle and walked right in. Before I got across the old bear got loose and shot for it through the cane. Well, I kept on, and once in a while I could hear my dogs fighting and baying just before me. I followed this way about four or five miles as near as I could guess, when the old bear couldn't stand it any longer and took a tree. I went up but at first it was so dark I could see nothing, but after looking about and getting the tree between me and a star I could see a very dark-looking place, and I raised old Betsey, and she lightened. Down came the old bear, but he wasn't much hurt.

Of all the fights you ever see that one beat all. I had six dogs, and for nearly an hour they kept rolling and tumbling right at my feet. I couldn't see anything but an old white dog I had, but every now and then the bear made 'em sing out right under me. After a while bear, dogs and all rolled into a crack just before me and I could hear 'em fighting like they was in a hole. I loaded Betsey and felt around in the hole with her till I got her agin the bear, and I fired, but I didn't kill him. Out of the hole he bounced, and the dogs fought harder than ever. They just formed a lump, rolling about, and presently they all went down into the hole again.

My dogs began to sing out mighty often now. It had been the hardest fight I ever saw. I found out how the bear was laying, and I looked for old Betsey to shoot him again, but I had laid her down somewheres and I couldn't find her, so I thought I would get down into the crack and kill him with my knife. I knew my bear was in a crack made by the shakes, but how deep it was and whether I could get out if I got in were things I couldn't tell. But my dogs would sing out as if they wanted help, so I let myself down into the crack behind the bear. Where I landed was about as deep as I am high, and I felt mighty ticklish. I couldn't see a thing in the world but I drew my knife and kept feeling about with my hands and feet till I touched the bear; this I did very gently. Then I got on my hands and knees and inched my left hand up his body with the knife in my right, though all the time he was twisting and turning with the dogs. I got pretty far up and then I plunged it into him. He sunk down, and for a minute there was a great struggle, but by the time I scrambled out everything was getting quiet. My dogs came out, one at a time, and laid down at my feet.

I didn't know the direction of my tent so I determined to stay the night. I took out my flint and steel and raised a little fire, but the wood was so cold and wet it wouldn't burn much. I had sweated so after the bear that I began to get very thirsty and felt like I would die if I didn't get some water, so I went to look for the creek I had waded in, and as good luck would have it I found the creek and got back to my bear. But from having been in a sweat all night I was now very chilly. So I set to work again to build me a fire but all I could do wouldn't make it burn. The excitement I had been laboring under had all died away and I was so cold I felt very much like dying, but a notion struck me to get my bear out of the crack, so down I went into it, and worked till I got myself into a sweat again, and just as I would get him so high that if I could turn him over once he'd be out, he'd roll back. It began to hail mighty fine, but I kept on, and in about three hours I got him out.

THE WORLD OF THE CHIPMUNK

BY ALAN DEVOE

Alan Devoe (1909–1955) was born and grew up in New Jersey, was educated at Columbia University. A dedicated naturalist and a writer with unusual skill in translating natural science to popular terms, he wrote for both popular and scientific journals and reported his own field findings from his farm near Hillsdale, New York. This selection, which appeared first as an article in Audubon Magazine *and later in* The Audubon Book of True Nature Stories, *shows his meticulous observation as well as his deceptively simple, effective style of writing.*

(*The Audubon Book of True Nature Stories,* edited by John K. Terres; Thomas Y. Crowell Company, 1958.)

At first, there is only an enveloping darkness. Darkness and the feel of warmth against him as his tiny newborn body lies intimately with the bodies of his litter-fellows, and in his nostrils the primal smell of the inner earth, root-damp, grass-sweet, humid, and utterly enclosing. This is the initial life experience of the chipmunk. These are the first uncomprehended knowings that in the May of the year come to newborn *Tamias* (the steward, the prudent husbandman), lying blind and naked in the central chamber of the burrow, a foot

or two underneath the blossoming bloodroots and yellow adder's tongue of the Outer World, but accessible only by a long and twisting tunnel through which no light can enter. Safety is here, in the friendly darkness: a dim contentment to pervade his uninstructed blood. This, and the already-stirring impulsions of instinct, of the hereditary unlearned lores which are the central wisdom of a little *Tamias* as much as of a hunting wolf or a migrating warbler or, not very differently, a chemically obedient milkweed that "knows" it must thrust its hairy stalk toward the hot sun.

In the quiet earth-darkness, blind and tiny, the baby chipmunk stirs and frets a little, and knows what he must know. He raises his infant muzzle, kneading and nuzzling the furry warmth that is the belly of his mother. He seizes upon a small teat and sucks a drop of chipmunk milk, and now an enormous peace, a quiet fulfillment, possess him utterly. He lies wholly tranquil now. There is a warmth, there is darkness, there is the smell of the enwombing earth, there is the taste of milk. He falls asleep.

This is the texture of the chipmunk's infancy, in the warm security of the grass-lined nest.

The weeks go by, and in the Outer World there is great change. Now is the season of tremendous happening, of the great annual thrust and drive and upward-rushing of the life-force in its myriad forms. The robins and bluebirds have nested now, the mayflies have danced their brief fantastic dance in the twilight, the woods and meadows have been caught up in an omnipresent tumult of greenness and aliveness and flowering and growing and singing. It is the time of the blue-winged warblers brooding; and the damsel-fly nymphs crawling from the brook water; and the young night herons, raucous and ungainly, making their first explorations of the mudflats and swamplands in the dusk.

It is nearly June. And in this time of metamorphosis and new life, of countless beginnings and maturings as earth draws toward its summer solstice, there has come change also to the chipmunk in his dark withdrawn birth-world. He has grown from the unknowingness of blind and naked infancy and is ready for adulthood. For many days now, since not long after his eyes opened, black and bright as little chokeberries, and his little squirrel-body took on the striated pelage that is the unmistakable coat of chipmunkhood, he has made explorations of his subterranean universe.

On swift scampering feet he has pattered, endlessly inquisitive, along the galleries of the burrow. He has explored that chamber, below the frostline, where there are mounded husks of hickory nuts, and that other chamber, reached by a long zigzagging route, where there are stored perhaps acorns and beechnuts; and he has been tempted to nibble at them, and so his weaning has come about. He knows now how to hold a nut in his adroit forepaws, twisting and turning it, and strip the husk from it with his sharp little incisors. He knows the uses of the pouches in his cheeks, and how they may be stuffed with foods that are to be carried from place to place; and he has acquired that curious and necessary chipmunk knowledge which tells him that when acorns are to be stuffed into his cheek pouches the sharp tips of the nuts must first be bitten off.

A little of all these things he has learned by experience, by trial and error, in his early explorings and investigations of the dark galleried world. But only a little. Mostly his knowledges have come to him as instinct. They have developed in him as his little lithe striped body has developed, will-lessly, without his taking thought of it. His acorn lore is as sure, and as uncalculated, as the instinct that prompted him a little while ago to suck the tiny milky dugs of his mother; or the instinct that a little later sent him pattering, curious and restless, through the galleries of the burrow; or the instinct that now in recent days has led him to engage in rough-and-tumble playings and frolickings with his brothers and sisters. These are the inheritance of his chipmunk blood. He obeys them. The sweet pungence of hickory nuts is meaningful to him, from the first; the scampering quickfooted gait he has developed now is not a privately decided thing, as a man's gait may be, but a hereditary and general chipmunk thing, inalienable from his blood, as a skunk's lumbering waddle is the changeless skunk way or a coon's heavy plantigrade plodding is the unreckoned and necessary movement of a coon.

To young *Tamias,* as to every other animal, the life experience presents itself as a series of external phenomena touching off spontaneous inner responses. In these last days of immaturity, now, the frolicking and anticking of his brothers and sisters arouses in him an excited urgency to tumble and tussle with them; and, as always, he follows impulse—"the subconscious faith of the animals"—and his education and development are carried one stage further. There are squeakings and chitterings and scamperings in the burrow now, and small furry body tumbling and wrestling with small furry body; and what is happening is that young chipmunk muscles are being made finally strong, and chipmunk coordinations made fully sure and quick, and the last preparation for life in the Outer World being effected.

Young *Tamias* has no knowing that this is so. The mind of a chipmunk is not a private mind. It is but participant in "the general intelligence of nature" (that *Mysterium Tremendum* ultimately no less inscrutable to philosophers than to chipmunks); and chipmunk destiny is forwarded by no private guesses, no deductive inferences, no shrewd concludings, but by the interior and unrealized impellings which forward likewise the destinies of negatively phototropic earthworms, positively phototropic bees, tactilely sensitive and obediently reflexive beavers when with unconscious and exquisite precision they fell a birch. The psyche of little *Tamias* is not made for thinking. No wild thing's is. It is made for feeling and acting. To play has a good feel; it fulfills an obscure desire. In the earth-darkness, under the tansy stems, *Tamias* plays.

The chipmunk looks nearly like his parents now. His squirrel body is almost six inches long, and his flattened furry tail almost four. The five black stripes that run from his shoulders to his rump are bright and sharp, as is the narrow little black stripe through his eye; and his short rounded ears are prominent on his tawny skull. His thick fur is warmly reddish and chestnut-colored now, clearest and warmest on his small rump and on his delicate little paws, and all his chipmunk powers that will fit him for the Outer World have come to their maximum development: the bright and watchful-eyed alertness, the sharpness of scent and hearing, the ingenuity of forepaws that are like little hands and that can dig a hollow in the sun-baked earth or hold delicately the smallest seed, the sharpness of twenty little chipmunk-teeth.

It is the time to go alone, to be an adult. The smell of his mother's fur has ceased now to attract him irresistibly, as the presence of light ceases in autumn to attract a wintering queen wasp; and the darkness of the burrow dimly oppresses him. There is a new impulsion now, urging him and tugging at his blood. It is the attraction of the sunlit world that lies outside the burrow-mouth—the free and windswept and sky-arched world where there are new foods to be found and hoarded, tree boles to be investigated, enemies to be outwitted and evaded, the unhampered and exultant life of an adult animal to be lived. On a summer morning, the young chipmunk patters to the burrow-mouth, peeps out, and is gone. He has come to his majority.

The lives of all animals, from the greatest to the least, are ruled by four chief necessities. These are the necessities to feed, to have a lair, to breed, and to be wary against death. There are other ingredients, of course, in the life pattern; there is play, for example, and there is the dim half-drowsing resting, the obscure and relaxed hours of inactive and dreaming peace, that are a major part of living in the woods and meadowlands. But the four great necessities are paramount; and to these, as every animal must do, the small chipmunk comes to devote his adult attentions.

His feeding is enormous and almost omnivorous. Unlike the gray squirrels and the red squirrels, he is not impelled to extensive climbing in the treetops, to nibble at sweet elm seeds and maple keys and greening hickory nuts. Mostly he is a ground feeder. Restless, quick-footed, with fuzzy little tail straight out behind, he scampers along old stone fences, patters through the meadow grass, scurries and scuttles in the underbrush, his keen inquisitive little muzzle alert for the scents that mean provender. Grains of all kinds are welcome to him; seeds of a hundred sorts, berries, and nuts.

To the chipmunk, as to most animals that are largely vegetarian, the procuring of food presents little of a problem. He need not hunt for prey, as a hawk must; his diet lies everywhere around him. Only rarely, as the weeks pass and he makes his scampering rounds of the weed tops and the berry bushes, does he feel an inadequacy in his diet, a need for a taste that grain and berries do not give. When this happens, he takes to the treetops. There are birds' nests there, some with fledglings in them in the latter summer, and *Tamias* is able, when he wants, to clamber up to them as ingeniously as any red squirrel. He is as deft with an egg as with a nut. With the taste of egg yolk or the taste of warm blood in his little gullet, he is satisfied and returns to the ground again to resume his vegetarian feeding. Not often does his periodical carnivorousness become such a habit that he presents a peril to birdlife. It is a hunger that comes to him only rarely, like his hunger for grasshoppers and crickets, and like the recurrent appetite which may sometimes send him creeping softly into a nest of the little deer mice, to pounce on the litter and devour them as eagerly as though he were a weasel. Mostly *Tamias* goes peaceably, harmlessly, through the woods-world, stuffing his cheeks with acorns, squeaking and chittering and flirting his tail at the astonishments and excitements of the universe, preparing the seed hoards which have earned him his Latin name of steward.

Second only to feeding, as a major rite in his life, is the chipmunk's making of his burrow It must be at once his storehouse and his refuge from enemies, and he has not been long an adult before he sets about its construction. In a secluded place—under a fallen log, perhaps, or in the shelter of a boulder—he begins to dig a hole. As he works, he throws the excavated earth behind him as a woodchuck does. Down sharply for a foot or so he tunnels, and then on a more gradual slope for a yard or two; and then, below the level to which the frost is likely to reach, the corridor is dug laterally. The chipmunk extends it yard after yard, making it only about two inches in diameter (an adequate accommodation for his own lithe little body, but readily barricaded against weasels); and presently he begins to work at ramifications that will be storage rooms. These he hollows and scoops until they are big enough so that any one of them can hold several quarts of seeds and nuts, and he may construct as many as three or four. In the root-smelling darkness, absorbed and furiously laboring little *Tamias* finishes the storage rooms, the long lateral corridors, the central sleeping place; and then he tunnels gradually upward to make the exit into the Outer World again.

Because this exit hole has been dug from below, there is no accumulation of excavated earth thrown out around it—no telltale sign which might let an enemy know of the burrow's presence. And so, when the chipmunk has come up through this unobtrusive orifice into the Outer World again, the instinctive wisdom of his ancestral chipmunk blood leads him to do an extraordinary and unconsciously very cunning thing, wise with that old earth-wisdom that is anterior to the intellect. He scampers to the original entrance hole, where earth perforce was thrown out as he excavated, and with swift dexterousness piles the earth into the hole again and scatters the surplus. Every sign of the telltale digging is obliterated, and the hole stoppered tight shut. As a final act of concealment, *Tamias* carries leaves and bits of grass to the site and layers it over until every evidence of his work has been hidden. His burrow now has only the inconspicuous entrance which was originally its exit, and over this the tangle of weeds and underbrush will quickly grow a concealing screen.

Tamias does not know the why of what he has done—any more than an orb-weaving spider knows the why, or a dauber wasp when it paralyzes the spider for its young, or infant *Tamias* when he suckled in the spring—but the inherited behests of his blood have been fulfilled, and he has now an obscure peace of accomplishment, and nature has been wise for him.

All the rest of the summer the chipmunk's life follows now a not greatly varying pattern. Very early in the morning, before dawn, he awakens in his sleeping chamber and comes scampering to the door of the burrow and sets forth for his day's feeding. His universe is a smell of hickory nuts, a pungence of weed seeds and of dawn-damp earth to which his little muzzle is so close, an exultancy in the unrationalized awareness of his little chipmunk aliveness.

Nibbling, scurrying, searching, gnawing . . . this is his preoccupation. Occasionally there comes to his rounded furry ears the squalling scream of a hovering hawk, or there is detectable in his small quivering nostrils the rank odor of a fox or the thin musky odor of a gliding snake; and he darts then back to his burrow or to one of the shallower auxiliary burrows which he may have dug in concealed places nearby and among which he has established, by repetition, a quite regular route of travel. If it is to his main burrow that he has recourse for safety, he approaches it in a curious fashion. He rushes to it in high leaping bounds, almost such leaps, in miniature, as a white-tailed deer makes; and he is careful not to follow the same track that he followed the last time he came home. It is chipmunk tactic, natively instinctive, to ensure that with the passing of time he will not beat a regular and visible trail to the burrow's hidden entrance hole.

Feeding and being watchful against enemies: these are the chipmunk's central activities. For the rest, there is endless exploration to satisfy his curiosity; there is dozing near the burrow entrance or atop an old stump when he is well fed with seeds and the dreamy contentment steals over him that steals over all wild things when they are well fed and unpursued; and, not least, there are sometimes playing and singing.

The life-exultancy can well up in a small chipmunk even as in a caracoling deer or a ceremoniously dancing caribou; and now and then little *Tamias,* stirred by that clamorous gladness, may frisk and frolic and tumble in an exuberance of play. Hearing the sharp "*Chip!*" of another of his kind, he may answer; and from elsewhere in near woods or fields others may likewise make their little chipmunk utterance; and for many minutes together there may be a chorus of callings and answerings. Partly, in latter summer, it is perhaps what biologically is called a "pseudo-mating," like the performance of the spotted newts. But much of the while it is something else, something simpler. Animal life, even the least and littlest, like *Tamias'*, has in it the element of a simple primal exultation.

On a day in the autumn the chipmunk feels a diminishing of his vitality. The coursing life force that has made him flirt his little tail and scrabble vigorously in the earth and chitter with his fellows has suddenly dwindled, with the coming of frost into the air. For several weeks now he has been filling his cheek pouches ever more busily, bringing back grains and seeds in loads of more than two tablespoonfuls at a time, storing them assiduously in his underground vaults until there has come to be a hoard of more than half a bushel. Instinctive chipmunk lore has served him again, in this gathering of his supplies; and he has brought into the burrow no berries or grains which may spoil from a long keeping. Now, with his granaries full and the sharpness of autumn in the air, he has felt the stealing over him of a growing lethargy. There is not the impulse, now, to be up before the dawn; there is no wanting to rush and scamper and chirrup and be endlessly inquisitive. There is a wanting only of quiet, and a love (as in infant days, six months ago in the spring) of the cool root-scented darkness of the under-earth. The blood says now: Be quiet. The drive of instinct says now: Hush, rest.

In the spring it will be time to mate. It will be time to wake, nibbling at grains and seeds stored prudently against that need, and time to scamper with all the rush and vitality of abounding chipmunkhood. But now it is the time to hibernate. It is the time for bats and bears and little five-striped beasts with flattened furry tails to have their winter sleep.

The chipmunk lies in his central sleeping chamber, curled into a ball, relaxed, motionless. Around him, as in babyhood, there is only the darkness, the smell of the grass-sweet earth, the enwombing silence. His breathing grows slow, slower. His heartbeat quiets. The winter has come now; and *Tamias,* the steward, the prudent husbandman, has done what he must do and known what he must know. It is very quiet here, dark and protecting. He sighs a little shallowly, and enters into an enormous nothingness.

LIKE CRUSOE, I DISCOVER AN ISLAND

BY LEONARD DUBKIN

Leonard Dubkin (1911 —) was born on Christmas day in Odessa, Russia, but was brought to this country as a small boy and has been a Chicagoan most of his life. Fascinated by nature, he began writing about the city's birds and insects while still in his teens. He looked for, and found, nature in the midst of busy streets and towering buildings, and has been writing about it ever since. A newspaperman on a Chicago daily, he writes a weekly column about nature, and in his spare time he continues to make his unlikely discoveries in unexpected places, and to write books about them. This selection is from Enchanted Streets, *which is subtitled "The Unlikely Adventures of an Urban Nature Lover." It represents the guileless way Mr. Dubkin writes as well as the way he sees the city's remarkable secrets through eyes that have never lost their young gleam of wonder.*

(*Enchanted Streets*, by Leonard Dubkin; Little, Brown and Company, 1947.)

The season was nearing its end, and I was still coming downtown every day to look for work. But the necessity for finding a job had somehow lost its extreme urgency, and my mind was no longer filled with foreboding, with fears of the future when I should be starving and homeless. The truth of the matter was that I had become adjusted to the state of being unemployed, and, though I did not like it, though it still embarrassed me to be asked by some acquaintance what I was doing these days, I was finding it not as unpleasant as I had thought it would be. I had been out of work all summer, and I could go on being out of work for another month or two, or as long as it took me to find a job.

I was bringing my lunch downtown with me every day now, a couple of sandwiches and an apple or an orange in a paper bag. It was a little inconvenient carrying a bundle under my arm while I went about applying for a job in answer to Help Wanted advertisements in the morning paper, but it was cheaper than eating in restaurants, and I enjoyed eating my noonday meal out of doors, sitting on a park bench or on the grass in Grant Park. The routine of my days was about as follows: I would buy a newspaper in the morning and look through the Help Wanted section on my way downtown on the streetcar. If there were any ads that looked promising (it could never be more than a promise, for Help Wanted ads are always couched in such devious, obscure terms, their offers and their requirements wrapped in such ambiguity, that only one who has answered the same ad before can be certain whether the offer is a good one, or contains a hidden "joker") I would go up to these places, fill out an application and answer a few questions. Then, if it was still early, I would go up to one of the newspaper offices to see the city editor or talk to some friend. About eleven o'clock, wherever I happened to be, I would start walking east, cross Michigan Boulevard and then one of the bridges over the I.C. tracks, and sit down in Grant Park, which was usually deserted at that time of day, to eat my lunch.

After lunch I would sit in the grass for an hour or two, with my back against a tree trunk or leaning on one elbow watching the insects. Sometimes I would lie on my back under a tree looking up through the branches. If you have never lain under a tree on a summer's day, looking up through the twirling leaves at the blue sky, then you have no conception of what complete and absolute repose is like. At first, when you have stretched out full length on the grass, it will seem a ridiculous position to be in, and there will be all sorts of minor annoyances, a pebble under your head, a little hill under your back, or an ant crawling up your ear. But as you continue to lie there gazing upward through the branches you will soon begin to lose all consciousness of the earth beneath you, there will be only the green leaves and the blue sky and perhaps a little white cloud floating by, with your body suspended in space just below them. If there are a few low clouds moving rather swiftly you will soon find yourself wondering whether it is actually the clouds that are in motion, or your body that is floating under the tree.

One day there seemed to be more people than usual in Grant Park, sitting about on the benches and walking over the grass, so rather than eat my lunch there I continued walking east and crossed the bridge onto Northerly Island. This island was built, I believe—that is, the lake was filled in to make it—for the World's Fair in 1933. Now there is only one building on it, the low, round-domed Adler Planetarium; the rest of the island is flat and desolate, with no trees or bushes, and bordered with huge rocks to keep the waves from washing over it. People who come to the island to visit the Planetarium, to watch the whole universe reflected in miniature on the dome of the lecture room, seldom step off the paved walk that circles the building. And why should they? They have just ranged the heavens, they have ventured into interstellar space while a lecturer explained the motions of the heavenly bodies. Would it not be ridiculously anticlimactic to exhibit any curiosity about the desolate, muddy little island on which the Planetarium stands?

After I had eaten my lunch on the island the first time, I spent the rest of the afternoon there, and in the days that followed I went there quite often with my lunch, for I found it very interesting. There was not the wealth of insect and bird life that could sometimes be found on the mainland, but on the other hand there were creatures there that were seldom or never seen in other parts of the city. A few rabbits hopped about among the rocks, field mice scurried through the grass, a small turtle sometimes came up to sun itself on the rocks, and a few times I saw garter snakes disappearing into holes in the ground. The turtle, of course, came from the lake, but the rabbits, mice and snakes had probably come over the bridge during the night, when the island and the bridge leading to it were dark and unfrequented.

Occasionally I saw some bird on the island that I had not seen before in the city, and I would carefully note its coloring, size, shape and other characteristics, and, when I got home that evening, try to identify it by the pictures and descriptions in a little worn bird guide I had used ever since I was a boy. This sounds simple—one had merely to look through the book until one found a picture of the bird one had seen. But actually it was a discouraging business. In the first place, the pictures showed mounted birds, which had probably been touched up with a little paint here and there to make them look more lifelike. If I had only seen a robin once in my life, a quick, hurried glance as it paused on a branch of a tree or flew by overhead, I could never have identified it from the picture of the large, sedate, crimson-breasted bird they called a robin in the bird guide. Other bird pictures, for example Audubon's, while they are fine works of art, are almost as ineffectual for purposes of identification. I have seen a number of the birds Audubon painted, and they have seemed drab and colorless compared to his pictures; nor have I ever seen any of them adopt the "natural" poses in which he painted them.

Another factor that makes identification difficult is the fact that one's memory can seldom be depended on to retain the minor but often important details of a bird's plumage and coloring. Did a small bird one saw for a few seconds this morning have a black bill, or was it yellow? Did it have brown stripes under its wings? Was it 5.2 inches long, or 5.8 inches? These details often determine whether the bird belonged to one species, or to another. As for the other descriptive details one finds in bird guides—number, color and markings of eggs, construction and placement of nest, type of food, range, and so on—I have never found this information of any value to me. Perhaps if I had actually become a naturalist, as I planned, the fact that I had memorized many of these descriptions when I was a boy would have stood me in good stead. I doubt it, though.

One afternoon as I sat on a flat rock on Northerly Island I saw a flock of ten or twelve fairly large birds fly over my head and land a short distance away. I got up and went toward them, then stood for a few minutes watching them as they walked about among the rocks, pecking at things on the ground. From their long legs and the odd way they walked about, their necks stretched straight out before them, I guessed that they were some sort of plover. I had never seen plover in the city before, though I have heard that they are common in some of the suburbs, and in the forest preserves.

As I turned to go back to the rock on which I had been sitting I noticed two women standing on the walk that circles the Planetarium, looking at me through field glasses and waving their arms frantically. I stood looking at them for a time, wondering what they were so excited about, and then, as they continued to wave their arms in the air, I walked up the hill toward them. They were both middle-aged women, smartly dressed, and I could see that the field glasses they were looking through were powerful and expensive.

"What's the matter?" I asked when I reached them.

"We were motioning for you to get away from those birds," one of the women said. "We were afraid you might frighten them off. You see, we're from the ornithological society."

"Oh," I said. "What kind of birds were they?"

"Black-bellied plover. We thought there might be a phalarope among them, but there wasn't. You haven't seen a phalarope around here, have you?"

I had only a vague idea of what a phalarope looked like, from having seen pictures of it long ago, but I was certain I had not seen one, so I said, "No, I haven't."

"Oh, dear," said one woman, "I suppose we never will see it. This is the third time we've driven out here to look for it."

"But why are you so anxious to see a phalarope?" I asked.

"Don't you see, it would be quite a feather in our caps. None of the other society members have ever seen a phalarope in the city, so when a young fellow told us Saturday that he had seen one out here on the island we hurried right over. But we haven't had any luck yet."

I said I hoped they would see it, and walked away, leaving them searching the island through their field glasses. As I walked back to my rock I smiled at the thought of these two smartly dressed matrons coming out to this island time after time in search of a bird no other member of the ornithological society had seen. It was amusing, and yet it was a little pathetic. I could not help feeling sorry for them. They were typical of all mankind in its seeking for the rare, the unusual, the exotic. People were always wanting to climb a peak that had never been scaled before, or to be the first to set foot in a new land, or to fly higher or faster than anyone had ever flown before. There was fame and glory in being the first, and yet it seems to me that little of any real worth to humanity has ever come from mere discoverers. If Columbus had not discovered this continent when he did, someone else would have found it soon afterward. Our debt is not to him, but to the patient, plodding, unimaginative men and women who came after him, who built their homes in the wilderness and endured the hardships of a hostile environment that they might lead a life of greater freedom from restraint.

But to most people Columbus and Lindbergh are greater men than Lincoln and Franklin Roosevelt, and the philosophy that makes this view possible permeates our civilization. A man is proud of being a citizen of the greatest country on earth, he lives in the largest meat-producing city in the world, would not miss going to the movies when they are showing the most stupendous production ever filmed, and is told after an operation that he had the largest appendix the doctor had ever seen. There are always enough "firsts" and "biggests" and "smallests" to go around; even the humblest of men can have a few.

Why should it be so important to be the first to do a thing, or the last? To grow the largest tomatoes in one's garden, or be the first to come to work in the morning? The important thing about an action one performs, it seems to me, is not its order in some external sequence, but its effect on oneself, and on one's environment. The pleasure I experience when I see a robin in March is not heightened by the fact that it is the first robin I have seen that year, even if I know that I am the first person in the north who has seen one. My pleasure is like that of meeting an old friend whom I have not seen for a long time, and of knowing that now I will see him frequently.

And so it seemed pathetic to me to see these two women who had come out to Northerly Island to see a bird, and to realize that their interest in birds was only a form of vanity, a desire for the adulation of their fellow society members. With all the birds about, with the city full of pigeons and sparrows and starlings and robins and grackles and nighthawks, each species having habits and a mode of life that was fascinating to study, they came out here day after day with their field glasses to look for a phalarope so they could have the honor of being the first to see one in the city.

For a few days I had been watching a certain spot between two boulders on the island, for once I had caught a quick glimpse of some brown fur disappearing between the rocks. Then one day a small brown head with a pointed face peered out at me as I sat a little distance away eating my lunch. I saw no more of it that day, but the following afternoon the animal came out in the open and took a few steps toward me, sniffing the air cautiously. As soon as I saw the lithe brown body, with the back humping upward as it walked, I knew it was a weasel. In the days that followed, this weasel and I became about as friendly as a wild weasel and a man can get—that is, if I sat perfectly still for an hour or so, he would deign to creep up and sniff at my shoe.

This weasel had a family somewhere, between those rocks, a female that was slightly smaller than himself and two half-grown cubs. Neither the female nor her cubs ever came out while I was sitting there, but sometimes as I came out to the island I would see the four of them frolicking on the ground or sunning themselves on a rock. As soon as I came close, however, they would all disappear.

I suppose I might have come to know this weasel family better, but I didn't think it was worth either the effort or the time that would have been required. It was difficult to sit motionless for long periods just to have the one weasel come out and sniff my shoe, and I suppose I might have had to sit even longer before the mother and cubs would come out. Furthermore, weasels are not normally inhabitants of a city, and they have no rightful place in this book. Out in the country they may be beautiful, interesting, delightful little creatures; but when they decide to make their home in the city one cannot have much respect or admiration for them: they are outlanders intent on preserving their own way of life in their new surroundings, like foreigners who come to this country but insist on keeping their old habits and speaking their native language.

Besides, it was at this time that I got a job.

A SHORT LIFE BUT A FULL ONE

BY GUSTAV ECKSTEIN

Gustav Eckstein (1890 —) was born in Cincinnati, educated at the University of Cincinnati and at Harvard. He summarizes his biography thus: "Born, practiced dentistry, studied medicine, taught physiology, learned not much, read two or three men, learned a little, came to know two or three women, learned a good deal, made friends with two rats, learned prodigiously, wrote about the rats, continued to write." Actually, Dr. Eckstein has taught, lectured and written a great deal, and now is a member of the Department of Psychiatry at the University of Cincinnati, "a slight job but interesting and new to me." He has written biography, fiction, plays, and three books about animals. This selection is from one of those books, Lives, *and shows what an unusual man he is and how quietly and eloquently he writes. It is one of the most poignant pieces of writing I know, and it is about nature observed on the desk of a researcher in his laboratory office.*

(*Lives*, by Gustav Eckstein; Harper & Brothers, 1932.)

I had got to be a doctor, a man of science, and took a tiny creature, a thing so small it sat with comfort in the palm of my hand,

and cut into its skull and removed a tip of its brain. Science has not got much by that, but possibly a few rats have, for he taught me, that little white rat, and I have changed my mind about many things.

The little white rat survived my cunning. There was no mutilation of any function that is commonly said to lodge in the brain. His thought was clear, his spirit brave, he could guide his body, and his length of life seemed even increased, for he reached what in our terms is a hundred years.

The moon tonight is full and flooding through the window. He runs from his chamber—a box that I have set at one end of my roll-top desk—to his granary, a drawer on the other side and below. Back and forth, back and forth. He has been running that way for a month of nights. In the day he sleeps, only with the darkening opens his amber nervous eyes, casts about him, wonders what he missed while away, then yawns, a mighty yawn, and scratches like a mountebank by the side of his ear, and scrubs his face. Scrubs rather his head, the whole of it, uses both hands and the lengths of his arm. And now he cleans his tail, cleans that particularly, knowing that never a healthy rat but a clean one. Then back and forth, back and forth, and back and forth again. Suddenly he stops, just in the middle of the top of the desk, and one would say he was porcelain did he not sway and lean far out. It is the moon. He is bathed in the moon's flood. He is struck. He is queer.

She I bring him is a tiny thing. In the half-dark she trembles like a patch of that very moonlight. She rushes, in those first hours, explores, all this new, is pleased, but vouchsafes him no solitary glance. He is gone to his corner. He watches steadily from there.

I had always said he might have the top of the desk and the upper three drawers, and he had always kept to that, but she now lives everywhere, bites through the back of the upper drawer, lets herself hang and drop, and by that strategy coming thus from the rear, is in possession of all, immediately bringing her belongings, really his belongings and my belongings—one leap from the top to where I drive my distracted pen, another leap to the drawer, and thereafter subterranean grumblings and thuds and perturbations.

He cannot understand it—this fine slender woman, that she should be so material. What can she think of doing with it all? What does she dream?

I cannot understand either—his bedding, his food, my pencil, my pens, the cork of my ink bottle, the eraser with the chewable rubber at one end, the chewable tuft of brush at the other. Hour after hour diagonally across my work she goes, head held high to keep what she carries above her flying feet. In human distances it must be twenty miles. Certainly more than the tiny burnings of that tiny body drive that machine. Only late does she cease. She looks where he huddles uncovered in his chamber. She seems to think him over. She comes to a conclusion. She waddles toward him, settles into him, drops her head, is ostensibly asleep. He cannot sleep. He does not even close his eyes, squats there motionless, almost breathless, is afraid he may disturb her. I pick up the few gnawed bits of my belongings, turn out the lights.

Three weeks ago was the wedding. So soon as I arrived this morning she made me comprehend it was newspaper she wanted. I brought her a newspaper. She put her foot on it, as if to establish possession, then looked at me hard.

"A single newspaper?"

I brought her an armful.

All day she stuck to the job, did not eat, did not drink. I placed food and drink before her. She ran around them. When I persisted she ran through them, trailed them. The paper she tore into strips, leaped with the strips into the drawer, there continued the tearing, each strip into squares. By noon an inch of squares bedded the bottom of the drawer. By evening, three inches. By midnight five. And now, shortly after, she is ready to rest. Still she has not eaten. I ask her again. She only turns her head.

Poor husband now and then has tried to tear a little paper too, but it was not in his character, a big bulging character. This new young wife has made great changes in our ways, his and mine. A hush lies over the establishment. I sit before my desk, but do not work. She sits by my side. She is thinking her thoughts. And so is he. And so am I.

Next morning the mother and father are moving about. Mother is thin. They are thirteen, if I count them right, and they wiggle and worm and topple and tumble. She will not eat even now, and he does not find it easy, either. He is bewildered. How can anything like that have happened? I try to explain to him, but I do not rightly understand, myself, and he climbs heavily out of the drawer, and on my arm, and in my pocket hides his confused head. By evening, however, he has talked it over with her, and she has told him something I could not, and in consequence he is licking her, and she is licking them, and he is so interested in what he is doing that he steps all over them, and they squeak and step over one another, the smallest the most stepped on. No one in the heap seems able to take in the whole of the heap. That is somehow sad.

Three out of the litter I intended to leave little mother, but she would have a big family or none. At least she was indifferent to three. Two I found when I came on the fourth morning, dead. The third I never found, though, fearing it might have got into difficulty, I looked under every square of paper. I regret they are gone. They had the color and somewhat the form of the fingers of the newborn baby. The little pink legs were so weak that they dragged, and the little pink tails dragged symmetrically between them. Boneless they seemed, and sightless they were, and they kept up an aimless motion.

Mother appears unconcerned about what has happened, but I am not sure, for mother is hidden deep under her white hair, and perhaps is hidden deeper even than that. At any rate, father, who knows her better than I, is more solicitous today than usual. He picks her vermin with a more insistent care. She lies there very flat, spreads a maximum of surface to the smooth cool table below, and the maximum of surface to the great father above. The exertion makes him pant. As to his feelings about the babies, I believe they were mixed. Thirteen was too many, and though they were lovely, it must be admitted they were restless.

Both are asleep. I reach into the chamber to pet the back of mother's heaving neck. She starts. She bites me. It is not much of a bite and she is grieved. She probably thought I was coming for one of the brood. She glances nervously about, finds it hard to recollect.

Toward ten every evening the two take turns to bathe. I have fitted a board across the basin under the tap where the water drips one drop at a time. To be wet all over makes them very weak and very unhappy, but to catch one drop, and wash vigorously with that, and then catch another, that is different. I myself also look forward to it—to see the way they rise from the board, put out those marvelous hands, and wait for the drop.

Father this morning is lying on his side, his two hands folded just under his nose, as if he had fallen asleep in prayer. Father's sleep is pictured with dreams. I can tell by the way he waves the tip of his tail, and when the dream gets too vivid he turns, settles on his belly, sidles over to where mother is sleeping on her belly. Then he scratches his head. A little later he scratches his head again. This time he wakens sufficiently to realize that though he is scratching his head he feels nothing. Promptly he scratches again, and still feels nothing. It is a condition so peculiar that it breaks his sleep. He opens one eye, not far, but far enough to make out what has happened, for he is scratching not his head but hers, she having pushed hers under his neck and brought it up just inside his right hand. The discovery does not anger him. It does not even surprise him. Gently he puts her head aside, and scratches his own.

Father grows older and older. Then one evening he leaves drawers and desk top. He goes to be an eagle. At least he goes to be an eagle if it is true that yearning has its way. His gaze was always at the edges of his universe.

I am filled with the pain of the shortness of everything. That is a common pain. But it is freshened by the shortness of this little life. His great events were a thirtieth the length of my great events, yet they make mine seem not long, but brief. When I saw his death coming, how truly frightful was the feeling that nothing could stop it. And that also is a common feeling. But this life lay right there in my hand and made my helplessness seem so much more helpless. Good care and good food and warmth would save him an uneasy week, perhaps, and were I able to add all the cunning in the world it would save him another week perhaps. How then must I know with a new strong draft of conviction that gentleness and gaiety are the best of life.

He knew that. He knew how to be affectionate to his friends. To mother he yielded not only what she needed but what she wanted, and what she did not want, what the sweet and lavish extravagance of her youth and sex made her wish only to cast to the winds, cast off the precipice into the dark empty spaces of the universe.

Every night the last months he and I used to play a game. He had too heavy a body, and his legs were too short, and where he walked he rubbed the earth, so it was difficult to pretend to flee ahead of my hand, then abruptly in the midst of that flight to rear on his hind legs, give the length of his body an exaggerated shiver, as in some barbaric dance, and then continue to flee. Yet that was the game.

I think of that now. I think as one does of everything, of the night he made it plain he needed a wife, and how she nevertheless confounded him when she came, and of the litters that passed one by one, and the signs of maturity, how they passed, and the signs of age, and all in my hand, he learning every day to be less a rat, and then the final sharpness, how he mastered even that, grew gentler and gentler, and one night went to be an eagle.

Poor little mother! Babies gone and father gone. I describe how it is with father this morning, how he is off to the Peruvian mountains, and how, a short distance below the highest peak, where there is a good shelter against the blasts of the south, under great wings, nudging his brothers and sisters, he is beginning again, is waiting, though perhaps he knows it not, for little mother.

I put my hand into the dark of the drawer, and she pretends my fingers are the whilom family. She scrubs them roughly one by one. She crawls under them, crawls over them, goes round the nails and up into the crotches. She scrubs them thoroughly, and when each is done bites it, bumps it aside. I talk to her. She answers out of the dark. Father never would use his voice. Hers is a kind of cluck, and after she has spoken she is quiet. And I am quiet. Each of us has it in mind to wait on what the other will do. But she never can wait, must at least turn round, shove her little self through a quarter of a circle, then fix me with one great glowing eye. What she sees of me with that eye I have no notion. Nor have I any notion of what she makes of what she sees, more than that it is an embodiment with which in her loneliness she finds it possible to commune.

MAMMALS WITHIN THE CITY GATES

BY JOHN KIERAN

John Kieran (1892 —) was born in New York City, educated at the College of the City of New York and Fordham University. A versatile scholar and prolific writer, he was a daily-newspaper reporter and sports columnist for many years and became a naturalist largely by chance. Once launched in that career, however, he became an accomplished ornithologist and a botanist of distinction though almost entirely self-taught. His later years have been spent in large part observing and writing about nature, and his Natural History of New York City *is as nearly definitive a popular work as we have in that field. This selection from that book shows his knowledge of animal life, still another facet of his wide-ranging interest, which was so well known during his brilliant years as a panelist on the "Information, Please" radio and television program. He now lives at Rockport, Massachusetts, and has become an authority on the shore birds of that area.*

(*Natural History of New York City,* by John Kieran; Houghton Mifflin Company, 1959.)

Just as a matter of record, the resident citizens outnumber any other kind of mammal to be found within the confines of New York

City. But our business is with the quadruped mammals, a group from which Man is separated by physical, mental, moral, and spiritual attributes best explained or expounded by poets, professors, philosophers, or theologians. In the field of anthropology it is enough to state that this city probably—yea, almost certainly—contains representatives or descendants of all the known races of Man under the sun. It also contains a great many more "wild animals" than most of the human inhabitants suspect. And a considerable number of tame or domestic animals, too.

It's curious how we have grown into the habit of using the term animal as though it applied exclusively to four-footed mammals. We forget or ignore the fact that fish, birds, insects, and oysters belong to the Animal Kingdom, too. This is thoroughly unscientific but quite clear to readers or listeners and thus no great harm is done. We also make another distinction based on civilization rather than the laws of nature. We have "domestic animals" and "wild animals." Although the wild kind are more interesting, we must take stock of the city supply of domestic animals such as farm animals and cats and dogs. Farm animals, of course, are a minor matter but cats and dogs often make the headlines in the city's newspapers.

Although some farms and truck gardens are still to be found within the city limits, with the steady increase of buildings for business and residential purposes, the comparatively few farm animals of the area—the horses, cows, sheep, pigs, and goats—are a vanishing group. Those that survive these days are kept under regulations and conditions set forth by the Department of Health. But dogs and cats are a problem and often a cause of personal or neighborhood warfare between those who own them or love them and those who, while they may or may not love them, wish to banish them from the pavements of the crowded sections of the city.

By arrangement with the city authorities, dogs are licensed ($2 for the first license, $1 per year for renewals) by the American Society for the Prevention of Cruelty to Animals, a humane society that has done long and faithful service in alleviating the hardships and cruelties that horses, dogs, cats or, for that matter, any other creatures may be subjected to by thoughtless, selfish, or brutal persons within the city limits. In one recent year the SPCA licensed 276,119 dogs in the city and doubtless there were some running around unlicensed, though the society and the police do their best to track down such tax dodgers. Since cats need no licenses, there is no accurate way of checking on their numbers in the city.

However, one of the functions of the SPCA is to destroy, humanely, unwanted animals or those suffering beyond hope of relief from accident or disease. In the same recent year that saw the licensing of 276,119 dogs, the SPCA humanely destroyed—usually by gas—59,413 dogs and 133,436 cats! From these figures we might arrive at an estimate of the number of cats residing in the city at any given time. Take the figures as normal for any year (there was no indication in the society report that they were unusual in any respect): the dog population runs to about four and one half times the number destroyed in a year. Cats breed faster than dogs and kittens are more often unwanted than puppies; thus the mortality rate in the painless gas chambers would run higher for cats than it does for dogs. Even if we double the death rate in the case of the felines it still would leave us with more cats than dogs—roughly 300,000 cats—in the city. It is a rare thing to find a dog without an owner or a legal place of residence, but hundreds of the city's cats are homeless prowlers.

As for "wild animals" within the city limits, New York has a far larger population of wild quadrupeds than most of the resident bipeds suspect. That's because so many of the wild mammals are small in size and nocturnal in habit, as a result of which they are rarely seen except by those who look for them. We do have, however, some fair-sized mammals that occasionally are seen by daylight. Probably the largest mammal definitely recorded within the city limits in the past century was a young Sperm Whale (*Physeter catodon*) that apparently had lost its mother, followed a steamer into New York Harbor, and suffered an untimely death when it became stranded in Brooklyn's famous Gowanus Canal. The Saddleback or Harp Seal (*Phoca groenlandica*) sometimes is seen offshore at Coney Island in winter and the Harbor Seal (*Phoca vitulina*) occasionally ventures into the Lower Bay in the winter months.

The most primitive mammal in North America is the opossum, a marsupial with the typical nursing pouch for the young and thus a relative of the wallabies, kangaroos, and other native mammals of Australia. Common in the South, the Virginia Opossum (*Didelphous virginiana*) until recently was a rare animal in our territory, but now it is a settled resident and, being a bounteous breeder, it is rapidly increasing in numbers in the vicinity. It is, in fact, extending its range northward and eastward into New England, as are some other forms of life in this retreating Ice Age on the North American Continent.

Our opossum would never take a prize for beauty. It looks too much like a large, blond, long-haired rat with a naked tail almost as long as its body. This tail is prehensile and the animal often hangs by it while feeding in fruit trees. Although it enjoys fruit, the opossum is not a finicky feeder. If need be, it will eat almost anything animal or vegetable, and has a fondness for eggs that makes it unpopular with poultrymen. Despite its sharp teeth, it is a timid animal and rarely puts up a fight if attacked. It is more likely to curl up and pretend to be dead—or, at least, it gives the appearance of putting on such an act, whatever the facts may be.

There are, however, exceptions to customs and family traits. At 2:45 A.M. of April 10, 1955, the police of the Wadsworth Avenue station on Washington Heights in Manhattan were notified that a noisy battle of some kind was raging along Audubon Avenue nearby. Two patrolmen were sent to investigate and found a Virginia Opossum engaged in what the *New York Times* reported to be "a glorious battle with nine alley cats." The plucky opossum was holding its own when rescued and sent to the SPCA shelter. Other opossums visiting the city or living here have not been so fortunate. Doing much of their foraging by night and being leisurely of gait, they occasionally become confused by headlights of autos on the highways at night and are struck and killed by the passing cars. Sometimes a mother opossum will move about in the darkness with half a dozen or more small offspring clinging to the fur on her back.

The Virginia Opossum is the only mammalian newcomer in our area. Most of the others have been natives of the region for thousands of years and even the imported species have been resident for several centuries. Moles, for instance, have been on the ground—or just under the surface—for ages. On park and private lawns and on the fairways of the municipal golf courses there will be found the raised roofs of the tunnels of the Eastern Mole (*Scalopus aquaticus*) and also, in many cases, the upright traps set like guillotines along the tunnels to execute the underground travelers. Moles actually do more good than harm to humans in their way of life, because most of their diet consists of injurious insects in adult or larval form; but they do raise unsightly ridges on otherwise smooth lawns and for that crime they are beset with traps or tempted with poisoned bait put out by indignant gardeners. They may eat some plant roots, as charged. More often the damage done to shrub roots or flower bulbs along mole tunnels is the work of mice who take advantage of the runways dug by the moles.

There is a widespread belief that moles are blind, but such is not the case. They have very small eyes either covered with a thin skin or so effectively concealed in the fur in which they are buried that they easily escape notice even when the animal is in hand. The fur screen undoubtedly obscures the vision of the mole but it also protects the eyes from loose dirt in its digging operations, which is more important. Eyesight is a minor matter to a mole that finds practically all its food by its senses of smell and touch. The Eastern Mole has a chunky roundish body, up to 6 inches or so in length, covered with a coat of thick velvety gray hair that is wonderfully soft to the touch. It also has a short naked tail, barely an inch or so in length and, in typical mole fashion, its front feet are twisted outward and clawed in a way to make them serve as remarkably efficient digging tools in the excavations of their tunnels.

The Starnose Mole (*Condylura cristata*), named for the really astonishing rosette of tiny protuberances at the end of its pinkish nose, is another resident of our region but it is by no means as abundant as the Eastern Mole, nor is it ordinarily a disturber of manicured lawns or treasured flower beds. It prefers wet meadows and the edges of swamps, though occasionally it is caught in traps set for the Eastern Mole. Although the two species are of about the same size, the Starnose is darker in color, almost blackish above, and has a much longer tail. Still another member of the clan that turns up in the area now and then is the Hairytail or Brewer's Mole (*Parascalops breweri*), much like the Eastern Mole in size and color but easily distinguished by the hairy tail that accounts for one of the names applied to this species.

Moles are reputed to be voracious feeders and ferocious fighters for their size. Shrews, which look like short-legged mice but are more nearly allied to the moles, have even worse reputations for gluttonous gorging and vicious dispositions. Some species are said to eat twice their own weight daily, and there are reports of shrew battles in which one contestant killed and ate the other—conduct that we, as humans, are likely to look upon as carrying a family quarrel too far. Shrews are insectivorous mammals, like moles. They differ, however, in that they do not live in tunnels nor are their front feet twisted outward for added efficiency in digging. They forage along the surface of the ground, often under dead leaves and other litter, and you will more often hear them than see them at such work. They do much scratching and no little digging in the pursuit of food, and their tiny but comparatively broad and sharp-clawed front feet are a big help to them in the pursuit of their prey.

Three or four species of shrew are regular inhabitants of our territory. They are seldom seen because they are quite small and generally are working under cover of one kind or another. Occasionally one will "break cover" to run across a path or even scurry across a paved road, but even then they probably are mistaken for mice by those who see them for no more than a few seconds. The Masked Shrew (*Sorex cinereus*) of moist ground in our territory is a tiny grayish-brown creature with a body length of about 2 to 2½ inches and a tail up to 2 inches in length. The larger and darker Shorttail Shrew (*Blarina brevicauda*), which usually is found on higher and drier ground, has a body 3 to 4 inches in length with a fine, close-fitting coat of dark gray fur that looks black at first glance. The tail that accounts for its common name is only an inch or so in length. I often found shrews of this species lying dead on woodland paths in the Riverdale and Van Cortlandt regions. Presumably they were left there by cats who caught them in the underbrush, started to carry them home and then decided to have no more to do with such prey. The proffered explanation is that something about the shrews—the odor or the taste—is disagreeable to cats, so they drop the matter and leave quietly. It is even said that the bite of the little creatures is slightly toxic but perhaps these bad reports about shrews are not due so much to the little animals themselves as they are to the parasitic mites that infest them and perhaps infect them. A third species found in our territory is the Least Shrew (*Cryptotis parva*) that wears a cinnamon or reddish-brown coat by which it may be distinguished from the Masked Shrew of the same approximate size but with a grayish-brown coat. The Least Shrew is a settled resident of Staten Island and the Smoky Shrew (*Sorex fumeus*), slightly larger and dull brown in color, is reported there, too, but I have encountered neither on my home ground at the north end of the city.

We turn swiftly to higher things. Nature anticipated Man in devising an effective sound-ranging system. The bats, our only mammals that can truly fly, are equipped with built-in sound-ranging systems that, by means of emitted high-pitched squeaks and the registering of their reflected echoes in remarkably efficient ears, enable them to avoid solid objects in space that might bring damage or death to them in their flights in the dark. Our species feed entirely on the wing and mostly on insects that are harmful. Bats are odd-looking creatures and possibly even a little frightening in appearance to females who view them as no better than flying mice. They are, however, not a bit dangerous but quite timid and actually beneficial. If by any chance one is discovered in the house, you may be sure it has no desire to entangle itself in a woman's hair, though folklore has charged it with this type of disorderly conduct.

The wings of these flying mammals are merely modified forelegs—or arms and hands, if you will—equipped with thin flexible membranes that, when outspread, serve the same purpose as the flight feathers of birds. At the outer joint of the wing one of the digits—the equivalent of the thumb on the human hand—has been developed into a sharp little hook by means of which the bats are enabled to cling in an upright position on a vertical surface of wood, stone, or brick if they wish, but they also can rest comfortably while clinging to an overhead support with their feet and hanging upside down. Many bats are gregarious and gather in great numbers, particularly for migration or hibernation, as the case may be according to the species.

Of this group of marvelous mammals four species are of common occurrence in New York City and one species at least has been so considerate as to hibernate in a wing of the American Museum of Natural History on Central Park West. That was the Big Brown Bat (*Eptesicus fuscus*), which is big only in comparison with the Little Brown Bat (*Myotis lucifugus*) that has a body about 3 inches or so in length and weighs little more than a five-cent piece. The Big Brown Bat has a body half again as large and a wingspread of a foot or more. Both these species hibernate in caves, barns, church steeples, or any such protected places in the area but the Red Bat (*Lasiurus borealis*), which is between them in size but readily distinguishable by its color, is migratory.

The one common bat of the area whose name gives no hint concerning the color of its fur coat is the Eastern Pipistrel (*Pipistrellus subflavus*). The color is yellowish brown though it looks black as this smallest of our local bats flutters overhead in the dusk. This is the one most often seen in the twilight or gathering dark flitting lightly and silently about the roofs and chimneys of old houses or outbuildings in the more open spaces on the fringe of the city. Often there are Chimney Swifts on the wing with them at twilight and then the noiseless zigzag fluttering of the bats stands out in contrast to the chattering flight of the birds in sweeping curves. A few other species may be encountered in our territory but the Big Brown Bat, the Little Brown Bat, the Red Bat, and the Eastern Pipistrel are the ones that justifiably may be encountered as regular residents of the area and, as far as most New Yorkers are concerned, unsuspected participants in the night life of the city.

If a-hunting he would go, actually it is still possible for a man to go "coon hunting" in the dark of night on the outskirts of the city with a fair chance of bagging some game. However, since it is illegal to hunt within the city limits, the Raccoons (*Procyon lotor*) of the region lead a protected and well-fed existence. They are still present in numbers in the outlying sections of Queens and the Bronx. A good-sized adult Raccoon may weigh fifty pounds or more. They are destructive around poultry yards and vegetable gardens but, aside from that, they are harmless, handsome, and quite amusing animals that tame easily if caught young. The "black domino" or mask across the eye region gives them a sinister appearance, as though they were wrinkling their brows for the plotting of some deep mischief, but it may be only a raid on a row of garbage pails in some sparsely populated section of the city.

They rarely venture out until dusk falls and for that reason they usually escape notice unless some chance encounter discloses their presence in the vicinity. Such was the case in Riverdale recently when, shortly before midnight, a resident turned his dog loose in the yard and a few minutes later heard it yelping excitedly. The householder investigated and found his dog making frantic leaps under an apple tree from which a large Raccoon was looking down, audibly and visibly expressing complete disapproval of the whole proceedings. Up to that moment the dog owner never had suspected the presence of a Raccoon in the vicinity, but for those who know the ways of the wild the long-toed tracks in the mud or the snow indicate that this ring-tailed night-prowler is still a permanent resident of the wilder reaches of the Bronx.

The same thing may be said of the Longtail Weasel (*Mustela frenata*) and the Mink (*Mustela vison*) except that they are not as numerous as the Raccoons and perhaps the Mink is only a visitor, though a regular one, in the region. Dr. William Beebe recounts how, during his years at the Bronx Zoo, he trapped eleven Mink along the Bronx River where it runs through the park and had the skins fashioned into a fur piece for his wife. A few years ago a man was caught trapping Mink in a marshy section of the East Bronx and was fined for doing so without a license. The Longtail Weasel, being a bold animal like all of its tribe, is not a bit afraid of hunting in broad daylight and I have met several of these fearless little fellows poking about in the Van Cortlandt swamp where I also found the telltale tracks of Mink though I never met one of these expensive fur bearers face to face in the area.

As for the Striped Skunk (*Mephitis mephitis*), the fatal and odorous evidence of its presence is found in the flattened corpses of the animals on the motor parkways in the outlying sections of the city. These handsome and harmless—if unmolested—animals trot about at night in leisurely fashion in search of food and, in crossing roads, make little effort to avoid cars. The result often is a strong odor in the dark and a messy mass of black and white fur on the concrete roadway in the morning. Skunks are largely beneficial in their way of life. They feed mostly on insects and fruit but they also catch mice and they are expert in finding the buried egg clutches of the Snapping Turtle. Like the Raccoon, they may do some damage around the poultry yard or the kitchen garden, but on the whole they are amiable creatures that do not turn loose their "liquid fire" unless they are frightened or provoked.

Probably the largest resident wild animals in the city are the foxes that are comparatively few in number but persistent in the northerly section of the Bronx where both the Red Fox (*Vulpes fulva*) and the Gray Fox (*Urocyon cinereoargenteus*) are found to this day. Every so often a resident of Spuyten Duyvil or Riverdale or the East Bronx sees a fox and reports it to the newspapers as something extraordinary in a big city, but the neat straight-line tracks in new-fallen snow each winter prove that foxes are as regular on their nightly rounds in the region as the postman is by day. In recent years a Gray Fox made itself at home in a rocky culvert under the river road in the Spuyten Duyvil region, and for all I know it may still be there.

At different times I have seen Red Foxes trotting steadily about their affairs through different sections of Van Cortlandt Park and I knew a fox earth that was obliterated by the building of the Henry Hudson Parkway on the west border of the swamp near the city line. Even so, the foxes refused to leave the neighborhood, for I saw some later in the area and a friend saw a vixen playing with young on the hillside west of the swamp ten years after the old earth had been run over and crushed by the wheels of progress. As a matter of fact, every fall of snow produces new evidence that foxes are still residents of the region, *anno Domini* 1958.

One encounter with a fox was most amusing. At 7:30 A.M. on the morning of April 7, 1955 (I keep a journal), I was walking up the railroad track on the east side of the Van Cortlandt swamp with Fred Nagler, the artist. It was a bright warm morning and we were looking for birds. About a hundred yards north of the parkway bridge we saw a fine, large, and well-groomed Red Fox standing motionless just inside the wire fence that separates the golf course from the railroad track. Master Reynard was almost under the protection of a clump of Forsythia fringing the golf fairway and it was apparent that he hoped we hadn't noticed him, though we were not fifty feet apart. But when we stopped and stared, he knew he was detected. There was a gate in the fence on either side of the track at that point so that Park Department workers could get through. Evidently the animal had come down from the wooded slope to the eastward and planned to slip through the partly open gates to hunt in the swamp on the west side of the track. It was reluctant to give up the expedition but it didn't trust us. It started to retreat across the fairway—stopped several times to look back at us and reconsider—then finally gave it up as a bad job and loped across the links to disappear in the undergrowth of the woods beyond.

It should be remembered that there is good foraging for foxes along the city's northern border and, even if all the resident foxes were destroyed, newcomers would drift in from Westchester to take up residence in a short time. It is not so with all outlying sections of the city, of course, nor with animals less wary than the proverbial fox. It is not so, for instance, with the familiar Woodchuck (*Marmota monax*) that retains a bare foothold in our territory but is losing ground steadily as more buildings go up and more pavement is laid down. It isn't as sly, as secretive, or as swift of foot as most of the other wild creatures of the area. It feeds by daylight, early and late, grows to an over-all length of 2 feet, stubby furry tail included, and is bulky of shape. It finds little nourishment and too much human traffic in our parks. It prefers cornfields, apple orchards, and kitchen gardens, items that are lessening year by year in the city. Small boys and large dogs are death to this short-legged, broad-beamed, daylight-foraging animal if it wanders far from any of the three or four entrances to its underground apartments. Though it has a threatening look and gives a defiant chattering whistle through gnashing teeth when cornered, it is timid at heart and not tenacious of life. And when the Woodchuck disappeared from Staten Island, the myriad Woodchucks of New York and New Jersey farmlands had no way of sending fresh individuals to represent the clan on an island girt by salt water. Thus Staten Island is missing most of these larger mammals that for many years to come will be found regularly and in fair numbers along the northern border of the Bronx which is, as has been mentioned previously, the only borough on the mainland of North America. A newcomer seeking the city from that direction doesn't have to swim for it.

Under another name—just in case some city dwellers do not know it—the Woodchuck is the "Ground Hog" that, according to folklore, comes out of hibernation on Candlemas (February 2) each year to take a weather observation. If the sun is shining and it sees its shadow—so runs the old wives' tale—it goes back into its den to sleep for another six weeks of hard weather. But if the sky is overcast or rain or snow is falling, the Ground Hog stays out, confident that fine spring weather is in the offing. However, modern farmers look to the Weather Bureau rather than the Ground Hog for meteorological information and, furthermore, I never knew a Woodchuck or Ground Hog that would so much as stick its nose out of its burrow that early in February. I never looked for it to appear above ground until

March made sweet the weather
With daffodil and starling
And hours of fruitful breath.

Perhaps both Woodchuck and Ground Hog are misnomers—it doesn't chuck wood and it isn't a hog—and the animal should be called the Overstuffed Ground Squirrel. It looks well fed to the point of bulkiness, actually is a member of the Sciuridae or Squirrel Family, and generally feeds on the ground though on a few occasions I have seen Woodchucks among the lower branches of old apple trees with slanting trunks. Another member of the family that prefers to stay on the ground is the Eastern Chipmunk (*Tamias striatus*) that, in the words of a small nephew, "looks like a little squirrel with a strip of bacon on its back." It also hibernates like the Woodchuck, but there the resemblance ends. The lively little Eastern Chipmunk is common enough in the larger parks of all five boroughs along with the tree-loving, acrobatic Eastern Gray Squirrel (*Sciurus carolinensis*) that is altogether too common in many parts of the city.

We must admit that the Gray Squirrel is a handsome and graceful animal and an arboreal gymnast of daring artistry but it is notorious for robbing the nests of birds of both eggs and young in the breeding season and in winter it is a pest around feeding stations designed to attract and nourish small birds through the months of snow and ice. A century ago the Red Squirrel (*Tamiasciurus hudsonicus*) was common in the area but it has not taken kindly to the growth of the city. I have not seen one on city territory since boyhood days in Kingsbridge groves and orchards. It has been stated that the Red Squirrel is more than a match for the larger Gray Squirrel in single combat but it is apparent that the Gray Squirrel can not only survive but thrive where the Red Squirrel dies out in a crowded region. Incidentally, if you see a black squirrel anywhere in the city, it will not be a new species for you but the Eastern Gray Squirrel wearing a fur coat of another color. Melanism—the occurrence of black individuals in species ordinarily of another color—is occasional over most of the range of this squirrel and quite common in some restricted area such as the northern section of the Bronx, where I have had as many as six black-coated Eastern Gray Squirrels in sight at one time.

By far the most attractive member of the family resident in New York City is the lovely and friendly little Southern Flying Squirrel (*Glaucomys volans*), whose presence is unsuspected by most of the human inhabitants of the area. Yet the large-eyed, gentle little creature—it is about the same size as the Eastern Chipmunk—is fairly common in the wooded outskirts of the northern and eastern sections of the city and perhaps in other sections. It is hard to be sure because it is so seldom seen, being almost completely nocturnal in its way of life. Dusk is the beginning of its working day, so to speak.

One summer evening when I was sitting on the verandah of our rambling old house in Riverdale—like the fox earth mentioned earlier, this dwelling was "run over" by the construction of the Henry Hudson Parkway—I saw a dark object sail downward through the dusk toward the base of a White Ash that stood about twenty feet away on the lawn. I heard a soft *plop* as the object landed. There was just light enough for me to see that it was a Flying Squirrel that had landed head-upward on the trunk of the tree just a few feet above the ground. Then it shot up the tree like a streak and disappeared.

Later I made closer acquaintance with other Flying Squirrels of our neighborhood. One of them—we named it "Chicot"—came nightly to a bedroom window sill that served as a feeding station for birds by day. How it discovered this table d'hote spread free of charge I have no idea, but my wife woke up one night to find a small dark form in outline on the window sill. Having associated only birds with that window sill, she thought it was one of the small owls and roused me to investigate, which I did. But as I came close to the window, there was a swift scurrying sound and the creature was gone. I borrowed from Hamlet to the extent of "A rat! A rat!" and was sorry I couldn't add "Dead for a ducat." But I thought better of it when I went back to bed. No rat could scurry as swiftly as that. I suspected a Flying Squirrel and was ready for it the following night. When the little form suddenly appeared on the window sill, I waited until I could hear it cracking sunflower seeds and then, with my wife in the dark behind me, I turned on a flashlight. Thus we made acquaintance with Chicot and soon we became firm friends.

We put out a special diet of shelled walnuts for the distinguished visitor each evening and it would sit there in the dark and nibble away calmly when we turned on the flashlight and even when we tapped on the glass an inch or so from its nose. I'm sure we could have tamed it to the point of handling it—others have done it easily —but we were afraid it would come into the house if we left the window open. The lady of the house, though delighted to have it as a window sill visitor, had no desire to have it as a house guest. So we all kept our respective distances and, since Flying Squirrels do not hibernate, we had Chicot as a nocturnal boarder at our window sill buffet all through the winter. It disappeared in the spring, probably intent upon family matters. And we never saw it again.

Telling the tale to others, we found that our experience was by no means uncommon in the region and that Flying Squirrels had made themselves free of bird feeding stations in other sections of the city. These creatures are almost incredibly agile and their swift scurries are almost like the swooping of birds. The "flying," of course, is mere gliding or volplaning from a high launching point to a lower landing place by means of the extra fold of skin along each side of the body that can be flattened out by the action of the fore and hind legs to which it is attached. This, in effect, makes something like a "sail plane" of the body of the animal. It must "fly" downward, of course, but it lands facing upward by a quick turn of the body and tail at the end of the "flight."

The Flying Squirrels are the quietest members of the family in the area. At most, all you hear from them is a series of little squeaks in the night. The Gray Squirrels, by far the most abundant members of the family, are also the loudest. They give off sustained volleys of hoarse, rasping coughs or barks that usually end on a squalling note. Such discordant noises command attention. The long, whirring rattle of the Red Squirrel or Chickaree is now a rare call in the region and the stout Woodchuck, another species on the way out, gives breath to its quivering downward whistle only when it is frightened or enraged. The Chipmunk utters chattering notes when it is excited or angry but its song of contentment—or its advertisement of its presence in a particular spot—is a slowly repeated and hollow-sounding *chock-chock-chock* that can be heard several hundred yards away of a quiet day in the woods or fields.

Roundish masses or clumps of dead leaves seen high up among the bare branches of trees in winter usually turn out to be the "summer homes" of the Gray Squirrels. In hard weather and for breeding purposes they prefer the hollows of trees and other protected nooks, but in late spring you will notice them climbing up trunks of trees with their mouths stuffed with fresh leaves and twigs with which to build these warm weather retreats for themselves. Flying Squirrels have the same habit on a smaller and lower scale. If you come upon a rounded mass of dead leaves in a crotch of a small tree or a tall shrub, give it a poke and perhaps a Flying Squirrel will pop out and scurry off like a shot. You never can tell what will happen when you look into such matters.

There are many square miles on the face of the earth where there are resident rats and mice and no human beings, but it is doubtful that there is a single square mile that contains resident human beings and no rats or mice. The common House Mouse (*Mus musculus*), the Norway Rat (*Rattus norvegicus*), and the Black Rat (*Rattus rattus*), originally immigrants from Europe, are now thoroughly at home on the North American Continent, particularly the House Mouse and the Norway Rat that have swept from the East Coast along which they were introduced all the way to the West Coast and up to Alaska. The Black Rat, so far, is largely coastal and there is a wide stretch from the Appalachians to the Rockies that is yet free of its depredations. As a matter of fact, it was thought to be comparatively scarce in our territory until recent collections by professional exterminators who gave infested sections a thorough going-over proved by irrefutable evidence—dead bodies—that it was on the premises in round numbers. Even so, it is far behind the House Mouse and the Norway Rat in abundance in all five boroughs.

Conditions are bad but they could be worse. Indeed, they were worse a century ago and even fifty years ago when most houses were made of wood and there were livery stables on almost every street in Manhattan. Livery stables meant board and lodging for any number of rats and the occupants of old-fashioned frame houses fought unending campaigns against the House Mouse. It isn't that bad in Manhattan and downtown Brooklyn now. Office buildings, hotels, apartment houses, and shops of all kinds now are constructed of steel, concrete, and glass. The increased use of plastics in offices and homes has been an important factor in reducing the number of rodents formerly holed up in private homes or business houses. But it must be admitted that rats still range the waterfronts and also the city dumps and even the swanky residential districts where the householders do not see to it that their garbage pails and cans are tightly covered as required by law. The Department of Health and the Department of Sanitation wage sporadic campaigns against the careless householders and the foraging rodents but, to date, they have not been able to reform one group or eradicate the other.

The more common of the smaller outdoor mice of the region are the Meadow Mouse (*Microtus pennsylvanicus*), the Whitefooted

Mouse (*Zapus hudsonius*), all harmless and even attractive little creatures, though it is difficult to bring most women to view them in any such light. The Meadow Mouse—or Meadow Vole, as some prefer to call it—is one of the most abundant small rodents of the northern half of North America. It is a chunky, short-tailed, well-furred little animal that varies considerably in color over its wide range. In our territory it runs to a dark brown color with a body length of about 4 inches and a tail about 2 inches long.

The mild Muskrat (*Ondatra zibethica*), which looks something like an aquatic Woodchuck, is really only an overgrown mouse or vole that prefers life in the water to life on land. It is a common resident of the slow streams, ponds, lakes, and freshwater marshes of the city and its heaped-up houses of piled vegetation are easy to spot when the surrounding greenery of summer falls away in the late autumn. The bulky body of the Muskrat is about a foot long and is covered with two kinds of hair; a short beautiful undercoat of soft and silky brown fur and a long coat of coarser hair. Its stout naked tail—almost as long as its body—is vertically flattened to aid in propulsion and steering when the animal is swimming. Its hind feet are partially webbed as another aid to progress in the water.

The lower end of the Van Cortlandt swamp often contains a dozen or more Muskrat houses. It was there, as a boy, that I had my first glimpse of a Muskrat when I was playing ice hockey or "shinny." As I was skating over the clear ice I saw this animal swimming directly ahead of me just under the ice and moving about as fast as I was. I pursued it to the edge of the "pond" or cleared zone, where it slipped among the cattail stalks below and disappeared. That was more than fifty years ago and it is pleasant to know that Muskrats still swim there under the ice in winter. They also swim there and in the nearby lake in summer, often with their noses and foreheads cutting the surface of the water. One day last June I was standing at the water's edge, looking for marsh birds, when a Muskrat quietly emerged from the water at my feet and, without looking up, began to nibble at some roots. This went on for about a minute while I stood perfectly still. Whether it was the sight of my shoes as it turned to graze in that direction or some other clue I do not know, but suddenly the animal realized that it was not alone. It threw up its head for a quick glance and turned and dived out of sight almost in one motion.

Muskrats are quite prolific and often raise two or more broods in a year. That's why they are able to survive within the city limits where their natural habitat is limited and their natural enemies are reinforced by stray dogs, local rowdies who think that all "wild animals" are fair game at any time of year, and, though it is strange to think of it going on in a big city, poachers who set trap lines in the winter months and make their rounds by stealth. I found and removed a number of such steel traps set by poachers in the Van Cortlandt swamp.

Rabbits are common in the fields and thickets of Staten Island and in the outlying sections of the Bronx and the Borough of Queens. The resident species is the Eastern Cottontail (*Sylvilagus floridanus*) that may grow to a length of 17 to 18 inches and a weight of 3 to 4 pounds. It is wonderful how they persist in the face of diminishing open ground and increasing hazards in the form of stray dogs, roaming cats, fast-moving cars, and illegal shooting. House cats on the loose probably are their worst enemies, at least in their younger days. The alert full-grown Cottontails usually are able to elude prowling cats but, since they do much moving around at night, they frequently are confused by the headlights of cars and many are killed on the parkways. Despite these casualties and the harrying and chivvying by their natural enemies in the woods and fields, the rapidity with which they breed keeps the Cottontail population fairly steady and there is no immediate threat of their extinction as residents of the region.

To the best of deponent's knowledge and belief, this completes the list of the common mammals that regularly occur in the area either as residents or migrants. There were others, of course, on the premises long ago. The Beaver (*Castor canadensis*), the Black Bear (*Ursus americanus*), the Gray Wolf (*Canis lupus*), the Mountain Lion or Catamount (*Felis concolor*), the Bobcat (*Lynx rufus*), and the Whitetail Deer (*Odocoileus virginianus*) were residents of the region in Indian times but, like the Indians, they were gradually driven out by the invading white men. The Gray Wolf retreated to Canada and the Mountain Lion fled far to the south and west, as far south as Florida on the Atlantic side of the continent. But the Black Bear still can be found within one hundred miles of the city and the Bobcat, the Beaver, and the Whitetail Deer hold the rank of next-door neighbors in Westchester County.

Occasionally one or two of the Westchester deer wander into the northern section of the Bronx. A few years ago two such visitors lingered among the lawns, gardens, and remaining groves of shade trees in the Riverdale region for about a week before they decided that life in the big city was not for them. They disappeared, presumably in the direction of the Westchester acres from which they came. On September 20, 1955, the New York *Herald Tribune* had a front page story about a six-point buck that was found the previous day in the Midland Beach section of Staten Island and was taken under the protection of the State Conservation Department. The supposition was that it reached Staten Island by swimming from the New Jersey shore across the Kill Van Kull. Despite these and other such occasional incursions, New York City no longer can be considered home territory for these animals. Any Whitetail Deer found within the city precincts may properly be charged with vagrancy.

WHICH WAY DID THE DINOSAURS GO?

BY IRVING PETITE

Irving Petite (1920 —) is a native of Oregon and except for intervals as a merchant marine sailor, has spent his life in the Pacific Northwest. For the past twenty years he has lived on a 165-acre ranch in the foothills of the Cascade Mountains, farming, logging, working part time as a rural mail carrier, and watching and writing about the wildlife around him. His first book, Mister B., *was about a year in the life of an orphaned black bear cub he raised. The selection I have chosen is a chapter from* The Elderberry Tree, *a book about the birds and animals in his own dooryard and just beyond. Petite is a good observer, writes in his own way, and makes his reader see his foothill woodland with fresh eyes. He also has a sense of humor.*

(*The Elderberry Tree*, by Irving Petite; Doubleday & Company, Inc., 1964.)

If animals pass on any cultural heritage besides the obvious facts of life such as how to find a roof for one's head, how to keep one's belly full, how to avoid untimely death, and how to rear the next generation, then one of the mountain beavers in his tunnel down the bank from the elderberry tree may at this moment be telling his grandchild what *really* happened to the dinosaurs.

For mountain beavers, who were contemporaries of the dinosaurs, have tunneled down to us, intact, between time's close-writ lines. Today they live along the west slope of the Cascade Mountain range, from California to British Columbia, and nowhere else on earth. *Aplodontia rufa* is their name and it is singular: they constitute the entire family of Aplodontiidae.

My first mountain beaver had gone head-first into a trap set at its burrow mouth by my cousin, Mary V., on her parents' ranch above the Oregon coast. It was a grayish, unprepossessing-looking creature about a foot long, weighing two to five pounds. The appearance, to my five-year-old eyes, was grotesque: squinched slits where the eyes should be; crinkly, bare ears; no tail worthy of the name; toes splayed out exactly like those in illustrations of dinosaurs (but otherwise no similarity to the giant reptiles); four curving front teeth stained as if from eons of conscientious tobacco chewing.

How had such a miserable creep lived down the centuries while Big-Bad-Dad Dinosaur, sometimes even armor-plated, had vanished altogether?

Later, the book *Dry Guillotine* taught me that one wizened Frenchman may escape Devil's Island while strong men perish in the same attempt, but brain was *his* secret weapon. Nothing brainy about a creature that steps into unbaited traps! It wasn't brawn and it wasn't brain—fool's luck, maybe? The armadillo, iguana, and the flightless birds of Australia also had survived since prehistoric times, but in their various structures and/or strengths one could see a reason; not so with the mountain beaver.

Mountain beavers, out of the burrow, were as helpless as a tame goose where predators were concerned. I learned this during the first years on the ranch when I found their teeth, undigested, in coyote scat and their skulls along the woods paths where coyotes had left them. The skull, about two inches across and three inches long, had huge bone "spectacles" where the squinchy eyes had been. They had nice, flat, even chewing teeth. But in front there were four long teeth, two at the top and two at the bottom, close together; the top two slid back into the skull for some distance; I could take my forefingers and slide them in and out, and I imagine that those teeth continue to grow out as the biting tips are blunted. They were the most spectacular thing about the animal, but not at all reminiscent of the gnashing fangs that *should* have preserved the dinosaur.

One night when a dog kept barking at a single location, out toward the main road, I went out with a lantern and discovered that she had cornered a mountain beaver between the legs of a stump. Backed up to solid wood, the little animal was weaving its blunt, low forehead back and forth and chattering its teeth; but the dog would have rushed in and taken it off with one quick snap of the neck had I not called her off.

The secrecy of its habits and its very nondescriptness may have helped the animal to survive. A naturalist (he had read about "our" mountain beavers in *Audubon Magazine*) came from California, expecting to get photographs. Mountain-beaver tunnels crisscrossed the ranch hillsides, and burrow mouths opened at almost any place one cared to part the underbrush and look; but to get a picture was a rodent of another color! Even when one *is* photographed (as I had found in my own experience), there isn't much to see: unkempt, long whiskers; large, bare ears; a fur without markings and without eye appeal. The pelt looks as if it would smell musty, like a rug thrown out into the yard after a long winter's use, moldering without dignity into the earth. The naturalist left without a picture, for mountain beavers are mostly nocturnal, and even at night they are uncouth about posing.

Lewis and Clark, on the West Coast leg of their cross-continent expedition in 1805–06, might have missed the animal altogether. They were introduced to him through Indian robes made of the short, brownish-gray fur of a nearly tailless animal. Little did they realize that with this discovery they had ventured backward in time as well as westward in space to meet "the unique surviving genus of the primitive rodents of the family Aplodontiidae" in his final habitat. Captain Meriwether Lewis thought the animal was a tailless squirrel, and for many years it was thought to belong to the squirrel family. Lewis gave it what he thought to be the Indian name: *sewellel* or *showt'l.* But that was probably the term for the robes made from its fur. *Ouka-la* and *chehalis* the Indians also called him. The Chehalis River, town of Chehalis, and former Chehalis County (now Grays Harbor County) in Washington State wear his name today; if time is any real tester, he will outlive them.

Washington Territory pioneers called him "whistler," perhaps confusing him with the whistling marmot. Some called him "kick willy," possibly because they heard him kicking ground (as I have) or rolling rocks along his subterranean tunnels and chambers—a labyrinth underlying much of the West, as travelers on foot or on horseback have discovered by stepping into such a tunnel's mouth or through its roof. Others called him "mountain boomer," "ground beaver," "underground beaver." Mountain beaver, the name which has stuck, is a misnomer like all the rest, because he lives from sea level to the mountains and isn't a beaver at all but a rodent, like the prairie dog, which isn't a dog.

To me, he is an underground farmer with vertical hay fields. On this ranch, one of my first experiences with a mountain beaver occurred while I was looking for down cedar logs for fence-post material and he was looking for upright cedar trees for fodder stuff. Down below the elderberry tree, in a shelf of land above a swamp, stood a gigantic cedar stump with cedar logs left over from logging days jackstrawed about its base. While I was marking one of the minor logs and preparing to saw, I sensed movement in a young, fourteen-foot living cedar tree nearby. Near its top, where only birds *should* be, there was a grayish animal—squat, industrious, with huge, naked ears—and he was gnawing at the base of a branch. He was "busy as a beaver" but otherwise not at all like one.

As I watched, he got the limb off and slid it along his mouth until his tusklike front teeth were clasping it on each side of the stem. Then he backed down the tree; turned; went to the road between me and the elderberry tree; scooted across with never a look up or down (he would have done the same had it been a main highway)—with his green-foliaged limb safely clutched. He worried the limb up a bank to a hole which opened (and does, to this day: that was fifteen years ago) near the base of the elderberry tree. He deposited the cedar limb, stem forward, at the burrow's mouth. Beside it there were other cedar boughs, but mostly (it was summertime) windrows of alder boughs—all curing in the sunlight that filtered down through overhanging bushes. I could see that his hay was air-cured, not burned by direct sunlight, and that was best, for it retained most of its food value that way.

Unaware of me, he stood up on his hind legs and stretched, like a farmer who straightens up after carrying a load of hay on his pitchfork. He took both forepaws and scratched his elephantine ears energetically, with a quick, circular rubbing motion that reminded me of a mouse's. I could almost *feel* his pleasure at laying down his burden and scratching himself. Looking more closely about the area (usually a man is *traveling* a road, not *looking above it,* even when walking), I saw that many of the short alder trees along the bank near his burrow's mouth were pruned. Some had only a few lower limbs missing; some were minus everything but a single stem or two near the top. "That saves me the trouble," I thought—for alders soon "take" a hillside where new evergreen trees would otherwise grow. I was less gleeful when, upon going to the garden one morning, I found that the potato plants along the upcreek side were also "pruned" and laid in a neat row at a burrow between two roots of a stump; but the fact did not lead me to set traps for, after all, the animal had problems of provisioning which were similar to my own. While this "beaver" had cut the potato sprouts, he never carried them into his burrow, and the next time the seed potatoes sprouted he left them alone, having discovered, I imagine, that they were not appetizing fodder. And I have never found an animal or fowl, wild or domestic, that *did* relish potato tops.

He reminded me, more than ever, of a blunderer down the ages. But, still, he outlived *Tyrannosaurus rex*—so why criticize?

The secret of his success had certainly not been *personality.* One April morning I found a mountain beaver off his course, chilled and shuddering, stumbling about the base of a stump whose flat top I used as a feeder table for kid goats. I put him into a rabbit hutch with hay for warmth. As the sun came out, he came to life. Within a few hours he had arranged the hay and some dried leaves, which were already in the hutch, in the form of an open-topped nest, the tight shape of the lower end of the "sock" nest of an oriole or brush tit. He sat inside the nest, on his tail that was only a few scraggly black hairs, and turned round and round, pulling the sides in toward him—the action being an approximation, I supposed, of his underground nest building somewhere at the dead end of his main tunnel or in a chamber off to one side.

I had seen such nests when a bulldozer, working in a thicket where the ground had not been disturbed for many years, uncovered a tunnel. The underground hay-storage chambers seemed to be separate. Once, in the front field, a bulldozer blade had just passed over the roof of an underground hayloft. Later in the day I went back over the new clearing and found a bucket-sized hummock of dried leaves and twigs, mostly alder, some willow. The "hay" had been packed in under pressure and had popped up through the ceiling once the weight of the ground above was removed. Dried, but still greenish in color, it would have filled a bushel basket.

But mountain beavers, who make hay while the moon shines (and in the dark of the moon too) don't stop haying just because the sun's season is over. In winter, even when the snow is on, I can expect to find fronds of brake fern, an evergreen shrub, hauled up to form an ornamental whorl—stems all pointed inward—around the burrow mouths of tunnels in the bank down toward the elderberry tree.

What comes out at the burrow mouths can be more interesting, to me, than what points in. On the shoulders of Tiger Mountain, up above the level of the logging grade, the mountain beavers push out rocks that are impeding their way or making their beds lumpy. When Mount Rainier was a volcano and its lava was running, molten, to form these minor mountains, a sky-blue agate bubbled and cooled in glass-thin sheets along certain surfaces of the andesite rock. Today's mountain beavers bring out pieces of this blue stuff, bubbled along one side; I pick them up and pocket a flat chunk of heaven.

Down below, on the ranch, where they work in banks of dirt, I take the wheelbarrow and shovel up the fine soil they have pushed out, putting it on the upper-level gardens, over the gravel.

In the uncleared, uncultivated portions of the ranch, mountain beaver runways and tunnels catch the water which would otherwise run off and down the rain-swollen creeks in winter, divert it in many directions, helping to conserve the moisture and what topsoil has been forming since the leaf mulch was burned off by fires that followed the logging.

In many ways the mountain beaver's minor industry aids and intrigues me. Mostly it says to me, whenever I walk out upon this segment of the earth, "You don't have to be *mighty* or even *clever* in order to prevail. Just keep on *making hay*."

WOLVES

BY MARY KIDDER RAK

Mary Kidder Rak (1889–1961) was a Californian of Massachusetts stock. Educated at Leland Stanford University, she taught school and did social work in San Francisco for fifteen years and, after she married Charles Rak in 1917, lectured on social science at the University of Arizona for a time. In 1919 the Raks bought and moved to the Old Camp Rucker Ranch in Cochise County, in the southeast corner of Arizona, directly north of Douglas on the Arizona-Mexico border. It is still rugged country and, when Mrs. Rak wrote her two books about life there in the 1930s, it was both wild and remote. Mrs. Rak's first book was A Cowman's Wife. *Her second,* Mountain Cattle, *from which this selection is taken, continued her story of the life the Raks lived there as cattle-ranch folk. Mrs. Rak wrote with color, vitality and humor, and with an observant eye for all the natural life of her area.*

(*Mountain Cattle,* by Mary Kidder Rak; Houghton Mifflin Company, 1936.)

Whenever Ramón has been out riding on the range by himself, he comes over to the house as soon as he has unsaddled his horse, eager to tell me in great detail all that he has seen or done. By the time he has walked halfway from the barn to the house, I know whether he is the bearer of good tidings or ill. If Ramón brings good news, his shrill, tuneless whistle precedes him and I am assured that he has encountered no dead calves, dry water-holes, lame horses, or cows with the pinkeye. If my first notice of his approach is the slow clump-scrunch, clump-scrunch, of his high-heeled boots on the gravel of the terrace, then I prepare myself to hear some tale of disaster.

'Will you come over to the barn with me, please, Senora,' he gloomily requested when he appeared in our doorway one morning after only an hour's absence. 'There is something I want to show you.'

An Indian can be exceedingly glum without half-trying. Ramón's beady black eyes were expressionless; his angular chin set like a rock. On his mouth there was not even a pucker of the lips where a whistle had once been. Without a word I started over to the barn, feeling positive that I was not going to like what I found there.

In the corral stood a drooping, dejected, three-year-old heifer, who looked up at me with sick, bewildered eyes. I walked around behind her and gasped with astonishment and pity. At the root of her tail and on her rump were long gashes, torn in her flesh by the fangs of a wolf that had tried to pull her down to the ground and kill her. Unlike most of our cattle, she had not been dehorned, and it was quite possible that her life had been saved because she still had horns to use for self-defense.

'Great grief!' I sighed. 'A lobo on the range to add to all our other troubles!'

I continued to mourn as I helped Ramón drive the poor creature into the chute where her wounds could be doctored and covered with pine-tar to keep off the blow-flies. We could tell by the condition of the wound that she had been attacked only the night before and Ramón had found her only half a mile from home. A wolf within a mile may be no worse than one five miles off, but it is uncomfortably near our door. There seemed to be an excellent chance of saving the life of the heifer, although we should have to doctor her for weeks, and during her long convalescence she would consume more hay and cake than she was worth. Later in the day her calf was prematurely born and died within an hour, chalking up another score against the lobo.

For all my love of dogs, starting with the noble Saint Bernards and ending with shivering, hairless Chihuahua terriers, I am still unable to encounter the friendliest of German police dogs without a shudder. They are far too much like the fierce gray lobo of the Southwest. Huge, ravenous wolves, singly, in pairs, and in packs, preyed upon our cattle in earlier years until the combined efforts of the United States Biological Survey and the State succeeded in so reducing their numbers that one was rarely known on an Arizona range. Down on the International Line the Government hunters maintained their own border patrol to halt the alien wolves that are forever trying to slip into this country from the nearby mountains of Old Mexico. The trouble was that these hunters were too efficient and presently found that they had worked themselves out of a job.

'Why should we pay hunters when there are no longer any wolves left in Arizona?' argued some of the town-dwelling members of the State Legislature, and they failed to make an appropriation for that purpose. The Federal appropriation for Arizona was withdrawn as soon as the State refused to match it, and the hunters were dropped from the payroll. Unmolested, mother wolves now raised their pups in Arizona caves. Gray shapes flitted across the Mexican Border at night to sample Arizona beef; lions stole through the mountains, stalking deer and colts; coyotes yammered and tittered on the foothills, while everywhere resounded the bawling of cows, mourning their lost calves.

'Who said we don't need hunters?' clamored the roused stockmen, and Governor Moeur searched his official pockets until he found money which he could use to put the hunters back on the payroll. Among those who returned to duty was 'Brother' Eddie Anderson, a transplanted Yankee, who devotes his traditional Connecticut ingenuity to outwitting wolves.

To him I wrote as soon as I returned to the house after seeing the poor heifer, and Ramón rode down the canyon to give the letter to a neighbor who was going to town the following day. I was not at all confident that Mr. Anderson would take the message seriously when he saw that it came from a woman. Men of the Southwest seem to have decided ideas with regard to 'woman's sphere.' With a few noteworthy exceptions, even those men who know that I help my husband with our cattle are still reluctant to talk with me 'about a cow.' In the light of this experience I foresaw that Mr. Anderson might not condescend to talk with me about a wolf. He might even be unwilling to believe, on my unsupported say-so, that there was a wolf on our range—if not in my sphere.

To be prepared to meet his doubts, Ramón and I rode out in the afternoon to make a wide search of the range. We looked, and sniffed the air, for earlier victims of the wolf, and rejoiced when we found none. We scanned the trails, the salt grounds, and the watering-places for wolf tracks, finding no sign. This puzzled us until we came upon one clear print of a huge forepaw, with pointed pads and two elongated middle toes. The print had been freshly made by a lobo that had merely crossed a cowpath instead of following it.

Around this one precious, distinct track of the lobo, Ramón and I built a miniature log cabin with walls and roof of small sticks, so that no animal could efface the print, nor wind blur its sharp outline. This track was Exhibit A, to uphold our case against the world. Exhibit B was the torn flesh of the unfortunate heifer, which gave mute evidence as to the width of the wolf's jaws and the length of his fangs. We had now done everything that we could and waited impatiently for word from the hunter.

The very first Government hunter that we ever summoned to help us, many years ago, traveled in primitive style, as befitted those times. He had covered the distance between the Rincons and the Chiricahuas, seated on the high spring seat of a high-wheeled, creaking farm wagon. On the uncomfortable backless wooden seat perched his wife, unsheltered from sun or rain. In the back of the wagon was their meager outfit, helter-skelter: bedroll, grain for the horses, traps, bait, cooking-pots, provisions, frames for stretching hides.

The hunter who came to help us a few years later, bounced along merrily in a *truckicito*, a little delivery truck, with his traps and Dutch ovens rattling together companionably in the box at the back of the car. A lion-hunter came in a battered, sputtering, boiling touring car, the mournful faces of his hounds thrust through the tattered curtains. Their eerie baying warned us—and the lions—of their approach.

On his previous visits to our range, Mr. Anderson had fetched his camping outfit, traps and guns, in a capacious trailer that bobbed along on two wheels behind his automobile. This time he drove up to our door in a neat roadster, and when I noted the absence of the trailer, I feared that he did not plan to stay.

He uncoiled his lean, putteed legs and crept out from the low-slung roadster to mount the steps of the terrace, his khaki riding-breeches and shirt as immaculate and creased as those of any army officer. Before the door he paused and wiped his high forehead, looking around appreciatively at the juniper trees and vines that surround the house.

'My! It's fine up here in the woods—even in a drought!' he exclaimed. 'I've been camped down on the border where there isn't a tree in miles.' His blue eyes gleamed as they rested on the wooded mountains.

Another car now appeared at the gate and, when it was driven into the yard by Mr. Anderson's helper, my anxieties were over. It was a housecar, a veritable perambulating mansion. Soon the proud owner was showing me all its devices and gadgets, bed, table, cupboards, and clothes closets. There was a sink, and a water-tank to supply it; a gasoline stove for cooking and a wood-stove for heating; radio, electric lights, bookshelves and desk. It was Bachelor's Hall on wheels. Mr. Anderson is so tall that there was little room between his blond head and the ceiling. To compensate for this disadvantage, he is also extremely thin and takes up little room sidewise. On a shelf in the cupboard were glass jars of fruit that he had put up himself. No spinster could have lived more tidily, and everything was in apple-pie order from the curtains at the windows to the little rug just inside the door. Mr. Anderson frequently moves at a day's notice and in this rolling home he is as snug as a turtle in its shell and able to travel far faster. In half an hour he was settled pleasantly by a pool in the river, shaded by a spreading juniper tree that has sheltered him before.

He looked at our heifer and nodded his head with satisfaction, enthusiastically agreeing that only a large lobo could have bitten her in that manner. Almost he congratulated us upon having a ravenous wolf on our range, and, while I did not consider this a matter for congratulation, I recognized his professional attitude, something like that of a skillful surgeon who is pleased with a serious case that is worthy of his best efforts.

He, Ramón, and I went up into Coal Pit Canyon and knelt beside the covered track of the lobo while Mr. Anderson's long, sensitive fingers daintily removed the log cabin of sticks that had preserved it. The print told the experienced hunter more than it had revealed to us.

'That is an old loafer,' he said with assurance, rising and fastidiously brushing the sand and leaves from his knees. 'Perhaps he is trap-wise.'

As always, when talking about a wolf, Mr. Anderson spoke softly. Now he looked up and down the trail cautiously, and I had a fleeting thought that the wolf might be hidden in the nearest manzanita thicket, listening to every word. Overhead were birds, and the hunter lowered his voice even more as he continued, lest the wolf say, 'A little bird told me.'

'This lobo's toe-nails leave only a faint mark at the end of his big toes because he has blunted them by rambling across the country through the rocks like lightning, instead of sticking to the cow-trails like the average wolf. That makes it very hard to tell from what direction he came or where he is going.'

Mr. Anderson looked down at the lone track, chin in his lean hand, pondering.

'They tell about an old horse-wrangler,' I suggested, 'who had no difficulty in finding the horses, no matter how rough and brushy the country was in which they ran. When someone asked him how he managed it, he said, "I just ask myself where I would go if I were a horse. Then I go to that place—and there are the horses." '

'That's just the way I aim to do with this wolf!' chuckled Brother Anderson.

Long familiar with every ridge, canyon, and watering-place in the Chiricahuas, Mr. Anderson needed little time to decide where he would prowl of nights if he were a lobo, rambling through the woods in pursuit of beef, venison, or excitement. Between towering cliffs and along the floor of deep canyons were narrow passes which a wolf could hardly avoid if he were roving through these mountains. In these strategic spots the hunter set his traps. After covering the steel jaws with earth, he artfully obliterated every visible trace of his work, leaving it to the wind and hot sun to destroy the scent of human hands before nightfall. As the last and most important preparation for the reception of the wolf, the hunter poured out a little of his precious, secretly compounded bait, a potent lure which had tempted many a lobo to draw near a trap, stop, sniff, and scratch—just once too often.

The traps were so widely scattered over our range that it was impossible to visit the whole line each day on foot. For mounts Mr. Anderson had the use of two small Mexican mules belonging to our neighbor, Aaron Cummings; skittish creatures with flashing heels and hostile eyes bulging beneath stiffly pointed ears. When these mules were not fastidiously picking their way over the rock-strewn trails, they were hee-hawing indignant protests to everyone who passed the Hermitage corrals where they spent their off hours. They seemed to consider themselves much abused, although they had hay and grain in abundance and a walnut tree for shade. Except for the daily round to inspect the traps and see that they were undisturbed, the hunter's part had been played and the next move must be made by the wolf.

Charlie Rak had been away from home while all this was going on, and we were almost out of grain when he drove in one evening after dark and backed up to the barn door to unload a truckful of cottonseed cake, bran, and rolled barley. Ramón and Maximo came from their house to unload the grain, and I hastened over to the barn, flashlight in hand.

'What do you suppose happened to me today?' Charlie burst out the moment I appeared. 'A man tried to have me arrested!'

'Arrested for what?' I cried. The flashlight betrayed my state of mind by wobbling in my trembling hand, casting a dancing flicker around the dark corral.

'He swore to a warrant for no reason at all! Just pure spite!' Charlie sputtered. 'I had told Santiago to take down a piece of fence and he got mixed up and started to take down an old, rickety, abandoned fence that belonged to another man. The fellow doesn't want me down there in the Valley, so he grabbed at the chance to make trouble for me and did his best to have me arrested for stealing a fence. That place down there is Hell's Hip Pocket!'

A reputation for honesty has a distinct, practical value in this sparsely settled country of Arizona where everyone knows everybody else. The justice of the peace readily believed Charlie's explanation that the fence had been taken down by mistake and was already being rebuilt. The warrant was not even served. None the less it was a disturbing experience and a warning of the hostility that we might expect. We realized that we were sure to be unpopular with men who had for years been grazing their cattle free of expense upon the land which we were now leasing, but we had not dreamed that their resentment would be shown in this particular manner.

'I shall have to ask Mr. Heyne to lend me his transit,' said Charlie. (Luckily he had plenty of experience in land surveying while he was in the Forest Service.) 'I'll find an established section corner and run each line before I take down any more fences or build any. I can't trust to landmarks, and the fences of our neighbors down there are as crooked as a dog's hindleg. If I set a post a foot or so over on another man's land there'll be more hell a-popping. It's a good thing the fellow did try to have me arrested. Now I know what I'm up against and I'll give them no chance to hang anything on me.'

After a snack of cold cornbread and milk, which was all the larder afforded that night, Charlie Rak continued his tale of Hell's Hip Pocket. His exciting experience with law and order had wound up a week that had been maddening, in view of our great need to have our new land fenced and our cattle located upon it. Up here in the mountains our cattle were in urgent need of feed, while in the Valley the cattle of other men were fattening on the range that we had leased. The owners of these stray cattle had seen our fences going up and were trying to use our range to the utmost before we could enclose it.

For two weeks my husband had been trying his best to make some sort of deal with an exasperating, unbusinesslike woman, who seemed incapable of deciding whether to lease her half-section of land to him, to someone else, or to no one at all. For years this land had lain unfenced, undesired; tenanted only by the stray cattle that grazed upon it. Now that Charlie Rak wished to lease it, several other men at once desired it also, and the dazzled owner played 'eeny, meeny, miny, mo' with all of them, hoping they would bid against one another. One day she accepted from Charlie a check for the first year's rent in advance, promising to sign the lease which he left with her. The next day she returned both lease and check, having changed her mind overnight. So long as there was any chance of securing this land, Charlie did not want to fence it outside of his pasture; and until he was surely in possession, he could not fence it inside.

In desperation, he offered to buy the land outright, and this move, instead of ending the agony, merely prolonged it. The owner wanted to find out if someone else would offer her a higher price before accepting this new offer. Finally Charlie induced this elusive lady to go with him to a lawyer, intending to have the deed drawn up, signed, sealed, and delivered all in one swoop while she was in the proper mood. It then developed, to the chagrin of all concerned, that she was not the actual owner of the land, although she had been paying the taxes for several years. The property was part of her dead father's estate which, because of her ignorance of legal matters, had never been probated. She could neither lease nor sell it. After all this delay we must now build a mile of fence between this land and ours, meanwhile seeing stray cattle by the bunches overrunning the range which we so sorely needed for our own cows.

On the two days that Charlie remained at home, we devoted every possible moment to the writing of letters to absentee owners of additional land that we wished to lease, and to making out lease agreements for the signature of those owners who had answered our previous letters favorably. Then Charlie departed with a towering load of fenceposts, a roll of stay-wire, a keg of staples, and shovels and crowbars which he had sharpened at the forge while I pumped the bellows. He utterly declined to add the wolf to his other worries.

'Brother Anderson will catch that lobo,' said my husband positively. 'He has never failed yet.'

No sooner had he left than the telephone rang imperatively and I took down the receiver with much reluctance. This is not a year in which ranchers indulge in idle chit-chat over the party line and a ring is apt to mean some species of grief. Sure enough. At the other end of the line was our neighbor, Frank Krentz, in a high state of excitement, urgently inquiring for Hunter Anderson. Two of the Krentzes' valuable registered cows, heavy with calf, had been killed by a wolf that very morning when they came to drink at the tank. The place where they watered was in the open, level country miles below the wooded mountains. Mr. Krentz had found the cows while they were still warm, showing that they had been attacked in daylight. Any wolf might have killed a single animal in order to satisfy his hunger, but this lobo had eaten very little of the first cow and had wantonly killed the second one without touching the meat. He was a 'killer' from sheer love of the chase, far more to be dreaded than an ordinary wolf because his depredations were out of all proportion to his appetite.

Word was sent to Mr. Anderson, and just as soon as he had made his daily round of the traps in Rucker, he started for the Spear E Ranch by automobile, seventy-five miles by the road around the foot of the Chiricahuas. At the Spear E he picked up Frank Krentz, and in the late afternoon they drove down the long gentle slope to the tank, the glare of the westering sun in their eyes. As they approached the watering-place they heard bawling and bellowing; saw a commotion among the cattle, and arrived just in time to find the brazen wolf in the very act of attacking a calf. He was snapping at it and pulling it down.

Hearing the motor, the lobo stood over the calf and looked calmly at the approaching car until it was almost upon him. Then he wheeled and loped away over the grassy plain. After the wolf sped the automobile at non-stop boulevard speed, driven by an eager, relentless hunter, who paid no heed to bumps, holes, and shallow washes, his eyes fixed upon the fleet, gray form ahead. They gained on the wolf. They were within shooting range when the lobo jumped into an arroyo, was lost to sight for an instant, then climbed the opposite bank. The car stopped and the men shot once—and missed.

There was no second chance, for the wolf had now reached the deep wash for which he had been heading, a narrow, rocky gash in the plain where no car could follow him. Into this he plunged and ran among the concealing boulders until he was well out of the range of a rifle. Then he emerged and stopped on a knoll to look back at the men who had vainly pursued him. Angry and frustrated, the men were forced to look on helplessly as the lobo leisurely ascended the rocky slopes and entered the sanctuary of the nearest rim-rock.

Around the watering-place where the wolf had killed the cows and attacked the calf (which later died), there were any number of tracks which corresponded with the lone print found on our own range. Away from the watering-tank the ground was hard and rocky. For all his searching Mr. Anderson was unable to find a trail which would show where the wolf had traveled when coming down to the plain. He had just 'fallen off the mountains,' and there was little use in setting traps because he might never again descend in the same place.

Within a few days the wolf again made a raid upon the Krentzes' cattle, maliciously choosing the registered, pure-bred cows as his victims instead of the less valuable 'grade-stuff.' This time he attacked his two helpless victims in the lower end of Tex Canyon, where the mountains meet the plain. Mr. Anderson hastened over to the Spear E range again and this time set out a few traps near the dead cows. He arranged for an experienced hunter to watch these traps for him, since it would have meant a ten-mile ride each way on his mule by way of the mountain trail, and that was too far from Rucker for him to visit the traps daily. On his way back from the Krentzes', Mr. Anderson stopped here—and, when I saw him plodding up the steps, soberly, wearily, I feared that he might be going to tell me that he had decided to take up the traps on our range and move over to the Spear E's. I asked him if that was what he intended doing.

'No, Mrs. Rak,' he replied thoughtfully. Then he sank down on the wooden bench before the house as though he felt too tired to go inside for the sake of a comfortable chair. 'Some folks might think that I ought to move over there, but I'm not going to do it.'

'I am awfully glad to hear that,' said I.

'This is the way I look at it,' he began.

There was a slight rustling sound by the honeysuckle vine, and Brother Anderson looked around suspiciously. Twirly, the gray ground-squirrel that lives in a hole under the house, was very near us, sitting up on its haunches, front paws hugged to its breast, head bent forward. Its eyes were full of eager curiosity and its ears were perked in a listening attitude.

Mr. Anderson instinctively lowered his voice so that the squirrel could not overhear our conversation and I was obliged to slide nearer to him on the bench to catch his confidential tones as he continued.

'You folks wrote to me that you had a wolf on your range ten days before it was reported by the Krentzes, and I know by the tracks that it is the same wolf. I have set out some traps in Tex Canyon, and I am going to have them watched and baited every day—but I shan't catch the lobo over there. I know where I should go if I were a wolf, and there I'll catch him.'

'Just because you like Rucker Canyon is no reason why the wolf should prefer it,' I remarked skeptically.

'Wait and see!' Brother Anderson murmured almost inaudibly. 'Wait and see!'

By now, even his breath was bated.

There was no longer any need of secrecy and silence when he drove up to our door with a flourish the very next morning, honking his horn, beaming and beckoning.

'Come on out and look at this, Mrs. Rak!' he cried with immense satisfaction.

Dramatically he lifted the lid of the storage compartment in the back of his roadster, and there lay the hide of a great gray lobo. We measured it, six and a half feet from tip to tip. The head was still intact, green eyes glaring balefully, yellowed fangs bared in a snarl.

At the end of the roughened pads of the large feet were the blunted toe-nails that had made the killer's sign distinct from that of lesser wolves.

Lifting my eyes from the long gray hide and terrifying head, now lying in a heap at my feet, I looked up at the lofty mountains that surround Rucker Basin, regarded the fringe of pines on the crest of Monte Vista, outlined against the blue sky; Turtle Mountain; Sage Peak; unnamed lesser mountains by the score, humbly surrounding the giants. Somewhere, amid this welter of peaks, canyons, ridges, precipitous slopes, and wooded mesas, Hunter Anderson had buried a steel trap in a space that he could cover with his two hands—and the wolf had set his paw upon a trigger that I could cover with one of mine.

THE PORCUPINE AND THE MARTEN

BY MAYNE REID

Mayne Reid (1818–1883) was born in Ireland but came to the United States while still a boy. After a wide variety of experience—as actor, soldier, Indian fighter, teacher, store-keeper—he became an author. He was a prolific writer, publishing some ninety books, most of them romances set in the Southwest or the prairie country of the West. He knew those areas at first hand, had traveled, hunted and lived there. He was a close observer of nature, though not schooled in any of the natural sciences, and nature was an important element in many of his books. This selection is from his novel The Desert Home, *and it shows Reid's strong story sense as well as his knowledge of wildlife. As novels, most of his romances are now forgotten; but their backgrounds and their frequent accounts of dramatic incidents involving animals are well worth reading. In writing about nature, Mayne Reid was a better naturalist than many of the avowed nature writers of his day.*

(*The Desert Home*, by Mayne Reid; 1864.)

It was in the middle of the winter. A light snow had fallen upon the ground—just enough to enable us to follow the trail of any animal we might light upon. Of course, the snow filled us with the idea of hunting; and Harry and I started out upon the tracks of a brace of Elk that had passed through our opening during the night. The tracks were very fresh-looking; and it was evident that the animals had passed in the morning, just before we were up. We concluded, therefore, that they had not gone far off; and we hoped soon to come up with them.

The trail led us along the side of the lake, and then up the left bank of the stream. Castor and Pollux were with us; but in our hunting excursions we usually led them on a leash, so that they might not frighten the game by running ahead of us.

When about half a mile from the house, we found that the Elk had crossed to the right bank of the stream. We were about to follow, when all at once our eyes fell upon a most singular track or tracks that led off into the woods. They were the tracks of human feet—the feet of children!

So thought we, at first sight of them; and you may fancy the surprise into which we were suddenly thrown. They were about five inches in length, and exactly such as would have been made by a barefooted urchin of six years old. There appeared to be two sets of them, as if two children had passed, following one another, on the same trail. What could it mean? After all, were there human beings in the valley besides ourselves? Could these be the footprints of two young Indians?

All at once, I thought of the Diggers—the Yamparicos—the root eaters—who are found in almost every hold and corner of the American Desert. Could it be possible that a family of these wretched creatures existed in the valley? "Quite possible," thought I, when I reflected upon their habits. Living upon roots, insects, and reptiles, burrowing in holes and caves like the wild animals around them, a family or more might have been living all this time in some unexplored corner of the valley, without our having encountered any traces of them. Was this really so? and were the tracks before us the footmarks of a brace of young Diggers who had been passing from point to point?

Of course, our Elk hunt was given up until this mystery should be solved; and we turned off from the trail of the latter to follow that of the children.

In coming out to an open place, where the snow lay smoothly, and the footprints appeared well defined, I stooped down to examine them more minutely, in order to be satisfied that they were the tracks of human feet. Sure enough, there were the heels, the regular widening of the foot near the toes, and the toes themselves, all plainly stamped upon the snow. Here, however, arose another mystery. On counting the toes, I found that in some of the tracks there were five,—as there should have been,—while in others there were only four! This led me to examine the print of the toes more carefully; and I now saw that each of them was armed with a claw, which on account of some hairy covering, had made but a very indefinite impression in the snow. The tracks, then, were not the footmarks of children, but those of some animal with claws.

Notwithstanding that we had come to this conclusion, we still continued to follow the trail. We were curious to see what sort of a creature had made it. Perhaps it might be some animal unknown to naturalists—some new species; and we might one day have the merit of being the first to describe it. We had not far to go: a hundred yards or so brought us in sight of a grove of young cottonwoods; and these we saw at a glance were "barked" by a Porcupine. The whole mystery was cleared up—we had been following in the trail of this animal.

I now remember that the Porcupine was one of the plantigrade family, with five toes on his hind feet, and only four on the fore ones. The tracks were undoubtedly his.

My companion and I were somewhat chagrined at being thus drawn away from our hunt by such an insignificant object; and we vowed to take vengeance upon the Porcupine, as soon as we should set our eyes upon him. We were not long in doing this; for, as we stole quietly forward, we caught sight of a shaggy animal moving among the branches of a tree about fifty yards ahead of us. It was he, of course. At the same moment, however, another animal "hove in sight," in appearance as different from the Porcupine as a Bull from a bluebottle.

This creature—tail and all—was not less than a yard and a quarter in length, and yet its body was not thicker than the upper part of a man's arm. Its head was broad and somewhat flattened, with short erect ears and pointed nose. It was bearded like a Cat, although the face had more of the Dog in its expression. Its legs were short and strong; and both legs and body denoted the possession of agility and strength. It was of a reddish brown color, with a white mark on the breast, and darker along the back and on the legs, feet, nose, and tail. Its whole appearance reminded one of a gigantic Weasel,—which in fact it was,—the great Marten of America. When we first saw it, it was crouching along a high log that ran directly towards the tree, upon which was the Porcupine. Its eyes were fixed intently upon the latter; and it was evidently meditating an attack. We stopped to watch it.

The Porcupine had not yet perceived his enemy, as he was busily engaged in splitting the bark from the cottonwood. The Marten, after reconnoitring him for some moments, sprang off from the log, and came running towards the tree. The other now saw him, and at the same instant uttered a sort of shrill, querulous cry, and appeared to be greatly affrighted. To our astonishment, however, instead of remaining where it was, it suddenly dropped to the ground, almost at the very nose of its adversary! I could not, at first, understand the policy of this strange tactic on the part of the Porcupine; but a moment's reflection convinced me it was sound policy. The Marten would have been as much at home on the tree as himself; and had he remained among the branches—which were slender ones,—his throat and the under part of his body—both of which are soft, and without quills—would have been exposed to the teeth of his adversary. This, then, was why he had let himself down so unexpectedly; and we noticed that the instant he touched the ground, he rolled himself into a round clew, presenting on all sides the formidable chevaux-de-frise of his quills.

The Marten now ran around him, doubling his long, vermiform body with great activity—at intervals showing his teeth, erecting his back, and snarling like a Cat. We expected every moment to see him spring forward upon his victim; but he did not do so. He evidently understood the peril of such an act; and appeared for a moment puzzled as to how he should proceed. All this while, the Porcupine lay quiet—except the tail. This was, in fact, the only "feature" of the animal that could be seen, as the head and feet were completely hidden under the body. The tail, however, was kept constantly in motion—jerked from side to side, and flirted occasionally upwards.

What would the Marten do? There was not an inch of the other's body that was not defended by the sharp and barbed quills—not a spot where he could insert the tip of his nose. Would he abandon the contest? So thought we, for a while; but we were soon convinced of our error.

After running around several times, as we have described, he at length posted himself near the hind quarters of the Porcupine, and with his nose a few inches from the tail of the latter. In this position, he stood for some moments, apparently watching the tail, which still continued to oscillate rapidly. He stood in perfect silence, and without making a movement.

The Porcupine, not being able to see him, and perhaps thinking that he was gone, now waved his tail more slowly, and then suffered it to drop motionless.

This was what the other was waiting for; and, the next moment, he had seized the tail in his teeth. We saw that he held it by the tip, where it is destitute of the thorny spines.

What would he do next? Was he going to bite off the end of the Porcupine's tail? No such thing. He had a different game from that to play as we soon witnessed.

The moment he caught the tail, the Porcupine uttered its querulous cries; but the Marten, heeding not these, commenced walking backward, dragging the other after him. Where was he dragging it to? We soon saw. He was pulling it to a tree close by, with low branches, that forked out near the ground. "But for what purpose?" thought we. We wondered as we watched.

The Porcupine could offer no resistance. Its feet gave way, and slipped along the snowy ground; for the Marten was evidently the much stronger animal.

In a short time, the latter had reached the tree, dragging the other after him to its foot. He now commenced ascending, still holding the Porcupine's tail in his teeth, and taking precious care not to brush too closely to the quills. "Surely," thought we, "he cannot climb up, carrying a body almost as big as himself, in that manner!" It was not his intention to climb up,—only to one of the lowermost branches,—and the next moment, he had reached it, stretching his long body out on the limb, and clutching it firmly with his Cat-like claws. He still held fast hold of the Porcupine's tail, which animal was now lifted into such a position that only its forequarters rested on the ground, and it appeared to stand upon its head, all the while uttering its pitiful cries.

For the life of us, we could not guess what the Marten meant by all this manoeuvring. He knew well enough, as he gave proof the moment after. When he had got the other, as it were, on a balance, he suddenly sprang back to the ground, in such a direction that the impetus of his leap jerked the Porcupine upon its back. Before the clumsy creature was able to turn over and "clew" itself, the active Weasel had pounced upon its belly, and buried his claws in the soft flesh, while, at the same time, his teeth were made fast in the throat!

In vain the Porcupine struggled. The other rode him with such agility, that he was unable to get right side up again; and in a few moments the struggle would have ended by the Porcupine's throat being cut; but we saw that it was time for us to interfere; and, slipping Castor and Pollux from the leash, we ran forward.

The Dogs soon drove the Marten from his victim, but he did not run from them. On the contrary, he turned round upon them, keeping them at bay with his sharp teeth and fierce snarling. In truth, they would have had a very tough job of it, had we not been near; but, on seeing us approach, the animal took to a tree, running up it like a Squirrel. A rifle bullet soon brought him down again; and his long body lay stretched out on the earth, emitting a strong odor of musk, that was quite disagreeable.

On returning to the Porcupine, which our Dogs took care not to meddle with—we found the animal already better than half dead. The blood was running from its throat, which the Marten had torn open. Of course, we put the creature out of pain, by killing it outright; and taking the Marten along with us for the purpose of skinning it, we returned homeward, leaving the Elk hunt for another day.

BEAVER

BY LEONARD LEE RUE III

Leonard Lee Rue III (1926 —) was born and grew up in New Jersey, where he still lives. He has been an outdoorsman all his life. His education was in vocational agriculture, but he soon turned to nature as a career. He is a woodsman who has conducted canoe trips in Canada, knows most of the eastern wilderness areas and is at home in the back country of New Jersey where for some years he has been chief gamekeeper for the Coventry Hunting Club. An expert nature photographer as well as a writer, he has contributed to the major outdoor and nature magazines. The World of the White-Tailed Deer *was his first book. This selection is taken from his* The World of the Beaver, *a definitive popular study of the beaver written from extended personal observation and detailed knowledge acquired in the field.*

(*The World of the Beaver*, by Leonard Lee Rue III; J. B. Lippincott Company, 1964.)

Although beavers are famous as engineers, their skills are often overrated. Their persistence is often just as important in getting the dam built, and in keeping it in shape, as is its actual location. Beavers are like people in that some are much more intelligent than others. Many of the dams of beavers have been washed away or broken, yet few people realize this. Often, by merely choosing a slightly different location for the dam, up or down the stream, only a fraction of the work that was expended by beavers would have been needed. They often construct dams that are 100 feet long, whereas if they had sought the ideal spot they could have held the same amount of water with a dam 25 feet long. Yet, once the beavers start to build, no other spot will do. By sheer hard work, they overcome all the obstacles that are presented. Also, there may be reasons why beavers build where they do that are obscure to a human being.

Dam building is actually a compulsion with beavers. If they decide to build their lodge in a manmade pond, where the water is already held back by a good solid concrete dam, they may still not be satisfied until they try to improve upon the job by attempting to cover the concrete with sticks and mud. When building in large natural lakes, beavers will forego the dam-building urge; however, they will dam the outlet streams of smaller lakes. Quite frequently, in Quebec, where most of the country is very flat, beavers will build their lodges on the long spits of land that are usually formed at each lake's entrance by sediment dropped as the flow of water slows down.

Constant persecution of beavers will cause them to completely abandon dam building. Originally the beavers of Europe built dams and lodges like those of the American beavers. Because of steady harassments and pressures by people they gradually stopped building dams, possibly to escape detection. Gradually they stopped building lodges, too, and reverted to living in dens in the banks of ponds and streams. Little by little, European beavers were eliminated. Finally, and just in time, they were given protection, and their numbers started to increase. At the same time, they began to build dams and lodges again, which proved that the age-old habits had not been lost, but were simply repressed.

When the damsite has finally been selected, the newly paired beavers set to work. They fell shrubs and saplings, and though larger pieces are used later, the bulk of the dam will be constructed of relatively small material. Alder, which usually grows in dense thickets by streamsides, is the most frequently used wood. Each piece is dragged to the damsite as soon as it is cut and is placed with the butt end facing upstream. The beavers work feverishly because until there is a pool of water into which they can retreat for safety, they are quite vulnerable to lynxes, wolves, and other predatory animals. Almost everything goes into a dam that the beavers can find—live wood, dead wood, mud, grasses, rocks, and, occasionally, even old railroad ties. A fairly substantial dam can be built by a pair of beavers in three or four nights.

One time, when beavers were building a dam that was flooding out a railroad culvert, officials of the company sent in a work crew to destroy the dam. In doing so, the men used a 9-foot-long iron poker to help pull the dam apart. When the crew departed for the night, they left the poker lying on the dam. On returning the next morning, the men discovered that the beavers had buried the poker in the dam, which helped to reinforce it.

Many times, when beavers have caused economic damage because of the location of their dams, men have tried to discourage their repair work at night by placing lighted lanterns or flare pots on top of the dam. Almost invariably, when they returned in the morning, they found that the lantern or the flare had been buried by the beavers in the dam itself. In fact, one of the men I talked with was convinced that the beavers enjoyed having the light and that it helped them to see better so they could complete their repair work before daybreak and thus keep ahead of the destruction by the work crews.

In building the dam, beavers raise the crest of it uniformly. Wherever a low spot develops, they place more materials and thereby gradually raise the height evenly. This also allows them to extend the wings of the dam as needed. If they built the dam in sections, much effort would be wasted because they would have no way of building it on the same level throughout. They have no levels as carpenters and builders do for guiding their work; therefore they use the waterline, which makes a perfect level.

At first the dam leaks badly, but the beavers soon overcome this. They dredge up mud from the bottom of the pond and plaster it on the dam's upstream side. The flow of the water downstream washes the mud in among the sticks, gradually clogging up the leaks. It is because of this dredging that the deepest part of a beaver's pond is usually directly above the dam. Rocks are used by them to compress and to weight down the brush in the dam. Some of the stones used by beavers in building their dams weigh as much as 30 to 40 pounds and require a tremendous amount of energy from the animals to put them in place.

Sediment and leaves washed downstream gradually collect against the upstream face of the dam, effectively sealing it shut. A dam in good repair will lose very little water through seepage. A beaver dam is built on good engineering principles, with the base always much wider than the top, which counteracts the greater pressures on the bottom of the dam. The upstream face of the dam is not steep, but is tapered upstream like a wedge. Beavers usually take advantage of any boulders, trees, or other natural obstructions that are already in the stream and make them a part of the dam. Because of this, some dams may actually be built "zigzag" across the stream and may look like a W, or have some other odd conformation.

Usually, on streams that are fairly open and deep, the dam will be bowed slightly *downstream.* This happens because the water is forcing the material downstream, and the beaver anchors it where it is. On very fast moving streams, particularly in the western United States where the water builds up great pressure rushing down from high altitudes, the beavers will deliberately bow the dam upstream to counteract it.

In a narrow stream bed, the dam may be comparatively short. In wide, flat meadowlands the dams may be hundreds of feet long. The longest dam I have ever seen was about 800 feet long, while another was 177 good paces (about 500 feet long), or as good a pace as I could make while walking along the crest of the dam. The tallest dam I have seen was 8 feet high from the top of the water on the downstream side to the top of the dam. It would have been even higher if I had measured it from the bottom of the stream itself.

The highest beaver dam that I can find records of was one on Taylor's Creek in Bayfield County, Wisconsin, measured in 1919. It was 12 feet high and 640 feet long. Grasse and Putnam, in their studies of beavers in Wyoming in 1955, photographed a dam that was only 30 feet wide but was 18 feet high. A dam on the Jefferson River near Three Forks, Montana, was 2,140 feet long, but the record must go to a dam built by beavers in New Hampshire near the present town of Berlin. It was 4,000 feet long and created a lake containing forty beaver lodges.

The width of the top, or crest, of the dam itself, varies in thickness. Sometimes it is only a few inches or so wide, or it may be 3 or

4 feet. The older the dam and the wider the crest, the more solidly packed the whole mass becomes. Often, the crest will be so narrow that you actually stand in water as you try to walk along the top because the crest sinks at each footstep. At other times, an old dam becomes a main bridge over a stream, used by all kinds of wild animals. Even moose will sometimes cross a stream on a beaver dam.

Beavers build several types of spillways to take care of the excess water that fills up behind the dam. Often, it is allowed to run over the dam's crest for almost its entire length; at other times it will pour over it at some reinforced point in the crest. Where possible, beavers will prevent water from flowing over the dam by channeling it away at one end so the water flows out harmlessly over solid ground. This is perhaps the safest way, since solid earth can withstand the constant scouring of water much better than the dam.

In times of floods, the pressure on the dam may become so great that it will be washed out. If there is time enough, beavers will usually cut a spillway in the dam itself to relieve the pressure. I have seen this done many times. After the flood waters have subsided, the beavers have only to repair the hole they have cut, which is less work than repairing flood damage to the entire dam.

In an effort to take some of the pressure off the main dam, particularly if it is a long one, the beavers often build subsidiary or reinforcing dams below the main one. These lower dams raise the downstream water up to the base of the main dam and greatly decrease the pressure there. Three or four lower dams built for this purpose may resemble the terraces in the rice paddies of the Philippines. Small dams built upstream from the main one by the beavers increase the accessibility to more food-trees by flooding a greater area.

Although almost everything handy is used by beavers in building a dam, by far the oddest material that I ever saw was in a dam in Van Campen's Brook, above my New Jersey home. There was no wood available, and the entire dam was made of cornstalks! This is not an isolated example, however, as I know of its being done on the same stream in the same locality during three different years. The cornstalks did not have the strength of wood, and the dam was easily broached. However, it was the only material available, and the beavers used it. They did not attempt to build a lodge, but lived in holes in the banks of the stream.

All beaver dams are not built alike. Some of them are very sloppy and are the result of the inexperience of the young beavers or the halfhearted efforts of an old bachelor. I have seen several dams that were of such poor construction that the entire mass of material looked as though it had drifted there.

At times, even the most energetic and intelligent beavers cannot cope with the force of the water. Occasionally, families in adjoining colonies may help each other in the repairs to a dam, but usually only one family builds the dam originally. Yet, there are so many reports of young beavers unable to complete their dams and requiring the help of adults that there may be some truth in them. I have heard that these young beavers try repeatedly to dam a stream. When they fail, they are said to seek out an adult whose superior knowledge and experience makes the building of the dam successful. While these stories seem logical, I have no proof they are true. I feel, however, that the beaver story would be incomplete if I did not tell of them.

It is in the building of its dams that the beaver comes into its greatest conflict with man. Often valuable timber is flooded out and water-killed by the beaver ponds, and roads are often inundated or weakened by the rising waters. To a beaver, one of the best spots to build a dam is on a stream above a road or railroad culvert. The flow of water is already restricted by the steel pipe or concrete culvert that carries it under the highway or railroad. All the beaver needs to do is to build a dam across this narrowed waterway instead of across the full width of the natural stream. There are countless stories and records of the warfare between man and the beaver over its natural instinct to build its dams in such spots. Thousands of dollars and hundreds of man-hours may be spent to oust the beavers. Sometimes the efforts of men are defeated because a challenge of this sort usually brings out the beaver's greatest talents in adapting to the obstacles or in some way circumventing them.

Creosote or oil of tar poured on trees, brush, sticks, the dam itself, or just all over the general area will act as a repellent to beavers, or at least prevent them from picking up the coated sticks in their mouths. However, even this may not deter a really determined beaver. Dams are dynamited, bulldozed, and razed by every means available, and still the beaver fights back. Often, if the beavers would move their dam just a short distance, they would be left in peace. However, it seems that when the beaver once makes up its mind where it wants to build its dam, nothing short of death is going to stop it.

Since beavers are usually protected by state law, outright killing of them because they are a nuisance is forbidden. Under such circumstances the only recourse left is to livetrap them and move them to an area where they are not likely to cause damage. This is not as easy as it might seem because beavers may be wary of traps. Some of them may even spring the trap with a stick and then use the trap as part of the dam.

Much controversy rages about whether a beaver dam is an asset or a detriment to trout fishing. The general opinion today is that most ponds created by the beaver are a help to trout production. It is true that occasionally, in the warmer regions of the country, the water held by the dam warms up so much that the temperature is too high for trout. Another disadvantage for trout is in the removal of trees along the shore of the stream by beavers, which allows more sunlight to strike the water, thus raising its temperature. Also, sediment coming down the stream may settle on the bottom of the pond and cover the gravel beds needed by trout when laying their eggs.

On the other hand, extensive studies have proved that beaver dams are very beneficial to trout. In Wyoming, where the water is too cold to provide adequate food for good trout growth, studies by Grasse and Putnam have proved that the beaver dams were of great benefit to trout. The water of the beaver ponds in these cold streams warmed up enough to allow plentiful hatches of insects on which trout feed, and the growth of the trout was exceptional. The investigators concluded that the beaver ponds were the vital link in trout production. Studies in California also bear this out, and proved that waters dammed up by beavers produced more food and more trout; also, the dams were not a hindrance to the movements of trout, since tagged fish were able to cross the dams at any season.

Besides the advantages to fish, beaver dams and their impounded waters are also a great asset to man. Beaver dams prevent floods by trapping the water high up in the headwaters of streams, preventing it from gaining the momentum that causes destruction. It is far more efficient to dam the smaller tributaries of a stream than to dam the main stream, and the beaver can do the job much better and far cheaper than man. Beaver dams also catch and so reduce the loads of soil sediment that the streams would carry into the manmade dams farther below. Ponds also force more water underground, thus helping low water tables of the land to rise. In addition to providing many wild creatures with an ideal habitat, the ponds also act as storage tanks for livestock in many of the Western streams, as well as providing water for fighting forest fires. Because the water pressure in the streams is reduced by the dams, erosion on lands below them is reduced also.

In order to transport beavers back into the mountainous areas where they can do the most good, many of our states have abandoned the old method of hauling them in by pack horse. Today, beavers are placed in specially designed crates, flown in by airplane, and then parachuted down to the desired spot. Now in a matter of hours the beavers can be put in areas that were once inaccessible, or would have required days of backbreaking work to reach.

One amusing incident involving a beaver dam occurred in the fall of 1962 on the Black River in central New Jersey. Earlier, when beavers moved in, built a dam, and flooded quite a large swamp area, most of the local sportsmen were pleased because of the attractiveness that the pond would have for migrating waterfowl. Everyone looked forward to the hunting season. However, there was a great deal of chagrin on opening day of the duck hunting season when cold weather froze the impounded water, forcing the ducks to go elsewhere.

I have learned to appreciate beaver dams especially when canoeing on some of the smaller streams. Although it requires extra effort for me to get the canoe across the dam, this is more than compensated for by the easy paddling over the long quiet stretch of the pond itself. In fact, ascending some of the swift-running, smaller streams is possible only because of the breaks provided by the quiet waters of beaver ponds.

THE KANGAROO RAT

BY ERNEST THOMPSON SETON

Ernest Thompson Seton (1860–1946) was born in England, grew up in the woodlands of Canada and the western plains of the United States. Both artist and writer, he produced many books about animal life and the outdoors. An able naturalist, he had a particular appeal for young readers, which fact has obscured his contribution to natural history. In books for younger readers he tended toward the romantic and the sentimental, but the core is sound and the natural history is well observed. This selection is from Lives of the Hunted, *and tells about kangaroo rats in Arizona.*

(*Lives of the Hunted,* by Ernest Thompson Seton; Charles Scribner's Sons, 1901.)

It was a rough, rock-built, squalid ranch-house that I lived in, on the Currumpaw. The plaster of the walls was mud, the roof and walls were dry mud, the great river-flat around it was sandy mud, and the hills a mile away were piled-up mud, sculptured by frost and rain into the oddest of mud vagaries, with here and there a coping of lava to prevent the utter demolition of some necessary mud pinnacle by the indefatigable sculptors named.

The place seemed uninviting to a stranger from the lush and fertile prairies of Manitoba, but the more I saw of it the more it was revealed a paradise. For every cottonwood of the straggling belt that the river used to mark its doubtful course across the plain, and every dwarfed and spiny bush and weedy copse, was teeming with *life*. And every day and every night I made new friends, or learned new facts about the mudland denizens.

Man and the birds are understood to possess the earth during the daylight, therefore the night has become the time for the four-footed ones to be about, and in order that I might set a sleepless watch on their movement I was careful each night before going to bed to sweep smooth the dust about the shanty and along the two pathways, one to the spring and one to the corral by way of the former corn-patch, still called the "garden."

Each morning I went out with all the feelings of a child meeting the Christmas postman, or of a fisherman hauling in his largest net, eager to know what there was for me.

Not a morning passed without a message from the beasts. Nearly every night a skunk or two would come and gather up table-scraps, prying into all sorts of forbidden places in their search. Once or twice a bobcat came. And one morning the faithful dust reported in great detail how the bobcat and the skunk had differed. There was evidence, too, that the bobcat quickly said (in Bobcat, of course), "I beg pardon, I mistook you for a rabbit, but will never again make such a mistake."

More than once the sinister trail of the "Hydrophoby-cat" was recorded. And on one occasion the broad track of the king wolf of the region came right up the pathway, nearly to the door, the tracks getting closer together as he neared it. Then stopping, he had exactly retraced his steps and gone elsewhere about his business. Jack-rabbits, coyotes, and cottontails all passed, and wrote for me a few original lines commemorative of their visit—and all were faithfully delivered on call next morning.

But always over and through all other tracks was a curious, delicate, lace-like fabric of polka-dots and interwoven sinuous lines. It was there each morning, fresh made the night before, whatever else was missing. But there was so much of its pattern that it was impossible to take any one line and follow it up.

At first it seemed to be made up of the trails of many small bipeds, each closely followed by its little one. Now, man and birds are the only bipeds, but these were clearly not the tracks of any bird. Trying to be judicial, I put together all the facts that the dust reported. First, here was proof that a number of tiny, two-legged, fur-slippered creatures came nightly to dance in the moonlight. Each one, as he pirouetted about, was closely followed by a much smaller one of the same kind, as though by his page. They came from nowhere and went again as they would. And they must have been invisible at will, or how else escape the ever-watchful coyotes?

If only this had happened in England or Ireland, any peasant could have explained it offhand—invisible pairs of tiny, furry boots, dancing in the moonlight—why, the veriest idiot knows that—*fairies*, of course.

But in New Mexico, I had never heard of such a thing. In no work on this country, so far as I knew, was there any mention of their occurrence.

If only it could be! Would it not be delightful? I would gladly have believed. Christian Anderson would have insisted on believing it, and then made others believe it, too. But for me, alas! it was impossible, for long ago, when my soul came to the fork in the trail marked on the left "To Arcadie," on the right "To Scientia," I took the flinty, upland right-hand path. I had given up my fayland eyes for—for I do not know what. And so I was puzzled, but the more puzzled, the more interested, of course; and remembering, from former experience, that it pays to offer a great deal of clear writing-space to the visitors who nightly favored me with their autographs, I made with unusual care a large extension of the clean-swept dust sheet, to which the sagebrush-scented evening wind added a still smoother finish, and which next day enabled me to follow out a single line of the point-lace pattern.

It went dimpling down the path, toward the six old corn-stumps called the garden, and then, leaving the clear written dust, it had turned aside, and seemed to end at a weed-covered mound, about which were several small holes that went in, not downward, but at a level. (Yes, of course, another pretty mystery nearly gone. How sharp the flints are on this upland path!) I set a trap by these holes, and next morning I had surely caught my "fairy." Just the loveliest, daintiest fawn-brown little creature that ever was seen in fur: large beautiful eyes like a fawn's—no, not like a fawn's, for no fawn that ever lived had such wonderfully innocent orbs of liquid brown, ears like thinnest shells of the sea, showing the pink veins' flood of life. His hind feet were large and strong; but his fore feet—his hands, I mean—were the tiniest of the tiny, pinky white and rounded and dimpled, just like a baby's, only whiter and smaller than the tip of a baby's smallest finger. His throat and breast were snowy white. However does he keep himself so sweetly clean in such a land of mud! Down the outside of his brown velvet knickerbockers was the cutest little silvery-white stripe, just like that on a trooper's breeches. His tail, the train that I suppose the page carried in dancing, was remarkably long, and was decorated to match the breeches with two long white stripes, and ended in a feather duster, which was very pretty but rather overdone, I thought, until I found out that it was designed for several important purposes.

His movements were just like what one might have expected from such an elegant creature. He had touched my heart before I had seen anything but his tracks, and now he won it wholly at first meeting.

"You little beauty! You have been so invisible and mysterious that I began to hope you were a fairy, but now I see I have heard of you before. You are *Perodipus ordi,* that is sometimes called the kangaroo rat. I am much obliged to you for all the lace designs you have sketched and for the pretty verses you have written for me, although I could not read them all; but I am eager to have you translate them, and, in fact, am ready to sit at those microscopic and beautiful feet of yours and learn."

It is of course well known that the daintiest flowers grow out of the dirt, so I was not surprised to find that the Perodipus's home is in a cave underground. No doubt those wonderful eyes and long feelers were to help him in the unlighted corridors of his subterranean house.

It may seem a ruthless deed, but I was so eager to know him better that I determined to open his nest to the light of day as well as keep him a prisoner for a time, to act as my professor in Natural History.

I transferred the plush-clad atom of life to a large box that was lined with tin and half full of loose earth. Then I went out with a spade, carefully to follow and pry into the secrets of the Brownie world of which my captive was a native.

First I made a scaled diagram of the landscape concerned, for science is measurement and exact knowledge was what I had sought since I made my choice of trails. Then I sketched the plants on the low mound. There were three large, prickly thistles, and two vigorous

Spanish bayonettes, or soapweeds, all of them dangerous to an unwary intruder. Next, I noticed there were nine gateways. Nine—I wondered why nine. Nine Muses? Nine lives? No, nothing of that sort (Perodipus does not live in the clouds). There were nine simply because there were nine. . . .

After hours of patient digging and measuring I got a map of the underground world where the Perodipus passes the daytime.

The central chamber could be *nearly* reached by any of the entrances, but one not knowing the secret would have passed by and come out into the air again at another door. No matter how often he went in, he would never have found the nest or any of the real treasure of the home, for the road to the nest was plugged with earth each time the owner left it. . . .

The chamber itself was very large, being twelve inches long and eight inches wide, with a high vaulted roof over five inches from the floor, and ribbed with the living roots of the grand old bayonette-trees at the door. Having discovered the entry to it, I thought I was in the nest; but not so. I was stopped now by a mass of interlaced, spiny grasses. . . . After I had forced my way through this I found that the real entrance was cleverly hidden near a corner. Then there was a thick felting of fine grass and weed silk, and inside of all a lining of softest feathers. I think that every gay little bird on the plains must have contributed one of its finest feathers to that nest, for it was as soft and pretty and warm as it should have been for the cradle of those pinky-white seed-pearls that the Perodipus's babies are when they first come from the land of the stars and the stork into their underground home.

Down in one corner of this great hall I found signs of another secret passage. It was like exploring a mediaeval castle. This passage went down at a slant when I got fairly into it, and before long it opened out into a large storehouse that was filled with over a pint of seeds of the prairie sunflower. This room was sunken deepest of all in the ground, and was also in the shadiest part of the mound, so that the seed would be in no danger of heating and sprouting. At one end of this chamber was another blind lead that possibly was used in filling the warehouse and afterward sealed up for safety. There were many of these blind alleys. They appeared to be either entrances plugged up or else deliberate plans to mislead an intruder who did not have the key to the secret door.

Yet one more chamber was found, and that was a second store-house, a reserve supply of carefully selected helianthus seeds, about half a gill of them, and yet not a bad one or a shrivelled one was to be found in the lot.

But I did not find any of the Perodipus family, and think it possible that when they heard my rude approach they all escaped by some other secret passage that I failed to discover.

This was the home of my nightly visitor, planned and carried out with wisdom for all the straits of his daily life and near future.

Its owner in the cage I now watched with double interest. He was the embodiment of restless energy, palpitating with life from the tip of his translucent nose and ears to the end of his vibrant tail. He could cross the box at a single bound, and I now saw the purpose of his huge tail. In the extraordinary long flying leaps that Perodipus makes, the tuft on the end does for him what the feathers do for an arrow. It keeps him straight in the air on his trajectory. But it does more, for it enables him slightly to change course if he finds it wiser after he has leaped. And the tail itself has other uses. The Perodipus has no pocket in his striped trousers to carry home his winter supplies, but he has capacious pockets, one in each cheek, which he can fill till they bulge out wider than himself—so wide that he must turn his head sidewise to enter his own front gate. Such a load added to his head totally displaces his center of gravity, which is adjusted for leaping with empty pockets. But here is where the tail comes in. Its great length and size make it a powerful lever, and by raising it at different angles he accommodates himself to his load and leaps along in perfect poise in spite of a week's provisions in his cheeks.

He was the most indefatigable little miner I ever saw. Those pinky-white paws, not much larger than a pencil-point, seemed never weary of digging, and would send the earth out between his hind legs in little jets like a steam-shovel. He seemed tireless at his work. He first tunneled the whole mass through and through, and, I doubt not, made and unmade several ideal underground residences, and solved many problems of rapid underground transit. Then he embarked in some landscape gardening schemes and made it his nightly business to change entirely the geography of his whole country, laboriously making hills and canyons wheresoever seemed unto him good.

There was one landscape effect that he seemed very fond of. That was a sort of Colorado Canyon with the San Francisco Mountains on its edge. He tried a long time to use a certain large stone for a peak for his mountain, but it was past his strength, and he resented, rather than profited by, any help I gave him. This stone gave him endless trouble for a time. He could not use it, not even get rid of it, until he discovered that he could at least dig the earth from under it, and so keep it going down, until finally it settled at the bottom of the box and troubled him no more.

He used to take a lot of comfort out of jumping clear from the top of the Frisco Peak across the Grand Canyon into Utah (two hundred miles), at the other side of the box, and back home again to the Peak (six thousand feet).

I watched, sketched, and studied him as well as I could, considering his shyness and nocturnal habits, and I learned daily to admire him more. His untiring devotion to his nightly geographical lesson was marvelous. His talent for heaving up new mountain ranges was astonishing, positively volcanic. When first I suspected his existence, I had been willing to call him a fairy. When I saw him I said, "Why, it's only a kangaroo rat." But after I had watched him a couple of weeks in the cage I realized fully that millions of little creatures with such energy, working for thousands of years, could not but change the whole surface of a country, by letting in the frost and rain, as well as by their own work. Then I was obliged to concede that Perodipus was more than rat or Brownie; he was nothing less than a Geological Epoch.

But one night there was a fresh upheaval of Nature, and my Immeasurable Force tried a new experiment in terrestrial convulsions. He started his mountain, not in the middle of his kingdom, as aforetime, but afar to the southwest, in one corner of the box, and a notable mountain he made. He simply ruined the Grand Canyon to use the materials of its walls.

Higher and higher those pink pawlets piled the beetling crags, and the dizzy peak arose above the sinking plain as it never had before.

It went up fast, too, for it was in the angle of the box, and it was rapidly nearing the heaven of heavens represented by the lid, when an accident turned the current of the Perodipus's ambitions. He was now at an altitude he had never before reached since his imprisonment, so high that he could touch the narrow strip on the wooden walls that was unprotected by the tin. The new substance tempted his teeth. Oh, new-found joy! it was easy to cut. He set to work with his usual energy, and in a very short time cut his way through the half-inch pine, then escaped from the tin-clad kingdom that had been forced upon him, and its Geological Epoch was gone. My professor had quit his chair. . . .

And now he is once more skimming merrily over the mud and sands of the upland plains; shooting across the open like a living, feathered arrow; tempting the rash coyote to thrust his unfortunate nose into those awful cactus brakes, or teaching the prairie owls they will surely come to grief on a Spanish bayonet; coming out by night again to scribble his lacework designs on the smooth places, to write verses of measured rhythm, or to sing and play hop-scotch in the moonlight with his merry crew.

Birds

So the snake became the bird, in some long-forgotten time and for some long-forgotten reason. Thus, we say, wings and feathers and song became a special part of our legacy. Or perhaps the birds, who were here first, inherited man and learned to live with him. Whatever the source and the sequence, the story sings and flashes what we call beauty, and we can leave beginnings to their own past.

Who cares whether a feather was once a scale when a cardinal in the apple tree whistles to his mate? Who would seek origins when a black-capped mite comes to the hand for a seed in a snowstorm and sings *chick-a-dee-dee-dee?* Who thinks of a pterodactyl when a skein of geese, chattering of far places and wide horizons, wings northward in the April moonlight? More than evolution is involved in the flash of an indigo bunting, the gleam of a goldfinch, or the darting flight and hover of a ruby-throated hummingbird.

Bird—what an inadequate name! Yet a name that sings simply because birds sing; because it means robin and wood thrush and brown thrasher as well as grackle and crow and eagle and awkward heron. We wait for the migrant birds to know it is spring. We soar with the swallows in the dusk of June. We hear the woodland in the drumming of the partridge. We sense night's shadowed mysteries in the voice of the owl.

Forget the fossils and the beginnings. Welcome the birds, fly with them, sing with them. Without birds, where would we have learned that there can be song in the heart?

H.B.

THE WHOOPING CRANE'S WORLD

BY ROBERT P. ALLEN

Robert P. Allen (1905–1964) was born and grew up in Lycoming County, Pennsylvania, but he spent the last twenty-odd years of his life in Florida. For thirty years he was Research Director of the National Audubon Society and wrote three of the Society's research reports, on the roseate spoonbill, the flamingo, and the whooping crane. A distinguished ornithologist, he was known as an authority on American wading birds. His book On the Trail of Vanishing Birds, *won for him the John Burroughs Medal. This selection is from* Discovery, *an anthology of original accounts of great moments in the lives of outstanding naturalists, and tells of his experiences with the rare whooping cranes at the Aransas Wildlife Refuge at Austwell, Texas.*

(*Discovery: Great Moments in the Lives of Outstanding Naturalists,* edited by John K. Terres; J. B. Lippincott Company, 1961.)

I knew that twenty-four of the big cranes had started north from Texas the previous April, as they and their kind had done for countless springs. They had responded to a rhythm and a pattern that had been old for long, long slumbering ages.

Now again, toward the end of the winter season there would be a shift in the prevailing wind direction, a new warmth in the damp Gulf Coast air. Since December, the big white whooping cranes on their wintering grounds at Aransas Wildlife Refuge had been solemnly demonstrating the strength of their marriage vows. For the union between these pairs is much more than an intense, temporary, sexual bond. It is a permanent mating, blindly and jealously guarded through innate structures that are firmly established in the character of the species. Even on the wintering grounds, where a relaxing of the strife of territorial defense is the general rule among other birds, there is seldom any letup in the fierce alertness with which the whooping crane pair resists the intrusion of others of its kind.

A neighboring pair that have, in their feeding, encroached a few yards beyond their own territory, will cause the next-door male and his mate to join voices in a shrill duet of violent protest. With bills pointed skyward they seem to stand on tiptoes in their desire to advertise their anger and disapproval. Even a young one of the previous summer, changing rapidly now from the russets and buffs of immaturity to a dirty, smudged sort of whiteness, raises his head with an air of surprising insolence for one of such tender age. But he only glares, for his voice is not yet very impressive, and it is seldom used.

If the invading pair fail to withdraw at the first series of warning notes, the male of our indignant family group struts about with anger in every wrathful line of his body. From my hiding place in my blind, 200 feet away, my binoculars reveal his baleful eyes in which is concentrated cold and furious suspicion. The iris, for all its yellow brilliance, is never warm. The Mexicans sometimes call the whooper the bird of the evil eye—*viejo del mal ojo*—and at close range one can understand why.

There is only a fractional lapse between the male's take-off crouch and that of his mate and offspring. Sometimes I have seen the young bird crook its extended neck just an instant before the male runs forward, wings spread and flapping. There is evidently some definite movement or posture or perhaps a shading of tone in the warning note of the adult male that releases the flight or chasing reaction. Perhaps it is a signal that is not discernible to me but that penetrates the releasing patterns of all three birds and results in a nearly simultaneous take-off.

All three run forward, heads lowered, necks outthrust, wings flapping rather heavily. Five or six running strides may be needed, and the business of getting each individual load of 16 or 18 pounds or more into the air impresses one as labored. Indeed, it seems probable that the wing manipulation of *Grus americana*, the whooping crane, is fairly primitive. Certainly the completely extended posture of the wings in flight, the stiff, "flicking" motion, and the narrow arc of the full beat are less efficient than the easy, graceful, effortless flight of other birds. The evident lack of wrist action suggests that this type of wing beat lies somewhere between the sailing or gliding flight of the earliest birds and the fully developed use of the principles of aerial dynamics exhibited in the flight of more modern species.

Following the lead of the male the trio swerves, banks, and heads straight for the pair that have invaded their territory. Twenty or thirty paces away they change stroke, still seeming to follow the imperceptible lead of the male, their legs thrust down and slightly forward. Then, as they make almost simultaneous contact with the ground, three pairs of wings are flapped in a slow backstroke that brakes the speed of actual grounding. Now the male of the family appears at his most male-ish. The mother and offspring stand stiffly in the background, alert to every movement in the formalized ethological drama before them, but merely a supporting claque, never active participants. The male again stands in the tiptoe posture and sounds his shrill challenge. Then he charges, half running, half flying, head and bill straight forward like a spear. The invading pair of whooping cranes, which have been standing perfectly still, their collective attitude one of guilty foreboding, retreat at once. Who wouldn't! Without apology or shame, they are up and off! The pursuing male is now in the air and bearing down on them. He gets on the tail of the nearest intruder and follows its swerving flight in much the manner of a gull or a tern harrying one of its kind.

The chase carries the two trespassers far into their own territory, even beyond it at times. When they attempt to land in what would seem to be an uncontested area, the relentless pursuer may charge a second time, his reaction still strong. Eventually he has chased the pair 2 miles or so, and, as if the rules of conduct have been satisfied, he returns to his waiting family. Their behavior seems to demonstrate a complete confidence in his ability, although it is more likely a simple lack of warlike male patterns in the female and the immature crane. Before the male has returned from his chase, they have lost interest and have been calmly poking about in the mud of a small temporary pond, looking for trapped crabs or killifishes. The master's return is modestly triumphant, his demeanor suitably arrogant but offhand. All in a day's work!

I suppose that in the solidarity, and the more or less permanent, year-around isolation of the family unit, one can find survival values. At least the evolution of behavior patterns intolerant of trespass by their own kind probably developed such values in the original, undisturbed population. At the present time, however, with the population greatly reduced, this aggressive defense of the wintering territories may actually limit the whooping crane's survival. In our current assortment of families—adult cranes with young; adult pairs without young; pairs that are not mated but are simply companions (perhaps second-winter birds and odd "pairs" of the same sex); and lone cranes—the chances of new breeding pairs being formed readily through close association of unmated birds on the wintering grounds appear to be more difficult. Sometimes this may even be impossible because of the defensive habits of males of established pairs.

For example, in 1947, an adult whooping crane arrived at Aransas Refuge from the [at that time] unknown northern breeding grounds with a young bird in tow, but without a mate. Throughout the winter this lone adult (I suspected it was a female) attempted unsuccessfully to establish a territory. Neighboring males were particularly vicious in driving off this whooping crane and its young one. Later this bird and its offspring joined company with two wandering whooping cranes that had no established territories. These two were probably subadults* in their second winter. The four were seen together on several occasions in later winter of 1948, wandering through the edges of various territories claimed by well-ordered pairs and whooping crane families. Eventually the attacks of the male birds in these territories separated this foursome, although I had hoped that from this situation, the "widowed" adult would find another mate. During the late winter and early spring the family of two was again alone and may have left for the northern breeding grounds by themselves.

Of course, since no observations had been made on the nesting grounds at that time, we did not know what possibilities existed

* A term used by ornithologists for birds that require more than one year to become mature.

there for renesting. Perhaps all pair formation, both the initial mating of three-year-olds and the remating of bereft adults such as the suspected female of our example, takes place at the nesting site. It seemed to be a difficult point to clear up.

There are periodic breaks in the defensive wall that normal groups throw around their winter territories. These relaxations result, perhaps, from the lowering of the physiological drive in typical male and family behavior. On occasion, especially toward the end of the winter season, a wandering pair or a single whooping crane will move slowly through a segment of a territory previously defended, and no challenge from the male and his mate will be forthcoming. The male seems aware of the intrusion, but he and his mate continue their preening or feeding without assuming any of the postures of aggressive defense.

Finally, with the arrival of spring, the southerly winds have set in for the season. Many other migrant birds have moved northward through Aransas Wildlife Range and have gone. Over the salt-flat grass the gull-billed terns search for insects, and on the edge of tidal ponds, brimful from recent rains, pairs of black-necked stilts stand demurely side by side. On the chain of islands offshore the herons, egrets, cormorants, and gulls are already incubating their eggs. Willets flash their splendid wings, and their wild melodious cries fill the warm air. What hereditary vision now penetrates the consciousness of our white cranes? Poised on the outskirts of all this excitement, they give only slight evidence that they are on the brink of their long journey north. Once, three weeks before their departure, I saw a pair fly aloft to an unaccustomed altitude and soar in wide circles, moving gradually and with what seemed reluctance back to the slough below them where they had passed the winter months.

Suddenly the whoopers begin to disappear. For some weeks I had noted subtle marks of change. Pairs with young had begun to show annoyance at the presence of their offspring, each pair driving its gangling hopeful away with sudden jabs and threatening lunges. All of the whooping cranes flew about more, and they seemed more nervous. Less and less were they concerned about defending their winter territories.

Then, by two's and three's they were gone! Whatever it is that has been given them, it is strong enough to send them aloft into an appalling space of sky, to carry them on their widespread wings over thousands of miles of land, across networks of highways, across busy farms and cities, through leagues of foul industrial haze, and dangers unnumbered. It is quite as if they have flown upward and outward to another universe.

The summer passes. Then in autumn it is time for their return. Will they come back? How many of them? Will any young birds return with their parents? Every day I cover the ground at Aransas Refuge. Every acre is scanned and then scanned again. The daily effort becomes routine, it grows stale. You come to hate every mudhole in the road, despise the necessity for climbing out of the jeep at every lookout. You grow irritable, peevish. Another day goes by and then another. You come home at night worried and silent. Your supper is tasteless to you, and your family watches you furtively, but without comment. The children are sent quietly to another room so that they can laugh and talk and be normal. You, miserable wretch, must be alone and let your mind go dead, blank, empty. No one can help. No one can do anything. We can only wait.

Then, on a dull morning that is without hope or fear, you pull up at one of the lookout stations and there they are! The first pair of whooping cranes has come back! There is no russet-colored young with them, but your heart pounds. You had almost forgotten how serene, how magnificently dignified and aloof they are. Scarcely daring to breathe, you watch them. Their heads are up and they are watching you, but the distance is considerable and they are not alarmed. Slowly, elaborately, they pick their way along the rim of the pond, pausing to turn their fierce, searching gazes sharply in your direction.

They have returned. This year they would all return, all but one, one that was lost somewhere in that unknown breeding place and migration route of danger and uncertainty. After the long waking nightmare of the past weeks it seemed a miracle. But there they were, flesh and blood, satiny feathers and great, stiff wings.

Is it an accident that these tall birds have survived beyond the Pleistocene? Perhaps, but they are vital and alive, and now only Man has been able to change their world until it seems nearly untenable. If anything can save the whooping crane from the final indignity of extinction, it must be our doing, a belated balancing of the account for the low numbers to which our guns and drainage of their nesting marshes have brought them. There may still be time.

THE WILD TURKEY

BY JOHN JAMES AUDUBON

John James Audubon (1785–1851), natural son of a French merchant and sea captain, was born in Haiti, educated in France, and came to America at the age of nineteen. On his father's estate near Philadelphia he hunted, fished, and became interested in birds. After various business failures he spent twenty years roaming the wilderness, drawing and painting birds, perhaps inspired by Alexander Wilson's earlier American Ornithology. *By 1826 he had finished the pictures for his* Birds of America, *and, when he failed to find an American publisher, took them abroad. The first volume, published in Scotland in 1827, brought immediate fame, but he did not start writing his* Ornithological Biography *to go with the pictures until three years later. With the help of William MacGillivray it was completed and published in 1839; MacGillivray is usually credited with much of its scientific information. Audubon's later years were spent on* Viviparous Quadrupeds of North America, *which his sons finished after his death. Audubon had rare skill as an artist but was less than a genius as a writer, often being mannered, romantic, or slap-dash. This selection, from the* Ornithological Biography, *is one of the better examples of Audubon's writing, though no one can say how much of a hand MacGillivray had in it. It is more matter-of-fact and less florid than much of the writing Audubon undeniably did alone.*

(*Ornithological Biography*, by John James Audubon; Edinburgh, 1839.)

About the beginning of October, when scarcely any of the seeds and fruits have yet fallen from the trees, these birds assemble in flocks, and gradually move towards the rich bottom lands of the Ohio and Mississippi. The males, or, as they are more commonly called, the *gobblers*, associate in parties of from ten to a hundred, and search for food apart from the females; while the latter are seen either advancing singly, each with its brood of young, then about two-thirds grown, or in connexion with other families, forming parties often amounting to seventy or eighty individuals, all intent on shunning the old cocks, which, even when the young birds have attained this size, will fight with, and often destroy them by repeated blows on the head. Old and young, however, all move in the same course, and on foot, unless their progress be interrupted by a river, or the hunter's dog force them to take wing. When they come upon a river, they betake themselves to the highest eminences, and there often remain a whole day, or sometimes two, as if for the purpose of consultation. During this time, the males are heard *gobbling*, calling, and making much ado, and are seen strutting about, as if to raise their courage to a pitch befitting the emergency. Even the females and young assume something of the same pompous demeanour, spread out their tails, and run around each other, *purring* loudly, and performing extravagant leaps. At length, when the weather appears settled, and all around is quiet, the whole party mounts to the tops of the highest trees, whence, at a signal, consisting of a single *cluck*, given by a leader, the flock takes flight for the opposite shore. The old and fat birds easily get over, even should the river be a mile in breadth; but the younger and less robust frequently fall into the water—not to be drowned, however, as might be imagined. They bring their wings close to their body, spread out their tail as a support, stretch forward their neck, and, striking out their legs with great vigour, proceed rapidly towards the shore; on approaching which, should they find it too steep for landing, they cease their exertions for a few moments, float down the stream until they come to an accessible part, and by a violent effort generally extricate themselves from the water. It is remarkable, that immediately after thus crossing a large stream, they ramble about for some time, as if bewildered. In this state, they fall an easy prey to the hunter.

As early as the middle of February, they begin to experience the impulse of propagation. The females separate, and fly from the males. The latter strenuously pursue, and begin to gobble or to utter the notes of exultation. The sexes roost apart, but at no great distance from each other. When a female utters a call-note, all the gobblers within hearing return the sound, rolling note after note with as much rapidity as if they intended to emit the last and the first together, not with spread tail, as when fluttering round the females on the ground, or practising on the branches of the trees on which they have roosted for the night, but much in the manner of the domestic Turkey, when an unusual or unexpected noise elicits its singular hubbub. If the call of the female comes from the ground, all the males immediately fly towards the spot, and the moment they reach it, whether the hen be in sight or not, spread out and erect their tail, draw the head back on the shoulders, depress their wings with a quivering motion, and strut pompously about, emitting at the same time a succession of puffs from the lungs, and stopping now and then to listen and look. But whether they spy the female or not, they continue to puff and strut, moving with as much celerity as their ideas of ceremony seem to admit. While thus occupied, the males often encounter each other, in which case desperate battles take place, ending in bloodshed, and often in the loss of many lives, the weaker falling under the repeated blows inflicted upon their head by the stronger.

I have often been much diverted, while watching two males in fierce conflict, by seeing them move alternately backwards and forwards, as either had obtained a better hold, their wings drooping, their tails partly raised, their body-feathers ruffled, and their heads covered with blood. If, as they thus struggle, and gasp for breath, one of them should lose his hold, his chance is over, for the other, still holding fast, hits him violently with spurs and wings, and in a few minutes brings him to the ground. The moment he is dead, the conqueror treads him under foot, but, what is strange, not with hatred, but with all the motions which he employs in caressing the female.

When the male has discovered and made up to the female

(whether such a combat has previously taken place or not), if she be more than one year old, she also struts and gobbles, turns round him as he continues strutting, suddenly opens her wings, throws herself toward him, as if to put a stop to his idle delay, lays herself down, and receives his dilatory caresses. If the cock meet a young hen, he alters his mode of procedure. He struts in a different manner, less pompously and more energetically, moves with rapidity, sometimes rises from the ground, taking a short flight around the hen, as is the manner of some Pigeons, the Red-breasted Thrush, and many other birds, and on alighting, runs with all his might, at the same time rubbing his tail and wings along the ground, for the space of perhaps ten yards. He then draws near the timorous female, allays her fears by purring, and when she at length assents, caresses her.

When a male and a female have thus come together, I believe the connexion continues for that season, although the former by no means confines his attentions to one female, as I have seen a cock caress several hens, when he happened to fall in with them in the same place, for the first time. After this the hens follow their favourite cock, roosting in his immediate neighbourhood, if not on the same tree, until they begin to lay, when they separate themselves, in order to save their eggs from the male, who would break them all, for the purpose of protracting his sexual enjoyments. The females then carefully avoid him, except during a short period each day. After this the males become clumsy and slovenly, if one may say so, cease to fight with each other, give up gobbling or calling so frequently, and assume so careless a habit, that the hens are obliged to make all the advances themselves. They *yelp* loudly and almost continually for the cocks, run up to them, caress them, and employ various means to rekindle their expiring ardour.

Turkey-cocks when at roost sometimes strut and gobble, but I have more generally seen them spread out and raise their tail, and emit the pulmonic puff, lowering their tail and other feathers immediately after. During clear nights, or when there is moonshine, they perform this action at intervals of a few minutes, for hours together, without moving from the same spot, and indeed sometimes without rising on their legs, especially towards the end of the love-season. The males now become greatly emaciated, and cease to gobble, their *breast-sponge* becoming flat. They then separate from the hens, and one might suppose that they had entirely deserted their neighbourhood. At such seasons I have found them lying by the side of a log, in some retired part of the dense woods and cane thickets, and often permitting one to approach within a few feet. They are then unable to fly, but run swiftly, and to a great distance. A slow turkey-hound has led me miles before I could flush the same bird. Chases of this kind I did not undertake for the purpose of killing the bird, it being then unfit for eating, and covered with ticks, but with the view of rendering myself acquainted with its habits. They thus retire to recover flesh and strength, by purging with particular species of grass, and using less exercise. As soon as their condition is improved, the cocks come together again, and recommence their rambles. Let us now return to the females.

After the middle of April, when the season is dry, the hens begin to look out for a place in which to deposit their eggs. This place requires to be as much as possible concealed from the eye of the Crow, as that bird often watches the Turkey when going to her nest, and, waiting in the neighbourhood until she has left it, removes and eats the eggs. The nest, which consists of a few withered leaves, is placed on the ground, in a hollow scooped out, by the side of a log, or in the fallen top of a dry leafy tree, under a thicket of sumach or briars, or a few feet within the edge of a cane-brake, but always in a dry place. The eggs, which are of a dull cream colour, sprinkled with red dots, sometimes amount to twenty, although the more usual number is from ten to fifteen. When depositing her eggs, the female always approaches the nest with extreme caution, scarcely ever taking the same course twice; and when about to leave them, covers them carefully with leaves, so that it is very difficult for a person who may have seen the bird to discover the nest.

Several hens sometimes associate together, I believe for their mutual safety, deposit their eggs in the same nest, and rear their broods together. I once found three sitting on forty-two eggs. In such cases, the common nest is always watched by one of the females, so that no Crow, Raven, or perhaps even Pole-cat, dares approach it.

The mother will not leave her eggs, when near hatching, under any circumstances, while life remains. She will even allow an enclosure to be made around her, and thus suffer imprisonment, rather than abandon them. I once witnessed the hatching of a brood of Turkeys, which I watched for the purpose of securing them together with the parent. I concealed myself on the ground within a very few feet, and saw her raise herself half the length of her legs, look anxiously upon the eggs, cluck with a sound peculiar to the mother on such occasions, carefully remove each half-empty shell, and with her bill caress and dry the young birds, that already stood tottering and attempting to make their way out of the nest. Yes, I have seen this, and have left mother and young to better care than mine could have proved—to the care of their Creator and mine. I have seen them all emerge from the shell, and, in a few moments after, tumble, roll, and push each other forward, with astonishing and inscrutable instinct.

Before leaving the nest with her young brood, the mother shakes herself in a violent manner, picks and adjusts the feathers about her belly, and assumes quite a different aspect. She alternately inclines her eyes obliquely upwards and sideways, stretching out her neck, to discover hawks or other enemies, spreads her wings a little as she walks, and softly clucks to keep her innocent offspring close to her. They move slowly along, and as the hatching generally takes place in the afternoon, they frequently return to the nest to spend the first night there. After this, they remove to some distance, keeping on the highest undulated grounds, the mother dreading rainy weather, which is extremely dangerous to the young, in this tender state, when they are only covered by a kind of soft hairy down, of surprising delicacy.

The young Turkeys now advance rapidly in growth, and in the month of August are able to secure themselves from unexpected attacks of Wolves, Foxes, Lynxes, and even Cougars, by rising quickly from the ground, by the help of their powerful legs, and reaching with ease the highest branches of the tallest trees. The young cocks shew the tufts on the breast about this time, and begin to gobble and strut, while the young hens pur and leap, in the manner which I have already described.

The old cocks have also assembled by this time, and it is probable that all the Turkeys now leave the extreme northwestern districts, to remove to the Wabash, Illinois, Black river, and the neighbourhood of Lake Erie.

The Wild Turkeys cannot be said to confine themselves to any particular kind of food, although they seem to prefer the pecan-nut and winter-grape to any other, and, where these fruits abound, are found in the greatest numbers. They eat grass and herbs of various kinds, corn, berries, and fruit of all descriptions. I have even found beetles, tadpoles, and small lizards in their crops.

Turkeys are now generally extremely shy, and the moment they observe a man, whether of the red or white race, instinctively move from him. Their usual mode of progression is what is termed walking, during which they frequently open each wing partially and successively, replacing them again by folding them over each other, as if their weight were too great. Then, as if to amuse themselves, they will run a few steps, open both wings and fan their sides, in the manner of the common fowl, and often take two or three leaps in the air and shake themselves.

When, after a heavy fall of snow, the weather becomes frosty, so as to form a hard crust on the surface, the Turkeys remain on their roosts for three or four days, sometimes much longer, which proves their capability of continued abstinence. When near farms, however, they leave the roosts, and go into the very stables and about the stacks of corn, to procure food. During melting snowfalls, they will travel to an extraordinary distance, and are then followed in vain, it being impossible for hunters of any description to keep up with them. They have then a dangling and straggling way of running, which, awkward as it may seem, enables them to outstrip any other animal. I have often, when on a good horse, been obliged to abandon the attempt to put them up, after following them for several hours. This habit of continued running, in rainy or very damp weather of any kind, is not peculiar to the Wild Turkey, but is common to all gallinaceous birds. In America, the different species of Grouse exhibit the same tendency.

When a Turkey is merely winged by a shot, it falls quickly to the ground in a slanting direction. Then, instead of losing time by tumbling and rolling over, as other birds often do when wounded, it runs off at such a rate, that unless the hunter be provided with a swift dog, he may bid farewell to it. I recollect coming on one shot in this manner, more than a mile from the tree where it had been perched, my dog having traced it to this distance, through one of those thick cane-brakes that cover many portions of our rich alluvial lands near the banks of our western rivers. Turkeys are easily killed if shot in the head, the neck, or the upper part of the breast; but if hit in the hind parts only, they often fly so far as to be lost to the hunter. During winter many of our *real* hunters shoot them by moonlight, on the roosts, where these birds will frequently stand a repetition of the reports of a rifle, although they would fly from the attack of an Owl, or even perhaps from his presence. Thus sometimes nearly a whole flock is secured by men capable of using these guns in such circumstances. They are often destroyed in great numbers when most worthless, that is, early in the fall or autumn, when many are killed in their attempt to cross the rivers, or immediately after they reach the shore.

Whilst speaking of the shooting of Turkeys, I feel no hesitation in relating the following occurrence, which happened to myself. While in search of game, one afternoon late in autumn, when the males go together, and the females are by themselves also, I heard the clucking of one of the latter, and immediately finding her perched on a fence, made towards her. Advancing slowly and cautiously, I heard the yelping notes of some gobblers, when I stopped and listened in order to ascertain the direction in which they came. I then ran to meet the birds, hid myself by the side of a large fallen tree, cocked my gun, and waited with impatience for a good opportunity. The gobblers continued yelping in answer to the female, which all this while remained on the fence. I looked over the log and saw about thirty fine cocks advancing rather cautiously towards the very spot where I lay concealed. They came so near that the light in their eyes could easily be perceived, when I fired one barrel, and killed three. The rest, instead of flying off, fell to strutting around their dead companions, and had I not looked on shooting again as murder without necessity, I might have secured at least another. So I showed myself, and marching to the place where the dead birds were, drove away the survivors. I may also mention, that a friend of mine shot a fine hen, from his horse, with a pistol, as the poor thing was probably returning to her nest to lay.

During spring, Turkeys are *called,* as it is termed, by drawing the air in a particular way through one of the second joint bones of a wing of that bird, which produces a sound resembling the voice of the female, on hearing which the male comes up, and is shot. In managing this, however, no fault must be committed, for Turkeys are quick in distinguishing counterfeit sounds, and when *half civilized* are very wary and cunning. I have known many to answer to this kind of call, without moving a step, and thus entirely defeat the scheme of the hunter, who dared not move from his hiding-place, lest a single glance of the gobbler's eye should frustrate all further attempts to decoy him. Many are shot when at roost, in this season, by answering with a rolling gobble to a sound in imitation of the cry of the Barred Owl.

But the most common method of procuring Wild Turkeys, is by means of *pens*. These are placed in parts of the woods where Turkeys have been frequently observed to roost, and are constructed in the following manner. Young trees of four or five inches diameter are cut down, and divided into pieces of the length of twelve or fourteen feet. Two of these are laid on the ground parallel to each other, at a distance of ten or twelve feet. Two other pieces are laid across the ends of these, at right angles to them; and in this manner successive layers are added, until the fabric is raised to the height of about four feet. It is then covered with similar pieces of wood, placed three or four inches apart, and loaded with one or two heavy logs to render the whole firm. This done, a trench about eighteen inches in depth and width is cut under one side of the cage, into which it opens slantingly and rather abruptly. It is continued on its outside to some distance, so as gradually to attain the level of the surrounding ground. Over the part of this trench within the pen, and close to the wall, some sticks are placed so as to form a kind of bridge about a foot in breadth. The trap being now finished, the owner places a quantity of Indian corn in its centre, as well as in the trench, and as he walks off drops here and there a few grains in the woods, sometimes to the distance of a mile. This is repeated at every visit to the trap, after the Turkeys have found it. Sometimes two trenches are cut, in which case the trenches enter on opposite sides of the trap, and are both strewn with corn. No sooner has a Turkey discovered the train of corn, than it communicates the circumstance to the flock by a cluck, when all of them come up, and searching for the grains scattered about, at length come upon the trench, which they follow, squeezing themselves one after another through the passage under the bridge. In this manner the whole flock sometimes enters, but more commonly six or seven only, as they are alarmed by the least noise, even the cracking of a tree in frosty weather. Those within, having gorged themselves, raise their heads, and try to force their way through the top or sides of the pen, passing and repassing on the bridge, but never for a moment looking down, or attempting to escape through the passage by which they entered. Thus they remain until the owner of the trap arriving, closes the trench, and secures his captives. I have heard of eighteen Turkeys having been caught in this manner at a single visit to the trap. I have had many of these pens myself, but never found more than seven in them at a time. One winter I kept an account of the produce of a pen which I visited daily, and found that seventy-six had been caught in it, in about two months. When these birds are abundant, the owners of the pens sometimes become satiated with their flesh, and neglect to visit the pens for several days, in some cases for weeks. The poor captives thus perish for want of food; for, strange as it may seem, they scarcely ever regain their liberty, by descending into the trench, and retracing their steps. I have, more than once, found four or five, and even ten, dead in a pen, through inattention. Where Wolves or Lynxes are numerous, they are apt to secure the prize before the owner of the trap arrives. One morning, I had the pleasure of securing in one of my pens, a fine Black Wolf, which, on seeing me, squatted, supposing me to be passing in another direction.

Wild Turkeys often approach and associate with tame ones, or fight with them, and drive them off from their food. The cocks sometimes pay their address to the domesticated females, and are generally received by them with great pleasure, as well as by their owners, who are well aware of the advantages resulting from such intrusions, the half-breed being much more hardy than the tame, and, consequently, more easily reared.

While at Henderson, on the Ohio, I had, among many other wild birds, a fine male Turkey, which had been reared from its earliest youth under my care, it having been caught by me when probably not more than two or three days old. It became so tame that it would follow any person who called it, and was the favourite of the little village. Yet it would never roost with the tame Turkeys, but regularly betook itself at night to the roof of the house, where it remained until dawn. When two years old, it began to fly to the woods, where it remained for a considerable part of the day, to return to the enclosure as night approached. It continued this practice until the following spring, when I saw it several times fly from its roosting place to the top of a high cotton-tree, on the bank of the Ohio, from which, after resting a little, it would sail to the opposite shore, the river being there nearly half a mile wide, and return towards night. One morning I saw it fly off, at a very early hour, to the woods, in another direction, and took no particular notice of the circumstance. Several days elapsed, but the bird did not return. I was going towards some lakes near Green river to shoot, when, having walked about five miles, I saw a fine large gobbler cross the path before me moving leisurely along. Turkeys being then in prime condition for the table, I ordered my dog to chase it, and put it up. The animal went off with great rapidity, and as it approached the Turkey, I saw, with great surprise, that the latter paid little attention. Juno was on the point of seizing it, when she suddenly stopped, and turned her head towards me. I hastened to them, but you may easily conceive my surprise when I saw my own favourite bird, and discovered that it had recognised the dog, and would not fly from it; although the sight of a strange dog would have caused it to run off at once. A friend of mine happening to be in search of a wounded deer, took the bird on his saddle before him, and carried it home for me. The following spring it was accidentally shot, having been taken for a wild bird, and brought to me on being recognised by the red ribbon which it had around its neck. Pray, reader, by what word will you designate the recognition made by my favourite Turkey of a dog which had been long associated with it in the yard and grounds? Was it the result of instinct, or of reason—an unconsciously revived impression, or the act of an intelligent mind?

WINTER ON HAWK MOUNTAIN

BY MAURICE BROUN

Maurice Broun (1906 —) was born and grew up in the heart of Boston and saw his first bird, really saw it, in a mid-city park. It was a magnolia warbler. Passionately interested, he began teaching himself and within five years had identified more than two hundred species of birds within five miles of the Boston State House. Soon he became a researcher for the Department of Agriculture, working under two great ornithologists, Edgar Howe Forbush and John B. May. Dr. May was an authority on hawks. Broun went from Boston to Lenox, Massachusetts, and developed the Pleasant Valley Sanctuary, then spent three years researching and banding birds on Cape Cod, and from there went to Shelburne Pass, Vermont, where he was supervisor of nature activities for the Green Mountain Club. And finally, in 1934, he became warden of Hawk Mountain, the first hawk sanctuary ever established, in the Pennsylvania mountains. In Hawks Aloft *he wrote the story of Hawk Mountain and the years he and his wife spent there. Broun is not only an outstanding ornithologist but a botanist of distinction and an authority on ferns. This selection is from* Hawks Aloft, *a memorable account of a unique achievement in conservation.*

(*Hawks Aloft: The Story of Hawk Mountain*, by Maurice Broun; Dodd, Mead & Company, 1949.)

Our nearest neighbor is two miles to the east, near the foot of the mountain, and an unbroken wilderness void of human beings extends four and a half miles south, to the nearest town, Hamburg [Pennsylvania]. We have no telephone and no electricity. We have never felt it a hardship to be without these amenities to living. Despite our oil lamps, despite the washtub in which we bathe with hot water dipped from the tank on the kitchen stove, we have lived well.

Our detachment from the world in these times of endless turmoil and crises intrigues some of our friends; they envy our "splendid isolation." Of course we are not as remote as some might think, for people from all over the continent, and at least fifteen foreign countries, nosing their cars up our mountain road eight months of the year, have enriched our lives. Often we are asked: "Aren't you lonely up there?" We reply emphatically, "No! there's never a dull moment." Not even in the depth of winter, when deep snow closes the road and we seldom see visitors, have we ever felt the slightest touch of loneliness.

A young truck driver once delivered cement to us and thought it remarkable that anyone could live up here on the mountain. Then he saw one of our goats, and exclaimed: "At least, you got something human up here!"

I am a lucky fellow, for it would go hard with me if my wife demanded to be taken to night clubs, or to the movies, or to bridge parties, or if she dashed off at every trumpet call of the Women's Political League. We are very simple people, with simple habits, free from the distractions which most people crave—or endure.

We enjoy people, but we also enjoy solitude—especially the solitude of the mountains in winter. This would be an unthinkable existence to the mass of people. I remember the woman who came to get her young son who had been staying with us. She could not get off the mountain quickly enough. "You can have it," she said tartly, "I'll take Atlantic City."

It is one of the tragedies of modern civilization, I think, that most people are unable to enjoy solitude. When I was in the Service I observed that almost all the stalwart young heroes whom I encountered were quite unable to endure solitude; indeed, they seemed to be afraid to be alone with their thoughts. Because I enjoyed solitary excursions into the jungles of the South Pacific islands I was considered eccentric. For perhaps a million years man must have been forced into solitude from time to time; his nervous system became attuned to the stimuli of nature: the sound of the wind, the lapping of waters, the green of plant life. Such things soothe the nervous system, allowing imagination and constructive thoughts to ripen in the individual. Christ, and all the truly great figures of history, recognized the value of solitude; they were able to pull themselves onto the right spiritual track by frequent contact with nature. So it is that because modern man has, for the most part, lost the ability to use solitude, he is quite unaware of the things he suffers. Perhaps a Sanctuary like ours has an additional function: to provide solitude and re-creation for the human soul.

As a youngster, city-bred, I yearned for the simplicities of country life; not merely rural living, but far-off wilderness living. I wanted to escape from the grating noises, the confusion, the artificialities of the city; I wanted to get as far as possible from the slavery of our machine civilization. I was inspired by Thoreau, who wrote: ". . . if one advances confidently in the direction of his dreams, and endeavors to live the life which he has imagined, he will meet with a success unexpected in common hours." I enjoyed my first taste of solitude during three years passed in the pioneer development of the Pleasant Valley Bird Sanctuary in the heart of the Berkshires. It was a salutary experience for me, in which I quickly learned the full meaning of self-reliance. For to breast the sudden transition from city living to life in the woods meant learning how to use my hands and tools. I then in part had achieved my dreams but, unlike Thoreau, I was a sorry bachelor. Three winters of complete aloneness could not entirely fulfill the "direction of my dreams." I wanted a marriage partner, but I despaired of ever finding one who would put up with me. But as all things supposedly come to him who waits, in due time I found my wife during another three years of comparative solitude on Cape Cod.

We have spent five winters on Hawk Mountain (two of them before the war), without ever once feeling any trace of "cabin fever." To both of us, winter is a season of deep contentment. And nearly complete isolation. We have been snowed in as much as seven weeks at a time. Once only have we seen a snowplow on our usually forgotten road. That was after a severe storm in late January, 1948—the winter which, according to the oldest inhabitants of the valley, was the worst and hardest in their memory. Except for the little runways of our dogs and our own imprints around the house, the snow lay deep and trackless. And then, wonder of wonders, the snowplow churned up the road. We could hardly believe our eyes. For a brief hour or so, we were excited and delighted with this consideration never shown to us before. But presently we reconsidered. We resented this intrusion! We were blissfully secure in our isolation. The unbroken road was beautiful. Who cared for a life-line to civilization!

Our winter preparations begin in late May, when the tender shoots of pokeweed, or pigeon-berry, appear along the roadside. The pokeweed shoots are delicious; like asparagus, but better, in my opinion. Pokeweed grows so abundantly near Schaumboch's that my wife cans quarts of it. She has also canned dandelion greens. It is a thrilling thing, in the dead of winter, to bring up from the cellar these tasty, nourishing Maytime products. Then, in June and July, she busily gathers and preserves the wild strawberries and blackberries (from the valley pastures), and the vegetables from our gardens. Later she makes the most savory jellies from the wild grapes which grow in dense tangles all about the edges of our little apple orchard. . . .

Sub-zero temperatures seldom strike the mountain. The house, situated in a dimple of the mountain, at 1100 feet, is exposed to the easterly gales, but it is reasonably well protected from the north and west. On only three occasions during the bitter winter of 1948 did the mercury at the house dip to just below zero. But in the Great Valley, where the cold air settles like a heavy blanket, the temperatures often sagged to as much as 18° or 20° below zero. On the other hand, the snow is usually gone from the valley floor, which is about 500 feet above sea level, by mid-March; and on the mountain it lingers into April.

Ice storms visit us three or four times each winter. Though they may spread across the mountain a sparkling, crystal mantle whose beauty beggars description, they are nevertheless the only dreaded features of our winter; they invariably spell real ice-olation, and sometimes wreak havoc to the forest. During the winter of 1947 there was a three-weeks' period when we could hardly move from the house, for to venture out on the glassy road or into the woods was an invitation to a broken neck. Yet 300 yards down the road, at an elevation of about 750 feet, there is a sharp line of demarcation, below which there is seldom any ice.

One Christmas Eve a furious ice storm struck. Sleet and snow piled up rapidly and a stinging east wind crackled the ice-burdened birches by the house. We were snug by the little wood stove in our living room. There was an odd scratching at the window. "Sleet," I remarked to my wife. The scratching persisted. Upon investigation we saw a small bird struggling against the windowpane. I went out and gently picked up a goldfinch. It might have perished within an hour, on the deep snow of the window sill. The goldfinch had room and board for the night, in a small wire cage which I placed in the cool, dark attic. Next morning we looked out on a glittering, fairyland world in which we were trapped securely. But not our goldfinch. It took off with a joyous song. Nothing could have given us deeper pleasure on that Christmas Day than the rescue of that terror-stricken little bird, lost in the night.

The ice storm of New Year's Day, 1948, will long be remembered. The devastation to trees, to telephone and electric installations throughout the Northeast was terrific, and brought with it real hardship to thousands of families. Though we were locked in as though in the heart of a glacier, we were not inconvenienced. Our friends in the valley, long accustomed to electrical conveniences, dug out their old oil lamps, put aside their radios, and for a month or more reverted to the simple ways of fifty years ago. At Schaumboch's our oil lamps and coal and wood stoves glowed cheerfully, and our battery-set radio kept us up to the minute on all the crucial happenings between man and weather. But the inch-and-a-half wall of ice that formed on our mountain literally crushed the forest, destroying or damaging most of the first-rate hardwood trees. It was ghastly. The rattling of the ice-sheathed branches sounded like the clashing of steel sabres.

Throughout that night we were awakened by the sharp, pistol-like sounds of branches and trees snapping under their burdens of accumulated ice. The next morning we could hardly believe our eyes. We looked out through ice-draped windows on an incredible world of ice and splintery trees bowed to the ground, of small trees flattened, of mangled trees everywhere—a frozen chaos! All day the impenetrable woods resounded with the cracking and snapping of oaks and poplars. I was awed to see a big poplar, and a fifty-foot oak, each snap into splinters, like matchsticks. The top of our big persimmon tree went and the tree looked as though it had been pruned by a maniac. Nearly every large tree about the house sustained ugly, irremediable damage. Interlacing branches and tops of trees folded over and settled athwart the road, making it impassable.

Snow, and chickadees all that day! The chickadees, bless their sturdy little souls, slid from icicle to icicle to reach the feeding stations which were well stocked with everything a chickadee loves. I heard a pileated woodpecker hammering (or chopping ice!) south of the house.

The radio was full of talk of the storm's havoc—"the worst storm of the century," with power lines down, trees littering all highways, motor traffic almost nil, and rampant devastation from Maine to Missouri. The ice of this one storm clung to the east side of Schaumboch's for six weeks.

A week later a gang of roadmen cleared our road of the storm-slashed trees. It required three days for twelve men to remove the debris from a three-mile stretch of the road. And as late as January 9th we heard the snapping and crashing of trees. For days the sun was in hiding. We would look out the window and wince with pain: gray, icy fog hanging like doom over a forest that looked as though it had been ravaged by war; chilling, clinging fog, producing a lost-world effect. Then, at last, eight days after the storm, the sun came out, coyly, tentatively, exposing diamond-studded horizons. The ice-armored trees took on sparkling life and lustre; a dead, gray world was transformed into matchless brilliance and beauty—but a beauty cruel and pain-inspired.

Bird life on our mountain, so excitingly abundant in the periods of migration, drops to its nadir during the winter months. Then far more birds may be found on the farmlands along the foot of the mountain, where there is a greater variety of natural foods, including weed-seeds. But our two pairs of "log-cocks" (pileated woodpeckers) are worth two hundred common birds. For three consecutive winters one pair has been wedded to the vicinity of Schaumboch's. Several times a week we are thrilled to hear the wild cry of one or the other of these big woodpeckers, and sometimes we see them in flight over the orchard. . . .

Our animal life during the winter months is far more varied and numerous than the bird life, but it is less obvious and must often be read and interpreted in the record of the snow. The winter begins with a large number of deer frequenting the Sanctuary. They come to us in early December, in the course of the detested deer-hunting season. I have often seen deer leaping over our boundary wire and into the Sanctuary when the surrounding forest was creeping with deer-hunters. By midwinter most of the deer have taken off for the sheltered ravines and rhododendron tangles of the lower flanks of the ridge, or to the proximity of the open fields. At least a score are residents, however. We have seen the deer stalk out of the woods in the gathering twilight and come to feast at our persimmon tree, pawing and shaking the lower branches to get at the fruit.

Gray squirrels and opossums also come to enjoy their share of the persimmons. The squirrels fearlessly spend long hours in the topmost part of the tree, where the fruit is abundant. The raccoons that help the robins to strip the big cherry tree in back of the house during June remind us of their neighborliness during the inclement season when, on mild days, we find their tracks quite close to the house. The timorous cottontail rabbit is everywhere, often in the most surprising places in the woods; but they also build their nests in the orchard and raise their young in spite of the daily trespass of our dogs. I suspect the perennial presence of our owls is possible only because of the ubiquitous cottontails and wood rats. A tramp through the woods nearly always reveals the presence of foxes, both the red and the gray. I have often in winter examined the faeces of the red fox, and invariably they have contained the remains of mice. Neither species is numerous, for in all the surrounding country the unfortunate creatures are harried and trapped relentlessly.

Red-backed mice and short-tailed shrews occasionally seek food right at our kitchen door. Marvelously alert little beasts, they can disappear into their snow-tunnels as fast as you can flick an eyelid. Some of the smaller furry creatures of the woods invade Schaumboch's regularly. White-footed mice are among the most winsome and attractive and courageous little animals that I know, but I prefer them in their own world, rather than when they intrude into ours. When they invade the house I set traps reluctantly. I have endeavored vainly to make the cellar walls mouse-proof. But the mice come, and we must keep controlling them everlastingly, or else suffer an endless repertoire of mouse-noises within our thick stone walls. A weasel took over the job of control for us in the late fall of 1947, for which I was grateful. It lived in a stone wall by our garden. His mousing activities were so wonderfully effective that we were practically free of mice all that winter. The weasel's work was further abetted, I am sure, by both short-tailed shrews and the tiny smoky shrews which also take up residence in our cellar.

Allegany wood rats and occasionally bats were former inhabitants of Schaumboch's, which we once tolerated, for they did help to enliven two of our earlier winters at the Sanctuary. When we renovated the old house and improved the cellar with a concrete floor, in the spring of 1946, all our relations with the rats ceased, for no self-respecting wood rat would deign to dwell with us. We have no regrets!

Our daily contact with the birds and animals leading their untrammeled lives has brightened our own lives immeasurably. There are men who earn their sustenance as "game protectors." But they must not be confused with animal lovers. The game protector is a breed I know well. Rarely does he have humility and love in his heart for the creatures of the wild. He slays the fox to save the rabbit; he kills the owl hoping to fill the hunter's bag with more partridges; and he resists and stamps out anything that might compete with the pleasures of the hunter. And rarely does he understand, or even care to understand, the delicate, complex inter-relationships of all wild things. The game protector is the minion of the hunter. And as Samuel Johnson has observed, "It is very strange and melancholy that the paucity of human pleasures should persuade us ever to call hunting one of them."

WINTER OWLS

BY JOHN BURROUGHS

John Burroughs (1837–1921) was born on a farm near Roxbury, New York, and grew up in the woods and fields of the Catskills. He had a good enough education to spend several years as a rural schoolteacher, after which he spent ten years as a government clerk in Washington. Then he returned to his native hills, bought a farm and settled down to observe nature and write. The greater part of his nature writing was done in the next twenty years, after which he became more interested in philosophy. He had in him a mixture of Emerson, Whitman and Darwin, salted with a dash of Thoreau. Though he posed as a simple countryman, he traveled much, made friends with the leading men of his day, and became a national figure. His nature observation was often acute and he wrote with a persuasive blend of the colloquial and the classic which pleased a large audience. Some credit Burroughs with establishing the "nature essay" as a literary form, though what he really did was revive it and take it outdoors again, breathe air and life into it. The selection I have included here is from the volume of his essays titled A Year in the Fields, *which was primarily about his own farm and the nearby area.*

(*A Year in the Fields*, by John Burroughs; Houghton Mifflin Company, 1896.)

The country is more of a wilderness, more of a wild solitude, in the winter than in the summer. The wild comes out. The urban, the cultivated, is hidden and negatived. You shall hardly know a good field from a poor, a meadow from a pasture, a park from a forest. Lines and boundaries are disregarded; gates and bar-ways are unclosed; man lets go his hold upon the earth; title-deeds are deep buried beneath the snow; the best-kept grounds relapse to a state of nature; under the pressure of the cold, all the wild creatures become outlaws, and roam abroad beyond their usual haunts. The partridge comes to the orchard for buds; the rabbit comes to the garden and lawn; the crows and jays come to the ash-heap and corn-crib, the snow buntings to the stack and to the barnyard; the sparrows pilfer from the domestic fowls; the pine grosbeak comes down from the north and shears your maples of their buds; the fox prowls about your premises at night; and the red squirrels find your grain in the barn or steal the butternuts from your attic. In fact, winter, like some great calamity, changes the status of most creatures and sets them adrift. Winter, like poverty, makes us acquainted with strange bedfellows.

For my part, my nearest approach to a strange bedfellow is the little gray rabbit that has taken up her abode under my study floor. As she spends the day here and is out larking at night, she is not much of a bedfellow, after all. I think she is some support to me under there,—a silent, wide-eyed witness and backer; a type of the gentle and harmless in savage nature. She has no sagacity to give me or lend me, but that soft, nimble foot of hers, and that touch as of cotton wherever she goes, are worthy of emulation. I think I can feel her goodwill through the floor, and I hope she can mine. When I have a happy thought, I imagine her ears twitch, especially when I think of the sweet apple I will place at her doorway at night. I wonder if that fox chanced to catch a glimpse of her the other night when he stealthily leaped over the fence near by and walked along between the study and the house? How clearly one could read that it was not a little dog that had passed there! There was something furtive in the track; it shied off away from the house and around it, as if eyeing it suspiciously; and then it had the caution and deliberation of the fox,—bold, bold, but not too bold; wariness was in every footprint. If it had been a little dog that had chanced to wander that way, when he crossed my path he would have followed it up to the barn and have gone smelling around for a bone; but this sharp, cautious track held straight across all others, keeping five or six rods from the house, up the hill, across the highway toward a neighboring farmstead, with its nose in the air, and its eye and ear alert, so to speak.

A winter neighbor of mine, in whom I am interested, and who perhaps lends me his support after his kind, is a little red owl, whose retreat is in the heart of an old apple-tree just over the fence. Where he keeps himself in spring and summer, I do not know, but late every fall, and at intervals all winter, his hiding-place is discovered by the jays and nuthatches, and proclaimed from the treetops for the space of half an hour or so, with all the powers of voice they can command. Four times during the winter they called me out to behold this little ogre feigning sleep in his den, sometimes in one apple-tree, sometimes in another. Whenever I heard their cries, I knew my neighbor was being berated. The birds would take turns looking in upon him, and uttering their alarm notes. Every jay within hearing would come to the spot, and at once approach the hole in the trunk or limb, and with a kind of breathless eagerness and excitement take a peep at the owl, and then join the outcry. When I approached they would hastily take a final look, and then withdraw and regard my movements intently. After accustoming my eyes to the faint light of the cavity for a few moments I could usually make out the owl at the bottom feigning sleep. Feigning, I say, because this is what he really did, as I first discovered one day when I cut into his retreat with an axe. The loud blows and the falling chips did not disturb him at all. When I reached in with a stick and pulled him over on his side, leaving one of his wings spread out, he made no attempt to recover himself, but lay among the chips and fragments of decayed wood, like a part of themselves. Indeed, it took a sharp eye to distinguish him. Not till I had pulled him forth by one wing, rather rudely, did he abandon his trick of simulated sleep or death. Then, like a detected pickpocket, he was suddenly transformed into another creature. His eyes flew wide open, his talons clutched my finger, his ears were depressed, and every motion and look said, "Hands off, at your peril." Finding this game did not work, he soon began to "play possum" again. I put a cover over my study wood-box and kept him captive for a week. Look in upon him at any time, night or day, and he was apparently wrapped in the profoundest slumber; but the live mice which I put into his box from time to time found his sleep was easily broken; there would be a sudden rustle in the box, a faint squeak, and then silence. After a week of captivity, I gave him his freedom in the full sunshine: No trouble for him to see which way and where to go.

Just at dusk in the winter nights, I often hear his soft *bur-r-r-r*, very pleasing and bell-like. What a furtive, woody sound it is in the winter stillness, so unlike the harsh scream of the hawk! But all the ways of the owl are ways of softness and duskiness. His wings are shod with silence, his plumage is edged with down.

Another owl neighbor of mine, with whom I pass the time of day more frequently than with the last, lives farther away. I pass his castle every night on my way to the post-office, and in winter, if the hour is late enough, I am pretty sure to see him standing in his doorway, surveying the passers-by and the landscape through narrow slits in his eyes. For four successive winters now have I observed him. As the twilight begins to deepen, he rises up out of his cavity in the apple-tree, scarcely faster than the moon rises from behind the hill, and sits in the opening, completely framed by its outlines of gray bark and dead wood, and by his protective coloring virtually invisible to every eye that does not know he is there. Probably my own is the only eye that has ever penetrated his secret, and mine never would have done so had I not chanced on one occasion to see him leave his retreat and make a raid upon a shrike that was impaling a shrew-mouse upon a thorn in a neighboring tree, and which I was watching. Failing to get the mouse, the owl returned swiftly to his cavity, and ever since, while going that way, I have been on the lookout for him. Dozens of teams and foot-passengers pass him late in the day, but he regards them not, nor they him. When I come along and pause to salute him, he opens his eyes a little wider and, appearing to recognize me, quickly shrinks and fades into the background of his door in a very weird and curious manner. When he is not at his outlook, or when he is, it requires the best powers of the eye to decide the point, as the empty cavity itself is almost an exact image of him. If the whole thing had been carefully studied, it could not have answered its purpose better. The owl stands quite perpendicular, presenting a front of light mottled gray; the eyes are closed to a mere slit, the ear feathers depressed, the beak buried in the plumage, and the whole attitude is one of silent, motionless waiting and observation. If a mouse should be seen crossing the highway, or scudding over any exposed part of the snowy surface in the twilight, the owl would doubtless swoop down upon it. I think the owl has learned to distinguish me from the rest of the passers-by;

at least, when I stop before him, and he sees himself observed, he backs down into his den, as I have said, in a very amusing manner. Whether bluebirds, nuthatches, and chickadees—birds that pass the night in cavities of trees—ever run into the clutches of the dozing owl, I should be glad to know. My impression is, however, that they seek out smaller cavities. An old willow by the roadside blew down one summer, and a decayed branch broke open, revealing a brood of half-fledged owls, and many feathers and quills of bluebirds, orioles, and other songsters, showing plainly enough why all birds fear and berate the owl. . . .

The only ones of my winter neighbors that actually rap at my door are the nuthatches and woodpeckers, and these do not know that it is my door. My retreat is covered with the bark of young chestnut trees, and the birds, I suspect, mistake it for a huge stump that ought to hold fat grubs (there is not even a book-worm inside of it), and their loud rapping often makes me think I have a caller indeed. I place fragments of hickory-nuts in the interstices of the bark, and thus attract the nuthatches; a bone upon my window sill attracts both nuthatches and the downy woodpecker. They peep in curiosity through the window upon me, pecking away at my bone, too, often a very poor one. A bone nailed to a tree a few feet in front of the window attracts crows as well as lesser birds. Even the slate-colored snowbird, a seed-eater, comes and nibbles it occasionally.

The bird that seems to consider he has the best right to the bone both upon the tree and upon the sill is the downy woodpecker, my favorite neighbor among the winter birds, to whom I will mainly devote the remainder of this chapter. His retreat is but a few paces from my own, in the decayed limb of an apple-tree which he excavated several autumns ago. I say "he" because the red plume on the top of his head proclaims the sex. It seems not to be generally known to our writers upon ornithology that certain of our woodpeckers—probably all the winter residents—each fall excavate a limb or the trunk of a tree in which to pass the winter, and that the cavity is abandoned in the spring, probably for a new one in which nidification takes place. So far as I have observed, these cavities are drilled out only by the males. Where the females take up their quarters I am not so well informed, though I suspect that they use the abandoned holes of the males of the previous year.

The particular woodpecker to which I refer drilled his first hole in my apple-tree one fall four or five years ago. This he occupied till the following spring, when he abandoned it. The next fall he began a hole in an adjoining limb, later than before, and when it was about half completed a female took possession of his old quarters. I am sorry to say that this seemed to enrage the male very much, and he persecuted the poor bird whenever she appeared upon the scene. He would fly at her spitefully and drive her off. One chilly November morning, as I passed under the tree, I heard the hammer of the little architect in his cavity, and at the same time I saw the persecuted female sitting at the entrance of the other hole as if she fain would come out. She was actually shivering, probably both from fear and cold. I understood the situation at a glance; the bird was afraid to come forth and brace the anger of the male. Not till I rapped smartly upon the limb with my stick did she come out and attempt to escape; but she had not gone ten feet from the tree before the male was in hot pursuit, and in a few moments had driven her back to the same tree, where she tried to avoid him among the branches. A few days after, he rid himself of his unwelcome neighbor in the following ingenious manner: He fairly scuttled the other cavity; he drilled a hole into the bottom of it that let in the light and the cold, and I saw the female there no more. I did not see him in the act of rendering this tenement uninhabitable; but one morning, behold it was punctured at the bottom, and the circumstances all seemed to point to him as the author of it. There is probably no gallantry among the birds except at the mating season. I have frequently seen the male woodpecker drive the female away from the bone upon the tree. When she hopped around to the other end and tentatively nibbled at it, he would presently dart spitefully at her. She would then take up her position in his rear and wait till he had finished his meal. The position of the female among the birds is very much the same as that of woman among the savage tribes. Most of the drudgery of life falls upon her, and the leavings of the males are often her lot.

ON THE HEELS OF THE DODO

BY DON R. ECKELBERRY

Don R. Eckelberry (1921 —) was born and grew up in Ohio. An artist since boyhood, he has painted nearly all the birds of the continental United States and illustrated many books. For the past several years he has been painting the birds of America's tropics, doing field research in Mexico, Central and South America, and the West Indies. Like so many artists, he writes with economy and color and with authoritative detail. This selection first appeared in Discovery, *a collection of personal experiences by thirty-six outstanding naturalists. There it was titled "Search for the Rare Ivorybill," but at the author's suggestion I have restored his original title, "On the Heels of the Dodo."*

(*Discovery: Great Moments in the Lives of Outstanding Naturalists*, edited by John K. Terres; J. B. Lippincott Company, 1961.)

My arrival on the Singer Tract in Louisiana in 1944 was the end of a chain of events. These began twelve years earlier in the offices of the Louisiana Department of Conservation when, on an April day in 1932, a dead bird arrived, shipped from the northeastern part of the state. It was a big woodpecker, larger than a crow, strikingly patterned black and white, with a long scarlet crest and a prodigious ivory-white beak. The Conservation Department pronounced it a male ivory-billed woodpecker, *Campephilus principalis,* possibly the rarest bird in North America. None had been seen since 1926, and museum men were ready to dust off their specimens and put them on that shelf of extinct species already crowded with birds eloquent in their glassy-eyed reproach at our misuse of a continent.

When rediscovery of ivory-billed woodpeckers in Louisiana came, and with it some hope of saving them, the National Audubon Society made an immediate investigation of the area and found that there were at least six living birds in the Singer Tract, perhaps more. In this largest remaining southern hardwood forest of 80,000 acres, it was well-nigh impossible to make an exact census.

Effort for protection of the ivorybills began, and the Louisiana State Conservation Department had wardens on the Singer Tract. They forbade the collecting of any more birds; however, in order to make their rarity and value appreciated by the American public, a newspaper story had put an estimated value of one thousand dollars on an ivorybill skin. Forthwith a young fellow appeared with one of the big woodpeckers dangling from his hand, to collect the one thousand dollars. Wardens in the Singer Tract thereafter kept stricter vigil.

When a few ivorybills were also discovered in a similar wilderness along the lower Santee River in South Carolina, things seemed to be looking up. By 1937 the National Audubon Society had established a research fellowship at Cornell University which began with an extensive search throughout the South for more birds. This was to be followed by a careful study of the Louisiana group to try to find the key to an intelligent program to save the species.

James T. Tanner, a graduate student at Cornell University, was granted the research fellowship. He traveled thousands of miles on this assignment to the wildest, most inaccessible places where the ivory-billed woodpeckers had been rumored to be, or might persist. In many a small village and on many a backwoods farm, Tanner might have been seen showing photographs of the ivorybill to old-timers, logging men, game wardens, native guides, and hunters, but no more birds were found. In fact, the South Carolina birds had vanished, but from his travels and conversations, Tanner believed there could still be a few, perhaps as many as two dozen, lurking in the murky recesses of such habitats as Florida's Big Cypress Swamp.

Tanner settled down to his study of the Louisiana birds. His findings indicate that the ivorybill is, among birds, something of a gourmet, dining almost exclusively on certain wood-boring grubs which infest the inner bark next to the sapwood. Nature gave this largest of our woodpeckers (second in size, incidentally, only to the similar imperial woodpecker of Mexico) the very specialized job of keeping these particular insect larvae in check. Sometimes epidemics of these wood-boring insects kill large stands of trees.

After two or three years a dead cypress tree loses its bark and with it the insect food supply of the ivorybill. This means that the lordly ivorybill must depend on a regular supply of dying trees. Even in mature or virgin forest with its more or less regular death rate, even in these food-plain forests where tree growth is especially rapid, the ivorybill needs plenty of range to satisfy its appetite. Perhaps the species was nomadic, and when natural catastrophes such as storm, fire, or drought killed many trees, the ivorybills would move into such places until the food ran out and they were forced to look for food elsewhere. This theory would explain the sudden appearances of ivorybills in new areas and its equally sudden disappearances from old haunts. It may be the reason why mated pairs have the habit of moving about together throughout the year except during the nesting season when females are tied down with their families.

However that may be, we know that the ivorybills retreated from their original range, which was principally the river-bottom forests from Texas to North Carolina and up the Mississippi Valley to Indiana. As the South was lumbered, and the wilderness melted away, the remaining isolated patches were so far separated that the remaining birds were restricted to them. Unless such areas met their exacting requirements, they disappeared. The Singer Tract evidently suited them.

Since 1926 the owners had leased the tract to the state of Louisiana as a game refuge, but this lease did not prevent commercial exploitation. Logging rights were sold in 1937 while Tanner was still busy in the tract with his research. The National Audubon Society worked rapidly with federal and state officials hoping that the area might be purchased and set aside as a park or refuge not only for the rare woodpeckers, but as a sample of primeval southern hardwood forest with its teeming wildlife intact, as a permanent living exhibit for the American people.

When the United States entered World War II, lumbering in this country was greatly accelerated. The last known home of the ivory-bills was coming down around their heads. A final effort to save them got under way. John H. Baker, President of the National Audubon Society, went directly to President Franklin Delano Roosevelt, whose interest in such matters had always been great. The President expressed his interest in writing to the Secretary of the Interior. Baker followed through with the Secretary, with the Director of the U. S. Fish and Wildlife Service, and with the Director of the National Park Service. He spoke with the Acting Chief of the U. S. Forest Service, who stated that in the light of his knowledge of the inventory of southern hardwood timber, he did not think it necessary to cut all of the Singer Tract. The head of the War Production Board stated that he saw no reason why the board should not rule that the cutting of some of the timber on this tract might not well be excluded from the war production program.

Baker then went to the Governor of Louisiana and his Conservation Commissioner. It was decided that the state of Louisiana would spend $200,000 in the purchase of as much of the area as this sum would buy and set up an inviolate wildlife refuge. At the instance of the Governor, a meeting was arranged at the offices of the lumber company in Chicago and was attended by the Chairman of the Board and President of the company, the Conservation Commissioner representing the state of Louisiana, the Chief of the Division of Wildlife Refuges of the U. S. Fish and Wildlife Service and his counsel, and Mr. Baker. The Wildlife Service was prepared to lease, with options to buy, a buffer area of cutover land.

Just prior to this meeting, the Governors of four states sent a joint letter of appeal to the lumber company and the owners. In spite of all this demonstrated interest, the officials of the lumber company took the position that they were unwilling to discuss any form of cooperation in setting up a wildlife refuge which would involve any limitation whatever on their plan to complete cutting of timber in accordance with their contract rights.

With negotiations still stalemated at the end of 1943, Richard H. Pough, who was then, like myself, on the staff of the National Audubon Society, went down to the Singer Tract to see how the ivory-bills were making out. After six weeks of careful investigation, Pough sent disastrous news: "I have been able to locate only a single female and feel reasonably sure that no other birds are here." Knowing Dick, I knew that "reasonably sure" meant "sure." With this report I was wild to be off to Louisiana, not just to see a living ivorybill, but to sketch and paint as an historic record the only one known to be alive.

Dick Pough told me that the best way to find the bird was to have Jesse Laird, a local man who was keeping tabs on it as best he could, show me the roost tree. As soon as I had established myself in a farmhouse within the tract, I visited Jesse and got the further bad news that during the three months since Dick had returned to New York, the lumbermen had been cutting in the immediate area and that the roost tree was down. Moreover, the Mississippi River had flooded, backing up the Tensas River, which meandered through the tract, and inundating most of the bottom lands. Temporarily at least, lumbering operations were going on in another section, but the water and the litter left by the lumbermen made it difficult to get through the woods. On the brighter side, Jesse said he had seen the bird a few weeks before in the vicinity of an old roosting tree he thought it might be using again, and that we might go in the next afternoon to see if that was the case. In the meantime, he said, he would arrange for a boat to take me up the Tensas to Greenlea Bend early in the morning in case the bird had moved over there. When Jesse left, I morosely turned to unpacking the art supplies I was beginning to doubt I would have any opportunity to use.

That evening Mr. Henry, my host, and I were on the back porch watching the deer come out of the forest one by one at the far end of the clearing, their white-lined ears twitching and now and then a tail flashing up like a white flag of surrender to apprehension.

I shall call him Mr. Henry though that was not his name and though he probably would see no reason for the disguise. My host ran the place, but, as it turned out, I saw very little of him during those two weeks, which was probably just as well, as a little of Mr. Henry went a long way with me. I suppose he was busy overseeing the tenant farms, or perhaps he spent most of his time in Tallulah.

"Never get tired watchin' them deer, though they eat up the grass somethin' fierce," he drawled. Then, swinging his solid bulk around to face the kitchen, he bellowed, "Liza, when we gonna eat? You gettin' lazier ever' day. You been catfishin' ag'in?"

"No suh, Mistah Henry, suh, I ain't," Liza answered.

"I just *bet* she ain't," he said, turning to me.

"We is 'most ready, Mistah Henry," said Liza, unperturbed.

"Well I'm hungry," he grumbled. "That ol' Liza can sure cook, though, I *got* to say."

When, shortly, we sat down to table, Liza served a large platter of lambfries and sweet potatoes, a bowl of greens, and a dish piled high with steaming hot biscuits. Mr. Henry was clearly right about Liza's cooking.

The next morning a fellow appeared with an outboard motor; we hitched it to a soggy old boat and went upriver. The day was mellow and smelled of spring, though in early April the bare trees were only hazed with the rusts and yellow greens of preleaf flowers. Some had clumps of mistletoe in their crowns like heron's nests; others wore manes of polypody ferns up their trunks and along their larger branches. Willows displayed chrome-yellow catkins, and gray rags of moss hung from the cypresses.

The river narrowed as we passed Alligator Bayou. Above the whine of the motor the only bird song I could hear was the thin trill of the parula warbler, though cardinals flashed past and an anhinga flew vulture-high in circles. Around each bend the soft-shelled turtles sunning themselves on drowned branches would scramble back to the opaque safety of the brown water.

Here and there we cut the motor to listen; on higher ground we got out and walked. I was sure I would recognize the short, toy-trumpet call of the ivorybill if I heard it. I caught my breath once when we saw a large bird flying back through the trees, but it was only what my companion called a "Lord God," or pileated woodpecker, of which there are plenty there. We went up to Baker's Ditch, Andrew's Bend, and Greenlea Bend, but nowhere was there any sign of an ivorybill. So we returned.

It rained early in the afternoon, but by the time Jesse picked me up and we drove to John's Bayou, where we left the car and started walking in, the sun was sending long shadows across the puddles and over the sodden leaves. Pushing branches aside, tripping over snarls of greenbrier, and grasping at dangling grapevines for support brought sudden little showers. Saw palmettos wiped their broad surfaces against us. The trunks of the remaining trees were black with wet. As we moved in to lower ground our boots stirred cream mud into coffee water. We made our way around the great brush piles of lopped-off treetops and dismembered prostrate trunks. I believe these logs were ash, which Jesse said the lumber company cut while they were in to get the sweet gum, but which they planned to haul out only if the price later made it worthwhile.

Jesse signaled to be on the alert as we sloshed on, our rhythmic splashes sounding louder and louder in the already quieting woods. After about a mile of this, he stopped and pointed to a hole about 60 feet up in a half-dead ash.

We sat on a large log with our boots dangling in water to wait for the ivorybill. It was 6:15 P.M., and the sun was slipping down fast. A number of birds were still busy with their vespers. A prothonotary warbler sang with great persistence, nearly drowning out the more distant and melancholic notes of a titmouse. Woodpeckers were tattooing. A Carolina wren's rich and syncopated voice ricocheted around us. Towhee, myrtle warbler, downy woodpecker—I sorted them by ear and mentally pushed them aside. I looked at my watch. It was 6:25. I turned questioningly to Jesse, who shrugged his shoulders.

The cool shadows were creeping up the gilded trunk of the roost tree. The small birds became quiet, but a red-bellied woodpecker called nearby and beat out some overtime on a resonant stub. Barred owls had a round of hooting as their hunting time approached. It was in the midst of their hooting that I heard it, a somewhat nuthatch-like note but distinctive, and I turned again to Jesse, jerking my thumb in the direction of the sound. Jesse cocked an ear and paused some time until the note came again, followed by a loud double rap; then he smiled and nodded.

6:33. Only the owls called now, except for five toots from the ivorybill, no closer. I pulled out my notebook and wrote down the sound as "*henk!* or *hank!*, an abrupt falsetto note." More loud double knocks, two or three of these, a long pause, and repeated. I was about convinced she had a roost tree elsewhere. The mosquitoes were getting worse. 6:46. Then I saw her!

She came trumpeting in to the roost, her big wings cleaving the air in strong, direct flight, and she alighted with one magnificent upward swoop. Looking about wildly with her hysterical pale eyes, tossing her head from side to side, her black crest erect to the point of leaning forward, she hitched up the tree at a gallop, trumpeting all the way. Near the top she became suddenly quiet and began preening herself. With a few disordered feathers properly and vigorously rearranged, she gave her distinctive double rap, the second blow following so closely the first that it was almost like an echo—an astonishingly loud, hollow, drumlike *Bam-am!* Then she hitched down the tree and sidled around to the roost hole, looked in, looked around, hitched down beneath the entrance, double-rapped, and went in.

At 7:20, after I had finished all my notes and we were about to leave, she popped out and raced up the trunk to its broken top where, bathed in rich orange light of the setting sun, she alternately preened and jerked her head about in a peculiar angular way, quite unlike the motions of any other woodpecker I knew. I was tremendously impressed by the majestic and wild personality of this bird, its vigor, its almost frantic aliveness. She flew off after five minutes and in another five returned, calling once and going in to roost at 7:30 on the dot. By the time we regained the road it was quite dark.

During the following two weeks it rained a good deal, which prevented my painting outside as much as I wanted to. But when the weather looked favorable, I'd take my paper, brushes, paint, pencils, note pad, and binoculars and tramp back into the roost area early in the morning when the wild turkeys were gobbling, or late in the afternoon. I gave up trying to follow the bird through the ground litter. She would go a quarter or half a mile in one flight, and by the time I would struggle up to her she would be off to other feeding places. So with a few exceptions my observations were made at the roost tree, "putting her to bed" or waiting for her to get up. I sometimes got lost coming out after dark and would have to sit in the blackness waiting for the moon to rise and give me my bearings. Once I nearly bumped into a black bear which, as startled as I was, splashed and crashed off through the brush.

One day on my way in I investigated some desultory hammering expecting to find a pileated woodpecker, but it was the ivorybill working on a broken stub not 15 feet above the ground. I watched her for a good ten minutes. I hope I am not dispelling belief in what I have said about the regal qualities of this bird to add that there was something comical about it too. That big pale bill sometimes looked almost like an ice cream cone jammed into her black mouth, and then the expression of her eyes seemed the natural one at such an occurrence. Call that anthropomorphism if you like, but it is just such impressions which give the bird painter the key to that "rightness" of expression for which he is always striving.

At work, she was not so much a woodpecker as a barkpeeler. She attacked the bark by rearing back, her head usually off to one side, and striking at an oblique angle. Often the loosened bark was flipped off, after one or two blows, by a quick movement which appeared to combine a slight twist and a lateral flick of the head. Hammering was not rapid or persistent, but the bird's long neck gave tremendous thrust, for when fully applied these glancing stabs knocked free pieces as much as half a foot long and 3 or 4 inches across, though the ground below her was mostly strewn with smaller chips. Now and again she would wedge her bill under the bark immediately following a stroke and rapidly on in, in two or three short pushes, spreading the bark against the broadening bill until that big chisel of hers was pretty well buried, as though rushing after retreating borers. After resting quietly for a time she suddenly flew off in straight ducklike flight in which there seemed to be very little movement of the "inner wing"—the secondaries—most of the action being beyond the wrist.

So the days slipped away. Gradually I got my sketches and notes. Liza and I became increasingly good friends to the point where I could help her with the churning without her standing behind me in that ridiculous paper-bag hat and the skimpy print dress over her bony frame, clucking and worrying about what Mr. Henry would say, and to the point where she could warn me about being in the woods after dark. The woods, she said, were full of "hants." But the only spirit I could hear was the voice of doom for this entire natural community, epitomized by that poor lone ivorybill (which should have been feeding well-grown young these days, had she a mate) and vocalized by the shrill squeals of the donkey engine which worked all night bringing out the logs.

Before leaving, I rode a gasoline car back into the cutting. It *putputted* along uneven narrow-gauge rails like a launch in choppy water and teetered precariously over the bayous. In the worst spots, two Negroes sitting in front, poured sand on the rails to increase traction. German prisoners of war were employed for much of the work, supervised by a lumberman and with one army guard for every four men. The guards had no eye for the beauty of primeval forest, and they didn't like the mosquitoes, the ticks, or the mud. They called it "Little Guadalcanal." But the prisoners were enjoying themselves, except that to a man they hated their Prussian sergeant, who still maintained discipline over them. They were, as any European would be, incredulous at the waste—only the best wood taken, the rest left in wreckage to rot. I watched one tree come screaming down and cared to see no more. Most of the wood was used for packing crates and tea chests, I understand.

Possibly there are still, at this writing, ivorybills in the South, though the Louisiana birds are gone. If you consider the Cuban ivorybill to be a small race of the same species, there may remain a few of these also. But it would take an optimist indeed to foresee any hope for the species.

We tend to place value on rarity at all levels of experience. Perhaps that is why these few days live so vividly in my mind. But I think not. I have seen other birds rarer in museum collections and about which much less is known. My experiences were in no way unique; others have seen ivorybills, and some have known them far more intimately. I have had higher adventures in more exotic places. No, it was the stamp of Fate which impressed this experience upon me. Nature is little concerned with the fate of the individual, but there is no greater tragedy in the scheme of things than the extinction of a species.

SPRING IN WASHINGTON

BY LOUIS J. HALLE, JR.

Louis J. Halle, Jr. (1910 —) was born in New York City and educated at Harvard, receiving a graduate degree in anthropology. A man of diverse talents, he has amply proved that one need not be a rural recluse to write wisely and authoritatively about nature. A specialist in international affairs, he was working in the U. S. State Department in Washington when his Birds Against Men *was awarded the John Burroughs Medal in 1941. Still in Washington, deep in the problems of the final, crucial years of World War II, he kept the journals from which he wrote* Spring in Washington, *a beautiful, perceptive book about man and nature in an urban area. Mr. Halle writes about many topics, including diplomacy; but he often turns to nature as a reassuring and healing aspect of the environment in which man wrestles with man-made problems, and he writes about it with acute knowledge and a sense of enduring matters.*

(*Spring in Washington,* by Louis J. Halle, Jr.; William Sloane Associates, 1947.)

Sunday, March 25, because it brought me the first warbler, long before I had expected it, stands out in the list of days. In the sunrise a milky mist was streaming up from the river, like a smoke screen laid down along the channel. The dew was still sparkling on the grass and visible as a soft radiance or ground mist over it. Today the singing of birds was everywhere continuous and uninterrupted; where before today the orchestra had simply been tuning up, the individual instruments sounding separately. From either side of the road, as I bicycled through the misty dawnlight, came the song of the field sparrow, beginning slowly, all on one pitch, a series of measured notes accelerating until the bird was trilling like a canary. Thoreau knew this song a hundred years ago, and from his description it is apparent that there has been no change, though so many sparrow generations have elapsed that it would take man from two to three thousand years to equal them. It is as though Homer still sang.

I had already put up my bicycle, preparatory to going into the marsh at Dyke, in fact I had climbed the roadside fence and was on my way, when I heard a song from the trees across the highway that transfixed me. I knew it well, and my subconscious being was immediately flooded with the recognition and the old associations that accompanied it, though my consciousness fumbled and for the moment I could not say what it was. I stood rooted to the spot with delight and wonder. To me the song was beautiful, not in itself, but as his master's voice must be wonderfully beautiful to the lost dog who has not heard it for a year. I had forgotten its quality even while I remembered it as a fact. Perhaps one should not call it a song, for it is not melodious or musical like the songs of thrushes, meadowlarks or sparrows. It is simply an insectlike notation in sound, a brief signature made up of two or three preliminary strokes and some modest flourishes, repeated at regular intervals without variation. This is the family habit of the warblers, to sign themselves on the air at established intervals for identification. Each species has its distinctive little song with which it keeps announcing itself to the world.

I found my bird quickly enough, through my binoculars, in the bare tops of the trees, flitting from twig to branch, from branch to trunk to branch again, intent on its business, peering under and over and about, pausing only at the established intervals to throw back its head and make its announcement with vibrating trill. The low morning sun shone full upon it among the treetops, the blue-gray wings, the black-and-white head of the yellow-throated warbler. Now that it was here, the warbler season had begun.

The family of wood warblers inhabits the New World exclusively, having no close relatives or parallels abroad. However, when the first settlers came to this country from England they brought with them the names of English birds to fasten, without any fine discrimination, onto the American birds. They called our big redbreasted thrush the robin, after the English redbreast or robin redbreast, and they called these dazzling little birds, the like of which they had never seen, warblers, though they do not warble at all and, for the most part, have songs like the buzzing and creaking of insects. These little birds are the principal glory of the North American spring, quick and dainty in their movements, incessantly active, as bright and varied in color as the butterflies. For a few weeks in spring, on their way north, they swarm through our woods, filling and transforming them with their variety and numbers. Each of the many species is distinct in its color and markings, each has its own vocal signature, which the observer comes to know in time, each is a separate object of delight. Coming from the tropics, they arrive with the first appearance of leaves on the trees, reach the peak of their abundance about the time the trees achieve their full foliage, and then diminish rapidly until only those that nest here remain. The flowering of the Japanese cherry trees is not so wonderful as the wave of warblers that passes through the countryside in mid-May, remaining sometimes only a day.

Earlier naturalists could not know the warblers as we know them, since they did not have the prism binoculars that are necessary to observe these quick little birds among the leaves in the treetops. For the most part they must have been aware only of innumerable little birds darting in and out among the trees and the abundance and variety of song that accompanied them. They knew the beauty of the individual birds chiefly by bringing them down with a gun and examining them in the hand, but here they missed all the beauty of their ways, the extreme delicacy and quickness of their flitting and fluttering movements.

The appreciation of warblers is a slow acquisition, since most of the species are to be seen and heard only for a few days each year, and the rarer may be seen only at intervals of several years. When I say that I have been acquainted with a warbler for ten years, it may be that the sum of that acquaintance is only a few minutes. Perhaps I have seen the bird and heard its song only a half-dozen times, and then I was distracted by the presence of its innumerable congeners. The appreciation of birds, indeed the appreciation of all the phenomena of spring, cannot be dissociated from the accumulations of memory. The appearance of a familiar bird immediately awakens a train of forgotten associations, and this makes each spring transcend its predecessor. The interest accumulates and is compounded. The first yellow-throated warbler next year will be more meaningful to me as it brings back that moment in the woods opposite Dyke. For one remembers clearly enough the fact of such a moment, but only an evocative sight or sound or smell can bring back the full emotion. The person who sees the bird for the first time cannot know what moves me.

The bird, or the event, must have a background to be appreciated, but not necessarily the background of one's individual memory alone, important as this is. It is the great function of nature literature and art to teach us how to see these things, for the beauty of an object, a song, or a dance can never be altogether intrinsic, independent of old associations and acquired understanding. I have never seen an upland plover, or heard its cry, but the experience when it comes will be the more meaningful for me because I shall recall that description of the bird as Hudson knew it, flying over the pampas on its long migration to North America. "Lying awake in bed," he wrote, "I would listen by the hour to that sound coming to me from the sky, mellowed and made beautiful by distance and the profound silence of the moonlit world, until it acquired a fascination for me above all sounds on earth, so that it lived ever after in me. . . . It was the sense of mystery it conveyed which so attracted and impressed me—the mystery of that delicate, frail, beautiful being, travelling in the sky, alone, day and night, crying aloud at intervals as if moved by some powerful emotion, beating the air with its wings, its beak pointing like the needle of a compass to the north, speeding on its seven-thousand-mile flight to its nesting home in another hemisphere." Thus I am furnished by Hudson with a vicarious memory of the bird, in lieu of personal experience.

This fact, that one must have a background in memory for the appreciation of birds, was first brought home to me when I first visited the American tropics and looked on birds as wonderful in their characters, their colors and movements, as any seen in the world. But there was nevertheless a strange emptiness and frustration in the experience. These were not my birds, I could not really know them at all, or know how to see them, at first sight. It was only with the lapse of time and the building up of my own recollected associations that I began to appreciate and understand them. I could not be moved by a cotinga as I was when, riding through uninhabited tropical forest, surrounded by parrots and toucans, with monkeys in the trees overhead, I came upon the familiar sight of a wintering catbird and watched it flitting among the tropical vines or catching caterpillars on the jungle floor. There is no delight like that of recognition. . . .

It is March 25 and the dawn of summer. A light bloom of green, as insubstantial as a mist, is on the distant, wooded hillsides now. The dogwood is on the verge of blossoming. In the moist darkness of the woods, some violets in a clump are just about to open. You hesitate to turn away from them. An old wagon track leads down and down through woods of Virginia pine, joining with other tracks and occasionally forking, to your confusion if you are not careful. A musical chippering, all on one pitch, of established duration and regular interval, comes from this side and then that. This is the song of the newly arrived pine warbler, the streaked brown and yellow mite, throwing his head back amid the bowers of pine needles and singing with his vibrating bill.

At the bottom of the slope lies a long open marsh sunk into the woods, with trees wading out from the borders ankle-deep in bog water. Here, overlooking the marsh, is a slight elevation with ancient gnarled beeches, and tumbled rocks to sit on, a Wagnerian stage setting. The sounds of the forge and the cry of *Nothung, Nothung!* would not be out of place. Instead, a hairy woodpecker utters a machine-gun burst of notes; two wood ducks, barely seen behind the trees, rocket away, crying *oo-eek, oo-eek*. . . . A heron has taken off silently and wings its way along the edge of the forest. This, obviously, is the spot for our picnic lunch, or for a sacrifice to the gods. You feel like a hero in it. What could be more appropriate, then, than that our binoculars should fix an eagle soaring over the trees at the far end of the marsh?—not the American eagle, bird of the New World, but the golden eagle of emperors, heraldic symbol of feudal Europe. That glint on its head is the gold of the Niebelung hoard, the gold of fallen empires. Tamerlane knew it on the steppes of Asia. Forty centuries look down upon you from that brow. Now the imperial bird soars upward and away, farther and farther, till it is lost to sight.

At its lower end, by way of a narrow neck through the infringing woods, this marsh opens into the main marsh, the long, sweeping, sunlit vista of reeds and rivulets, between the high hills, that in turn gives into Gunston Cove. While the company keeps inside the woods where the footing is firm, I choose to wade knee-deep on the outside through cold water and quagmire, where I can see about me. The greater yellowlegs, one here and one there, are calling in their excitement from open mud flats. This, however, is pre-eminent as the home of the American eagles. They break from the big trees at the border as we advance, flapping with slow beat across the open, soaring into the sky. I count eleven in sight at one time, and there are more. One folds its wings and falls from the sky upon another, which almost at the moment of collision rolls over in one complete revolution, letting the attacker glance by; then both flap upward to see which, this time, shall rise above the other. These are giants at play. Another, white head and white tail gleaming in the sunlight, drops to the sparkling surface of the cove, splashes, and makes off with a fish in its talons.

Somewhere in the mists of time the eagle and the warbler had a common ancestor. Now the warbler sings in the pine woods, the eagle soars above the marshes, the ducks swim in the bay, gulls wheel. How extraordinary if this were altogether uninspired! We live ourselves in the mists of time, and cannot cast our vision beyond it. The world of our senses is purely spectacular. . . .

Every season is exceptional, and this spring is no exception. Flower and foliage were well ahead of schedule, and the warblers with them. During the week of March 25 to April 1 the woods everywhere were springing into leaf. You could see in the morning how much the leaves had grown overnight. This, of course, was measurable, and I measured it. In two days the leaves of a tulip tree had more than doubled their size and were already some two inches across. Like everything else, they responded to and were the outward manifestation of the perennial life that was flowing and surging in the earth. We take this for granted because so we have always seen it happen, just as the starlings heading for the city in the late afternoon take it for granted that night will fall. We make provision like the starlings, and buy our summer clothes in late winter. The starlings, of course, take these things for granted because they have not the gift of questioning and contemplation. Modern men often take life and the seasons for granted because they fondly believe that science has the explanations, that everything is known. In the same way we used to believe, when little, that grownups knew the answers to all questions. Hence no mystery! Science, however, follows back along the chain of physical causation to the brink of darkness and discovers nothing. It simply takes more steps to reach the unknown. The scientist who has explored the farthest is the most likely to believe in gods and demons. . . .

On March 27, the day that the first swallow appeared on the Tidal Basin, a roughwing, two violets bloomed in a crack in the paving of Rock Creek Parkway. I thought then that I could view the crumbling of our civilization with equanimity if violets were to spring up in the cracks. They would, too. All the flower shops in Washington do not hold as many flowers as may someday grow naturally here, out of the stonework. The mark of mortality is on everything man builds, but the violets and their kind are immortal. The vast and busy cities that once flourished in Central America are hardly to be found under the masses of foliage and bloom that cover them today, though the men who occupied them appeared to have conquered the wilderness. The government officials speeding to work past this spot in the early morning, if they only knew, would regard this clump of violets with awe. It was not planted by the United States Park Service.

MYSTIQUE

BY VICTOR PAUL HASS

Victor Paul Hass (1909 —) was born on Isle of Pines, West Indies, where his father had taken the family from Waupun, Wisconsin, to seek a fortune logging teak. The venture failed and the family returned to Wisconsin, where Hass grew up, went to Marquette University on a football scholarship and got "a pretty good education, but a better one in the Milwaukee Public Library." After editing small newspapers in New York and Wisconsin, he taught journalism for a year at Creighton University in Omaha, Nebraska, found that he disliked teaching and returned to newspaper work. He has been with the Omaha World-Herald *since 1937 as a news editor and since 1942 has been in charge of the book pages. "I've never had any desire to move," he says. "The town is nice, the hours are good, and the Nebraska quail- and pheasant- and goose-shooting are magnificent." Between hunting seasons he grows rare roses. And in his weekly column, "From a Bookman's Notebook," he occasionally writes a perceptive essay about the Missouri Valley countryside that he knows so well as an outdoorsman. This selection is one of those essays. I have included it because it captures that subtle kinship of man and nature the true sportsman feels but so seldom finds the words to express.*

("From a Bookman's Notebook," by Victor Paul Hass; Omaha, Nebraska, *World-Herald*, September 6, 1964.)

In "Tranquillity Regained," the third volume in Col. Harold Sheldon's delightful trilogy of hunting and fishing stories, there is a chapter called "One to Get Ready—." It is, I must concede, no great shakes as literature, but I always turn to it first for my annual rereading of the "Tranquillity" books.

"One to Get Ready—" is an account of a pleasant early-September day spent out of doors by "The Captain" and "The Judge," two ardent shotgunners who live in a hamlet near the shore of Lake Champlain in Vermont.

Their day, one of medium exertion and a great deal of pleasurable companionship, is devoted to building a duck blind in the alluvial marshes that are the haunt of mallards, teal, pintails, and (later on) the elusive woodcock. The shooting season is not open as yet but these two friends are the kind of hunters who dislike messing around with a blind on opening day while good shots are going to waste.

Besides, and this is what is important, their activity is a perfect safety valve to ease the pressure that builds up in every dedicated hunter from the time the seasons are announced until opening day. I can vouch for this therapy because I have been doing it for years with my friend Walter Olsen of Fremont, ably assisted for a long time by my son, Paul, and now by my son, Kit, since Paul has left the parental nest.

Our day is always the same and always one of contentment. We pack a hearty lunch, tools for making whatever repairs are needed on our blind, pruning shears to cut willows to improve the camouflage, shotguns for a bit of blue rocks shooting and fly rods and lures for that time in the afternoon when telltale bubbles on the surface of the lake announce that the bluegills and bass are beginning to feed and can be fooled with a fly or a popper.

It is always a leisurely day and I think that is a part of its charm. We manage to bear down enough to do what needs doing in and around the blind but we are never so busy that we cannot knock off work to watch a circling duck come to see what's going on, call attention to a cruising bittern, note an eagle planing high against the blue sky or simply chew the fat around the campfire over which we toast (perhaps "char" is a better word) the sandwiches we have brought along.

There are few times when food tastes as good as it does under conditions such as these and few times, too, when a pipeful of fragrant tobacco fits in so beautifully. Inevitably, we recall great days we have had in this blind—days when you couldn't seem to miss, no matter how difficult the shots. It is only human nature, I suppose, that we are able to forget those days when we couldn't seem to hit anything at all, though they are more frequent than the can't-miss days.

Indeed, the whole mystique of hunting is probably unintelligible to the non-hunter. Certainly it is to my wife, who inclines to the opinion that a kind of madness comes over me every year from the moment the open seasons are announced to that final day when waterfowl and upland birds are no longer legal quarry.

The English call the opening of their grouse season "The Glorious Twelfth" (of August). I find this understandable because, to me, as to all Nebraska hunters, October 1 (geese), October 3 (ducks), and October 17 (quail and pheasants) stand out on the calendar this year as though they were ringed with neon lights.

Hunting is shooting game, of course, and expensive vittles they are, but it is infinitely more. It is pleasure in perfecting an elusive skill with a fowling piece; it is a glorious sunrise or a vivid sunset; it is a retreat into solitude; it is a special kind of companionship with men you enjoy and admire.

More, it is the thrilling burst of a covey of quail, the unnerving clatter of a pheasant rocketing from sere corn, the haunting call of wild geese, the wonder of brilliant mallards cupping their wings over a blind. But, most of all, it is being abroad in autumn, when Nature is at her beautiful best. Until you have sat in a duck blind and watched an autumn day unfold, develop and then decline, you have missed one of life's greatest pleasures.

PEREGRINE FALCON

BY ROBERT MURPHY

Robert Murphy (1902 —) *was born near Philadelphia, but when he was eight the family moved to Richmond, Virginia, and there he got acquainted with the woodland and water he later described so well in his book* The Pond. *He spent two years at Washington and Lee University, but "didn't seem to like education very much, which wasn't very bright of me. I ran to the woods every chance I got. I've spent a fair amount of time in the Rockies; I've been to Baffin Island, and so on. I have been, off and on, a falconer; I love to see a falcon in the air, I like to have one around. Now, I like them more free. . . . I don't know where the nature interest came from, for my parents were lukewarm toward it. My father, recognizing it in me, did all he could to encourage it, for which I am grateful. I like to go down, or up, a trout stream with a flyrod, taking plenty of time to see what's going on around me. I like to sit still in the woods for the same reason." After various jobs, Murphy settled down as an editor of* The Saturday Evening Post *for twenty years before he quit to be a full-time writer. He has written three novels about the outdoors, one about a boy's growing up in Virginia, one about a peregrine falcon, one about a golden eagle. He lives in rural Pennsylvania. This selection is from* The Peregrine Falcon, *and tells about a part of the bird's first migration. The peregrine falcon, also called the duck hawk, is the fastest-flying hawk in the world.*

(*The Peregrine Falcon,* by Robert Murphy; Houghton Mifflin Company, 1963.)

The weather grew warmer toward morning as the wind shifted to the south; ground mist swirled like a ghostly and sluggish sea around the rocks, shrubs, and windfall timber of the opening, and it began to rain. Varda tightened her feathers and sat it out, rousing only momentarily from her hunched and semi-somnolent state when a mink surprised a rabbit, whose despairing screams rang out eerily in the mist below her. She was thoroughly wet when the sun came out at noon, and spent an hour with her wings drooping, her feathers loose and her tail spread out to dry, preening herself afterward and pulling each tail feather through her beak to dress it.

Dry and comfortable once more, she set out again. The spruces laid a shadow on her mind, and she wanted to get away from them. The wind was still against her and she stayed low, flying just above the trees; the miles fell behind her. She was flying so close to the ground and so swiftly that she went through each opening she came to like an arrow. Most of them were barren of life, but in one a dozen blue jays were mobbing a great gray owl, flitting about and screaming in raucous excitement. They were having a splendid time and their attention was concentrated upon their victim, but one of them saw her when she was almost among them and screeched the alarm. They scattered wildly in all directions, but she had already picked one out; she rolled over on her back, swept upward between it and the safety of a spruce, and picked it out of the air.

She plumed it and ate it on the topmost branch of a dead tree, and went on. The wind changed in the afternoon and the sun warmed the earth; rising air currents took her high again, and beneath her the country began to change. The massed pines and spruces gave way increasingly to more deciduous trees, their somber greens to the counterpoint of bright gold and crimson. Here and there little farms broke up the woodlands, and narrow roads ran between them.

As the country grew more open and rolling, more stony and barren with the glacial rocks of the Laurentian shield and the concealing, secret spruce forest thinned out, Varda felt more at home; in a measure it resembled the Barrens, where all the vast sweep was open to the sky and the eye could see what moved around on it. She hadn't liked the close growing spruces, hiding everything in their dense and tangled shadows, where prey could only be happened upon accidentally and nothing could be pursued for more than a few feet. It was not her way to hunt in this fashion; it was the realm of the goshawks and the sharpshins, which lurked like cats in the thick growth and made short, swift dashes at their victims. They were supremely maneuverable with their short rounded wings and long tails; they were made for such hunting and she was not. She needed the open, where the eye could see for miles and where speed counted the most and there was room for the long, swift stoop or the headlong, slashing pursuit, where her quarry could not get into the thick cover in which her long, narrow wings put her at an overwhelming disadvantage. She would have gone hungry if she had been forced to spend much time in the spruce country, except for luck; another year she would probably remember this and follow the open seacoast.

She went on, flying fast and not inclined to soar and waste time in the pleasure of it; when the wind was against her she dropped low to be shielded from it. She did not consciously know it but she was longing for the sea, the great wide restless plains of the Atlantic and the pale beaches that contained it, and the mysterious intuition that guided her took her toward it. Her lonely way took her down over the farmland and across the wide St. Lawrence between Ottawa and Montreal and into the Adirondacks, that vast state park once haggard from careless lumbering and now preserved and restored, mountainous, covered with forest and filled with glacial lakes. The hardwoods flared in their autumn glory among the pines, and their bright colors dyed the wind-rippled surface of the lakes; the mountains marched off and faded into October haze. The evening caught her and she came down to rest for the night in a high dead tree at the edge of a beaver pond. Chipmunks ran busily about beneath her, filling their storerooms; three deer came quietly to drink and raised their heads together, ears cocked, at a red fox that came to drink as well across the pond from them. The trout in the pond began to dimple the water in their evening rise, and presently the first beaver's head broke the surface as he emerged from his house to set about his night's work. His mate came soon after to join him and they fell to cutting sticks and ferrying them to the vicinity of their house, to sink them to the bottom for winter provender when ice covered their world. The kits of the summer came out last, to swim ashore and play together among the fallen leaves until darkness blotted them out, and far off a barred owl greeted the night.

She was off early the next morning and went hungry, for the forest made poor hunting for her; nearly an hour later, flying strongly, she was a little east of the farm where the bones of John Brown, who hated slavery, had long since gone back into the earth. She could see the bulk of Mt. Marcy to the west, and later dropped down into the trough where Lake George lay and took a bufflehead drake close to the water.

She rested for an hour on an islet of gray rocks and spruces like a dish-garden made by the Japanese and circled high again. The valley of the Hudson River would have been easier, but the shifting winds of mountain flying exhilarated her. She cut through the Appalachians and the rolling Green Mountains at the corner of Vermont, above stone-fenced, hard-won fields and the foundations of farmhouses long abandoned and fallen down and hidden from her by the glow of maples in the sun, the deep old-gold of hickories and pale, gleaming clumps of white birch.

As the land dropped and leveled she saw a red fox running through a field of rosy-brown grass, mobbed by a great, screaming flock of wheeling crows; in the little calm villages white church steeples stood above the maples and elms. The villages grew closer together and gathered into cities, where factory smoke towered up and flattened and spread long plumes of haze over the land and people went about their concerns below it beside their dirty rivers.

No one saw her except a farm boy who was hunting rabbits after school in the underbrush along the lane of a hilltop farm, and she was upon him and gone before he had time to raise his old single-barreled shotgun, but he retained for a long time a confused impression of her golden coloring shining in the slanting sunlight and her quick, purposeful wingbeats that left him with a feeling of her splendid vitality and power; she seemed to have the stamp of strange and faraway places upon her, for he had never seen her like before. He often thought of her at night in the drowsy time just before he fell asleep and was finally glad, in a half-ashamed way, that he had been unable to shoot her.

The remembrance of him remained with Varda as she traveled, re-enforcing the shadow cast on her mind by the ominous image transmitted through the germ plasm of generations which had encountered man and escaped him, by the memory of similar creatures seen from a distance who had brought the geese dead out of the air at James Bay; his involuntary movement as he turned and half raised the shotgun somehow held more menace than any other animal's approach to attack.

She didn't brood upon the encounter; animals do not live forever with the fear of death; it became a part of her education, of her pattern of behavior for the future, which would make her react quickly when the necessity arose. Some creatures never learn this, some have no opportunity, and some learn it incorrectly; they do not usually live very long. Varda was better prepared than those and avoided people. She came over Long Island Sound and crossed it and Long Island itself and Great South Bay to drop on the barrier well east of Ocean Beach. The beach was lonely and the Atlantic was in front of her, its combers curling green in the autumn sun. She bathed in a small pool of rainwater and dried herself in the cool breeze off the ocean, and for the moment was content.

GHOULIES AND GHOOSTIES

BY ROGER TORY PETERSON

Roger Tory Peterson (1908 —) was born in Jamestown, New York, grew up with an interest in all wildlife but especially in birds, and was educated as an artist. After several years as a decorative artist and a teacher, he turned to bird painting as a full-time occupation. To this he soon added writing, with birds his major topic. He has illustrated a score of books and written and illustrated more than a dozen of his own. His classic Field Guides *are based on methods of bird identification he originated. He has received many honors as a naturalist and has been one of the foremost advocates of conservation. This selection is taken from* Birds Over America, *a collection of his own experiences with birds. He now lives in Connecticut, near Long Island Sound.*

(*Birds Over America,* by Roger Tory Peterson; Dodd, Mead & Company, 1948.)

Guy Emerson had not yet seen a white-crowned sparrow for a year. This in itself seemed excuse enough for our drive into rural Maryland that October Sunday. As if by appointment, we found our bird, a young one, tan with a pink bill, right where we parked the car outside the Fish and Wildlife Research Laboratories at Bowie. Our objective attained, we sauntered into the narrow brick building where the millions of bird banding records are kept. There we found Joseph Hickey hard at work, as he always seemed to be, day or night, on his doctor's thesis. Emerson, fascinated by the intricate filing system, asked Hickey if he might see the barn owl cards, particularly those from Massachusetts. Joe dumped the stack of barn owl cards into the IBM sorting machine and, with a rapid shuffling motion, the Massachusetts cards dropped out. The first card that popped forth was that of a young bird banded near Emerson's home on Martha's Vineyard. He had seen this very bird, and, by a curious coincidence, so had I, a year later, but not at Martha's Vineyard. The card recorded that the owl was recaptured as a nesting female in an old coal elevator in the Bronx nearly 200 miles away.

The card with its formal telegraphic data evoked memories of a full moon shining on the water along the dark river wharves, on the night that Irving Kassoy took me up the rickety ladder into the tower to see his new owl family. I remember how excited he was when he discovered later that the female wore a band—one that he had not put there! For weeks he tried to catch the owl to read its number. We all offered advice, but it was not until Mike Oboiko set one of his squirrel traps that the mystery of the bird's origin was solved.

Kassoy is the historian of the few barn owls known to live in the Bronx; he has watched these mystery birds for years, and some of his friends in the Linnaean Society say (much to his irritation) that he is beginning to look like an owl. Perhaps his glasses and the look of quiet wisdom create this illusion. Like Huxley, Kassoy believes we should "smite every humbug," and in the past few years he has dispelled more notions and unearthed more facts about the barn owl than any other man before him.

Kassoy once worked in a midtown Manhattan jeweler's firm. After long days devoted to diamond rings and Swiss watches he would hurry to his owl observatory in the Bronx—in the old Huntington mansion at Pelham Bay. Night after night he kept his lonesome vigil, under the eaves with the "ghoulies and ghoosties, long-leggy beasties, and things that go bump in the night."

I met him one evening after work. He had a necklace to deliver on Park Avenue before we plunged below the street level and boarded the IRT subway for the Bronx. At 125th Street we changed from the lurching local to the Pelham Bay express. While we hung from

the swaying straps, shoved and pushed by the evening crush of commuters, Kassoy told me something of the history of his birds. There was a new female, he said. The previous female had been frightened from the building by some workmen. It was daytime, and crows mobbed the bewildered bird. They drove her to the water of Eastchester Bay; then the gulls closed in and finished her off. Apparently even the birds look upon *Tyto* with suspicion, as a bird of ill omen, to be attacked and destroyed. Perhaps that is why barn owls live in church belfries so often, I mused—for like outcasts of old who sought sanctuary in the temple, they can find refuge there. Certainly, I reflected, they are nonsectarian, for I had seen barn owls in the square tower of a synagogue in Alexandria, Virginia, in a fashionable Episcopal church at Rye, New York, in a little white Baptist church on the east coast of Florida and in a famous old Franciscan mission in California.

But whereas some barn owls seek sanctified, holy places, others live in a gloomy, almost evil atmosphere. Such a place was the abandoned Huntington estate, five minutes' walk from the end of the Pelham Bay line. We had long known the place, because it was there that, on a Christmas census, we always saw our night herons, a hundred or more, crouched disconsolately in the somber branches of the Norway spruces inside the wall. We never climbed that wall because into its broad top had been cemented thousands of pieces of broken glass, a jagged hint to trespassers. But now the estate is park property and Kassoy had permission to enter the big house. He flashed a light into the spreading, silvery limbed beech tree where the owls often perched, but they were not there. He swung the light beam over to the eaves of the house. There was the ventilator hole through which the birds gained access to the ivy-covered building. We could hear the young ones calling for food, a rasping, sucking sound that has been likened to an ill-mannered person imbibing soup.

We passed through the big gate and Kassoy went over to the caretaker's house to get the key which hung on a nail inside the door. The caretaker believed the house was haunted, and I am sure he thought Kassoy was quite mad, sitting up there night after night by himself. We went up two flights, lifted a trap-door and tiptoed across the attic floor. In the corner, Kassoy knelt over a box. He turned a switch attached to a dry cell battery and a tiny light illuminated the dark interior of the box. Huddled there were five of the most grotesque owlets I had ever seen, like little monkeys with white caps pulled about their ears. In size they were like stepping stones, for young barn owls usually hatch two days apart.

The top of the box was a pane of glass treated so that the owls saw only their reflections, while we could see them and remain unseen ourselves—a sort of two-way mirror—the same device that has been used in zoos to make monkeys act natural, unstimulated or uninhibited by their unseen audience. Kassoy is probably the only man alive who has ever been eye-witness to some of the intimacies of the adult barn owls—even their actual mating. He was amazed to find how closely the courtship cycle was synchronized with the full of the moon. Indeed, he found he could predict within a day or two when the first egg would be laid.

When I called the owlets grotesque, he was indignant. To him they were beautiful babies. Perhaps they were. But no one, seeing an adult barn owl at close range, can deny that it is beautiful. When painting it I have marveled at the soft blendings of rufous and gray, sprinkled with tiny dots, and the liquid brown eyes set deep in the white heart-shaped face. I can see why some people call it the "monkey-faced owl," but a monkey, by contrast, is wizened, wrinkled and homely. If it must have a nickname, I prefer "golden owl."

For many months Kassoy had been climbing up there. His heart would skip faster at the scampering of rats or the sudden thunderclap of a summer storm, but usually all was empty silence broken only by the periodic rumble of a distant train pulling into the station. . . . Night after night, 200 or more, he hunched over his box like some immobile Buddha, his face, reflecting the wan light, the only thing visible in the blackness. A loud rasping cry, like a banshee with laryngitis, told him that one of the old birds was in the beech outside. In a moment, it would magically appear in the box, like an apparition, a meadow mouse (*microtus*), dangling from its beak, or a rat from the garbage dump out on the Eastchester marshes.

The nest was strewn with bits of fur and bones. Although owls swallow their mice whole, the strong digestive action soon rolls the bones up in a felt-like wad of fur and this the bird coughs up with a struggle. These pellets have a wet, varnished look at first but are soon broken up and trodden into a foul carpet by the young birds. The pellets on the attic floor were the best contact Kassoy had with his pets between seasons when they were not nesting. Like a detective, he would dissect each one for clues. He could tell how well the birds had been eating and how lately they had been roosting in the attic. Most of the pellets held two skulls apiece, nearly all of them rodents with their long, curved incisors; but occasionally he found an English sparrow, and once a phoebe.

With no brood of his own at the time, the young owls became to Kassoy as his own family. When two or three of the babies toddled out of the ventilator shaft one night and were dashed to their death on the hard ground below, he was grieved for days. When the owls laid again he built a little porch and railing as a safeguard.

One brood was started so late that it was early January before they flew and starvation faced the family. Worried about his charges, he broke track through the deep snow one blustery night with two pounds of raw beefsteak under his arm, only to find that the keeper had locked up his house. He could not get the key, so he scattered the pieces of meat over the snow.

Year by year Kassoy grew to love the old place more and more. While waiting for the owls he spent long hours with his thoughts. There were times, though, when his subconscious seemed to be playing tricks on him. For example, once he had stayed in the mansion long past midnight. It was possibly two or three o'clock but it was a Sunday morning and he could sleep late. He had fallen into a doze when a door slammed downstairs. He knew he was the only one with a key. Footsteps crossed the empty library. Step by step they came up the first flight of stairs and started up the second. Kassoy's hair stood out above his ears, like the back hairs of a dog at bay. The sounds paused just below the trap-door. Just then one of the owls popped through the ventilator into the nest, and Kassoy, like a true scientific investigator, put all else from his mind and concentrated on the little drama in the lighted box below him. When the owl left, he listened again. The footsteps had stopped, nor did he hear them after that. He had wondered about it ever since. . . .

All owls are weirdly beautiful, from the big white snowies that come down along the beaches on their cyclic winter invasions, to the mysterious little fellows that live in the desert mountains, but the barn owl is more truly "owlish" than any of the others. At Cape May, New Jersey, lying on my back among the dunes near the boardwalk, I have squeaked them overhead, while their ghostly forms reflected the light from the street lamps. Some day I would like to see a phosphorescent barn owl, a rare but authenticated phenomenon. The phosphorescence is not an illusion but is believed to be caused by fungi that impregnate the rotten wood of cavities where the owls hide in the daytime. The oxidation of the mycelium of these fungi causes the unearthly glow or cold light that has been called "fox fire."

I cannot imagine how such an owl would look, but a barn owl always seems as eerie as a golliwogg, whether it is hunting amongst the rows of stately palms in southern California where it snatches up the palm rats as they clatter over the dead fronds, or is perched high on the rafters of a rickety ice house along the Hudson (they say the invention of the automatic refrigerator, and the consequent abandonment of these ice houses, extended the range of the barn owl to Albany).

One of the most widely distributed birds in the world, the barn owl is found on every continent. There are caves in South America, which, to judge by the thick deposits of debris, have probably been occupied by them for centuries, perhaps for thousands of years. In 1934, Sir George Courthope wrote in the foreword to *The Barn Owl in England and Wales*, by G. B. Blaker:

"There is an old tree near my home where barn owls have bred all my life. Some fifty years ago, my grandfather told me that his grandfather told him they had bred in the same tree all his life—he was born in 1737."

Two centuries of continuous occupancy!

In Flushing, New York, owls inhabited a church belfry from 1880 to 1926—forty-six years. That is quite a record, but the most famous barn owls in this country are the ones that live in the northeast tower of the old Smithsonian building in Washington. An egg in the National Museum was taken from there over eighty years ago, and barn owls have been in residence there ever since. Dr. A. K. Fisher, in making his classic study of the food habits of the hawks and owls, gathered great numbers of pellets that littered the floor of the loft. One small species of rodent, the harvest mouse, was first known to occur in the District of Columbia when its skull was found in a pellet. Today, Alexander Wetmore, the Secretary of the Institution, has issued instructions that no one is to clean up the tower. It is to be left just as it is—a permanent haven for owls.

THE WOODCOCK

BY OLIN SEWALL PETTINGILL, JR.

Olin Sewall Pettingill, Jr. (1907 —) was born, grew up and was educated in Maine and took graduate work in zoology at Cornell University. Specializing in ornithology, he became an international authority in that field and has written and lectured about birds for many years. He is also a distinguished photographer of birds. Since 1960 he has been Cornell University's Director of Ornithology. He has known and studied woodcocks since his Maine boyhood, and still maintains a home at Wayne, Maine, close to some of the best woodcock areas in the world. This selection is an article he wrote for Down East, *a regional magazine devoted to Maine's wealth of natural outdoor resources.*

("The Woodcock," by Olin Sewall Pettingill, Jr., first published in *Down East* in the issue of May 1963.)

"That was a woodcock!" No doubt it was, but you hardly saw it. To most of us, unless we have been lucky enough to find it sitting quietly on its nest, the woodcock is a robin-sized chunk of dark feathers that startles us in some alder thicket by jumping straight up at our feet, its wings whistling, then disappearing straight ahead the instant it reaches the tops of the trees.

Except for its close relative by the same name in Europe, there is no other bird quite like the woodcock. A shorebird by ancestry, it has found its niche away from shore water, in moist alder thickets and other brushy habitats. Occasionally forest edges attract it, as long as the ground is soggy, but rarely if ever deep woods. To this somewhat restricted environment it has become remarkably adapted in a multitude of ways. It is cryptically colored to match the dead leaves and twigs of the ground it occupies. On legs shortened to bring it close to the leaves and twigs, it moves unhurriedly and noiselessly; if alarmed, it squats, motionless. As though conscious of the infallibility of its protective coloration, it flushes only when about to be stepped on.

The woodcock's most conspicuous physical feature, the long bill, is an efficient device for obtaining earthworms—with which its habitat is ordinarily well supplied. Whereas the robin, notorious for its predilection to earthworms but without special equipment, must rely on skill in capturing such prey at their burrow entrances, the woodcock forces its bill into the ground, feeling for them in any promising soft spot. Once a worm is located, the bill is opened slightly at the tip, providing a pincers for grasping and pulling out its find.

Although earthworms provide its principal food, the woodcock will occasionally take beetle grubs and other small, subterranean animals that the bill may chance upon. A late-summer drought, which inevitably causes a paucity of earthworms, forces the woodcock to accept millipedes, centipedes, ground-surface insects, spiders, and sometimes seeds. Hard pressed, the bird may leave its favorite habitat for shaded streamsides to wade in shallow places for aquatic insects and snails. During a dry season more than one Maine resident has been surprised to see a woodcock on his lawn, in the early morning or late afternoon, hopefully probing for night crawlers in a spot recently watered. Hunger begets boldness, even in the normally shy woodcock!

Officially called American woodcock, our species is by no means as wide-ranging as the name would imply. It is actually confined to eastern North America, mainly from the Maritime Provinces of Canada and Maine, west to eastern Minnesota, and south to north Florida and northeastern Texas. When winter approaches, the more heavy northern population simply moves in on the more sparse southern population, beginning in southeastern Virginia and northern Arkansas.

Unquestionably more woodcock breed in Maine—particularly in Hancock and Washington counties—and parts of Nova Scotia and New Brunswick than anywhere else. In 1937 the Moosehorn National Wildlife Refuge, near Calais in Washington County, was established specifically for the protection and management studies of this important game bird. Here several wildlife biologists at the University of Maine began intensive investigations which have been carried on over the years since by Dr. Howard L. Mendall. The wealth of significant information which he and his associates have gathered on the woodcock's habits, behavior, and survival problems would fill a huge book.

Woodcock return to Maine with the disappearance of snow in late March and early April. Some of the bigger drifts may still remain when the males appear for the first time on their respective singing grounds—always open places such as fields, pastures, and forest clearings. Each singing ground is a male's sole domain, to be vigorously defended against intrusion by other males of his kind. Here during the ensuing three or four weeks, in the twilight of early morning and evening and on moonlit nights, he performs courtship displays that are unique among American birds.

Part of his performance involves a peculiarly harsh nasal *peent* at leisurely intervals. Rasping and penetrating when heard near by, it has great carrying quality, enabling you to spot his singing ground a considerable distance away. But the truly extraordinary part of his total performance is the flight song. This involves the bird's slow spiral ascent, wings all the while whistling or trilling musically, to a point slightly over 200 feet from the ground where he hovers momentarily, wings still trilling, and then a rapid zigzag descent accompanied by vocal chirping notes in groups of five or six. The flight song alternates with sessions of peenting. The first two or three songs in the evening usually take place when there is enough light to permit your seeing the flights, provided you first hide quietly at the edge of the singing ground.

Both nasal sounds and flight songs are in a sense advertising media, partly to attract females for nesting purposes. Thus the singing grounds become the meeting places of the sexes and, strangely enough, the only place where the sexes are regularly in contact with each other during the nesting season.

When I began studying woodcock, I thought that the nests would be not far from the singing grounds; that to find them, all I had to do was locate the singing grounds, and the rest of the job would be comparatively easy. Such was not the case, however, as most of the nests, ultimately discovered by random searching over a vast area, were so far distant from the singing grounds that the peents and flight songs were beyond my hearing range. By hard experience I learned that woodcock do not establish anything like a mating bond. The female mates with the male on his singing ground and then is off on her own, to nest and rear her young without any assistance from the male.

The fact that each male woodcock always performs on just his own singing ground and uses it regularly and alone throughout the breeding season makes it possible for wildlife biologists to make a census of the breeding population of woodcock in a given area. By counting the number of singing males and multiplying that number by two for the females that presumably attend them, a fairly accurate estimation can be made. Information of this sort has proven to be highly valuable to game authorities in keeping track of population trends and regulating hunting laws accordingly.

The woodcock's nest, invariably on the ground, is a mere depression in the dead leaves, twigs and grasses, molded by the female's body. It has no real structure. In it the female deposits her protectively colored eggs, one a day, until there are four. These she arranges symmetrically, with their smaller ends pointing toward the center of the nest and their long axes forming a Greek cross. The eggs consequently occupy the least possible space and, when she sits on them, two are warmed by one side of her breast and the other two by the other side.

In northeastern Maine the majority of nests, according to Dr. Mendall, are in young, second-growth woodlands, primarily birch and aspen, frequently mixed with spruce and fir. Farther southwest in the state, pine may replace the spruce and fir in most nesting habitats. Occasionally, nests are discovered in brushland and even in open fields.

Woodcock in Maine usually begin nesting the third week in April, but there are instances of a few starting earlier in the month. In any case, they run the risk of an occasional late snowstorm.

Years ago I was making daily observations on an April-nesting woodcock when, one afternoon while I was away, it began to snow and by nightfall three inches lay on the ground. Curious as to the fate of the nest, I made my way to it after dark, using a flashlight. There they were, four eggs in a cup of dry leaves completely surrounded by snow. Several snowflakes had turned to droplets on their warm surfaces. No tracks of any sort led away from the nest, so obviously the bird had flown from it, probably taking temporary leave in search of an evening meal. I crept into the blind, which had been put up close by, and, directing the flashlight on the nest, awaited the bird's return. Heretofore, under normal conditions, she had always walked to the nest from a distant point. Minutes passed; all I could hear was the sifting of falling flakes and the clattering of bare tree branches disturbed by the wind. Finally I sensed shrill wings circling overhead and soon descending, not far away but out of view. Moments later the bird appeared, her big eyes shining in the beam of light, her long, downward-projecting bill and her belly cutting a trough in the snow as she wallowed ahead on her stubby legs. Now and then with a vigorous, resentful shake of her head she dislodged the snow which persisted in piling up on the front of her bill. Her nest almost reached, she quickened her efforts in a last-minute dash. But alas, she tripped over a buried twig, and lunged forward, her bill, head and shoulders going out of sight. Recovering and dispatching the snow with one indignant shake, she was soon in the nest and settled comfortably. The snow, it seemed, was no more than a petty annoyance in her regular routine.

The habit of woodcock to "freeze" when approached, flushing only as a last resort, is often carried to extremes by incubating females. They will allow you to get close enough to take lens-filling pictures; some will even permit you to touch them, to stroke their backs, and occasionally lift them up slightly so that you can see their eggs. Dr. Mendall relates an instance of a nest in an area that was being opened up for a gravel pit. Discovered by the workmen, the nest and two square yards around it were left untouched. For days the area buzzed with activity. The female was repeatedly flushed from the nest and sometimes kept off six or more hours. Yet the bird persisted in her efforts to incubate, however discouraging the conditions, and her eggs ultimately hatched. Such tenacity can also work to the disadvantage of the species. For example, Dr. Mendall reported a nest in an area swept by fire. The female was driven off by the flames which burned the surrounding cover, even the rim of the nest, and fatally scorched the eggs. The female nevertheless returned while the fire still smoldered and continued for days to incubate the eggs which would never hatch. She did not re-nest, so no brood was brought forth by her that season.

The downy chicks, which appear in the nest after the usual 20 to 21 days of incubation, leave with the female within 24 hours, and soon go a great distance from the nest, never to return. In cool or stormy weather they are brooded, mother-hen fashion, by the female. If she and her brood are chanced upon by a human being, quickly she responds with a "broken-wing" act—a performance that serves effectively to distract attention from her charges, which by this time are crouched and motionless, relying on their camouflage coloration rather than running away. The chicks require their parent's assistance in getting earthworms, as they are unable to probe successfully until they can fly, beginning at about 14 or 15 days of age. By the time they are 25 days of age—about mid-June in Maine—they are practically full grown and independent of parental attention.

Woodcock generally migrate from Maine during October and nearly all have departed by mid-November. From what we have learned through recoveries of banded specimens, there is a strong possibility that the bulk of the Maine population moves to the lower Mississippi valley—chiefly Louisiana—for the winter. The journey to and from wintering grounds is fraught with mortal dangers from storms, high winds, and sudden drops in temperature. Worse still, because woodcock migrate at night at altitudes below 50 feet, they often run into utility wires, television towers, and other man-made obstructions to their passage. It is not unlikely that more woodcock are killed during migration than during all their other yearly activities combined.

In recent years has come another man-made danger to woodcock—the poisons that accumulate in the soil through promiscuous use and re-use of pesticides and herbicides. We know that these poisons eventually reach the digestive tract of earthworms and we have evidence that robins—earthworm-feeders—have been decimated by earthworm-borne poisons. Can woodcock endure this threat in addition to the already existing hazards of migration and the hunting season? We may soon have the answer.

BIRD SONGS

BY ARETAS A. SAUNDERS

Aretas A. Saunders (1884 —) was born in Avon, Connecticut, educated in science and forestry at Yale, and spent five years in the U. S. Forest Service in Montana. Returning to Connecticut, he taught biology and natural history for many years, spending his summers as field ornithologist for the Roosevelt Wildlife Forest Experiment Station and as instructor in bird study at the Allegheny School of Natural History. A pioneer in the study of bird songs, he made thousands of graphic records before the advent of sound recording in this field and became an outstanding authority on the subject. But he is that modern rarity, an all-round naturalist with wide field experience backed by scientific knowledge. I have spent many hours in the field with him and know at first hand his definitive knowledge not only of ornithology but of botany, zoology and entomology as well. He has written hundreds of scientific articles as well as many popular studies of nature. This selection is from his The Lives of Wild Birds, *originally published in 1954 and more recently revised and published under the title* An Introduction to Bird Life for Bird Watchers.

(*The Lives of Wild Birds,* by Aretas A. Saunders; Doubleday & Company, 1954.)

The bird lover values a knowledge of bird songs because it helps him to identify birds. The field ornithologist values it because it aids him in following the migration or in making a list or census of the birds in a particular area. But aside from these aims, there is reason for paying more careful attention to songs and to their details for the sake of the study of songs themselves. There are many things we wish to know about the songs of birds but few serious scientific students in the field attempting to discover them.

Anyone who has learned to recognize the songs of different species in the field can add to our knowledge by keeping notes on the seasons of songs; the time of day when singing is most or least abundant; the succession of species in the morning awakening, or the ceasing of song in the evening; the number of songs per minute or hour under different conditions; the relations of singing frequency to weather, light intensity, or other factors; the relation of song to the nesting cycle, and many similar things. But the study of variations in song, which may be seasonal, geographical, or local, and the descriptions of songs require an especially good ear for song and a training in musical principles and the physics of sound.

People vary greatly in the ear they possess for musical sounds, in distinguishing differences in pitch, time, loudness, quality, and phonetics. One who cannot recognize tunes and sing or whistle them accurately, even though he can recognize bird songs, should not attempt descriptions of songs or study of variations, except perhaps through the indoor study of records made by a mechanical recording device. Such a study does not require use of the ear, but an analysis of the sound track on film by microscopic observation.

But there are many people who possess good ears for music and know bird songs who might contribute to this study but do not do so because of lack of musical knowledge. Frequently such people think it is a lack of ear that is the handicap, when it is only a lack of knowing how to describe what the ear hears. They are in the same position as one who might try to describe bird plumages without knowing the names of colors. We have learned to name colors from early youth and, unless we are actually color blind, have no difficulties. But most of us have not learned to name pitches of sounds. When in the field I might remark that the interval between two notes in a bird song is a tone and a half or a minor third, someone is likely to remark, "You have an unusual ear for music." But it is not that my ear is better than a great majority of others, but that I know what to call the pitch interval I hear. Anyone who is not "pitch-deaf," if I may use such a term to correspond to color blind, may learn to know these things. He may learn to recognize an octave, a fifth, a tone, a half tone, or other interval. He may study the simple principles of the physics of sound, apply it to bird songs, and thus be equipped to describe songs accurately, make records of them, and launch forth into the field of study of variations in bird song.

Among some bird lovers there seems to be a bit of confusion as to what is a bird song and what is not. Birds produce many sounds that are more or less musical, but not all of them are songs. A song, to be such, must fulfill two conditions. It must be chiefly or entirely a performance of the male, and it must be used mainly, or entirely, at a definite season of the year, the season of reproduction. It is difficult, however, to make a more absolute statement than this, for there are numerous cases of performances that are unquestionably songs yet do not fulfill one or the other of these conditions perfectly. In a number of species, the female sings more or less, but I know of no species in which the female sings as definitely, frequently, and certainly as the male. There is probably more female singing than we know, for it is impossible to distinguish sexes in the field in many species. But it still seems true that song, in every species, is mainly a masculine character.

There is also great variation in the extent to which song is confined to a definite season. Such species as the song sparrow and the meadowlark may be heard singing in every month of the year. But they are silent for a time, in the period of postnuptial molt, and song is never so frequent and certain in fall or winter as it is in the season of mating and nesting. Consequently songs do fulfill these two conditions mainly, and in every species, even though there are occasional exceptions.

A song need not be musical to our ears, nor is every musical bird sound a song. The "conqueree" of the redwing is undoubtedly a song. It is strictly confined to the male and the season of nesting. It is given from a perch, or on the wing, in a singing manner, accompanied by display of the red wing patches, and it is pleasingly musical. The yellow-headed blackbird goes through a very similar performance in every way, except that the final sound produced is not pleasingly musical, but a ludicrous squawk. Many would be unwilling to call such a sound a song, but from our definition it undoubtedly is.

Whenever a bird sings normally, its song is recognizable as to species. Anyone who knows the song of that species will be able to name the bird. Because of this, there seems to be an idea on the part of many bird students that the songs of all birds of a species are alike and that the description of one song is a description of the song of the species. This idea has unfortunately been fostered through the recording of songs by sound-reproducing devices, for in most cases a single song has been recorded and announced as *the* song of *the* species, whereas it is actually *a* song of one individual of that species. Other individuals would sing the song somewhat differently, and that individual would probably have several more ways of singing. When a recorded song is fairly typical of the species, it is helpful in teaching students to know songs. But when that song is not very close to the more typical form, as is frequently the case, it is likely to confuse the student who attempts to hear the same song again from a living wild bird. Though most songs have something about them that is characteristic of the species and are recognizable, there is great variation. It is often difficult to find two songs of the same species that are alike. The song of the Baltimore oriole, for example, is exceedingly variable. Birds in one locality may sing songs that are rather similar to each other, but in another locality, only a short distance away, the songs are quite different. Yet the basic notes of which they are composed, and the quality of these notes, are such that a song is practically always recognizable to the experienced bird student.

In most species not only do individuals differ from each other in their songs, but each individual has a number of songs, and these are somewhat varied, sometimes with the season and sometimes with the time of day. Each individual song sparrow has a whole repertoire of songs, and each one is likely to be different from the songs of other individuals. In the height of the nesting season, after the nest is established and incubation has begun, each male sings his songs with considerable regularity in the early morning. Each song is repeated a dozen times or so and then another taken up. Studying one individual for a number of mornings will generally reveal about the limits of its song variations. The number of different songs may vary from six to twenty or more, but the extreme of variation is a matter of interpretation of the observer. Just how much variation constitutes a different song? Some individuals are likely to make performance of a song slightly different by variations, particularly in the terminal notes. Yet when a really new song is sung, it is different throughout.

Many other species besides the song sparrow have varied songs and a particular manner of singing. Each species is a study in itself, and comparatively little has been recorded about these manners of singing. One surprising thing is the likeness in form of song in totally unrelated birds. The habit of alternating two different songs is common to the towhee, redstart, and meadowlark, and probably other species. A long vocal performance, beginning with rapid notes and ending with retarded slurs or two-note phrases is found in such unrelated birds as the pie-billed grebe, common gallinule, laughing gull, and yellow-billed cuckoo, but I know of no passerine species that sings in this way. The habit of repeating a song two or three times in succession, without a pause, is common to the purple finch and the ruby-crowned kinglet. If we classified birds by the likeness in their songs instead of their anatomy, our classifications would be totally different.

A good many of the variations in the singing of individual birds are seasonal, or vary with the conditions of the nesting cycle. Thus the meadowlark sings regularly for nearly two months before the season of mating begins, and it is during this period, in late March or early April, that it is likely to alternate two different songs. In late April, when courtship and mating begin, it sings one song after another, repeating each song a number of times and producing a much greater number of songs than the song sparrow. But unlike the song sparrow, these songs are not distinctly different from those of other meadowlarks. Certain of them are very common songs of the species, apparently sung by every meadowlark in the region and often repeated by first one bird and then another. After nesting is established, song becomes somewhat less abundant and variable but may be heard regularly till August, when the nesting is over and the postnuptial molt begins. Song is generally resumed in September and may be heard fairly regularly through the fall and even occasionally in winter months.

The commonest and best known song of each species is the territory song, the song first used when the male has selected a territory and is singing to warn away other males and to advertise his need of a mate. To accomplish these purposes this song must be loud, frequently repeated, and distinctive of the species. Such songs, heard frequently in the spring and earlier part of the nesting season, become extremely familiar to bird students. Those students who search for birds mainly in the May migration are often acquainted with the fact that some birds sing other and sometimes quite different songs later in the season.

A good many of the warblers have two distinctive types of songs, singing sometimes one and sometimes another. With some warblers, such as the black-throated green, these two types are both common, and there seems to be no rule of season, time of day, or individuality that determines which song will be used. Apparently both can serve as a territory song. But with some of the other warblers there is a fairly definite seasonal difference in the two songs. It is well marked, for instance, in the black and white, blue-winged, and chestnut-sided warblers. In the spring these birds arrive, singing the common territory song; the "weesy weesy" of the black and white, the two wheezy notes of the blue-winged, and the "pleased to meet you" song of the chestnut-sided. But as the season advances, evidently after nesting is established, a new song begins to be heard now and then. The black and white breaks its chain of "weesys" for some irregular, lower-pitched notes; the blue-winged sings an altogether different song of four or five varied notes rather than two; and the chestnut-sided has a special song, with some notes near the end still high and accented, but with no definite "meet you" at the end. These songs are less well known but not uncommon, and can be heard by any observer who keeps watch through the season in localities where these species breed. Such songs, coming when the birds are actually nesting, are probably best termed the nesting songs. Just what their significance is, is a matter to be worked out. It is noticeable that the common territory song is not entirely abandoned at this season, and with the little blue-winged warbler the nesting song is used in late summer, after the postnuptial molt.

In the very brief period of courtship there are sometimes songs of peculiar character that are little known because they come so infrequently and last for so short a time. With a number of species, such songs are likely to be faint, of the type that have been called "whisper songs," and except for that, they are much like territory songs in form. In a few cases courtship songs are flight songs, though most flight songs seem to be something else that comes later in the season. With the meadowlark the courtship song is a flight song, coming in April, a peculiar performance of different and less musical character than the territory song. This is true in both eastern and western meadowlarks. The song is not common, however, and sometimes years go by without my hearing it.

Flight songs, whether they are courtship songs or not, are of considerable interest. Each species that sings in flight is worthy of special study, for the conditions are different in almost every one. Some birds sing only occasionally in flight, but it seems quite likely that almost every species may sooner or later be observed in flight song. Many of these, however, are apparently mere accidents. A bird in migration, and singing as it feeds in the treetops, now and then happens to sing as it flies from one point to another. But other species, particularly ground and low-bush nesters, vary the song and prolong it when in flight, rising in flight and singing in a sudden ecstatic outburst.

A few birds, such as Sprague's pipit, sing mainly, if not entirely, in flight. Bobolinks and longspurs sing more frequently in flight than from a perch. Birds like the ovenbird, yellow-throat, and mourning warbler have a special flight song, quite different from the more common territory song. Such songs are generally sung as the bird rises, ceasing when it reaches a certain height and drops back to the ground silently. The longspurs, however, rise silently and begin singing at the high point, floating downward to the grass as they sing. The ovenbird rises above the treetops and progresses a long distance as it sings, usually turning about and flying back at a lower level when the song is over. The Townsend solitaire may go through elaborate twisting and turning flights or hover in one spot for a long time, singing continually. The ludicrous clownlike flight song of the chat is still another variation.

One may observe some species for years without knowing that they sometimes have a flight song. Such has been my experience with several species: first with the seaside sparrow, and more recently with the Canada warbler. Yet there are some birds that apparently never sing in flight. I have never observed a flight song from any of the thrushes or vireos. Why certain birds do not sing in flight is just as interesting a question as why others do.

With a good many species flight song is a phenomenon of late summer and evidently has no relation to the nesting. There is perhaps good reason to think that such songs are of more or less primitive nature. Their rambling, indefinite character would also indicate this.

Therefore, flight song may be regarded as a phenomenon of past ages that today is gradually disappearing.

There is a tendency of some species of birds to elaborate their songs in late summer, at the time the nesting season is about to close and before the postnuptial molt has begun. Some species simply lengthen their songs, while others add notes of a somewhat different character. Some, like the field sparrow, may sing their regular song over and over without pause. These kinds of songs need study, for little has ever been noted about them, and there are only vague surmises as to why such songs exist.

In late summer, early fall, and occasionally early spring, one may hear faint warbling songs that are rambling, indefinite and often prolonged. They may be twitters, warbles, or trills, or all three mixed. Such songs are usually inaudible from any great distance. When we succeed in identifying the singer, we may find it to be a wren, sparrow, catbird, or almost any species. These songs have been referred to in literature as "whisper songs," but the term that gives a better idea of the meaning is "primitive songs." The theory is that once the ancestors of singing birds sang a song like this, before the development of more definite territory songs took place. Today birds return to these songs at seasons when regular singing is ceasing or just beginning. Evidently young birds that have never sung before may begin their singing with such primitive songs. Birds that are not singers, such as jays and magpies, indulge at times, usually in fall, in primitive song. In contrast to territory songs, these primitive songs are infrequently heard, have no definite form, are not loud, and are not distinctive of species. We can do little more in studying them than to determine which species use them, the season when they do, and the question whether young birds or adults are the chief or possibly the only ones to use them.

Song is seasonal, but the particular season, the definite date when it begins or ends, varies greatly with species. Some birds, such as the song sparrow, meadowlark, cardinal, and Carolina wren, sing more or less throughout the year. Others, such as the brown thrasher, rose-breasted grosbeak, and Louisiana water thrush, sing for a short time. Most of our migratory species sing on migration and are singing when they first arrive on the breeding grounds. A few arrive silently and do not begin singing for some days, or even weeks, after their arrival. Songs of some summer residents cease in June or July, while others continue till late August. Certain species commonly revive the song in late summer or fall, after the postnuptial molt. Others do so very rarely or perhaps never. There is a large field for study of this matter and need for prolonged studies through a period of years in numbers of different localities.

In studying the cessation of song after the nesting season, it is not merely enough to record the last date on which a song is heard from a particular species. With a species that is a common breeder and singer in the region of the observer, notes should be made also on the date when the first sign of cessation is noticed; when the species as a whole has ceased singing; and when the last straggler has finally ceased to sing.

Examining records over a period of years shows that there is great variation from year to year. In some years, songs cease early. In others, they are continued to later dates than usual. With species that are rather irregular singers, there is great variation in the volume of song from year to year. Nonpasserine species, such as the cuckoos and the mourning dove, show surprisingly different conditions in different years. Variations in temperature, rainfall, humidity, and food supply all probably have effects on the season of song, but which is the most potent factor is not easily determined.

The manner in which song varies through the day in the height of the season is a matter of considerable interest. As a rule, the greatest amount of singing comes in the early morning and the next greatest in the evening. At times there is considerable singing all through the day. Weather from day to day has something to do with the abundance of song, and the season of the year much more.

Another problem that has been studied a little by a few students is the order in which species begin singing in the early morning and the order in which they cease singing at night. To observe it, one must be up and out where birds are to be found before the first daylight. As a rule, finches, thrushes, and flycatchers begin to sing quite early, warblers a little later, and vireos still more so. There are also differences between birds that inhabit forests and those that live in thickets or open grasslands.

Some birds have special ways of singing in the early morning that differ from daytime singing. This is particularly true of the flycatchers. Many of the flycatchers have songs, known as "twilight songs," that are generally sung between the first beginning of daylight till a short time before sunrise. Twilight songs have been reported for most of the flycatchers but not, to my knowledge, for the olive-sided flycatcher. This bird may have such a song waiting to be discovered and described.

The best known of the twilight songs, and perhaps the most musical of them, is that of the eastern wood peewee. A co-operative study of this song has been made and the results published. This is the first co-operative study of a bird song that has yet been made, and brings to light a great amount of detail about this bird's singing habits and serves as a model for other possible co-operative studies in the future.

Occasional individuals of almost any species of bird may have unusual songs, so different from the normal song of the species that the bird stands out and can readily be identified as an individual. Sometimes the song is so different that it is not recognizable until the bird is seen. The student must depend on chance to hear and study such singers, but they are common enough so that one or more examples can be found nearly every year. How such individuals come to sing so differently from the rest of their kind is a matter about which we can theorize. Perhaps they are geniuses, improving the song of their species. Perhaps they have inherited this genius from somewhere back in their ancestry. Perhaps they are merely imitating some song or other sound that they heard in early youth.

A question that has been discussed a great deal and is still not definitely settled is that of how young birds get the ability to sing, whether by imitation or heredity. A young bird begins to sing the song of its species. In a majority of cases its song is more or less individual; like that of its species in a general way, but with certain peculiarities that are all its own. It undoubtedly inherited the ability to sing, but it hardly seems as if it could inherit its individual peculiarities. Studies of acquirement of song by young birds in captivity have, in some cases, shown that the young bird inherits its song and in others that it imitates some sound it hears. We may learn much by a study of captive birds, but a number of results of such studies seems to show that when birds are kept in captivity they often produce sounds that are not the original, natural ones. The study of the sounds made by a caged parrot will not teach us much about the sounds its species makes in the wild state. Man inherits the ability to make sounds but has to acquire speech. Foreign-born Americans usually speak with an accent, but their children born in this country do not. So birds, living in nature with their own kind, sing the song of their species, but when brought up in captivity may acquire something else. Probably singing what we have called primitive song is inherited, but singing the normal songs of the species is acquired. . . .

For those who possess a good musical ear and wish to try making accurate, scientific descriptions of bird songs and studying variations in bird songs, I would suggest the following procedure. Listen carefully to some comparatively simple bird song and ask yourself questions about it. I would suggest the eastern meadowlark as a good species to start with. How many notes are in the song? Are all these notes the same in the length of time they take? If not, which notes are shorter and which longer? Are the shorter notes just half as long as the longer, or is there some other proportion in length? Next consider pitch. Are all the notes on the same pitch, or are some notes higher or lower than others? Which notes are higher and which lower? How many different pitches are in the song? Suppose there are as many as four, could you number them, making the highest note 1 and the lowest 4? Can you write these numbers in the order in which they occur in the song? For example, a common five-note song might come out 23134 or 13234. Now listen to another meadowlark, or perhaps to a different song from the same bird, and try to determine its time and pitch. If you try this a number of times, you will begin to appreciate how much variation there is in meadowlark songs, and perhaps you will find a fascination in seeing how many variations you can hear and record, or how often you hear the same song you have once recorded from a different meadowlark.

There is not much variation in the loudness of meadowlark songs, but if you try the method on other birds, you may soon find one in which there is, and record which notes are loudest and which soft. Ovenbirds, blackpoll warblers, cardinals, and white-eyed vireos will show interesting variations in loudness.

Quality in sounds is the difference we note in the tones of the different instruments in an orchestra. Bird songs differ in quality. For example, the most noticeable difference to the beginner, in the songs of the robin and the scarlet tanager, is quality. The robin's song is a clear whistle. That of the tanager is a harsh whistle. For other kinds of bird songs, can you write a word or words that describe the quality of its tones? At the present time we cannot describe or measure the quality of a bird song as accurately as we can time and pitch. Some birds change the quality of their songs. One of the characters of the song of the yellow-breasted chat is the change in quality between notes or groups of notes.

A good many bird songs have sounds in them, at the beginnings or ends of notes, that suggest consonants. The recording of these is what I mean by phonetics. Listen to a bird song, and record, in the field, just what the bird seems to say. I do not mean fit some English words to it, but write down such things as "tweet" or "chick" or "wheeoh" or "Ayleelo." Some of these consonant sounds are liquids, like *l* or *r*, as we hear them in the songs of the robin and the wood thrush. Others are explosives, like *t* or *ch*, as heard in the songs of such birds as the cardinal and white-eyed vireo. Some sounds are sibilant, like *s* or *z*. If we write vowel sounds in accordance with pitch, *ee* for the highest and *oo* for the lowest, and other vowels in between, we will have a good phonetic rendition of the song.

Call notes and alarm notes should also be studied as well as songs. These are often too short to measure their time, but the pitch can be recorded and they can be written phonetically. It is surprising how many different calls one species of bird may have. Usually one call and one alarm note are the most commonly heard, but when we make intimate studies around a nest, we may hear quite a number more. The common call notes are as useful in identifying species as are the songs, when they are distinctive, but in some cases, such as the warblers, the call notes of most of the species are so much alike that I doubt if any field student could name all the warblers by the "tsick" sounds they produce.

THE WILD PIGEON

BY ALEXANDER WILSON

Alexander Wilson (1766–1813) was born in Scotland, had only a meager education, and came to America in 1794. He settled near Philadelphia, became fascinated by American bird life, and soon found William Bartram, who lived nearby and was the foremost naturalist of that day. From him he learned basic natural history. Dreaming of writing the first comprehensive ornithology of America, he schooled himself as an artist, made wilderness expeditions, and within ten years produced both the pictures and text for his remarkable American Ornithology. *He covered only the eastern United States north of Florida, but his work was so comprehensive that in the next hundred years only twenty-three indigenous land birds were added to his list. Audubon, whose work was not published until twenty years later, was the greater artist, though I prefer some of Wilson's plates. But as a writer, Wilson was a craftsman of considerably greater stature. He fancied himself as a poet, but his poems are prosy; his prose is classic, fresh, vivid and economical, much better than most of the prose of his day. And his nature observation is accurate and unsentimental. This selection, from his* Ornithology, *is typical of his style and substance, which, after Wilson died, was rarely equaled until Thoreau began to write his close-grained prose about the natural world.*

(*American Ornithology*, by Alexander Wilson; seven volumes, 1808–13.)

The Wild Pigeon of the United States inhabits a wide and extensive region of North America, on this side of the Great Stony [Rocky] Mountains, beyond which to the westward, I have not heard of their being seen. According to Mr. Hutchins, they abound in the country round Hudson's Bay, where they usually remain as late as December, feeding, when the ground is covered with snow, on the buds of juniper. They spread over the whole of Canada—were seen by Captain Lewis and his party near the Great Falls of the Missouri, upwards of two thousand five hundred miles from its mouth, reckoning the meanderings of the river—were also met with in the interior of Louisiana, by Colonel Pike; and extend their range as far south as the Gulf of Mexico; occasionally visiting or breeding in almost every quarter of the United States.

But the most remarkable characteristic of these birds is their associating together, both in their migrations, and also during the period of incubation, in such prodigious numbers as almost to surpass belief; and which has no parallel among any other of the feathered tribes, on the face of the earth, with which naturalists are acquainted.

These migrations appear to be undertaken rather in quest of food, than merely to avoid the cold of the climate, since we find them lingering in the northern regions around Hudson's Bay so late as December; and since their appearance is so casual and irregular; sometimes not visiting certain districts for several years in any considerable numbers, while at other times they are innumerable. I have witnessed these migrations in the Genesee country—often in Pennsylvania, and also in various parts of Virginia, with amazement; but all that I had then seen of them were mere straggling parties, when compared with the congregated millions which I have since beheld in our western forests, in the states of Ohio, Kentucky, and the Indiana territory. These fertile and extensive regions abound with the nutritious beech nut, which constitutes the chief food of the Wild Pigeon. In seasons when these nuts are abundant, corresponding multitudes of Pigeons may be confidently expected. It sometimes happens that having consumed the whole produce of the beech trees in an extensive district they discover another at the distance perhaps of sixty or eighty miles, to which they regularly repair every morning and return as regularly in the course of the day, or in the evening, to their place of general rendezvous, or as it is usually called the roosting place. These roosting places are always in the woods, and sometimes occupy a large extent of forest. When they have frequented one of these places for some time, the appearance it exhibits is surprising. The ground is covered to the depth of several inches with their dung; all the tender grass and underwood destroyed; the surface strewed with large limbs of trees broken down by the weight of the birds clustering one above another; and the trees themselves, for thousands of acres, killed as completely as if girdled with an axe. The marks of this desolation remain for many years on the spot; and numerous places could be pointed out where for several years after, scarce a single vegetable made its appearance.

When these roosts are first discovered, the inhabitants from considerable distances visit them in the night, with guns, clubs, long poles, pots of sulphur, and various other engines of destruction. In a few hours they fill many sacks, and load their horses with them. By the Indians, a Pigeon roost, or breeding place, is considered an important source of national profit and dependence for that season; and all their active ingenuity is exercised on the occasion. The breeding place differs from the former in its greater extent. In the western countries above mentioned, these are generally in beech woods, and often extend in nearly a straight line across the country for a great way. Not far from Shelbyville in the state of Kentucky, about five years ago, there was one of these breeding places, which stretched through the woods in nearly a north and south direction, was several miles in breadth, and was said to be upwards of forty miles in extent! In this tract almost every tree was furnished with nests, wherever the branches could accommodate them. The Pigeons made their first appearance there about the tenth of April, and left it altogether, with their young, before the twenty-fifth of May.

As soon as the young were fully grown, and before they left the nests, numerous parties of the inhabitants, from all parts of the adjacent country, came with wagons, axes, beds, cooking utensils, many of them accompanied by the greater part of their families, and encamped for several days at this immense nursery. Several of them informed me, that the noise in the woods was so great as to terrify their horses, and that it was difficult for one person to hear another speak without bawling in his ear. The ground was strewed with broken limbs of trees, eggs, and squab Pigeons, which had been precipitated from above, and on which herds of hogs were fattening. Hawks, Buzzards, and Eagles, were sailing about in great numbers, and seizing the squabs from their nests at pleasure; while from twenty feet upwards to the tops of the trees the view through the woods presented a perpetual tumult of crowding and fluttering multitudes of Pigeons, their wings roaring like thunder; mingled with the frequent crash of falling timber; for now the axe-men were at work cutting down those trees that seemed to be most crowded with nests; and contrived to fell them in such a manner, that in their descent they might bring down several others; by which means the falling of one large tree sometimes produced two hundred squabs, little inferior in size to the old ones, and almost one mass of fat. On some single trees upwards of one hundred nests were found, each containing one young only, a circumstance in the history of this bird not generally known to naturalists. It was dangerous to walk under these flying and fluttering millions, from the frequent fall of large branches, broken down by the weight of the multitudes above, and which in their descent often destroyed numbers of the birds themselves; while the clothes of those engaged in traversing the woods were completely covered with the excrements of the Pigeons.

These circumstances were related to me by many of the most respectable part of the community in that quarter; and were confirmed in part by what I myself witnessed. I passed for several miles through this same breeding place, where every tree was spotted with nests, the remains of those above described. In many instances, I counted upwards of ninety nests on a single tree; but the Pigeons had abandoned this place for another, sixty or eighty miles off, towards Green river, where they were said at that time to be equally numerous. From the great numbers that were constantly passing over head, to or from that quarter, I had no doubt of the truth of this statement. The mast had been chiefly consumed in Kentucky, and the Pigeons, every morning, a little before sunrise, set out for the Indiana territory, the nearest part of which was about sixty miles distant. Many of these returned before ten o'clock, and the great body generally appeared on their return a little after noon.

I had left the public road, to visit the remains of the breeding place near Shelbyville [Kentucky], and was traversing the woods with my gun, on my way to Frankfort, when about one o'clock the Pigeons, which I had observed flying the greater part of the morning northerly, began to return in such immense numbers as I never before had witnessed. Coming to an opening by the side of a creek called the Benson, where I had a more uninterrupted view, I was astonished at their appearance. They were flying with great steadiness and rapidity, at a height beyond gunshot, in several strata deep, and so close together, that could shot have reached them, one discharge could not have failed of bringing down several individuals. From right to left as far as the eye could reach, the breadth of this vast procession extended; seeming everywhere equally crowded. Curious to determine how long this appearance would continue, I took out my watch to note the time, and sat down to observe them. It was then half past one. I sat for more than an hour, but instead of a diminution of this prodigious procession, it seemed rather to increase both in numbers and rapidity; and, anxious to reach Frankfort before night, I rose and went on. About four o'clock in the afternoon I crossed the Kentucky river, at the town of Frankfort, at which time the living torrent above my head seemed as numerous and as extensive as ever. Long after this I observed them, in large bodies that continued to pass for six or eight minutes, and these again were followed by other detached bodies, all moving in the same south-east direction, till after six in the evening. The great breadth of front which this mighty multitude preserved, would seem to intimate a corresponding breadth of their breeding place, which by several gentlemen who had lately passed through part of it, was stated to me at several miles. It was said to be in Green county, and that the young began to fly about the middle of March. On the seventeenth of April, forty-nine miles beyond Danville [Kentucky], and not far from Green river, I crossed this same breeding place, where the nests for more than three miles spotted every tree; the leaves not being yet out, I had a fair prospect of them, and was really astonished at their numbers. A few bodies of Pigeons lingered yet in different parts of the woods, the roaring of whose wings was heard in various quarters around me.

All accounts agree in stating, that each nest contains only one young. This is so extremely fat, that the Indians, and many of the whites, are accustomed to melt down the fat for domestic purposes as a substitute for butter and lard. At the time they leave the nest they are nearly as heavy as the old ones; but become much leaner after they are turned out to shift for themselves.

It is universally asserted in the western countries, that the Pigeons, though they have only one young at a time, breed thrice, and sometimes four times, in the same season; the circumstances already mentioned render this highly probable. It is also worthy of observation, that this takes place during that period when acorns, beech nuts, &c., are scattered about in the greatest abundance, and mellowed by the frost. But they are not confined to these alone; buckwheat, hempseed, Indian corn, hollyberries, hackberries, huckleberries, and many others furnished them with abundance at almost all seasons. The acorns of the live oak are also eagerly sought after by these birds, and rice has been frequently found in individuals killed many hundred miles to the northward of the nearest rice plantation. The vast quantity of mast which these multitudes consume, is a serious loss to the bears, pigs, squirrels and other dependents on the fruits of the forest. I have taken from the crop of a single Wild Pigeon, a good handful of the kernels of beech nuts, intermixed with acorns and chestnuts. To form a rough estimate of the daily consumption of one of these immense flocks, let us first attempt to calculate the numbers of that above mentioned, as seen in passing between Frankfort and the Indiana territory. If we suppose this column to have been one mile in breadth (and I believe it to have been much more), and that it moved at the rate of one mile in a minute; four hours, the time it continued passing, would make its whole length two hundred and forty miles. Again supposing that each square yard of this moving body comprehended three Pigeons, the square yards in the whole space, multiplied by three, would give two thousand two hundred and thirty millions, two hundred and seventy-two thousand pigeons! An almost inconceivable multitude, and yet probably far below the actual amount. Computing each of these to consume half a pint of mast daily, the whole quantity at this rate, would equal seventeen millions four hundred and twenty-four thousand bushels per day! Heaven has wisely and graciously given to these birds rapidity of flight, and a disposition to range over vast uncultivated tracts of the earth; otherwise they must have perished in the districts where they resided, or devoured up the whole productions of agriculture, as well as those of the forests.

A few observations on the mode of flight of these birds must not be omitted. The appearance of large detached bodies of them in the air, and the various evolutions they display, are strikingly picturesque and interesting. In descending the Ohio, by myself, in the month of February, I often rested on my oars to contemplate their aerial manoeuvres. A column, eight or ten miles in length, would appear from Kentucky, high in air, steering across to Indiana. The leaders of this great body would sometimes gradually vary their course, until it formed a large bend of more than a mile in diameter, those behind tracing the exact route of their predecessors. This would continue sometimes long after both extremities were beyond the reach of sight, so that the whole, with its glittery undulations, marked a space on the face of the heavens resembling the windings of a vast and majestic river. When this bend became very great, the birds, as if sensible of the unnecessary circuitous course they were taking, suddenly changed their direction, so that what was in column before became an immense front, straightening all its indentures, until it swept the heavens in one vast and infinitely extended line. Other lesser bodies also united with each other, as they happened to approach, with such ease and elegance of evolution, forming new figures, and varying these as they united or separated, that I was never tired of contemplating them. Sometimes a Hawk would make a sweep on a particular part of the column, from a great height, when almost as quick as lightning, that part shot downwards out of the common track, but soon rising again, continued advancing at the same height as before; this inflection was continued by those behind, who on arriving at this point, dived down almost perpendicularly, to a great depth, and rising followed the exact path of those that went before. As these vast bodies passed over the river near me, the surface of the water, which was before smooth as glass, appeared marked with innumerable dimples, occasioned by the dropping of their dung, resembling the commencement of a shower of large drops of rain or hail.

Happening to go ashore one charming afternoon, to purchase some milk at a house that stood near the river, and while talking with the people within doors, I was suddenly struck with astonishment at a loud rushing roar, succeeded by instant darkness, which, on the first moment, I took for a tornado about to overwhelm the house, and everything around, in destruction. The people observing my surprise, coolly said, "It is only the Pigeons;" and on running out I beheld a flock, thirty or forty yards in width, sweeping along very low, between the house and the mountain or height that formed a second bank of the river. These continued passing for more than a quarter of an hour, and at length varied their bearing so as to pass over the mountain, behind which they disappeared before the rear came up.

In the Atlantic States, though they never appear in such unparalleled multitudes, they are sometimes very numerous; and great havoc is then made amongst them with the gun, the clap-net, and various other implements of destruction. As soon as it is ascertained in a town that the Pigeons are flying numerously in the neighborhood, the gunners rise en masse; the clap-nets are spread out on suitable situations, commonly on an open height, in an old buckwheat field; four or five live Pigeons, with their eyelids sewed up, are fastened on a movable stick—a small hut of branches is fitted up for the fowler at the distance of forty or fifty yards; by the pulling of a string, the stick on which the Pigeons rest is alternately elevated and depressed, which produces a fluttering of their wings similar to that of birds just alighting; this being perceived by the passing flocks, they descend with great rapidity, and finding corn, buckwheat, &c., strewed about, begin to feed, and are instantly, by the pulling of a cord, covered with the net. In this manner ten, twenty, and even thirty dozen, have been caught at one sweep. Meantime the air is darkened with large bodies of them moving in various directions; the woods also swarm with them in search of acorns; and the thundering of musketry is perpetual on all sides from morning to night. Wagon-loads of them are poured into market, where they sell from fifty to twenty-five and even twelve cents per dozen; and Pigeons become the order of the day at dinner, breakfast and supper, until the very name becomes sickening. When they have been kept alive, and fed for some time on corn and buckwheat, their flesh acquires great superiority; but in their common state they are dry and blackish, and far inferior to the full grown young ones, or squabs.

Insects

They fly, they hop, they creep, they crawl; they hum and buzz and rattle and scratch and stridulate. Far back in the beginning, it is said, they were children of the water who fled or escaped to land and air; some still hatch in the water and recapitulate eons of life and evolution. What strange urgencies or forces shaped them, no one really knows. But the insects are so numerous in kind that, though he already numbers them in hundreds of thousands, man has not yet catalogued them all. More than 22,000 species of beetles alone are known on this continent.

They are small, six-legged, boneless creatures, full of instinct but almost devoid of intelligence, packed in a chitin skin that can be soft as tissue or hard as horn. They vary in form from the butterfly to the carrion beetle, from the ant to the praying mantis, from the midge to the katydid and the cricket. Some live only a few days; others survive seventeen years. The queen bumblebee, fertile with next summer's colony, hibernates. The monarch butterfly migrates. Many flies and moths survive the winter only as eggs. The incredible aphids possess the secret of parthenogenesis. The wasps made the first paper and the bee makes honey.

They are scavengers, midwives to flowering plants, harvesters, devastators, boon and bane to everything else on earth. The ant and the bee were colonists, efficient and ruthless beyond belief, two hundred million years ago. The insects learned the secret of survival before the first lizards crawled out of the tepid sea.

H.B.

INSECTS OF THE OLD WEST

BY HIRAM MARTIN CHITTENDEN

Hiram Martin Chittenden (1858–1917) was born in the Chautauqua Lake region of New York and was educated at Cornell and West Point. As an Army Engineer, he was in charge of road building in Yellowstone National Park and there developed a deep and abiding interest in the history of the West. Although continually occupied as an engineer, building roads, reservoirs and river improvements, he found time for much writing. He wrote a history of early steamboat navigation on the Missouri, collaborated on a biography of Father De Smet, wrote two technical volumes on reservoir systems, and produced the first history of Yellowstone National Park. But his most enduring work was his The American Fur Trade of the Far West, *the first comprehensive history of that memorable era of discovery and exploration. His personal knowledge of the area, its geography, its wildlife, its whole natural aspect, was supplemented by vigorous research of original sources. He vitalized all this material and produced a classic history of a then little-known period. All subsequent studies of that time and place have leaned heavily on Chittenden, and while they have broadened the documentation and made some corrections, they have not lessened the basic scope and validity of Chittenden's remarkable history. I might add that Chittenden was an excellent field naturalist*

and a practical conservationist. This selection is from Volume III of The American Fur Trade of the Far West.

(*The American Fur Trade of the Far West,* by Hiram Martin Chittenden; New York, 1902.)

The winged portion of the animal creation in the Far West filled a very small place in the life of the hunter and trapper. In a land of large game, the hunting of birds had little attraction, for ordinary meat could be much more easily procured from other sources. On the lower Mississippi and in the Southwest the wild turkey abounded, and was extensively used for food. Everywhere upon the water courses wild geese and the several varieties of ducks were met with and were often captured by the hunters when nothing better was at hand. The same was true of the numerous varieties of ground birds, such as prairie chickens, sage hens, grouse, pheasants, and the like. For the capture of winged game, whether birds of the bush or water fowl, the hunters attached to the large parties regularly carried fowling pieces.

As to the other birds, they have no practical connection with the business of the fur trade. The swan, eagle, crane, hawk, raven, magpie, and buzzard abounded, some very generally, others in certain localities, but the hunter had little use for them, unless he sought to imitate the Indian by ornamenting his person with their plumes and feathers. . . .

Among insects, by far the most important, because of its intolerable annoyances, was the mosquito (*Culex mosquito*). Scarcely any other member of the animal kingdom received more attention than this from the early traveler. It abounded everywhere except upon the naked prairie, and was particularly numerous in those places which were most frequented by man, the river valleys and the forests which lined the streams. So fierce and incessant were their attacks that at times they completely absorbed the energies of the individuals, and have been known to cause the death of horses.

Strange as it may seem, their strength and voracity increase with the latitude, and they are more terrible the farther north they are met. It is as if all their energies were concentrated into the shorter season, and that their power increased inversely with the length of time in which it was exercised. With these explanations the reader of the literature of this period will be less inclined to belittle the virility of the mountaineer and explorer for giving so much space to the consideration of so diminutive a creature. He will see how far-reaching may be its influence when it destroys the aim of the rifle, interferes with the explorer when making important observations, causes the pilot to let slip his wheel when in dangerous places, to say nothing of destroying sleep and so inflaming the skin as to unfit one for work. Of all the pests of the prairies the mosquito was incomparably the worst. With it must also be classified the various kinds of flies that annoyed the horses at certain seasons.

In the Great Basin the more degraded nations used ants for food. They were collected in large quantities, washed free from the dirt in which their mounds were built, and then crushed into a kind of pastry, which was much relished by the Indians. It is also recorded that these insects were frequently eaten alive by the handful as scooped up from the anthills.

Father De Smet gives an interesting account of the use which these same Indians make of grasshoppers and of their method of catching them. They begin by digging a hole ten or twelve feet in diameter and four or five feet deep. They then take long branches of sage brush and surround a field of three or four acres, more or less, according to the number of persons engaged in the work. They stand about twenty feet apart and commence thrashing the ground to frighten up the grasshoppers, thus continually driving them towards the pit, until all fall into it. It often happens that a few acres will yield enough of these insects to fill the hole prepared for them. "They (the Indians) have their tastes like other people," observes Father De Smet. "Some eat the grasshoppers in soup; others mash them and make a kind of pie of them, which they harden and bake in the sun or dry by a fire; others still take pointed sticks, on which they string the larger grasshoppers, and as fast as they are sufficiently roasted the poor Indians regale themselves until the repast is entirely consumed."

Another interesting insect that played no inconsiderable role in the pioneer period of the country along the lower half of the Missouri River, was the common honey bee. Like the white man, the bee was an intruder into these remote solitudes, where he preceded the settler by only a few years. The Indians were accustomed to say that they could tell that the white man's advance was near whenever the honey bee came. The abundance of these insects was astonishing, if we may accept the many corroborated accounts of the explorers. Their hive was almost always in hollow trees, occasionally, however, in hollows in rocky bluffs. So plentiful were the "bee trees" in early times that search for them in certain localities was as much a part of the hunter's labor as was the search for game. Honey was a common article of food on the frontier and considerable quantities were at one time shipped to St. Louis.

WILD HONEY

BY HECTOR ST. JOHN DE CRÈVECOEUR

Hector St. John de Crèvecoeur (1735–1813) was born in France, educated in England, and came to America at the age of twenty. After a time in Pennsylvania he became a gentleman farmer in Orange County, New York. He traveled widely, through New England, the South and the Midwest, interested in agriculture, natural history and social conditions. Tory in sympathy, he returned to Europe during the latter years of the American Revolution and did not come back till after the war. Letters from an American Farmer, *the book from which this selection is taken, probably was written before he went abroad; it was published in England in 1782, but not in America until 1793. It deals with rural life and conditions and only incidentally with nature; but the nature parts are some of the best of his day, though he accepted much dubious folklore and was basically romantic in approach.*

(Letters from an American Farmer, by Hector St. John Crèvecoeur, 1782.)

My bees, above any other tenants of my farm, attract my attention and respect; I am astonished to see that nothing exists but what has its enemy, one species pursues and lives upon the other: unfortunately our kingbirds are the destroyers of those industrious insects; but on the other hand, these birds preserve our fields from the depredation of crows which they pursue on the wing with great vigilance and astonishing dexterity.

Thus divided by two interested motives, I have long resisted the desire I had to kill them, until last year, when I thought they increased too much, and my indulgence had been carried too far; it was at the time of swarming when they all came out and fixed themselves on the neighboring trees, from whence they catched those that returned loaded from the fields. This made me resolved to kill as many as I could, and I was just ready to fire, when a bunch of bees as big as my fist, issued from one of the hives, rushed on one of the birds, and probably stung him, for he instantly screamed, and flew, not as before, in an irregular manner, but in a direct line. He was followed by the same bold phalanx, at a considerable distance, which unfortunately becoming too sure of victory, quitted their military array and disbanded themselves. By this inconsiderate step they lost all that aggregate of force which had made the bird fly off. Perceiving their disorder he immediately returned and snapped as many as he wanted; nay, he even had the impudence to alight on the very twig from which the bees had driven him. I killed him and immediately opened his craw, from which I took 171 bees; I laid them all on a blanket in the sun, and to my great surprise 54 returned to life, licked themselves clean, and joyfully went back to the hive; where they probably informed their companions of such an adventure and escape, as I believe had never before happened to American bees!

I draw a great fund of pleasure from the quails which inhabit my farm; they abundantly repay me, by their various notes and peculiar tameness, for the inviolable hospitality I constantly show them in the winter. Instead of perfidiously taking advantage of their great and affecting distress, when nature offers nothing but a barren universal bed of snow, when irresistable necessity forces them to my barn doors, I permit them to feed unmolested; and it is not the least agreeable spectacle which that dreary season presents, when I see those beautiful birds, tamed by hunger, intermingling with all my cattle and sheep, seeking in security for the poor scanty grain which but for them would be useless and lost. Often in the angles of the fences where the motion of the wind prevents the snow from settling, I carry them both chaff and grain; the one to feed them, the other to prevent their tender feet from freezing fast to the earth as I have frequently observed them to do. . . .

If in a cold night I swiftly travel in my sledge, carried along at the rate of twelve miles an hour, many are the reflections excited by surrounding circumstances. I ask myself what sort of an agent is that which we call frost? Our minister compares it to needles, the points of which enter our pores. What is become of the heat of the summer; in what part of the world is it that the N.W. keeps those grand magazines of niter? When I see in the morning a river over which I can travel, that in the evening before was liquid, I am astonished indeed! What is become of those millions of insects which played in our summer fields, and in our evening meadows; they were so puny and so delicate, the period of their existence was so short, that one cannot help wondering how they could learn, in that short space, the sublime art to hide themselves and their offspring in so perfect a manner as to baffle the rigors of the season, and preserve that precious embryo of life, that small portion of etherial heat, which if once destroyed would destroy the species! When that irresistable propensity to sleep so common in all those who are severely attacked by the frost? Dreary as this season appears, yet it has like all others its miracles, it presents to man a variety of problems which he can never resolve; among the rest, we have here a set of small birds which never appear until the snow falls; contrary to all others, they dwell and appear to delight in that element.

It is my bees, however, which afford me the most pleasing and extensive themes; let me look at them when I will, their government, their industry, their quarrels, their passions, always present me with something new; for which reason, when weary with labor, my common place of rest is under my locust tree, close by my beehouse. By their movements I can predict the weather, and can tell the day of their swarming; but the most difficult point is, when on the wing, to know whether they want to go to the woods or not. If they have previously pitched in some hollow trees, it is not the allurements of salt and water, of fennel, hickory leaves, etc., nor the finest box, that can induce them to any hive. When that is the case with mine, I seldom thwart their inclinations; it is in freedom that they work: were I to confine them, they would dwindle away and quit their labor. In such excursions we only part for a while; I am generally sure to find them again the following fall. This elopement of theirs only adds to my recreations; I know how to deceive even their superlative instinct; nor do I fear losing them, though eighteen miles from my house, and lodged in the most lofty trees, in the most impervious of our forests. . . .

After I have done sowing, by way of recreation, I prepare for a week's jaunt in the woods, not to hunt either the deer or the bears, as my neighbors do, but to catch the more harmless bees. I cannot boast that this chase is so noble, or so famous among men, but I find it less fatiguing, and full as profitable; and the last consideration is the only one that moves me. I take with me my dog, as a companion, for he is worthless as to this game; my gun, for no man you know ought to enter the woods without one; my blanket, some provisions, some wax, vermillion, honey, and a small pocket compass. With these implements I proceed to such woods as are at a considerable distance from any settlement. I carefully examine whether they abound with large trees, if so, I make a small fire on some flat stones, in a convenient place; on the fire I put some wax; close by this fire, on another stone, I drop honey in distinct drops, which I surround with small quantities of vermillion, laid on the stone; and then I retire carefully to watch whether any bees appear. If there are any in that neighborhood, I rest assured that the smell of the burnt wax will unavoidably attract them, they will soon find out the honey, for they are fond of preying on that which is not their own; and in their approach they will necessarily tinge themselves with some particles of vermillion, which will adhere long to their bodies.

I next fix my compass, to find their course, which they keep invariably straight, when they are returning home loaded. By the assistance of my watch, I observe how long those are returning which are marked with vermillion. Thus possessed of the course, and, in some measure, of the distance, which I can readily guess at, I follow the first and seldom fail of coming to the tree where those republics are lodged. I then mark it; and thus, with patience, I have found out sometimes eleven swarms in a season; and it is inconceivable what a quantity of honey these trees will sometimes afford. It entirely depends on the size of the hollow, as the bees never rest nor swarm till it is all replenished; for like men, it is only the want of room that induces them to quit the maternal hive. Next I proceed to some of the nearest settlements, where I secure proper assistance to cut down the trees, get all my prey secured, and then return home with my prize. The first bees I ever procured were thus procured in the woods, by mere accident; for at that time I had no kind of skill in this method of tracing them. . . .

This business generally takes up a week of my time every fall and to me it is a week of solitary ease and relaxation. . . . There is nothing very material to do at home, and this additional quantity of honey enables me to be more generous to my home bees, and my wife to make a due quantity of mead. The reason, Sir, that you found mine better than that of others is, that she puts two gallons of brandy in each barrel, which ripens it, and takes off that sweet, luscious taste, which it is apt to retain a long time.

THE SECRET OF LIFE

BY LOREN EISELEY

Loren Eiseley (1907 —) was born, grew up and got his basic education in Nebraska, took graduate degrees in anthropology at the University of Pennsylvania, and returned to the West to teach and search for evidence of early man. In 1947 he returned to the University of Pennsylvania to head the Department of Anthropology. A naturalist in the full meaning of the term, Dr. Eiseley, who writes poetry as well as distinguished prose, is constantly aware of the long spans of time and change and of life's enduring mystery. His books are a unique blend of scientific truth and philosophical speculation. This selection, from The Immense Journey, *illustrates both his viewpoint and his broad concept of life, as well as his virtuosity as a writer.*

(*The Immense Journey*, by Loren Eiseley; Random House, 1957.)

I am middle-aged now, but in the autumn I always seek for it again hopefully. On some day when the leaves are red, or fallen, and just after the birds have gone, I put on my hat and an old jacket, and over the protests of my wife that I will catch cold, I start my search. I go carefully down the apartment steps and climb, instead of jump, over the wall. A bit further I reach an unkempt field full of brown stalks and emptied seed pods.

By the time I get to the wood I am carrying all manner of seeds hooked in my coat or piercing my socks or sticking by ingenious devices to my shoestrings. I let them ride. After all, who am I to contend against such ingenuity? It is obvious that nature, or some part of it in the shape of these seeds, has intentions beyond this field and has made plans to travel with me.

We, the seeds and I, climb another wall together and sit down to rest, while I consider the best way to search for the secret of life. The seeds remain very quiet and some slip off into the crevices of the rock. A woolly-bear caterpillar hurries across a ledge, going late to some tremendous transformation, about which he knows as little as I.

It is not an auspicious beginning. The things alive do not know the secret, and there may be those who would doubt the wisdom of coming out among discarded husks in the dead year to pursue such questions. They might say the proper time is spring, when one can consult the water rate or listen to little chirps under the stones. Of late years, however, I have come to suspect that the mystery may just as well be solved in a carved and intricate seed case out of which the life has flown, as in the seed itself.

In autumn one is not confused by activity and green leaves. The underlying apparatus, the hooks, needles, stalks, wires, suction cups, thin pipes, and iridescent bladders are all exposed in a gigantic dissection. These are the essentials. Do not be deceived simply because the life has flown out of them. It will return, but in the meantime there is an unparalleled opportunity to examine in sharp and beautiful angularity the shape of life without its disturbing muddle of juices and leaves. As I grow older and conserve my efforts, I shall give this season my undivided attention. I shall be found puzzling over the saw teeth on the desiccated leg of a dead grasshopper or standing bemused in a brown sea of rusty stems. Somewhere in this discarded machinery may lie the key to the secret. I shall not let it escape through lack of diligence or through fear of the smiles of people in high windows. I am sure now that life is not what it is purported to be and that nature, in the canny words of a Scotch theologue, "is not as natural as it looks." I have learned this in a small suburban field after a good many years spent in much wilder places upon far less fantastic quests. . . .

It was only with the rise of modern biology and the discovery that the trail of life led backward toward infinitesimal beginnings in primordial sloughs, that men began the serious dissection and analysis of the cell. Darwin, in one of his less guarded moments, had spoken hopefully of the possibility that life had emerged from inorganic matter in some "warm little pond." From that day to this biologists have poured, analyzed, minced, and shredded recalcitrant protoplasm in a fruitless attempt to create life from nonliving matter. It seemed inevitable, if we could trace life down through simpler stages, that we must finally arrive at the point where, under the proper chemical conditions, the mysterious borderline that bounds the inanimate must be crossed. It seemed clear that life was a material manifestation. Somewhere, somehow, sometime, in the mysterious chemistry of carbon, the long march toward the talking animal had begun.

A hundred years ago men spoke optimistically about solving the secret, or at the very least they thought the next generation would be in a position to do so. Periodically there were claims that the emergence of life from matter had been observed, but in every case the observer proved to be self-deluded. It became obvious that the secret of life was not to be had by a little casual experimentation, and that life in today's terms appeared to arise only through the medium of preexisting life. Yet, if science was not to be embarrassed by some kind of mind-matter dualism and a complete and irrational break between life and the world of inorganic matter, the emergence of life had, in some way, to be accounted for. Nevertheless, as the years passed, the secret remained locked in its living jelly, in spite of larger microscopes and more formidable means of dissection. As a matter of fact the mystery was heightened because all this intensified effort revealed that even the supposedly simple amoeba was a complex, self-operating chemical factory. The notion that he was a simple blob, the discovery of whose chemical composition would enable us instantly to set the life process in operation, turned out to be, at best, a monstrous caricature of the truth. . . .

If the single-celled protozoans that riot in roadside pools are not the simplest forms of life; if, as we know today, these creatures are already highly adapted and really complex, though minute beings, then where are we to turn in the search for something simple enough to suggest the greatest missing link of all—the link between living and dead matter? It is this problem that has kept me wandering fruitlessly in pastures and weed thickets even though I know this is an old-fashioned naturalist's approach, and that busy men in laboratories have little patience with my scufflings of autumn leaves, or attempts to question beetles in decaying bark. Besides, many of these men are now fascinated by the crystalline viruses and have turned that remarkable instrument, the electron microscope, upon strange molecular "beings" never previously seen by man. Some are satisfied with this glimpse below the cell and find the virus a halfway station on the road to life. Perhaps it is, but as I wander about in the thin mist that is beginning to filter among these decaying stems and ruined spider webs, a kind of disconsolate uncertainty has taken hold of me.

I have come to suspect that this long descent down the ladder of life, beautiful and instructive though it may be, will not lead us to the final secret. In fact, I have ceased to believe in the final brew or the ultimate chemical. This is, I know, a kind of heresy, a shocking negation of our confidence in blue-steel microtomes and men in white in making such a statement. I would not be understood to speak ill of scientific effort, for in simple truth I would not be alive today except for the microscopes and the blue steel. It is only that somewhere among these seeds and beetle shells and abandoned grasshopper legs I find something that is not accounted for very clearly in the dissections to the ultimate virus or crystal or protein particle. Even if the secret is contained in these things, in other words, I do not think it will yield to the kind of analysis our science is capable of making. . . .

It is not, you understand, disrespect for the laudable and persistence of these dedicated scientists happily lost in their maze of pipettes, smells, and gas flames, that has led me into this runaway excursion to the wood. It is rather the loneliness of a man who knows he will not live to see the mystery solved, and who, furthermore, has come to believe that it will not be solved when the first humanly synthesized particle begins—if it ever does—to multiply itself in some unknown solution.

It is really a matter, I suppose, of the kind of questions one asks oneself. Some day we may be able to say with assurance, "We came from such and such a protein particle, possessing the powers of organizing in a manner leading under certain circumstances to that complex entity known as the cell, and from the cell by various steps onward, to multiple cell formation." I mean we may be able to say all this with great surety and elaboration of detail, but it is not the answer to the grasshopper's leg, brown and black and saw-toothed here in my hand, nor the answer to the seeds still clinging tenaciously to my coat, nor to this field, nor to the subtle essences of memory, delight, and wistfulness moving among the thin wires of my brain.

I suppose that in the forty-five years of my existence every atom, every molecule that composes me has changed its position or danced away and beyond me to become part of other things. New molecules have come from the grass and the bodies of animals to be a part of me a little while, yet in this spinning, light and airy as a midge swarm in a shaft of sunlight, my memories hold, and a loved face of twenty years ago is before me still. Nor is that face, nor all my years, caught cellularly as in some cold precise photographic pattern, some gross, mechanical reproduction of the past. My memory holds the past and yet paradoxically knows, at the same time, that the past is gone and will never come again. It cherishes dead faces and silenced voices, yes, and lost evenings of childhood. In some odd, nonspatial way it contains houses and rooms that have been torn timber from timber and brick from brick. These have greater permanence in that midge dance which contains them than ever they had in the world of reality.

If the day comes when the slime of the laboratory for the first time crawls under man's direction, we shall have great need of humbleness. It will be difficult for us to believe, in our pride of achievement, that the secret of life has slipped through our fingers and eludes us still. We will list all the chemicals and the reactions. The men who have become gods will pose austerely before the popping flashbulbs of news photographers, and there will be few to consider —so deep is the mind-set of an age—whether the desire to link life to matter may not have blinded us to the more remarkable characteristics of both.

As for me, if I am still around on that day, I intend to put on my old hat and climb over the wall as usual. I shall see strange mechanisms lying as they lie here now, in the autumn rain, strange pipes that transported the substance of life, the intricate seedcase out of which the life has flown. I shall observe no thing green, no delicate transpirations of leaves, nor subtle comings and goings of vapor. The little sunlit factories of the chloroplasts will have dissolved away into common earth.

Beautiful, angular, and bare the machinery of life will lie exposed, as it is now, to my view. There will be the thin, blue skeleton of a hare tumbled in a little heap, and crouching over it I will marvel, as I marvel now, at the wonderful correlation of parts, the perfect adaptation to purpose, the individually vanished and yet persisting pattern which is now hopping on some other hill. I will wonder, as always, in what manner "particles" pursue such devious plans and symmetries. I will ask once more in what way it is managed, that the simple dust takes on a history and begins to weave these unique and never recurring apparitions in the stream of time. I shall wonder what strange forces at the heart of matter regulate the tiny beating of a rabbit's heart or the dim dream that builds a milkweed pod. It is said by men who know about these things that the smallest living cell probably contains over a quarter of a million protein molecules engaged in the multitudinous coordinated activities which make up the phenomenon of life. At the instant of death, whether of man or microbe, that ordered, incredible spinning passes away in an almost furious haste of those same particles to get themselves back into the chaotic, unplanned earth.

I do not think, if someone finally twists the key successfully in the tiniest and most humble house of life, that many of these questions will be answered, or that the dark forces which create lights in the deep sea and living batteries in the waters of tropical swamps, or the dread cycles of parasites, or the most noble workings of the human brain, will be much if at all revealed. Rather, I would say that if "dead" matter has reared up this curious landscape of fiddling crickets, song sparrows, and wondering men, it must be plain even to the most devoted materialist that the matter of which he speaks contains amazing, if not dreadful powers, and may not impossibly be, as Hardy has suggested, "but one mask of many worn by the Great Face behind."

THE SOCIAL REGISTER

BY HOWARD ENSIGN EVANS

Howard Ensign Evans (1919 —) was born in Hartford, Connecticut, educated at the University of Connecticut, and received a doctorate in insect taxonomy from Cornell University. After teaching at Kansas State University and Cornell, he became Associate Curator of Insects at the Museum of Comparative Zoology at Harvard. He has done field research, primarily on wasps, in the western United States, in Mexico, and in Florida, as well as on the eight-acre tract in upstate New York that he calls Wasp Farm. A one-time chicken farm, it had largely gone back to brush and brambles when he bought it both as a place to live and a wasp laboratory, since its variety of soils and natural growth attracted many of those insects. Out of his year-round life there, and his wasp studies in all seasons, he wrote Wasp Farm, *an informal but highly informed book about the life cycles of wasps, their behavior and their infinite ways of meeting the problems of survival. The insistently individual digger wasps are his favorites, but this selection from* Wasp Farm *is about the social wasps, known to every suburban and rural householder. Dr. Evans has written a textbook about wasps, articles about them for many scientific journals, and is a frequent contributor to the natural history magazines. This selection shows how scientific material can be made thoroughly readable without sacrificing accuracy or indulging in romance.*

(*Wasp Farm*, by Howard Ensign Evans; The Natural History Press, 1963.)

Life is full of frustrations, large and small: and small ones repeated continually are as bad as large ones. I would hate to say how many times I have been introduced to someone as an authority on wasps only to have the person remark, "Oh, you must come and see the wasps in my attic!" It is a sad fact that to most people the word "wasp" conjures up an image of only one particular kind of wasp, the common black paper wasp. It is understandable that to such persons my enthusiasm for wasps seems perverted. Polistes fuscatus, the black paper wasp, is interesting enough in its own way, but will hardly rate as beautiful or sweet-tempered. And here in the temperate zone, Polistes is hardly a "typical" wasp, being an invader from the tropics and one of our very few "social" wasps: that is, the nests are communal affairs, in which several females live together and exhibit a division of labor. . . .

Polistes fuscatus is our most domestic wasp, even more so than the mud daubers, which also nest in the eaves of buildings but which spend the cooler months of the year dormant in their nests. The social wasps are different in that they overwinter as adult wasps in various sorts of protected places. Since Polistes fuscatus generally nests about human habitations, it is natural enough that in the fall those individuals that are seeking a place to hibernate get into houses. Here they may loaf about in the bathroom or perch precipitously over the baby's crib, causing much more concern than is really justified. They can, of course, sting, but at this season they are sluggish and have no nests to defend, so it takes a great deal of provocation to get them to sting. Throughout most of the winter they are rarely in evidence, though on unseasonably warm days they may creep out of their crevices and fly about the house or even out of doors. By late February and March they are more often in evidence, and by late April those that have survived the winter have begun their nests. Apparently these overwintering females often revisit their old nests on these winter and early spring flights, and when they are ready to build they often return to the same area where they themselves were reared. But they never reuse an old nest, even though they might save themselves a great deal of labor by so doing.

On Wasp Farm we usually have a few Polistes nesting under the eaves in various parts of the house. But the major nesting areas are under the garage roof, at each end, where there are vents which provide convenient flyways for the wasps. During some springs I have numbered the various nests here and marked some of the wasps with colored spots so that I could keep track of them. Then I have kept records of individual nests, starting very conscientiously in late April and early May, then tapering off when it came time to grade final examinations in late May and early June, and finally giving up altogether with the great flux of solitary wasps—my true loves—in mid-June. But I have studied them enough, and have read enough about them in books, to know that there are many riddles to be solved concerning these most common of all wasps.

Although the wasps which invade houses in the fall include males and females, the only ones to survive the winter are some of the hardier females which developed late in the season and mated at that time. They emerge from hibernation with live sperm stored in their bodies and with their ovaries beginning to swell, shortly to begin producing eggs which, as in all insects, will be fertilized just as they are about to be laid. At first these females seem to "loaf about" in the sun, visit their old nesting sites, and in general try the patience of naturalists who, also recently emerged from hibernation, are eager to read the book of nature. But one fine day things begin to happen: a few females begin scraping the surface of old boards and logs, chewing up and moistening the pulp, and applying the first blobs of it to the spot they have selected for a nest. At first a small disc is prepared, then a slender pedicel extending downward from it, finally a small cup facing downward. The paper made by paper wasps is remarkably tough stuff, as anyone knows who has tried removing or dissecting the nests. This one small pedicel may eventually hold a flat comb of many cells. But at first there will be only one, then two and three very short cells. By this time the female will have begun laying her eggs; one egg is glued into the bottom (or top, I suppose, since the cup is inverted) and only later is the cell expanded to its full length by the addition of further paper. A small nest with about three cups, one or more of them with eggs, is about par for the first week of May in our area.

By this time the picture is already becoming a bit confused. Here and there one finds a basal disc that was never drawn out into a pedicel, a pedicel that was never expanded into a cell, and small abandoned nests of one or a few cells. And suddenly a second or even a third or fourth female shows up on an established nest. Up until about the first of July the picture is a fluid one: females shifting from one nest to another, disappearing mysteriously, abandoning nests, and so forth. Yet some of the nests persist and grow. Their growth is not steady: a week of rain, and nothing much happens; then a couple of warm, sunny days and the nest is suddenly several cells larger. In general, the number of active, growing nests becomes somewhat narrowed down by June. A typical nest in early June may be about fifteen cells, attended by four or five females, one or two of which may have been on the nest for quite some time, the others more recent arrivals. On each nest one female, often the original founder of the nest, will "stay put" most of the time and do most of the egg laying (we suppose, though this is hard to prove). The others will be in and out, making paper, building cells, and bringing food for the growing larvae. The primary female—this major and perhaps sole egg-layer, often also the founder of the nest—is often called the "queen," the other associated females "workers." The queen and workers differ not at all in appearance, and even their behavioral differences are not spectacular. Unless one has marked the individuals in a nest and watched the nest almost continually, he may be hard put to decide which is the queen. Some workers may spend much time on the nest, and the queen may be away for short periods; all individuals perform various manipulations of the cells and their contents and react to each other in various ways.

An Italian worker, Pardi, studying the European species Polistes gallica, has described a definite hierarchy or "peck-order" among the females on the nest. The female on top of the peck-order dominates the others psychologically, employing various threatening postures, and thus wrangles food from the others and is able to remain on the nest most of the time, develop larger ovaries, and become the major egg-layer. The next one down the peck-order, just as in a flock of chickens, is able to dominate all but the queen, and if the queen dies she quickly assumes the queen's role. The wasps at the bottom of the peck-order presumably lead a rather harried existence and never get to lay an egg. If one kills all the wasps on a given nest and dissects out their ovaries, he finds that the queen has large ovaries full of eggs, the next one down the peck-order slightly smaller ovaries with perhaps a few developing eggs, the next one still smaller, and so on.

This makes a very nice story, but the fact is that hardly anyone who has studied Polistes has found it to be quite that simple and clear-cut. Even if there is an element of truth in the "peck-order" theory, it leaves many things unexplained. Once a hierarchy has been set up, the dominant wasp can perhaps wheedle the most food and thus develop larger ovaries. But how does the queen acquire her original psychological dominance? Is there a real tie-up between ovary size and behavioral dominance, and if so what is it like? Why do some females establish a nest, where they are "boss," then suddenly leave it and become an underling on another nest? What is the real significance of the various behavioral interactions between the females on the nest? To what extent do the individuals second and third in the hierarchy contribute to egg-laying, and if they contribute at all can one really use the terms "queen" and "workers"?

I remember once, when I was discussing social insects before a group of undergraduates, one of them spoke up and asked: "Dr. Evans, how does a honeybee get to be queen?" What a stupid, naive question, I thought. Like asking why the sky is blue. But come to think of it, why is the sky blue? And how does a honeybee, or a Polistes wasp, get to be queen? The question is simple, the answer complex and uncertain.

The honeybee is a rather different matter. But in the case of Polistes, I would venture to guess—without any proof at all—that success in hibernation is tied up with many of these matters. Females go into hibernation with a certain limited amount of stored fat in their bodies, fat that will in part be converted into ovaries and eggs in the spring. A wasp that spends the winter at an optimum temperature and is not lured out time and again during the winter may emerge in the spring in prime condition. On the other hand a wasp that is badly chilled or exposed to occasional periods of warmth, making her body more active, may emerge in the spring with the fat in her body depleted and unable to produce large ovaries. In one area there will be a whole gamut from vigorous females, because of their developing eggs ready to start nests and "assert their dominance," all the way down to females which have barely survived the winter—and of course some that haven't. Some of the females in between the two extremes might start nests but be unable to maintain them long, so would abandon them and join other groups of females. But this is all quite theoretical, and even if it should prove true, it still leaves many things unexplained.

Along about the first of July, in our area, the picture changes considerably. About this time the first capped cells appear on the nests; that is, some of the cells have convex, whitish tops on them. This means that the first larvae have reached maturity and will become pupae. In a few days the first of the new wasps appear. These will all be females . . . wasps can control the sex of their offspring, and in this case all develop from "female" eggs. These females will have a "new look" about them; they will be a little brighter and lack the tattered wings and worn mandibles of the original occupants of the nest. They will also average slightly smaller, perhaps because they didn't get fed quite as well here, in the spring, as their mothers and aunts did last summer. These females have small ovaries and, of course, don't have any sex life at all, since there aren't any males around. They remain with the nest and assume the duties of papermaking and brood rearing; there is no question that we can safely call them "workers." By the time the new workers begin to emerge in numbers, the females of the older generation have begun to become depleted in numbers. The hierarchy, such as it is, will often have shifted many times, and if there have been many deaths a female well down the "peck-order" may now be queen, her ovaries now well developed and productive. Such a colony may, by mid-July, be a thriving community of a few "elders" and thirty or more new workers. The comb may now be quite large, with perhaps fifty to a hundred cells. But from now on the nest will not grow very much if at all. Unlike solitary wasps, the social wasps may use the same cell twice or even three times. The builders become housekeepers, cleaning out old cells, and the eggs and young larvae, which were once found around the edge of the comb, are now found in the middle, in combs which have been used before.

With this large group of workers, freed from the need to build new cells, hunting in the lush world of midsummer for the caterpillars and other insects which, chewed up into a ball, provide the food of Polistes, it is natural that the larvae are very well fed. The wasps which begin emerging in August are, in fact, a bit larger than those that emerged earlier, and they have much more stored fat in their bodies. And some of these are males, for the old queen has, for some time, been laying some unfertilized or "male" eggs. As the end of summer approaches, the old queen becomes senile and finally dies, the workers lose their attachment to the nest and begin to die off, too. The larger females which emerged in August and early September fly about, feed at the flowers of goldenrod, and mate with the males. It is these females that will survive the winter—some of them anyway—to start the cycle over again in the spring.

Social wasps, as you can see from this rather sketchy account, are vastly different and more complicated creatures than solitary wasps. And yet Polistes has hardly gotten into the social register; its societies are of a very primitive sort as compared with those of some other insects. True, the nests are communal affairs in which there is a division of labor and in which females feed larvae which are not their own offspring—the true test of a "social" animal. But some say that insects must have a "caste" system in order to be considered truly social. This means that there have to be on the one hand "workers" and on the other hand "queens." Now the first group of females to emerge from Polistes nests are, on the average, a bit smaller than the others, and we can perhaps call them "workers" even though they are otherwise no different from Polistes emerging at other times. But later there will be a slight increase in their size, and finally a crop of females that will mate and survive the winter. Should we call all these "queens," and if so, where shall we draw the line? A good many will, of course, fail to survive the winter; are these then disqualified as "queens"? Of the ones that survive, some will not found nests or will abandon their incipient nests to join other groups of females; in these groups, some will lay eggs consistently, others perhaps occasionally, others perhaps later in the season, some perhaps not at all. When is a queen not a queen? When she is a worker, I suppose. But it's a rare day in June that you can put your finger on a Polistes and say: This is a queen. Come to think of it, putting your finger on a Polistes isn't a particularly good idea anyway.

Luckily, for purposes of comparison, we have right around us some wasps that have reached the very apogee of the social evolution (though no wasps can be said to rank with the honeybee or the ants as social creatures). I am referring to the hornets and yellow jackets. The words "hornet" and "yellow jacket" both apply to the truly social wasps (subfamily Vespinae); there is really no need for two terms, as hornets are merely large yellow jackets (which may or may not be yellow), or conversely yellow jackets are merely small hornets. The term hornet is usually applied to the white-faced hornet, a native wasp that builds large paper nests in trees and bushes, and to the European hornet, a recent arrival from the Old World which nests in accessible places between the walls of houses. The latter, a huge orange-and-black creature, now ranges throughout most of the northeastern states. The more familiar yellow jackets are best known as unwelcome visitors to picnics; there are several common kinds, some of which nest above ground. In every case the nest consists of horizontal combs, one above the other, all of them enclosed in a surrounding carton made up of several layers of paper. These wasps are all rather similar in their over-all biology, but they differ in several ways from their distant relatives, the Polistes.

As in Polistes, only mated female hornets and yellow jackets survive the winter. They hibernate chiefly beneath the bark of logs, where they can sometimes be found in midwinter, completely rigid and apparently "frozen stiff." But warm days in March and April slowly bring them out of their torpor, and by May they are out hunting for a place to start a nest. The species Dolichovespula will start their nest on the branch of a tree or bush. The commonest Dolichovespulas in the Northeast are maculata, the white-faced hornet, and arenaria, a common yellow jacket. The species of the closely related genus Vespula seek out cavities in the ground, chiefly old rodent burrows, later expanding these by digging as the nest grows in size. Two of our commonest yellow jackets in the Northeast, maculifrons and vulgaris, belong to this group. All four of these wasps are common on Wasp Farm. One year we had a huge nest of white-faced hornets in a currant bush, and I paid for our currant jelly that year with a few stings. Another time a nest of Dolichovespula arenaria in a closed-in portion of our porch eaves got too large for the space available and began to spill out of the crevices in the boards. The wasps plastered the whole area with paper; at the end of the season I had to scrape off all the paper and repaint the entire area.

Although the nests of these wasps are eventually much larger and rather different than the nests of Polistes, they start out in much the same way. The female, having selected a place to nest, makes a small basal disc of paper, then a pedicel, and finally several cells in a flat comb at the end of the pedicel—almost exactly like a new Polistes nest. But at some point during or immediately following the construction of these initial cells, the wasp does something different: she builds a paper envelope from the pedicel completely around the cells, leaving an opening in the bottom. This envelope will eventually consist of several partial or complete layers of paper. Having done this, the female ceases to do any more building; she lays eggs in the cells, and when they hatch she feeds the larvae with chewed-up insects. The larvae apparently develop more rapidly than they do in Polistes; soon there are capped cells in the nest, and shortly thereafter the first new wasps appear. These wasps are females which are very much smaller than their mother, the queen. They immediately begin to feed the remaining larvae and expand the nest so that the queen may have more cells in which to lay eggs. From then on until the end of the season the queen becomes strictly an egg-layer; she is fed by the workers and rarely if ever has occasion to leave the nest. Incidentally, one never finds two or more mated, overwintered females working together in the same nest as one does in Polistes. It is not uncommon to find incipient nests which have been abandoned, but in these cases the queens have presumably died or built another nest somewhere else. As in Polistes fuscatus, the nests are strictly annual affairs, never used a second year. However, individual cells may be used two or more times during the same season.

In the hornets and yellow jackets, there is never any question which is the queen and which are the workers. The queen is very considerably larger than the workers and even shows minor differences in structure; in some species she even has a decidedly different color pattern. The first workers to be produced are very small, since the queen has to feed the larvae herself and doesn't overdo it. After the workers take over the feeding of the larvae there is a slight increase in their size, though they are still much smaller than the queen. Late in the season, the workers build some unusually large cells, and feed the larvae which develop in them a correspondingly larger amount of food. About the same time the old queen lays unfertilized, "male" eggs, in either large or small cells, and thus a crop of males (called drones) is assured. After mating, the new queens enter hibernation and those that survive are ready to start things off the following year.

At the height of its activity, in July and August, a hornet or yellow jacket colony has all the hustle and bustle of a great city. A large nest may have many hundreds, even thousands, of workers. One large nest in California was found to have 4768 workers and a queen at midseason; this nest contained over 10,000 cells, most of which had been used more than once, and would surely have had more cells added. The life of the workers is fairly short, so the population at any one time is much less than the total population for the whole season. In the northeastern states, most nests have only a few hundred workers at their peak. A surprisingly large number of queens and drones, sometimes several hundred, are produced in late summer. After these leave the nest, the workers begin to behave erratically, and soon there is a complete breakdown in the social structure of the colony, even though there may still be several weeks of warm weather ahead. The workers often consume any larvae remaining in the nest and spend much of their time wandering about, feeding on dropped fruit, decaying meat, and so forth. The old queen by this time has died, and the new queens, after mating, seek out places in which to spend the winter, even though the first frost may not yet have arrived. Generally speaking, the species that build aerial nests tend to have smaller colonies which break up sooner; the subterranean nests of Vespula maculifrons and other species are often very large and may persist into early fall.

As can be well imagined, a prodigious amount of labor is involved in the gradual expansion of the small "queen nest" into a massive city of paper. A series of combs is constructed, each new one attached to the one above it by several pedicels. As new combs are added, and as the combs are enlarged by adding cells at their periphery, the paper carton surrounding them has of course to be continually enlarged. The wasps do this by simply tearing down the inner layers of paper and adding others at the outside. The inner envelope of aerial nests such as those of the white-faced hornet normally contains many layers of tough paper. If such a nest encounters an obstacle, such as another branch, as it expands, it simply envelops it. Subterranean nests, protected from the elements as they are, have thinner surrounding envelopes and are made of generally weaker paper. As subterranean nests grow, of course, the wasps have to dig out the soil around them to provide room for expansion. It is a common sight to see great numbers of yellow jackets flying out of a hole in the ground, each carrying a small load of earth which is dumped on the ground some distance from the nest.

With these insects, there is no question of whether or not there is a "caste" system: the queen is larger than the workers and differs to some extent in structure and color—and surely in behavior. The workers also show a marked division of labor among themselves; the younger ones stay in the nest, receiving food and paper from the older field workers and distributing it within the nest. If anyone doubts that these are highly efficient and thoroughly social creatures, let him disturb the nest of a yellow jacket! The stings no longer play an important part in paralyzing and preserving the prey, which is macerated with the mandibles; they function primarily as weapons for defending the colony. And even man, the lord and master of the world, must admit that the stings of social wasps are not to be taken lightly.

The common yellow jacket, she who licks up the jam at the picnics, is very much the elite of the wasp world. Even in the tropics and in the far corners of the earth there are no wasps that have achieved a higher social organization than these back yard urchins. And we still know very little about the inner workings of their societies.

CONSIDER THE EGG

BY LORUS J. AND MARGERY J. MILNE

Lorus J. and Margery J. Milne are a husband-and-wife writing team, both biologists and college professors. Lorus Milne has been professor of biology at the University of New Hampshire since 1948. Margery Milne retired from teaching to full-time writing several years ago. They have traveled widely, on research projects, and they have written technical articles, textbooks and popular books about nature and conservation. Their first nature book, A Multitude of Living Things, *from which this selection is taken, deals with lesser known aspects of life that go unnoticed though close at hand. Their writing is vivid and scientifically impeccable. It has won for them many well-deserved honors and awards.*

(*A Multitude of Living Things*, by Lorus J. and Margery J. Milne; Dodd, Mead & Company, 1947.)

If you ask a dozen people chosen at random to tell you what they know about eggs, all will stare at you in amazement that you should inquire on such a subject. Eleven of the twelve may oblige briefly and inform you that eggs are laid by hens, are sold by the dozen, contain concentrated nourishment, and come in white or brown shells. The final friend may have additional ideas—all birds lay eggs, and they range from pea-size in the hummingbird to cantaloupe-size in the ostrich. Penguins lay one, pigeons two and wild turkeys about a score to make up a "clutch." Robins' eggs are a peculiar shade of blue. Each egg has an air pocket at one end. Easter, rabbits and eggs are traditionally associated. So are ham and eggs. Angelfood cake requires many eggs—so do egg-nogs, but the eggs are not the source of flavor. The list comes to a disjointed and largely irrelevant finale. Why do you want to know anyway? Are you writing a book?

There ought to be a book about eggs—not just a Department of Agriculture bulletin classifying them by weight into "pullet," "medium" and "large" or by surface garnishings as "U.S. Extra Dirty." Nor is it sufficient to go into the many difficulties revolving about the endless sequence of hen—egg—hen, as at least one extremely popular book has done. There should be a proper account of the many thousands of different kinds of eggs. Hens have no monopoly on them; neither have birds. Almost every creature large enough for us to see starts out as an egg. You did yourself although you can't remember the experience.

Each egg contains a single cell with the potential ability to grow into a reasonable facsimile of the parent. Accompanying this single cell is a greater or lesser quantity of food in the form of clear, oil globules, or of yellow yolk granules. The amount is determined largely by the number of hours or days that the embryo must grow before it is large and vigorous enough to obtain nourishment outside the egg—either by tapping a new food supply from its parent, or by actively foraging as does a tadpole or chick. Another important feature in most egg designs is a water supply, but again the degree of difficulty to be experienced by the embryo in obtaining further water decides how much of an aquarium will be provided by the parent. The white of a hen's egg is the water store. The albumin it contains is a protein that preserves the neutral nature of the aquarium in spite of toxic acids added by the hemmed-in embryo. Quite incidentally the albumin is nourishing, but it is one of the least important of proteins in terms of food value.

The single cell in a snail's egg is not very different in size or appearance from that with the potentialities of becoming a man, a mouse or a mackerel. The frog, the fowl and the fishworm start from a single cell that is scarcely bigger or smaller than that giving rise to a hummingbird or a whale. Yet the eggs of these creatures are obviously unlike—in over-all dimensions, amount of stored food and water, and in the protective covering or shell. But the shell is governed by the way in which the parent handles her eggs. Its presence generally means that the egg is designed to be deposited on land, exposed to air, without the buoyant support of water. The parchment-like covering of a turtle egg and the limy shell of a bird's, are mechanical structures that keep the contents from spreading out like a pancake on a griddle. They serve, too, in deflecting chance blows, and in reducing water loss by evaporation.

An egg shell is not all gain. Its presence slows down the important exchange of carbon dioxide from the growing embryo for oxygen from the surrounding air. This process must go on or the egg will never hatch. The thinner and more porous the shell is, the better the exchange can take place, but also the poorer is the protection it affords. Each kind of creature seems to produce a shell that is as light as can be, considering the size of the egg. For the larger the egg, the heavier it is, and the stronger must be the shell that keeps it in shape. There is a definite limit to the size of an egg, because of the mutually incompatible requirements of strength and respiration. Without internal struts or partitions to aid in the support (and offer additional complications for the embryo), an egg cannot be successful if much larger than that of an ostrich. For years there were claims that the non-existence of much larger eggs was due merely to the inability of any living bird to put into one shell a larger proportion of its own body materials. Then someone found the goose-sized Kiwi—a flightless bird of New Zealand—that is so profligate in egg-laying that its products weigh almost a third as much as the bird itself. Two such eggs in rapid succession (the normal clutch) is the physical limit of possibility. Yet the Kiwi hen survives. A corresponding effort on the part of an ostrich would yield 100-pound eggs that would either fall apart because of their own weight, or suffocate because of the increased thickness needed in the shell. The actual limit in size was approached more closely by the ostrich-like *Aepyornis* of Madagascar—now extinct for several centuries—which laid the largest known eggs—nine and a half inches in diameter and thirteen long, with very thick shells.

The single living cell of a bird's egg comes to lie centrally on the upper surface of the massive yellow yolk, as a small grayish white spot. Around this are wrapped successive layers of the white of the egg, then a tough membrane and the limy shell. Down the tube connecting the ovary to the outside world, the whole is driven by contraction of ring after ring of strong muscles. This rough treatment leaves its mark on the egg. The walls of the tube drag on the shell while it is still flexible, polishing its surface everywhere except over the two ends. The muscles impress a taper on the egg, giving it a streamlining like a tear-drop. The "round end" and the air cushion inside are at the front—to be laid first. The "pointed end" trails in conformity with the best principles of dynamic design. The eggs laid by young birds are not only smaller but also more pointed or elongated, because the passageways have not yet been stretched. An old hen, with distended oviduct, lays more nearly spherical eggs.

A chick must develop for many days in its egg shell before it is ready to brave the outside world. A wide variety of creatures are able to fend for themselves in as many hours. A corresponding reduction in the amount of food required in each egg often means that the parent can produce more eggs in a single season. This in turn allows far less parental care, and survival of the offspring is left largely to chance. It is easier to throw out a few hundred more eggs than to protect the large number already laid. Thus it is that great numbers of sea worms, sea urchins, sea squirts, starfish and other animals liberate thousands of sex cells each spring, and all of these potential young float upward toward the ocean's surface. The sea becomes a sort of thin soup, but somehow the eggs are fertilized properly. A significant number of them escape enemies, develop into feeding larvae and begin a new generation. Many members of each kind attain maturity and repeat the cycle. This is the simplest kind of egg production and development. The parents never meet each other. The eggs are provisioned for only the few hours until each can begin feeding itself on microscopic creatures in the surrounding sea. A thin membrane is sufficient protection, and the ocean itself is the aquarium so that no water store need be included with the single egg cell.

Somewhat similar egg-laying methods are used by the degenerate parasitic worms in the digestive tracts of animals with backbones. These too are in a liquid that is chiefly water. Many of them broadcast tiny eggs, either separately or in bags. But these eggs need shells—not from danger of collapsing so much as from likelihood of being digested by the parasite's host. To resist the potent ferments in an intestine requires a particularly impervious coating. Tapeworms and roundworms provide their young with such protection. Eggs of *Ascaris*, the roundworm of the horse that became a classical case for the geneticist, have been kept for years in formaldehyde, or alcohol, or fairly strong toxic solutions of other kinds, only to awaken and begin development as soon as taken into the stomach of a new host.

None of these simple eggs have much character. Even their parents don't appreciate them. But many of the higher animals go to considerable pains to place a smaller number of eggs where they will have a better chance for survival. These eggs are often distinctive, one kind from another. Yet so different in appearance are they from hen's eggs that few people notice them at all. Commonly they are not recognized as being even eggs.

Instinct no doubt guides an animal in deciding where to lay its eggs, but occasionally the outcome is nothing short of ridiculous. A hen at the Mountain Lake Biological Laboratory specialized in wastebaskets. Countless green katydids have spent the night cementing their flat, overlapping eggs to the cords of windowshades. Many a gardener has found these strange gray objects stuck in rows to his tomato stakes. Usually no one thinks of them as eggs or suspects their origin. Nor do the brilliant, jewel-like eggs of butterflies and moths suggest the insects that placed them with such great care. Some have highly ornamented surfaces, with microscopic ridges and pits in fantastic patterns. Others are so smooth and clear that features of the embryos can be seen through the shell long before they are ready to hatch. Lace-wing fly eggs are a shining white, but the pale green parent supports each on a fine, hair-like, transparent stalk. It has always been supposed that this isolation prevented the first born from satisfying its hunger by cannibalizing its unhatched brothers and sisters.

Most children bring home each spring a pailful of eggs of frogs and toads, and through the transparent jelly-like whites, watch the embryos develop and transform into black tadpoles. Some youngsters carry into adulthood the memory that toad eggs are in ropes like pearls while frog eggs are in masses. A few recall some special occasion when a trip to the pond resulted in finding a little clump of salamander eggs glued to a submerged twig. All of these eggs start out as tiny spheres with a black-pigmented upper surface, and a yellow or gray bottom. The embryos change form slowly and acquire a magic ability to revolve within their jelly while moving no visible muscles.

By the time they are ready to emerge into the pond, the frog and toad tadpoles have sucker-like, puckered mouths; vegetation is their first food. But the salamander young have broad mouths and extended feathery gills. They are ready to catch small insects and other minute creatures in the water. Spasmodically each tadpole wriggles to get from one place to another, only to rest there for minutes on end, motionless on the bottom.

Among the vegetation to which the tadpoles cling are full-grown nymphs of dragonflies. As the weather becomes warmer, these brownish gargoyles creep out of the water up cat-tail leaves and change into the graceful, flying adults. Soon they are darting about, hawking for midges and mosquitoes over the pond surface. Well-laden females hover over selected spots of quiet bay while they bring a single, pellet-like egg to the tip of the abdomen. Then they tilt their glassy wings a trifle and descend slantwise through the air as though backing quickly down a staircase. The abdomen drops into the water momentarily and washes off the extruded egg. At once the insect zooms upward to regain its original stationary vantage point, and begin maneuvering another egg into position.

Many of the dragonfly's eggs live to hatch. But toll is taken by various water bugs with sharp beaks and powerful sucking muscles. One of these—a diminutive cousin of the Giant Electric Light Bug—has solved some of the problems of protection for its own eggs. The female holds down her unwilling mate while she cements a cargo of eggs to his back. Nothing he can do will shake them free before they hatch, and he forms a living, though seemingly sulky perambulator for her brood. Other aquatic bugs glue their eggs to submerged vegetation. Some of the so-called Water Boatmen in the lakes near Mexico City are so prolific and so abundant that natives gather the annual incrustation of insect eggs and prepare them for human food.

In big cities, there are many people who still practice the medieval custom of blood-letting for therapeutic purposes by application of "medicinal" leeches. For this market, live leeches are advertised by various down-town drug stores. The leeches themselves are interesting creatures, but their eggs are even more so. Yet when a naturalist first finds and recognizes leech eggs in the field, he is likely to give himself a little pat on the back. They are not uncommon under stones in slow streams. Each is enclosed with several more in a brownish envelope that is translucent, about half an inch long, and very much flattened. Just as the leech has a sucker at each end, so also the leech egg packet has two adhesive disks below by means of which it is stuck to the rock. In an aquarium the leech young can be seen developing in their envelope, until the day when they are ready to emerge and swim gracefully through the water or loop about like inchworms.

Some eggs are sold by the quart. Earthworm eggs can be purchased that way from special supply centers. They are "grown" for farmers who see the need for more earthworms in their soil. The eggs come in packets less than a quarter of an inch long, each capable of producing from one to a dozen tiny pink worms. Loam such as is packed around houseplants in flower pots often contains a packet or two. Colored like the soil, they are overlooked when the earth is examined, yet some weeks later they hatch—to the annoyance of the flower fancier. The eggs and the packets are produced separately by the worm, and the finished product is put together with assembly-line precision. The brownish translucent sheath is secreted by the "saddle" —the band of smooth glandular tissue everyone has seen part way back on a big fishworm. Between this tough cylinder and its soft skin, the worm lays its eggs and adds a supply of albumin-rich water. Then the cylinder and its contents are worked forward by the worm. As the sleeve approaches the creature's head region, sex cells (obtained in swap from another worm) are added to the eggs, and the "cocoon" closes automatically by pinching together as it slips off over the worm's front end. Sometimes the egg capsule has a lemon-shape. Often it resembles more an orange tied by two drawstrings in a short length of Christmas stocking. Ragged edges of the tube project at each extremity, but the package is egg-tight.

One couple, who now know about earthworm eggs, had planted too much parsley in their garden. When fall approached they could not bear to see it freeze, so they made a narrow metal box to fit an indoor window sill, and transplanted about a yard of parsley and soil to last through the winter. The parsley did well enough, but the earth produced one crop of creatures after another. First came earthworms. Then a few dozen very ambitious grasshoppers appeared. They were gray and quite tiny. But before their emergence was noticed, they were well distributed in the box, the window, Venetian blinds and on the nearby walls and floor! Like the earthworm cocoons, one or two small masses of grasshopper eggs had gone unnoticed when the box was filled in the garden. These were short-horned grasshoppers or locusts that bury their eggs, in contrast with the long-horned grasshoppers such as katydids that attach their products above ground. Each female locust is able to work her abdomen down into the soil, and secrete there a mass of brownish froth in which she packs a double row of eggs, all standing upright parallel to one another. More froth protects the top eggs, and frequently the grasshopper takes no trouble to conceal the hole leading downward to her brood. Curiously enough, the top eggs (laid last), hatch first. As the young emerge they leave space for the next eggs to use in hatching. So it goes until all, or almost all, have escaped to the surface and are ready to chew some vegetable food.

Spiders often give their eggs better care. Wolf spiders lay a bagful and then trail the sphere after them wherever they go. When the young emerge, they creep up on their mother's back and ride along, staying with her until after they have had a meal or two and have grown larger and more independent. Other spiders build a silken chamber under some stone or bit of bark, and remain in it with their eggs until the young have hatched and are ready for a foraging expedition. Web weavers commonly attach their eggs to a protected part of the net, and may stand guard over the cluster when not actively engaged in winding a shroud around a fly or repairing some rent in the web.

Like the wolf spider, cockroaches drag their eggs around with them for a while. But the insects show far less interest in guarding the future generation. Roach eggs are packed snugly in a seed-like brown envelope, and this remains partly unlaid in the female's body while the greater bulk of it protrudes behind her. Like a letter stuck in an overcoat pocket—as though she had forgotten to put it in the mail box, the parent carries the egg packet around with her for several days, paying no attention to it. Then casually she drops it while creeping through some dark cranny. After that, the eggs are on their own.

As fall approaches, and leaves drop away to expose bare branches, the peculiar egg masses of the praying mantis become conspicuous. Somewhat earlier the female can be found spouting froth and eggs from the end of her abdomen as she clings head downward to some golden rod or shrub of medium height. The mass hardens in the air and protects the closely packed eggs through the winter. A month of warm weather allows development to the hatching stage. Then as many as two hundred gangling, greenish yellow mantids issue from the lower surface of the mass, and let themselves down on fine threads before commencing to scramble about in search of living animal food.

About the same time that the mantis mothers are whipping up a frothy mass, walking-stick insects among hazelnut bushes are noisily sowing their seed-like eggs—extruding them one at a time and allowing them to bounce and patter from leaf to leaf until they reach the ground. There the smooth brown pellets lie until spring, when a stick-insect young pushes open a trap-door in the end of each egg. Newly hatched stick-insects are among the most awkward animals imaginable. After crawling through the hole in the shell, they seem to have no idea about which leg goes after which. Six legs is about five too many, and they get completely tangled up with their long appendages. The creatures even stand with one foot on top of another while they strain and struggle to move the lower leg!

Through the winter, the bare branches of wild cherry are usually studded with blackish-brown swellings that appear to have been varnished. These are egg masses that will hatch to tent caterpillars in the very early spring. It is a great temptation to pluck every one within reach and mash it so that the ugly webs with their myriads of crawling worms will not mar the fresh beauty of the tree just when its leaves are most attractive and its flowers should be having a chance. But unless *all* the eggs on any one tree are destroyed, no good is done and there is danger of considerable harm. Even one egg mass remaining will produce enough caterpillars to destroy the tree's first crop of leaves. The worms will not be crowded and most of them will reach maturity. But if all the egg masses hatch and there is terrific competition for that first crop of leaves, great numbers of the caterpillars will die of starvation and of diseases that thrive under crowded conditions. Parasites will have a field day, and there will be even more of them to hold next year's tent makers in check. Natural methods of control are far more effective in most situations than any hasty, though well-meant, move of man's. Tent caterpillars have been plaguing wild cherry trees since long before Columbus found America. The trees recover by the simple expedient of holding a second crop of leaves and flowers dormant until after the tent worms have either died or reached the mouthless pupal stage. Then the tree bursts forth once more. And although the unsightly tents remain, the tree fits into the remaining summer days the essential tasks that make it a successful plant.

Eggs cast up along the seashore have many forms that intrigue the beachcombing naturalist. Some of them have names that call a shape to mind but tell nothing of the makers. The "sand collar" is a thin curved sheet, some four inches across, that seems to be all sand grains until it is held up to the light. Then the limp material is seen to be studded with transparent dots—the eggs of the "moon snail." This animal rests its great foot on the ocean bottom and secretes a sheet of mucus in an incomplete circle over the body surface. To this the eggs and sand adhere, and the whole hardens to the consistency of thin wet cardboard. It holds its shape when the snail moves on and gives a false impression of fragility. A sand collar makes a fairly good indicator of humidity. In sea air or on a damp day inland, it is dark gray, quite flexible, and tends to settle down on any supporting surface. But in dry air, it becomes lighter colored, hard and very brittle, and curls up stiffly away from its stand like a starched collar.

Whelks that prey on oysters and other shellfish leave even more spectacular objects behind them in the breeding season. Each of these large snails secretes a rope of horny yellow material, and affixes the end to some solid support. Then as it produces an extension of this cord, the whelk adds packets of eggs at regular intervals, all attached to one side of the strand. The first egg packets are small, but successively they increase in size until some degree of uniformity is maintained. Toward the end of the egg supply, the packets dwindle again and the string terminates, perhaps a foot from its attachment point. The whole is often torn loose by waves and cast up on the beach as a "sea necklace" suggestive of a broken chain with a series of charms attached. But each charm is a flattened oval bag an inch across, with a scalloped outer rim, containing as many as three dozen eggs. Under proper conditions these develop into tiny whelks complete with shells. Soon the creatures open a pore in the edge of the packet and emerge through it exactly opposite the attachment point to the rope.

Everyone has been trained to fear sting-rays, but seldom do visitors to the shore realize the relationship between skates or rays, and the black or brown "sea purses" they find. These fish enclose each egg in a horny case, two to three inches long, with extended filaments at four corners. The twisted arms become tangled in seaweed and form anchors for the egg so that it will not be cast ashore by waves. But in spite of these precautions, the eggs do work loose, or are torn out by predatory fish, or the seaweed itself is ripped free by a storm and the eggs are found along the high tide mark or in the drift debris. Most of them have hatched from a small slit between the two filaments at one end, and the similarity to a purse or bottle is not overlooked by the naturalist who has exhausted his supply of containers. Insects or beach fleas can be imprisoned in a skate egg by merely plugging the opening with a wad of seaweed.

One generalization is safe concerning eggs. All are defenseless. Since most are very acceptable as food to hungry animals, eggs are seldom left in conspicuous places. Not many are as carefully camouflaged as those of beach-nesting sea birds. But unless their very small size renders them practically invisible, each parent hides her eggs or guards them in some way. They may be slid into crevices or concealed under leaves. It takes ingenuity, even detective ability, to find them in the first place. It requires resourceful reference to books or patient persistence in observation to learn what creature comes from each kind. Any watchful outdoorsman can soon collect a basketful of information about eggs he will never meet on the table.

OUT OF THE SOFT, BLACK NIGHT

BY WILLIAM BYRON MOWERY

William Byron Mowery (1889–1957) was born and educated in Ohio and was a college teacher in Illinois and Texas until 1929, when he became a full-time writer. Most of his work was fiction, but it had a strong outdoor flavor and from time to time he wrote nonfiction about the outdoors and wild life. This selection originally appeared in Audubon Magazine *and is taken from* The Audubon Book of True Nature Stories, *selected by John K. Terres. It tells about the night world of the big native moths.*

(*The Audubon Book of True Nature Stories,* edited by John K. Terres; Thomas Y. Crowell Company, 1958.)

It was a beautiful midsummer night, soft, sultry, and velvety black, with an occasional flare of heat lightning on the horizon but not a breath of air stirring. You could smell the rich, moist earth of the rocky, wooded hollow. Here and there, on stump and rotting log, we saw the eerie, ghostly glow of foxfire, in pale yellow, reddish and amethyst. Except for the high-pitched squeak of a flying squirrel now and then, the dark woods of the upstate New York hill country seemed wholly deserted and asleep.

But it only seemed so. A woods on a summer night is teeming

with life, far more than in the day; a silent, pulsing life of myriad strange winged creatures, big and little. Their lives are brief and feverishly busy. Into only one night or two they must crowd the whole span of emerging, feeding, mating, egg-laying, dying. Though this night life of the woods is there for anybody to go and see who wants to, it's something that most people never have glimpsed or even thought existed—a queer, nocturnal world like nothing else on earth.

I was particularly on the lookout that trip for a certain species of Pandorus hawk-moth. Using only our small hand flashes, we went quietly up along the brook that came down the hollow. In a patch of hydrophila or waterplant I showed little Helen, my friend Chris's nine-year-old daughter, a colony of sleeping butterflies, silver fritillaries, hundreds of them. Big Chris, who lives on a small farm way back in these headwater hills, was carrying his little girl in a slingseat he'd made for that purpose. You see, Helen had been all crippled up by infantile paralysis.

By the glow of our flashes we began seeing white tigers, rosy maples, and other small tame moths. Out beyond the periphery of our lights I could see, vaguely and dimly, the flip of bigger wings; glimpses of spectral white, vanishing blurs of ruby and brown; and the tiny, brilliant gleam of moth eyes, the most jewel-like things in nature. The August night was right, the woods were right, and I knew we were in for a fine hunt.

On a small open flat a few hundred yards up the hollow we made our first stand. I merely set my searchlight on the ground, pointed it straight up and adjusted the focusing for a diffused floodlight instead of a beam. Then we crouched down, sat quiet, and waited.

Hardly ten seconds had passed when in fluttered one of the beauties among the woods moths, the so-called Io, a medium-sized species, its forewings a light, bright yellow, its aft-wings yellow and wine. The Io is a common species, comparatively; there were literally hundreds of them there in Chris's hollow, close by his house; but neither he nor Helen had ever seen one or imagined such a creature lived. You should have seen Helen's fascinated stare as the Io lit on the moss near her, its wings atremble, and her joy when I caught the moth and told her she could take it home to mount and keep.

Out of the soft, black night other woods moths came drifting in, light-drawn, till in half an hour we had several dozen of them fluttering around us or sitting on the sphagnum moss. Most moths don't have any common names, so I'll just have to tell you that we were practically snowed under by Catocalas, Ios, silver-and-purple Apanteses, and many others. All of these were sort of old-hat with me, but with Chris and particularly little Helen each pretty, strange-hued arrival was something new and spectacular—creatures from a world that lay right at their back door but which they'd never known a whisper about.

I caught several of the finer specimens for Helen to take home. You can be sure I kept a sharp eye out for the Pandorus I wanted, but none showed up. However, I did have one piece of utterly unexpected good luck there at that stand. For four summers I'd been hunting high and low for a certain very rare, bullet-swift, extremely wild "hummingbird moth." Ordinarily you look for this species in the open fields, and catching one in your net is like shagging a winged bullet. But just as I was snapping off our big light to move on, in came a fine specimen of this prize species and lit on a sprig of clubmoss right in front of my nose. With no trouble, without even using the net, I popped her into my best-padded live bottle, and by morning she was laying her eggs.

Here maybe I should explain that a "live bottle" is any sort of small, wide-mouth jar—mayonnaise jars do fine—with a couple of air holes punched in the top. To avoid breakage, wrap them in some kind of padding. A "killing bottle" is an airtight jar with a wad of absorbent material in the bottom, this material charged with a little chloroform, cyanide, or tetrachloride. For large moths I've always preferred chloroform. An ordinary butterfly net, a light, and a six-volt battery are all the rest of the equipment necessary. A five-cell flashlight will do for the beginner, but the stronger light is really needed to "shoot down" the bigger and wilder moths.

As we started on up the hollow I smelled walnut on the heavy night air. Then I remembered, from my daytime field trips, that in the next open flat above us there was a walnut tree, with the low-crowned, roundish shape that trees assume when they grow solitarily. Speaking mostly to little Helen, I said:

"If we sneak up quietly, and if we're lucky, you're going to see a real sight. I want you to take a good look at it and then tell me what you think it is."

Keeping our flashlights pointed down at the ground, we slipped up to within forty feet of the tree and stopped. I adjusted my big beam to a broad, diffused light and swung it slowly onto the walnut. I'd been afraid that the season was a few weeks too late for the spectacle I wanted Helen to see, but no, there it was!

At the walnut in the open glade about a dozen little Tom Thumb creatures were executing a slow, weird-looking dance up and down and around and around the tree. Against the dark green walnut foliage their white bodies, about the size of your thumb, were strikingly conspicuous. They had big graceful wings of apple green; and their eyes were brilliant, flashing rubies.

Helen was so bug-eyed and speechless that I had to poke her with a finger and repeat: "Tell me what it is."

She got out just the one word: "*Fairies!*"

That was the honest, naive, instinctive reaction of a child. But it's also the reaction of most adults the first time they see this walnut-tree tableau of the woods on a summer night. I've seen this sight myself half a hundred times and still it always reminds me cogently of fairies. Of the Little *White* Folk. I always have to blink my eyes a time or two before I realize that it's only a troupe of Luna moths, gravid females, laying their eggs on the outer foliage of the tree.

There's always a small core of fact or reality to fantasies, like the grain of sand that a pearl forms around. And there's no doubt in my mind—and other observers have said the same thing—that the big, wild, showy moths were the originating factor of our fairy lore. Europe has several races of Luna moth—the Irish, Apennine, Alpine, Carpathian; and these became the Little White People, who go in troupes, aren't too wild, and never do any mischief.

The Little *Brown* People—the pixies, brownies, elves, gremlins—are entirely different. According to the traditional lore about the Wee People, the brownies don't go in troupes but individually; they're so shy and wild that all you usually see of them is the flip of a vanishing wing; and there are many different kinds of brownies, whereas the Little White People are all one kind.

All of these folklore descriptions match up, amazingly, with the actual traits of the big brown moths, such as the Polyphemus, Samia, Rothschild, etc. These moths never gather in egg-laying groups, but are solitary; they're very wild, and are swift and erratic in flight; and the different species vary a great deal in size, habits, and other characteristics. No doubt whatever about it, the Wee Brown People originated from the big brown moths of the summer-night woods.

I wanted to show Helen some of these big browns, and as we went on up the hollow I specialized on them. Believe me, capturing those boys can take some doing. With your light adjusted to a narrow, blinding beam, you pick up one of them out in the dark woods and try to keep the beam trained on them as he zooms and dives, zigs and zags, to get away. If you're good you can "shoot down" about one in a dozen that you flush and get your beam on.

In that section of the hollow there were plenty of spicebush thickets along the brook and scrub sassafras up against the hillsides. It was a perfect night for moth ovipositing (egg-laying) and I knew there were lots of the big browns all around us, working those aromatic bushes and trees. But mostly all I could catch of them was a vanishing blur, a zip and a flop of brown. I gunned around for half an hour before I finally managed to shoot down and capture a Polyphemus, a very large, fawn-and-brown moth with a single eye, like an isinglass window, in each of its four wings.

It was long after Helen's bedtime, but she was as wide awake as a barn owl and thoroughly entranced with the strange world she was seeing for the first time. As for Chris, her daddy, he wasn't making any more remarks about moth-hunting being a pantywaist and slightly balmy business. In fact, it got so that half the time I was toting Helen and he was cat-footing it around in the woods trying to stalk and shoot down a big brown. One surprising thing was the way those two people caught onto moth identification. When we started up that hollow they didn't know one moth from another, didn't really know the name of a single one. But by now they were calling out, like old China hands at the game: "Looky, there's an Io!" Or "I've got a Catocala!" Or "Daddy, there goes a Polyphemus—shoot him!"

Although you have the richest and most pleasant hunting in the months of June, July, August, and September, you can begin mothing in mid-April and continue till the first hard freeze. In fact, after you've had some experience and worked up some know-how about it, mothing is a year-round pleasure. When I go out in wintertime for a snootful of fresh air I always take along a couple of live bottles and bring back some moth pupae or cocoons. You find these hanging in silken shrouds on bushes, under stones and logs and loose bark, in the ground, or just about anywhere you look. A few days in your warm house and they emerge, and you have a perfect specimen for your collection or for mounting in plastic as an *objet d'art.*

I'll tell you one more incident about that night up Chris's hollow. We had many thrills, many glimpses of winged prettiness; but this incident was the beat of them all, by a mile and a toad hop. I'd seen this same thing before, a few times. Mostly it happens more by accident than through planning or good stalking. But however it happens, there's nothing outdoors by day or night, summer or winter, that can touch it for sheer, outlandish, out-of-this-world, breath-taking beauty.

We were up near the head of the hollow, standing halfway up against the south hillside. I had the searchlight focused to a sharp, small beam, and was playing this beam up at some tall hickories across on the north slope. Away up at the top of a hickory, at a steep slant and about three hundred feet distant, I picked up a large moth. The white of its body, tiny at that distance, and the ruby glint of its eyes, told me it was a Luna. She was up there ovipositing, high in the hickory top.

When my light caught her, she fluttered this way and that for a few moments trying to escape. But I managed to hold her in the beam, and pretty soon she gave up, turned and faced the light, fixed her wings, and without further protest came gliding down that bright shaft of light toward us. With her long green wings outstretched, her white body gleaming, her eyes like ruby stars, no Wee White Person was ever prettier, no diminutive angel could stun you more with its loveliness. . . .

It was two o'clock in the morning when we got back to the house. Helen was so dead asleep that Chris just put her in bed, clothes and all. While the coffee warmed up, Chris and I talked about the night's doing. Moth-hunting had taken hold of him, from merely the one trip. On top of that he realized that Helen had fallen for it hard; that it was something at which his crippled girl could spend long and pleasurable hours. So I explained a few of the rudiments to him. Also, I left them one of my manuals, some bottles and other gear, and hoped these would be put to good use.

That, by all means, is how a person ought to learn moth-hunting. Right out in the fields and woods. Not out of books. To be sure, a person needs a moth manual, which you can get at any good-sized book store, to identify your catches. But put the field work—the chasing and catching, the delightful, unforgettable hours in the summer-night woods—put that first.

BEE PASTURES

BY JOHN MUIR

John Muir (1838–1914) was born in Scotland, came to the United States at the age of eleven, and grew up in Wisconsin. Interest in botany made him an outdoorsman and he traveled widely, often on foot, before he settled in California, first as a fruit farmer, then as a naturalist and conservationist. He was largely responsible for the creation of Yosemite National Park and had much to do with saving California's redwoods and mountain wilderness areas. An able field naturalist, he wrote a number of descriptive books as well as many pamphlets and magazine articles urging conservation. His writing was vivid and accurate, sometimes tinged with the purple phrase, often sharply critical of enemies of conservation. He was a dedicated crusader, but he was also a knowing naturalist. This selection is from his The Mountains of California, *which celebrates the beauties of that area.*

(*The Mountains of California*, by John Muir, 1894.)

When California was wild, it was one sweet bee garden throughout its entire length, north and south, and all the way across from the snowy Sierra to the ocean.

Whenever a bee might fly within the bounds of this virgin wilderness—through the redwood forests, along the banks of the rivers, along the bluffs and headlands fronting the sea, over valley and plain, park and grove, and deep, leafy glen, or far up the piny slopes of the mountains—throughout every belt and section of climate up to the timber line, bee flowers bloomed in lavish abundance. Here they grew more or less apart in special sheets and patches of no great size, there in broad, flowing folds hundreds of miles in length—zones of polleny forest, zones of flowery chaparral, stream tangles of rubus and wild rose, sheets of golden compositae, beds of violets, beds of mint, beds of bryanthus and clover, and so on, certain species blooming somewhere all the year round.

But of late years plows and sheep have made sad havoc in these glorious pastures, destroying tens of thousands of the flowery acres like a fire, and banishing many species of the best honey plants to rocky cliffs and fence corners, while, on the other hand, cultivation thus far has given no adequate compensation, at least in kind; only acres of alfalfa for miles of the richest wild pasture, ornamental roses and honeysuckles around cottage doors for cascades of wild roses in the dells, and small, square orchards and orange groves for broad mountain belts of chaparral.

The Great Central Plain of California, during the months of March, April, and May, was one smooth, continuous bed of honey bloom, so marvelously rich that, in walking from one end of it to the other, a distance of more than four hundred miles, your foot would press about a hundred flowers at every step. Mints, gilias, nemophilas, castilleias, and innumerable compositae were so crowded together that, had ninety-nine per cent of them been taken away, the plain would still have seemed to any but Californians extravagantly flowery. The radiant, honeyful corollas, touching and overlapping, and rising above one another, glowed in the living light like a sunset sky—one sheet of purple and gold, with the bright Sacramento pouring through the midst of it from the north, the San Joaquin from the south, and their many tributaries sweeping in at right angles from the mountains, dividing the plain into sections fringed with trees.

Along the rivers there is a strip of bottom-land, contersunk beneath the general level, and wider toward the foothills, where magnificent oaks, from three to eight feet in diameter, cast grateful masses of shade over the open, prairie-like levels. And close along the water's edge there was a fine jungle of tropical luxuriance, composed of wild-rose and bramble bushes and a great variety of climbing vines, wreathing and interlacing the branches and trunks of willows and alders, and swinging across from summit to summit in heavy festoons. Here the wild bees reveled in fresh bloom long after the flowers of the drier plain had withered and gone to seed. And in midsummer, when the "blackberries" were ripe, the Indians came from the mountains to feast—men, women, and babies in long, noisy trains, often joined by the farmers of the neighborhood, who gathered this wild fruit with commendable appreciation of its superior flavor, while their home orchards were full of ripe peaches, apricots, nectarines, and figs, and their vineyards were laden with grapes. But, though these luxuriant, shaggy river-beds were thus distinct from the smooth, treeless plain, they made no heavy dividing lines in general views. The whole appeared as one continuous sheet of bloom bounded only by the mountains.

When I first saw this central garden, the most extensive and regular of all the bee pastures of the State, it seemed all one sheet of plant gold, hazy and vanishing in the distance, distinct as a new map along the foothills at my feet.

Descending the eastern slopes of the Coast Range through beds of gilias and lupines, and around many a breezy hillock and bush-crowned headland, I at length waded out into the midst of it. All the ground was covered, not with grass and green leaves, but with radiant corollas, about ankle-deep next the foothills, knee-deep or more five or six miles out. Here were bahia, madia, madaria, burielia, chrysopsis, corethrogyne, grindelia, etc., growing in close social congregations of various shades of yellow, blending finely with the purples of clarkia, orthocarpus, and oenothera, whose delicate petals were drinking the vital sunbeams without giving back any sparkling glow.

Because so long a period of extreme drought succeeds the rainy season, most of the vegetation is composed of annuals, which spring up simultaneously, and bloom together at about the same height above the ground, the general surface being but slightly ruffed by the taller phacelias, pentstemons, and groups of Salvia carduacea, the king of the mints.

Sauntering in any direction, hundreds of these happy sun-plants brushed against my feet at every step, and closed over them as if I were wading in liquid gold. The air was sweet with fragrance, the larks sang their blessed songs, rising on the wing as I advanced, then sinking out of sight in the polleny sod, while myriads of wild bees stirred the lower air with their monotonous hum—monotonous, yet forever fresh and sweet as everyday sunshine. Hares and spermophiles showed themselves in considerable numbers in shallow places, and small bands of antelopes were almost constantly in sight, gazing curiously from some slight elevation, and then bounding swiftly away with unrivaled grace of motion. Yet I could discover no crushed flowers to mark their track, nor, indeed, any destructive action of any wild foot or tooth whatever.

The great yellow days circled by uncounted, while I drifted toward the north, observing the countless forms of life thronging about me, lying down almost anywhere on the approach of night. And what glorious botanical beds I had! Oftentimes on awaking I would find several new species leaning over me and looking me full in the face, so that my studies would begin before rising.

About the first of May I turned eastward, crossing the San Joaquin River between the mouths of the Tuolumne and Merced, and by the time I had reached the Sierra foothills most of the vegetation had gone to seed and become as dry as hay.

All the seasons of the great plain are warm or temperate, and bee flowers are never wholly wanting; but the ground springtime—the annual resurrection—is governed by the rains, which usually set in about the middle of November or the beginning of December. Then the seeds, that for six months have lain on the ground dry and fresh as if they had been gathered into barns, at once unfold their treasured life. The general brown and purple of the ground, and the dead vegetation of the preceding year, give place to the green of mosses and liverworts and myriads of young leaves. Then one species after another comes into flower, gradually overspreading the green with yellow and purple, which lasts until May.

The "rainy season" is by no means a gloomy, soggy period of constant cloudiness and rain. Perhaps nowhere else in North America, perhaps in the world, are the months of December, January, February, and March so full of bland, plant-building sunshine. Referring to my notes of the winter and spring of 1868–69, every day of which I spent out of doors, on that section of the plain lying between the Tuolumne and Merced Rivers, I find that the first rain of the season fell on December 18. January had only six rainy days—that is, days on which rain fell; February three, March five, April three, and May three, completing the so-called rainy season, which was about an average one. The ordinary rainstorm of this region is seldom very cold or violent. The winds, which in settled weather come from the northwest, veer round into the opposite direction, the sky fills gradually and evenly with one general cloud, from which the rain falls steadily, often for days in succession, at a temperature of about 45° or 50°.

More than seventy-five per cent of all the rain of this season came from the northwest, down the coast over southeastern Alaska, British Columbia, Washington, and Oregon, though the local storms from the northwest blow from the southeast. One magnificent local storm from the northwest fell on March 21. A massive, round-browed cloud came swelling and thundering over the flowery plain in most imposing majesty, its bossy front burning white and purple in the full blaze of the sun, while warm rain poured from its ample fountains like a cataract, beating down flowers and bees, and flooding the dry watercourses as suddenly as those of Nevada are flooded by the so-called "cloud-bursts." But in less than half an hour not a trace of the heavy, mountain-like cloud structure was left in the sky, and the bees were on the wing, as if nothing more gratefully refreshing could have been sent them.

By the end of January four species of plants were in flower, and five or six mosses had already adjusted their hoods and were in the prime of life; but the flowers were not sufficiently numerous as yet to affect greatly the general green of the young leaves. Violets made their appearance in the first week of February, and toward the end of this month the warmer portions of the plain were already golden with myriads of the flowers of rayed compositae.

This was the full springtime. The sunshine grew warmer and richer, new plants bloomed every day; the air became more tuneful with humming wings, and sweeter with the fragrance of the opening flowers. Ants and ground squirrels were getting ready for their summer work, rubbing their benumbed limbs, and sunning themselves on the husk-piles before their doors, and spiders were busy mending their old webs, or weaving new ones.

In March, the vegetation was more than doubled in depth and color; claytonia, calandrinia, a large white gilia, and two nemophilas were in bloom, together with a host of yellow compositae, tall enough now to bend in the wind and show wavering ripples of shade.

In April, plant life, as a whole, reached its greatest height, and the plain, over all its varied surface, was mantled with a close, furred plush of purple and golden corollas. By the end of this month, most of the species had ripened their seeds, but undecayed, still seemed to be in bloom from the numerous corollas-like involucres and whorls of chaffy scales of the compositae. In May, the bees found in flower only a few deep-set liliaceous plants and eriogonums.

June, July, August and September is the season of rest and sleep,—a winter of dry heat,—followed in October by a second outburst of bloom at the very driest time of the year. Then, after the shrunken mass of leaves and stalks of the dead vegetation crinkle and turn to dust beneath the foot, as if it had been baked in an oven, Hemizonia virgata, a slender, unobtrusive little plant, from six inches to three feet high, suddenly makes its appearance in patches miles in extent, like a resurrection of the bloom of April. I have counted upward of three thousand flowers, five eighths of an inch in diameter, on a single plant. Both its leaves and stems are so slender as to be nearly invisible, at a distance of a few yards, amid so showy a multitude of flowers. The ray and disk flowers are both yellow, the stamens purple, and the texture of the rays is rich and velvety, like the petals of garden pansies. The prevailing wind turns all the heads around to the southeast, so that in facing northwestward we have the flowers looking us in the face. In my estimation, this little plant, the last born of the brilliant host of compositae that glorify the plain, is the most interesting of all. It remains in flower until November, uniting with two or three species of wiry eriogonums, which continue the floral chain around December to the spring flowers of January. Thus, although the main bloom and honey season is only about three months long, the floral circle, however thin around some of the hot, rainless months, is never completely broken.

GRASSHOPPER ROAD

BY EDWIN WAY TEALE

Edwin Way Teale (1899 —) was born and grew up in Illinois and his early years were spent in the woods, fields and lakeshore area of the Midwest. Educated there and at Columbia University, he worked for some years in writing and editorial jobs in New York before becoming a full-time nature writer and photographer. First from a base on Long Island, later from the woodland of northeastern Connecticut, he has written many books about wildlife close at hand. Specializing first in insect life, he later reached out to all phases of nature and conservation. Among his notable books is the series about the seasons and their aspect all over America. This selection is from one of that series, Journey into Summer, *and deals with insect life on the High Plains of the West.*

(*Journey into Summer*, by Edwin Way Teale; Dodd, Mead & Company, 1960.)

A mile of grasshoppers led us to the center of the United States. At Grand Island (Nebraska), we left the Platte and our route to Iowa, to drop south ten miles into Kansas. East of Smith Center, just above Lebanon, we came to a mile-long spur of hardtop. It extended across rolling land to a simple monument of field stones which, at that time, marked the exact geographical hub of the nation. Since then, the admission of Alaska as the forty-ninth state has carried this center point 439 miles north and west into upper South Dakota and the acceptance of Hawaii as the fiftieth state has moved it six miles west by southwest to its final location hear Castle Rock, S.D., about twenty miles east of the point where the boundaries of Wyoming, Montana and South Dakota meet. But on this August day, the monument in the Kansas field marked the center of America. It also seemed, on that day, to mark the center of concentration of America's grasshoppers.

Nowhere else did we see locusts congregating so densely. All that mile of highway was covered with them. They paved the road with a second surface. They spread before us in a living carpet continually in motion. As we advanced slowly, thousands upon thousands rose, filling the air with their shining bodies. Like hail, they drummed on the metal roof of the car. When I stopped and stepped to the roadside, the vegetation appeared to dissolve into winged fragments as the multitude of insects swarmed upward with a dry roaring of wings around me. Once more we were in the presence of summer's overwhelming fecundity of insect life.

Before we reached the end of that mile of grasshoppers, the hood of our car was covered with the insects clinging in place by the adhesive pads of their feet. So firm is a grasshopper's grip on a smooth surface that it can maintain such a position on a car even at relatively high speeds. I remember once in North Dakota trying an experiment. I speeded up until I was traveling fifty miles an hour. A large grasshopper, facing straight ahead like an ornament near the front of the hood, still retained its hold. Chickens in the West have learned to come running when a car stops in a farmyard in the summertime. They recognize it as a source of clinging or dead grasshoppers.

Watching the locusts endlessly parading back and forth over the blistering pavement that afternoon, we noticed how, more and more as the day grew hotter, they tended to walk like crabs, with their bodies held high. Many seemed advancing on tiptoe. In these days when the fires of summer burn brightest, numerous insects thus reduce the temperature of their bodies by lifting them away from the heated ground, by letting more air circulate between them and the surface over which they are advancing.

Among the Indiana dunes I have watched field crickets venture out a little way onto the hot sand. Invariably their bodies appear lifted higher than usual. Certain leafhoppers in the desert regions of the Southwest possess abnormally long, thin legs that raise their bodies well above the ground when they have to walk about. Again, in the dry portions of the West, harvester ants can be seen lifting their abdomens higher and higher as the heat of the day increases.

Science has divided all living creatures into two groups, the *poikilotherms* and the *homeotherms.* The former, including the reptiles and the insects, are cold-blooded. They are unable to control their temperature internally. Their bodies have roughly the same warmth as the medium that surrounds them. The *homeotherms,* comprising only the birds and the mammals, are warm-blooded. Their bodies maintain a relatively constant temperature the year around. It is interesting to note, in view of the bird's evolution from the reptile, that for the first nine days of its life a young passerine bird is unable to control its temperature. Its body heat may drop as much as 20 per cent when the parent bird leaves the nest.

Summer, for the cold-blooded, represents the Elysian days. Warmth brings life and animation. Their blood responds, literally, to every rise and fall of the mercury. Chill is synonymous with sluggishness, cold with immobility. The sun directly regulates the intensity with which they live.

In West Africa the natives refer to the early morning sun as "the lizard's sun." For it is then, after the cool of the night, that all the small lizards are out basking in the warmth. Both lizards and grasshoppers have been observed regulating their body temperatures by changing their position in relation to the rays of the sun. Early in the morning, grasshoppers tend to place their bodies broadside to the sun, at right angles to its rays. In this position they gain the maximum effect of solar radiation. In this way, they sometimes raise the internal temperatures of their bodies as much as twenty degrees above that of the surrounding air. Like a man warming himself before a fireplace on a chilly day, the insects change their position from time to time.

Later, when the sun has risen higher and the heat has mounted, the grasshoppers face directly toward or away from the sun, placing their bodies parallel to the rays. In this position they receive a minimum of solar radiation. Dark-colored species, naturally, warm up most rapidly. One entomologist found, by means of delicate electric thermocouples, that during the same period of time the temperature of a brown grasshopper rose more than eight degrees F. above that of a buff-colored one when the two basked side by side in the sun.

But even for cold-blooded creatures, stimulated by summer's warmth, there is a limit to the heat their bodies will endure. All along the way, as we roamed the mid-portion of the continent during the mid-portion of the season, we saw various creatures, cold-blooded and warm-blooded alike, adjusting themselves in diverse ways to the rigors of summer heat.

Fish descended into the cooler water of the deeper pools. Dogs lolled out their tongues. Rabbits panted. Unable to sweat, these animals cool their bodies by increasing the flow of air over their moist tongues and lips. Burrowing spiders were avoiding the heat by going to the bottoms of their silk-lined holes. So were ground squirrels and other tunneling rodents. In the depths of their holes, they spent the day surrounded by temperatures that rarely rose into the upper eighties no matter how hot the air grew outside. Gray squirrels, at times in summer heat, sprawl like miniature bearskin rugs on the cool, moist open ground of shaded places. Once we passed fifteen tan piglets in a barnyard, all huddled together in the shade of a wagon. Where small digger wasps excavated tunnels in sand that was burning hot under the glare of the sun, they often flew about in the air to cool off after every few seconds of feverish burrowing.

By the time the mercury neared 100 degrees, we noticed all the perching birds let their wings down, holding them out from their sides. The plumage of a bird is less dense during the summer months. The creature is more lightly clad. In effect, birds wear lightweight suits in the summertime. A goldfinch, for example, has about 1,000 fewer feathers in summer than in winter. By wearing lighter colors during months when the sunshine is more intense, the colored lizard of Arizona reduces the effect of solar radiation. In winter it is dark-hued, absorbing more of the warmth of the sun; in summer its body becomes lighter in color, reflecting the sunshine.

Another creature of the desert, the kangaroo rat, has a unique water-cooling system that saves its life during peaks of abnormal heat. Unlike humans, who are fortunate in being able to perspire and thus cool their bodies, this rodent has no sweat glands. Instead it possesses a curious substitute. The highest internal temperature the kangaroo rat can endure is about 107 degrees F. As the animal approaches this lethal limit, a sudden and copious secretion of saliva occurs. It runs down its chin and the front of its body, wets the fur, and by its swift evaporation lowers the animal's temperature sufficiently to save its life. Research workers who have studied this emergency heat regulation have found that it may result in a loss of as much as 15 per cent of the creature's body water. This is perilously close to the 20 per cent which is considered the limit of desiccation that the animal can survive. In such circumstances, the desert dweller saves its life between two deadly hazards, approaching close to both —the hazard of heat that cannot be endured and the hazard of water loss beyond the point of recovery.

Because the relative surface area is greater in small animals than in large ones, the rate of evaporation increases as size decreases. This explains why the smaller creatures do not possess sweat glands. Their body fluids would be lost too rapidly. Loss of moisture is the great problem of summer heat. Insects have shown that they can stand markedly higher temperatures in moist surroundings than they can stand when the air is dry. The grasshoppers that swarmed over the monument road wore a thin outer coating of waxy material that reduced moisture loss through evaporation. Above about 111 degrees F., this wax begins to soften and melt, resulting, in very dry air, in a loss of body water. On the hottest days, grasshoppers climb vegetation to escape the heat being radiated from the ground. How swiftly this heat is dissipated is indicated by the fact that there may be a drop of twenty or even thirty degrees in the first half inch above an asphalt road and a further reduction of several degrees for each additional inch. In times of great heat, the shaded sides of western fenceposts are sometimes fringed with densely packed masses of clinging grasshoppers.

It is in desert lands, dry and hot, that special adaptations for moderating the rigors of summer heat attain some of their most striking forms. One of the *Meloidae*, or oil beetles, of the Southwest, for example, has its elytra, or shards, fused together over its back, providing an air space, like an empty attic, above its abdomen. The insect has a swollen, enlarged appearance, suggesting half a miniature green orange. This globular shape presents the smallest surface to the sun, while the dead-air space beneath the shards provides a certain amount of insulation.

The strange Gila monster, the orange-and-black venomous lizard of the Sonoran desert of the Southwest, overcomes heat in another way. Birds nest early in this area. During the spring the Gila monster gorges itself on eggs. Its blunt tail swells into a larder of stored-up fat. Then, during the hottest time of summer, it lives on this accumulated food. Retreating to some hiding place, it falls into the torpor of estivation, that hot-weather counterpart of winter hibernation. This particular creature estivates in summer and hibernates in winter. Thus it spends much of the year in a state approaching suspended animation.

Various creatures, ranging from ground squirrels to snails, tide themselves over periods of intense, dry heat by sinking into a state of estivation. During this summer sleep, the functions of their bodies almost cease. Breathing is shallow, heartbeats slow down, digestive processes are almost suspended. So deep is its dormancy that the creature approaches closely to the borderline of life and death. Thus it sleeps away the weeks of oppressive heat.

In Australia, R. J. Tillyard, the famous dragonfly expert, discovered one nymph that estivates in the beds of evaporated pools and streams during the hottest, most arid weeks of the year. It can live for months in dry sand. In its dormant state, Tillyard reports in *The Biology of Dragonflies,* it becomes so desiccated it crackles when handled. Yet it recovers in a few minutes when placed in water.

A desert dweller that seems particularly able to endure great heat is the chuckwalla. This vegetarian lizard, sometimes attaining a length of a foot and a half, will rest for as long as twenty minutes unshaded from the burning midsummer sun. It can remain without any apparent discomfort on rocks that are too hot for human hands to touch. Among mammals, the antelope of the Great Plains gives the impression of being among the least affected by the blaze of the sun. It remains in the open when other creatures around it have sought the shade.

Shade is the lifesaver for a host of animals—including man. When we wear a hat or walk under a summer parasol or, for that matter, open the door and enter a house, we are making use of shade. So, in other ways, a myriad of wild creatures turn to shade for relief from the midsummer sun. One noon, on a sun-drenched street in a South Dakota town, we watched a house sparrow picking insects—grasshoppers and yellow butterflies mainly—from the fronts of parked automobiles. Each time it would flutter up, snatch a dead insect in its bill, then alight and hop rapidly across the sidewalk out of the torrid rays of the sun. There, in the shade of the stores, it would eat its prize at leisure before venturing out into the white glare once more.

Amid open rangeland, we saw cattle huddled in the sparse shade of cottonwood and once, on the long, dry road down eastern Montana, we passed a forlorn sheep, with no tree to turn to, that was using the narrow shade of a fencepost. It stood with its body exposed to the burning sunshine but with its head carefully placed behind the upright post so the shadow strip ran across it. It seemed to be wearing the shade like a bonnet.

Mary Austin, in *The Land of Little Rain,* tells of a boundary fence that ran for a long way across rangeland in the Little Antelope country of the dry interior of southern California. "Along its fifteen miles of posts," she relates, "one could be sure of finding a bird or two in every strip of shadow; sometimes the sparrow and the hawk, with wings trailed and beak parted, drooping in the white truce of noon."

Many times, as we rode across the open prairies, we saw birds perching on wire fences at the exact spots where the shadows of posts cut across them. Later, in northern Texas, a government naturalist told us of coming upon a line of fenceposts with a jack rabbit stretched out in the shade of each post. They all pointed outward with their backs against the upright wood, ready for an instant getaway if danger appeared. As the position of the sun slowly altered in the sky, swinging the post shadows over the ground, the animals kept shifting their places so they remained extended exactly within the narrow band of the outstretched shade.

The swiftest serpents in America are the racers and whip-snakes of the Southwestern deserts. They are day hunters. The slower snakes of the dry country come out mainly at night. For few reptiles can stand any prolonged exposure to the summer sun. The swift desert species streak from bush to bush, from shade to shade, their speed lessening the time they are exposed to the direct rays of the sunshine. In Death Valley, where the thermometer once reached the record height of 134 degrees F. in the shade, small harvester ants die in less than half a minute when they are outside in the open during the hottest hours of the summer. Yet these insects continue to carry seed husks to refuse piles outside the nest. But a scientist who timed these forays into the full sunshine found that the insects, in some way, gauged precisely the period they were without shade. The trips always ended before the danger point was reached.

Because, in the sandy stretches of desert country, the soaring heat of the day dissipates swiftly and is replaced by the cold of the night, many animals, particularly small cold-blooded creatures, avoid both extremes by becoming crepuscular. They emerge and feed in the twilight after the sun has sunk below the horizon. They are, in effect, using the shade of the planet to protect them from the heat of the summer sun.

In our own way, later that afternoon when we left the road of the grasshoppers behind and turned toward Nebraska again, we took advantage of the cooling shade. We were driving on a long, straight stretch of highway in the full blaze of the sun when we were overtaken by the moving shadow of a drifting cloud. I fed the engine a little more fuel and adjusted our speed to the pace of the shadow. For several miles we ran in this manner, with the sun veiled, bowling along at more than fifty miles an hour, riding under the awning of a cloud. All the way there was the sense of a sudden lessening of the pressure of the midsummer heat. We wore the shade of the cloud as gratefully as the Montana sheep had worn the bonnet of the fence-post shadow.

MAY-MONTH

BY WALT WHITMAN

Walt Whitman (1819–1892) was born and grew up on Long Island, where he had only a public school education. He worked as carpenter, printer, teacher and editor and made long, wandering tours north into Canada, south to New Orleans. His first collection of poems, Leaves of Grass, *was published in 1855, and throughout the rest of his long life he revised and added to it. As a poet he was both praised and censured, but he was an enduring influence on American prose as well as poetry. He wrote several volumes of prose which, while not as sharply at odds with traditional form and subject as his poems, were marked by his own rhythms and his fresh though sometimes lush descriptions. Not a naturalist, he was a good observer and he captured a freshness of detail and a warmth of emotion when he wrote about nature. Among the best of his writing about the outdoors is that in* Specimen Days. *This two-part selection about spring is from that book, the first part about rural Timber Creek and the second about nearby Camden, New Jersey. Both have the vivid detail and the discriminating choice of words I find in the best of his poetry.*

(*Specimen Days,* by Walt Whitman; David McKay, 1882.)

May-month—month of swarming, singing, mating birds—the bumblebee month—month of the flowering lilac—(and then my own birth month). As I jot this paragraph, I am out just after sunrise, and down toward the creek. The lights, perfumes, melodies—the bluebirds, grass birds and robins, in every direction—the noisy, vocal, natural concert. For undertones, a neighboring woodpecker tapping his tree, and the distant clarion of chanticleer. Then the fresh earth smells—the colors, the delicate drabs and thin blues of the perspective. The bright green of the grass has receiv'd an added tinge from the last two days' mildness and moisture. How the sun silently mounts in the broad clear sky, on his day's journey! How the warm beams bathe all, and come streaming kissingly and almost hot on my face.

A while since the croaking of the pond-frogs and the first white of the dogwood blossoms. Now the golden dandelions in endless profusion, spotting the ground everywhere. The white cherry and pear-blows—the wild violets, with their blue eyes looking up and saluting my feet, as I saunter the wood-edge—the rosy blush of budding apple trees—the light-clear emerald hue of the wheat fields—the darker green of the rye—a warm elasticity pervading the air—the cedar bushes profusely deck'd with their little brown apples—the summer fully awakening—the convocation of blackbirds, garrulous flocks of them, gathering on some tree, and making the hour and place noisy as I sit near.

Later. Nature marches in procession, in sections, like the corps of an army. All have done much for me, and still do. But for the last two days it has been the great wild bee, the humblebee, or "bumble," as the children call him. As I walk, or hobble, from the farmhouse down to the creek, I traverse the before-mention'd lane, fenced by old rails, with many splits, splinters, breaks, holes, etc., the choice habitat of those crooning, hairy insects. Up and down and by and between these rails, they swarm and dart and fly in countless myriads. As I wend slowly along, I am often accompanied with a moving cloud of them. They play a leading part in my morning, midday or sunset rambles, and often dominate the landscape in a way I never before thought of—fill the long lane, not by scores or hundreds only, but by thousands. Large and vivacious and swift, with wonderful momentum and a loud swelling perpetual hum, varied now and then by something almost like a shriek, they dart to and fro, in rapid flashes, chasing each other, and (little things as they are) conveying to me a new and pronounc'd sense of strength, beauty, vitality and movement. Are they in their mating season? or what is the meaning of this plenitude, swiftness, eagerness, display? As I walk'd, I thought I was follow'd by a particular swarm, but upon observation I saw that it was a rapid succession of changing swarms, one after another.

As I write, I am seated under a big wild-cherry tree—the warm day temper'd by partial clouds and a fresh breeze, neither too heavy nor light—and here I sit long and long, envelop'd in the deep musical drone of these bees, flitting, balancing, darting to and fro about me by hundreds—big fellows with light yellow jackets, great glistening swelling bodies, stumpy heads and gauzy wings—humming their perpetual rich mellow boom. (Is there not a hint in it for a musical composition, of which it should be the background? some bumblebee symphony?) How it all nourishes, lulls me, in the way most needed; the open air, the rye fields, the apple orchards. The last two days have been faultless in sun, breeze, temperature and everything; never two more perfect days, and I have enjoy'd them wonderfully. My health is somewhat better, and my spirit at peace. (Yet the anniversary of the saddest loss and sorrow of my life is close at hand.)

Another jotting, another perfect day: forenoon, from 7 to 9, two hours envelop'd in sound of bumblebees and bird music. Down in the apple trees and in a neighboring cedar were three or four russet-back'd thrushes, each singing his best, and roulading in ways I never heard surpass'd. Two hours I abandon myself to hearing them, and indolently absorbing the scene. Almost every bird I notice has a special time in the year—sometimes limited to a few days—when it sings its best; and now is the period of these russet-backs. Meanwhile, up and down the lane, the darting, droning, musical bumblebees. A great swarm again for my entourage as I return home, moving along with me as before.

As I write this, two or three weeks later, I am sitting near the brook under a tulip tree, 70 feet high, thick with the fresh verdure of its young maturity—a beautiful object—every branch, every leaf perfect. From top to bottom, seeking the sweet juice in the blossoms, it swarms with myriads of these wild bees, whose loud and steady humming makes an undertone to the whole, and to my mood and the hour.

May 21. Back in Camden. Again commencing one of those unusually transparent, full-starr'd blue-black nights as if to show that however lush and pompous the day may be, there is something left in the not-day that can outvie it. The rarest, finest sample of long-drawn-out clear-obscure, from sundown to 9 o'clock. I went down to the Delaware, and cross'd and cross'd. Venus like blazing silver well up in the west. The large pale thin crescent of the new moon, half an hour high, sinking languidly under a bar-sinister of cloud, and then emerging. Arcturus right overhead. A faint fragrant sea-odor wafted up from the south. The gloaming, the temper'd coolness, with every feature of the scene, indescribably soothing and tonic—one of those hours that give hints to the soul, impossible to put in a statement. (Ah, where would be any food for spirituality without night and the stars?) The vacant spaciousness of the air, and the veil'd blue of the heavens, seem'd miracles enough.

As the night advanc'd it changed its spirit and garments to ampler stateliness. I was almost conscious of a definite presence, Nature silently near. The great constellation of the Water-Serpent stretch'd its coils over more than half the heavens. The Swan with outspread wings was flying down the Milky Way. The northern Crown, the Eagle, Lyra, all up there in their places. From the whole dome shot down points of light, rapport with me, through the clear blue-black. All the usual sense of motion, all animal life, seem'd discarded, seem'd a fiction; a curious power like the placid rest of Egyptian gods took possession, none the less potent for being impalpable. Earlier I had seen many bats, balancing in the luminous twilight, darting their black forms hither and yon over the river; but now they altogether disappear'd. The evening star and the moon had gone. Alertness and peace lay calmly couching together through the fluid universal shadows. . . .

Plants and Trees

A root, a stem, a leaf, some means of capturing sunlight and air and making food—in sum, a plant. The green substance of this earth, the chlorophyll, is all summed up in the plants. Without them we perish, all of us who are flesh and blood.

The plant is as humble as a blade of grass. It is as majestic as the towering redwood. It is the buttercup and the poisonous ivy leaf. It is the bean, the cabbage and the parsimonious desert cactus. It is the symbiotic lichen and the succulent seaweed. It is the infinitely complex blossom, the brief-lifed pollen, the eager ovule, the consequent seed. It is root and bulb and tuber and cion. It is life, throbbing with the great rhythms of time and the seasons, waiting, sprouting, burgeoning, flowering, ripening, waiting again, endless life encapsulated in the seed and vitalized in the leaf.

Where it came from, we can only guess. Why it evolved as it did, we shall never know. Rooted, it takes what is in reach from where it is anchored. Breathing the poisons our lungs reject, it gives back the sustaining oxygen we need. At the mercy of water, it moistens the air. Dying, it creates the soil for its own seedlings. Without brain or nerves or animate senses, it yet sustains flesh and blood and covers the earth with its nourishing plenty.

And when we have walked our trodden paths the last time, the plants will root there and make them green again, green as the hills when spring comes whispering to every root and seed.

H.B.

FLOWERS: POLLEN AND SEED

BY HAL BORLAND

This selection is from a book I wrote some years ago largely because I wanted to read such a book and could not find one in print. The book I wrote is no longer in print, either, but I like this chapter and think it has things to say and says them clearly.

(*The Enduring Pattern,* by Hal Borland; Simon and Schuster, 1959.)

The flowering plants are often spoken of as the most advanced form of plant life, with the blossom itself as the evidence. In this sense, the flowering plant is the plant world's equivalent of the mammal in the animal world.

I am not sure I can agree with this unless the word "advanced" is taken in a rather restricted sense. Man has a habit of calling any complex form of life or complex life process advanced, with the clear implication that it is better or more admirable than its predecessors. From man's point of view, the highest achievement of evolving life is man, with his intricate arrangement of cells, specialized organs and members, elaborately complex nervous system and remarkable brain. But the very simplest forms of life still persist. They may never have "advanced" very far, but they proved long ago that simplicity can

endure and that it long, long ago solved the basic problem of life, which is to live and produce. Man, endowed with intelligence and strong emotions, has other ideas about the purpose of his own life, but we have yet to verify any purpose in nature beyond life's own persistence. And in that sense, the blossom on a buttercup or on an orchid is no more than a complex means of continuing life from one generation to the next. This should not lessen man's aesthetic or intelligent interest in a flower, but it does mean that man, not nature, invented aesthetics.

Since the original division of primitive life into the two branches, plant and animal, there has been relatively little change in the basic processes of living, maintaining life. Plants manufacture their food from inorganic substances, using the sun's energy to convert air and water into sugars and starches; and animals maintain their life processes by consuming organic matter, plants and other animals. These are fundamental processes that have been elaborated but not basically changed over hundreds of millions of years.

But the processes of reproduction, though based on a common fundamental, have diverged in many directions. This has been particularly true in the plant world, with the most complex reproductive mechanism of all in the blossom.

Stripped of detail, the fundamental of reproduction is a division of the original life form. At its simplest, the single-celled plant or animal divides itself, nucleus and all, into two parts, both of which grow and in turn reproduce, always by self-division. As one moves down the eons of life history, this self-division becomes more and more complex. In both plant and animal the parent individual, itself an elaborate organization of cells, achieves the power of creating special reproductive cells which are separated from the parent and grow into new reproductive units. Essentially, this is still a form of self-division. In animals this special reproductive cell is the egg. In plants it is the spore or seed.

In most instances, the egg or seed must be fertilized before it can grow. Fertilization is accomplished by the union of two dissimilar cells, the egg and the sperm, each produced by a separate parent, the female and the male. This necessity and this differentiation of cells and parents constitutes sex. The word "sex" comes from the Latin and seems originally to have meant to cut, to divide. It really means that there is a difference between the two parent organisms, the male and the female.

In animals and in most insects the male and female cells are produced by separate individuals. In some plants this is also true, but in many plants both the female and the male cells are produced in the same flower or in different flowers on the same plant. If a flower produces both kinds of cells it always has both the female and the male organs. In a sense, the bisexual flower, which produces both kinds of reproductive cells, is one of nature's economies, a simplification of the basic means of reproduction. The simplification, of course, is in the method, not the means, since any flower is a complex of specialized organs.

There is a scientific explanation of the seed-egg process that is important to the specialist and perhaps interesting to the layman. This interpretation is called "the alternation of generations." It points up the idea that life is continuous even though it passes through a variety of forms even in the same species. It applies to all forms of life except the very lowest, the single-celled. Perhaps the most graphic example is in the life of a butterfly, which proceeds through the form of egg, larva, butterfly, then egg again. Each of these forms constitutes a "generation," and each is quite different from the others. Yet all are necessary in the life history of a butterfly.

In a flowering plant there are equivalent steps. The common field mustard, a weed in the pastures of my valley, is a green and leafy plant which forms clusters of buds at its tip and comes to blossom in May. The mustard flower has four small yellow petals and is bisexual, with one pistil, the female organ, surrounded by six stamens, the male organs. In the ovary at the base of the pistil are produced special female reproductive cells or ovules. In the anthers at the tip of the stamens is produced the pollen, the male reproductive cells.

According to the alternation of generations interpretation, the individual grains of pollen, the male cells, are short-lived individual plants, though they are unable to reproduce alone. And the ovules, the female cells in the ovary, are also short-lived individual plants also unable to reproduce alone. They constitute a "hidden" generation in the plant's life.

When these minute male and female plants, pollen and ovules, meet and fuse, they produce a fertile entity, the seed. The seed in turn will grow into a leafy, budding mustard plant, and when its yellow blossoms open the whole process will be repeated. In this sense there is an unending continuation of life which passes through alternate forms, generation by generation. And the flower, the blossom, is no more than a mechanism for producing those minute "plants," the pollen and the ovules, which join to form the seed.

To the paleobotanist this interpretation explains, at least in part, the basic part of evolution. Plants, all life, apparently originated in single-celled ancients. In even the most complex plants and animals of today, life still goes through that primitive form where minute flecks of parent life divide and unite in the creation of the seed or the egg. Male sperm and female ovules are created by the parent. These two basic units, the male and the female, must unite to create a more complex unit, the fertile egg or seed. Unless they meet and fuse, they cannot duplicate the parent and carry on the life process, including reproduction.

Broadly speaking, the female cells, the ovules, are quiet but hungrily receptive bits of life. They remain in the flower's ovary awaiting the arrival of the pollen, the male element. The ovule's whole purpose, so far as we can comprehend purpose, is to be fertilized. The male pollen is vigorous and active. In one sense, the pollen is a spore. Its purpose is to find an ovule and fertilize it. This impulse of necessity in both ovule and sperm is one of the most urgent and yet one of the most persistently hidden of all the life processes, since it usually occurs at the microscopic level.

An excellent example can be found in any cornfield, on my neighbor's farm or in my own sweet-corn patch. Corn produces its pollen, its male cells, in the tassel at the tip of the plant. The ovules, the female cells, are on the young ear farther down the stalk. The ovules are ranked on the cob, hidden beneath several layers of husk; but each ovule, each potential kernel of corn, has a long "silk," a hollow strand of soft vegetable fiber that reaches out into the open at the tip of the ear.

At a proper time, the pollen is mature and the ovules are ready for fertilization. The pollen begins to fall from the tassel. Gravity urges it downward and the breeze distributes it. One grain of that male pollen, one spore, falls on the tip of one strand of silk. It is held there by a kind of adhesive. The tip of that silk is an ideal place for growth of that particular kind of spore. It grows into a male plant too small to be seen by the naked eye, a plant that thrusts a fine thread down that hollow silken strand toward the waiting ovule. That pollen grain, that spore, is endowed with enough energy to thrust that thread eight inches or a foot down that silken tube to reach the ovule. The ovule is reached, male and female cells fuse, fertilization occurs, and a kernel of corn begins to take form beneath the protective husks. The female ovule extended its silken invitation. The male pollen grain found that particular silk. In a matter of hours pollination, fertilization, had been accomplished. A fertile seed, from which another corn plant can grow, had been created.

This elaborate process has been evolved over millions of years. It began with the first plants that crept or were washed by the waves onto land. They were spore-bearers. The spore itself was a result of long evolution, a means of dividing the parent plant without destroying or greatly impairing the strength of the parent.

The spore is minute, often microscopic, and it is not always distinguished by sex. In the simplest form of spore plants, an intermediate form of plant grows from the spore, a bisexual plant, and from that plant is reproduced still another plant substantially like the original spore-bearing parent. Mushrooms are among the most prolific of the spore-bearers, a single mushroom often producing two or three billion spores. Mushroom spores are sexed, but they can scarcely be called male and female because there are four "sexes" among them and they will pair off only in certain groupings, say number one and number three, or number two and number four. In a favorable environment these spores grow into minute filaments, and if two filaments of the proper "sexes" meet they fuse and grow into a mushroom capable of bearing more spores. But the unmated filaments that grow directly from the spores are plants, intermediate forms and an essential part of the whole reproductive process. They are broadly equivalent to the pollen grain with its searching thread thrust down the corn silk and the waiting ovule at the base of the silk.

Many plants still reproduce by means of spores. Most of them are water dwellers, but ferns, horsetails and fungi are among the land dwellers that cling to the spore system. Spores of most water-dwelling plants have hairlike means of movement, but the spores of most land-dwelling plants have no means of self-movement and usually are distributed by the wind. And most of them go through an intermediate stage of individual growth before they re-create a plant like the parent. The fern spore, to take one example, is more direct in its process than that of the mushroom. The fern spore grows into a tiny, inconspicuous plant called a prothallium—from the Greek words meaning "before" and "young shoot"—and the prothallium has both male and female organs from which a plant like the parent fern is eventually produced.

No one knows exactly why or when the primitive spore-bearing plants moved over toward the process of reproducing by means of a fertilized seed, but by the Carboniferous period, some 300 million years ago, there were trees that had begun to produce seeds. Apparently a plant of the fern type condensed the intermediate generation, the growth of the spore into a bisexual prothallium, and created a cone in which the essentials of this process could take place. Out of this evolved the fertile seed.

The blossom of a plant has only a few essentials. There is the pistil, the female organ, equivalent to the ovaries and the uterus of the female mammal. In it are the female cells, the ovules, awaiting fertilization. And there are the stamens, the male organs, equivalent to the testes in the male mammal. They produce the sperm cells, the pollen, full of urgency to find and fertilize the ovules.

Those are the essentials. They can be found in notable simplicity in the inconspicuous flowers of most grasses, many of which consist of little more than an ovary and three stamens. The grasses have achieved this simplicity because they are pollinated by the wind and need no assistance from insects or birds. More complex blossoms, especially those depending on insects to help in pollination, have elaborate sepals and petals. The sepals are the leaflike outer coverings of the flower, often the bud sheath, and in some ways resemble leaves. They may have evolved from leaves. Usually the sepals are green and have chlorophyll in them, just as do leaves. The petals are the divisions of the corolla, the cup which usually surrounds the pistil and stamens.

Some flowers have no sepals, some no petals, but the great elaboration and variety of floral forms have been in petals and sepals, in their shapes and colors. Some flowers have nectar to lure insects. Some have deep pockets in which pollen or nectar or both are hidden so that the visiting insect must invade or reach inside to get the treasure, and thus unwittingly leave pollen from another flower to fertilize the ovules. Some have their stamens and pistil so arranged that the insect visitor simply releases the pollen for self-fertilization. Whatever the arrangement, the blossom's design seems dictated by a need to insure pollination of the ovules.

The whole architecture of a flower, whatever its shape, has only one basic purpose—production of fertile seed that will insure perpetuation of the species. This urgency toward reproduction is characteristic of all flowering plants. Typical of it is the profusion of pollen. The sperm cells, the male pollen, vastly outnumber the egg cells, the ovules.

I am struck by this prodigality of pollen each Spring when a big Norway spruce beside my house comes into flower. There are hundreds of catkinlike clusters of male flowers, but only a relatively few female flowers, or potential cones. When the pollen begins to fall it comes in a golden mist. We must at that time keep windows closed on that side of the house or floors and furniture would be filmed with golden-tan spruce pollen. The floor of the porch is covered with it so thick that I sweep it into windrows for the dustpan. All this from one big tree, and all waste pollen, pollen that failed to find a female ovule to fertilize. It is that one spruce tree's extravagant outpouring of male sperm cells to insure that perhaps one hundred cones shall be fertilized.

Every flowering plant does this, to some degree, from ragweed to columbine, from tulip to apple blossom. Wind-pollinated species, such as conifers and grass, are most lavish with their pollen, but in all flowering plants there is an unbelievable prodigality of pollen production, a tremendous excess of male cells over female cells.

It is usually taken for granted that the petals of a flower were evolved to serve as landing platforms for the insects that pollinate it. This may be correct, but the reasoning is not necessarily absolute. It is also taken for granted that the petals are colored to attract insects. This too may be subject to challenge. Some researchers say that the insect eye cannot distinguish color. Others, with perhaps more persuasive evidence, insist that bees and certain other insects can see color, particularly in the red end of the spectrum.

When we speak of color we think of it in terms of our own vision. But color is a matter of wave length, and the human eye has a limited range of reception for such wave lengths. The color spectrum was devised as a gauge of man's visual range, but we now know that there are color waves beyond that rather limited range. It is conceivable that an insect eye—or the eye of a bird or animal—could be unable to see color as we see it, and yet be capable of distinguishing color, even colors that we cannot see, in some other way. We know, from experiment, that at least some birds and animals react to color visually much as human beings do. It is possible that through their eyes, or even through some other organs they "hear" color or "smell" it, color of which the human eye is unaware. And it is possible that many of them are totally unaware of color.

When we say that a flower's petals are colored to attract insects, then, we are speculating on cause and effect. The color we see may be incidental to some emanation of which we are unaware. Or it may have still another purpose.

It is conceivable that the color of a flower has something to do with the plant's own vital need. We know, for instance, that when a plant is germinating, flowering, or maturing seeds the plant's temperature is somewhat higher than at other times. Isn't it possible that a flower's petals trap heat or other forms of radiation, much as leaves trap energy from sunlight? I have noticed that many flowers that bloom in the shade have darker colored petals than flowers of the same species that bloom in full sun. The jack-in-the-pulpit that blooms in deep shade has dark brownish-purple stripes on its green spathe, but the jack that blooms in full sun has faded or completely green stripes. I find the deeper-colored violets in the shade. And when I find wild anemones in bloom in April, those in the open are normally white but those in the shade are often flushed with pink. The same is true of bluets, those in the open usually white, those in the shade often tinged with lavender. I cannot see that this variation has anything to do with attracting pollinating insects.

I also see something of the same thing seasonally in wild flowers. In the Spring there is a preponderance of yellow. Yellow is toward the long-wave, or warm, end of the spectrum. In the Fall there is a predominance of blues and purples, at the opposite end of the spectrum. And the same thing can be seen geographically. The warm colors, the rich reds, oranges and yellows are typical of the tropics, while the blues and purples are typical of the temperate zones. The colors at the red end of the spectrum tend to reflect the long, hot waves of light, and the colors at the blue end tend to absorb those hot, infrared rays.

One can only speculate on the meaning of this. Perhaps someday someone will investigate it and learn some of the answers. It may be that the plant at the time of its fertility, the time of flowering, needs extra heat and acquires it at least in part through the petals. The temperature in the female mammal rises at the time of fertility and the body provides it by slightly increased metabolism. Life has its mysterious parallels, plant and animal, in more surprising ways than this.

The variation of colors in a blossom is baffling, no matter what theory is used to explain them. For instance, where I live the wild Eastern columbine grows profusely. It is a beautiful wild flower, rich golden yellow and deep red. In the mountainous parts of Colorado where I once lived the wild columbine grows also, a plant obviously of the same parent stock as the columbine of the East. But the Colorado columbine is usually blue and white instead of red and gold. Both flowers have substantially the same shape, though the sepals and petals of the Colorado variety are much larger than those of the Eastern native. Both are aided in pollination by the long-tongued moths and butterflies. Why did they evolve in such sharply divergent colors? One is at one end of the spectrum, the other at the opposite end. Can it be that the Colorado columbine needs to absorb more red heat rays of the sun to complete its seeding cycle? Does a mile's difference in altitude create such a divergence of color to meet some special need?

This whole matter of color in flowers is shot through with fascinating questions. But the blossom itself is really not at all mysterious. It is a rather complex arrangement of specialized organs designed to do a particular job—to produce male and female cells, to bring them together, and to create fertile seeds from which plants substantially like the parent will grow.

This is a process typical of all life. In one form or another it is found throughout both the plant and animal kingdoms. I see it going on all around me each year, from the time the first colts-foot comes to blossom in a sheltered hollow till the last aster fades and the witch hazel comes to bloom. I see it in the drift of "cotton" from the poplars and the blow of milkweed floss, in the pollen haze over the cornfields and the swarming of bees in the apple trees in May. I smell it when the lilacs bloom and the basswood drips its honey, when the clover whitens the meadow and when goldenrod makes September acrid.

It may be that the blossom is the highest achievement of the whole plant world. I find it fascinatingly complex. And it may be that members of the composite family—sunflowers, asters, goldenrod, thistles and all their kind—are the most advanced of all the flowering plants. I have already registered my reservations about that word "advanced." I would add only that to me the composite flowers, with their tightly packed heads of dozens of individual florets, have merely achieved a kind of community system, a "social organization" something like that of the ants. Perhaps this is advancement, of a kind. Perhaps it is an example of social efficiency. But each season I still celebrate the fact that there are individuals, the wild lilies, the wild roses, the anemones, the columbines, who have thus far resisted such evolution. The flower is not only an efficient achievement; it is beautiful, and it is entitled to be as much of an individual as I am.

WHAT SEEDS ARE AND DO

BY VICTOR R. BOSWELL

Victor R. Boswell (1900 —) was born, grew up and was educated in Missouri and took graduate degrees in Maryland where he taught until he entered government service in the Bureau of Plant Industry of the Department of Agriculture in Washington. He is a horticulturist with special interest in vegetable plants and when this selection was written was Chief of the Vegetable and Ornamentals Research Branch in the Crops Research Division of the Agricultural Research Service. It was first published in Seeds, *the U. S. Department of Agriculture yearbook for 1961.*

(*Seeds: The Yearbook of Agriculture,* 1961. Government publication.)

SEEDS are many things.

Above all else, they are a way of survival of their species. They are a way by which embryonic life can be almost suspended and then revived to new development, even years after the parents are dead and gone.

Seeds protect and sustain life. They are highly organized fortresses, well stocked with special supplies of food against long siege.

Seeds are vehicles for the spread of new life from place to place by the elements and by animals and people.

Seeds are food for man and animals and other living things.

Seeds are raw material for the fashioning of myriad products by people.

Seeds are wealth. They are beauty. They are a symbol—a symbol of beginnings. They are carriers of aid, of friendship, of good will.

Seeds are a source of wonder. They are objects of earnest inquiry in man's ceaseless search for understanding of living things.

Seeds of unwanted kinds are as enemies; they are a source of trouble.

Seeds are many things, but everything about seeds—their numbers and forms and structures—has a bearing on their main purpose, to insure continuing life. Seeds are containers of embryonic plants, the embryos of a new generation.

SEEDS are borne by two great and different classes of plants.

One group, less highly developed than the other, produce "naked" seeds that develop from "naked" ovules.

In plants of the more highly developed and much larger class, the ovule and the seed develop within an ovary, the seed vessel. The ovary is the part of the flower that contains the ovule with its egg, or female sex cell. The ovary later becomes a fruit with the developed ovule or ovules—seeds—inside. This group of plants we call angiosperms, a word that means vessels for seeds.

Plants of the other group, the gymnosperms, the "naked seed" plants, have no ovaries, no flowers, and no fruits, although they do have seeds. Gymnosperms include the cone-bearing trees, the conifers. Their seeds are borne in pairs at the bases of the scales of the cones.

Deep within the ovary of the mother flower (or between the scales of seed cone) lies the ovule, which contains an embryo sac and its tiny egg. The egg must be fertilized by a sperm cell from a pollen tube before it can start to develop into an embryo and so perpetuate the parent's life.

Along with the embryo there develops a special store of food, the embryo's own special "formula" or diet for its use after it is separated from its mother plant.

Every seed contains carbohydrates, proteins, fats, and minerals to nourish the embryonic plant within. The nature and proportions of each of them differ among the many kinds of seeds. Some seeds, like corn, are predominantly starchy. Seeds of flax and sunflower are oily or fat. Others, such as peas and beans, are notable for their high content of protein.

Some seeds (such as the seeds of orchids, which are like specks of dust) contain only tiny bits of stored food because they are so small. Large seeds may contain a billion times more food than the smallest ones.

Some kinds of seed have most of their reserve supplies packed inside their seed leaves. Others have it packed in tissues developed from the embryo sac, called endosperm, or from the cells of the ovule that surrounded the embryo sac.

The seed usually is well protected through its development. This protection differs greatly among different kinds in degree and in the way it is provided.

The ovary and the tissues that are attached to it become the fruit of the plant. The seeds (formed by ovules in the ovary) of plants having large or fleshy fruits are deeply protected therefore so that we never see them before maturity unless we open the fruit to find them.

Although the seeds of gymnosperms are said to be naked, they nearly always have some protection during development. The seeds of the pine tree and other conifers, for example, are hidden at the bases of the scales of the cone. The cone scales of some pines separate to release the seeds as soon as they are mature. Others remain closed for years.

The fruit tissues that enclose some seeds are scanty and are attached to the coat of the seed. A kernel of corn, for example, is more than a seed—it is a one-seeded fruit. The kernel is nearly all seed, but a thin layer of ovary tissue surrounds the seed and has grown together with the seedcoat in such a way that we can hardly see the tissue.

Many structures that we call seeds are actually fruits. Most of them, such as the fruits of the cereals and other grasses, lettuce, and spinach, contain only one seed. Members of the carrot family produce two-parted fruits, each with one seed. Some fruits, such as those of beets, have one or several seeds.

Botanists identify the various types of fruits and give them specific names, but our purpose here is served if we deal with the small, dry, one- or few-seeded fruits, which we are accustomed to plant like seeds, as though they were seeds.

Seeds of some species develop in the mother plant with amazing speed. Some others are surprisingly slow. A chickweed plant that is pulled from the garden and thrown aside at the time its flowers first open may form some seeds before it withers and dies.

Most familiar plants form their seeds during a period of several days to a few weeks following pollination. Pine trees, however, take 2 to 3 years to mature their seeds. The fruit of the sea palm is said to need 7 to 10 years to mature.

Another aspect of the survival of plants is that the seed-bearing species can be perpetuated in two ways.

One, which we have been discussing, is sexual—that is, by means of seeds, which develop from fertilized egg cells.

The other is asexual, or vegetative, as we usually say, by means of such parts as buds, pieces of root, and pieces of stem with attached buds, bulbs, and tubers.

The seeds of some plants—like potatoes, cultivated tree fruits, grapes, berries, and many ornamental garden plants—do not come true to variety. Their seeds therefore are worthless for perpetuating the varieties we plant in gardens and orchards.

For them, we must use vegetative propagation. We can grow apple trees, grapevines, potatoes, or strawberry plants from seeds, but the plants and their fruits (or tubers) will be unlike those of the varieties that produced the seeds.

That is because most seeds, as we have seen, develop after the union of male and female reproductive cells. The seeds perpetuate the hereditary characteristics contributed by both the male and female cells. Seeds of plants like potatoes, apples, pears, and tulips fail to come true to variety because their sex cells carry random assortments of mixed-up sets of characters. Among the offspring of the numberless chance unions that occur in such plants, hardly any two are alike. The plants from seeds of most species come reasonably true to variety if precautions are taken to keep the pollen of undesired types from reaching the flowers of desired types.

We must note a rare exception. A few kinds of plants, such as some species of grasses and of Citrus, produce asexual seeds, whose embryos develop entirely from cells of the ovule outside the egg apparatus. No fertilization of the egg cell is involved. There is no mixture of characters from pollen cells with those of the mother cells. The embryo is formed entirely from mother-plant cells and therefore is identical with the mother plant in its hereditary makeup. Such asexual seeds, therefore, come true to variety and afford the unusual opportunity of accomplishing "vegetative" propagation by means of seeds. Except for such rare instances, however, seed propagation means sexual propagation, and asexual or vegetative propagation means propagation by some means other than seeds.

Plants that do come true to variety from seed of sexual origin can also be propagated asexually from stem cuttings or other appropriate parts of the plant under favorable conditions.

Why, then, do we consider the seeds of such plants of great importance? Why are seeds essential if we can perpetuate the plants without seeds?

The answer is that conditions rarely are favorable or practicable for their vegetative propagation.

A prohibitive amount of work would be required for the vegetative propagation of the billions upon billions of such plants that we need to grow every year. An even greater obstacle is that there is no feasible way to keep these "vegetative" plants alive through periods of great cold, drought, or flood. If such plants are killed before they produce seed, that is the end of their line.

The kinds and varieties of plants that fail to produce viable seeds —that is, seeds that can grow or develop—must be perpetuated by asexual means. There is no other way. Such diverse plants as certain grasses, bananas, and garlic produce no seeds, but each has an asexual feature (a vegetative structure) by which it can be multiplied.

Sometimes, for a particular reason, growers resort to vegetative propagation of a kind of plant that is normally grown only from seeds.

Small farmers in the hills of Vietnam grow cabbage year after year without the use of seeds. The climate there is not cool enough at any time to induce flowering and seed production in cabbage, and the farmers cannot import seeds for each planting. The farmers therefore make cuttings from the stumps of the cabbage plants after the heads are harvested. They plant the pieces of stump, each of which has one or more side buds. Roots soon develop. The buds form and produce new cabbage plants that will develop heads. The process is repeated for each crop.

This method of growing cabbage would be impossible where the seasons become too cold, too hot, too wet, or too dry for the continued survival of the vegetative stage of the plant.

The enormous numbers of seeds that single plants of some species produce make it feasible to increase seed supplies at almost fantastically rapid rates. Single plants of other species produce few seeds, and the rates of increase are ploddingly slow.

One tobacco plant may produce as many as 1 million seeds. The average is about 200 thousand seeds. The garden pea plant produces a few dozen seeds at best.

The possible rate of spread of some plants over an area by seeds therefore is astronomical. With other plants, the rate is modest or slow.

Even the relatively slow rates of seed increase among annual and biennial plants are fast and easy, compared to most vegetative propagation.

Species and varieties of hardy perennial plants that spread by runners (creeping stems about the soil surface), stolons (creeping stems below the soil surface), bulbs (arrangements of fleshy leaf bases on a drastically shortened stem), and tubers (greatly thickened underground stems), are especially adapted to survival for long periods without depending on seeds, although they may also produce seeds. Seeds of these kinds of plants often do not come true to variety.

Plants are able to spread naturally only very slowly if seeds are absent. They can only creep. Their vegetative structures do not fly on the wind, float on the water, or ride on animals to distant sites as easily as seeds do. Vegetative reproductive parts may be torn from parent plants by animals or by storms and later may take root after being carried some distance. Vegetative spread nevertheless is slow and cumbersome in nature, compared to spreading by seeds.

Seeds are the protectors as well as the propagators of their kinds. Thousands of kinds of plants have evolved in such ways that they cannot survive, even in the regions where they are best adapted, if they produce no seeds.

Seeds of most plants are the very means of survival of the species. They carry the parent germ plasm, variously protected against heat, cold, drought, and water from one growing season that is suitable for growth of the species to the next.

Most kinds of seeds will live considerably longer than the time from one growing season to the next if their surroundings are not too extreme for their respective characteristics. Some seeds normally keep alive under natural conditions above ground only a year or two.

Others can keep alive for a score of years or more. A few, such as the seeds of silver maple, remain viable only a few days if they are not kept moist and cool.

Some kinds can survive deep burial in the soil, dry or moist, for 10 to 20 years or longer. In one famous experiment, started in 1902, J. W. T. Duvel, of the Department of Agriculture, placed some seeds in soil in flowerpots, so he could find them later. He then buried the pots and all. At intervals he dug up the pots, recovered the seeds, and then planted them under favorable conditions for germination. More than 50 of 107 species tested were viable after 20 years. Many weed seeds remain viable for a very long time if they are buried deeply.

Seeds of common evening-primrose and mullein have been known to remain viable after 70 years in soil.

Most crop seeds keep best for one or a few years when they are stored in a dry place. Exposure to warm, moist air shortens their life. Repeated wetting or submergence in water soon kills most of them. Seeds of plants that grow in water, on the other hand, are not soon harmed by water.

Onion seeds kept in a warm, humid place will lose their life in a few months. When they are well dried and sealed in glass, they remain viable more than a dozen years at room temperature. If seeds are relatively dry, most kinds will tolerate for years extreme cold that would quickly kill their parent plants.

Most seeds also tolerate prolonged hot weather if they are dry. Seeds of muskmelon have produced good plants in the field after storage in a hot, dry office for 30 years. Seeds of Indian-mallow, a common weed, have germinated after 70 years of dry storage. Seeds of Mimosa, Cassia, and some other genera have germinated after being kept in a herbarium more than 200 years.

The seeds of Lagenaria, a gourd, are not harmed by the immersion of the fruits in sea water for a year, long enough for the fruits to float across an ocean. Water may enter the fruits and wet the seeds. Lotus seeds estimated to be 800 to 1,200 years old have germinated.

The stories, however, about the finding of viable seeds 2 thousand to 3 thousand years old in Egyptian tombs are not true. Viable barley seeds found in the wrappings of a mummy were traced to the new straw in which the mummy was packed for shipment to a museum. Viable seeds of corn, squash, and beans found in caves and ancient ruins of cliff dwellings had not lain there for hundreds of years—

pack rats or other creatures had carried them in not long before the archeologists found them.

The long "storage" life of the embryo within the seed not only helps insure survival of the species, it makes possible the distribution or spread of the species over long distances, either in the wild or by the agency of man.

Viable seeds probably are never completely inactive. Vital processes go on as a seed awaits conditions favorable for germination and plant growth. If we knew how to arrest or suspend all these processes completely, it would be possible theoretically to retain viability indefinitely. We do not know how to do that.

Activity within the seed may be so low that we cannot measure it by any known method. In time, however, if the seed does not encounter conditions that will permit it to grow, unidentified substances become exhausted or they deteriorate, and germinating power is lost. The seed dies. Warmth and moisture hasten the exhausting life processes and shorten the life of the seed. Dryness and cold slow down activities, conserve vital substances, and protect the delicately balanced systems within the seed.

Seeds possess remarkably complex and effective protective mechanisms that help insure survival.

Consider a tender plant that grows in a region of sharply different seasons and matures its seeds and drops them to the ground while the weather is still favorable for growth. If those seeds grow promptly, the new plant surely will be killed when winter comes.

In such situations, seeds that grow promptly are wasted because they fail to perpetuate the parents.

Many seeds therefore have a rhythm of ability to grow that coincides with the rhythm of the seasons. They have a delayed-action mechanism, a natural timeclock, which insures that the seeds will remain dormant until another growing season rolls around—a season long enough to permit another generation of seeds to mature.

Many kinds of seeds remain dormant—fail to grow upon planting—for a while after separation from the mother plant. The length of the dormancy and the nature of the delaying mechanism differ greatly among species and varieties.

Dormancy that is due to water-resistant ("hard") seedcoats may last for years, until enough water has soaked into the seed for it to germinate. Tiny nicks or scratches in the seedcoat will permit water to enter, thus breaking the dormancy. Natural abrasion of the seeds —by the freezing and thawing of soil or by their movement among rock particles by water—permits water to enter the seed. Hard seeds of crop plants are abraded artificially to induce germination. Dormancies due to some other mechanisms may be overcome less easily.

Some dormant seeds, before they will grow, must go through a long period of cool temperature while they are moist. They must go through conditions that simulate a cold, moist soil during autumn or winter. The rhythm of the seasons must be simulated in the environment of the seeds if they are to grow.

Some seeds lie dormant, although they are in moist soil, until they are exposed to light. Certain weed seeds never germinate deep below the soil surface, but grow quickly after they are brought to the surface when the soil is worked.

Still other seeds fail to grow soon after separation from the mother plant because they are immature. Structural developments or chemical processes, or both, must be completed before they can grow. The naked seed of the ginkgo tree drops to the ground in the autumn long before its embryo is fully grown. The embryo must continue its development for many months, nourished by the foods stored around it, before it is mature enough to break out of the seedcoat and grow.

Some seeds in a nondormant state after harvest can be pushed into a dormant state. Upon exposure to unfavorable warm and moist conditions, some varieties of lettuce seed become dormant, although they are capable of germinating under favorable conditions. It is as though their growth processes recoiled, or went into reverse, in the face of a situation that would be unfavorable for the plants developed from those seeds.

Witchweed, a semiparasitic seed-bearing plant, has an unusual survival device. Witchweed is a parasite on many species of crop plants and weeds. Its almost microscopic seeds may lie dormant in the soil for many years if no suitable stimulator plant grows close to them. When the root of a stimulator plant grows close to them, some substance from the root causes the seeds to germinate. The young witchweed plants promptly become parasitic on the roots of any host that caused the seeds to germinate. If a nonhost should cause the seeds to germinate in the absence of a host, the witchweed seedlings die.

Many species of plants are widespread because their seeds are great travelers. Besides the special features that insure perpetuation of their respective species, plants have other features for spreading the species as far and wide as they are able to grow.

Most of the familiar structures that aid in the natural transport of seeds involve fruits rather than the seeds alone. (As I said, a large proportion of the plant parts we call seeds are actually tiny, dry fruits containing one or a few seeds.)

The windblown dandelion and thistle "seeds" are one-seeded fruits, called achenes. To each is attached a feathery pappus that serves as a sail and a parachute.

The "sticktights" of Spanish-needle and barbed achenes that catch in the coats of animals and people to be carried afar.

A "tickseed" of the beggarweed plant is a one-seeded fragment of its leguminous pod (fruit). It is covered with minute hooks that make it "sticky."

The flying "seed" of the maple tree is a samara, a one-seeded, one-winged fruit.

The water-resistant seeds in buoyant fruits, large or small, one-seeded or many-seeded, may be carried great distances by water. Coconuts, gourds, and the tiny berries of asparagus are examples.

A few kinds of plants distribute their seeds widely as the entire aboveground part of the mature plant tumbles about over the land, blown by the wind. The Russian-thistle is noteworthy among these tumbleweeds. They sometimes roll for many miles, even over fences and other obstructions, scattering seeds as they go.

Some seeds travel on their own. They need not depend on features of their enclosing fruits or of their mother plants as aids to transportation. The coats of some seeds resemble certain surface features of fruits.

The coat of the pine seed is expanded into a wing, which carries it a short distance.

The seed of the milkweed has a tuft of long, silky hairs attached to its coat. The wind carries this seed far.

When a seed of flax becomes wet, as by rain, its surface becomes gelatinous. It adheres to whatever touches it and is carried away.

The coats of many seeds are resistant to moisture and to the digestive fluids of animals. If such seeds happen to escape grinding by stones in the crops of birds or by the teeth of animals that eat them, the seeds will pass unharmed through the alimentary tract. Some of them reach congenial soil many miles from where the animal got them.

The seeds of the mesquite tree have been distributed by cattle over millions of acres of formerly good grazing lands in the Southwest.

Seedlings of cherry, dogwood, and holly commonly appear where seeds have been dropped by birds far from any parent tree.

Unwanted plants make seeds, too.

It seems that undesirable or unwanted plants generally are more prolific seed producers than most of the crop plants that we strive to grow. One investigator estimated that one large tumbling pigweed produces more than 10 million seeds. Many kinds produce 100 thousand to 200 thousand seeds per plant.

Weeds are the pests they are partly because they produce so many seeds. More than that, though: The seed and the plants that grow from them have a remarkable capacity for survival. Reproductiveness and survival value have evolved to a high level by natural selection. Seeds of many weeds are such potent survivors and successful travelers that their species have become nuisances over much of the world.

Farmers and gardeners must contend with weeds that arise from seeds. They appear to come suddenly from nowhere—or everywhere. They arrive unnoticed by air, by water, by animals, and by man's devices.

Earlier arrivals have accumulated in the soil and lie there waiting for the husbandman to stir them up to the surface, where they seemingly explode into growth. One investigator recovered 10 thousand to 30 thousand viable weed seeds in patches of soil about a yard square and 10 inches deep. Various kinds of seeds kept dormant a long time by their respective mechanisms persistently produce successive waves of noisome seedlings each time the soil is cultivated.

Weeds thus continue to appear although the grower has not allowed a parent plant to produce seed on the site for years. Survival value! Many weed seeds will survive in the soil 20 years and some for longer than 70 years.

Many weed seeds have nearly the same size, shape, and density as the crop seeds with which they may become mixed. The complete removal of such weed seeds from crop seeds is difficult and expensive. Weed seeds that contaminate seeds for food or industrial use lower the grade and value of the latter. Weed seeds will continue to pose problems for gardeners, farmers, and processors.

Seeds are an aid in efforts to improve plants.

It is said sometimes—incorrectly—that plant improvement can occur only through seeds. Many improved varieties of plants have originated as mutations in vegetative (asexual) cells and have been perpetuated vegetatively (asexually). No seeds are involved in such instances, although the plants may be seed producers.

Most purposeful plant "improvements," however, have come about through sexual reproduction and the consequent formation of seeds. Useful variations in hereditary characteristics occur much oftener in incidental or sexual propagation than in asexually propagated plants. Plant improvement would be extremely slow and uncertain, indeed, if we could only sit and wait for useful mutations to occur.

Man learned long ago that like begets like among annual and biennial plants. He learned that he could gradually upgrade the plants he grew year after year by saving and planting the seeds produced by the most desirable plants.

We speak of "seed selection" when we really should say "parent selection." Man nevertheless has made productive use of the capacity of seeds to contain, preserve, and perpetuate the properties of selected parent plants. For thousands of years he has been gradually improving plants by the parental characters he has helped to perpetuate.

As research has revealed more and more about how plant characters are inherited, seeds have become an increasingly valuable element in the purposeful modification of plants. Seeds are not only a means of perpetuating and multiplying plants but an essential feature of the most rapid and practicable way of progressively improving them.

As additional desirable plant characters (or more desirable degrees of existing traits) are found in a potential parent plant, they can be combined with other desirable characters in a second potential parent by mating the two. Through the seed that results from this planned union, the desired combination of characters is captured and retained. A step upward is taken.

Large progenies generally can be developed rather quickly and inexpensively through the agency of seeds. Large numbers greatly increase the probability of finding truly superior plants for further increase and selection or for further mating with other desirable parent plants.

The compactness and longevity of most seeds enable the plant breeder to store collections of germ plasm in small space at small cost and safely and also to distribute germ plasm readily to distant points. Seeds thus help man in his efforts to produce better plants so that he may live better.

Somewhat different but related aspects of survival have to do with the utility and beauty of seeds—the reasons why we grow them, breed them, and husband their spark of life.

Seeds are the world's principal human food. The American Indians, for example, gathered the seeds of about 250 species in more than 30 families of plants for food. Among these were seeds of more than 50 kinds of pine, nut trees, and oak; more than 40 kinds of grasses, of which corn is most important; 30-odd members of the thistle family (like sagebrush and sunflower), and 20 of the goosefoot family (like saltbush and lambsquarters).

Seeds of the wild species used by the Indians are no less wholesome and nutritious today than in the distant past. Most of those species, however, are less productive or are more trouble to grow or harvest than our present crop plants. Or, the seeds are more trouble to prepare or less attractive to our tastes than the ones we now depend on.

All dry edible seeds are highly concentrated foods.

For human food, the seeds of certain grasses, the cereals, are by far the most important group. The seeds of wheat provide more human food than any other plant or animal product, and the seeds of rice are second in importance the world over.

The seeds of rye, barley, corn, sorghums, millets, and oats are also important for human food in different regions of the world. Rye and corn are most important in the Americas and Europe. Rice, wheat, and sorghums are dominant in the Far East.

About one-fourth of the supply of human energy in the United States comes from seeds of the cereals; in Europe, about one-half; and in the Far East, about three-fourths. These seeds are relatively easy to grow, harvest, and store. One or another of them can be grown wherever there is any agriculture at all.

Seeds are the raw materials for making a great diversity of important products for use in industry and the arts and for making pharmaceuticals, cosmetics, and alcoholic beverages.

Among these various purposes, the oilseeds have the widest range of uses.

Millions of tons of both oily and starchy seeds are used every year in this country for products other than food and feed.

Most seeds are objects of beauty of form, proportion, surface, and color.

Many seeds are so small that their beautiful features escape us. Many others, although large enough to see easily, are such common, everyday objects that we do not really see them. They are, however, worth our careful observation.

The first and most obvious beauty in most true seeds is in the perfection of their simple forms. Their outlines or silhouettes exhibit endless variations in the curve of beauty. In their entirety, too, we find wide ranges of proportion and different graceful and simple masses that are pleasing to look upon.

The sphere is a thing of beauty in itself, although quite unadorned. Artists have tried to produce nonspherical "abstract" forms that possess such grace and proportion as to call forth a satisfying emotional or intellectual response in the beholder. Some of the nicest of such forms lie all about us, unnoticed, in seeds. The commonest are such basic forms as the sphere, the teardrop, and the ovoid and other variations of the spheroid.

Some of these curving shapes are flattened, elongated, or tapered in pleasing ways. Sometimes they are truncated or sculptured into somewhat rough and irregular form. They may bear prominent appendages, such as wings, hooks, bristles, or silky hairs. Most seeds show a smooth flow of line and surface that is perfection itself.

The details of the surface relief of many seeds are even more beautiful in design and precision than the mass of the seed as a whole. Often you can find minute surface characters of surprising kinds. Surfaces that appear plain and smooth to the unaided eye may be revealed under a good hand lens to have beautiful textures.

Surfaces may be grained or pebbled. They may have ridges like those of Doric columns. They may bear geometric patterns in tiny relief, forming hexagons, as in a comb of honey, or minute dimples may cover the surface. Some irregular surface patterns of surprising beauty sometimes appear under the lens. Surfaces may be a dull matte, or highly glossy, or anywhere in between.

Last but not least in the beauty of seeds are their surface colors. They may be snow white or jet black. The color may be a single solid one, or two or more may be scattered about at random. Colors may form definite patterns that are distinctive and characteristic of the species and variety. The colors may be almost any hue of the rainbow—reds, pinks, yellows, greens, purples—and shades of ivory, tan, brown, steely blue, and purplish black.

Look for all you can see with the unaided eye. Then look at smaller seeds and the surfaces of large seeds with a good hand lens. You will be delighted with what you find.

There is still another beauty, a potential beauty in seeds, that can be seen only as the seed fulfills its ultimate purpose—the production of a new plant possessing its own beauty. This is perhaps the greatest of all: Beauty of general form; grace of stem; the shape, sheen, and color of the leaf; and finally the loveliness of the flower or the lusciousness of a fruit. The cycle is complete, and so we are back to the beauty of a seed.

Seeds are a symbol. They color our language and habits of thought.

From prehistoric times man has understood the role of seeds. Ancient languages, ancient cultures, and our own contain many words and concepts based on this understanding. The Bible contains several such examples, including the parable of the sower, the use of the word "seed" to mean offspring or progeny, and references to good and bad seed.

Our language contains both common and technical terms involving "seed," although the meanings are quite unrelated to the subject of plants.

The meanings recognize, however, some metaphoric connection in one way or another. "Seed" is a noun, an adjective, and a verb.

Watermen speak of seed oysters, seed pearls, and seed fish. The optician speaks of seeds in glass. The chemist seeds a solution with a crystal to induce crystallization. We speak of the seed of an idea or a plan.

We know a great deal about how seeds are formed and what they do, but we know only a little about why that is so. Many purely practical questions still cannot be answered. We wonder about many features of seeds and their behavior.

Scientists study seeds for two kinds of reasons. It is desirable to learn everything possible about seeds in order that man can produce and use them more efficiently and effectively. Seeds or parts of seeds are especially convenient forms of living material for the study of the fundamentals of life processes in plants.

Researchers are conducting more inquiries into seeds today than ever before, and still our wonder grows.

Why does a very dry seed become so well protected and so insensitive that it can tolerate sharp, deep-freeze temperatures for years, with no harm and no loss of vigor?

A light-sensitive seed, while dry, may be so well protected and so insensitive that it is quite unaffected by daylong exposure to sunlight, yet, after it becomes moist, it may respond to a light exposure from a flash lamp as short as one one-thousandth of a second. Exactly what chain of events is set in motion by that flash, and how?

Why do some seeds require alternating temperatures in order to grow, while others do not?

Why do some seeds live for decades and scores of years, while others, apparently as well protected, die in 2 or 3 years?

Why do some small plants produce seeds that are much larger than the seeds of some much larger plants?

Why does one kind of seed develop completely in a few days while another takes years?

How is it that seeds are so wondrously different among species, and yet all are quite evidently evolved to accomplish the same thing?

Seeds are a source of wonder.

Seeds are many things.

VIRGIN COAST, 1602

BY JOHN BRERETON

John Brereton (1572–16??) was an obscure English cleric, a Cambridge graduate, who at the age of thirty had his one fling by voyaging to America with Bartholomew Gosnold. After the voyage he wrote a pamphlet titled A Briefe and True Relation of the Discouerie of the North Part of Virginia in 1602, *then settled down as a village rector so little known that the date of his death is uncertain. There is even some confusion about his name, which is sometimes spelled Brierton. On the voyage, made five years before Captain John Smith founded Jamestown and eighteen years before the first settlers landed at Plymouth, Gosnold's first landfall was the southern coast of Maine, near Cape Porpoise. From there the expedition went southward and landed near a "mightie headland" which Gosnold named Cape Cod. The first island explored is now called No Mans Land. Gosnold called it Martha's Vineyard, honoring his eldest child, but the name later was transferred to the larger island which bears it today. The island the party chose for its base is now called Cuttyhunk, though Gosnold called it Elizabeth's Isle, honoring another of his daughters. This selection, from Brereton's pamphlet, is one of the first English descriptions of the New England coast. I have retained Brereton's antique spelling.*

(*A Briefe and True Relation of the Discouerie of the North Part of Virginia in 1602*, by John Brereton; 1602.)

Upon the sixe and twentieth of March, 1602, being Friday, we went from Falmouth, being in all, two and thirtie persons, in a small barke of Dartmouth, called *The Concord*, holding a course for the North part of Virginia. . . . On Friday the fourteenth of May, early in the morning, we made the land, being full of faire trees, the land somewhat low, certeine hummocks or hilles lying into the land, the shore ful of white sand, but very stony or rocky. And standing faire alongst the shore, about twelve of the clocke the same day, we came to an anker, where sixe Indians, in a Baske-shallop with mast and saile, an iron grapple, and a kettle of copper, came boldly aboord us, one of them apparelled with a waistcoat and breeches of blacke serdge, made after our sea-fashion, hose and shoes on his feet; all the rest (save one that had a paire of breeches of blue cloth) were all naked. These people are of tall stature, broad and grim visage, of a blacke swart complexion, their eiebrowes painted white; their weapons are bowes and arrowes; it seemed by some words and signs they made, that some Basks or of S. John de Luz, have fished or traded in this place, being in the latitude of 43 degrees. But riding heere, in no very good harbour, and withall, doubting the weather, about three of the clocke the same day in the afternoone we weighed, and standing Southerly off into the sea the rest of that day and the night following, with a fresh gale of winde, in the morning we found ourselves embayed with a mightie headland; but coming to an anker about nine of the clocke the same day, within a league of the shore, we hoisted out the one halfe of our shallop, and captaine Bartholomew Gosnold, my selfe, and three others, went ashore, being a white sandie and very bolde shore; and marching all that afternoon with our muskets on our necks, on the highest hilles which we saw (the weather very hot) at length we perceived this headland to be a parcell of the maine, and sundrie Islands lying almost around it: so returning (towards evening) to our shallop (for by that time, the other part had been brought ashore and set together) we espied an Indian, a young man, of proper stature, and of a pleasing countenance; and after some familiaritie with him, we left him at the sea side, and returned to our ship, where, in five or sixe hours absence, we had pestered our ship so with Cod fish, that we threw numbers of them overboord againe: and surely, I am persuaded that in the moneths of March, April and May, there is upon this coast, better fishing, and in as great plentie, as in Newfoundland: for the sculles of mackerell, herrings, Cod and other fish, that we dayly saw as we went and came from the shore, were woonderfull; and besides, the places where we tooke these Cods (and might in a few daies have laden our ship) were but in seven faddome water, and within less than a league of shore; where, in New-found-land they fish in fortie or fiftie faddome water, and farre off. From this place we sailed round about this headland, almost all the points of the compasse, the shore very bolde; but as no coast is free from dangers, so I am persuaded, this is as free as any; the land somewhat lowe, full of goodly woods, but in some places plaine: at length we were come amongst many faire Islands, which we had partly discerned at our first landing; all lying within a league or two of one another, and the outermost not above sixe or seven leagues from the maine: but comming to an anker under one of them, which was about three or foure leagues from the maine, captaine Gosnold, my selfe, and some others, went ashore, and going round about it, we found it to be foure English miles in compasse, without house or inhabitant, saving a little old house made of boughs, covered with barke, an olde piece of a weare of the Indians, to catch fish, and one or two places, where they had made fires. The chiefest trees of this Island, are Beeches and Cedars; the outward parts all overgrowen with lowe bushie trees, three or foure foot in height, which beare some kinde of fruits, as appeared by their blossomes; Strawberries, red and white, as sweet and much bigger than ours in England, Rasberries, Gooseberries, Hurtleberries, and such; an incredible store of Vines, as well in the woodie part of the Island, where they run upon every tree, as on the outward parts, that we could not goe for treading upon them; also, many springs of excellent sweet water, and a great standing lake of fresh water, neere the sea side, an English mile in compasse, which is maintained with the springs running exceeding pleasantly thorow the woodie grounds which are very rockie. Here are also in this Island, great store of Deere, which we saw, and other beasts, as appeared by their tracks, as also divers fowles, as Cranes, Hernshawes, Bitters, Geese; Mallards, Teales, and other fowles, in great plenty; also, great store of Pease, which grow in certeine plots all the Island over. On the North side of this Island we found many huge bones and ribbes of Whales. This Island, as also all the rest of these Islands, are full of all sorts of stones fit for building; the sea sides all covered with stones, many of them glistering and shining like minerall stones, and very rockie; also, the rest of these Islands are replenished with these commodities, and upon some of them, inhabitants; as upon an Island to the Northward, and within two leagues of this; yet we found no townes, nor many of their houses, although we saw manie Indians, which are tall big boned men, all naked, saving they cover their privie parts with a blacke tewed skin, much like a Black-smithes apron, tied about their middle and betweene their legs behinde: they gave us of their fish readie boiled (which they carried in a basket made of twigges, not unlike our osier) whereof we did eat, and judged them to be fresh water fish: they gave us also of their Tabacco, which they drinke greene, but dried into powder, very strong and pleasant, and much better than any I have tasted in England: the necks of their pipes are made of clay hard dried (whereof in that Island is great store both red and white) the other part, is a piece of hollow copper, very finely closed and semented together: we gave unto them certeine trifles, as knives, points, and such like, which they much esteemed. From thence we went to another Island, to the Northwest of this, and within a League or two of the maine, which we found to be greater than before we imagined, being 16 English miles at least in compasse; for it containeth many pieces or necks of land, which differ nothing fro severall Islands, saving that certeine banks of small bredth do like bridges joyne them to this Island: on the outsides of this Island are many plaine places of grasse, abundance of Strawberries and other berries before mentioned: is mid May we did sowe on this Island (as for triall) in sundry places, Wheat, Barley, Oats and Pease, which in fourteen daies were sprung up nine inches and more: the soile is fat and lustie; the upper crust, of gray colour, but a foot or lesse in depth, of the colour of our hempe-lands in England; and being thus apt for these and the like graines; the sowing or setting (after the ground is cleansed) is no greater labour, than if you should set or sowe in one of our best prepared gardens in England. This Island is full of high timbered Oaks, their leaves thrise as broad as ours; Cedars, strait and tall; Beach, Elme, Hollie, Walnut trees in abundance, the fruit as bigge as ours, as appeared by those we found under the trees, which had lien all the yeere ungathered; Haslenut trees, Cherry trees, the leafe, barke and bignesse not differing from ours in England, but the stalke beareth the blossomes or fruit at the end thereof, like a cluster of Grapes, forty or fifty in a bunch: Sassafras trees plentie all the Island over, a tree of high price and profit; also divers other fruit trees, some of them with strange barks, of an Orange colour, in feeling soft and smoothe like Velvet: in the thickest parts of the woods, you may see a furlong or more round about. On the Northwest side of this Island, neere to the sea side, is a standing Lake of fresh water, almost three English miles in compasse, in the middest whereof stands a plot of woodie ground, an acre in quantitie or not above: This Lake is full of small Tortoises, and exceedingly frequented with all sorts of fowles before rehearsed, which breed, some lowe on the banks, and others on low trees about this Lake in great abundance, whose young ones of all sorts we tooke and eat at our pleasure: but all these fowles are much bigger than ours in England. Also, in every Island, and almost in every part of every Island, are great store of Ground nuts, fortie together on a string, some of them as bigge as hennes egges; they grow not two inches under ground: the which nuts we found to be as good as Potatoes. Also divers sorts of shell-fish, as Scallops, Muscles, Cockles, Lobsters, Crabs, Oisters, and Whilks, exceeding good and very great. But not to cloy you with particular rehearsall of such things as God and Nature hath bestowed on these places, in comparison whereof, the most fertil part of al England is (of it selfe) but barren; we went in our light-horsman fro this Island to the maine, right against this Island some two leagues off, where comming ashore, we stood a while like men ravished at the beautie and delicacie of this sweet soile; for besides divers cleere Lakes of fresh water (whereof we saw no end) Meadowes very large and full of greene grasse; even the most woody places (I speake only of such as I saw) doe grow so distinct and apart, one tree from another, upon greene grassie ground, somewhat higher than the Plaines, as if Nature would shew her selfe above her power, artificiall.

LIFE CYCLE OF A FERN

BY BOUGHTON COBB

Boughton Cobb (1894 —), son of an architect who believed in country living, was born on a farm near Chicago and grew up there and on subsequent farms near Washington, D.C., and Brewster, New York. His knowledge of nature, he says, was forced on him by his younger brother, "a very inquisitive boy. He and I were in the woods and fields continually, and he had thousands of questions about the whys and wherefores of nature. It was up to me to provide the answers." After graduating from Harvard he studied architecture at Columbia, but after service in World War I he entered the textile business, which led to extensive travel here and abroad. But his interest in nature, particularly in birds, continued. After accumulating a sizable life list of birds he switched to botany and specialized in ferns. Some years ago he followed his father's example and bought a farm, in northwestern Connecticut, where he has a fern garden containing virtually every native fern of the Northeast. Now retired from business, he spends full time on his life-long interest, "a depth study of nature, particularly research in pteridology and ornithology. Philosophically I find this attitude of co-operation with nature, as opposed to competition and conquest of nature, satisfies my early constructive training as an architect." This selection is from his A Field Guide to the Ferns, *one of the best, most readable books of its kind I know.*

(*A Field Guide to the Ferns and Their Related Families,* by Boughton Cobb; Houghton Mifflin Company, 1956.)

Each of the four classes of the Pteridophytes has its own characteristic behavior in producing, bearing, and propagating its spores. In turn the subdivisions, orders, families, genera, and species all have their own different distinctive behavioral patterns. It is by these differences that we commonly classify the various ferns and their allies.

The life cycle pattern within which ferns produce spores, spores develop into gametophytes, and the gametophytes produce the new fern plants is extremely interesting and little understood by many.

Even though the characteristic reproductive behavior of each family, genus, and species is given later in this handbook, an overall understanding will be enhanced by a brief and simple description of the reproductive behavior of one of the more common ferns—*Dryopteris marginalis,* the Marginal Woodfern.

In summer, on the undersides of the subleaflets of the fertile leaves of this woodfern, there appear tiny greenish round specks. These specks mature rather rapidly and turn into dark brown spots. They are called sori, from the Greek word meaning "heaps." These sori, or *fruitdots,* are tiny masses of spore cases, or sporangia, which contain the spores. In the case of the Marginal Woodfern, the sori are covered by a thin membrane, or a part of the skin of the leaf. This protective membranous covering is called the indusium, or *fruitcover.* When the spore cases are ripe and fully developed, they push off this protective covering. The *spore case,* or sporangium, is a small round capsule made of a single layer of sterile skin mounted on a tiny stem. The capsule is almost completely belted vertically by a jointed ring, called the *annulus,* which is unjoined at about "four o'clock." When the spores are ripe and the spore case is dry, the annulus breaks and bursts the spore case. The ring snaps backward rapidly to below a horizontal position and then snaps forward even more rapidly and catapults the spores some distance away. As the spore case and the annulus are most sensitive to moisture, breakage only occurs under dry conditions. The spores, therefore, are freed only when the air is dry, or when there is a dry wind which can better disperse them and give them more opportunity to land in suitable spots to develop first into their *prothalli* and later into their *gametophytes*. The spores of the Marginal Woodfern develop into gametophytes in about two weeks, and the gametophytes develop into the new young fern after about three and one half months. This varies, of course, in different ecological regions and with varying climatic conditions.

The Marginal Woodfern is not one of the largest ferns, nor has it many fertile, or spore-bearing, leaves. It produces, however, many hundreds of thousands of spores each season. Some of the larger ferns with many fertile leaves and more spore cases to their leaves produce millions of spores each season. (One botanist estimated 52 million spores on one *Dryopteris marginalis* plant.) This is hard to believe but can be readily appreciated when we take into consideration that each spore case contains, usually, 64 spores, and each fruitdot, or sorus, contains scores of spore cases with each tiny leaflet containing a dozen or more fruitdots. There are hundreds of leaflets on each fertile leaf and many leaves on a full-grown fern plant.

When a spore finds itself in a suitable place in the form of a tiny bit of shady moisture at the proper temperature, it begins developing into a *prothallus*, or gametophyte. The prothallus starts as a one-celled body and promptly puts down a tiny rootlike hair to anchor it to the soil. Then by adding one cell to another, it enlarges into a small heart-shaped, green, membranous body about ¼ inch in size. The notched end is several times thicker than the apex, forming a kind of cushion. The sexual organs develop on the underside.

The male organs, or *antheridia*, are near the apex, and the female organs, or *archegonia*, are near the notch. Both male and female organs are microscopic in size. The female organ consists of a sterile neck, or chimneylike tube with its base imbedded in the cushion part of the gametophyte. The base holds one single egg. There are twenty or more female organs in one gametophyte. When the female organs are fully developed, they all bend toward the apex better to receive the sperms, or *antherozoids*. The male organs are more numerous than the female. They are short and bulbous, and each contains several sperms. The sperm is shaped like a corkscrew, with hairs, or *cilia*, at one end for propelling itself through moisture.

When the gametophyte is fully grown and the sex organs are fully developed, the thin skin of the male organ bursts if, and only when, there is contact with a tiny bit of moisture. At the same time the necks of the female organs open and exude a chemical that is attractive to the sperms and causes them to swim toward the open necks and enter and fertilize the egg. As soon as the one egg is fertilized the neck closes, as, it is believed, do all the other necks on that particular gametophyte. (Customarily only one plantlet develops from each gametophyte.) If, however, there is enough moisture present, sperms may swim to adjacent gametophytes and fertilize their eggs.

The time development of the gametophytes varies for different species. If the time development for two different species of the same family synchronizes exactly and their gametophytes are adjacent in the same tiny bit of moisture, one species can fertilize another species, and produce a hybrid. But even though it is common for several species of ferns to grow close together, hybrids are not as common as we imagine.

After fertilization, the egg develops. At first it is anchored to the base of the female organ in the cushion of the gametophyte. Then it grows a root downward into the soil and a stem upward, which curves through the notch of the heart-shaped gametophyte. From the stem grows the first tiny leaf. Nutrition from the cushion lasts only long enough to have the root and the leaf develop sufficiently to become the independent plant again, with multiple roots, stems, and leaves, ready for the next cycle.

Such is the life cycle for the *True Ferns.*

The *Fern Allies* differ somewhat from this in general. Their spores are not born on the underside of the leaves, but are usually in cone-like spikes—i.e., Horsetails and some Clubmosses; or in special chambers between the leaves—i.e., some Spikemosses and Quillworts; or in special individual cases, or *sporocarps*—i.e., Water Ferns. The spores of the Clubmosses, like those of the True Ferns, are all alike, at least in outward appearance, and their gametophytes have both male and female sex organs, whereas the Horsetails have spores of one kind but gametophytes of two kinds, male and female. The Water Ferns have two kinds of spores and two kinds of gametophytes. The Quillworts and Spikemosses also have two kinds of spores and two kinds of gametophytes, which are small, or minute, and rudimentary; but the female gametophyte in the megaspore (large female spore) retains the fertilized egg and nourishes it until it has attained sufficient growth and strength for independence. Even though the alternation of generations exists here, it is of a highly modified form and close to that of the seed-bearing plants.

NATURE

BY RALPH WALDO EMERSON

Ralph Waldo Emerson (1803–1882) was born in Boston, educated at Harvard. After several years as teacher and preacher, he went abroad, met Europe's leading literary figures, and came home a dedicated American, one of our first major advocates of American sources for writers and thinkers. His religious ideas were influenced by the writings of Emanuel Swedenborg and he became a leader in the Transcendentalist movement. The distinguished group of thinkers and philosophers at Concord looked to him as their chief spokesman. His essays and his lectures were of a piece and were essentially philosophical rather than literary. He loved nature though he knew little about it beyond its surface aspects; nature, to Emerson, was essentially an object lesson. Thoreau built his Walden cabin on land owned by Emerson and was a member of the Emerson household from time to time; his early writing was patterned on that of Emerson, but he soon developed patterns of both thought and writing distinctly his own. This selection is from Emerson's Essays: Second Series, *first published in 1876. Its style is pure Emerson, vigorous, assertive and full of the platform speaker's rhythms.*

(*Essays: Second Series,* by Ralph Waldo Emerson; Ticknor & Fields, 1876.)

There are days which occur in this climate, at almost any season of the year, wherein the world reaches its perfection; when the air, the heavenly bodies and the earth, make a harmony, as if nature would indulge her offspring; when, in these bleak upper sides of the planet, nothing is to desire that we have heard of the happiest latitudes, and we bask in the shining hours of Florida and Cuba; when everything that has life gives sign of satisfaction, and the cattle that lie on the ground seem to have great and tranquil thoughts. These halcyons may be looked for with a little more assurance in that pure October weather which we distinguish by the name of the Indian summer. The day, immeasurably long, sleeps over the broad hills and warm wide fields. To have lived through all its sunny hours, seems longevity enough. The solitary places do not seem quite lonely. At the gates of the forest, the surprised man of the world is forced to leave his city estimates of great and small, wise and foolish. The knapsack of custom falls off his back with the first step he takes into these precincts. Here is sanctity which shames our religions, and reality that discredits our heroes. Here we find nature to be the circumstance which dwarfs every other circumstance, and judges like a god all men that come to her. We have crept out of our close and crowded houses into the night and morning, and we see what majestic beauties daily wrap us in their bosom. How willingly we would escape the barriers which render them comparatively impotent, escape the sophistication and second thought, and suffer nature to intrance us. The tempered light of the woods is like a perpetual morning, and is stimulating and heroic. The anciently-reported spells of these places creep on us. The stems of the pines, hemlocks and oaks almost gleam like iron on the excited eye. The incommunicable trees begin to persuade us to live with them, and quit our life of solemn trifles. Here no history, or church, or state, is interpolated on the divine sky and the immortal year. How easily we might walk onward into the opening landscape, absorbed by new pictures and by thoughts fast succeeding each other, until by degrees the recollection of home was crowded out of the mind, all memory obliterated by the tyranny of the present, and we were led in triumph by nature.

These enchantments are medicinal, they sober and heal us. These are plain pleasures, kindly and native to us. We come to our own, and make friends with matter, which the ambitious chatter of the schools would persuade us to despise. We never can part with it; the mind loves its old home: as water to our thirst, so is the rock, the ground, to our eyes and hands and feet. It is firm water; it is cold flame; what health, what affinity! Ever an old friend, even like a dear friend and brother when we chat affectedly with strangers, comes in this honest face, and takes a grave liberty with us, and shames us out of our nonsense. Cities give not the human senses room enough. We go out daily and nightly to feed the eyes on the horizon, and require so much scope, just as we need water for our bath. There are all degrees of natural influence, from these quarantine powers of nature, up to her dearest and gravest ministrations to the imagination and the soul. There is the bucket of cold water from the spring, the wood-fire to which the chilled traveller rushes for safety,—and there is the sublime moral of autumn and of noon. We nestle in nature, and draw our living as parasites from her roots and grains, and we receive glances from the heavenly bodies, which call us to solitude and foretell the remotest future. The blue zenith is the point in which romance and reality meet. I think if we should be rapt away into all that and dream of heaven, and should converse with Gabriel and Uriel, the upper sky would be all that would remain of our furniture.

It seems to me as if the day was not wholly profane in which we have given heed to some natural object. The fall of snowflakes in a still air, preserving to each crystal its perfect form; the blowing of sleet over a wide sheet of water, and over plains; the waving rye-field; the mimic waving of acres of houstonia, whose innumerable florets whiten and ripple before the eye; the reflections of trees and flowers in glassy lakes; the musical, streaming, odorous south wind, which converts all trees to wind-harps; the crackling and spurting of hemlock in the flames, or of pine logs, which yield glory to the walls and faces in the sitting-room,—these are the music and pictures of the most ancient religion. My house stands in low land, with limited outlook, and on the skirt of the village. But I go with my friend to the shore of our little river, and with one stroke of the paddle I leave the village politics and personalities, yes, and the world of villages and personalities, behind, and pass into a delicate realm of sunset and moonlight, too bright almost for spotted man to enter without novitiate and probation. We penetrate bodily this incredible beauty; we dip our hands in this painted element; our eyes are bathed in these lights and forms. A holiday, a *villeggiatura*, a royal revel, the proudest, most heart-rejoicing festival that valor and beauty, power and taste, ever decked and enjoyed, establishes itself on the instant. These sunset clouds, these delicately emerging stars, with their private and ineffable glances, signify it and proffer it. I am taught the poorness of our invention, the ugliness of towns and palaces. Art and luxury have early learned that they must work as enchantment and sequel to this original beauty. I am over-instructed for my return. Henceforth I shall be hard to please. I cannot go back to toys. I am grown expensive and sophisticated. I can no longer live without elegance, but a countryman shall be my master of revels. He who knows the most, he who knows what sweets and virtues are in the ground, the waters, the plants, the heavens, and how to come at these enchantments,—is the rich and royal man. Only as far as the masters of the world have called in nature to their aid, can they reach the height of magnificence. . . .

But it is very easy to outrun the sympathy of readers on this topic, which schoolmen called *natura naturata,* or nature passive. One can hardly speak directly of it without excess. It is as easy to broach in mixed companies what is called "the subject of religion." A susceptible person does not like to indulge his tastes in this kind without the apology of some trivial necessity: he goes to see a wood-lot, or to look at the crops, or to fetch a plant or a mineral from a remote locality, or he carries a fowling-piece or a fishing-rod. I suppose this shame must have a good reason. A dilettantism in nature is barren and unworthy. The fop of the fields is no better than his brother of Broadway. Men are natural hunters and inquisitive of wood-craft, and I suppose that such a gazetteer as woodcutters and Indians would furnish facts for, would take place in the most sumptuous drawing-rooms of all the "Wreaths" and "Flora's chaplets" of the bookshops; yet ordinarily, whether we are too clumsy for so subtle a topic, or from whatever cause, as soon as men begin to write on nature, they fall into euphuism. Frivolity is a most unfit tribute to Pan, who ought to be represented in the mythology as the most continent of the gods. I would not be frivolous before the admirable reserve and prudence of time, yet I cannot renounce the right of returning often to this old topic. The multitude of false churches accredits the true religion. Literature, poetry, science are the homage of man to this unfathomed secret, concerning which no sane man can effect an indifference or incuriosity. . . .

Nature is always consistent, though she feigns to contravene her own laws. She keeps her laws, and seems to transcend them. She arms and equips an animal to find its place and living in the earth, and at the same time she arms and equips another animal to destroy it. . . . If we look at her work, we seem to catch a glimpse of a system in transition. Plants are the young of the world, vessels of health and vigor; but they grope ever upward towards consciousness; the trees are imperfect men, and seem to bemoan their imprisonment, rooted in the ground. The animal is the novice and probationer of a more advanced order. The men, though young, having tasted the first drop from the cup of thought, are already dissipated; the maples and ferns are still uncorrupt; yet no doubt when they come to consciousness they too will curse and swear. Flowers so strictly belong to youth that we adult men soon come to feel that their beautiful generations concern not us: we have had our day; now let the children have theirs. The flowers jilt us, and we are old bachelors with our ridiculous tenderness. . . .

If we consider how much we are nature's, we need not be superstitious about towns, as if that terrific or benefic force did not find us there also, and fashion cities. Nature, who made the mason, made the house. We may easily hear too much of rural influences. The cool disengaged air of natural objects makes them enviable to us, chafed and irritable creatures with red faces, and we shall be as grand as they if we camp out and eat roots; but let men be men instead of woodchucks and the oak and the elm shall gladly serve us, though we sit in chairs of ivory on carpets of silk.

This guiding identity runs through all the surprises and contrasts of the piece, and characterizes every law. Man carries the world in his head, the whole astronomy and chemistry suspended in a thought. Because the history of nature is characterized in his brain, therefore is he the prophet and discoverer of her secrets.

LET NATURE GROW HER OWN

BY LEWIS GANNETT

Lewis Gannett (1891 —) was born in Rochester, New York, educated at Harvard and in Germany. After many years as reporter, foreign correspondent and daily book reviewer, he retired to the hills of northwestern Connecticut where he had summered and vacationed for more than twenty years. He has written about many topics but never with more affection than when he is discussing the Cream Hill area of Connecticut's Cornwalls, whose woods and fields he knows intimately. A field naturalist of long experience, he has grown most of the native flowers and edible plants on his own rocky acres and practically speaks their language. In this selection, a chapter from Cream Hill, *his book about life on a Connecticut hilltop farm, he speaks his mind about natural bounty.*

(*Cream Hill,* by Lewis Gannett; The Viking Press, 1949.)

According to popular superstition the Indians were lazy folk. They planted corn in virgin soil, sometimes thrusting a dead fish into the hills, and otherwise let Nature thrust her bounty upon them. But after a very slight experience with the business of letting Nature grow her crops for us, we have come to the conclusion that the Indians must have been a neurotically over-busy people.

It is a pretty theory: that the woods are God's own garden, and that one may find nourishment by walking the hillsides without the weary pother of planting, hoeing, weeding, and cultivating. In twenty years of book reviewing I have read a lot about the bounty of the wayside and living off the wild. But it sounds better in books than it proves to be when one works at it; and even in books, when one reads between the lines, it is a bit of a hoax.

Take acorns, for instance. Our woods are full of oak trees, and in good years the ground is littered with acorns. It seems a shame to waste them. "Although bitter and somewhat astringent when raw," the learned Dr. M. L. Fernald says in his *Edible Wild Plants of North America*, the most erudite as well as the saltiest of the let-Nature-grow-it-for-you books, "acorns lose these properties by being leached and there is left a nutty meat rich in oil and starch."

So far, so good. And we all know that some of the Indian tribes almost lived on acorn meal. They mixed the meats with hardwood ashes and water, according to Dr. Fernald, or powdered the dried kernels and either poured boiling water through the flour, thus removing the tannin, or placed the powdered mass in a basket or in a hollow pocket of sand and allowed the running water to trickle through the mass. This, some authorities say, explains why the Indians had such bad teeth.

But, Dr. Fernald continues, it is unnecessary to mix sand with acorn flour and thus sandpaper the teeth. All that is necessary is to dry the kernels thoroughly, boil them for two hours, pour off the darkened water, soak the blackened kernels in cold water, with occasional changes, for a few days, then grind them into a paste. Acorn flour, Dr. Fernald holds, makes good muffins when mixed with wheat flour in the fifty-fifty conventional recipe for corn bread. But it sounds to us as if someone about the tepees had to work for days to get a little acorn meal, and someone else had to gather the acorns.

We have never tried it. We have never had that much time.

We have tried candied wild ginger, nettle greens, creamed milkweed shoots, and boiled fiddle fronds of assorted varieties of ferns, and, of course, the far less esoteric nourishment of wild strawberries, wild raspberries, wild blackberries, hickory nuts, and butternuts. We have even tried the groundnuts—actually a kind of tuberous-rooted wild bean—on which the Pilgrims are said to have lived in large part during their first winter in New England. These, the books say, were so cherished that plants were exported to France, and one Yankee town is alleged to have passed a law forbidding Indians to dig groundnuts on English land, on pain of being whipped.

Groundnuts are as easily cooked as potatoes, though not as easily pared, and they taste like fair turnips. The trouble is to find enough of them. The only place I know where they could be dug in sufficient quantity to make them really worth gathering is beneath my neighbor Ted Gold's porch trellis. His grandfather planted them there, and they flourish. Their fragrant chocolate-colored flowers in midsummer are almost as handsome as the trumpet vines that screen our own south porch. But my neighbor Ted has never encouraged my hints that it might be well to thin his groundnut patch, and I have never found any comparable masses of them in the wild. My experience with groundnuts—I spent half a day spotting and digging a small mess for two—added to my conviction that the Indians worked overtime.

Nettles and milkweed, on the other hand, are among the most abundant crops on Cream Hill. From May until October our hands habitually sting from misencounters with nettles, and only since we learned of the miraculous selective murder accomplished by the chemical known as 2.4D have we begun to get our nettles under control. (2.4D is the herbicide which spares narrow-leaved grasses and day lilies while working foul vengeance on assorted broad-leaved weeds—also, as we learned by painful experience, on the broad-leaved flowers which you accidentally spray when on a nettle-slaughtering campaign.)

Nettles, the books say, made Pliny's favorite pudding in old Roman days. Sir Walter Scott celebrated their virtues in *Rob Roy,* and Victor Hugo in *Les Misérables.* They are still eaten with pleasure by the peasants of France and Scotland, but seldom in America. And in these days when Americans are boasting so constantly about the superiority of our ways of life, it is curious that no one has ever pointed, as another sign of the superiority of American civilization, to the fact that we Americans don't eat nettles. The Gannetts have tried them. We know.

Perhaps I should say that I have tried them. Ruth, generally a gastronomical experimenter, willing to try anything once and usually three times, has never evinced the slightest interest in boiled nettles, and Michael and Ruthy both had the normal child's "I-call-it-spinach-

and-to-hell-with-it" attitude toward any greens. The three times that we tried nettles Ruth graciously permitted me to gather, wash, and cook them myself. She watched me with a distant air; and for her, each time, one spoonful of boiled nettles was enough—it was for me, too, though I didn't admit it. I tried them straight the first time; they were unpleasantly bitter. I added sugar the second time; the resulting taste was terrible. I changed the water repeatedly on the third experiment. The nettles still weren't worth eating—let alone picking and washing.

Milkweed is different, and we have one of the finest fields of volunteer milkweed in all New England. During the war, when the newspapers were full of propaganda about the potentialities of milkweed as a source of a rubber substitute, we used to gaze speculatively on our milkweed crop and discuss our chances of wealth. We never cashed in on it; neither, so far as we learned, did anyone else. But, for a week or two in May, young milkweed stalks make good eating.

We have sampled a variety of field greens—mustard greens, young dock, certain varieties of pigweed, "pussley," and others. We have always intended to sample marsh marigold greens, which are said to be good, if a trifle mucilaginous, just before the flower buds break into gold. But it seems something of a crime to boil marsh marigold for greens just before it comes into its golden glory, and we have never been able to steel ourselves to the offense. Milkweed is something else. The root stalks run deep and horizontal underground. When you pull a young stalk you do no more harm to the plant than when you cut asparagus; it soon replaces itself. Besides, it tastes good. It has a tang of its own. It doesn't just have a generic flavor of vitamins and "greens"; it tastes, in fact, almost precisely like asparagus.

You pull it before the leaf buds separate from the stem. I hesitate to correct the great botanical gastronomer Dr. Fernald, but the illustration in his *Edible Wild Plants of North America* is of a milkweed with the leaves already expanded. At that stage the milk has begun to form, and the taste is bitter. It is not milkweed in its prime.

Sometimes we eat milkweed by itself, with drawn butter or a cream sauce. (Ruth disapproves of cream sauces, but I like them on almost anything.) Sometimes, when guests turn up beyond the capacities of our asparagus patch, we add milkweed to our asparagus, and we have yet to find a guest who detected the difference until told of it. Milkweed is one of the few wild crops which are easy to harvest and worth the effort.

Fiddle fronds are another. Of late years fiddleheads have received extensive newspaper publicity; a firm in Maine cans them. We first heard of them from Charlie, the famous chef of the Rapids Hotel in Analomink, Pennsylvania. Charlie, a Frenchman and an epicure, insisted that bracken made the most appetizing fiddleheads, and bracken are usually mentioned in the newspaper stories. Professor Fernald recommends cinnamon fern, and we agree with him that cinnamon fern is preferable to the rather stringy bracken. But ostrich ferns are best. Picked before the fiddleheads uncoil, boiled, and served with salt and butter, they are a noble dish, and it is almost as easy to pick a mess of them as to pull a bunch of carrots. All you have to do is to know where they grow.

As to dandelion greens, or, even more, dandelion salad, anyone liking them is welcome to them. You can find plenty on any roadside, and that, in our judgment, is where dandelions belong. We feel the same way about dock, wild mustard, the slippery purslane, and Good King Henry.

Woods gourmets find all manner of foods in the forests. Oliver Perry Medsger, for instance, author of *Edible Wild Plants,* tells with enthusiasm of the thrice boiled and thrice strained skunk cabbage, which he eats with relish. We read of his experiments with interest; we have not imitated him. Dr. Fernald has proved that while the raw roots of the Jack-in-the-pulpit puckers the mouth worse than a green persimmon, the same root stock boiled, drained, baked, and mellowed—apparently with more effort than is required to make crepes suzette—is quite edible. He may be right; we have not tried. Why should anyone?

Dr. Fernald, indeed, is a glutton for work. I cherish with particular delight his account of a meal he once served to a group of visiting botanists; indeed, it is such an impressive evidence of botanical and gastronomic zeal that I venture to quote it in full:

> Planning for a meeting of botanists in [my] study, [I] set to work on the menu to follow the business meeting: purée of dried fairy-ring mushrooms, escalloped canned purslane, salad of cooked blanched pokeweed and sorrel from the cellar, etc. A bread of pigweed-seeds was decided upon. Proceeding in Janu-

ary to the border of a frozen truck-farm, a peck of seeds with husks and other fragments was quickly gathered. Winnowed by pouring back and forth from containers out-of-doors, so that the lighter husks and debris blew away, a yield of a full quart of the black and drab fruits was left. When supper was served, Mrs. Fernald brought in the soup which found favor, with thin biscuits of Jack-in-the-pulpit flour, then the purslane and salad, with a plate of intensely black muffins.

I explained that, having no cook, I had volunteered to make the muffins. The plate went round the table, regularly to receive a polite "No, I thank you," until it reached the late Emile Williams, half-French and with more than usual Yankee consideration for others. Everyone else having declined my black muffins, Williams took one, put on his eyeglasses and inspected it, then sniffed at it.

"Ah, *Chenopodium album*," was his immediate diagnosis. Asked how he guessed, he replied: "I've just been reading Napoleon's Memoirs. Napoleon at times had to live on it." The plate was promptly cleared and returned to the kitchen for more, to nibble with the beach-plum preserve.

Dr. Fernald, obviously, is an outdoors cook who really cares.

The woods and fields about us are full of butternuts and shagbark hickories. Each autumn we pick up a bushel or two. Sometimes we crack a few. They are good, but somehow we usually find other ways to spend our long winter evenings. In fact, without electricity, we usually go to bed.

Ruth is a fanatic for berries of all kinds. I like wild strawberries, but to me it seems rather gluttonish to eat a lot of them at table. Eaten as they are picked, one by one, one gets the full individual flavor. Other berries, I feel, clutter up the teeth with seeds beyond all real enjoyment. I am willing to pick as many quarts of raspberries or blackberries as Ruth and her friends will eat, but I prefer not to be asked to eat them in the raw. Cooked and strained, the juices make delicious jelly. It is Ruth's contention that jelly is a lot of work.

We have tried choke-cherry jelly, which is an interesting effort, though not one to be indulged in when sugar is short; and Ruth regularly puts up a little elderberry jelly. The elderberry is one of the most neglected of Nature's gifts. Even Dr. Fernald, who is almost omnivorous, casts a slur upon its flavor. We like it. And the birds, notably the cedar waxwings, which gather about the ripening elderberries in great flocks, agree with us.

But in general, it is our tested opinion that the man who tries to let Nature do his gardening for him works harder than the man who grows his own. There are a lot of things in life which are not as simple as they sound.

JOHNNY APPLESEED

BY W. D. HAILEY

W. D. Hailey seems to have disappeared into the fog of the past; I can find no record of him beyond a few magazine articles in periodicals now brittle with almost a century's age. But I salute him as a writer of skill and economy in a time when so many other journalists were both florid and wordy. This selection is from an article Mr. Hailey wrote about Johnny Appleseed and which appeared in Harper's New Monthly Magazine's *issue for November 1871. Various authors have written about Johnny Appleseed since then, but virtually all of them owe a debt, at first or second, or even third hand, to the mysterious W. D. Hailey, who so obviously knew both the background and the firsthand stories about old Johnny, whose christened name was Jonathan Chapman. As for Johnny Appleseed, I need add only that he is now as firmly embedded in our folklore as Paul Bunyan, but with the difference that Johnny Appleseed was real, not mythological, a unique, eccentric outdoorsman who left a legacy such as no one else who ever wandered the frontier woodlands of this country.*

("Johnny Appleseed: A Pioneer Hero," by W. D. Hailey; *Harper's New Monthly Magazine,* November 1871.)

Among the frontier heroes of endurance that was voluntary, and of action that was creative and not sanguinary, there was one whose name, seldom mentioned now save by some of the surviving pioneers, deserves to be perpetuated.

The first reliable trace of our modest hero finds him in the Territory of Ohio, in 1801, with a horse-load of apple seeds, which he planted in various places on and about the borders of Licking Creek, the first orchard thus originated by him being on the farm of Isaac Stadden, in what is now known as Licking County, in the State of Ohio. During the five succeeding years, although he was undoubtedly following the same strange occupation, we have no authentic account of his movements until we reach a pleasant spring day in 1806, when a pioneer settler in Jefferson County, Ohio, noticed a peculiar craft, with a remarkable occupant and a curious cargo, slowly dropping down with the current of the Ohio River. It was "Johnny Appleseed," by which name Jonathan Chapman was afterward known in every log-cabin from the Ohio River to the Northern lakes, and westward to the prairies of what is now the State of Indiana. With two canoes lashed together he was transporting a load of apple seeds to the Western frontier, for the purpose of creating orchards on the farthest verge of white settlements. With his canoes he passed down the Ohio to Marietta, where he entered the Muskingum, ascending the stream of that river until he reached the mouth of the Walhonding, or White Woman Creek, and still onward, up the Mohican, into the Black Fork, to the head of navigation, in the region now known as Ashland and Richland counties, on the line of the Pittsburgh and Fort Wayne Railroad, in Ohio. A long and tiresome voyage it was, as a glance at the map will show, and must have occupied a great deal of time, as the lonely traveler stopped at every inviting spot to plant the seeds and make his infant nurseries. These are the well-authenticated facts in the history of Jonathan Chapman, whose birth, there is good reason for believing, occurred in Boston, Massachusetts, in 1775. According to this, which was his own statement in one of his less reticent moods, he was, at the time of his appearance on Licking Creek, twenty-six years of age, and whether impelled in his eccentricities by some absolute misery of the heart which could only find relief in incessant motion, or governed by a benevolent monomania, his whole after-life was devoted to the work of planting apple seeds in remote places. The seeds he gathered from the cider-presses of Western

Pennsylvania; but his canoe voyage in 1806 appears to have been the only occasion upon which he adopted that method of transporting them, as all his subsequent journeys were made on foot. Having planted his stock of seeds, he would return to Pennsylvania for a fresh supply, and, as sacks made of any less substantial fabric would not endure the hard usage of the long trip through forests dense with underbrush and briers, he provided himself with leathern bags. Securely packed, the seeds were conveyed, sometimes on the back of a horse, and not unfrequently on his own shoulders, either over a part of the old Indian trail that led from Fort Duquesne to Detroit, by way of Fort Sandusky, or over what is styled in the appendix to "Hutchins's History of Boguet's Expedition in 1764" the "second route through the wilderness of Ohio," which would require him to traverse a distance of one hundred and sixty-six miles in a west-northwest direction from Fort Duquesne in order to reach the Black Fork of the Mohican.

This region, although it is now densely populated, still possesses a romantic beauty that railroads and bustling towns cannot obliterate —a country of forest-clad hills and green valleys, through which numerous bright streams flow on their way to the Ohio; but when Johnny Appleseed reached some lonely log-cabin he would find himself in a veritable wilderness. The old settlers say that the margins of the streams, near which the first settlements were generally made, were thickly covered with low, matted growth of small timber, while nearer to the water was a rank mass of long grass, interlaced with morning-glory and wild pea vines, among which funereal willows and clustering alders stood like sentinels on the outpost of civilization. The hills, that rise almost to the dignity of mountains, were crowned with forest trees, and in the coverts were innumerable bears, wolves, deer, and droves of wild hogs, that were as ferocious as any beast of prey. In the grass the massasauga and other venomous reptiles lurked in such numbers that a settler named Chandler has left the fact on record that during the first season of his residence, while mowing a small prairie which formed a part of his land, he killed over two hundred black rattlesnakes in an area that would involve an average destruction of one of these reptiles for each rod of land. The frontiersman, who felt himself sufficiently protected by his rifle against wild beasts and hostile Indians, found it necessary to guard against the attacks of the insidious enemies in the grass by wrapping bandages of dried grass around his buckskin leggings and moccasins; but Johnny would shoulder his bag of apple seeds, and with bare feet penetrate to some remote spot that combined picturesqueness and fertility of soil, and there he would plant his seeds, place a slight enclosure around the place, and leave them to grow until the trees were big enough to be transplanted by the settlers, who, in the mean time, would have made their clearings in the vicinity. The sites chosen by him are, many of them, well known, and are such as an artist or a poet would select—open places on the loamy lands that border the creeks—rich, secluded spots, hemmed in by giant trees, picturesque now, but fifty years ago, with their wild surroundings and the primal silence, they must have been tenfold more so.

In personal appearance Chapman was a small, wiry man, full of restless activity; he had long, dark hair, a scanty beard that was never shaved, and keen black eyes that sparkled with a peculiar brightness. His dress was of the oddest description. Generally, even in the coldest weather, he went barefooted, but sometimes, for his long journeys, he would make himself a rude pair of sandals; at other times he would wear any cast-off foot-covering he chanced to find—a boot on one foot and an old brogan or a moccasin on the other. It appears to have been a matter of conscience with him never to purchase shoes, although he was rarely without money enough to do so. . . . His dress was generally composed of cast-off clothing, that he had taken in payment for apple-trees. . . . In his later years, however, he seems to have thought that even this kind of second-hand raiment was too luxurious, as his principal garment was made of a coffee sack, in which he cut holes for his head and arms to pass through, and pronounced it "a very serviceable cloak, and as good clothing as any man need wear." In the matter of head-gear his taste was equally unique; his first experiment was with a tin vessel that served to cook his mush, but this was open to the objection that it did not protect his eyes from the beams of the sun; so he constructed a hat of pasteboard with an immense peak in front, and having thus secured an article that combined usefulness with economy, it became his permanent fashion.

Thus strangely clad, he was perpetually wandering through forests and morasses, and suddenly appearing in white settlements and Indian villages, but there must have been some rare force of gentle goodness dwelling in his looks and breathing in his words, for it is the testimony of all who knew him that, notwithstanding his ridiculous attire, he was always treated with the greatest respect by the rudest frontiersman, and, what is a better test, the boys of the settlements forebore to jeer at him. . . . The Indians also treated Johnny with the greatest kindness. By these wild and sanguinary savages he was regarded as a "great medicine-man," on account of his strange appearance, eccentric actions, and, especially, the fortitude with which he could endure pain, in proof of which he would often thrust needles into his flesh. His nervous sensibilities really seem to have been less acute than those of ordinary people, for his method of treating the cuts and sores that were the consequences of his barefooted wanderings through briers and thorns was to sear the wound with a red-hot iron, and then cure the burn. During the war of 1812, when the frontier settlers were tortured and slaughtered by the savage allies of Great Britain, Johnny Appleseed continued his wanderings, and was never harmed by the roving bands of hostile Indians. On many occasions the impunity with which he ranged the country enabled him to give the settlers warning of approaching danger in time to allow them to take refuge in their blockhouses before the savages could attack them. . . .

He was a most earnest disciple of the faith taught by Emanuel Swedenborg. . . . He entertained a profound reverence for the revelations of the Swedish seer, and always carried a few old volumes with him. These he was very anxious should be read by everyone . . . and devised an original method of multiplying one book into a number. He divided his books into several pieces, leaving a portion at a log-cabin, and on a subsequent visit furnishing another fragment, and continuing this process as diligently as though the work had been published in serial numbers. By this plan he was enabled to furnish reading for several people at the same time, and out of one book; but it must have been a difficult undertaking for some nearly illiterate backwoodsman to endeavor to comprehend Swedenborg by a backward course of reading, when his first installment happened to be the last fraction of the volume. . . .

Next to his advocacy of his peculiar religious ideas, his enthusiasm for the cultivation of apple trees in what he termed "the only proper way"—that is, from the seed—was the absorbing object of his life. Upon this, as upon religion, he was eloquent in his appeals. He would describe the growing and ripening fruit as such a rare and beautiful gift of the Almighty with words that became pictures, until his hearers could almost see its manifold forms of beauty before them. To his eloquence on this subject, as well as to his actual labors in planting nurseries, the country over which he traveled for so many years is largely indebted for its numerous orchards. But he denounced as absolute wickedness all devices of pruning and grafting, and would speak of the act of cutting a tree as if it were a cruelty inflicted upon a sentient being. . . .

Theoretically he was as methodical in matters of business as any merchant. In addition to their picturesqueness, the locations of his nurseries were all fixed with a view to a probable demand for the trees by the time they had attained sufficient growth for transplanting. He would give them away to those who could not pay for them. Generally, however, he sold them for old clothing or a supply of corn meal; but he preferred to receive a note payable at some indefinite period. When this was accomplished he seemed to think that the transaction was completed in a business-like way; but if the giver of the note did not attend to its payment, the holder of it never troubled himself about its collection. His expenses for food and clothing were so limited that . . . he was frequently in possession of more money than he cared to keep, and . . . it was given to some poor family whom the ague had prostrated or the accidents of border life impoverished. In a single instance only he is known to have invested his surplus means in the purchase of land, having received a deed from Alexander Finley, of Mohican Township, Ashland County, Ohio, for a part of the southwest quarter of section twenty-six; but with his customary indifference to matters of value, Johnny failed to record the deed, and lost it. Only a few years ago the property was in litigation. . . .

Some of the pioneers were disposed to think that Johnny's humor was the cause of an extensive practical joke; but it is generally conceded now that a widespread annoyance was really the result of his belief that the offensively odored weed known in the West as the dog-fennel, but more generally styled the May-weed, possessed valuable antimalarial virtues. He procured some seeds of the plant in Pennsylvania, and sowed them in the vicinity of every house in the region of his travels. The consequence was that successive flourishing crops of the weed spread over the whole country, and caused almost as much trouble as the disease it was intended to ward off; and to this day the dog-fennel, introduced by Johnny Appleseed, is one of the worst grievances of the Ohio farmers.

In 1838—thirty-seven years after his appearance on Licking Creek —Johnny noticed that civilization, wealth and population were pressing into the wilderness of Ohio. Hitherto he had easily kept just in advance of the wave of settlement; but now towns and churches were making their appearance, and even, at long intervals, the stage-driver's horn broke the silence of the grand old forests, and he felt that his work was done in the region in which he had labored so long. He visited every house, and took a solemn farewell of all the families. Little girls who had been delighted with his gifts of fragments of calico and ribbons had become sober matrons, and the boys who had wondered at his ability to bear the pain caused by running needles into his flesh were heads of families. With parting words of admonition he left them, and turned his steps steadily toward the setting sun.

During the succeeding nine years he pursued his eccentric avocation on the western border of Ohio and in Indiana. In the summer of 1847, when his labors had literally borne fruit over a hundred thousand square miles of territory, at the close of a warm day, after traveling twenty miles, he entered the house of a settler in Allen County, Indiana, and was, as usual, warmly welcomed. He declined to eat with the family, but accepted some bread and milk, which he partook of sitting on the door-step and gazing on the setting sun. Later in the evening he delivered his "news right fresh from heaven" by reading the Beatitudes. Declining other accommodation, he slept, as usual, on the floor, and in the early morning he was found with his features all aglow with a supernal light, and his body so near death that his tongue refused its office. The physician, who was hastily summoned, pronounced him dying, but added that he had never seen a man in so placid a state at the approach of death. At seventy-two years of age, forty-six of which had been devoted to his self-imposed mission, he ripened into death as naturally and beautifully as the seeds of his own planting had grown into fiber and bud and blossom and the matured fruit.

A TIME REMEMBERED

BY BESSIE F. JOHNSON

Bessie F. Johnson (1878 —) was born and has lived virtually all her life in Rhode Island. Beyond that, I know little about her except what she tells in this selection. She is not a professional writer, and she lays no claim to being a naturalist; but she is one of those rare people who learned and remembered and can make others see. Several years ago, after reading one of my books, she wrote a long letter to me about her girlhood in rural Rhode Island. When I replied and asked questions, she wrote another letter. With her permission, I have combined these two letters and am using them here because they say so well the things that are a part of America's remembering; they bring back the curiosity and delight of childhood and the shine of young discovery in the outdoors.

Eighty years ago, when I was six years old, we moved to a farm in western Rhode Island, not far from the Connecticut line. My mother, a semi-invalid, loved nature in all its forms but had to rely on others to bring it to her. So as little children my sister and I were taught to keep our eyes open and bring flowers, pretty stones, etc., to her. Then out would come the microscope, a geology textbook or Gray's Botany, and in a little while Mother would tell us their names. Every summer Mother would take up a different phase of nature, one year ferns, mosses and lichens, another astronomy. But each year the flowers and the stones were the favorites.

One year she wrote a children's story, or perhaps a household article, and sent it off to some magazine. In payment she received a book, "Birds Through an Opera Glass," and she gave it to me for my birthday. Someone else gave me the opera glasses. With book and glasses and a pencil and notebook I would hie me off to the fields. The directions in the book were simple, so I became acquainted with most of the local birds. I was allowed to take one egg for a collection if I found a nest. I once found a cowbird's white egg in the nest of a brown thrasher, whose eggs are thickly speckled. The cowbird prefers to have some other bird hatch and bring up her family.

I loved the meadowlark, with its sweet, plaintive song, but I think the bobolink was my favorite. I remember one June Sunday morning as we sat in church. It was a warm, drowsy day and through the open doors and windows came whiffs of new-mown hay and the scent of wild grape blossoms on the stone wall down the road. Uncle George, Grandfather's brother and the minister of the little white church for forty years, was droning along when all at once the most ecstatic burst of song filled the room as a bobolink flew up from the meadow just across the road. He was so gay and joyous, so overflowing with bubbling drops of music, he seemed to be saying thanks for the summer day. I would love to hear one once more.

We learned to go in early spring to the maple swamp for the Jack-in-the-pulpits, the trilliums, the long-stemmed blue violets, and to the little brook flowing in the meadow for the yellow cowslips. In that same meadow in the fall the grass was blue with fringed gentians. At the foot of a huge chestnut tree grew the fairy-like Indian pipes. Before we could get them home their pearly pink color would have turned to black.

Along the Ice Pond grew wild cotton, the only name we knew for the plant with cotton-like tufts which grew atop the long stems. There were also masses of tiny blue-veined white violets, slow picking but Oh, so sweet! And at the end of the pond grew blue flag. A neighbor used to dig the roots, wash and scrape them, boil them until tender in a heavy syrup, then spread them on plates till the sugar coating was dry—blue flag candy. It had a bitter-sweet taste.

Some nights when I cannot sleep I start out in memory from our stone doorstep and walk down the lane to the main road where we got our mail, and try to recall the flowers which grew on either side. Flat in the dust, so tiny it could scarcely be seen, grew a five-petaled purple flower. I still do not know its name. There was mouse-everlasting, toad flax, St. Johnswort. Close to the wall grew the woolly, dark blue violets, and loosestrife with its small yellow flowers blooming up the stem with a cluster on top. In its season, rosy-pink hardhack, and the creamy puffs of New Jersey tea in bloom. And across the wall were five-fingers and star flowers and the dainty wind flowers.

A culvert had been built for the little brook which crossed the road, and underneath grew purple monkey flower, closed gentian, snakehead, monkshood and, in late summer, the beautiful, deep red cardinal flower. On the edge of the brook were meadow rue with its misty white flower tufts and jewel weed, whose leaves turned silver when we put them in water and whose seed pods we loved to pop off in our hands. For years there was a clump of four- and five-leafed clovers on the brook bank.

All these flowers and plants we brought home to Mother to identify. She was a remarkable person. Probably I realize it more now than when I was growing up. She was never without pain, but never complained. She filled her mind with other things. She could read only a little at a time, but her books were always at hand. She'd read a bit, lean back, eyes closed, in her old Boston rocker (the last years in a wheel chair). In her lap would be a pad and pencil with which to jot down a thought which would afterward become a poem or a farm article, some piece of writing to be sent to some magazine. For these she received not much money, but subscriptions and many books. She used to wish sometimes there was more money, but as I think of it now perhaps it was better so, for that would have gone into the daily living and we would never have had those wonderful years of study. With the Psalmist, I often say to myself, "Yea, I have a goodly heritage."

Our house was burned down, a few years later, so all Mother's records and our lovely collections are gone. The farm was long since sold, my parents are gone long ago, and I have lived in the city for many years. But, especially in the spring, I miss most of everything the running in the fields.

WILD RICE

BY SIGURD F. OLSON

Sigurd F. Olson (1899 —) was born in Chicago, educated in Wisconsin and Illinois, and taught biology for a time. An ecologist and conservationist, he is a former president of the National Parks Association and a consultant for the Izaak Walton League, the President's Quetico-Superior Committee, and the Department of the Interior. He writes often about all phases of conservation and especially of the U.S.-Canadian border wilderness area, which he has explored many times. This selection, from his Runes of the North, *tells about the wild rice harvest.*

(*Runes of the North*, by Sigurd F. Olson; Alfred A. Knopf, Inc., 1963.)

When I look at my bag of wild rice, I feel rich. Food of the north, this is nature's wheat, the traditional staple of Indians in the lake states. True, they have many other foods, but this wild grain, gathered in the shallow, mud-bottomed lakes and rivers of the north Middle West, is more important to them than any other. Bloody tribal wars were once fought for its possession, and those whose lands included strands of it were considered wealthy and insured against starvation and want.

Wild rice is easy to prepare; it needs only to be washed, to have boiling water poured over it and be allowed to steam to make it palatable. It should never be boiled, for that may result in a gray, gluey mass, unless mixed with meat or fat. As a stuffing for wild ducks, as a side dish, or cooked with game or fish, it is superb. Even for breakfast with berries, cream, and sugar, it could give modern cereals severe competition. It can even be popped like corn in a skillet, or mixed with bacon, mushrooms, or cheese; wild rice can be served as an entire meal or in infinite combinations with other foods. A purely American dish, it is indigenous to the north.

"Give me five hundred pounds of rice," said my friend Henry Chosa, "and I can feed my family for a year. A few fish now and then, some snared rabbits, a bear and some venison, and there's nothing to worry about. Rice, bear fat, and fish, are all an Indian needs to keep him strong and healthy."

When the fur trade began some three hundred years ago, it did not take the *voyageurs* long to discover the virtues of wild rice, and soon after it was used for barter. They looked forward to it after their monotonous diet of parched corn, pea soup, and salt pork, and eagerly awaited the time when their canoes entered the rice country of northern Wisconsin, Minnesota, Michigan, and southern Ontario where it thrived. While wild rice never attained the prominence of that western plains mixture of dried buffalo meat and tallow known as pemmican, it nevertheless contributed greatly to exploration and trade.

Father Marquette, on his expedition with Joliet in 1673, spoke of the tall grass growing in small rivers and swampy places which "The Savages Gather and prepare for food in the month of September." He told how they shook the ears from the hollow stems into their canoes, dried them on a grating over a slow fire, and trod the grain to separate the straw.

Radisson, in the journal of his expedition into this area in 1660, left this account:

"Our songs being finished, we began our teeth to work. We Had a kind of rice much like oats. It grows in the water three or four feet deep. They have a particular way to gather up that grain. Two take a boat and two sticks, by which they get the ear down and get the grain out of it. Their boat being full, they bring it to a fit place and dry it, and this is their food for the most part of the winter, and they do dress it thus: for each man a handful of that they put in the pot, that swells so much that it can suffice a man."

Many explorers and traders spoke of wild rice as excellent and tasty food. Alexander Henry stated in 1775, "The voyage could not have been prosecuted to its completion" without the supply of wild rice acquired from the Indians at Lake of the Woods, and Daniel Harmon mentioned in 1804 that each year, they bought from 1200 to 1500 bushels.

The French called the plant, known scientifically as *Zizania aquatica, folle avoine* meaning wild or foolish oats, and from this came the name of a Wisconsin tribe of rice gatherers. Early records always speak of them as the "Folles Avoines," though their real name was Menominee, coming from *Omanomen,* meaning rice, and *Inini,* person—people of the rice. The name Wisconsin may also have stemmed from association with the grain—*Weese-coh-seh*—meaning a good place in which to live, the good place may well have meant where wild rice grows and game and fish are plentiful.

When I see my bag of rice, I think of many things, for it holds far more than food. In addition to high nutrient value and flavor, it has certain intangible ingredients that have to do with memories, and for those who know the country where it grows and have taken part in the harvesting, it has powerful nostalgic associations that contribute as much to the welfare of the spirit as to the body.

There are many legends and stories about how wild rice came to the Indian people, but this is the one I like best. In the days of long ago, it was the custom for the chief to send young boys approaching manhood into the woods to live alone and prove their strength and courage. They existed on berries, roots, and anything they could find, and were told to stay out many days. Sometimes they wandered very far, got lost, and did not return. During these long and lonely journeys, spirits spoke to them and they had dreams and visions from which they often chose a name. If they returned, they became hunters and warriors, and in time took their places in the councils of the tribe.

One year a young boy wandered farther from the village than all the rest. It was a bad time for berries and fruits and he was sick from eating the wrong kinds. This boy loved all that was beautiful and, though hungry, always looked about him for flowers and lovely plants. One night in a dream, he saw some tall, feathery grass growing in a river. More beautiful than any he had ever seen, it changed color in the wind like the waves on a lake. Upon awakening he went to the river and there was the grass, tall and shining in the sunlight. Though starved and weak, he was so impressed that he waded into the river, pulled some plants from the mud, wrapped their roots in moss and bark, and started at once toward the village.

After many days he saw the tepees before him and when at last he showed what he had found, his people were happy and planted the still wet roots in a little lake nearby where it grew for several years until it became a field of waving grass in the bay. One fall a wise old Indian, who had traveled in many countries and knew all things, came to visit the village. He was taken to the lake to see the beautiful tall grass one of their young men had found. Seeing it, he was amazed, raised his arms high and cried in a loud voice:

"Manomen—Manomen—a gift from the Manito."

He explained that the seeds were good to eat, showed them how to gather it and separate the chaff from the grain. Before he left, he advised them to plant it everywhere, guard it well, and use it forever. The Indians have never forgotten—and now all over the north country it grows in golden fields.

In the old days each family had a portion of a rice field as its own, outlined by stakes and established as a claim long before the rice was ripe. Sometimes as an aid in harvesting, and to protect the grain from the ever present threat of being blown off by the wind, the Indians tied it into small sheaves. Basswood fiber was used, one length fastened to another until a large ball was made. The ball was placed on a birchbark tray behind the woman doing the tying, one end of the fiber going over her shoulder through a birchbark loop to her hand. As the canoe was pushed through the rice, she gathered it in with a hoop and with a deft motion tied it together. The rows were long, their straightness a matter of pride. Now the rice was claimed, and safe from the storms.

At harvesting time, a camp was set up on the shore of a lake or river where wild rice grew; often several families banded together. Equipment was simple: canoes propelled by long, forked poles, rice-beating sticks, birchbark, woven matting of cedar, canvas, kettles or tubs from parching, trays for the winnowing, bags or bark containers for storage.

Few food supplies were taken along on these expeditions, the natives depending almost entirely on rice with fish, game, and berries; maple sugar from the spring gathering was often the only seasoning. At night the women set their nets and in the morning drew them out. If fishing were good, drying and smoking racks were set up and fires kept going constantly. The men hunted the fat, rice-fed ducks, shot moose, bear, or deer wherever they could find them. Snares were set for rabbits and partridge, blueberries were picked and dried, a great supply of food laid by for the all important days when harvesting took all their time.

Each day after work around camp was done, they started for the rice fields, usually not to return until midafternoon. A canoe full of rice was considered a day's harvest if there were any distance to go, but if the field were close, several loads could be picked in a day.

Warm, still days were ideal for harvesting, as winds and rain could ruin an entire crop within an hour, a catastrophe not unknown. This was the reason for tying the heads, for then the storms could come without danger of losing all. Not all the rice was picked; some was left for seed and some for the ducks, who were not only good to eat, but planted the rice, as they believed, in many places.

In small camps the parching and threshing was done in the afternoon and evening, and those who did the harvesting assisted; but in large camps where several families worked together, this all important activity was carried on by trusted experts who did nothing else.

Some years ago, in early September, I carried my canoe across the Basswood portage to Hula Lake where I knew the Indians were camped. Long before I reached the tents and tepees along the shore, I could smell the rich pungence of the parching fires, for their haze hung over the woods and blended with that of fall. Just before I reached the camp I stopped and rested my canoe in the crotch of a tree. A dog barked—someone was chopping—and then I heard what I was listening for, the modulated voices of Chippewas talking. It was a pleasant sound, rising and falling, an obligato to the rustling of leaves and to the lazy smoke drifting through the trees, part of the hush which seems to lie over the rice beds before they turn to gold.

Continuing the portage, I walked through the camp, dropped my canoe at the landing and returned. The men were sitting around resting and smoking after their day in the rice fields, women tended parching kettles, some tossed winnowing trays in an open place.

Over a central fire was a tripod of white birch poles and from it hung a great iron kettle. An old woman was stirring and the fragrance of a wild rice stew made me hungry for the evening meal. Just beyond, another woman was chopping wood. Dogs and children ran happily about. Some canoes were still out, others returning loaded to the gunwales with green rice.

The field lay greenish gold in the light and the aspen where the camp was pitched took up the color, deepened and spread it all over the shores. Flocks of ducks were over the rice with a constant movement and flashing of wings; they paid little attention to the harvesters. Mostly black ducks, they were heavy and sluggish with the rice they had been gorging. When canoes came close, the ducks rose reluctantly to alight a short distance away, only to hurdle the canoes on their flight back. The harvest of succulent water-soaked kernels on the bottom was also theirs. Already fat as butter, they had a flavor no other fowl could equal.

David Thompson, a famous explorer in the late seventeen hundreds, spoke not only of the rice but of the ducks, stating in his diary:

"Mr. Sayer and his Men passed the whole winter on wild rice and maple sugar, which keeps them alive, but poor in flesh. It was a weak food, those who live for months on it enjoy good health, are moderately active, but very poor in flesh."

However, when he wrote about the ever present ducks, he was more enthusiastic for he said, they "become very fat and well tasted."

Had he known what the Indians knew, that wild rice must be eaten with fish, game, bear fat, or mixed with berries, to be a complete food, he might have changed his opinion of its nutrient value.

The scene before me had a certain timelessness. Except for the fact that Indians now had iron kettles, canvas, and modern tools, instead of birchbark canoes, matting, and utensils made of cedar and other woods, it was little different from the age of copper and stone. These people were enjoying themselves. Rice gathering was never work, it was the occasion for a festival, with a sense of good feeling and industry that seemed to permeate the camp, the sea of tall grass out on the lake, and the very air itself.

I paddled out where some of the canoes were still harvesting. Joe and Frances were working down one of their rows, Joe poling the canoe, Frances using her rice sticks to gather in the grain. I sat quietly, watching. What a smooth and even rhythm, first the bending of the stalks to the gunwale, then a stroke with the beating stick, never a waste motion, the action almost hypnotic in its effect. Already there were several inches of the long, green kernels on the bottom. In a short time they would be ready to return.

"Good rice," said Joe without stopping the movement of his pole, "nice big rice and clean."

He leaned down, held up a handful for me to see, let it run between his fingers into the canoe. I paddled close, felt it myself. The kernels were long and heavy, as fine a crop as I had ever seen.

"I save some for you," he said, and that fall it was his bag of rice that hung from my rafter.

Later I followed the canoes back to camp and watched the preparations. First the green rice was spread on canvas in partial shade where the sun would not shine on it directly. Heating and mold could destroy it so it was stirred and dried evenly, a process that took most of a day depending on the weather.

After the first drying, the rice was parched, over a slow fire, in a large kettle or tub placed in a slanting position so it could be stirred by someone sitting beside it. The heat was carefully regulated, but skill was required so the kernels did not burn or scorch. The quantity done at one time was seldom more than a peck and it usually required an hour before it was finished. The woman doing this work felt her responsibility, for a moment's neglect or carelessness could destroy the work of many hours. She wielded her slender stirring paddle with a sense of importance, knowing the contents of her kettle might be the last should a storm or wind blow up before the harvest was finished.

Parching loosened the husks and imparted a smoky flavor to the rice. The paddle went round and round, through the rice and underneath, never still for a moment. A stick at a time was pushed into the fire, no large ones or any that might flame. The heat must be constant and slow.

But there was another and far more ancient process in use that day: green rice placed on a rack lined with marsh grass over a smoldering fire. Slower than the kettle method of parching, it dried the grain as one might dry vegetables, berries, or meat. This was "hard rice," greenish black when finished, requiring longer to cook. Keeping indefinitely, it was stored against emergencies and long trips.

After the rice was thoroughly parched by either process, it was put into a barrel or tub for the pounding which loosened the sharp husks and prepared the grain for treading. A wooden pestle, somewhat pointed at one end, was moved gently up and down near the edge of the mortar, never pushed, but allowed to drop of its own weight. It was considered an art to finish the pounding so most of the rice was whole. Broken and shattered grain was the mark of an amateur. While as good for eating as the other, something was lost in quality and appearance that was a matter of pride to the Chippewas.

The final step in the process was the treading to dislodge the fragments of husk. For this, a wooden receptacle holding about a bushel was partially sunk in the ground. A strong cross-pole was tied between two trees at a height of about four feet directly in front of it. The treading was done by a young man wearing a clean pair of new moccasins especially made for this purpose and tied tightly around the ankles. The sole of the foot, so Indians believe, is particularly adapted to this work, is soft, gentle, and firm in its movements.

I watched a man do this all important work; his treading like that of a dancer, his entire being in action. Leaning on the cross-pole and taking the weight off his feet, his body moved with undulating rhythm and sinuous grace. He felt the rice beneath his feet, massaged it, turned it over, almost caressed it in his attempts to separate the precious kernels from their hard and flinty husks. Before the days of wooden tubs, a hole was dug in the ground and lined with deer skin, but the process was exactly the same, a work of care, devotion, and artistry. Many Indians look with favor on the old ways, feel that to deviate too much from ancient customs means a loss not only in flavor, but in the meaning of the food.

After the treading came the winnowing and for this the threshed rice was carried to an open place where wind could sweep away chaff and hulls. It was either tossed and caught in a tray or poured from a height onto a canvas underneath. If the wind was dry and strong, and if parching, pounding, and treading had been well done, the chaff was all blown away, leaving the greenish, black kernels clean and ready for use.

The finished product was now poured carefully into bags, sewn tightly, and placed under cover. Some was for sale to whites, or for trade with other Indians, but most was saved for winter food. Once birchbark or woven matting was used for containers, but now the bags are of burlap or canvas. Their contents were always precious and guarded well.

One night there was a dance, the rice or harvest dance. Everyone dressed for the occasion and there was much excitement and laughter. Kettles were steaming with new rice, game, and berries. The bags were placed under cover where all could see and admire them, for the harvest was almost over. This was a night to be happy and to thank the Manito for his largesse and for a fine harvest season.

After dark when everyone was fed and the fire built up, the drums began their rhythmic beating and the dancers took their places. At times only men danced in a circle around the fire, sometimes only women, often both, the usual stepping and stomping to the steady beat of the drums. That night after the dancing had gone on for several hours, I saw a young man, possibly more gifted and imaginative than the rest, begin to imitate the actions of the harvest, the motion of poling a canoe through the water, the graceful swinging of the rice sticks, the circular motion of the paddle in the parching, the dance of the treader holding on to his balancing pole, the final winnowing with a tray. Others soon followed the inspired one until there was much confusion, each attempting to interpret some part of the many aspects of harvesting and preparation. Finally, tiring, they relapsed into the ancient broken half-step of all native dances, a ritual looked forward to by all the band.

I have not seen a harvest dance for a long time now, and it is possible younger Indians do not remember, or if they do would think it old-fashioned and beneath their dignity to indulge, but those who have seen and taken part, cannot forget the deep joy and meaning of such celebrations.

In the fall when the rice harvest is on, I think of canoes going through golden fields of it against the blue of the water, the flash of ducks above and the whisper of their wings, the redolent haze from parching fires over some encampment. I remember the drums and the dancers under a big September moon, the soft voices of the Chippewas, the feeling of these Indian harvesters of the lake country for this gift of their Manito, long ago.

SPRING AT WALDEN POND

BY HENRY DAVID THOREAU

Henry David Thoreau (1817–1862) was a gnarly, opinionated man who wrote a great deal but published only two books and a handful of magazine articles during his lifetime. Born in Concord, Massachusetts, he went to Harvard, returned to Concord and, as he said, traveled widely there. He had grown up knowing the outdoors intimately and continued to study it all his life. Walden *was not prepared for publication until six years after he left the cabin in which he lived for two years on the shore of Walden Pond, though it was based on the journals he kept there. He was an exceptional nature writer, though he is now most often quoted as a social critic. I doubt, though, that one in a hundred of those who quote him today ever read one of his books from cover to cover. He was an excellent field naturalist and I find his nature-writing superb, sinewy and specific. In shaping this selection from* Walden *I have omitted some of his social comment and philosophizing, which distract from the wonderfully perceptive things he has to say about the natural world around him. Concord and Boston were full of social critics and theorists in Thoreau's day, but there was only one Naturalist Thoreau.*

(*Walden, or Life in the Woods,* by Henry David Thoreau, first published privately in 1854.)

One attraction in coming to the woods to live was that I should have leisure and opportunity to see the spring come in. The ice in the pond at length begins to be honeycombed, and I can set my heel in it as I walk. Fogs and rains and warmer suns are gradually melting the snow; the days have grown sensibly longer; and I see how I shall get through the winter without adding to my wood-pile, for large fires are no longer necessary. I am on the alert for the first signs of spring, to hear the chance note of some arriving bird, or the striped squirrel's chirp, for his stores must be now nearly exhausted, or see the woodchuck venture out of his winter quarters. On the 13th of March, after I had heard the bluebird, song-sparrow, and red-wing, the ice was still nearly a foot thick. As the weather grew warmer, it was not sensibly worn away by the water, nor broken up and floated off as in rivers, but, though it was completely melted for half a rod in width about the shore, the middle was merely honeycombed and saturated with water, so that you could put your foot through it when six inches thick; but by the next day evening, perhaps, after a warm rain followed by fog, it would have wholly disappeared, all gone off with the fog, spirited away. One year I went across the middle only five days before it disappeared entirely. In 1845 Walden was first completely open on the 1st of April; in '46, the 25th of March; in '47, the 8th of April; in '51, the 28th of March; in '52, the 18th of April; in '53, the 23rd of March; in '54, about the 7th of April.

Every incident connected with the breaking up of the rivers and ponds and the settling of the weather is particularly interesting to us who live in a climate of so great extremes. When the warmer days come, they who dwell near the river hear the ice crack at night with a startling whoop as loud as artillery, as if its icy fetters were rent from end to end, and within a few days see it rapidly going out. So the alligator comes out of the mud with quakings of the earth. One old man, who has been a close observer of Nature, and seems as thoroughly wise in regard to all her operations as if she had been put upon the stocks when he was a boy, and he had helped to lay her keel,—who has come to his growth, and can hardly acquire more of natural lore if he should live to the age of Methuselah,—told me, and I was surprised to hear him express wonder at any of Nature's operations, for I thought that there were no secrets between them, that one spring day he took his gun and boat, and thought that he would have a little sport with the ducks. There was ice still on the meadows, but it was all gone out of the river, and he dropped down without obstruction from Sudbury, where he lived, to Fair-Haven Pond, which he found, unexpectedly, covered for the most part with a firm field of ice. It was a warm day, and he was surprised to see so great a body of ice remaining. Not seeing any ducks, he hid his boat on the north or back side of an island in the pond, and then concealed himself in the bushes on the south side, to await them. The ice was melted for three or four rods from the shore, and there was a smooth and warm sheet of water, with a muddy bottom, such as the ducks love, within, and he thought it likely that some would be along pretty soon. After he had lain still there about an hour he heard a low and seemingly very distant sound, but singularly grand and impressive, unlike anything he had ever heard, gradually swelling and increasing as if it would have a universal and memorable ending, a sullen rush and roar, which seemed to him all at once like the sound of a vast body of fowl coming in to settle there, and, seizing his gun, he started up in haste and excited; but he found, to his surprise, that the whole body of the ice had started while he lay there, and drifted in to the shore, and the sound he had heard was made by its edge grating on the shore,—at first gently nibbled and crumbled off, but at length heaving up and scattering its wrecks along the island to a considerable height before it came to a standstill.

At length the sun's rays have attained the right angle, and warm winds blow up mist and rain and melt the snow-banks, and the sun dispersing the mist smiles on a checkered landscape of russet and white smoking with incense, through which the traveller picks his way from islet to islet, cheered by the music of a thousand tinkling rills and rivulets whose veins are filled with the blood of winter which they are bearing off.

Few phenomena gave me more delight than to observe the forms which thawing sand and clay assume in flowing down the sides of a deep cut on the railroad through which I passed on my way to the village, a phenomenon not very common on so large a scale, though the number of freshly exposed banks of the right material must have been greatly multiplied since railroads were invented. The material was sand of every degree of fineness and of various rich colors, commonly mixed with a little clay. When the frost comes out in the spring, and even in a thawing day in the winter, the sand begins to flow down the slopes like lava, sometimes bursting out through the snow and overflowing it where no sand was to be seen before. Innumerable little streams overlap and interlace one with another, exhibiting a sort of hybrid product, which obeys halfway the law of currents, and halfway that of vegetation. As it flows it takes the forms of sappy leaves or vines, making heaps of pulpy sprays a foot or more in depth, and resembling, as you look down on them, the laciniated, lobed, and imbricated thalluses of some lichens; or you are reminded of coral, of leopards' paws or birds' feet, of brains or lungs or bowels, and excrements of all kinds. It is a truly *grotesque* vegetation, whose forms and color we see imitated in bronze, a sort of architectural foliage more ancient and typical than acanthus, chicory, ivy, vine, or any vegetable leaves; destined perhaps, under some circumstances, to become a puzzle to future geologists. The whole cut impressed me as if it were a cave with its stalactites laid open to the light. The various shades of the sand are singularly rich and agreeable, embracing the different iron colors, brown, gray, yellowish, and reddish. When the flowing mass reaches the drain at the foot of the bank it spreads out flatter into *strands*, the separate streams losing their semi-cylindrical form and gradually becoming more flat and broad, running together as they are more moist, till they form an almost flat *sand*, still variously and beautifully shaded, but in which you can trace the original forms of vegetation; till at length, in the water itself, they are converted into *banks*, like those formed off the mouths of rivers, and the forms of vegetation are lost in the ripple marks on the bottom.

The whole bank, which is from twenty to forty feet high, is sometimes overlaid with a mass of this kind of foliage, or sandy rupture, for a quarter of a mile on one or both sides, the produce of one spring day. What makes this sand foliage remarkable is its springing into existence thus suddenly. When I see on the one side the inert bank,—for the sun acts on one side first,—and on the other this luxuriant foliage, the creation of an hour, I am affected as if in a peculiar sense I stood in the laboratory of the Artist who made the world and me—had come to where he was still at work, sporting on this bank, and with excess of energy strewing his fresh designs about. I feel as I were nearer to the vitals of the globe, for this sandy overflow is something such a foliaceous mass as the vitals of the animal body. You find thus in the very sands an anticipation of the vegetable leaf. No wonder that the earth expresses itself outwardly in leaves, it so labors with the idea inwardly. The atoms have already learned this law, and are pregnant by it. The overhanging leaf sees here its prototype. . . . The feathers and wings of birds are still drier and thinner leaves. Thus, also, you pass from the lumpish grub in the earth to the airy and fluttering butterfly. The very globe continually transcends and translates itself, and becomes winged in its orbit. Even ice begins with delicate crystal leaves, as if it had flowed into moulds which the fronds of water plants have impressed on the watery mirror. The whole tree itself is but one leaf, and rivers are still vaster leaves whose pulp is intervening earth, and towns and cities are the ova of insects in their axils.

When the sun withdraws the sand ceases to flow, but in the morning the streams will start once more and branch and branch again into a myriad of others. You here see perchance how blood vessels are formed. If you look closely you observe that first there pushes forward from the thawing mass a stream of softened sand with a drop-like point, like the ball of the finger, feeling its way slowly and blindly downward, until at last with more heat and moisture, as the sun gets higher, the most fluid portion, in its effort to obey the law to which the most inert also yields, separates from the latter and forms for itself a meandering channel or artery within that, in which is seen a little silvery stream glancing like lightning from one stage of pulpy leaves or branches to another, and ever and anon swallowed up in the sand. It is wonderful how rapidly yet perfectly the sand organizes itself as it flows, using the best material its mass affords to form the sharp edges of its channel. Such are the sources of rivers. In the silicious matter which the water deposits is perhaps the bony system, and in the still finer soil and organic matter the fleshy fibre or cellular tissue. What is man but a mass of thawing clay? The ball of the human finger is but a drop congealed. The fingers and toes flow to their extent from the thawing mass of the body. Who knows what the human body would expand and flow out to under a more genial heaven? Is not the hand a spreading *palm* leaf with its lobes and veins? The ear may be regarded, fancifully, as a lichen, *umbilicaria,* on the side of the head, with its lobe or drop. The lip—*labium,* from *labor* (?)—laps or lapses from the sides of the cavernous mouth. The nose is a manifest congealed drop or stalactite. The chin is a still larger drop, the confluent dripping of the face. The cheeks are a slide from the brows into the valley of the face, opposed and diffused by the cheek bones. Each rounded lobe of the vegetable leaf, too, is a thick and now loitering drop, larger or smaller; the lobes are the fingers of the leaf; and as many lobes as it has, in so many directions it tends to flow, and more heat or other genial influences would have caused it to flow yet farther.

Thus it seemed that this one hill side illustrated the principle of all the operations of Nature. The Maker of this earth but patented a leaf. What Champollion will decipher this hieroglyphic for us, that we may turn over a new leaf at last? This phenomenon is more exhilarating to me than the luxuriance and fertility of vineyards. True, it is somewhat excrementitious in its character, and there is no end to the heaps of liver, lights, and bowels, as if the globe were turned wrong side outward; but this suggests at least that Nature has some bowels, and there again is mother of humanity. This is the frost coming out of the ground; this is Spring. It precedes the green and flowery spring, as mythology precedes regular poetry. I know of nothing more purgative of winter fumes and indigestions. It convinces me that Earth is still in her swaddling clothes, and stretches forth baby fingers on every side. Fresh curls spring from the baldest brow. There is nothing inorganic. These foliaceous heaps lie along the bank like the slag of a furnace, showing that Nature is "in full blast" within. The earth is not a mere fragment of dead history, stratum upon stratum like the leaves of a book, to be studied by geologists and antiquaries chiefly, but living poetry like the leaves of a tree, which precede flowers and fruit,—not a fossil earth, but a living earth; compared with whose great central life all animal and vegetable life is merely parasitic. Its throes will heave our exuviae from their graves. You may melt your metals and cast them into the most beautiful moulds you can; they will never excite me like the forms which this molten earth flows out into. And not only it, but the institutions upon it, are plastic like clay in the hands of the potter.

Ere long, not only on these banks, but on every hill and plain and in every hollow, the frost comes out of the ground like a dormant quadruped from its burrow, and seeks the sea with music, or migrates to other climes in clouds. Thaw with his gentle persuasion is more powerful than Thor with his hammer. The one melts, the other but breaks in pieces.

When the ground was partially bare of snow, and a few warm days had dried its surface somewhat, it was pleasant to compare the first tender signs of the infant year just peeping forth with the stately beauty of the withered vegetation which had withstood the winter,—life-everlasting, goldenrods, pinweeds, and graceful wild grasses, more obvious and interesting frequently than in summer even, as if their beauty was not ripe till then; even cotton-grass, cattails, mulleins, Johnswort, hardhack, meadow-sweet, and other strong stemmed plants, those unexhausted granaries which entertain the earliest birds, —decent weeds, at least, which widowed Nature wears. I am particularly attracted by the arching and sheaf-like top of the wool-grass; it brings back the summer to our winter memories, and is among the forms which art loves to copy, and which, in the vegetable kingdom, have the same relation to types already in the mind of man that astronomy has. It is an antique style older than Greek or Egyptian. Many of the phenomena of Winter are suggestive of an inexpressible tenderness and fragile delicacy. We are accustomed to hear this king described as a rude and boisterous tyrant; but with the gentleness of a lover he adorns the tresses of Summer.

At the approach of spring the red squirrels got under my house, two at a time, directly under my feet as I sat reading or writing, and kept up the queerest chuckling and chirruping and vocal pirouetting and gurgling sounds that ever were heard; and when I stamped they only chirruped the louder, as if past all fear and respect in their mad pranks, defying humanity to stop them. No you don't—chickaree—chickaree. They were wholly deaf to my arguments, or failed to perceive their force, and fell into a strain of invective that was irresistible.

The first sparrow of spring! The year beginning with younger hope than ever! The faint silvery warblings heard over the partially bare and moist fields from the bluebird, the song-sparrow, and the red-wing, as if the last flakes of winter tinkled as they fell! What at such a time are histories, chronologies, traditions, and all written revelations? The brooks sing carols and glees to the spring. The marsh-hawk sailing low over the meadow is already seeking the first slimy life that awakes. The sinking sound of melting snow is heard in all dells, and the ice dissolves apace in the ponds. The grass flames up on the hill sides like a spring fire,—"et primitus orbitur herba imbribus primoribus evocata,"—as if the earth sent forth an inward heat to greet the returning sun; not yellow but green is the color of its flame;—the symbol of perpetual youth, the grass-blade, like a long green ribbon, streams from the sod into the summer, checked indeed by the frost, but anon pushing on again, lifting its spear of last year's hay with the fresh life below. It grows as steadily as the rill oozes out of the ground. It is almost identical with that, for in the growing days of June, when the rills are dry, the grass-blades are their channels, and from year to year the herds drink at this perennial green stream, and the mower draws from it betimes their winter supply. So our human life but dies down to its root, and still puts forth its green blade to eternity.

Walden is melting apace. There is a canal two rods wide along the northerly and westerly sides, and wider still at the east end. A great field of ice has cracked off from the main body. I hear a song-sparrow singing from the bushes on the shore,—*olit, olit, olit,—chip, chip, chip, che, char,—che wiss, wiss, wiss.* He too is helping to crack it. How handsome the great sweeping curves in the edge of the ice, answering somewhat to those of the shore, but more regular! It is unusually hard, owing to the recent severe but transient cold, and all watered or waved like a palace floor. But the wind slides eastward over its opaque surface in vain, till it reaches the living surface beyond. It is glorious to behold this ribbon of water sparkling in the sun, the bare face of the pond full of glee and youth, as if it spoke the joy of the fishes within it, and of the sands on its shore,—a silvery sheen as from the scales of a *leuciscus,* as it were all one active fish. Such is the contrast between winter and spring. Walden was dead and is alive again. But this spring it broke up more steadily, as I have said.

The change from storm and winter to serene and mild weather, from dark and sluggish hours to bright and elastic ones, is a memorable crisis which all things proclaim. It is seemingly instantaneous at last. Suddenly an influx of light filled my house, though the evening was at hand, and the clouds of winter still overhung it, and the eaves were dripping with sleety rain. I looked out the window, and lo! where yesterday was cold gray ice there lay the transparent pond already calm and full of hope as in a summer evening, reflecting a summer evening sky in its bosom, though none was visible overhead, as if it had intelligence with some remote horizon. I heard a robin in the distance, the first I had heard for many a thousand years, methought, whose note I shall not forget for many a thousand more,—the same sweet and powerful songs as of yore. O the evening robin, at the end of a New England summer day! If I could ever find the twig he sits upon! I mean *he;* I mean *the twig.* This at least is not the *Turdus migratorius.* The pitch-pines and shrub-oaks about my house, which had so long drooped, suddenly resumed their several characters, looked brighter, greener, and more erect and alive, as if effectually cleansed and restored by the rain. I knew that it would not rain any more. You may tell by looking at any twig of the forest, ay, at your very wood-pile, whether its winter is past or not. As it grew darker, I was startled by the *honking* of geese flying low over the woods, like weary travellers getting in late from southern lakes, and indulging at last in unrestrained complaint and mutual consolation. Standing at my door, I could hear the rush of their wings; when, driving toward my house, they suddenly spied my light, and with hushed clamor wheeled and settled in the pond. So I came in, and shut the door, and passed my first spring night in the woods.

In the morning I watched the geese from the door through the mist, sailing in the middle of the pond, fifty rods off, so large and tumultuous that Walden appeared like an artificial pond for their amusement. But when I stood on the shore they at once rose up with a great flapping of wings at the signal of their commander, and when they had got into rank, circled about over my head, twenty-nine of them, and then steered straight to Canada, with a regular *honk* from the leader at intervals, trusting to break their fast in muddier pools. A "plump" of ducks rose at the same time and took the route to the north in the wake of their noisier cousins.

For a week I heard the circling groping clangor of some solitary goose in the foggy mornings, seeking its companion, and still peopling the woods with the sound of a larger life than they could sustain. In April the pigeons were seen again flying express in small flocks, and in due time I heard the martins twittering over my clearing, though it had not seemed that the township contained so many that it could afford me any, and I fancied that they were peculiarly of the ancient race that dwelt in hollow trees ere white men came. In almost all climes the tortoise and the frog are among the precursors and heralds of this season, and birds fly with song and glancing plumage, and plants spring and bloom, and winds blow, to correct this slight oscillation of the poles and preserve the equilibrium of Nature. . . .

On the 29th of April, as I was fishing from the bank of the river near the Nine-Acre-Corner bridge, standing on the quaking grass and willow roots, where the muskrats lurk, I heard a singular rattling sound, somewhat like that of the sticks which boys play with their fingers, when, looking up, I observed a very slight and graceful hawk, like a night-hawk, alternately soaring like a ripple and tumbling a rod or two over and over, showing the underside of its wings, which gleamed like a satin ribbon in the sun, or like the pearly inside of a shell. This sight reminded me of falconry and what nobleness and poetry are associated with that sport. The Merlin it seemed to me it might be called: but I care not for its name. It was the most ethereal flight I had ever witnessed. It did not simply flutter like a butterfly, nor soar like the larger hawks, but it sported with proud reliance in the fields of air; mounting again and again with its strange chuckle, it repeated its free and beautiful fall, turning over and over like a kite, and then recovering from its lofty tumbling, as if it had never set its foot on *terra firma.* It appeared to have no companion in the universe,—sporting there alone,—and to need none but the morning and the ether with which it played. It was not lonely, but made all the earth lonely beneath it. Where was the parent which hatched it, its kindred, and its father in the heavens? The tenant of the air, it seemed related to the earth but by an egg hatched sometime in the crevice of a crag;—or was its native nest made in the angle of a cloud, woven of the rainbow's trimmings and the sunset sky, and lined with some soft midsummer haze caught up from earth? Its eyry now some cliffy cloud.

Besides this I got a rare mess of golden and silver and bright cupreous fishes, which looked like a string of jewels. Ah! I have penetrated to those meadows on the morning of many a first spring day, jumping from hummock to hummock, from willow root to willow root, when the wild river valley and the woods were bathed in so pure and bright a light as would have waked the dead, if they had been slumbering in their graves, as some suppose. There needs no stronger proof of immortality. All things must live in such a light. O Death, where was thy sting? O Grave, where was thy victory, then?

Our village life would stagnate if it were not for the unexplored forests and meadows which surround it. We need the tonic of wildness,—to wade sometimes in marshes where the bittern and the meadow-hen lurk, and hear the booming of the snipe; to smell the whispering sedge where only some wilder and more solitary fowl builds her nest, and the mink crawls with its belly close to the ground. At the same time that we are earnest to explore and learn all things, we require that all things be mysterious and unexplorable, that land

and sea be infinitely wild, unsurveyed and unfathomed by us because unfathomable. We can never have enough of Nature. We must be refreshed by the sight of inexhaustible vigor, vast and Titanic features, the sea-coast with its wrecks, the wilderness with its living and its decaying trees, the thundercloud, and the rain which lasts three week and produces freshets. We need to witness our own limits transgressed, and some life pasturing freely where we never wander. We are cheered when we observe the vulture feeding on the carrion which disgusts and disheartens us, and deriving health and strength from the repast. There was a dead horse in the hollow by the path to my house, which compelled me sometimes to go out of my way, especially in the night when the air was heavy, but the assurance it gave me of the strong appetite and inviolable health of Nature was my compensation for this. I love to see that Nature is so rife with life that myriads can be afforded to be sacrificed and suffered to prey on one another; that tender organizations can be so serenely squashed out of existence like pulp,—tadpoles which herons gobble up, and tortoises and toads run over in the road; and that sometimes it has rained flesh and blood! With the liability to accident, we must see how little account is to be made of it. The impression made on a wise man is that of universal innocence. Poison is not poisonous after all, nor are any wounds fatal. Compassion is a very untenable ground. It must be expeditious. Its pleadings will not bear to be stereotyped.

Early in May, the oaks, hickories, maples, and other trees, just putting out amidst the pine woods around the pond, imparted a brightness like sunshine to the landscape, especially in cloudy days, as if the sun were breaking through mists and shining faintly on the hill sides here and there. On the third or fourth of May I saw a loon in the pond, and during the first week of the month I heard the whippoorwill, the brown thrasher, the veery, the wood-pewee, chewink, and other birds. I had heard the wood-thrush long before. The phoebe had already come once more and looked in at my door and window, to see if my house was cavern-like enough for her, sustaining herself on humming wings with clinched talons, as if she held by the air, while she surveyed the premises. The sulphur-like pollen of the pitch-pine soon covered the pond and the stones and rotten wood along the shore, so that you could have collected a barrelful. This is the "sulphur showers" we hear of. Even in Calidasa's drama of Sacontala, we read of "rills dyed yellow with the golden dust of the lotus."

And so the seasons went rolling on into summer, as one rambles into higher and higher grass.

Thus was my first year's life in the woods completed; and the second year was similar to it. I finally left Walden September 6th, 1847.

Bibliographical Index

Ackerman, William C. (with E. A. Colman and Harold O. Ogrosky). "Water," from *Water: The Yearbook of Agriculture*. Published by the U. S. Department of Agriculture, 1955.

Allen, Durward L. "Boom and Bust," from *Our Wildlife Legacy*. New York: Funk and Wagnalls Company, 1954.

Allen, Robert P. "The Whooping Crane's World," from *Discovery: Great Moments in the Lives of Outstanding Naturalists*, edited by John K. Terres. Philadelphia: J. B. Lippincott Company, 1961.

Audubon, John James. "The Wild Turkey," from *Ornithological Biography*. Edinburgh: 1839.

Austin, Mary. "Cactus Country," from *The Land of Journeys' Ending*. New York: D. Appleton-Century, 1924.

Bartram, William. "Flora and Fauna of Spanish Florida," from *Travels*. Philadelphia: 1791.

Beston, Henry. "The Year at High Tide," from *The Outermost House*. New York: Doubleday, Doran & Company, 1928.

Borland, Hal. "Flowers: Pollen and Seed," from *The Enduring Pattern*. New York: Simon and Schuster, 1959.

Boswell, Victor R. "What Seeds Are and Do," from *Seeds: The Yearbook of Agriculture*. Published by the U. S. Department of Agriculture, 1961.

Brereton, John. "Virgin Coast, 1602," from *A Briefe and True Relation of the Discouerie of the North Part of Virginia in 1602*; 1602.

Broun, Maurice. "Winter on Hawk Mountain," from *Hawks Aloft*. New York: Dodd, Mead & Company, 1949.

Bulkeley, Morgan. "Neighbors of the Night," from "Our Berkshires" column in the *Berkshire Eagle*, Pittsfield, Massachusetts: 1963–64.

Burroughs, John. "Winter Owls," from *A Year in the Fields*. Boston: Houghton Mifflin Company, 1896.

Carrighar, Sally. "The Deer Mouse," from *One Day on Beetle Rock*. New York: Alfred A. Knopf, Inc., 1945.

Carson, Rachel. "The Enduring Sea," from *The Edge of the Sea*. Boston: Houghton Mifflin Company, 1955.

Catlin, George. "Minataree Village," from *North American Indians*. Published by the author in London, 1880.

Chittenden, Hiram Martin. "Insects of the Old West," from *The American Fur Trade of the Far West*. New York: 1902.

Clark, William. "To the Great Falls," from *Original Journals of the Lewis and Clark Expedition*, edited by Reuben Gold Thwaites. New York: Dodd, Mead & Company, 1904–05.

Clemens, Samuel Langhorne. *See* Twain, Mark.

Cobb, Boughton. "Life Cycle of a Fern," from *A Field Guide to the Ferns and Their Related Families*. Boston: Houghton Mifflin Company, 1956.

Colman (with William C. Ackerman and Harold O. Ogrosky). "Water," from *Water: The Yearbook of Agriculture*. Published by the U. S. Department of Agriculture, 1955.

Crèvecoeur, Hector St. John de. "Wild Honey," from *Letters from an American Farmer*, 1782.

Crockett, David. "Davy Crockett Kills a Bear," from *A Narrative of the Life of David Crockett . . . Written by Himself*, 1834.

Devoe, Alan. "The World of the Chipmunk," from *The Audubon Book of True Nature Stories*, edited by John K. Terres. New York: Thomas Y. Crowell Company, 1958.

Douglas, William O. "Olympic Mountains," from *My Wilderness: The Pacific West*. New York: Doubleday & Company, Inc., 1960.

Dubkin, Leonard. "Like Crusoe, I Discover an Island," from *Enchanted Streets*. Boston: Little, Brown and Company, 1947.

Eckelberry, Don R. "On the Heels of the Dodo," from *Discovery: Great Moments in the Lives of Outstanding Naturalists*, edited by John K. Terres. Philadelphia: J. B. Lippincott Company, 1961.

Eckstein, Gustav. "A Short Life but a Full One," from *Lives*. New York: Harper & Brothers, 1932.

Edwards, Everett E. "The Settlement of Grasslands," from *Grass: The Yearbook of Agriculture*. Published by the U. S. Department of Agriculture, 1948.

Ehle, John. "Autumn Harvest," from *The Landbreakers*. New York: Harper & Row, 1964.

Eifert, Virginia S. "The Rainy Day," from *Land of the Snowshoe Hare.* New York: Dodd, Mead & Company, 1960.
Eiseley, Loren. "The Secret of Life," from *The Immense Journey.* New York: Random House, 1957.
Emerson, Ralph Waldo. "Nature," from *Essays: Second Series.* Boston: Ticknor & Fields, 1876.
Errington, Paul L. "Of Marshes and Fall," from *Of Men and Marshes.* New York: The Macmillan Company, 1957.
Evans, Howard Ensign. "The Social Register," from *Wasp Farm.* New York: The Natural History Press, 1963.
Farb, Peter. "Sea of Grass," from *Face of North America.* New York: Harper & Row, 1963.
Flagg, Wilson. "Pine Woods," from *The Woods and By-Ways of New England,* 1872.
Flint, Timothy. "On the Beautiful Ohio," from *Recollections,* 1826.
Fosburgh, Hugh. "Adirondack Hunt," from *One Man's Pleasure.* New York: William Morrow & Company, 1960.
Frémont, John Charles. "Crossing the Sierra in Winter," from *Report of the Exploring Expedition to the Rocky Mountains in the Year 1842, and to Oregon and North California in 1843–44.* An official government report, 1845.
Gannett, Lewis. "Let Nature Grow Her Own," from *Cream Hill.* New York: The Viking Press, 1949.
Graves, John. "The Island," from *Goodbye to a River.* New York: Alfred A. Knopf, Inc., 1960.
Gregg, Josiah. "The Prairies," from *Commerce of the Prairies.* New York: 1844.
Grinnell, George Bird. "Man and Nature," from *The Story of the Indian.* New York: D. Appleton & Company, 1895.
Hailey, W. D., "Johnny Appleseed," from "Johnny Appleseed: A Pioneer Hero," in *Harper's New Monthly Magazine,* November 1871.
Hall, Leonard. "White Water and Blue Heron," from *Stars Upstream.* Chicago: University of Chicago Press, 1958.
Halle, Louis J., Jr. "Spring in Washington," from *Spring in Washington.* New York: William Sloane Associates, 1947.
Hass, Victor Paul. "Mystique," from "From a Bookman's Notebook," in the *World-Herald,* Omaha, Nebraska: September 6, 1964.
Horgan, Paul. "Great River: Prologue," from *Great River: The Rio Grande.* New York: Rinehart & Company, 1954.
Irving, Washington. "Up the North Platte," from *The Adventures of Captain Bonneville.* New York: G. P. Putnam, 1849.
Johnson, Bessie F. "A Time Remembered," from personal letters, 1964.

Kieran, John. "Mammals Within the City Gates," from *Natural History of New York City*. Boston: Houghton Mifflin Company, 1959.
Krutch, Joseph Wood. "The Contemplative Toad," from *The Desert Year*. New York: William Sloane Associates, 1952.
Lavender, David. "Mountain Winter," from *Bent's Fort*. New York: Doubleday & Company, Inc., 1954.
Leopold, Aldo. "Wilderness," from *A Sand County Almanac*. New York: Oxford University Press, 1949.
Lewis, Meriwether. "Up Jefferson's River," from *Original Journals of the Lewis and Clark Expedition*, edited by Reuben Gold Thwaites. New York: Dodd, Mead & Company, 1904–05.
Milne, Lorus J. and Margery J. "Consider the Egg," from *A Multitude of Living Things*. New York: Dodd, Mead & Company, 1947.
Mirov, N. T. "A Tree Is a Living Thing," from *Trees: The Yearbook of Agriculture*. Published by the U. S. Department of Agriculture, 1949.
Mowery, William Byron. "Out of the Soft, Black Night," from *The Audubon Book of True Nature Stories*, edited by John K. Terres. New York: Thomas Y. Crowell Company, 1958.
Muir, John. "Bee Pastures," from *The Mountains of California*, 1894.
Murphy, Robert. "Peregrine Falcon," from *The Peregrine Falcon*. Boston: Houghton Mifflin Company, 1963.
Ogrosky, Harold O. (with William C. Ackerman and E. A. Colman) "Water," from *Water: The Yearbook of Agriculture*. Published by the U. S. Department of Agriculture, 1955.
Olson, Sigurd F. "Wild Rice," from *Runes of the North*. New York: Alfred A Knopf, Inc., 1963.
Oñate, Juan de. "Oñate Goes East," from *True Account of the Expedition of Oñate Toward the East—1601*.
Parkman, Francis. "Journey to the Arkansas," from *The Oregon Trail*, 1849.
Peattie, Donald Culross. "The Nest in the Cave," from *Singing in the Wilderness*. New York: G. P. Putnam's Sons, 1935.
Peterson, Roger Tory. "Ghoulies and Ghoosties," from *Birds Over America*. New York: Dodd, Mead & Company, 1948.
Petite, Irving. "Which Way Did the Dinosaurs Go?" from *The Elderberry Tree*. New York: Doubleday & Company, Inc., 1964.
Pettingill, Olin Sewall, Jr. "The Woodcock," from *Down East* magazine. Camden, Maine: May 1963.
Powell, John Wesley. "The Canyon," from *The Exploration of the Colorado River*. An official government document, published in 1875.
Rak, Mary Kidder. "Wolves," from *Mountain Cattle*. New York: Houghton Mifflin Company, 1936.

Rawlings, Marjorie Kinnan. "Big Storm," from *The Yearling*. New York: Charles Scribner's Sons, 1938.

Reid, Mayne. "The Porcupine and the Marten," from *The Desert Home*, 1834.

Richardson, Wyman. "Wind and Weather," from *The House on Nauset Marsh*. New York: W. W. Norton & Company, Inc., 1955.

Roberts, Elizabeth Madox. "A Promise Land," from *The Great Meadow*. New York: The Viking Press, 1930.

Roosevelt, Theodore. "Dakota Plains," from *Hunting Trips of a Ranchman*. New York: Charles Scribner's Sons, 1885.

Ruark, Robert. "Shame to Waste a Boy," from *The Old Man and the Boy*. New York: Henry Holt and Company, 1957.

Rue, Leonard Lee, III. "Beaver," from *The World of the Beaver*. Philadelphia: J. B. Lippincott Company, 1964.

Saunders, Aretas A. "Bird Songs," from *The Lives of Wild Birds*. New York: Doubleday & Company, 1954.

Seton, Ernest Thompson. "The Kangaroo Rat," from *Lives of the Hunted*. New York: Charles Scribner's Sons, 1901.

Sutton, George Miksch. "Dust Storm," from *Discovery: Great Moments in the Lives of Outstanding Naturalists*, edited by John K. Terres. Philadelphia: J. B. Lippincott Company, 1961.

Teale, Edwin Way. "Grasshopper Road," from *Journey into Summer*. New York: Dodd, Mead & Company, 1960.

Terres, John K. "A Pond in His Life," from *The Wonders I See*. Philadelphia: J. B. Lippincott Company, 1960.

Thomson, Betty Flanders. "New England's Mountains," from *The Changing Face of New England*. New York: The Macmillan Company, 1958.

Thoreau, Henry David. "Spring at Walden Pond," from *Walden*, 1854.

Tonti, Henri de. "La Salle on the Mississippi," from Tonti's account of La Salle's expeditions, c. 1683.

Twain, Mark. "High Water on the Mississippi," from *Life on the Mississippi*, 1883.

Van Dyke, Henry. "Ice Fishing," from *Fisherman's Luck*. New York: Charles Scribner's Sons, 1899.

White, Stewart Edward. "The Ordeal," from *Folded Hills*. New York: Doubleday, Doran & Company, 1934.

Whitman, Walt. "May-Month," from *Specimen Days*. New York: David McKay Company, 1882.

Wilson, Alexander. "The Wild Pigeon," from *American Ornithology*, 1808–13.